# Equality in Theory and Practice

Ronald Francis

# Equality in Theory and Practice

## A Moral Argument for Ethical Improvements

Springer

Ronald Francis
Victoria University
Melbourne, Australia

ISBN 978-981-15-3487-4 ISBN 978-981-15-3488-1 (eBook)
https://doi.org/10.1007/978-981-15-3488-1



This Springer imprint is published by the registered company Springer Nature Singapore Pte Ltd.
The registered company address is: 152 Beach Road, #21-01/04 Gateway East, Singapore 189721, Singapore

*Dedicated to the memory of my late wife*

Gloria Lesly Francis

# Preface

This book is an account of the concept of equality. It considers the arguments and evidence and notes that equality is of different kinds: among such items are the different forms that it might take, including economic equality, education, equality before the law, and equality of opportunity; and it goes on to consider both gender equality and the appropriate incentives in the light of personality differences. It also concludes that inequality is a profoundly moral question, as well as notes that there are good practical reasons for its adoption. Among the contributions is a consideration of classical theories from Aristotle to Hume, as well as contemporary approaches such as Rawls' distributive justice and approaches from Haidt, Temkin, and Parfit: it also considers such issues as the naturalistic fallacy and what is different about the Goleman view of moral sensitivity and the ethical personality. The array of evidence includes such issues as the effect of wind, climate, various plants (such as sugar and cotton) and their impact on the slave trade, the concept of Gaia, Darwinism, sex inequality, personality, culture, psychological issues, and the quantification of ethics. There are two appendices: one giving the relationship of "contentment with one's lot in life" to longevity, the Gini index, peace, female legislators, and corruption and the other a demonstration of paired comparisons. It is concluded that they form a complex whole. What is original about this work is the array of arguments and evidence supporting equality. It provides methods of quantifying values and looks at various approaches to equality. The book concludes with some practical suggestions for improving equality and also involves the use of the twin methods of education and legislation, and they both become more effective when combined with the gradualist approach.

Melbourne, Australia — Ronald D. Francis

# Acknowledgments

Grateful thanks are given to Professor Arthur Tatnall, owner of Heidelberg Press, for permission to quote, as has also been done by Tom Lloyd. The *Journal of Financial Crime* has also given permission to quote from the "Assumptions" article. If I have forgotten to acknowledge anyone, it is simply by failure to recognize. It will be appreciated that the views expressed here are those of the author and, as such, may be problems of interpretation.

# Contents


1 **Introduction to Equality** 1
The Nature of Equality 1
What This Work Sets Out to Do 2
Ethics and Morals and Committees 2
Ancient Injunctions 2
Types of Equality 3
Chief Seattle 3
Economic Equality 4
Topics 5
Abuse 5
Climate Change and Politics 5
Colonialism 6
Corruption & Open-Ness 6
Excellence 6
Factors in Equality 7
Globalisation 8
Income 9
Industrial Consequences 9
Lovelock & Darwin 9
Marxism 10
Migration 10
People Smugglers 11
Personal Privacy 11
Population Growth 12
Precepts Change Over Time 12
Race and Power 13
Slavery 14
Social Equality 15
The British Empire 15
UN Reference to 'Mankind' 16
Utopias 16

- Violence ... 17
- Women ... 18
- Conclusions ... 18

**2 Physical Matters** ... 19
- Introduction ... 19
- Ancient Injunctions ... 19
- Theorists ... 20
  - Malthus ... 20
  - Darwin ... 21
  - Lovelock ... 22
  - Hobhouse ... 23
  - Health Accounts ... 24
- Topics ... 25
  - Aesthetics ... 25
  - Climate ... 26
  - Maps ... 27
  - Media ... 27
  - Personal Finances ... 27
  - Population Control Policy ... 28
  - Racism ... 30
  - Statistics ... 31
- Technological Solutions ... 31
- Education and Legislation ... 32
- Conclusions ... 32

**3 Psychological Approaches** ... 33
- Introduction ... 33
- Psychological Bases of Behaviour ... 35
  - The Ecstatic Phenomenon ... 35
  - Maslow's Hierarchy of Needs ... 38
  - The Phi Phenomenon ... 39
- Cross Cultural Aspects ... 39
- Time Has Two Aspects ... 40
- Fashions in Science ... 41
- Topics ... 42
  - Altruism and Prisoner's Dilemma ... 42
  - Applications ... 43
  - Empathy ... 44
  - Excellence ... 44
  - Gurus ... 45
  - Human Relations ... 46
  - Personal vs Public Interests ... 46
  - Violence ... 47
- Conclusions ... 48

4 **Personality** .... 49
Introduction .... 49
Approaches to Personality .... 50
General Theorists .... 51
Tests Not Yet Devised .... 51
Legislation to Ban .... 53
Aspects of Personality Approaches .... 53
Assumptions .... 54
Etiquette .... 55
Formal Testing .... 56
Psychopathy .... 57
Mental Illness as a Criminal Defence .... 58
Approaches .... 58
Political Rectitude .... 58
Habit and William James .... 59
Moral Approaches .... 60
Physical Abuse .... 61
Logical Rules and Cultures .... 61
Conclusions .... 62

5 **Culture** .... 63
Introduction .... 63
Definition of Culture .... 64
Confounding of Race and Culture .... 65
Culture Shock .... 66
Logical Rules and Cultures .... 66
Cultural Values .... 67
Cultural Attitudes .... 67
Cultural Modifications .... 68
Attributes of Culture .... 68
Cultural Oddities .... 70
Special Cases of Cultural Applications .... 70
Comparing Cultures .... 71
The McSally Case .... 72
Expatriates .... 73
The Mozart Effect .... 74
Suggestions for Cross-Cultural Socialising .... 74
Finding Out More (HRAF) .... 75
Conclusions .... 75

6 **Business** .... 77
Introduction .... 77
Early Attempts .... 77
New Lanark .... 77
Cadbury .... 78
Unionism .... 79

The Marlowe Declaration . . . 80
Money Matters . . . 81
General Progress Indicator . . . 83
Factors in Business . . . 84
Business Decisions . . . 84
Freedom of Expression . . . 85
Metaphors . . . 85
Prescriptions . . . 86
Robots . . . 86
Stremes . . . 86
Succession Planning . . . 87
Commentary and Cautions . . . 88
Conclusions . . . 89

**7 Communication** . . . 91
Introduction . . . 91
Aesthetics . . . 91
Non-verbal Communication (NVC) . . . 92
Face . . . 93
Words . . . 95
Translation . . . 96
International Language . . . 97
Developmental Studies . . . 98
Assumptions . . . 98
Media . . . 99
Cultural Differences in Communication . . . 99
Styles and Skills . . . 100
What Makes a Good Communicator? . . . 101
Six Degrees of Separation . . . 101
Music as Communication . . . 102
Taking out Anti-feminine Bias . . . 103
Choosing a Course of Study . . . 103
Conclusions . . . 104

**8 Corruption** . . . 105
Introduction . . . 105
Definition of Corruption . . . 106
Hong Kong Anti-corruption Commission . . . 106
Transparency and Courtesy . . . 107
Corruption Types . . . 108
Casualisation of the Workforce . . . 109
Bribery . . . 110
Conflict of Interest . . . 111
Cultural Mores . . . 111
Deceit and Underhandedness . . . 113
Dimensionality of Corruption . . . 113

Hypocrisy . . . 114
Loyalty . . . 115
Misuse of Power . . . 116
Towards a New Definition. . . . 116
United Nations . . . 117
Conclusions. . . . 118

**9 Politics** . . . 119
Introduction. . . . 119
Structural Approaches. . . . 120
National Matters . . . 121
Political Remedies . . . 122
Reliance on Consultants . . . 122
Sortition. . . . 123
Acting on the Wishes of the Electorate. . . . 123
Political Rectitude. . . . 124
Special Cases . . . 127
Women's Votes . . . 127
Independence . . . 127
Incumbency. . . . 128
Gay Marriage . . . 129
Health and Education . . . 130
Moral Obligations. . . . 130
Whistleblowing. . . . 131
General Observations . . . 132
On Being Cautious . . . 133
Independence . . . 133
Women's Votes . . . 134
Health and Education . . . 134
Moral Obligations. . . . 135
Whistleblowing. . . . 136
On Being Cautious . . . 137
Conclusions. . . . 137

**10 Sex Differences** . . . 139
Issues Differentially Affecting Women. . . . 140
Facial Recognition and Communication. . . . 140
Ambiguous Data . . . 146
Prostitution . . . 146
Polygamy . . . 146
Imprisonment and Faith . . . 147
Law and Custom and Norms. . . . 148
The Use of Referenda . . . 149
Conclusions. . . . 149

**11 Slavery** ... 151
Historical Comments ... 152
William the Conquerer ... 153
Enslaving Africans ... 154
Definition of Slavery ... 155
Villeinage ... 155
Human Trafficking ... 156
Economy ... 156
Countries ... 157
Press Ganging ... 157
Blackbirding ... 158
Contemporary Example ... 158
UN Declaration ... 158
Law ... 159
Wilberforce ... 159
Websites ... 160
Borgen Surveys ... 160
End Slavery Now ... 160
Free the Slaves ... 161
The Global Slavery Index ... 162
The Walk Free Foundation ... 163
Commentary ... 163
Grading of Slavery ... 163
Conclusions ... 164

**12 Quantification of Social Variables** ... 167
Happiness ... 167
Further Quantification ... 171
Principle ... 172
Comparisons ... 172
Ranking and Rating ... 172
Paired Comparisons ... 173
Other Techniques ... 173
Methodological Issue ... 173
Discriminant Analysis ... 174
Factor Analysis ... 174
National Character ... 174
Delphi Technique ... 175
Conclusions ... 176

**13 Theories** ... 179
Introduction ... 179
Classical Theories ... 179
Virtue Ethics ... 180
Kantian Analysis ... 180
Deontology ... 180

Utilitarianism & Hedonism . . . 181
Consequentialism . . . 181
Pantisocracy . . . 182
The Naturalistic Fallacy . . . 182
Modern Approaches . . . 183
Rawls . . . 183
The Rio Declaration . . . 184
Kohlberg . . . 184
Parfit . . . 185
Temkin . . . 185
Haidt . . . 185
Distributive Justice . . . 186
Social Attitudes . . . 186
Attitude to Death . . . 187
Numerology . . . 187
Social Indicators . . . 188
Applications . . . 189
Moral Dilemmas . . . 189
Whistleblowing . . . 190
Religious Encyclical . . . 191
Physical Constants . . . 192
Assumptions as Critic . . . 192
By Elimination . . . 192
Assumption of Equal Competence . . . 192
The Offensive Prize . . . 193
The Basis of Humour . . . 193
Wrong but Socially Useful . . . 193
Challenging Assumptions . . . 193
Knowability . . . 194
The Missing Item . . . 194
Comment on Theory . . . 194
Rationality . . . 195
Logical Paradoxes . . . 195
Easterlin Paradox . . . 195
The Cantril Ladder . . . 196
The Research Paradox . . . 196
Description of Minimal Principles . . . 197
Excellence . . . 197
Conclusions . . . 199

**14 General Conclusions** . . . 201
Factors in Equality . . . 202
Solutions . . . 203
Theories . . . 203
Psychological Contributions . . . 204

Hidden Truths and Research . . . 204
Moral Dilemmas . . . 205
Naturalistic Fallacy . . . 206
Politics. . . . 206
Population Policy . . . 207
Rights . . . 207
Social Approaches. . . . 208
Women and Fertility . . . 209
Relation to Religion . . . 209
The Republic Debate and Referenda . . . 210
Oxymorons and Paradoxes . . . 210
The United Nations. . . . 211
The Indigenous Peoples . . . 211
The Moral Personality. . . . 211
Types of Inequality . . . 212
Final Commentary . . . 213
Recommendations. . . . 214
Ethics Is a Changeable Condition. . . . 217
Two Types of Intervention . . . 217
The Overall Conclusion . . . 218

**Appendix** . . . 221

**References** . . . 223

**Index**. . . . 231

# Chapter 1
# Introduction to Equality

This book argues the case of equality, and does so by presenting both the moral arguments and the evidential bases. When combined, these two telling features add up to a persuasive argument: the twin methods of legislation and education being the bedrock; that, combined with the principle of gradualism (the principle of persistence and a determination to succeed eventually); those methods present a persuasive argument. The book examines the proposition that there is a movement toward equality, although far from steady toward such a state.

## The Nature of Equality

Equality is a matter of objective fact, for example one might compare the income of males and females and the answer will be a matter of numbers. Equity is more of a philosophical term and refers to the morals of equity and, basically, is personal and subjective, which is not to say that there should not be equal pay. The confounding of the two terms often gives rise to considerations of difference whereas equivalence is not applicable. Most specifically, this work argues that our common humanity is governed by principles which are universal, and which cross cultural boundaries. The expression of these well-established principles is intended as an insight into human interchanges, and should be of practical help. At the end of the book suggestions are offered for improving equality.

It is not a book in the pop psychology genre. That genre has been the subject of recent justifiable criticism in that many of the works are opinions as to action based on no knowledge of the circumstance This work of Justman is not one of the analyses of conflict, as that work is already done by Stohl et al. (2017). It is, rather, a work that calls on a diminution of violence: in other words a kinder and more equitable world.



R. Francis, *Equality in Theory and Practice*,
https://doi.org/10.1007/978-981-15-3488-1_1

## What This Work Sets Out to Do

This work then attempts to buttress the argument with evidence. Not the least of the movement toward equality rests with increasing respect for life and suffering. We are, rightly, exhorted to be mindful of being aware of minor infractions, and less concerned with major ones or, as is said, strain at gnats and swallow camels. There is an apt seventeenth century quatrain:

> The law locks up the man or woman
> Who steals the goose from off the common
> But leaves the greater felon loose
> Who steals the common from the goose

The purpose of ethics is to allow moral argument's sway over more mundane considerations. It invokes the idea that, no matter what the justification, economic considerations do not prevail over such issues as work-safety or slavery: it is, essentially, about the application of moral values to these considerations: it is about treating all people as equally worthy of life and limb.

## Ethics and Morals and Committees

The essential difference between ethics and morals is that the latter, morals, is a general understanding of which values are worthy of pursuit. A code of ethics, on the other hand, is a codified set of values, and of particular application (thus legal ethics applies to lawyers and their ancillaries only, medical ethics to medical practitioners and their ancillaries, etc.). Ancient populations: were very small compared to present populations. As such the notion of 'kings' was vastly different from what we understand today.

## Ancient Injunctions

The moral precepts that were formulated then may, or may not, have application in the modern world. A prime example is that the Hippocratic oath forbade, noting that Hippocrates asserted that.

Nor shall any man's entreaty prevail upon me to administer poison to anyone; neither will I counsel any man to do so. Moreover, I will give no sort of medicine to any pregnant woman, with a view to destroy the child.

That is a view that appears to be inconsistent with modern legislation on the dying-with-dignity movements and abortion in many countries, the current predominant view being it is a person's right to choose, as we shall see in the chapter on theories of ethics (see, for example, Abortion in References). Old Testament texts expressed the view that it is admirable to 'Increase, multiply and replenish the earth'. In KJV Genesis (1:28) God said

> ... be fruitful, and multiply, and replenish the earth, and subdue it: and have dominion over the fish of the sea, and over the fowl of the air, and over everything living thing that moveth upon the face of the earth'.

Presumably this does not mean that 'every living thing that moveth' since it also includes other people. It is easy to be a critic, but one ought to bear in mind the intentions of the writer. This injunction, in context, may be taken to mean that when the earth was underpopulated there was reason to multiply. It also implies that 'dominion over' means using non-humans always for human's benefit. Just such an injunction might be taken to mean that other creatures are not to be considered as sentient beings. Furthermore, the move to allow rational adults, who are terminally ill, to end their lives with peace and dignity. They will choose to do so at a time of their own choice: a proposition that runs counter to the Hippocratic Oath.

## Types of Equality

One might ask equality of what? Equality of opportunity? Outcomes? Income? Gender equality? Social standing? Equality before the law? It is just such questions that need to be addressed. There will, in the foreseeable future, a need for regulation to further curtail the excesses of unbridled wants. Without regulation there will always be urban decay, low educational standards, racism, and low self-esteem. One of the essentials of a code is to have in two parts: a code of ethics and a code conduct. The first sets out the values to which one aspires; the second is what to do in particular situations (such as accepting gifts up to a certain value).

In an ideal situation one would also have an ethics committee. The idea of the committee is to have it comprised of a variety of experts: not, as someone once suggested, as to have every minor group represented (we are short of one-legged lesbians!). The expertise would, ideally, consist of a group of (say) seven experts, all from different fields such as biology, medicine, psychology, physics – and perhaps a clergyman or tribal elder. The essential is their individual commitment to ethics and chapter 5, desirably, a knowledge and commitment to ethics. That committee would also do double deliberation, being deciding on cases, and also reviewing the code. It should be clear that the one function also invests the other.

## Chief Seattle

We quote the alleged Chief Seattle on environmentalism wherein he quotes:

> Every part of this earth is sacred to my people. Every shining pine needle, every sandy shore, every mist in the dark woods, every clearing and humming insect is holy in the memory and experience of my people.

And

> The Earth does not belong to man; man belongs to Earth. Man did not weave the web of life; he is merely a strand in it. Whatever he does to the web, he does to himself.

And

> If all the beasts were gone man would die from a great loneliness of the spirit. For whatever happens to the beasts soon happens to man.... all things are connected. Although there is difficulty in attributing this authorship to Chief Seattle, it does summarise the situation most aptly.

## Economic Equality

While there are works that deal with economic equality, Stiglitz (2013) for example, it also deals with the morality of equality. It argues that there are significant advantages to equality, with several resting on human rights grounds. Indeed, the book dedication includes the notion that the hope is expressed that '... they will inherit a world and a country that are less divided'. That leaves us with the clear understanding of where his sympathies lie. As Stiglitz is an American economist it is understandable that the orientation should be thus, but does not ignore the rest of the world. Indeed, we must recognise that many of the financial devices were American in origin (derivatives, hedging, futures, etc.), as was ably recorded by Lanchester (2010). The Stiglitz book lays understandable emphasis upon the economic consequences of inequality, and does so at the expense of other forms of inequality (such as the rule of law and opportunities other than economic), and emphasises the value of social capital, and of trust.

It is held here that there is a thread that runs through social development. Among the significant advantages to developing equality is that it values life more highly, it results in the diminution of violence, it gives equal rights to women, it conduces to prosperity, and advances the democratic process (see, for example, Callinicos 2000, Stivers 2008, and Smith 2011). By way of contrast there are arguments against the subversion of equality: among such are that it:

- Breeds distrust
- Cements power structures
- Diverts resources that could be gainfully employed elsewhere
- Entrenches poverty
- Fosters civil unrest
- Gives a wrongful sense of entitlement
- Wrongfully enriches the few

# Topics

## *Abuse*

Two of the most recent instances of inegalitarianism are those of child abuse, and of slavery. The misuse of positions of responsibility for sexual gratification has led to investigative commissions, indicting churches, state systems, orphanages, schools, media figures, and various other allegedly protected institutions. In the Western world there are, increasingly, fewer places to hide. It is, rightly, the protection of the vulnerable that is an impressive development. One could be aware that the vulnerable may insist on rights that they do not legitimately have (such as the right to privilege): nevertheless, the move is one toward equalisation. As to the second it is a dimensional, and extreme, form of coercion.

## *Climate Change and Politics*

On the issue of climate change it seems clear that some island states, such as Kiribati and Tuvalu will disappear under the rising ocean. As such they will lose their sovereignty. What is to be done in such cases has yet to be determined. Other places, particularly those such as India, have better options. Whereas a place such as the Ganges delta may become uninhabitable there are places on the sub-continent that, previously inhospitable, have now become habitable. The governments of such countries have a genuine option of relocating those populations. It is the circumstance of climate change that forces us to consider options for better social circumstances for disappearing states, and of relocation.

In the Fragile States index (see References) it is worthy of note that the most fragile states were in sub-Saharan Africa. They did not fare well in the Index. The countries that fared best were those of Scandinavia and Western Europe, Australia, Canada, Britain, USA, and New Zealand. The Index also listed trends, such as Turkey deteriorating to an autocracy.

The glib use of such concepts as ‘globalisation’ often obscures what are some fundamental changes to human life on earth. Such issues as climate change, the loss of biodiversity, and of gross population growth, are changing the world into something not yet contemplated. Taking the last concept, for example, the growth of human population to currently over seven billion makes the issue of food production, living space, the disposal of waste, and the overuse of earth’s resources of pressing need for consideration (see World Population in References). Further, it has even been suggested that, rather than curb population growth we might seek to relocate to other planets.

## *Colonialism*

In that sense it is the modern form of colonialism in that it is exploitation of the vulnerable, and uses methods based on unequal power. In such a comparison, foreign aid by Western countries is both corrupted, and trivial in principle, with few exceptions, The World Bank website estimates that corruption costs money to each person on the planet, and asks a number of pertinent questions, such as why should Western countries increase foreign aid when developing countries corruptly tolerate, and even foster corruption? (see World Bank and corruption in References).

One of the major points here is that anti-corruption bodies fail to address the issues that are plainly in their brief. For example, the use of tendering for public works projects. They are dubbed, wrongly, with such terms as 'market-led infrastructure proposals' or the like. What that amounts to is a failure to engage in competitive proposals, and obviates the need for such time-consuming processes as getting competitive quotes. The spurious use of such terms as 'commercial in confidence', and the presumption 'intellectual property' are ways of obfuscating; the basic fact of not being competitive.

## *Corruption & Open-Ness*

We might also note that where there is corruption it flourishes in secrecy: the antidote is transparency, as was argued by the *Transparency International* movement. While we recognise that such issues as personal privacy, intellectual property, and state secrets are acceptable privacy issues: yet still, transparency is the default mode. Frankfurt, in 1987, argued that equality would matter less if people had enough: under such circumstances, disparities would matter less (he called it the 'doctrine of sufficiency'). As he went on to note, crime rates are higher in regions with greater disparities of wealth (even controlled for absolute levels of wealth) 'partly because chronic low status leads men to become obsessed with rank and to kill one another over trivial insults'.

## *Excellence*

In most professional work excellence is judged, in part, by the ethical codes. Excellence is, however, more easily recognised than codified. It is seen as a journey as well as a destination; a process as well as an achievement. As Peters and Austin so aptly put it, '... excellence happens when high purpose and pragmatism meet'. Judgments are not made on single issues, but on overall evaluation. The difference between statesmen and party hacks is that the former has a broader vision, substantial confidence in their own insight, a constructive approach and, most of all. a moral tone to their views and behaviour.

There are some forms of professionalism in which sheer competence and art, dreamtime, and artistry are sufficient; musicianship, for example. In most forms of professionalism, however, values become significant. We do not accord to dictators the notion of excellence, despite their efficiency, dedication and list of accomplishments. Those to whom we accord excellence have commonly acted according to commonly accepted ethical standards. Over recent decades various theories of management have, as one of their unstated premises, the search for more ethical ways of doing things. Team work theories, Theory X and Theory Y, primary social motives, and the application of Swedish and Japanese methods have a common motivation.

One of the characteristics of excellent professionals is that they feel they live in an imperfect world; things are rarely as good as they should be. Given the frailties of human nature, the demands of time and of competing values, the solutions to almost all problems are less than perfect. The current commitment to total quality management, and best international practice, is a recent expression of that idea, transferred to the business context. There is no doubt that quality sells goods and services: it benefits an organisation in the longer term, but not the shorter term.

Excellence may be construed in the negative rather than the positive sense. A story that illustrates the unusual employment of the negative is that of a job applicant who, when asked to nominate two referees of good standing, named the Commissioner of Police and the Chief Magistrate. On the applicant's return interview he was told that neither the Commissioner nor the Chief Magistrate had ever heard of him. 'There,' said the applicant triumphantly, 'isn't that an excellent reference?' It is worth noting that the companies on the Peters and Waterman criteria were also market leaders in their respective and diverse fields. Excellence, including ethical excellence, is clearly profitable. To achieve potential, some values need to be emphasised and these include:

- The value of personal worth and self-esteem based on the uniqueness, significance and importance of the individual;
- the value of loving our neighbours, of esteeming them and promoting their growth and well-being rather than pursuing our own interests at the expense of those around us;
- the value of community and the responsibility of businesses to take the social and human dimension into their areas of shareholder accountability;

## *Factors in Equality*

There are a number of factors that may influence equality: apart from the twin processes of legislation and education are those of political arrangements and of personality. At the national level one might be concerned at the idea that lobbying is done at all. Bearing in mind that MPs are responsible to their electorates it does seem odd that their loyalty should be to a party line rather than to the people who elected them, although it may be argued that 'a party' represents certain aspirations. It is thus that the notion of having lobbyists may be inappropriate, an interesting question. At the general level one might (or might not) be concerned that all refugees are welcome, and that may be at odds with the idea that political decisions affecting the electorate (and the country) should be at variance with the welcoming-all argument. This is clearly a debate that every country should have (provided that all adult women are included in the electorate).

It is instructive to note that human values follow a normal distribution. At one extreme is that of personal psychopathy where a dominant individual misuses power to foster their own interests and ideas. At the other extreme are those whose saintly style is constructive, helpful, and well-intentioned. While we can do less about the dominating psychopath we can, and should, provide the safeguards of the rule of law. The requirement that no-one may occupy a position of political power for more than an agreed period (restricted incumbency), and that member-nations of the UN may be required to conform to all of the principles lest they be expelled (or not).

## *Globalisation*

To all of this we might add the increasing globalisation of markets, and is of particular relevance to countries with, respectively high and low standards of living. The inequality of the cost of labour, and of production, gives economic favour to some nations at the expense of others. The press for developers and entrepreneurs to have their way may be regarded as a press to inegalitarianism. Most recently it has even been suggested that, due to the intervention of robots, human labour will not be as necessary as heretofore, and therefore everyone deserves a minimal living wage regardless of whether they work or not.

The notion of 'commercial in confidence' is to be viewed with suspicion. On one view, if public money is involved the people have the right to know how it is being spent. Once a contract is signed it should be public and therefore available. *The Golden Rule* has 'been rewritten as 'He who has the gold makes the rules'. That notion that 'might is right' has been overturned as a basis of morality. In addition to the power of ruling elites there is the issue of disparity of wealth. This comes in at least two forms: one is where individuals are given salaries that are a factor of many times the average income. Millions of dollars a year are allotted to CEOs of major companies, in some cases many many times the average national salary. The other case is where multi-national corporations have an effect on government policies. Their power is not in the ballot box but, rather, in the economic power that they wield. It is potentially disturbing that much of the economic power is owned by a relatively small proportion of the population.

## *Income*

In a 2008 paper 'Household wealth' (Davies et al. 2008b in References: see also Davies, Lluberas & Shorrocks) referred to the world's distribution of income. While one may be aware of factors other than wealth, but it does provide both security and opportunity. The absence of social safety-nets is also of importance. A substantial part of the world's wealth is located in North America and Europe. More importantly these areas contain the top 1% of all wealth-holders. It is that feature that is a concern that such a disparity is inimical to equality.

## *Industrial Consequences*

For example, one could institute safe procedures (as in workplace safety) but do not. Both kinds of case show a contempt for life, as though life is measured in terms of profit rather than valued for itself. One calls to mind the case of the time just prior to the French revolution a carriage speeding through a village and, on the way, killing a child of one of the local peasants. On realising what had been done the aristocrat threw a coin through the window for 'compensation' as though a coin was compensation enough for the life of a child.

One of the significant moves to equality was the notion, during the industrial revolution, was the move by the Cadbury family of Quakers to make life more agreeable to workers. Instead of treating them as industrial fodder they were treated as human beings, with all that that entails. Among the items that were introduced by Cadbury was that of good housing: without such a background, all else would seem to be trivial. The improvements not only included housing but also such issues as a living wage and the encouragement of a social life. What was most instructive was the improvement in production when workers were treated well, thereby showing the beneficial consequences of recognizing a common humanity.

## *Lovelock & Darwin*

The one-world proposition found an impressive exponent in Lovelock had already coined the term Gaia - named for the Greek Goddess of the Earth. This notion embraces the idea that the physical, biological and chemical environments form a complex whole, and that life and the environment interact rather than exist as separate systems. It is recognition of the idea that organic and inorganic forms are interdependent. As Lovelock put it, the earth must be seen as a whole, as a single organism it keeps this world as a place fit for life. This hypothesis, this model, in which the Earth's living matter, air, oceans, and land surface form a whole and complex system which can be seen as unitary, which has the capacity to keep our planet as a fit place for life. in other words, we are exhorted to see the unity of nature as well as that of humanity (see Lovelock in References). Reference is also made to Darwin, whose epoch-making discoveries, led to the common acceptance to the theory of evolution.

## *Marxism*

There was a brave attempt to give power to workers: in other words, to give power to the proletariat – Marxism. That powerful movement resulted in the Russian revolution of 1917 that deposed Tsarist rule. It was ultimately seen to lead to the tyranny of the party, and to Stalinist rule. There have been other attempts at socialism, which have been more successful: one has in mind the adoption of the Scandinavian approach.

## *Migration*

The general trend of migration has been to move from countries in which scant value is put on human life; where tyrants abound, and dictatorships prevail, and circumstances are most troublesome. Moves to countries where the rule of law is commonplace, where equal value is put upon lives, are seen as desirable destinations. Corruption involves not only inequalities but also the misuse of office for private gain, and has deceit as one of its major components. It is small wonder that millions of the displaced seek asylum elsewhere. Later in this work an analysis, and some solutions, are proffered.

For millions living in abject poverty, and often in tyrannies and turmoil, there is a wish to seek a better life. The number of displaced people in the world: that circumstance includes refugees, the internally displaced, the stateless, victims of natural disasters, and asylum seekers. In all such categories involve over 59 million (or thereabouts) people - more than enough to start a new state. In noting this one has to recognise that any one country has a limited capacity to absorb migrants, while imperilling the right of existing citizens to enjoy the fruits of previous objections, riots, and civil disobedience.

One is mindful of the nuances of allowing in an excess of migrants. As a matter if nuance, among such concerns is that of migrants tolerating lesser conditions than were previously available to existing citizens, and that on the grounds of would-be immigrants being so pleased with social improvements as to not object to the finer points of freedom currently enjoyed by existing citizens. Where those displaced from their homeland go is one question: another is what drives them to seek a new life elsewhere. Among such factors are those of corruption. Where corruption abounds, other things follow in train. For example, it exacerbates inequality, it enhances the income and power of ruling elites, and tends to political instability.

## *People Smugglers*

Most recently the concept of people smugglers came to the fore. In that 'enterprise' people were treated as profit-making entities rather than as ends in themselves. To treat humans thus is to degrade them to the level of chattels to be traded for profit. This brings out the qualities that make for humanity: ingenuity, desire for a better life, avoiding corruption, and persistence. All of those qualities are evident in the whole process of wanting to emigrate.

It is an interesting question of why the rich Gulf states are not taking in refugees from either Syria nor Myanmar (Bahrein, Kuwait, Oman, Qatar, Saudi Arabia, and the UAE). There may be good reasons why they are not signatories, but one would wish to hear of such reasons. The combined GDP is trillions for a combined population of just under 43 million. It is noted that none of the six Gulf monarchies have ever signed the International Convention on Refugee Rights and Statelessness, as of 2017 (see References for International Convention on Refugees: also see Reference to Gulf monarchies): though they contribute huge sums of money and do things, but do not seem to take in their co-religionists. That leaves their co-religionists, and those of like culture, to seek refuge in Europe. Germany has welcomed tens of thousands of Syrian refugees where Australia has a closed borders policy (at least as far as 'boat people' go – but not for those who enter legally and overstay their visas).

## *Personal Privacy*

Part of the egalitarian move is to give personal privacy, where before it was absent. Indeed, it is argued here that the diminution of violence owes its origins to the concept of developing egalitarianism. The idea that 'if you have nothing to hide you have nothing to fear' is anathema. Some issues, such as that of personal privacy, is may be regarded as a breach of human dignity.

Uncurtailed commercialism may be at odds with some features of life values. It is just such an argument that requires that we examine the concept of equality to see what it offers as a guiding principle. No longer do we forbid trade unions, fail to give universal franchise, force little boys up chimneys, no longer condone slavery. It is seen that there is a continuous movement to abolish the death penalty. According to *Amnesty International* 140 countries have abolished the either the legality or the practice of state executions.

Unlike this work, the book on *Freakonomics* has no theme. It is worthy of note that the work of Levitt and Dubner (2005) simply questions that are worth asking. As they noted, '… morality represents the way we would like the world to work and economics represents how it actually does work …'. The questions that they pose are highly varied, and encompass sumo wrestlers, criminology, the naming of minorities, and real estate agents. The one caveat that we do need to enter is that, in the long term, morality does come to dominate other considerations. It is just such a consideration that we see improvement in the human condition, notwithstanding the point of massive population increases.

## *Population Growth*

It is argued here that one of the major problems of the world has to do with unchecked population growth. The move from a population of 1650 billion in 1900 it was over 6000 billion in the year 2000, and in 2050 is estimated to exceed 9300 billion. This planet cannot support such a growth rate: to that we must add the idea that the capacity of the Earth is finite, and the increasing growth of consumption, and of waste disposal, will shortly exceed the capacity of the Earth to cope. In this some cultural expectations are prominently at variance. Whatever the more precise figures, the general argument still stands.

The steady change, dating from abject slavery through various improvements, including the abolition of apartheid, we have seen the move to equality as one that is inevitable but has frequent reversions. The political system, the unequal distribution of economic power, and the force of personality, are among such. A concept of one-world is an underlying precept of the UN, yet it is comprised of many regimes that flout the UN *Declaration of Human Right*s.

## *Precepts Change Over Time*

The notion that precepts may change is evident, express or implied, although this may challenge in the works of Temkin (1993), White (2007), Parfit (2011), Dorling (2012), and Haidt (2012), although Works common to the area question whether equality is desirable. If it is then what type of equality to which we should aspire. Temkin's question is fundamental, and questions when is one situation worse than another with respect to inequality? He imagines three situations: many are free and prosperous and few badly off; a number are not free or well off; and a situation where the number of well off and badly off are about equal. At first glance it would seem that a minority are strongly disadvantaged, the second is where many are oppressed, the third is where the oppressed and the free and prosperous are about equal. Here the fundamental question is 'are they equal'. Parfit's cases pose similar problems. In his work, that of a philosopher, many issues are canvassed, and some solutions contemplated. It is a work that would be of inestimable value to specialists in philosophy.

Haidt's (2012) contribution to the debate on equality has his suggestions as six-fold, they are:

- Care (as distinct from harm)
- Fairness (as opposed to cheating)
- Liberty (as opposed to oppression)
- Loyalty (as opposed to betrayal)
- Authority and respect (as opposed to subversion)
- Sanctity (the opposite of degradation).

The basic message here is moral precepts may well change: what is acceptable at one time may be quite unacceptable at another. His approach puts less pressure on rationality and more on intuition, and may be subsequently modified by discussion. Three recent decisions have played a part in denying the previously endorsed principles: one is the notion of being terminally ill and allowed, with physician help, to die with dignity: a second one is that of putting legislative strictures on the treatment of animals: a third is the right to abortion under certain specified conditions (for example, in cases of rape). Such instances serve to remind us that moral precepts are fluid, and in constant need of re-consideration. It will be seen in the text that various views, the basis of morality are canvassed: all have merit, some more than others.

The overall conclusion to be reached here is that, in the longer term, morals triumphs over economics. For example, slavery is now outlawed in every sovereign state (notwithstanding, slavery persists to this day). It is an irony that one of the countries strongly opposed, and indeed was engaged in a revolt against enslavement, is now one of the countries reputedly has one of the largest portions of enslavement. It is clear that the United Nations is implacably opposed to enslavement and carries it into one of the 1948 principles (Article 4).

## *Race and Power*

Moving now to the topic of race, more recently a more austere scientific approach has been published. It will be seen from the previous comments that there is a wide understanding that humanity has not only a common heritage, but that a ready recognition of that concept that has non-measurable benefits. It is not to be denied that there are nay-sayers, and that psychopaths exist. It is doubly unfortunate that some psychopaths find their way into positions of political power, with consequent serious damage to the quality of life, and destruction of a desirable social fabric.

MPs, too, may be brought down by such matters. Ashley, writing in 1992, noted that 'Few sights equalled the incredulity and dismay of the over-mighty when they were transformed overnight from government to opposition'. As we would now say 'today a proud rooster – tomorrow a feather duster'. Some things endure while others are evanescent – and the move toward equality is one of the enduring ones.

During the period of power of Margaret Thatcher as PM she was asked why, during the life of that Parliament the gap between the richest 10% and the poorest 10% had widened. Her reply was to the effect that one does not make the poor richer by making the rich poorer. This rebuke was not, in fact, originally Thatcher's: economist Milton Friedman had sent different versions of the attack throughout his influential career, but it did tidily sum up the argument Margaret Thatcher enjoined on the British public on her way to Downing Street. The obvious problem with the statement is that it simply assumes some political policies can't improve the incomes of the poor.

The flaw in the Thatcher response: it presumes that nobody could ever seriously support making the poor poorer to make the rich less rich. Admittedly, the idea seems ridiculous, but there's substantial evidence that suggests inequality, in and of itself, generates a whole combination of social problems that are harmful to individual and collective wellbeing. It is therefore conceivable that policies that reduce inequality could be worth pursuing even if they leave everyone, the poor included, with less income than they would otherwise have.

## *Slavery*

One of the most obvious manifestations of inequality is that of slavery. It will be recalled that the skilful legislation of William Wilberforce resulted in the passage of the *Slave Trade Act* of 1807, being finalised in 1833. Indeed, the same precept was promulgated by Governor Arthur Phillip when he was the founding Governor of the newly founded penal settlement in New South Wales. The notion of 'owning' another human is a both a curious, and a gross concept.

Attention is drawn to the work of Wilkinson and Pickett (2009). Their book is entitled *The spirit level*, and addresses the concept of equality, with the sub-title of the book indicating an answer to the question of why countries dedicated to equality almost always do better than do those with lesser concern for equality: they thus provide an economic justification for the adoption of equality. Their work, too, deals with changes over time.

Perhaps we need to draw the conclusion that egalitarianism is an essential of civilised discourse, and is manifest in such features as common courtesy. Indeed, they do hold that there may be a relationship between obedience and being employed to do someone else's bidding. As they say that if you are hired to 'advise on how your company can expand its markets, improve profits, avoid press attention, the chances are that you are not being asked for an ethical opinion' (Wilkinson and Pickett 2009: p. 255).

## *Social Equality*

None of this is not to say that equalisation does not work: some forms of socialism do seem to function better. The best examples of socialist equality seem to be in Nordic countries, and the one in the UK seems moderately, though less successful. This leads to the need for caution in that doctrinaire forms of socialism may lead to ideology. This is a prime example of using the theory itself to deny critics. From this the principle emerges that doctrines are always to be challenged from outside.

To all of this we might add the way in which the microchip has changed the way that humans interact. This includes the storage, and data matching, of enormous amounts of information. Added to this is the interconnectivity of people who now interact electronically where before it was interpersonal. As the modern saying has it, they seek refuge from people in things, thereby changing the nature of human relationships.

## *The British Empire*

The British Empire was, arguably, one of the most successful empires ever seen. It must be recognised that the changes it wrought is a balance of benefits and drawbacks. It is the only Empire which has converted to a Commonwealth of Nations, currently involving over a quarter of the world's sovereign states. It is considered desirable to join, and being expelled is a moral negative (since the inception of the Commonwealth, four nations have been suspended: Fiji (twice), Pakistan (twice), Zimbabwe and Nigeria (or, to technically correct, suspended).

In its earlier history it sent convicts to settle Australia, England dominated many other nations and used 'gunboat diplomacy' to enforce its wishes. Against this one might keep a sense of balance: for example, it outlawed the Indian practice of Suttee (the immolation of a wife on the funeral pyre of the dead husband). The benefit of built infrastructure is balanced against some exploitation of Indian resources: the child marriage was outlawed in 1929, but is to be balanced against the failure to outlaw the caste system. Even on that topic there is ambiguity. Under British rule Brahmins had certain privileges restored: on the other hand, British administrators did not sanction the use of harsher punishments for lower castes – that is, for the same offence. From all of this, the major offence was not allowing India to be self-determining.

India was seen as a whole but, in other parts of the world, there was national ambiguity. European administrators constructed 'countries' by lines on a map. They did so without regard to racial, tribal, or religious boundaries. It is just such a circumstance that is one of the sources of conflict in contemporary Africa. Where substantial social disparities exist, there must be a tendency to follow the majority view, leading to the sorry treatment of minorities. It is just such a moral approach that is the basis of modern judgment.

## *UN Reference to 'Mankind'*

It is also worth noting that in the third paragraph of the Preamble it refers to 'man' rather than to humanity. One presumes that this is meant in the generic sense whereas, as seen in the chapter on sex differences (it would have been improved by the clear understanding of 'man' embracing 'woman') as a fundamental press for equality. There are arguments in favour of such a conclusion, but the most fundamental is that of morality: people should be equal, taken as a basic proposition.

The general conclusion to be reached is the fundamental importance of the desirability of equality. The different kinds of equality so matter, is regarded as independent yet connected. Although there are different kinds of equality they are mutually dependent – one could argue that they are mutually dependent. One could not have one without the other.

It will be argued in this work that the desirability of equality is a premise that supersedes others. The various arguments in support of equality are outlined: in the longer term, ethics trumps economics. The view is held that that which unites us is far more powerful than that which divides. We share a common human history in its wider sense, and we share· a common biological heritage. In all of this we are agents of time: we do not exist in an eternal now, and do not function in the world as entities that perceive the world afresh on every new occasion. The history we carry is common to our biology, and of the concept (even if not the content) of our cultural heritage: we are moved by commonly held passions, concerns, and motives.

## *Utopias*

In a world that demonstrates its imperfections there have been various attempts to show how an ideal world would operate. Shangri Las, Utopias, and 'come the revolution' have small impact on this world except as speculations. Indeed, one needs to go back to Plato's *Republic* to see an early instance. Plato's division of society into instances as 'men of bronze, men of silver, and men of gold' is non-egalitarian. In more modern parlance one may be better with guiding principles that invest our understanding, guide us as to what to do, and generally act as beacons of hope: that would be egalitarian. In a similar vein one might argue that the Mozarts, the Michael Angelos, and the Shakespeare of this world are unique.

In a similar vein we have the case of Machiavelli in *The prince*. He is often criticised on the grounds that he is politically cynical, and even subversive. In his defence one would have to say that he was simply recording the best way for a prince to behave to be successful. It is plain that the descriptive and the moral realms are different realms of discourse (see Machiavelli 1532).

There have been cases where writers have attempted to define an ideal society. Perhaps the best-known is the already mentioned *Utopia* by Thomas More, set on an island. The plot revolves around the notion of how to maintain a 'good' society, and is an account of how Thomas More envisaged a society so ideal that medical practitioners are starving. His early account is one of the best-known in the Western canon (although it is noted in *Utopia* that enslavement is the fate of those who, for instance, are captured in battle, although their children are not enslaved, it is also the fate of adulterers) (see More and *Utopia*).

Another one, also well-known is that of Shangri La in a story called *Lost horizons* by James Hilton. His epic is set in the Himalayas, and is a confected account of the ideal place to live. As it is a more recent account the passengers in a plane were stranded in the ideal valley. What makes the account unusual is the criteria of what constitutes satisfaction. What we are to make of this is that it concentrates our attention of what it means to be satisfied with social circumstances. In an ideal world the construction of an ideal society is instant: in practice it seems to be the result of slow change and development.

One is taken with idea that perfect societies are basic and relatively unchanging. That view is contradicted by the proposition of Toffler (1970), who noted that it is not change that is disturbing as much as the accelerating rate of change. We are consuming the earth's resources at an alarming high rate, and there will come a time when such use exhausts the capacity of the planet to sustain such use. Consideration might be given to containing unbridled population growth on the grounds of unsustainability.

## *Violence*

Of like kind is the Pinker book, *The better angels of our nature* (2011). In that work he outlines the case for the steady diminution of violence over the centuries. This seemingly debatable proposition is convincingly argued. One might argue that it is the concept of quality that invests many other concepts. Here the notion of egalitarianism one of the geneses of the diminution of violence: it may also be a long-term trend that conduces to civilised society.

It might also be said of Pinker's work that in the chapter 5 (*The Long Peace*) he addressed the issue in terms of the population at the time that cruelty and slaughter were committed. He concluded that the Lushan Revolt of the eighth century ranked first; the Mongol conquests of the thirteenth century ranked second; and the Middle East slave trade of the seventh to the nineteenth century ranked third. The millions of dead in the Second World War ranked 9th.

This raises the question that, since there are more people, then the quantum of pain and suffering might increase. Having noted that it is apt to point to Pinker's conclusion that, in the section on 'Reason' he said '… people might be dumbfounded when asked whether we should burn heretics, keep slaves, whip children, or break criminals on the wheel, yet those very debates took place several centuries ago.

## *Women*

One of the most deeply entrenched prejudices is that against women. It will be seen in the relevant chapter that some states do severely discriminate against women. Some countries even deprive them of many human rights already accorded to men, restricting the rights to do even the simplest things. In Western societies it is known as the glass ceiling whereby women may look through it to better aspirations, but be often denied the actuality. Recent moves to ensure that women represent a due proportion of (say) boards is one way of making that happen.

When the current writer was on a committee that had called for expressions of interest, and one of the applicants was a woman. The discussion was, understandably, wide ranging. One person said of the strongest applicant that it is all very well to consider that applicant, 'but it is still a woman'. One of the arguments was that, despite the clear qualifications for membership 'they did not need the money as they had a husband' – clearly a denial of merit.

## Conclusions

The notion is that there are two kinds of relative contempt, of inequality, for consumers: one example is the active one of allowing a car to be marketed which is known to be unsafe on the active calculation that compensation in litigation is cheaper than manufacturing a safety device for inclusion. The second kind is the passive one where preventative action could be taken, but is not, one example being the use of unsafe machinery.

# Chapter 2
# Physical Matters

## Introduction

This chapter makes mention of several physical factors that either intervene or promote equality. Among the various issues nominated are those of physical attributes, genes, DNA, the environment, geographical location, climate, and available resources. Amongst other things is the issue of physical over-crowding. The mere fact of population surge, of climate change, and of the complex relationships between those variables, make the mix a heady brew. The idea of physical factors in the search for equality commonly founders on the rock of commercial viability. It is argued here that moral arguments in favour of equality eventually may take precedence over those of commerce, witness the relatively recent invention of ethics committees.

There can be little doubt that local conditions significantly influence a peoples' circumstances, and thus their approach to life. While it is recognised that no race is superior to any other overall it must be recognised that some races have an inherent ability to cope with what was, to them, a hostile environment. For example, the Australian Aborigines were superb at desert survival, as were the Bedouin. Eskimos splendid at cold weather coping, as were Laplanders. Each race developed its own methods of surviving and prospering in the environment in which it found itself. Climate change factors impact more upon the poor rather than the wealthy, for the wealthy have the option of moving, of making life easier with the appropriate use of technology, and the financial ability to cope in an ever-changing world.

## Ancient Injunctions

In the first book of the Bible (KJV Genesis 1: 28) it was held that God said



R. Francis, *Equality in Theory and Practice*,
https://doi.org/10.1007/978-981-15-3488-1_2

> … be fruitful, and multiply, and replenish the earth, and subdue it: and have dominion over the fish of the sea, and over the fowl of the air, and over everything living thing that moveth upon the face of the earth.

This injunction, in context, may be taken to mean that when the earth was underpopulated there was reason to multiply. It also implies that 'dominion over' means using non-humans always for human's benefit. Such an injunction could be taken to mean that other creatures are not to be considered as sentient beings.

## Theorists

There are significant theorists to provide explanations of what occurs, and what will occur. The ideas of Malthus, Darwin, Lovelock, and Hobhouse, accommodate some of our ideas. The notion of economic equality is given in the Gini index (where 10 or 100 equals maximum inequality). Notwithstanding, one cannot have genuine social equality without there being economic equality. It is to that end that we bend our thoughts. The one idea that is canvassed here is that the constant growth of humanity presents a continuing problem – and is most pressing in the absence of practical justification. Examples of four theorists are given; Malthus, Darwin, Lovelock, and Hobhouse. Each deal with a wider aspect of less apparent implications.

### *Malthus*

Malthus' essay (*An essay on the principle of population*) in 1798, and of the eugenics movement is seminal. The Malthusian concern centred upon population growth, in which he held that populations tend to increase geometrically whereas the food supply only increases arithmetically: the result being the reduction of wealth, and the suffering of the population: disease, starvation, and war being endemic. Such a view was one of the earliest classical expressions of population size, and a critique of unbridled population growth.

The seminal essay of Thomas Malthus held that, of the various forms of birth control, abstinence from sexual congress, and delayed marriage were viable solutions (see Malthus in References). Here the dilemma was that of directing birth control to a populace inured to unchecked births without consideration of infant mortality. The population increase is not of the well-educated but, rather, of those of lesser educational accomplishments. It is thus that eugenics was proposed. What one might say is that unchecked population growth might delay equalising social structures. Unchecked eugenics means that some are breeding stock while others are not. Here one of the dilemmas is 'which stock'.

## *Darwin*

Darwinism is one of the most impressive arguments in the history of science. It is a doctrine in which nature is 'red in tooth and claw' (as Tennyson put it). One might argue that morality is a human invention, and is one fully deserving of credit for being concerned. The notion of competition within and between species is one which, as has been put poetically 'so careful of the type she seemed, so careless of a single life'). The idea of personal morality is a more recent concern: the value of individuals is now to the fore as distinct from the universal benefits. To note that Darwin was unconcerned with individual morality is to do him an injustice, (as it is with Machiavelli): he was simply reporting that way that nature appeared to operate.

In 1859 Charles Darwin published On the origin of species. That epoch-making work was formally titled On the origin of species by means of natural selection. The subtitle was given as ' ... preservation of favoured races in the struggle for life'. From his use of the term 'races' an accusation of racism has been levelled. The term 'race' had a different meaning then, and included molluscs. What is important here is the notion that survival characteristics may, or may not, conduce to equality. Regrettable as it may seem, the notion of fitness for survival is critical. It appears that the world is a place without compassion: as Tennyson noted in his poem In memoriam.

> Who trusted God was love indeed
> And love Creation's final law
> Tho' Nature, red in tooth and claw
> With ravine, shriek'd against his creed

So much for ethics. The works of Darwin are seminal in that they present a new view of the world. One cannot think of substantive arguments against his major thesis on evolution. Indeed, the presentation on such issues as evolution, and facial expressions are ground-breaking. Although one would have to recognise the press to understand facial expression at about the same time (as is evident in the early work of Piderit and the later work by Ekman 1985). One of the reasons why we believe so strongly in Darwin's thesis is that it is buttressed by such an array of empirical evidence. It is as though morals is a human invention, being absent in nature.

It was recently pointed out by Parkinson (2017) that it is rare for us to make judgements of facial expression with knowing both the context and accompanying gestures and stances. One is tempted to suppose that morality has no place in evolution.

It is to be noted that Darwinism makes a point of natural inequality. The mere existence of some advantageous quirk confers a survival advantage on a species, and seems a form of inequality, but that is the nature of evolution. The dying out of a non-viable benefit is part of its nature.

One final observation needs to be made concerning morality. Nature, it seems, is indifferent to suffering: some animals become prey, suffering seems to have no curbs, and the quantum of suffering in the world knows no bounds. One does not blame Darwin for this but, rather, was simply recording facts. With this goes the Darwinian idea of the feeling of mutuality, of group cohesion, and togetherness.

## *Lovelock*

James Lovelock invented that concept of what he came to call *Gaia*: a name was originally given to the primal earth Goddess. The idea stems from Lovelock's original work, and has since proposed several new ideas; it included temperature self-regulation, made determinations on ocean salinity, on the regulation of oxygen, and the regulation of carbon dioxide.

It holds that organisms interact with their surroundings in formerly unexplained ways: it proposes that planet Earth is a self-regulating system. The theory sees life as a whole: as a totality of all of the interacting factors that comprise our being. The relevance to the current theme is that morality might be seen as an imposition onto the physical environment and should not interfere with physically ordained events. That said, the relevance here is to what extent may one morally intervene into the physical order: how one must act.

Lovelock (1979) wrote one of the significant books that changed our view of the world. In that work he rightly pointed out that we live on an inhabitable planet that needs nurturing. The *Gaia* principle is that organisms interact with inorganic matter. These form a synergistic form of self-regulation. The biosphere is a self-correcting mechanism consisting of temperature / salinity / oxygen / hydrosphere, all of which lead to evolution, and thus terrestrial habitability. In a series of works he outlined his main contentions, and proposed solutions to such problems as do exist.

For example, the ocean's having areas which are nutrient-rich and other areas which are nutrient-poor. For that problem he proposed ocean pipes to convey nutrient-rich areas to nutrient-poor ones. That also has the advantage of having a cooling effect. The coldness of ocean depths, and of the coldness of the Arctic regions could offset the heating of the Earth, as the oceans are repositories more so than is the atmosphere. All of this is an attempt to help the Earth heal itself, and make it more amenable to human existence.

The concept of *Gaia* has received impetus from work by Sheldrake who wrote in argument against a simple mechanistic approach. His approach is a holistic one in which organisms are more than disposable means by which lineage continues: they transcend simple mechanism and form part of the unity of nature. Living things differ only in degree, not kind – and so it is with non-living things.

Everything, from crystals to societies, is organised by fields. Morphogenesis is one aspect of morphic wholes. Crystals arrange themselves as they do because they have done so before: morphic resonance is the influence of like on like. What is interesting here is that Sheldrake' s approach, it is claimed, is capable of empirical demonstration. Thus, drugs that never existed before may be tested for their capacity to reorganise, and the case with which they do is a function of the number of times they have done so before. As if it were that they conformed to some superordinate law of nature they would not 'learn' so. As Sheldrake noted, 'mother nature is not an empty fable'. A strong example of this interdependence theme is that of the effect of climate on social and political institutions. (see Heylighen, also for a further discussion of the Sheldrake work see him in References).

In an updated version of *Gaia*, Lovelock (2006) has given us a further analysis. The new book emphasises the importance of the Earth as a pattern of evolution. Where Darwin was concerned to address the evolution of species, Lovelock is concerned to address the role of the Earth, itself a most complex entity. A homeostatic Earth is an essential entity on a living planet. Lovelock's thesis here is that a recognition of the Earth as a total and complex ecosystem is crucial both to our understanding evolution in its widest context, and to our survival as a species. His later book has a valuable glossary which readers will find most helpful. The title of this later work, *The revenge of Gaia,* is particularly apt. The Earth's homeostatic mechanisms continue to operate, and must be allowed to do so despite human industrial and consumer intervention.

## *Hobhouse*

In 1985 a book was published that listed seeds of change (Hobhouse 1985). That work outlined instances of plants that changed the world. Those nominated were:

- Cocoa
- Cotton
- Potatoes
- Quinine
- Sugar
- Tea

What is interesting about this selection is the social ramifications, whatever they may be that each plant engendered. Quinine, for example, derives from the bark of the cinchona tree. Its implications were both as a specific drug to treat malaria thereby making it possible to live in places which were previously uninhabitable (and, among other things, to build the Panama Canal): one of the two major aspects to overcome. It also gave rise to many synthesising experiments: in biochemistry for example, in order to identify the active components. They in turn led to experiments that yielded results that produced new items ranging from pharmaceuticals to plastics, and made commonly available rather than being the preserve of the holders of wealth.

Sugar was, in the eighteenth century, the most traded commodity in the world, and now forms the basis of criticism for its roles in obesity and in diabetes. It is a staple of making foods attractive, it is included in many soft drinks, in sweets, and commonly taken with tea or coffee. It is still the basis of many foodstuffs: indeed, it is hard to avoid taking it when so many foods include it.

Cotton fostered the slave trade (and led to the dark satanic mills, then found in Lancashire towns). Such towns in Lancashire were considered to be ideal as they endured rainfall, and was ideal for cotton spinning. The story of cotton mills in Lancashire have been given prominence, and are still to be seen. Though fading into lesser significance there is still a museum outlining the contribution that the Lancashire cotton mills made. Indeed, Britain was once the largest processor of cotton in the entire world. In 1860 there were 2650 cotton mills in Lancashire, but by the 1930s 800 mills had closed, thereby leaving 345,000 workers to quit the industry.

Tea was implicated in the opium wars in that trading in tea in return for opium. The Amerindian pipe met the Chinese use of opium, and became other than a pipe dream. As the British took to tea so too did the Chinese to opium and thus a lucrative trade was born.

The humble potato, so beloved by the Irish citizenry, led to famine when it blighted – and thus to a large migration. One in minded of the displaced crofters in Scotland who were priced off the land by changes in agricultural practice.

The cocoa plant, the basis of chocolate, was fostered by Quaker families in the UK (Cadbury, Rowntree, Fry) and led them to develop model villages wherein the workers were treated with dignity and respect – and thus to the other significant factories, as outlined elsewhere in this work.

That thesis is clearly a sustainable one in that it shows the social implications of particular plants, and the role that they played in the promotion of human equality. This meaningful but seemingly abstruse connection, draws our attention to the role that some specific plants have had on social consequences. Just as in biology the gene is the transmitting unit of inheritance, so in social matters the meme (the mimic theme), or so it is postulated. Bell-bottom trousers, navel piercing, curious haircuts, and hula hoops were all instances of what was 'fashionable'.

These ideas, like varied instances of karyotypes are put forth by nature to see if they are viable. The imitation of such an inclination would the idea of it being worth a try. The craze is then replicated to see if it continues to be viable and, if so, to become part of the ideas and value system of the culture, as Blackmore (1999) has noted). The purpose of the meme is to propagate itself, just as Dawkins has argued that it is the function of the gene (a chicken is an egg's way of making another egg).

## *Health Accounts*

In an article by Thomas (2017) he entitled it *A scientific strategy for life chances.* The general point that he was making was the connection between cognitive neuroscience and socio-economic status. The general thrust of the point was that there is a critical relationship between early life experience and our life as adults. There is a causal connection between what he called 'life chances', early experience, and cognitive neuroscience. The then British Prime Minister, David Cameron, drew connections between socio-economic status and brain development – with frequent references to neuroscience. The point here being that life chances are not equal for all, there being a connection, particularly with poverty, between such early experience and life chances.

One relevant recent discovery is that of mirror neurones, defined as a nerve cell that fires both when an animal is acting, and also when an animal observes that same action performed by another – hence they are called 'mirror neurones'. Whether they exist in humans may be demonstrated, but what their exact function is remains to be seen. The demonstrated existence of mirror neurones was discovered by Rizzolati & Craighero (2004) at the University of Parma in Italy in the 1980s. Why they are important is because they give a neurological explanation of vicarious behavioural learning.

It is possible, although we do not know how possible, that there are peoples or groups who have a biologically determined drive to wander. This is more than the wanderlust that affects the young but is, rather, a group drive. Among those we might nominate are Romanies, the Bedouin tribes, Australian Aborigines, and some of the Kurdish tribes. Tramps are those within a culture who seem unable to articulate why they behave so. Perhaps it is a tolerance of uncertainty, ambiguity, change, and a life style. Maybe the 'wandering gene' has a complementary one for the 'unchanging life'. That whole issue of cross-cultural uncertainty has been addressed by Phillips and Wright (1979).

In *The Lancet* there was an article by Marmot (2005) on the social determinants of health inequalities. His expressed concern related to substantial differences in life expectancy of 48 between countries, and 20 within. The gross inequalities in health that we see within and between countries present a challenge to the world. A burgeoning volume of research identifies social factors at the root of much of these inequalities in health. Social determinants are relevant to communicable and non-communicable disease alike.

Health status, therefore, should be of concern to policy makers in every sector, not solely those involved in health policy. As a response to this global challenge the World Health Organisation (WHO 2003) launched a Commission on social determinants of health, which reviewed the evidence, raise societal debate, and recommend policies with the goal of improving health of the world's most vulnerable people. A major thrust of the Commission is turning public-health knowledge into political action.

## Topics

### *Aesthetics*

It is a given that much thought and devotion is humanly given to the aesthetics of language, of music, of dance, and of scenery. To deny that such influences exist is to impoverish human experience. It is a commonplace that the appreciation of such enterprises can bring a sense of fulfilment to many lives. Those who aspire to language (such as a Shakespeare), to music (such as a Mozart), to navigation (such as a James Cook), and to painters (such as a van Gogh) seem to be 'sports' in the proper sense of that term. Neither the fathers nor the offspring were geniuses (language constructors, composers, navigators, painters): each of the mentioned experts existed as a one-off, and are accorded due recognition as outstanding talents.

## *Climate*

Human relations are affected by various external factors, including climate, political regimes, and industrialisation. So too do factors interact: thus, climatic changes affect the political scene. Global warming would swamp Pacific island nations, and cause widespread disaster in Bangladesh. It will certainly have implications for sovereignty as they want to move to a land less swamped.

Napoleon, it is said, was defeated at Waterloo by Wellington and Blucher: one could equally well argue that because of Napoleon's inability to get his artillery in place due to the heavy rain, he was defeated as much by climate as by strategy. As the Duke of Wellington so famously remarked of the battle, 'It was a damn close-run thing'.

Another example is that *El Nino* is responsible for periodic famines, floods, and pestilence. The French revolution was brought about by several items: one of them was adverse climatic conditions bringing famine and misery. Equally one could make a point about its impact on agriculture in Ireland leading to potato blight, the great potato famine, and thus to mass emigration. Climatic variables produce a variety of consequences. Temperature affects the rate of crime, particularly personal violence. Early criminologists, Quetelet and Lombroso, dubbed this the 'Thermic law of delinquency'. Rain changes social conditions of outdoor/indoor living, strong wind is upsetting, as school playground minders (and horse breeders) well know.

In parts of Europe there is a well-founded view that particular winds are associated with mood states. Thus, the significance of *Fohn* winds in Europe which are warm, dry, and gusty on the leeward side of mountains: the *Mistral* in France which is a jet stream that runs· up the Rhone valley; the hot oppressive *Sirocco*; and equally hot and oppressive *Hamshin* in Egypt; and the wet and the dry *Monsoons* of India. The effect of powerful winds (such as hurricanes) and of steady and reliable winds (such as the trade winds) is too obvious to need labouring. The associated variables of temperature, relative humidity, sunshine, rain, and barometric pressure all have their effects. The length of dark and light seasons is reputed to have an effect on the national psyche – as is reputed in northern Russia and Finland. The point here is that nature works on the principle of equity: that there has to be harmony and balance in the world or else it is reduced to imbalance, becomes out of control, and would self-destruct. Temperature, humidity, sunshine, rain, and barometric pressure all have their effects. The length of darkness and light all have their effect. One might suppose that in such zones there is a tendency to affect the national psyche (is that why much Russian music tends to be in a minor key?)

## *Maps*

It seems to be an artefact that our maps are politically drawn: those are the maps most familiar to us. One could imagine maps that drew boundary changes that compare 200 years ago with current ones. One could also imagine maps that outline geological features, mineral deposits, of race, or roads, of flora and fauna, of topography, of language, of wealth, and of pollution.

In recent times one of the map ideas is that of geological maps. In his book *The map that changed the world,* Winchester (2002) has detailed the argument for different kind of maps, and illustrated the point by noting that William Smith eventually drew a map of the underground geological structure of Britain. Such a map tells us much about origins of the land, its age, and its composition. It brought into being a wider understanding of the way that people thought about landscapes.

## *Media*

Media, too, has a role to play in perpetuating prejudice, as does the role of entrepreneurs. Media because in yellow journalism they perpetuate myths: entrepreneurs because they favour population growth at the expense of a better quality of life. The idea of the 'need' for a growing population fills the pockets of entrepreneurs who, in turn, lobby governments to foster such growth (increase encouragement to the birth-rate, foster migration). One might contemplate a time when populations are stable. In the shorter term this will result in an ageing population but, in the long term will overcome the problems endemic in the present policy. The notion of migration as a solution is as temporary as is the notion that technology, will become yet more innovative and efficient. There is a physical limit to the number of people this planet will support, and it becomes us to venture solutions. Counter to this is the notion that some peoples are reluctant to allow migrants to enter. Japan, for example, has a low birth-rate but is not keen to allow in migrants: who knows, they may be right.

## *Personal Finances*

It is difficult to determine which way causality goes. Perhaps a critical variable is whether you are making informed decisions about your finances. The virtuous circle question is whether being in financial control makes you happy and healthy, or whether being happy and healthy puts you in better financial control. After the financial crisis, it was noted that fewer people trust financial advice, and with good reason. Maybe the younger generation use the net to get financial advice. It is clear that different generations have varying degrees of financial planning and different methods of acquisition.

## *Population Control Policy*

The emergence of population control is quite recent, and involves contraception. The notion of recreational sex, of infertility being linked to such events, makes it a new concept. The prospect of banning sex is risible: one might as well ban the tides. It appears to be one of the fundamental drives, most particularly of younger humans – and fosters the notion of prostitution (with a consequent increase in venereal disease). Dating from early times, the idea of contraception has had a chequered history. What follows is a list of contraceptive methods:

- Infanticide (safer for the mother, and one knows the sex before 'exposing')
- War as a means of birth numbers
- Homosexuality
- Physical methods: Abortion: needle, purgatives, diuretics, emetics, pessaries, acidulous medicaments, direct pressure, punching, lifting heavy weights, jumping, riding a cart along a rough road, magical recipes.
- Condoms (vulcanisation of rubber in 1844)
- Spermicides
- Abstinence
- Coitus interruptus
- The use of sterile periods

There are reasons for such a press to increase the population. It is interesting to note that both Hitler and Mussolini favoured large families (as a means of replacing the war-dead?). The use of polygamy might also favour population growth where males are in short supply. Consistent with this is the fundamentalist religious view that there is a duty to procreate, with contraception being banned.

From this the term Eugenics is relevant: it means, amongst other things, 'the production of fine offspring', and thus takes one of two forms. Positive eugenics which endorses the production of positive qualities, and negative qualities which endorse the breeding out of undesirable qualities. Here the problem is twofold. One is never quite sure when a genius will arrive.; second, there is the problem of what is an 'undesirable' quality.

Despite such a worthy idea, it carries more dangers than is justified. What exactly would the criteria be for inclusion in any sterilisation programs? Why should certain people be adversely discriminated – particularly by such a questionable criterion? It also assumes that intellect may be the ultimate determiner. We have seen the consequences of the adoption of such an idea, and find it fraught with danger.

The idea that state-sanctioned killing as a means of population control was re-examined recently by Ball (2016). He argued that it cements power structures by giving special exemptions to those senior in the social hierarchy. It is, in other words, a means of propping up the social order. He made reference to the Watts study of (2003), showing the prevalence of sacrifice increased with greater social stratification. Plainly an argument supportive of the notion of equality. As Ball noted '...how rituals could be abused for prosaic gain'. There are several factors that foster growth, of which the role of entrepreneurs is one, others include such items are migration; in all of this, political lobbying must figure prominently. The problem is clearly one of compound growth.

If one were to look for reasons for population growth there would be several candidates. For example, the pressure to grow is a matter of fundamental economics. Entrepreneurs favour such a press because of the way that it fills their pockets. There is a corresponding concern about the donations made to political parties, with the expectation of reward. For economic reasons too, there is a press to migration as a means of increasing the working population. Without continued such growth the population would become, temporarily, and increasingly, aged.

One of the major problems is rate of reproduction of some peoples There is clearly a pressure, on the part of some, to have more children. Without social security children are a means of ensuring that one is minded in one's later years. Plainly there needs to be a system of minding the young in one's age before one can work on the notion of birth control. The Wilkinson (1979) account is that retails the views of the ancients regarding fertility: mention has been made of the concern about over-population in Malthus' essay of 1798.

One of the possible solutions to a low birth-rate is using adoption as a means of increase. Such a surplus of people does point to 'overproduction' of infants in some places. It could be that places do not welcome outsider children. There may a time when underpopulated countries incur an obligation to offer haven to the world's surplus children. The penchant for children of one's own seems to be largely entrenched in prospective parents, but without regard for the sex of the child (at least in some countries). The notion of having an heir, of limiting inheritances, and of primogeniture, are all relevant. It is instructive to note that British Parliament has enacted legislation that guarantees the first-born of royalty succession will have precedence, regardless of their sex, no doubt in response to the job well-done by the British Queen.

As populations grow, and the world becomes more prosperous, such problems will be exacerbated. Migration of itself is not a long-term solution. It is also curious that, for example, the problems in Afghanistan, Iraq, Iran, etc. have not managed to find sanctuary in adjacent Gulf states (Bahrein, Kuwait, Oman, Qatar, Saudi Arabia, and the UAE). With the growth in populations there is a need to foster equality. The European Union, for example, requires certain human rights undertakings before being admitted to the Union.

An instance of effective legislation is given in the case of China where the one-child policy was then introduced because of fecundity: by way of contrast Japan had a declining birth-rate, and introduced a policy of increasing birth-rates. It is evident that such policies do work. In China, for example, there were those who monitored children per couple: that was a necessary step to ensure that people conformed to government rule.

The glib use of such concepts as 'globalisation' often obscures what are some fundamental changes to human life on earth. Such issues as climate change, the loss of biodiversity, and of gross population growth, are changing the world into something not yet contemplated. Taking the last concept, for example, the growth of human population to currently over seven billion makes the issue of food production, living space, the disposal of waste, and the overuse of earth's resources of pressing need for consideration (see World Population in References).

Ancient populations were very small compared to present populations. As such the notion of 'kings' was vastly different from what we understand today. The moral precepts that were formulated then may (or may not) have application in the modern world. A prime example is that the Hippocratic oath forbade abortion. That is a view that appears to be inconsistent with modern legislation on abortion, the current predominant Western view being it is a woman's right to choose. Notwithstanding, the available abortifacients, then available, made it a much riskier business.

## *Racism*

One of the drawbacks of the social world is its tendency to persist with out-of-date attitudes: one such is racism. There have been many attempts to define 'race', with none successful so far. One could suppose that one can tell extremes. Someone with a very dark skin colour is discriminable from someone with a very fair skin. But that problem is rather like the problem of rain. When it is tropical downpour it is clearly raining. When it is a cloudless sky with the sun shining it is clearly not raining: but when does one say it is raining? (two drops per square centimetre per minute? Five drops? 100 drops?).

While there is no sustainable argument in favour of racism, it may lead to a moral dilemma. One would not wish to make racial distinctions, yet not to do so means that indigenous peoples lose their identity. The dilemma here is that racial distinctions are not acceptable, yet to deny an Aboriginal of his/her identity is to do them a disservice, and is a denial of their heritage. Indeed, the whole issue of social justice for the Aboriginal inhabitants is outlined by Behrendt (2003).

It was recognised that some races had an inherent ability to cope with what was, to them, a hostile environment. Each race developed its own methods of surviving and prospering in the environment in which it found itself. It is only recently that the doctrine of *Terra Nullius* (the empty land) was rejected in Australia, and so ruled the High Court (see the Mabo Case in References). One must recognise the existence of the Aboriginal peoples.

### *Statistics*

Any idea of population estimates and control has to be accommodated by statistics. It allows inferences to be drawn, and is the basis of actuarial studies. As the information is collected under obligatory conditions it represents a relatively reliable estimate of social composition and related variables. Before the invention of such the mode of dealing with population was a non-event, thus one needs to make assessments of which statistics are ideal. One might also observe that actuarial predictions are the lifeblood of such issues as insurance (in actuarial studies). It also allows predictions to be made about population growth, and shows that the present rate of population growth, if unchecked, would eventually lead to standing room only on this planet.

Before the invention of such the mode of dealing with population was a non-event. At the present rate of population growth must be subject to some sort of check. Part of that concern is rooted in the Gini index. That indicator was named after Corrado Gini in a paper of 1912. It is commonly used to measure inequality of income but may be used for other purposes, such as any form of uneven distribution. In that index the number 0 corresponds to perfect equality (where everyone has the same income): the number 1 refers to inequality (where someone has all the income and no-one else has any). That has now been extended to 100 for easier comparison. As instances some countries have the following indices: The Scandinavian countries commonly top the list. By way of comparison, using international comparisons; in Latin America Panama ranked 60, Peru 87, and Bolivia 118 – truly a great disparity.

## Technological Solutions

Those with substantial technological power might tend to think of problems as having technological solutions (people might starve so let's build a dam – rather than curb population growth or modify agricultural processes?).

Those with large military establishments tend to resort to military solutions – thereby supporting the doctrine of 'if you wish for peace, you must prepare for war', small countries tend to use their expertise, or to resort to special pleading (we value education and will be a knowledge-based nation), or (we are suffering from our colonial past so consider treating us with redress in mind). It is not suggested here that this is so much a clear hypothesis as an invitation to think that those who consider themselves as hammers are likely to see the world as nails.

Dating from early times, the idea of contraception has had a chequered history. The idea, in early times, of infanticide was one of the preferred methods of reducing the number of adults. It has, at once, two advantages: one is that it is safer than non-medical abortion; second one can determine the sex of the foetus prior to 'sacrifice'.

Among other methods of contraception were those of homosexuality, abortion, various maternal interventions, human sacrifices of adults, and war.

As has been mentioned, there were behavioural methods such as abstinence, coitus interruptus, spermicides, condoms. No story would be complete without reference to the oldest profession in the world, wherein the methods of contraception were well understood. Before that is the idea that it is a function of the way that the economy expresses itself. There is a responsibility for feeding the famished millions. It does, however, seem that different countries have different needs.

## Education and Legislation

There are two basic ways in which one may change the way that people operate: one is by legislation; the other is by education. In an ideal world, they would both be used. It is a truism that early education is more effective than is later learning, known as the Jesuitical seven years (give me the child, and the man is mine). Educating for equality is one of the effective means of inducing and fostering it. It is the unconscious messages that are so effective. If one were to play 'when I am dictator' one of the items one might address is that of equalising education, particularly in schooling. It is clear that inculcating attitudes of equality in the early years is most important. It is thus that, for example, Finland does have local governmental schools which pupils attend. Such an education runs from age 7 to age 16. Such a notion of is basic to equality, particularly in the relative absence of private schools of various kinds.

## Conclusions

Does one help individuals in the here and now, or have the long-term view (such as birth control). Food, water shortage, sewage and waste disposal are many of the problems of over-population. This leads to the question of whether sustainable economic growth is possible? Among the variables that one would identify are the ones of climate, terrain, local resources and wealth. Here it is apt to note that the richest billionaires control as much wealth as the world's poorest 50%: a circumstance that unbalances the social equation. Various theorists have each made their contribution-insights into the issues, and we find such contributions invaluable.

# Chapter 3
# Psychological Approaches

## Introduction

Unless there are human commonalities the world would be idiosyncratic to the point of being impossible to understand. Without our commonalities there would be no art, no world literature, no United Nations, no basis of any communication and, indeed no major religions. The works of Plato, the *Bible,* the *Koran*, the *Bhagavad Gita*, Tolstoy's *War and peace*, Hiroshige's *Tokkaido*, no Charles Dicken's *David Copperfield*, Machiavelli's *The Prince*, and classical fairy tales are all examples of trans-cultural and trans-temporal appeal. Psychobiology would make no sense, comparative psychology would be equal nonsense, religion would be idiosyncratic, international trade unachievable, and human interchange impossible.

Instances include that ordinary Americans could be persuaded to electrocute someone to death if instructed to do so by a man in a white coat (as in the *Studies in Obedience*: Milgram 1963); that the institution of sight to a formerly blind person results in instant accurate sight and perception; that there is a willingness to endorse contradictory statements (out of sight, out of mind, and absence makes the heart grow fonder); that over one third of people report hallucinations (where it is common only expressed that such a phenomenon is confined to the disturbed); and that teenagers working during high school is helpful (whereas some studies show that work harms teenagers' academic work – a moot point). The major point here is that whether something is 'obvious' or not it is still worth exploring. Even if 90% of what we do turns out to be useless it is the only way in which we will discover the useful 10% residue.

Those with substantial technological power might tend to think of problems as having technological solutions. Those with large military establishments tend to resort to military solutions. Small countries tend to use their expertise, or to resort to special pleading. It is not suggested here that this is so much a clear hypothesis as an invitation to think that those who consider themselves as carpenters are likely to see the world as timber.



R. Francis, *Equality in Theory and Practice*,
https://doi.org/10.1007/978-981-15-3488-1_3

News is timeliness. Not all crises are reported on the 7 o'clock news, and the reporting of news items is, of its nature, highly selective. The death of 3000 in the New York World Trade Centre was reported about as extensively as could be. The death of ten times that number in an earthquake in Asia, or that number of victims of a famine elsewhere, are not seen as equally newsworthy. Perhaps the reporting of those places where mega-deaths are commonplace has exhausted our emotional empathy so that we no longer relate to them as human problems. News, by its nature, is a high-turnover enterprise: hyperbole is the order of the day, and every other day.

Wars on the Horn of Africa, famine in Pakistan, fighting in Afghanistan become so commonplace that we feel inured to them. The wrecking of the Berlin wall, Israeli tanks at the Church of the Nativity in Bethlehem, and a balloon flight around the world have novelty. While most news is of the woe and tragedy kind there are numerous instances of positive humanitarian acts, commentaries on the oddities of life, and the occasional positive assertion – even if only symbolic. On a more constructive note it is pleasing to see that the Council of European Ministers meeting in Strasbourg in 1972 creatively adopted the Beethoven *Ode to Joy* as the anthem of European unity.

It is interesting to note that we call our common past 'culture', but have no word for our common future. While it is so that different cultures have differing attitudes to time, that might be better exemplified by considering those who have internalised two cultures, as is the case with the children of migrants. It would require them to 'time-switch' depending upon the context of their social interactions: are they 'clock-oriented' or 'sun-oriented': is it a 'make-it-happen' culture? Precision in one culture may be an unacceptable obsession in another.

Culture is the way in which we remember our social heritage. There is too the complementary view that nations need to forget in order to move on. Thus, how could a proud nation such as the French recover from the humiliation of their almost prompt capitulation to the Germans in WW II; how could the British recover from the early excesses of colonialism; and how could the Japanese remit the atrocities they committed within the last 80 years. There are recoveries from shamed memories: thus, the Germans' recovery from the Nazi era uses a self-conscious. Recognition of atrocities and a determination to prevent a recurrence: indeed, the German Constitution is a model. It recognises that the essence of a constitution is its recognition of the rights of individuals. It is also the source of public power and sets the limits of state power.

One aspect of some cultures is their capacity not to forget and not to forgive. Ancient wrongs, hatred of particular religious groups, remembrance of battles fought and lost from hundreds of years before, and vendettas are all manifestations of this notion. Given our life span, and the fixity of early educational experiences it is apt to remind ourselves that the institutions we see in current time are relatively evanescent.

Conquering nations was the way to economic imperialism, now economics has been added as a means: the extinction of sovereignty may be by any one of several causes: union, conquest, economic power, agreement, or civil war. The notion of secession (as, for example, from the European Union) is given new meaning, though it derived from the Hanseatic League to the modern European Union: sovereignty is a changing concept.

## Psychological Bases of Behaviour

One idea that spans both the physiological and psychological realms is that of the existence of 'pleasure centres'. The physiological work that identified the 'pleasure centres' of the brain may be, in part, an explanation of the phenomenon. In the 1950s there was a remarkable discovery by Olds and Milner (1954), leading to the existence of cortical localisation of 'pleasure centres'in the brain. This discovery, found in rats, was that electrical stimulation in certain septal areas of the cortex led to behaviour that was so impressive that it led to bar pressing for stimulation at the rate of many presses per hour. For work on that study see Kringelbach and Berridge 2010).

The original conception of 'pleasure centres' must now give way to the notion of pleasure systems. In just that same way we must now recognise that stimuli to such systems involve external rewards as well electrical and chemical stimuli. The appearance of such an experience was the subject of a survey and report by Laski (1961). She noted that it seemed to be a spontaneous occurrence, often a mystical union between two people, often couples, and was more widespread than previously thought. What is of interest here is that the intellectual expression of our unity seems distinctly mundane by comparison (see Hammersely et al. 2002, in References). What follows are three illustrations of the contributions of psychology.

### *The Ecstatic Phenomenon*

The now hackneyed expression 'deep and meaningful' would be appropriate here were it not so hackneyed. This notion of an overwhelming experience, of a spiritual insight and of ineffable peace and divine union seems to be common to humanity, even though its expression may vary. It is also reported in many cultures. Such ecstasies do not commonly seem to be induced at will, nor are they currently quantifiable. The raptures of religious mystics seem to be part of that genre of experiences, as do the insights of some seers.

There are relatively common instances of peak mental experiences reported, sometimes as individuals and sometimes between couples. The concept of ecstasy is common to many cultures. The feelings of unutterable peace, of divine union, and of ineffable ecstasy, have been expressed in many different ways. The mystical experience reported by many is epiphanic. It is a feeling of one-ness, of unsurpassed joy, and of rapture. It has been reported variously by writers, such as Koestler, and C S Lewis. Mariners, too, report it, one of whom was Sir Francis Chichester (a navigator) which he, with unintended pun, nominated as the 'oceanic feeling'. The unity with nature appears in various works, such as *Childe Harold's Pilgrimage* of which Byron wrote, 'Are not the mountains, waves, and skies, a part of me and of my soul, as I of them'; and Wordsworth noted (with reference to the French Revolution) that 'Bliss it was in that dawn to be alive, and to be young was very heaven'.

Such ecstasies do not commonly seem to be induced at will, nor are they quantifiable. The raptures of religious mystics seem to be part of that genre of experiences, as do the insights of some seers, some mediators, and of authors. Aldous Huxley, writing in *The doors of perception* (1954) was under the influence of mescaline and reporting on the Van Gogh painting of a chair. What we, in our ordinary state, regard as a common chair may be seen quite differently by others. Huxley's view of the chair was that it was invested with unutterable meaning: his words to describe it were 'empty, yet charged with the meaning and mystery of existence'. There may well be cultural ways of inducing such transcendental states. Among these are meditation, whirling (as with the Dervishes), incantations, drugs, posture, and particular experiences.

More recent work has focussed upon the chemical bases of such behaviour (see, for example, Albert 1985). The important issue here is, what is the survival value of such reward systems? Clearly, there must be some rewards and punishments that have survival value: equally clearly there are reward systems that do not have survival value – nicotine addiction in smoking, for example. This is a commonplace example of how chemical rewards, with no demonstrable value may be counterproductive to survival. That general approach is confirmed in the study of neurology (see Neurology in references) where it was demonstrated the diversity of the neural signal, and with the psychedelic state.

Another variant of an epiphanic experience is that of setting up possible Utopias. That Utopian dream has found expression in many ways. It could be of a kind that emerges from a rational debate, as in Plato's *Republic*, or of the fanciful way of Sir Thomas More in his book *Utopia*: it could be the cultural myths of a *Shangri La*. An economic version of an attempt at an economic utopia is given in such places as Robert Owen's *New Lanark*. What is important here is that the practical expressions which are democratically based, as in the *Mondragon* combine in Spain (see Mondragon in references) seem to be most effective. The high-level ideological aspirations seem to be too lofty to be of such practical long-term benefit except, perhaps, as exemplars of perfection.

The transcendence of nationalism, international culture, and the withering of cultural roots are the hopes and aims of rationalist liberals. Urbanisation, vulnerability, and exploitation lead to the need to protect one's brethren. There is a tension and an opposition between the scientific and impersonal government and the personalised and incommensurable feeling of identity and connectedness. The perfectibility of humanity, and the foundation of a *Utopia* are unlikely to happen because it would involve yielding ethnicity and nationalism – two of the major forms of loyalty, and of our self-concept, and of practical importance … the two main shows in town.

There are relatively common instances of peak mental experiences reported, sometimes as individuals and sometimes between couples. The concept of ecstasy is common to many cultures. The feelings of unutterable peace, of divine union, and of ineffable ecstasy, have been expressed in many different ways. The mystical experience reported by many is epiphanic. It is a feeling of one-ness, of unsurpassed joy, and of rapture. It has been reported variously by writers, such as Koestler, and C S Lewis. Mariners, too, report it, one of whom was Sir Francis Chichester (a navigator) which he, with unintended pun, nominated as the 'oceanic feeling'. The unity with nature appears in various works, such as *Childe Harold's Pilgrimage* of which Byron wrote, 'Are not the mountains, waves, and skies, a part of me and of my soul, as I of them'; and Wordsworth noted (with reference to the French Revolution) that 'Bliss it was in that dawn to be alive, and to be young was very heaven'.

Such ecstasies do not commonly seem to be induced at will, nor are they quantifiable. The raptures of religious mystics seem to be part of that genre of experiences, as do the insights of some seers, some mediators, and of authors. Aldous Huxley, writing in *The doors of perception* (1954) was under the influence of mescaline and reporting on the Van Gogh painting of a chair. What we, in our ordinary state, regard as a common chair may be seen quite differently by others. Huxley's view of the chair was that it was invested with unutterable meaning: his words to describe it were 'empty, yet charged with the meaning and mystery of existence'. There may well be cultural ways of inducing such transcendental states. Among these are meditation, whirling (as with the Dervishes), incantations, drugs, posture, and particular experiences.

More recent work has focussed upon the chemical bases of such behaviour (see, for example, Albert 1985). The important issue here is, what is the survival value of such reward systems? Clearly, there must be some rewards and punishments that have survival value: equally clearly there are reward systems that do not have survival value – nicotine addiction in smoking, for example. This is a commonplace example of how chemical rewards, with no demonstrable value may be counterproductive to survival. That general approach is confirmed in the study of neurology (see Neurology in references) where it was demonstrated the diversity of the neural signal, and with the psychedelic state.

Another variant of an epiphanic experience is that of setting up possible Utopias. That Utopian dream has found expression in many ways. It could be of a kind that emerges from a rational debate, as in Plato's *Republic*, or of the fanciful way of Sir Thomas More in his book *Utopia*: it could be the cultural myths of a *Shangri La*. An economic version of an attempt at an economic utopia is given in such places as Robert Owen's *New Lanark*. What is important here is that the practical expressions which are democratically based, as in the *Mondragon* combine in Spain (see Mondragon in references) seem to be most effective. The high-level ideological aspirations seem to be too lofty to be of such practical long-term benefit except, perhaps, as exemplars of perfection.

The transcendence of nationalism, international culture, and the withering of cultural roots are the hopes and aims of rationalist liberals. Urbanisation, vulnerability, and exploitation lead to the need to protect one's brethren. There is a tension and an opposition between the scientific and impersonal government and the personalised and incommensurable feeling of identity and connectedness. The perfectibility of humanity, and the foundation of a *Utopia* are unlikely to happen because it would involve yielding ethnicity and nationalism – two of the major forms of loyalty, and of our self-concept, and of practical importance … the two main shows in town.

## *Maslow's Hierarchy of Needs*

On a slightly different note, Maslow published his development of the hierarchy of needs model in 1943. Basically, it is a five-stage model. The lower levels are deficiency needs and the top level is growth needs. One of axioms that Maslow espouses is that the lower needs must be satisfied before the next level in the hierarchy is satisfied (proposition 7). One would question that original proposition: many people will die for a cause, no matter (for example) how hungry they are. Further, one sees altruistic behaviour without lower needs being met. A parent will personally starve in order to feed their child. One could hold, with Maslow, that a person may fluctuate between levels of the hierarchy: not every movement in the hierarchy will move in only one direction. The five basic levels are:

- The physical needs (air, drink, warmth etc).
- Safety need include security, law, stability, etc.
- The third level involves belongingness, and includes love, friendship, and being part of the social body.
- The fourth level are called esteem needs, and involve reputation, respect, and independence.
- The highest level involves being self-actualised, fulfilled, growth, and the feeling of ecstasy.

It is interesting, and perhaps parochial, to suggest with Maslow, that Eleanor Roosevelt was a self-actualised person, although he did nominate Abraham Lincoln and Albert Einstein as self-actualised (Gandhi? Helen Keller?). The behaviour that is characteristic of being self-actualised includes being absorptive and concentrative, being totally honest, and sticking to a belief if their views did not match those of the majority (see Maslow in References).

In a later stage model the five-point hierarchy was expanded to seven, then an eight-stage model. Between stages four and five he inserted two more – cognitive needs and aesthetic needs. After the seventh stage (self-actualisation) he inserted 'transcendence'. For Maslow, the emphasis was on the process: it will also be noted that the focus is upon the positive aspects of personality rather than upon psychopathology. One would have to be aware of the work generated by such a theory (see, for example, Lester 2013).

## *The Phi Phenomenon*

Psychology sometimes offers something seemingly minor but which turns out to be of major importance. In the early days of psychology in Germany, in the nineteenth century, one early worker was investigating the phenomenon of apparent movement. The notion under investigation was that if one had two lights that could go on and off under carefully timed control, they could be arranged to make movement seem to appear. Suppose that a left-hand light was on and then went off and the right-hand light, which was off, went on. If the timing was right, an apparent movement from left to right was reported.

The researcher devised a set of laws that seem to govern such movement. Korte's laws held that the distance between the lights, the distance of the observer from the plane of the lights, and the timing of the lights all influenced perceived movement – even though nothing moved. That phenomenon was called the *Phi phenomenon.* Five other forms of apparent movement were investigated. *Beta Movement* was an example – the apparent movement of an object from one position to another.

These seemingly esoteric findings found later expression in one of the world's now major enterprises – the moving image: nothing moves on the screen in a cinema or on a TV screen, yet movement is apparent. It is near impossible to overcome the illusion that something moves. and even that the sound of a voice is coming from elsewhere in the room is perceived as coming from the image that seems to move. The findings, and their later developments, gave rise to the motion picture industry, to making animated cartoons possible, to seemingly moving neon signs, and to television. It is a prime example of how academic psychology has unknowingly contributed to an enterprise that has given so much pleasure to so many millions. Such findings are of great value, but not if any new discovery, or confirmation or disconfirmation, are from a point of view that brooks no argument.

To hold that psychology is common sense dressed up is to do it an injustice. What psychology does do is to find that sometimes empirical conclusions that run counter to common expectations. Further, it discovers new principles, such as the phi phenomenon are illustrative, and provide an overview of the salient issues. When considering the evolutionary aspects of human behaviour it is difficult to distinguish between biological and psychological perspectives. That may not be a problem as one fades into the other and, overall, provide a rich overarching view.

## Cross Cultural Aspects

At a concert in a Western country a counter-tenor performed: the concert hall was full, and fully seated with over 2000 people heard an Afro-American, a Japanese American, and an Australian orchestra playing and singing music of previous centuries, composed by people from another continent: all heard in awed silence and appreciation. Without our commonalities there would be no art, no world literature, no UN, no basis of any communication and, indeed, no major religions. Of all recent inventions, it is probably the internet that has created the sense of commonality. It transcends national boundaries, bypasses many forms of censorship, and affords a wealth of information formerly unavailable· so widely (although some of dubious provenance: see Naughton 2001, in references). The availability of the telephone, and the relatively inexpensive air travel have all added to the global village (to re-coin a cliche).

## Time Has Two Aspects

Time is viewed quite differently in some cultures. Some divide time into at least two separate aspects: time passing, and the sequencing of events. One of the classic comments of someone recovering consciousness after trauma is 'what happened, where am I?' This need for reorientation in time and space seems to be fundamental. Our personal history, our family history, and our culture, are all part of our orientation. Time is both objective and subjective. Our notions of time and space are inextricably entwined. We seem to see time, with reference to our own being, but it is not so for all. An example of this is when one of the Dalai Lama's monks said to him, 'As your Holiness will recall saying 200 years ago'.

Time sequencing is one of the essences of being human. That point is graphically illustrated by what happens when a person becomes demented. The loss of temporality takes them out of relationships with both the physical world and with their social and familial relations. One might even give consideration to the notion of future time as being evolution-related; related to biological information systems, and to evolved intellectual capacity. Some languages have terms that distinguish time from sequence. In Italian, for instance, the word for time is 'tempo' but the term of occasion of sequence is 'sequenza' or 'volta'. There is a delightful story about James Joyce: engaged, as was usual, in his writing. He lamented to a friend that he had written only seven words that day, to which the reply was 'but think of the sequence'.

Alibis are time statements: and are inferred from temporal sequence, just as cause and effect is inferred from temporal sequence. Our judgment of others is partly dictated by the sequences they are inferred to have undergone (as in judgments of maturity, of worldliness, and of recent of political experience). Our biorhythms are time matters, as are our views on the cyclical nature of larger scale events (such as the night-day, the lunar cycle, the seasons, sunspot activity, and the metonic (lunar) cycle.

In politics, there is the cycle of the rise, consolidation, and decay of mighty empires: in economics there is the alternation of bull and bear markets, of regular fluctuations in commodity prices, all moods and fashions have their cycles; and thus are sequence-bound. It is not so much time that is the issue but, rather, the processes that occur in time: one might say that time heals all wounds but we might more accurately say that the processes of healing require time for them to operate. Time sequences are of the essence of being: we constantly put ourselves in the temporal position: witness the pleasure of school children have in putting their name and address as John Smith, 5 Williams Way, Candaville, British Columbia, Canada, North America, Northern Hemisphere, The World, The Solar System, The Universe.

Previous events in our lives have an effect, and sometimes a salience. In other instances the past is seen as an outside entity: time is another country. As Marlowe put it in *The Jew of Malta*, 'but that was in another country: and besides, the wench is dead'. Some of the great stories are ones of sequences out of joint. Thus, the story of Bizet's *Carmen*, and the story of *Romeo and Juliet* are instances of relationships occurring at times out of sequence. Carmen's attraction to Don Jose is reciprocated too late when Carmen has formed a new attraction towards Escamillo, leading to· Carmen's murder. Juliet's feigned death deceives Romeo who then suicides leaving Juliet bereft, thus leading to her own self destruction.

Books on human relations have much to offer, particularly that of Peterson (2018): his book is aptly named *The twelve rules of life.* One might dispute any one of the propositions: for example Principle 8 (work with the right motives). One might dispute what 'right' means. Principle 12 is 'keep close to God'. Many atheists would find this a curious inclusion. Notwithstanding, it is still a worthy attempt to formulate rules for living. This is a typical instance of a perspective from a psychological or a management perspective. They may do so from a principled but non-research basis. One needs to be cautious about the provenance of such works: many are worthy attempts, but one must decide which.

## Fashions in Science

There are fashions in science just as there are fashions in clothes – although not so readily admitted. Psychology is replete with instances of circumstances who have been the subject of intense high-level investigation to be replaced in another period by an equal application to other areas of interest. Thus, in the 1950s the extraordinary amount of work on sensory isolation fell into relative desuetude and was replaced by other interests. The intense work on ethology was period-specific just as the work on psychophysics characterised the early beginnings of psychology. One can never be sure of the consequences, and thus is a justification for fostering blue-sky enterprises.

Lea et al. (2002) in a concise article have addressed the issue of the worldly and important (everyday things that matter) using psychological principles. They took the notion of the way that psychological insight could have useful application for macro-economic policy. Among the issues they address are income tax evasion (using prospect theory). crime (using the monetising of behaviour). and notes and coins (money is more than an abstract symbol, the form, and its other attributes, do matter). The authors offer a bold plan with direct advice about implementing processes designed to improve the economic aspects of people's everyday lives.

# Topics

## *Altruism and Prisoner's Dilemma*

A more realistic goal might be to increase the quantum of altruism. Perhaps one of the most famous of illustrations of the benefits and drawbacks of altruism and loyalty is that of the *Prisoner's Dilemma.* Ridley's (1996) social account includes the creative use of games theory in general, and the *prisoner's dilemma* in particular. The *Prisoner's Dilemma* game involves two players (masquerading as prisoners) each of whom has two choices (co-operate or defect). Neither player knows what the other will do. Two individuals are detained by the police and charged with a bank robbery, which carries a hefty jail sentence. There is no solid evidence, so if neither says an incriminating word, the charges will have to be reduced to that of carrying firearms, attracting a much lighter penalty. However, each is offered the chance to plea bargain – to go free by turning in the other.

Two alternatives are available to each prisoner: whether to co-operate, with the motive of increasing benefit to both players jointly; or to compete as to increase individual benefit at the expense of the other. The best individual outcome is to go free and keep the money: the worst individual outcome is to be betrayed and languish in jail in the irksome knowledge that the other is disloyal, free, and rich.

In this 'game' the opportunity to make their sentences lighter is fostered by their silence. Defection by one will make a jail term unlikely, but increase their partner's jail time. With both silent they are collectively better off than if both defect. Since they do not communicate they cannot know what their accomplice has decided. Axelrod's analysis of tit-for-tat (TFT) seems to be the best strategy. Co-operation is assumed unless evidence to the contrary is given. Under this strategy prospect of defection is minimised to the mutual benefit. The essential point here is that co-operation is conditional: we tailor our responses to the behaviour of those toward whom we indicate a willingness to co-operate. The notion of unconditional co-operation is plainly one that has no survival value, and is thus not practised.

The best joint outcome (where both prisoners remain silent) is to receive a light sentence for carrying arms: but that is unstable since either individual can do better for himself by deviating (securing the best individual outcome for himself – but producing the worst individual outcome for the other). The worst joint outcome (where each betrays the other) lands them both in jail, though with a lighter sentence than a solitary burglar would receive. If both betray then both lose – hence the dilemma. Such dilemmas clearly implicate ethical values. Thus, the seeming, and real, advantage of the TFT strategy is that it is basically 'nice'. While defection receives a reaction, it is a forgiving and clear modus operandi. Defection yields a better immediate payoff but co-operation yields a better long-term game.

Axelrod (1980) found that the TFT strategy was a consistent best long-term winner. TFT strategists are not envious of other's scores; they never defect first; they respond to defection with a mild rebuke (not an irate one); they forgive readily when the rebuke has been accepted; and provides reward rather than punishment. It is not a strategy that fails to recognise defection, for it does so immediately; but is slow to anger and ready to forgive.

Understanding dyadic interaction in relationships represents an enduring challenge to reciprocity research. The application of many paradigms has been used to discern patterns of reciprocity in dyadic interaction: interpersonal, inter-group, inter-organizational, and international interaction. The advancement of dyadic relations and reciprocity research requires both theoretical and methodological innovations to further our understanding of the elusive nature of patterns of reciprocity.

Not all the relevant articles are the models of clarity one would expect. Some interesting ideas may become buried in difficult prose. For example, Bogumil (2001) wrote on reciprocity of relations that '... research in international relations requires the exegesis of conceptual issues of the nature of actions pertinent to the process of reciprocity'. That paper, presented an innovation in reciprocity research by the introduction of the Attribution Reciprocity (AR) model.

## *Applications*

The power to persuade may need to be exercised in the face of determined resistance – the will to go ahead despite powerful opposition. People will have entrenched views and, with such a view, goes what seems a paradoxical humility. Knowing how things ought to be induces in the convinced the idea that they must cope in a flawed world. This imperfection may be seen as something that invites adverse judgement. Exactly who is to bring judgement, or why such a judgement might be brought, is not fully explained. It is the inchoate sense of imperfection that lies at the heart of the concern. Lesser operators do not seem to be troubled by the notion of imperfection, and therein may lie the core of the issue.

There are works that apply psychology to practical situations. One such is that of Singer and Hudson (1992). That useful work has a cognitive science orientation in its first section; while its second section contains a personality-based analysis (birth-order and the development of attitudes to power, for example); and a group-dynamics approach in its third section. The general thrust of that work is to find expression in the context of international relations. What is interesting about that work is that it deals in sections. In the event six principles emerged: consistency, reciprocation, social proof, authority, liking, and scarcity.

Remoteness of relationship makes it easier to behave unethically. Dropping a bomb is a less harrowing way of killing than is stabbing, at least to the perpetrator and the victim. Politicians remote from their electorates may find it easier to behave with less consideration for their constituents than they would to someone with whom they have day-to-day contact; cheating the tax office (assuming there is small prospect of being caught) is seemingly less harrowing to the conscience than is cheating a brother. Public autopsies are not widely held nor widely attended. Watching operations on humans, wincing at seeing a violent accident, and the sympathy pains felt by the husbands of women in childbirth (*couvade*), are all illustrations of how empathy is a compelling illustration of the way in which we see our common humanity.

## Empathy

A kind of empathy may become evident in such belief systems, and may be bent to serve a purpose. The empathy that many feel extends to all sentient things. Psychology students are constantly exhorted not to engage in anthropomorphism – the attribution of thoughts and feelings to other animals, yet students sometimes do behave as if those creatures were sentient.

One could well argue that a failure to recognise sentience is, itself. a human diminution. In an engaging book by Lorenz (1949), *King Solomon's ring*. He recounted how popular legend has it that King Solomon had a ring which, when worn, allowed him to converse with animals. Lorenz has taken that theme and transformed it in such a way that he infers those qualities from observations of behaviour rather than in being simply anthropomorphic. What Lorenz did was to show that behaviour makes it possible to make good inferences about animal sentience.

One of the pieces of evidence about empathy was given in a recent study of World's worst sounds (see References). The 'winning' sound was that of vomiting. The authors did discuss the valuable point that our common humanity dictates what we hear as being repugnant. One of the most compelling everyday observations about our commonality is the distress and aversion felt by the average person when confronted with mutilation or with a corpse long dead.

## Excellence

As was mentioned previously, among the laudable aspiration of humanity is that of its perfectability. That idea has found expression in various times and places. It is put, with the religiously inclined, as the 'brotherhood of man under the fatherhood of God', as 'fellow workers and comrades in the struggle against imperialism', or that humankind may be made perfect by education, or by selective breeding. Plato's *Republic* has the political nirvana stemming from when kings become philosophers or when philosophers become kings. This seeming chimera of perfectibility is never short of new proponents and new ideas. One of the underlying elements of an approach to perfectibility is that of someone having an insight and imposing upon those not privy to the revelation.

One of the characteristics of excellent professionals is that they feel they live in an imperfect world: things are rarely as good as they should be. Given the frailties of human nature, the demands of time and of competing values, the solutions to almost all problems are less than perfect. A not uncommon expression of their concern is captured in the phrase 'they will find me out'. Their self-perceived inadequacies will become evident to the external critic. An essential precondition of intellectual or artistic eminence is the vision to see how things might be – to have an insight into ways of doing things better, of perceiving failings, and the power to persuade others.

As such, one might consider them to be not so much revelations as they are tyrannies. To ask common humanity to become perfect is to ask them to abandon the human condition, to rise above existential angst, and to be what they are not. Apocalyptic views on humanity may be dangerous, and may be doomed to failure, but that is not a reason for not trying. Without aspirations to improvement, rather than aspirations to perfection, we would be less than we are: with such aspirations we take on the process of improving without falling into the error of believing it to be too readily achievable.

The ultimate condition which affects us all eventually, is death. To some it may come as a welcome relief; to others it is something to be deferred until 'one's time has come'. To some it must seem that death is a welcome release from intolerable situations; to ideologies it must seem like a promise of paradise. The idea of changing attitudes to being dead is given in Seale (2000), giving an account on a world basis and over centuries. A further account, is given in Kubler-Ross (2011). There are various other accounts from the point of view of nurses, registered medical practitioners, religious authorities, etc. Notwithstanding one would have to say that it is a well-covered topic, and approached from various points of view. Further, the attitude towards death and dying has changed over the centuries, treating death as either something to be deplored, or as a welcome relief. One is ever mindful of the argument on the diminution of violence corresponds to such changed attitudes.

## *Gurus*

Among the dangers of the vulnerable is that of a total belief in some idea of which one has no personal knowledge. Well-illustrated here is a belief that someone, somewhere has a divine insight. The dangers of believing in a 'guru' who has a hot line to the 'truth' is well illustrated in Storr's (1996) book. His recipe for determining the value of gurus rests upon several suggestions. As he warned, 'The charisma of certainty is a snare which entraps the child who is latent in us all' (p.233). His suggested criteria for assessing self-styled gurus are with questions such as: Do they listen rather than preach? Do they encourage us to look inward and find what he or she finds unique? We should add: Do they try to dominate? Are they sexually and socially exploitative? Do they collect vast sums which are not put to proper charitable purpose? Are they a closed system that resists social and ideational interchange with the wider community? The gurus of the self-help movement can, paradoxically, make people more helpless – a point that has been argued by Salerno 2005.

## *Human Relations*

Books on human relations have much to offer but, as mentioned, many give a management viewpoint, and do so from a 'first principle' As such they are helpful, but do not have the same status as those based on evidence, unless they are. Seen in the context of games theory, there came a realisation that zero-sum games are advantageous. The use of mutually advantageous trade. of the value of co-operation, and the merits of the division of labour, are all instances. Pinker put it most aptly when he noted that '... instead of asking 'why is there war?' we might ask 'why is there peace?' As he noted, the developing concern for human rights, for justice, for man-made systems of improved law, all point to the fact that we are doing something right: what is it? In the common dealings with our friends and relatives, our work and social life, and in cross-cultural relations we need to include the application of psychology to such topics as propaganda, or intelligence work, and insights into world leaders.

## *Personal vs Public Interests*

Putting the common good ahead of personal interests does have benefits. To use one of Ridley's metaphors, personal fate is tied to the interests of each member of the group. He put it in terms of a sterile ant's best hope of immortality being through vicarious reproduction. 'just as an aeroplane passenger's survival is through the survival of the pilot' (one is reminded of that seeming paradox, death is the first prerequisite of immortality).

This point of the use of altruism as the best tactical approach to Utopia provides an argument stemming from the value of symbiosis. Trust and honesty, altruism and goodwill are all internationally marketable commodities. There are social advantages in flocking, caring, altruism, and the division of labour. Natural selection appears to serve the might-is-right principle, but the notion that the good of others is an operating principle exercised Darwin. His proposed solutions were that altruism might benefit family members (on the basis that they share the same family characteristics); the second principle is the notion that in the longer-term altruistic behaviour towards non-kin would be reciprocated and beneficial; the third idea is that the natural selection of some groups or communities would be more beneficial than direct competition. In the nominated 'game' the opportunity to make their sentences lighter is fostered by their silence.

There are lines of evidence from Ridley. Firstly, that brain injuries to frontal lobes produced emotional non-responsiveness even though their reasoning is unaffected; second, that reasoning about numbers is less easy than is reasoning about the violation of a social contract between people. We (rightly) trust those who have earned our trust, and tend to trust our own clan. The entail here is that we have a lesser trust of the outsider – a nascent xenophobia. It is a testament to the neural plasticity of humans that one-time enemies become transformed into allies. Ridley noted that 'Selfishness is almost the definition of vice. Murder, theft, rape and fraud are considered crimes of great importance because they are selfish or spiteful acts that are committed for the benefit of the actor and the detriment of the victim' (p 39).

This point of the use of altruism as the best tactical approach to Utopia provides an argument stemming from the value of symbiosis. Trust and honesty, altruism and goodwill are all internationally marketable commodities. There are social advantages in flocking, caring, altruism, and the division of labour. Natural selection appears to serve the might-is-right principle, but the notion that the good of others is an operating principle exercised Darwin.

## *Violence*

Violence, in general, is now regarded more lowly than it was formerly. The idea if burning someone alive for not believing is grossness in the extreme. The burning of non-believers, the roasting of cats, cock fighting, bear-baiting. The condemnation of 'bull-fighting'. and of vendettas, criminalising 'honour' killing of daughters, and the substantially lessened severity of criminal punishments are all part of that diminution of violence. In one respect Hobbes was right: as he noted in *The Leviathan,* in a state of nature, life really is what he said (solitary, poor, nasty, brutish, and short). This does not stem from any fundamental principle of anarchy: it is simply a result of the nature of nature.

The old adage of 'Three times blessed is he who knows his cause is just, but three times three blessed is he who gets his blow in fust' is not true. Fear will generate a feeling of self-interest and self-preservation, thus inviting the conclusion that a pre-emptive strike is advantageous. The recognition that retaliation only for an actual attack is more economical as well as self-preserving, thus might become a principle. Without that principle we have a deterioration to a system of vendettas – thereby exacerbating the situation – forever. Violence is fostered, amongst other things, by resentment, by inherited feuds, and by anarchy.

In the application of these principles there is always the ethical dimension. Because of that there will always be a tension between power and morality. The use of naked raw power and the unfettered use of force have no moral place in modern society. If the only answer to violence is force, violence will escalate. As we might put it, 'With an eye for an eye everyone ends up blind' (a variant of the fight fire with fire, and all the world will burn').

As Churchill so aptly said appeasement consists of saying nice pussy to a hungry tiger in the hope that you will be the last to be eaten. It follows that we have the question of when the use of force is justified, and when such use should be contained. Thus, we have the dilemma of the application of the highest ethical principles with the need to be self-protective.

## Conclusions

The general conclusion must be that psychological research has much to offer. In part that may involve a rebuttal of previously valued views: it may also involve a confirmation of insights accorded to us by seers. Further, it provides valuable new information. As one writer noted, it is not that we know much, it is that we believe inaccurate things. The affirmation and rejection of some such insights is a valuable function which is a substantial aid to our understanding. The chapter which follows give a succinct account of an essential of psychology – that of individual differences. We must have laws to contain the looters in life: there is no such legal restraint needed for the saints.

# Chapter 4
# Personality

## Introduction

We do need to recognise that individuals exhibit a wide variety of behaviour, the moral stance particularly. In disasters, there are those who go the disaster area to render aid and comfort, while others go to see what can be looted: a variation that is a constant source of wonder. There can be no doubt that culture may have a significant impact on personality, but it is not an overwhelming assumption that personality must follow. Within each culture there are substantial variations: as the old saying has it, there is no accounting for taste.

It is instructive to note the variety of classical studies that bear upon personality: amongst such is the *Oracle of Delphi*, an example of how physical factors can influence personality. The individuality of the *Sybil* (or the *Pythia*) is emphasised: it is speculated that a gas secreted by the junction of tectonic plates was responsible for the assertions of the *Pythia* (The Virgin Oracle). The speculation is that the *Oracle of Delphi* was inspired both literally and metaphorically by a gas secreted by a geological fault in the fissure in the rocks at Delphi. The priestess was apt to give cryptic ascriptions foretelling events and causes of action (and interpreted in excellent hexameters by the priests of Apollo). The attestation of durability showed that from its founding in 586 BC until a Thracian tribe burned the temple in 83 BC. It foundered on until toward to the end of the Roman empire. This is an example not only of differences, but also veneration: two very human qualities.

That there are varieties within any culture makes Darwinian evolution possible. If there were no varieties then evolution could not select favourable traits. Human relations are affected by various external factors, including climate, political regimes, and industrialisation. One would also wish to discriminate those cultures in danger of being literally swamped by rising seas and those driven out by war.

We must not yield our views to the decisions of others, but set about human relations from our own perspective. Human relations are not the exclusive province of some group, sect, political party, or professional expertise – whatever their


R. Francis, *Equality in Theory and Practice*,
https://doi.org/10.1007/978-981-15-3488-1_4

qualifications. There are many 'pop' psychology books on the market, and of vastly varying quality. The intention here is to lift the book above the level of 'Dr X advises', to draw upon the work of serious scholars, and to give those principles application in four areas: physical, personal, organisational, and the wider social context.

It is a common observation that when we know something we often assume that others know it too. A fundamental variant of this notion is that of experts who assume that those less expert have the same skilled frame of reference. An excellent example is someone who just copes with (say) word processing asking a geek how one does X. The answer is often 'Like this', accompanied by a blur of fingers. It is almost supererogatory to assert that there are variations both within and between cultures: there is the concept of national character, of cultures, and of organisational styles. While the basic theme of this present work is an exploration of our common humanity, it would be absurd to deny the differences that are so apparent. Most human qualities are distributed 'normally', according to the Gaussian curve. This includes such qualities as intelligence, extraversion, hypnotisability, generosity, energy level, emotional lability, deference, aggression, etc.

In looking for commonalities we are presented with the issue of dealing with individual differences. It is a truism that there is wide variety in the human condition. We have introverts and extraverts, saints and sinners, the balanced and the unbalanced, and the bright and the not-so-bright. Dealing with that variety brings complexity, and so acknowledgement is given to such diversity, followed by the recognition of commonalities of diversity.

## Approaches to Personality

As we have noted, there are fashions in theory and in research. Among such is the notion of Sharpeners and Levellers. Sharpeners are alert to distinctions thus, in presenting two pictures and asked for the differences between them the Sharpeners will see them relatively easily while Levellers will not see differences, even where they exist. That approach, popular in the 1960s now seems to have fallen into disuse. Another kind of theoretical approach is that of using the Pavlovian conditionability as a basis. In that it is linked to the four 'humours' of Hippocrates. (sanguine, phlegmatic, melancholic, and choleric), based upon the twin processes of excitation and inhibition. The responses to conditioning applications is one of the determinants of character (see Pavlov 1964: see also Smith in References).

Yet an instance is that of Freudian theory (with Id, Ego, and Superego). This last approach, as an example, suffers from the possible defect of being in total empathy (with a colleague who was a total doctrinaire devotee). For example, in dealing with a dedicated Freudian, and being a critic of (say) child sexuality one might say that one could see no universal evidence of it. To this the reply might be by a doctrinaire follower that it was because one has not resolved the issue of child sexuality. This leads to the general proposition in refutation that in research that every theory must be evaluated externally. These general approaches to the analysis of personality theory are in a state of constant flux, and rightly so. It also leads to the notion that there must be fundamental rules on evaluation.

One of the gravest difficulties in pencil & paper testing is not responding as one would act. For example, in a test of what one would do ethically is not quite the same as what one should do. The question might be 'what would you do if a close friend breached a confidence?' A response might be 'confront him/her to ascertain the facts'. What one might do in the circumstances is never to trust them again. That disparity bedevils research into pencil & paper responses.

## General Theorists

It is probably a good thing to have Lockeans and Leibnitzians, positivists and personalists, objectivists, and phenomenologists; those who favour mathematical models, animal models, mechanical models, psychiatric models – or no models. As Allport (1955) noted, one understands better if one looks at the process of becoming rather than at just cross-slices of personality.

## Tests Not Yet Devised

A possible basis of morality what came to be called the 'Zeigarnik Effect'. Kurt Lewin and Bluma Zeigarnik were accustomed to go to Kaffeeklatsch in Berlin. On one occasion, in 1936, they were at one such, and so engrossed in their conversation that they forgot to pay. Realising that they went back and settled the bill, and eventually came to realise the importance of the tension that is aroused when there is an uncompleted task – hence the term 'the Zeigarnik effect'. Having committed an offence it is feasible that the concern about being found out may generate a tension of incompletion, and prevent further infractions. At that it does seem possible that it may be involved in breaches of ethics. All of this assumes that one has a conscience.

One could imagine that committing such a breach would be betrayed by conscience – it is thus that significant breaches, and even criminal behaviour, could emanate from the notion that there is a tension in some people that renders them subject to conscience. Those of violent psychopathic tendencies would be less troubled by the prospect of being found out, and thus more likely to commit breaches. It's connection to morality may be so.

Another instance is that of the personality factor that has recently come to be called *The Teflon Factor*. (Teflon, after the coating applied to the inside of some cooking pans so that nothing sticks to them). This description is applied to characters who, despite actions which would be judged as objectionable in others, do not attract the odium that would result were the actions to be made by someone in whom this quality is absent.

There is also the observed phenomenon of those who are generous spirited in all things except money (generous spirited but money mean GSMM). Those who do favours for others are not always regarded with gratitude. When refugees are not treated as well as they would wish, the target countries get the criticism rather than the countries which drove them from their homeland.

Other un-investigated concepts are those of determination and strength of will, those who are unequivocally committed to a particular place, and whose quality of life depends upon being there, and those with a sense of the ridiculous (a variant of Somerset Maugham's precept that 'life is a comedy to those who think, and a tragedy to those who feel'. Others of interest are those able to constantly achieve successfully but we are unable to articulate why (as in Napoleon's 'I want lucky generals' – the military equivalent of the 'green thumb'.

Psychology has yet to capture some human qualities, by analysis, by name, or by measurement. Among the issues that psychology does not seem to have canvassed empirically is the concept of retaining psychological balance. In order to keep such balance, one needs to take most seriously what one does professionally, but not take oneself personally too seriously lest it lead to pomposity and self-righteousness. Another concept not formally examined is that of conceptualising those who love humanity, but not specific people: those who love specific people but not humanity; those who love neither, and those who love both.

Amongst other missed opportunities is the temporal integration test. This resulted from a paper published by Hearnshaw in 1951. He examined the concept of temporal integration. Although specifying that it may not be a unitary phenomenon he did claim that cognition is an important part of our psychological make, noting that British psychologists had already debated whether there was a general factor in intelligence (g factor). Among the issues that he mentioned was an index of phylogenetic continuity. It does appear to discriminate creatures of higher or lower intelligence, and acts as a mediator of intelligence. The ability to make temporally critical judgments is vital.

Yet another example of a principle that has no name is when those who do nothing are often held blameless while those who do something, though little·, are castigated. For example, a small financial contribution in response to a request for a donation to a worthy cause is labelled as 'mean', while those who do not contribute are held less accountable. It is as if the offered sum is demonstrably derisory and therefore judged to be so, whereas a refusal to contribute might be construed as a matter of some higher-level principle. These points are meant to illustrate how psychology has yet to accommodate a number of concepts. It is not that it is so capricious a discipline but, rather, that there is so much work to do that the uncovering of concepts such as are outlined will be aeons in the making. It is thus that one appreciates the human variety, and realises that more standardised tests are needed.

In most forms of professionalism, however, values become significant. We do not accord to dictators the notion of being morally excellent, despite their efficiency, dedication and list of accomplishments. Those to whom we accord excellence have commonly acted according to commonly accepted ethical standards. Over recent decades various theories of management have, as one of their unstated premises, the search for more ethical ways of doing things. Doing it morally well is construed in the positive rather than the negative sense. There is even an approach which addresses the issue of a sense of humour (and self-deprecation) to be found in Svebek (1996).

## Legislation to Ban

All of this is an interesting example of Acts of the legislature which ban the incitement to hatred, it is as though one is not allowed to scorn an idea. It is an essential tension between the right to be critical and the right not to be offended. The recent experience in Paris of the massacre of journalists who criticised an idea is one such case in point (the case of Charlie Hebdo).

Caregiving and good manners are much undervalued, but form a significant part of social life. The need to understand people is, in part, the need to appreciate different types of people. It is interesting to note that there is a divide between concern for humanity and a concern for individuals. That is evident in concern for those in parlous situations: on the one hand, there is concern for them as suffering individuals and, on the other hand, a concern for them as breeding more than is so for those in Westernised countries, thereby exacerbating the amount of suffering.

## Aspects of Personality Approaches

There is the consideration of rationality. Of like kind is the concept of evidence-based-medicine, as was clear in the germ concept of Ignaz Semmelweis in Vienna, in 1847. He thought that going from cadavers to baby delivery would introduce something that could result in baby deaths. He was reviled at the time, and even ended up in a madhouse where he died of pyaemia (a kind of septicaemia) within two weeks of admission. Later his exoneration was demonstrably vindicated, even having a prestigious university named after him in Hungary. It is thus that the alternation of rationality and irrational beliefs, with the addition of beliefs for which there is no evidence, variously prevail. To be concerned with evidence, to draw appropriately valid conclusions, and to have reasonable discourse is the essence of rationality.

Both between and within society there is a substantial variation. As such, relationships are under constant test, the limits being under special challenge by social deviants who do us a service by offering continuous challenges to accepted standards; thus, not all deviant acts are harmful to group life. This point of view is provided in Erikson' s analysis of the *Pilgrim Fathers* in America (1966), and the general way in which that society treated deviants. He noted that deviants provided pressure toward making clear the basic social standards. The expulsion of extreme deviants cemented the remaining community in its agreed lifestyle and standards.

The drawback of the harsh treatment of deviants is that it reduces social diversity and tolerance; it also reduces civil liberties in that society, and deprives modest dissenters from enjoying the benefits of their right to be different.

## Assumptions

The notion of the categorisation of assumptions was the subject of a paper by Francis (2014a). It is just such a challenge of assumptions that makes for scientific progress. The Aristotelean notion of all celestial motion being circular was questioned by Kepler, who observed that, as a matter of observation, that the path of a planet in orbit was an ellipse, with the sun at one focus – and expressed as Kepler's three laws of planetary motion – and in direct contradiction of Aristotle.

By way of contrast, Aristotle's analysis of chick embryos was classical, in yet some other respects his assumptions were mistaken. For example, the assumption that the Earth was the centre of the universe, and that all heavenly motion was circular, was in error. With our present knowledge, one must recognise that we carry our assumptions around with us: it is part of our mental furniture, and they deserve to be made explicit.

That paper categorised assumptions, the first being that one cannot legislate physical laws: they are what they are, and no change will be effected by legislating. Among them are included that one cannot legislate certain physical laws. In the American state of Indiana in 1897 a Dr. Edwin Goodwin's attempt at immortality met with failure. He attempted to legislate the value of pi, thinking it was untidy at 3.14159 – and rounded it to the number three. The result was, for example, that pendulum clocks went awry, and car manufacturers were unable to calculate the circumference of wheels, using the diameter. Physical constants are fixed, and no legislation is going to change them.

To those assumptions one might also add that assumptions are often the basis of humour (for example. Ken Dodd in London looking up at the Royal box and saying 'That reminds me, I must buy some stamps'. And again, an aspirant young actor gets role as part of husband and tells his father. The reply was 'Congratulations son, next time you might get a speaking part'. Thus, one of the bases of comedy is the recognition of a wrong assumption that so amuses us (when I am older I won't need glasses – I shall drink from the bottle). The paper by Francis (2014a) analysed the different categories of assumptions, and left out one of the most important and dangerous assumptions 'I know that I am right, and you must agree with me'.

One of the difficulties facing legislatures is that of framing rules that accommodate different personality types. An over-riding consideration is necessity of framing laws that are universal. One of the main aims of legislatures is that of keeping the rule of law. The basic precept here is to have laws of the widest possible applicability. There is to be no hypocrisy, the law aims to treat all equally. It is an essential tension being to accommodate differences but, at the same time, to make rules of universal applicability.

What appears here is a revisit of an article by Francis (2014a). He made an analysis of assumptions. Some issues simply need standard criteria. For example, the shiny coachwork of Rolls Royce cars seemed unstandardised until the criterion was established (someone with good normal eyesight could read *The Times* by the reflection of an image held at 15 inches from the coachwork). Another kind of assumption was when Gottlieb Daimler was asked if cars would ever become popular he replied, in effect 'Don't be ridiculous, there aren't more than 500 chauffeurs in Europe'.

Yet another kind of assumption is that there is an institution known as the British football pools. On one occasion, when the weather was particularly inclement a team of experts was established to determine who won. This bizarre arrangement does suggest that we could save a lot of money by not building the America's Cup boats, and have an expert team decide who would win (best out of six court cases?).

Galton's *Memories of my life* he reported that one day to see if he could induce a mental state artificially. He imaged the hansom cab horses were secretly regarding him, and with evil intent. Galton came to believe that it was true and had a sneaking caution about them subsequently. On another occasion, using his walking stick he also ensured that he used it to tap every rail on the park that he passed. Eventually he came to be seriously concerned when a rail was missed, thereby showing the importance of attitude.

What follows is a revised version of that article, with a caveat that one of the most important assumptions is missing, that of 'You must agree with, for I have a hot-line to the truth. If you do not agree with me I will kill you', as was done with heretics.

## *Etiquette*

Etiquette is a valuable part of specific professions. Etiquette says what to do in particular circumstances, and is a vital part of how to behave professionally. In the professions, for example, it is considered etiquette to treat all fellow professionals as equal, and do them equal honour, whereas we do know that they are not all equally competent. In law, for example, it is considered to be good etiquette to regard all lawyers as equally competent in their own areas, when this is patently wrong.

A number of items are well covered by standard testing, among them are extraversion-introversion, neuroticism, and psychopathy. There can be little doubt that many aspects of personality have failed to attract theories. Among them is that of predicting who will suddenly change character and, separately, who will become radicalised.

In professional interpersonal relationships we are often obliged to work with people whom we do not admire, and would prefer to avoid. For such situations there are helpful guide lines to be found in principles such as the use of courtesy, limiting the time of interaction, and restricting the interactions to professional or commercial issues. A work aptly titled *Dealing with people you can't stand* might commend itself to those with a bent for how-to books (Brinkman and Kerschner 2012).

There are, in history, those individuals who are outstandedly gifted. One has in mind such people as Aristotle, Shakespeare, Mozart, Einstein, and Michaelangelo. Their contributions are so extraordinarily insightful that one can only look on in admiration. How such people derive their contributions to the human condition is an eternal mystery: they just are. One cannot allow that they are the product of their time, or had extraordinary experiences: they just seem to occur.

In this there are those who make contributions of a nature that is significant, but not of quite the same calibre as those rightly accorded the title of 'genius'. One has in mind the holders of one of the Nobel Prizes, and of those unsung heroes who make their quiet contribution to human constructions. Human relations are affected by various external factors, including climate, political regimes, and industrialisation. So too do factors interact: thus, climatic changes affect the political scene. Global warming would swamp Pacific island nations, and cause widespread disaster in Bangladesh.

## Formal Testing

These tests mentioned below represent different approaches to testing, but often fail to capture a personality trait that is of importance. What is missing here are two types of test: one is that of testing non-verbal communication; the other is a test of the ethical personality. There have been various types of tests of personality: included are pencil and paper (eg. the Minnesota Multiphasic Personality Inventory (MMPI), and the Eysenck Personality Inventory [EPI]).

Intelligence tests were first developed by Alfred Binet in France at about the turn of the last century. One of his concerns was to classify, and stream children, into appropriate categories to assign them to fitting groups. His methods included tests using pencil and paper, pictures, and portable objects. In effect his approach to classification was the basis of what we still do today, with some variations. There are 'projective' tests in which the person projects themselves for an interpretation to take place. Instances of such tests are the Rorschach Inkblot Test, and the Thematic Apperception Test. Projective tests require that the respondent 'project' themselves into situation, and reveal to the administrator the qualities and concerns of the respondent. A typical test is the Blacky Pictures. That test consists of 12 pictures, and is psychoanalytical based. How it is interpreted gives clues as to personality. Perhaps the most famous projective test are the ten items of the Rorschach inkblot test. Again, the respondent tells what s/he sees, and the presenter makes the assessment.

Personality tests are designed to measure characteristics there vary, as between people. One of the best known is the Minnesota Multiple Personality Inventory (also known in shorthand as the MMPI). The MMPI 2 contains a list of 567 items: questions which, if answered correctly, give an outline of one's personality makeup.

Such a valuable test also has generated quite a literature and is the subject of further research on items, such as validity scales in civil forensic settings, and feigned memory impairment.

Other tests are situational (such as the British War Office Selection Boards: WOSBs); there are 'tests' of overall assessments based on talking to people. Situational tests are designed to assess such issues as creativeness and leadership skills. A standard one is to give a small group some items (a piece of rope, a ladder, a plank, and a small {and awkward] squad, with the stated aim of getting a large gun across a river). The assessment is done in terms of the stated creativeness, leadership skills, and time taken to solve the problem.

## Psychopathy

Psychopathy It is recognised that no concept is evident in isolation, there being strong connections to other concepts. One such issue is that of politeness, and requires that we sometimes dissimulate. To do so requires that we put ourselves into the shoes of others. None of that is to say that some personalities are not toxic, because some are. There is the outright active psychopath who deliberately sets out to hurt, the delaying psychopath (who harms by constant deferral of decisions), the messianic, the paranoid, those who attribute shabby motives and misinterpret data to others, the self-server, and the pathetically inadequate. Corruption in such cases inheres in their actions as well as in their intent. The appropriate formal test here us the Hare self-report *Psychopathy Scale* (the latest edition).

Psychopathy has a cluster of variables, including being guiltless, loveless, amoral, having impulsivity, superficial charm, the intention to exploit, and mendacity. As such one might ask if psychopaths are born rather than made: and there may be a genetic tendency. The over-riding consideration, the superordinate concept, is that of selfishness. Their world is constructed around their wishes and desires rather than that of being considerate, outgoing, and helpful. It may seem obvious but the answer must be an 'it depends'. One can readily imagine someone being born with psychopathic tendencies, but not having them develop because of the particular environment in which they are reared. With this goes the concept of the toxic personality. Blowhards, bigots, and bullies: if rich or influential they allow themselves to be surrounded with sycophants.

It is interesting to note that there is a concept now called 'passive psychopathy'. The essential attribute here is that damage is done by not making decisions, rather than making selfish ones. Not doing an action on time, failing to appoint someone when they are clearly qualified, and omitting to do what was promised. It does appear that harm can result from committing certain acts; it also appears that failing to do what is required is also a form of psychopathy.

There was a term, now fallen into disuse, known as 'moral insanity'. Just as there are people whose rationality is so minimal as to cause us to make the judgement of intellectually subnormal (for example, idiocy, imbecility, cretinism), so too might we regard moral imbecility. As we have those whose moral-cognitive ability is negligible so there are those whose moral notions are so lacking that we might regard them as moral imbeciles.

Their notions of altruism, and of selfless contributions, are so minuscule as to lead the ordinary person to regard them as unbalanced, and to be avoided where possible. This quality (or lack of moral quality) is a characteristic of dictators, low-grade politicians, and sundry psychopathic apparatchiks. We must recognise the existence of some unworthy motives, psychopaths, tyrants, and callousness. That is not to deny that but, rather, seeks to put the case for the more constructive aspects of human relations.

On the other hand, there are those who have lives dedicated to the loving service of others. The psychopathy exhibited by some in the community is a counterpoint to the altruism displayed by others. The public commonly distinguish the real from the pretence (if you can fake sincerity, you have got it made!). Saints, both religious and secular, act as an inspiration to most. We admire and accord acclaim; we cite secular saints as role models. and we use them to justify our commonality.

## Mental Illness as a Criminal Defence

The notion of mental illness is too common a defence for it to be totally effective. If someone is flagrantly mad it would be an excuse, but is not so often. One is taken by the Barbara Wootton's (1963) idea that a court should determine the guilt of the action first and then, and only then, determine what is best to be done. It is worth noting that while we are aware that many who damage, others pretend it is in the name of an ideology. What is less clear is the number who are drug addicted. Their stance is to pretend that it is for lofty motives whereas it is otherwise. Young people as victims do nothing for any ideological alleged cause, and could well alienate moderates. One might consider (or one may not) that those who act for assumed motives may need to have their attention drawn to an idea. That the causing significant harm to innocent youth is significantly at odds with the notion of an Eternal Merciful Being.

## Approaches

### *Political Rectitude*

People are more concerned at losing rather than at winning. That was particularly evident in the economic slump of 1929 where the 'haves' committed suicide because of having lost what they formerly enjoyed. It is thus that a deprivation is seen to be more punitive than is a reward for goodness. In the matter of luck (Frank 2016), reported, with considerable justification, how luck is a significant component of enterprise and success.

There is a test for Machiavellianism, being one devised by Christie et al. (1970) (with the title MACH IV). The test consists of 20 items and should take no more than five minutes to complete. Although not suitable for giving practical guidance to individuals but it is a useful research tool. The main point of the test is to use the less scrupulous means of achieving what we want in life. The common critique of Machiavelli is that he was not a moral person: one would have to qualify that by noting that his book, *The prince*, used the indicative mode rather than the moral one. He should not be criticised on the grounds that he did not prescribe but, rather, told it as he saw it.

### Religion and Secular Approaches

Possibly ascribing defects of character to religion is too facile. Millions of believers do not subscribe to the ‘be reasonable, see it my way’ point of view. They get on quietly with their own forms of worship without the need force others to conform. Time was, when a form of conformity was burning people alive because they did not conform to the principles formulated by others. The notion that we should immolate people because they disagree, indulge in public hangings, torture people in the foulest ways imaginable, and exploit them without regard to their safety are long going, and fortunately so, as Pinker has noted.

When it is done in the name of a specific ideology, it appears to be accepted as comprehensible. If it allied to a specific point of view and put into ‘cultural’ terms it is accepted; if it inheres in an individual it would be regarded as a curious form of deviation. The actions of such people should be seen as what it is – coercion to conform to someone else’s ideas. One is indoctrinated at birth in the religion of one’s parents: it often succeeds, and sometimes fails: too many have fought for the liberty to differ.

## Habit and William James

All of this points to the significance of habit. William James, in his classic two volume work (1981, and first published in 1890) recognized the heavier hand that inertia plays in social life. In his two-volume work, *The principles of psychology*, he noted on habit that it is:

> … thus the enormous fly-wheel of society, its most precious conservative agent. It alone is what keeps us all within the bounds of ordinance, and saves the children of fortune from the envious uprisings of the poor. It alone prevents the hardest and most repulsive walks of life from being deserted by those brought up to tread therein. It keeps the fisherman and the deck-hand at sea through the winter; it holds the miner in his darkness, and nails the

countryman to his log-cabin and his lonely farm through all the months of snow; it protects us from invasion by the natives of the desert and the frozen zone. It dooms us all to fight out the battle of life upon the lines of our nurture or our early choice, and to make the best of a pursuit that disagrees, because there is no other for which we are fitted, and it is too late to begin again. It keeps different social strata from mixing. Already at the age of twenty-five you see the professional mannerism settling down on the young commercial traveller, on the young doctor, on the young minister, on the young counsellor-at-law. You see the little lines of cleavage running through the character, the tricks of thought, the prejudices, the ways of the shop, in a word, from which the man can by-and-by no more escape than his coat-sleeve can suddenly fall into a new set of folds. On the whole, it is best he should not escape. It is well for the world that in most of us, by the age of thirty, the character has set like plaster, and will never soften again.

## *Moral Approaches*

There is, as the reader will be aware, tests for intelligence. There is also the recent work of Goleman (1997) wherein he proposed the notion of ‘emotional intelligence’. That concept addresses the issue of being aware of, and in control, of emotions. It is the ability to handle relationships with empathy and understanding: it is being aware of the emotions of others.

To these twin concepts of intelligence and emotional intelligence we might add that of a third concept – ethical intelligence. It differs from emotional intelligence in particular respect, that emotional intelligence refers to sensitivity and understanding of others whereas ethical intelligence refers to being aware of values and standards, and being sensitive and committed to them. It is to be noted that ethical intelligence involves components of emotional intelligence. While one may be cognisant of ethical intelligence it may be used inappropriately. For example, the correlation with actual intelligence is less than perfect (the position that it occupies with other tests). Second it may be used in selection processes where it may emphasis be inappropriate.

In ethical intelligence one would hive both sympathy and empathy for those who are victims of disasters or injustice: in emotional intelligence one might be able to use EI to gain advantage; in moral intelligence it is empathy and help for those hard pressed. In particular ethical intelligence commits one to acting ethically. One of the aspects of EI is that capacity to be sensitive of the needs of others. One of the problems here is that it may lead to an understanding of ethical needs (but using them to advantage). Social skills is one of the components if of EI, and it will be interesting to see how this distinction works out.

## Physical Abuse

Physical abuse may take any one of several forms, including the above enslavement, extortion, and torture, the formal terms are:

- Physical abuse
- Disregard for safety issues
- Enslavement
- Extortion
- Torture

It may also include slavery where the enslaved are forcefully deprived of their liberty (see the Chapter on slavery). The continuation of slavery is commonly regarded as corrupt by virtually all nations. Even slavery has its grades ranging from indentured labour, through Royal Naval press gangs of the eighteenth century, to outright ownership of human beings. To physical abuse we might also add mental abuse; bullying; undue criticism; and sneering. This does not accommodate fair criticism but does affect it when it goes over the line.

Another clear instance is that of political corruption where there is a usurpation of democratic political power by someone in the military. An example is the repeated power grabs in Fiji wherein someone takes over government in the interests of 'good government', and resulted in the dismissal of Fiji from the British Commonwealth of Nations. Another instance are allegations of rigging of elections by someone trying to stay in power (as allegedly did Mugabe in Zimbabwe. It must be said that Mugabe was eventually deposed by the electorate in 2017, and after 37 years in power (since Zimbabwe was declared independent from Britain in 1980. see Mugabe in References). One is also mindful of the seizure of power by the military in Thailand (see Connors and Hewison 2008).

## Logical Rules and Cultures

The rules of logic do not vary between Aden and Auckland. They have a universality that transcends all. It is thus with cultures: all cultures use courtesy towards strangers, even though its form may vary; all cultures value appearances ('face'or 'shame'); all cultures value generosity; and all cultures value loyalty to family. As E. M. Forster asserted, if one had to choose between national betrayal and betraying a friend he hoped to have the courage to betray his country. Cultural differences may come to matter less than principle, when one of these common features holds undue sway (profit to one's family gained from slavery, exploitations of the disadvantaged, the infliction of suffering, for example). The widely accepted canon and reference point for human values is the 1948 UN *Declaration of Human Rights.*

## Conclusions

There are conclusions to be drawn from the above considerations. One is the variety of humankind: indeed, its very diversity is of great significance. Apart from talent and hard work there is a strong element of luck in all human enterprises. Talent and hard work are seen as necessary, but not sufficient conditions, for success; though we do have to say that it plays a differential role in human endeavours. Luck may consist of being born in a highly developed country. Being basically illiterate, and having so few other advantages disposes one to being regarded as 'unlucky'. Further, luck plays an important role in success. Success is comprised of at least three related items; talent or merit, hard work, and luck. To have either talent or to work hard is necessary but not sufficient. Luck also has a role to play. In politics, for example, Hitler's rise to power is combined hard work, some political talent, and with a huge does of luck – the circumstances of the time. (for further development of that theme see Frank 2016, in References).

Rectitude is a damning force and could well prevent discussion of some fundamentals: when it becomes dogma it thereby becomes change-anathema. To add to this, it is noted that people are more averse to losing rather than winning. Notwithstanding, the general conclusion is that our mental furniture largely determines who we are, and what we think.

The defining characteristic here is whether one is free to choose. One cannot choose whether one is short or tall, has a hooked or an upcurving nose. There is no element of choice in being born in Israel, Britain, Patagonia, or Iceland. On the other hand, there is a choice in being Christian, Moslem, Atheist, or Zoroastrian. Here the legislation, it is argued, should make such a distinction between matters of non-choice and choice.

Above all we need to recognise the variety in the human condition. There are saints and sinners, looters and helpers, takers and givers, leaners and lifters. As such there is no change in the human condition, and we need to curb the negative excesses with appropriate legislation and education. There are a number of tests available, and yet more to be devised. As was noted in the business chapter, for the meek to inherit the earth the greedy will be forced to yield.

# Chapter 5
# Culture

## Introduction

It is recognised that there are variations of individuals within societies and nations, and that there are demonstrable national differences. War and conflict, cruelty and dispossession, famine and flood are an essential part of history, and told often and graphically. Such events are relatively unambiguous, but that may not be so for race, culture, and religion. Those attributes are often confounded. One might argue that they should be separate entities, and be treated as such in legislation. Being mindful of the decision is not only useful, but also instructive to legislatures. The confounding of race and culture, for example, confounds that over which we have no control, and things over which we do.

Notwithstanding, culture is a set of assumptions that invests our very thought: it is the way that we look at the world: it is the idiosyncratic knowledge and attitudes of a specific peoples: it may be defined by language, the arts, religion, cuisine, and social habits. They, in other words, shared patterns of behaviour and attitudes.

Just as we have biological evolution so too do we have cultural evolution. Cultures, like language, mores, and technology, have evolution. It is instructive to note from migrants of many countries that when they return to their native land for a visit, their memory of it is frozen but the reality is not. Indeed, the present writer has met people who have returned to their native land after many decades on another continent, have found it difficult to make themselves understood in their mother tongue, even though they readily adjust.

Just as we have a disposition to learn coping mechanisms for molecular forms of behaviour so too do we have a disposition to learn cultural ways of coping – culture being the macro-adaptation. Cultures are our common past, but we have no name for our common future. Culture may be defined, in part, as the way that a group of people solve problems: now we would have to add that it institutionalises approach to problem solving.



R. Francis, *Equality in Theory and Practice*,
https://doi.org/10.1007/978-981-15-3488-1_5

One cannot change one's race, whether one is Asian, Indian, Caucasian, or Indigenous. It is fixed permanently and is a part of who we are. On the other hand, we can hold the views that we do, but subject to reasonable debate. Most specifically, this work argues that our common humanity is governed by principles which are universal, and which cross cultural boundaries.

O'Neil (2016) has given us an expression of what she calls *Weapons of math destruction.* In that work she outlines the anti-democratic consequences of such weapons, and how the misuse of algorithms leads to regrettable consequences (although more appropriate ones have the potential to be beneficial). How such weapons may be used counterproductively, and how the process is past-oriented rather than future oriented. The process is, she avers, is basically unfair, paying less attention to being 'just' than being 'efficient'. In her concluding chapter there is a brief code of ethics, enjoining those espousing such view to be appropriately cautious, as well solutions to problems that are so ably outlined.

The book is an expression of these well-established principles is intended as an insight into human interchanges, and should be of practical help. The work is one that depends ultimately on evidential principles as well as morals; and is one that is explanatory, giving suggestions for application. Justman (2005), for example, traced the pop psychology movement from the utopianism of the 1960s. He avers, quite rightly, that the whole movement ignores the rhetoric of human rights and, as noted above, '... promises liberation from all that interferes with my power to create the self I want'.

Culture is one of the most pervasive influences on human development. One must recognise that not all cultural ways are equally appealing. There are some that are admirable, family feeling on belonging: others are to be condemned. Here one must also recognise the deleterious effects of prejudice against females. The notion that they 'belong' to someone else is morally abhorrent. Here we need to recognise that cultures that adversely discriminate against women do themselves the harm of excluding half of the human race, and thus an immense pool of talent.

## Definition of Culture

Culture has to do with custom and with belief. There are common customs and beliefs in many countries, and instances. Further, where a wide variety of beliefs are held. In such places there is diversity, tolerance, and a ready recognition that beliefs not only vary, but need to be given room to grow. As mentioned, there are some beliefs that are execrable, and not tolerated. The fashions that prevail in Westernised societies, although distinctly lesser, must have an impact. As fashions change, so too does culture. What impact fashion has upon culture is problematical, but it does undoubtedly have some.

Some cultures see actions as belonging to their peoples, and thus all are part of the consequences: other more individualistic cultures see more of personal responsibility – although this may not be so easy when the problem stems from a collective (a corporation, for example). In this latter case it is easier (though not always easy) to point to the action of some one person and hope to induce a change; in the former case the collective is the entity with which one must deal.

In some cultures, it is the family, not the individual, that is the basic unit. Shame and ill fortune seem to beset the family rather than the individual. Should one, therefore, allow access to information for the immediate family, as distinct from the individual? Under such a view one would not have such matters as medical privacy. The family might feel itself entitled to be privy to other members' financial situations, and the notion of individual privacy would be of much less importance than that which obtains in Western society.

In many countries what is now emerging is the multi-cultural society, largely consistent in a fusion of different cultures, and in which tolerance of differences is a key concept: cultures are always evolving, as does language.

## Confounding of Race and Culture

There are legislatures in the world that confound race and culture. In the UK, for example, there is the Equality Act of 2010. In that place, in the Introductory section it nominates the following characteristics as protected:

- Age
- Disability
- Gender reassignment
- Marriage and civil partnership
- Race
- Religion or belief
- Sex
- Sexual orientation

For example, one's race cannot be altered: one is what one is. On the other hand, one can choose to be tolerant and kind or intolerant and malicious. Taking an instance from the UK *Equality Act of 2010* one cannot choose one's age but one can choose religion or belief. It is regrettable that such a compound of items does not make such a distinction at least they are differed.

While one may criticise race, quite rightly at peril of ridicule, no such inhibitions should bar culture from being criticized. As mentioned, the essential difference here is that in the case of race, one has no control over it. One has a pink skin or a brown skin, aquiline or snub nose, blue eyes or brown, tall or short, etc. and no amount of argument is going to change it. With culture, however, one does have a choice. One can choose to be a murderer, a saint, a non-assertive believer or an intolerant: that is a choice. It provides an excellent reason for non-discrimination on racial grounds, but not for the non-admirable aspects of culture.

## Culture Shock

Culture shock occurs when placed in an unfamiliar environment where the values and standards are at variance with those held. Indeed, there are various models that seek to explain the phenomenon. They include culture learning, stress and coping, and social identification, as Zhou et al. (2008) has outlined. To this one would add that personality is also a critical variable.

Another analysis has complexity of culture as status with particular reference to criteria; for example, sedentary-nomadic; preliterate-literate; food producers-food gatherers. In an earlier seminal study Murdock and Provost (1973) listed scales: writing and records; fixity of residence; agriculture; urbanisation; technological specialisation; land transport; money; density of population; level of political integration; and social stratification.

These issues were addressed using a five-point scale (0–4) thus urbanisation would score 0 for fewer than 100 persons and 4 for a community of more than 1000 persons. Money would be 0 for no recognisable medium of exchange and 4 for coins of standard weight and their paper equivalents. Understandably, these scales were inter-related. Clearly such criteria are useful ways of looking at social complexity, but some might doubt the application of Western concepts to cultures where such criteria might be used in a judgmental way.

## Logical Rules and Cultures

The rules of logic do not vary between Aden and Auckland. They have a universality that transcends all. It is thus with cultures: all cultures use courtesy towards strangers, even though its form may vary; all cultures value appearances ('face' or 'shame'); all cultures value generosity; and all cultures value loyalty to family. As E M Forster asserted, if one had to choose between national betrayal and betraying a friend he hoped to have the courage to betray his country. Cultural differences may come to matter less than principle, when one of these common features holds undue sway (profit to one's family gained from slavery), exploitations of the disadvantaged, the infliction of suffering, for example). The widely accepted canon and reference point for human values is the 1948 UN *Declaration of Human Rights*.

## Cultural Values

In determining values one of the first considerations is 'what are fundamental values'. One might consider the view of cultural relativism: that is a view that cultural mores exist in relation to a press for solutions to problems occurring within that culture. It is a view that values are not absolute but, rather, stem from places and have no absolute value. If one disputes that, then the position is one whereby there are fundamental values that over-ride cultures, such as the belief in human rights – a position endorsed by the United Nations. It needs to be noted that one form of cultural relativity is that all cultures are equal. Plainly that is not so: there are some forms of culture that are abhorrent by being destructive, involve hatred, downgrade the rights of minorities, and the like.

## Cultural Attitudes

Turning now to the subject of war. As Pinker (2011) has shown, the overall conclusion drawn there is that, confounding conventional wisdom, all forms of political violence have decreased since the early 1990s, except for international terrorism, drones, and data matching. It is necessary to find such facts since differential reporting can so readily convey a false impression, just as reporting violent crime may induce a siege mentality when the risk is quite low. Much publicised failures are not a true picture.

Further, the onset of a war is reported: more recently its cessation has occasioned less reporting. To this rather melancholy caveat is to be added the notion that many human rights abuses occur without there being a war. The imposition of the military rule of tyrants, of corrupt political systems, and of the seizure of lands, are all instances of concern.

As mentioned, one particularly interesting conclusion is that the number of genocides and violent conflicts has dropped markedly in the wake of the Cold War. Not only are wars less frequent but also less deadly. What is less cheering is the finding that 90% of those killed in today's wars are civilians, and that women are disproportionate victimised by such armed-conflict. At least three reasons might be adduced for this diminution of war violence. One is the reduction of colonialism; the second is increasing globalisation; the third is that of the timely intervention of the UN.

There is, too, legislative approaches. One such is the most recent *Geneva Convention* on the treatment of Prisoners of War was adopted in 1949, and came into force in 1950. It is a most comprehensive document with 143 Articles, and four Annexures. That document is a moral statement that recognises the common humanity of all Prisoners of War: it is not culture or religion specific - and is testimony to the widely-held belief that we have common concerns, aspirations, and should have common rights.

To this we might add a concern for universal principles. The notion of the seven deadly sins originated with the desert fathers. As Cherry (2016) has remarked, while lust and gluttony are obvious there are others less obvious, such as control, and certainty. If one were to extend the list of the seven deadly sins it would be a matter of concern as to what might be included.

## Cultural Modifications

The notion that climate change may deprive some peoples of sovereignty. Among such was that of (1) the right to self-determination, (2) where the self-determination was threatened, and (3) those displaced and dispossessed become candidates for sovereignty over an acquired territory. Why, exactly, should current owners give up their new territory is not explained. One could well imagine that it could be used for the benefit of existing citizens.

Most importantly, it will involve a balancing of interests. Here the balance is between the claims of submerged states, and an acquired need versus the desire to help. That acquired need and, as we conclude to ignore the claims of refugee states. One might consider the problems of some countries being reluctant to yield land in to accommodate ocean-submerged states.

### *Attributes of Culture*

Reminders of cultural variations tend to distract us from the differences that exist within our own society. Cultures do not come as an invariant unit. The guidelines that apply to inter-cultural interchange can apply with at least some force to dealing with the substantial personality variations we see in our own everyday lives. None of this is to say that there are not cultural differences, because there plainly are. There are dimensions of cultural difference, and ways to attempt to measure these. For example, Smith et al. (1996) have given us relevant dimensions, as has Hofstede et al. (2010). To attempt to measure these. For example, the relevant dimensions are:

- Universalism versus Particularism
- Individualism versus Communitarianism
- Neutral versus emotional
- Specific versus diffuse
- Achievement versus ascription
- Sequential versus synchronous time
- Internal direction versus outer direction

In addition to formal taxonomies there are conceptual differences to be observed. Some cultures are what Ruth Benedict called ‘shame cultures’ – the ones driven by social appearances: others are what she called ‘guilt cultures’ (Benedict 1947). This distinction is one of emphasis. All cultures, guilt or not, have 'face' as a significant social component: all cultures have internalised concerns about values. It is just getting the understanding of the mix right that matters (see 'Facing up to' expression in References).

There are instances of cultures being analysed along certain dimensions: sometimes the categorization stems from a conceptual approach, and sometimes it emerges from the data itself. Examples of such categorization are (a) relations with others (b) collective versus individual responsibility (c) universalism versus particularism (d) focused versus diffuse.

Diversity may mean acceptance of difference, but not necessarily so. Writing in 2007, Mayer put the case for cultural variations in its approach to human rights. One would wish to qualify this in terms of stating fundamental rights first, and then looking at what different cultures do. It is held that there are fundamental issues that are superior to culture, and they are subverted at main risk to the proponents of such basic rights. Among the questions to be posed is, to what extent are various approaches, such as Confucianism, Christianity, Communism, Capitalism, etc. vested in human rights? It would be interesting to have modern exponents reach such considered conclusions.

In the international forum, in corporate forums, and in interpersonal exchanges, displays of tolerance are often essential: the reverse of it would undermine all that social transactions try to do. To be intolerant of culturally different ways is the way to social transactional failure; to be intolerant of outcomes not totally to one's liking, is also regarded as intolerant. We may not necessarily regard such variations from tolerance as failures.

The moral dimension may reverse that judgement. If an alien culture were to hold that the use of slavery, be totally acceptable then we would morally condemn: thus, the constant tension between tolerance and the moral imperative (indeed it is considered to ambiguous whether Napoleon banned the slave trade (see 'Napoleon: did he reintroduce slavery' in references).

Those polities that ban the use of the internet may be regrettable. One of the most recent manifestations of culture is that of social media. Yet again, to make a justifiable criticism, being commonly available, and not subject to censorship, it allows people to make unfounded disparaging remarks about another, often to their detriment and to their reputation. At its best it allows study on-line so that anyone may study for a degree, although not all complete and graduate. At least no-one is prevented from trying. Between these two extremes lie a variety of issues.

It needs to be asserted that in Westernised societies personal privacy is widespread. In some cultures there is no such concept: individuals are in someone's company from birth to death. Whereas Westerners often value privacy and time alone, there are some cultures where they are not alone from birth onwards. Such living is communal rather than individual, and not easy for Westerners to understand.

The observed dimension on which cultures may differ is that of collective responsibility. In some sense we all have a collective responsibility. In issues such as marine pollution or the use of fossil fuels, no one person is responsible for the larger picture. Many would like to contribute to constructive ways of reducing the problem yet each gain by making more pollution. If others use their cars less the temptation is to use one's own car more on roads thus less crowded: if common grazing land is depleted by overuse then collectively farmers should use it less – yet an individual farmer gains more by grazing his cattle more than their share (an interesting example of the Prisoner's Dilemma).

## Cultural Oddities

We can appreciate the oddity of comparisons when seeing a film such as the Italian *Mondo Cane* (It's a dog's world), and its sequel *Mondo Pazzo* (it's a mad world [or it is a crazy world]). It is the cross-cutting that makes it so powerful. For example, we see an African tribal woman putting decorative colours on her face: that seemingly primitive ritual is cross-cut to an American woman putting on makeup. We hear about the English love of animals; cross-cut to the practice of removing the vocal chords of dogs so that we do not hear the bark. While it may be tempting to think of the oddity of 'primitive' peoples we should not be blind to our own oddities.

One of the good features of a multi-cultural society is its promotion of tolerance. It should be pointed out, that in such diverse-oriented countries the limits of tolerance are often tested. What is plainly unacceptable is the notion of violence used to further political ends (or does violent resistance become the only means of protest? Is there a justification for a necessary war?).

Further, the idea that non-rational beliefs should hold sway, and is quite different from (say) the evidence on medical procedures, climate change, or nutrition. The UN 30 principles of the UN *Declaration of human rights* are a reference point, but it may not go far enough in asserting (say) the rights of women to be free of male coercion. It bears repetition that total confidence in the culture is to be regretted: what is acceptable is that cultures can, and do, learn from each other.

## Special Cases of Cultural Applications

No account would be complete without the observation that on most ranking criteria, and for whatever reason, sub-Saharan Africa fares badly. Perhaps it is there that we ought to concentrate humanitarian efforts. Finally, as mentioned, one is concerned over the justification for war. There may be some few cases where it seems perfectly justified, the second World War for example which sought dominance of one country over another.

One might also study diverse expression within a culture. One may look at popular culture from a variety of its expressions, including music, comedy, entertainment, etc. Clearly the discretionary use of time is a valuable indicator of changing values. The amount of time we choose to spend on various activities is a strong measure of how much we value them. A love-struck young swain would hardly be likely to argue that he had no time for his beloved because he was too busy cleaning his shoes.

Just as there are cultural inclinations so too are there national characteristics. This tendency finds expression in different ways: thus, Japanese and Germans are seen as formal; Australians not respectful of authority; Russians as soulful and sombre; and West Indians as light-hearted. These national stereotypes are not, of course, true of all members of those nations - nor are such qualities absent in other nations. The statement is merely one of tendency.

Although more specific than the United Nations *Declaration of Human Rights*, it does exist within that general framework of human rights, dignity, and the recognition of our common humanity. The commonality of humanity includes dramatic demonstrations of common origins. The outstanding achievement of Thor Heyerdahl and his crew, crossing the Pacific on a balsa raft, showing how great distance migrations were possible, is an ample illustration.

## Comparing Cultures

Plainly one must decide for one's self where priorities lie. There are various types of guides to cultures. One unusual approach is the listing one. Nwanna (1998) is an example of that genre. This approach is a purely tabular, and is so set-out. For example, that taking photos of people is illegal in Cyprus, and that whistling for the attention of a waiter in Turkey is not customary (or so it is claimed). While one can see merits in a comprehensive listing it seems unlikely that such detail will be recalled and used. What may be more helpful would be to set out some basic principles (and perhaps the issues which Nwanna raises, and then capture those in a principle).

Cultural values may collide on several issues. Among such are the notion of collective responsibility, attitudes to women, judgments about body shape, usury, secret commissions, and loyalty-to-family versus loyalty-to-principle. Among the important themes in international dealings are those of the need to resolve issues of values in relation to different cultures, and to try to find principles that transcend culture. At a personal level one might make the same observation: people do not necessarily come in fixed packages. Not all people from one culture hold the same degree of value attachment to different objects, issues, and principles.

The search for perfection is evident in many cultures, and exists within our framework of dreams and aspirations. It has found expression in that near formless yearning for the 'Golden age' the 'Dreamtime', the 'Garden of Eden', the search for the philosopher's stone, for the elixir of life, and for the state of enlightenment. The current commitment to total quality management, and best international practice, is a recent expression of that idea, transferred to the business context. There is no doubt that quality sells goods and services, and benefits an organisation in the longer term (as Mr. Rolls and Mr. Royce well knew).

Although culture is commonly, and rightly, seen as national or regional differences it can also be attributed to organisations. There can be no doubt about the commitment of organisations as the *Red Cross* or *Medecins sans frontieres:* on the other-hand there are nameless organisations whose main role seem to be profit at any cost, and where dishonesty is a desirable trait that contributes to a 'good' outcome. That point may also be true of specific companies, where the prevailing attitude may be one of honesty or dishonesty. 'Creative' accounting may prevail in some instances, either as downright dishonesty or as devious practices.

Some countries have less regard for human rights; their abrogation being justified by the need to rule such a diverse and large population. Other countries regard some categories as second-class citizens. Yet other places are ones in which the economics of survival are problematic. The problems seem to inhere in the specific circumstances that are dictated either by cultural mores, by ruler's inclinations - or even by something else.

## *The McSally Case*

One might also challenge cultural ways, as was the case of Colonel Martha McSally of the US air-force. Serving in Saudi Arabia she found the status of women appallingly low: the local practices there might best be described as gender apartheid. While stationed in Saudi Arabia she challenged a discriminatory Pentagon policy that required servicewomen to wear Muslim garb when traveling off-base in Saudi Arabia.

These ways of taking out bias bears repetition: one is the obvious one of legislation, as happened in the McSally case. If one were to give women equal opportunity then the talent pool would increase by 50%. One might also challenge cultural ways. While stationed in Saudi Arabia she challenged a discriminatory Pentagon policy that required servicewomen to wear Muslim garb when traveling off-base in Saudi Arabia.

There are strict rules that govern what women may or may not do. Women do not have the same rights as men in the matter of divorce, nor may they marry outside Islam. If a Saudi woman wants to go to hospital, she needs permission from a male relative, women must attend separate schools and, until very recently, not allowed to drive although change is imminent.

Although it is a corporate instance, religious authorities in Saudi Arabia ensure that women are 'appropriately' clad with an enveloping dress in public. The original US ruling was that women who leave the US base must wear the Abaya. Her argument was that the standards she espouses, and for which she fights, are superordinate to culture, a point which she eventually won. There is no doubt that issues, such as this, will continue to arise.

As she noted, she was the first woman to fly a combat mission in a fighter aircraft, but was not then allowed to drive in Saudi Arabia. Eventually she took on Donald Rumsfeld, then Secretary of State for Defense: she won the right to dress conventionally off base, as a Western woman would. It is interesting to note that female embassy staff in Riyadh do not wear the Abaya when representing the US. The argument is that the standards she espouses, and for which she fights, are superordinate to culture, a point which she eventually won. There is no doubt that issues, such as this, will continue to arise (see McSally in References).

## *Expatriates*

The problem of expatriates is one that deserves reconsideration. One might also be concerned that such shock will differentially affect those whose motives for moving might vary. Those who are sent abroad by their organisation, and purely temporarily, will react differently from those long-term sojourners, of those who emigrate with the expected outcome of eventual citizenship. All this reaction to culture shock will, in large part, depend on the personality of the incumbent. One would expect that the more ebullient a character, a willingness to learn, and a cheery outlook would all be a help. In this, flexibility is vital.

There are those whose expertise is needed in other countries, and who are sent by their company or organization. There are others who volunteer to go abroad for the experience, and whose stay is temporary. There are yet others who go with the intention of staying and working in a new environment. For each of such groups different conditions apply, and culture shock affects them differentially, as does the degree of preparation.

An account of some of the ways in which expatriates have to cope is evident. It applies particularly to non-corporates who do not have the organisations' backing or commonality. Of all ways of thinking, and of doing things, culture is the agreed common way. Culture is shared values, ideas and ideals: it is the common frame of reference that allows people to cope with their daily lives. As such, culture is a metonym for a significant part of our identity.

We do need to recognise that cultural adjustment and imposition are significant variables in coping by expatriates. The most obvious challenge is that of language. Not being able to communicate ideas and information is a highly important variable. Having a rudimentary knowledge of the language is vital, but that misses out on the nuances of speech. An instance is that of translating from one culture to another. An example is having a last drink in Mexico is called *La penultima*: even though it is the ultimate drink there is a tradition that the last drink is with the devil, or the last drink on earth (or some other variant explanation).

What is important here is that expatriates may move from one kind of culture to another kind, thereby exacerbating problems of adjustment. The problems arising from cultural insensitivity include such issues as attitude to time and punctuality, the importance of personal relationships, loyalty, gifting, and social responsibility. It is instructive to recall that when the Australian psychologist Porteus was testing Aborigines for cognitive ability they wanted help him, after all he was their blood brother.

## The Mozart Effect

In some Western cultures there is a commitment to what is called (catchy title) *The Mozart effect*, which refers to one of the expressed ideas that listening to Mozart's music enhances intelligence. Their three explanations involved the amount of media attention, particularly outside science; the second was a reflection of contemporary human concerns; the third was about the way that such legends evolved over the course of time. Just because there are various such explanations, does not negate that there may be substantial evidence for the idea: what it does show is the need for caution in believing too readily.

Many cultures have a concept of a dream of an ideal society, and, indeed, it often finds expression in their concept of heaven. Wassailing and drunken fighting, nymphs of unearthly beauty, the sense of ineffable peace, and the unity of humanity are among these. The theme here is the various ways in which the dream of perfectibility is expressed: it is the theme itself that is most interesting. An explanation of the propagation of rumours and legends has been given by Bangerter and Heath (2004). The improvements to the human condition abound. Among them is the idea that one can improve intelligence.

## Suggestions for Cross-Cultural Socialising

Courtesy and etiquette are often critical to an understanding of cultural practices. When dealing with alien cultures there are certain principles that, if followed, would lead to better diplomatic relations. They include:

- It is always safe to shake a proffered hand
- Admire in due season (rather than be critical)
- Do not assert the superiority of one's own culture
- Use formal names unless it is indicated otherwise
- Use honorifics unless told otherwise
- Be careful of sexual behaviour, particularly towards collegial relationships
- Be wary of miscueing, and explain and apologise if mistaken
- React generally to a compliment, and return it if appropriate
- Be wary of interpersonal distance (some cultures stand closer than is the norm in Western cultures).
- If an assertion is made that is plainly negative to the values that you hold dear then give a refutation that is both explains why you disagree, and do so diplomatically.

## Finding Out More (HRAF)

Just as there are inter-personal variations so too are there national and cultural ones. One might study diversity across cultures in such sources as the *Human Relations Area Files* (HRAF) or *The encyclopedia of anthropology* (Birx 2005). HRAF is a private and non-profit organisation that is affiliated with Yale University. In 1995 it had almost one million pages of text containing historical and descriptive information '... on ways of life in 358 different cultural, ethnic, religious and national groups around the world'. This derived from about 8000 source documents. From 1995 onwards, the annual instalments are distributed on CD (known as electronic HRAF).

This massive databank on cross-cultural psychology contains significant information on a variety of topics from over 300 cultures. These data are cast into more than 700 subject categories grouped into 70 major topical sections. The data are on issues as diverse as marriage, sorcery, cannibalism, litigation, incest and humour - with cultures ranging as widely as Zuni Indians, the rural Irish, to the Yoruba tribe of Nigeria. (The website of the Human Relations Area Files is to be found in the References under *Human Relations Area Files*).

## Conclusions

One should draw a distinct difference between racial and cultural factors. The essential difference here is between being free to choose - or not free to choose. One cannot choose to be a race other than that with which one is born: one is free, however, to choose to be culturally bound or not-bound. One is free to choose not to immolate oneself, to not indulge in murder. The essential difference is between choice and non-choice.

Further, extreme caution is recommended as a miscue could have difficult consequences. There have been successful approaches to the taxonomy of cultures; to cultural values; to adjustment; to the self-concept; and, most importantly, to the notion of the categorisation of assumptions. Suggestions are also offered to deal cross-culturally, and to do so without compromising one's own values. People plainly differ on some values which may be fundamental to both. Provide the arguments with their justifications – and do so with diplomacy.

The issue of expatriates and of culture shock is seen as a salient issue, as is the problems of assumptions. An essential conclusion is that the issues of ethnic ways are fraught with the possibility of misunderstanding. To that end some suggestions are offered in dealing cross-culturally.

There can be little doubt that being sensitive and/or well educated have an effect upon culture. One is mindful that the insensitive, particularly as migrants may garner no credit for their respective places of origin. The tendency to spit in public, to barge into others, and possible loudness of speech are intrusions into personal space and privacy. Culture is an evanescent phenomenon: it too evolves and, what was once true, then may become something questionable.

There are some aspects of cultures that are seen as admirable. The unity of the family for one, and business relationships for another. The present writer recalls talking to someone who valued family relationships so highly that she regarded such deprivation as almost insupportable. In some cultures, relationships are paramount. A good instance is that of Guanxi in China. Far from being corrupt is their way of doing business. The term translates as 'connections' or 'networks', and involves more of 'who you know' rather than 'what you know'. One would qualify this by noting that knowing people may be to the detriment of the best decision.

Dealing with known people has its distinct advantages, but we must be mindful that the transactions are honest ones, an example of a non-cultural difference. The British 'the old boy network', the collegiality of professionals, and the connections of freemasonry are all examples. In some cultures it is more overt than in others, but collegiality prevails. This is an instance of a cross-cultural indifference, but has a different emphasis with respect to its being plain and discussed.

One must conclude that cultural variations are matched by variations within cultures. One must also conclude that many cultural practices are such that me be regarded as valuable; by the same token one must also conclude that some practices are contrary to human rights, and to be shunned.

# Chapter 6
# Business

## Introduction

The aspect of business, as it is understood, is to make a profit. We might qualify that by saying the aim is to make a profit while dealing ethically. There has been a myriad of attempts to ameliorate working conditions by making the work safe, remunerated, and agreeable. Three instances are chosen: one is of changes due to the industrial revolution and the experiment of New Lanark and of Cadbury innovations: the second is an illustration of the growth of unionism: the third is the proclamation of the *Marlow Declaration*'.

## Early Attempts

### *New Lanark*

One of the first attempts in the English-speaking world to make labour dignified rather than exploitative was done by Robert Owen in New Lanark experiment. The mill was started by David Dale in 1785: his daughter Caroline, fell in love with Robert Owen. They were married and, in 1799, Robert Owen bought out his partners in the mill, and instituted a utopian colony that involved humane treatment, His major concern was to curb the power of capitalists to dictate the conditions of work – including long hours and dangerous working conditions.

Robert Owen preceded the Cadbury initiative by some time. Owen's view was that a person's character is formed by circumstances, often beyond their control, and thus life circumstances determine outcomes. Originally the manager of a mill in



R. Francis, *Equality in Theory and Practice*,
https://doi.org/10.1007/978-981-15-3488-1_6

Manchester, he founded New Lanark in Scotland in 1799, based on the principle that treating workers well would ameliorate the poor circumstances, and the crime rate: in that, he was successful. This preceded the Cadbury initiatives by over 100 years. The Cadbury initiative is to be admired, being based on the same principles as was New Lanark.

## *Cadbury*

The subsequent venture by the Cadburys ventured into treating workers well showed surprisingly good results. Initially the company built 16 houses, naming the village as Bournville. Eventually they added more homes, a school, and a hospital. By 1900 the village had 313 houses, being administered by a Trust. The important issue here was that of civilised living. The chocolate producing factory was formerly located in Birmingham, and then relocated to Bournville just a few miles out of the city.

The Cadbury brothers had found the slums of Birmingham depressing to the extent that they felt compelled to move the factory to a more salubrious place, also for the reason given above. One might also add that there was a need to find a place suitable for the factory to expand. There they started with a few houses and, eventually, it became a model village with all the healthy amenities associated with rural life. Importantly, the village showed that treating workers in an enlightened fashion was profitable.

The scheme also pioneered such enterprises as a pension scheme, joint work committees, sports grounds and changing rooms, and medical facilities. What is most interesting is that treating workers with dignity and worth did not diminish their profitability, witness that they remained in business. The complexities of the cocoa/chocolate trade was given in Cadbury (2012). As the Cadbury's were Quakers they built a 'meeting house' rather than a church: in accordance to their religious precepts there are no licensed premises or public houses on the estate. In 2010 Cadbury's was bought by the American company Kraft, and who may, or who may or may not, modify the enterprise. For views on maintaining Fair Trade principles see (References under Cadbury).

Early attempts by the Quaker families (among others they include, Cadbury, Fry, and Rowntree). Finding that they were barred from universities (as were all dissenters) and many professions they sought outlets in trade, essentially sought enterprises in non-military business. One instructive instance is that of what came to be known as the 'Chocolate wars' (Cadbury (b) 2012). As was mentioned, the core of what they did was to make labour an attractive prospect rather than one that was exploitative. As a model village was built, so too was a corresponding regard for human enterprises. In other words, the aim was to provide a whole-of-life experience by treating the workers as worthy people. The essence of what they did was to create agreeable conditions that made work a pleasure rather than a chore.

## *Unionism*

moving to the start of unionism; in 1834 farm workers in Dorset formed an early trade union, six of their leaders were tried and sentenced to seven years transportation (Tolpuddle, named after the village in Dorset whence these agricultural labourers originated). There was a massive protest campaign, and those sentenced returned home in triumph. The notion that the economy will suffer if we no longer, metaphorically, put little boys up chimneys was now totally unacceptable. The humane approach had its adherents whereas other approaches did not. Witness the enterprise actions were in the early days of union organisations: Chartism was another such. It was a movement devoted to parliamentary reform, and had a platform that was designed to encompass that ideal. The industrial revolution undoubtedly brought in its wake the slums, dreary labour, and the use of humans as a means of turning a profit.

Indeed, there was a movement to ban workers banding together to form a union. The Blakean view of the 'dark satanic mills' is an apt one, and led to disparities of wealth and influence. The Tolpuddle Martyrs were the six mentioned Dorchester labourers who, in 1833, were convicted of taking 'unlawful' oaths when they united to oppose a cut in wages. They were subject to transportation and were so sent, eventually being pardoned in 1836. The stood for a set of propositions which included:

- Annually elected parliaments
- Equal electoral districts
- Payment to MPs
- The abolition of property qualifications for membership
- Universal manhood suffrage
- Vote by ballot

equalising, and stemmed from growing discontent with the degradations of industrialisation. During the 1830s and 1840s many trade unionists were transported, including a group of Canadian rebels who tried to free Canada from British rule. This general approach gave rise to many attempts to assert the dignity of labour, to provide a secure living wage, and to make working safe in both the short-term and the long-term. It finds expression in such issues as human suffrage, the equality of the sexes, and safe working conditions (see Equality of the sexes in the Torah in References). Many employers today still resist the notion of union membership. They do make the point that since businesses are not allowed cartels why should labour not be subjected to the same restrictions? Notwithstanding, it did lead to the growth of unionism.

First the moves of the industrial revolution: the urbanisation of population movement is one where rural dwellers moved to cities to be near work, and to receive a weekly wage. The danger, and conditions of squalid living, eventually led to the growth of the union movement: one in which industrial safety became a paramount issue. Losing people in preventable industrial accidents, at least in Western societies, became a notable intervention. All lives are equal was a fundamental precept, and no-one had the right to profit from carelessness or the saving of essential expense.

The sweatshops, so ably recounted by Dickens, became a movement that eventually led to the diminution of industrial accidents. Notwithstanding, one hears stories of continuing carelessness in the case of Third World countries labour, where lives are expendable. That general trend toward safety and survival in Western societies is evident in the case of reported instances of exploitation in Pakistani factories in 2012, where a fire killed 257 people and injured more than 600. The general tenor of this concern is that lives are to be equally valued, a circumstance which appears to be in breach of some extreme right political views.

## *The Marlowe Declaration*

It is instructive to note that the general move to more humane business dealings has, of late, given rise to codes of ethics and codes of conduct. Among the early attempts to formulate ethical principles for business was in Britain in the early sixties. A copy of that document was obtained many years ago by the author, and is mentioned here (Fogarty 1963).

That document held that ethics is a unity, and indivisible. It also held that the purpose of industry was to fulfil human needs, and not the just make profits for entrepreneurs. The essentials of business include fair wages, security, status, comradeship, scope for self-development and fulfilment. Good safe working conditions are part of the package, as is pride in skill, a sense of belonging, and value to others of the work done. In addition to the principles already mentioned it is desirable that organisations be good neighbours, taking a constructive interest in local and national affairs. The document advocated a balance between the proper and productive use and development of resources, both human and material.

The original *Declaration* was drafted and circulated by 18 men at Marlowe in Buckinghamshire: their origins included the churches, the boardroom, trade unions, and the teaching profession. They came together because of their common conviction that our generation has within its grasp a great opportunity to shape a new society sustained by the rightness of its purpose and based on the justice of its institutions.

Among the points that they made was that the golden age is not past: qualities such as justice, ability, integrity still have strong currency. The continuation of human effort is both current and required. To this end actions, including business actions, must be based on clear ethical principles, and become a part of custom and practice. Among the principles that they addressed and endorsed were the importance of community, balanced with the notion that responsibility is always based on the individual. Their second point concerned social responsibility in which developing values enrich all our lives, and is an obligation placed upon all of us.

The declared goal of the *Declaration* was to direct public opinion toward society getting a better understanding of the nature of individual and economic realities within which it must function. It held that the most valuable asset of any organisation is best measured by the skill, knowledge, loyalty, enthusiasm, and goodwill, of those whom it employs, and those with whom it does business.

To that end aspects such as education, technical training, safety, induction, stress, and redundancy are all critical aspects. To this should be added the proper use of leisure, and of early retirement. There is an indivisibility of work/home life, each of which has a significant impact on the other. Consultation and negotiation are also both vital to a successful enterprise.

A final point by the Declarants was that authority is a trust. Leaders do so by force of example, and thus have a strong in influence on people's lives: to that end they must be held accountable. Further, such leading by example should bring attendant humility. The leader must be the servant of those they presume to lead. It is a demonstration that they do not just hold power for its own sake.

One would need to conclude that the English-speaking world were among the pioneers of the dignity and worth of labour. It was understood (or mis-understood) that the dictatorship of the proletariat would lead to something quite different, including Stakhanovite workers who were exhorted to yet greater outputs.

## *Money Matters*

The avowed intent of business is to make a profit. That is a totally worthy notion provided it is done in a manner consistent with dignity and safety uppermost in an employer's mind. While one cannot legislate to make the workers capitalists one can ensure that there is continuity of employment. If one were to single out one variable it is that of executive salaries. The point of 'the city' is that it is there, and unashamedly so, to make money. It is not there to improve life or run social issues. Return on capital is one of the main drivers.

While workers receive a certain salary the CEOs receive an amount that may be many times that of the average worker. For example, after VW was shown to cheat on emissions tests the CEO (Mr. Martin Winterkorn) resigned with a payout of millions of Euros (he has since been charged). This raises the question of should the salary of anyone be more than (say) ten times the national average, or some other moderate proportion. There is movement elsewhere to limit the salary and bonuses of CEOs, but it is a problem as to how successful such a move might be. The claim that it is competitive with overseas salaries, and could not attract business talent, with such inducements being a moot point. (see Volkswagen in References).

Where an executive gets (say) over $10 million dollars per annum, with customers funding it, is possibly dubious. Further, some of those in directorships are members of multiple boards, and receive a salary from each. While one has to recognise the value of such experience it is quite possible that such positions are not only financially rewarding but also may form a clique which places further barriers to board appointments.

Another finance issue is how one measures GDP. Its common definition is commonly defined as:

> The monetary value of all the finished goods and services produced by a country within a specific time period.

One also need to be aware that there is more than one form of GDP: there is the national one, the one on military spending or advertising, internationally (although one might call international figures 'expenditure'). It is curious that 'defence' always has a fully funded call upon the public purse whereas hospitals and schools have to run cake stalls to raise funds. The legislature determine such issues, but make it no less curious as to priorities. Clearly external defence outranks hospitals and schools. If defence were to rely on cake-stalls, and hospitals receive priority funding, it would amount to a reversal of priorities. The question here is, would it be a moral act?

What is curious about the definition of GDP is that it includes all legal activity and any measurable illegal activity. One could well imagine circumstances which include a lot of illegal activity which would boost GDP in undesirable ways. One could well ask what proportion of GDP is spent on such issues as military matters. As may one readily see, the proportion of GDP so spent has quite a variation. Haiti, for instance, is recorded as spending virtually nothing on the military while Israel spends over 5%. In business one could ask what percentage of GDP is spent on advertising.

A renascent interest in corporate performance may be driven by commercial imperatives. As competition increases so too does the need to strive for excellence. It is curious that we expect, and get, 'total quality management' (TQM) in symphony orchestras (no sour notes, excellent performance, prompt starting times, etc). Why can we not get the same from car repair garages, computer repair people, and airlines? Perhaps it is the 'luxury' nature of the product that demands such quality; one would not otherwise pay such money for a non-necessity. One pertinent question is whether Western values are consistent with the search for excellence. The conclusion is that there is such a set of values, and identified them being as follows:

- The inherent value of mankind; people is seen as an asset, what it is, and what it can become.
- It is our destiny to serve and to improve. The joy of good work; the satisfactory completion of something demanding brings fulfilment.
- The importance of service is not only service to customers, it is service to all – customers; neighbours; subordinates, etc. It is better to give than to receive; performance is judged by the stewardship of assets.

It might seem that these values are more philanthropic than commercial. Cormack (1991) argued that it is only by the adoption of these wider community values that we can become excellent. The relatively recent work on excellence (in the US) by Peters and Waterman (1982) is, arguably, one of the most important business books to appear in recent times. Even though the terms ‘ethics’ and ‘business ethics’ do not appear in the index, that work on excellence is clearly devoted to the subject.

One might be concerned that talent may be lost through the imposition of tertiary fees, thus in Germany university education for a first degree incurs miniscule fees. The German legislature did so on the basis that nothing conduces more to equality than that of equality of opportunity. In contrast we may view the alternative approach of the seeming conferral of privilege on graduates incurs a cost, which has to be met by those qualifying at higher levels. It is such debates that are at the heart of democracy.

Among other considerations is the notion of unpaid labour and unpaid support. Folbre (1994) has pointed out the missing aspect of Adam Smith’s work (*The wealth of nations*), is that Mrs. Smith was always there to support Mr. Smith, with children being a financial expense. This point needs to be emphasised that parents are often parents through choice. Economics apart, children are an emotional asset that is incalculable, a point that economic indicators often fail to accommodate.

The percent of GDP devoted to overseas aid is determined by government, and quite rightly so. What is less obvious is the way that it is spent. One country might use it as donations to worthy recipients, another might use it for immigration, and yet a third to cover the cost of refugee camps. Again, it is up to the legislature to determine. One is yet uncertain how much of the aid goes in corruption, and would it make a difference to its allocation if it were known? Would one be swayed by the argument that unless a proportion goes in bribes none of it would reach worthy recipients?

## General Progress Indicator

There are alternatives to the GDP: amongst such is the Genuine Progress Indicator. It is comprised of a number of components and measures, as it says, Genuine Progress. At present GDP is a measure of the health of an economy, but that is an economic indicator, and fails to measures progress in other areas. There is no doubt that GDP will be around for some time to come, but eventually will be replaced by some measure that will record progress in other relevant areas.

With respect to general funding there is a problem in that in a democracy there are many calls on the public purse. Among such are education, hospitals, and publicly funded broadcasters. The basis would be very difficult if the notion of independent broadcasters were to be so starved of funding that critics of the government were silenced, just becoming mouthpieces for the status quo – we call that 'government propaganda'. One of the essences of democracy is a vigorous and independent press.

## *Factors in Business*

Corporations have done much that is positive, and much that makes our lives better than almost any other human enterprise. As Lloyd noted 'The corporation has' ... created order out of chaos, wealth out of rubble and work out of idleness'. Despite it having been predatory it has never been 'cowardly or indolent'. As Lloyd put it, 'the admirable qualities of boldness and vigour that have inspired great achievements. Corporate activity has "tamed the elements" and has had a significant in influence in moulding our environment' (Lloyd 1991: p. xiii).

The comparatively recent development of the concept of the corporation parallels that of the evolution of living organisms. Corporations are subject to modification, and benefit in the same way from competition and co-operation. The basic thrust of Lloyd's argument is that it is now appropriate to be concerned with business ethics; he also argues that this is in the best long-term interests of an organisation. He noted that, at least by human standards, the organization has 'feral energy', and went on to say that '… the company unfettered and rampant, is a familiar villain in the dystopian visions of the future depicted in our literature'. Lloyd described the company as a non-moral entity '… motivated by greed… companies are monsters created by decent human Frankensteins, which monsters we need to control.' That is why we need such infrastructure as company law, various governmental agencies, and regulatory bodies.

Companies collectively constitute a conscious, intelligent, non-human species at a relatively early stage in their evolution. The theory of evolution represents a powerful, ready-made model for a dynamic theory of business economics. Recent changes in the chemistry of the corporate medium favour the emergence of strategies, internal as well as external, that are 'nicer' than traditional strategies?

## *Business Decisions*

The professions do have connections to the business world, to state the obvious. For example, one could not imagine an architect who was not connected to business decision making. The awkward balance involves such issues as privileged communications, the salience of professional codes over company codes, and the salience of professional ethics, and the role of research. Among the question we could pose, are human rights a Western imposition? A final point in business related matters is to what extent should business take into account those who are aged-employees?

Another quantification insight to us is the potential for crimes committed within the corporation. One might compare the numbers of crimes to cities of the same size. Within a giant corporation there will be a proportion of murders, rapes, assaults, thefts and embezzlement. While it is true that the populations at risk may be different, and offenders differentially detectable, the force of comparison is still there. It would be impossible to believe that any corporation hires only the saintly, has employment practices so perfect that HR only employs those who will not lie, cheat, steal, or assault.

## *Freedom of Expression*

Article 19 of the UN Declaration holds that all have the right to expressing their views on various matters. It goes on to assert that everyone has the right to freedom of opinion and expression; this right includes freedom to hold any view that they wish, and may do so without external influence. They are enjoined through any medium, to use whatever system they like to acquire and impart information as they see fit, and to do so without regard to national frontiers. That is a view tempered by the capacity to criticise anonymously.

Although this reference is to information generally it may be construed in various ways. At the basic level one might consider if potential talent may be squandered if that talent is not nurtured. Not all are suited to proceed to higher education, to make in obvious point: nor is it an aspiration of many who might otherwise have qualified. The fundamental point here is that of ‘caring for others’ and fostering the equality of opportunity to a higher education without an individual incurring a lifetime of debt: that is an issue worthy of debate.

## *Metaphors*

One of the difficulties of using the evolutionary metaphor – all metaphors limp, and some are legless (i.e. no metaphor is exact, and many vary in aptness). It is possible that the inheritance of acquired characteristics is a more appropriate explanation of the development of corporate behaviour than the Darwinian one.

That cannot be true of the corporation. In its place he proposed that strategic themes (stremes) are the building blocks of corporate evolution. Corporate life evolves by the natural selection of those who engage in the differential use of strategic themes. Just as genes propagate themselves in the gene pool via sperm and eggs, so ‘stremes’ are propagated in the streme pool by the propensity to emulate winning strategies (Lloyd 1991, p. 142).

## *Prescriptions*

We might consider whether or not to make employees part owners. There are some principles that might be implemented, notable among them are:

- Make courtesy mandatory (eg. ensure that adequate warnings are given, and remedies instituted, before terminating employment)
- Ensure total probity of banks. Either they are independent entities, or they are government backed. One might be concerned at the 'too big to fail' phenomenon: the dishonesty of banks is now almost legendary. No matter what a bank might not be allowed to do is to become insolvent. One method of ensuring greater honesty is to make the senior executives personally liable if there is dishonesty, even to the point of imprisonment.
- Reintroduce tenure of employment (an assured income of [say] $50K is better than an uncertain one of [say] $70K).
- Recognise that economic indicators and wage justice do not capture a child's smile, health, wellbeing, and education. Economic indicators, while important, may be distant from real human concerns.

## *Robots*

The advent of machines that do assembly work, and do it more efficiently, means that fewer people are employed, or the same number with a lesser working week. There is thus a shift from productivity toward service industries without there being commensurate corresponding changes in training and employment. The problem here is that the definition of being prosperous is materialistic. One could well imagine that such a change could have distinct advantages. For one thing, it would recognise that equality may have a substantial input into the quality of life, leaving people freer to enjoy relationships with family and friends. For instance, on

## *Stremes*

An example of an advantageous streme is that competitive advantage is a matter of producing new products quickly rather than existing products cheaply (Lloyd 1991, p. 147). Those corporations able to adapt are the ones most likely to prosper. An example of a streme is that of using a 'hollow corporation'. Such a corporation is entrepreneurial in that it has the business idea but contracts out the work. This allows for speed of response, reduces its need for infrastructure and capital, and makes it easier to contract with suppliers of goods and services who have an ethical standpoint. Among recent changes in corporate functioning are the ways in which information is being substituted for capital equipment and money, and the recurrent theme that people are the prime consideration.

## Succession Planning

Among the issues that confront businesses there are several such. They include mobility, succession planning, and the relationship to the professions. Professional and business mobility works against developing a loyalty to one organization. How does one promote loyalty in a shifting set of commercial and industrial alliances? If national espionage is permissible, why not industrial espionage? Are company mergers for personal protection to be ethically permitted? Should ethical statements be cast in culturally appropriate terms? Under what conditions is it ethical to accept gifts in a business context?

For a comparative account of teaching business ethics in several countries see White and Taft 2004. More recently there is a paper that considers the importance of the impact of religious beliefs on the teaching of business ethics (Ruhe and Lee 2008).

Succession planning involves issues of appointments, staff retention, family arguments, promotion, KPIs, resignations, talent spotting, and the 'glass ceiling'. It is relatively commonplace to find that the driving entrepreneur founds a company and makes it successful. Eventually they need to retire, and then come the problem of succession. Business planning ought to take place, and sometimes does. This notion of succession planning can be fraught with danger in that one offspring may be passed over, one offspring could so a better job, or one offspring is the 'wrong' sex. Agreeing on the method of deciding, and then employing that method, has much to commend it. Thus, one might decide in plenty of time what should take place.

The same point might also be made of someone taking over a business as CEO, and being under-qualified. The problem of succession-planning is more common in smaller private companies than it is in larger ones. There an appointment may be made on an objective basis, but always subject to those in the 'old boy network'. Following the proposition of wider and non-economic responsibility is that of what can be done. First and foremost is society, often in the form the legislature, to determine what kind of society we want. The rich sometimes get rich by political favours (such as rezoning) rather than by innovation, invention, or talent. Given that, then (and only then) can we determine the means by which it is to be achieved.

## Commentary and Cautions

Among the kinds of issues that business might address include once having determined that kind of society we want it is then that we must look to economy to see how it is to be achieved. The means might include:

- plugging loopholes in the tax system
- having a turnover tax that would prevent the artificial lowering of taxation
- make bullying the in the workplace a criminal offence (with personal sanctions)
- Have a clear system whereby whistleblowers are given maximum protection – and in highly practical ways
- put a cap on executive salaries (eg. no more than ten times the national average?) It is noted that in George Orwell's book *The lion and the unicorn* he made the recommendation that no-one should earn more than ten times the salary of anyone else (one might ask, what does 'anyone else' mean?)
- The stages of business planning and starting can be hazardous, and many governments have business bureaux which can be of assistance. The processes of running a business and, indeed, of exiting such a venture can benefit from advice. For some governments, there are grants available, such as for the arts or for farming. It is only by inquiring within the country that one would know if such schemes exist.

One might be justly critical of Credit Agencies. They are a business that seeks to contain risk while maximising profit. They assess financial assets, primarily bonds and stocks, rather than being concerned for consumers. As such they are investor-oriented. It is not argued that credit ratings are irrelevant, indeed the capacity to repay is critical, but it is not the only variable; one might also be disposed to help the genuine needy.

It is instructive to consider the principle of 'who will guard the guardians', a problem neatly outlined in Plato's *Republic*. Those who monitor issues may, themselves, not be free of taint, as in a conflict of interest. One might consider such cases as negative gearing (the offsetting of the costs of property owned being a deduction that is legally acceptable). Where the legislature contains people who benefit from its continuance, should they be allowed a vote on the issue? Further, how does one ensure that such a conflict of interest arises, and how to deal with it.

On the matter of a verbal 'dressing up' Denniss (2016) accused politicians and economists of using econo-babble to obfuscate issues. That point is true of psycho-babble and politico-babble. Misused, it excludes the common person from conversation about choices, it is often cryptic and uses elitist and belittling language. First, we must decide what kind of society we want and then, and only then, are we in position to set about making it effective. It is one in which it is possible to conceal truths from the public. According to Denniss there can be one or both processes; 'incomprehensible jargon, and words stripped of their ordinary meaning'. It, in modern terms, gives rise to 'spin doctoring'.

Of a slightly different kind is an account given by Levitt and Dubner (2005). Their work concerns questions about the way the world should work, and the way that it does. They pose such questions as the truth about real estate agents, campaign finance, the Ku Klux Klan. It is, in other words, a way of seeing through the clutter, and poses some very difficult questions – as it properly should. As mentioned, the essence of the argument is that economics is the way the world does *work*, and morality is the way that it *should* work.

It is worthwhile recording that entrepreneurship still pays dividends. Taking the case of Bill Gates, it was interesting that he chose to be paid royalties rather than selling outright. Who knows what would have happened had he sold? There are various strategic decisions made in business that have a powerful impact on the outcome. Such decisions are distinctly strategic rather than tactical. It is such decisions that have a profound impact on the development of businesses. All of this is predicated on the assumption that business size is not relevant, yet in other respects it most certainly is (as in economies of scale, for example).

One of the pressing problems, as ever, is that which bedevils practical research. Taking the case for mobile phones causes brain cancer. One could hypothesise that they do (or do not) have such an effect. One could imagine cases where a research department of a corporation commissioned university research. If the results showed that it might be implicated does the company then pressure the researcher to 'interpret' the results, or does the researcher resist? This is not to say that it happens, it is just that it is a serious dilemma. The resolution is an empirical one, fostered by independent research. The question of whether mobile phones cause cancer is something to be determined by factors other than the strict research methodology.

## Conclusions

One must conclude that treating workers as fellow humans instead of entities to be exploited is a relatively recent innovation. The value of such actions is both humanitarian and commercially advantageous. One is also persuaded that the presence of a code of conduct and a code of ethics is commercially advantageous. This would be supplemented by an ethics committee which would consider amendments to the Code as well as determining cases. The advantages to commerce include the value of stremes, of successional planning: to which are added some legislative suggestions, among which are the capping of executive salaries and multiple directorships. Overall the trend has been to greater equality of humans, despite the many reversions. Most importantly, the general trend is toward greater equality, and is shown to be profitable.

# Chapter 7
# Communication

## Introduction

One might ask about common-humanity, to which a response might be about the things that are common knowledge. In the field of aesthetics there are constants. For example, harmony and counterpoint in music seem to be universally appreciated, although the form it sometimes takes may vary. The notion of 'golden section' has come to us from the ancient Greeks. There is a ratio of length to breadth that seems to be most pleasing. Thus, a picture is rarely square nor very long and thin (when it is we then call it a frieze, or some other word, and apply another judgement: a very long box is no longer a box, it is a square tube).

### *Aesthetics*

The ratio that seems most pleasing is in roughly the ratio of three is to five. Indeed, one of the most famous buildings in the world is the Parthenon. Apart from its historical significance there are abundant aesthetically pleasing properties built in. Thus, the floor plan is golden section: the floor looks perfectly level but is slightly domed to make it look level; the supporting columns look straight, but are really thicker halfway along the column (noting that that is where they are mostly likely to break: thus, aesthetics and practicality go hand-in-hand). The slight doming of the floor ensures that it drains outwards rather than inwards.

The A4 paper with which we are now familiar comes with a beneficial characteristic. When an A3 sheet is folded to become two A4 sheets, the ratio of length to breadth remains constant: when an A4 sheet is folded in half to make an A5 those same proportions are preserved, and thus is both practical as well as aesthetically pleasing.



R. Francis, *Equality in Theory and Practice*,
https://doi.org/10.1007/978-981-15-3488-1_7

The notion of female beauty also finds form and function in unison. Thus, the most pleasing ratio of female waist to hips is in the ratio of 0.7:1.0 for a whole variety of cultures (excepting, perhaps, where steatopygia is present). Perhaps the attractive (to males) part is that a slender waist indicates youth and fitness. The way in which evolutionary biology has governed perceptions of human attractiveness has been examined by Gangestad and Scheyd (2005). Their conclusions included the notion of evolutionary adaptiveness as a driver: their study ranged more widely to Western ideas about modifications of the body to enhance attractiveness.

The whole notion of the science of attraction has been variously addressed. Their approach is based not only on the existing literature but also on psychological research. In this context the idea of body metrics is particularly apt (there is an excellent discussion of that idea to be found in Swami and Furnham 2007). For an evolutionary psychology perspective the work of Jones (2013) is appropriate.

The ability to communicate is vital to social life. Apart from its sociological significance it is also vital to citizenship and residence. One could not live in countries where (say) Arabic, or Mandarin, or Spanish, rather than English, is not spoken. In order to be part of the wider social network one needs a working knowledge of the local language. To be able, for example, to take part in the political process one needs to be able to read the platforms of prospective candidates. Quite apart from the political process one needs to be able to read such elementary items such as road signs and to shopping items. It is commonplace to find that communication may go awry.

## *Non-verbal Communication (NVC)*

It is estimated that much of our communication is non-verbal. This may include items such as body language and gestures, the use of tone of voice: it may also include such issues as significant silences. One might, for example, say pleasant things about someone whom your interlocutor does not share: a significant silence may be eloquent of disagreement, as may a locked gaze.

There are various systems by which one might interpret body language but it is also the province of charlatans who purport to give the 'answers' to what various bodily indications mean. A good question here is 'what is the evidence, and for which particular cultures?' One might also encounter those adept at covering the NVC, as in the card game of poker where one might develop a 'poker face' so as not to give anything away about the hand one holds.

Sometimes gestures are positive, as in sticking out the tongue or giving the thumbs-up, and negative as in making a vomiting gesture, or giving the thumbs-down. On occasion, they may also be an absence of gesture or comment, as in the case given above. An indication may also be given by body posture, as in standing arms-akimbo, or placing a hand over the mouth in a simulated yawn. Being attentive may be indicated by intensity of gaze, or by constant questioning, as if one wished to be well-informed.

Some time ago it was shown by Hess (1965) that the pupil dilated in response to pleasurable stimuli, and the drug Belladonna indicated a sexual interest by having enlarged pupils (Belladonna, meaning beautiful woman). Conversely the pupils narrowed under negative stimuli ('his eyes contracted to pinpoints of hatred'), Since that novel topic, it has been shown that it appears to be a robust finding. Between styles of writing and voicing. In a classic study, Morris (1977) went so far as to draw attention to certain international comparisons concerning the use of gestures – 'gesture maps' of Europe. For example, the common manner of summoning a waiter in some Latin countries would be regarded as peremptory and offensive to an Anglo-Saxon.

The size of the interlocutor group has a bearing on what is communicated. If one were talking to a trusted friend it would be quite a different enterprise from (say) giving a lecture. The largest group to which one might talk is the media: the understanding being that was is conveyed is to be used for public consumption unless it was said with caution (off the record). With this goes the concept of 'fake news'; fabricated information designed to put an alternative, and possibly false, interpretation on what was already disseminated. Running across that is the notion of confidentiality. Confidentiality may not be found in general talks, but may be available with trusted friends.

## Face

Zimmer's (2008) basic idea is that facial expression allows us to spy upon the intimate connections between brain and face. That topic has also been addressed by Finzi (2013), who substantiated the view that facial expression (or the inability to make it) can affect such issues as mood states. The overall conclusion to be drawn here is that facial concealment is a socially disabling act. In Western culture one might tolerate headscarves, hair over the eyes, and various other forms of concealment. What does seem to be the stopping point is that facial evidence in social situations is crucial to our form of interaction, and deviations from that norm, such as full-face covering, are marginally acceptable (see Face recognition in references).

The absence of the capacity to provide facial cues is both distressing for the sufferer and, in the longer term, makes them unable to take up professions in which interaction is critical – medicine, psychology, the ministry, law, teaching. It is salutary, in passing, to draw parallels between an incapacity to communicate via facial expression, and the denial of facial feedback arising from wearing a veil. More importantly, an inability to communicate via facial expression could lead to misunderstandings that may then lead to offending.

Prosopagnosia is a condition where the ability to recognise faces is significantly impaired, although the recognition of other objects seems to be normal: it is, in other words, a form of face blindness. A socially disabling phenomenon, it must cause distress to sufferers, although many learn to cope. A complementary condition is one known as 'Möbius Syndrome' in which a paralysis of cranial nerves leads to sufferers losing the capacity for facial movement and expression (see Cole and Spalding 2009).

More importantly, for this work, an inability to communicate via facial expression could lead to misunderstandings that may then lead to offending. One might argue that, where women are adversely discriminated one might even up the score by providing the veil. The difficulty here is that such an approach is historical (they are advantaged, have been adversely discriminated: but does not provide a justification for continuing such discrimination).

The use of face coverings by females in some cultures is contrary to the Westernised usual norms and forms of social interaction. Much of our social life depends upon facial recognition, on feedback in conversation, and in mutual gaze; without these our social life is impoverished, and an advantage is conferred on the covered one, who has access to information denied to her (or his) interlocutor. It also has criminal implications. If people were to be permitted to wear a total facial covering, it could conceal the identity of someone intent on committing an offence.

In this context, it is significant that for some time banks have required that motorcyclists remove their helmets when entering their premises so that recognition is possible. Further, the notion that men might be consumed with uncontrollable lust at the sight of a female face is not sustainable. It maintains, in effect, that men are not to be trusted; such a lack of trust is inimical to conventional social relations and courtesies. Furthermore, the idea that women's faces are to be concealed, whereas men's faces are not, may be contrary to Western notions of equality.

Here the issues involve not only facial recognition but also facial expression. Much of our social interaction is based on reading clues from others: their appearance and movement are as important in communication as the words they use. Our social interaction is predicated on being able to see faces, interpret expressions, and interact. *The Man in the Iron Mask* is a literally faceless character, the *Elephant man*, with his horribly disfigured visage, was the subject first of horror, then of pity. The popularity of emoji on the computer confirm that point.

To indicate particular emotions we 'pull a face', in showing courage we 'face the music', and withdrawal from sociability involves 'self-effacement'; in Blake's *Songs of Innocence* pity has a human face. Additionally, the vast international cosmetics industry provides a material testament to the importance we attach to the face. As W.H. Davies so aptly put it in his poem, 'What is this life if, full of care, we have no time to stand and stare'. The apt couplet here is 'No time to wait till her mouth can/enrich that smile her eyes began'.

Interpersonal distance, and percentage and direction of gaze are further examples of non-verbal communication that may be the subject of inter-ethnic misunderstanding. One wonders how often annoyance, sexual availability and general comprehension are misinterpreted in inter-ethnic conversation, and to what extent that generates criminal acts.

While one may question the existence of universal expressions of emotion (with the possible exception of the 'startle response'), there can be no doubt that facial expressions of whatever kind are of enormous significance. Because of this, we have come to stylise them and use them as a significant source of social information.

Here one has caution about universal expression of emotion. Some of it is facial, other views hold it to be an overall body language expression. Notwithstanding, one may still legitimately ask if there are universal and acceptable such expressions.

The importance of the connection between facial expression and emotion was highlighted by a study at Cologne University (Zimmer 2008). Women who had had Botox injections in the facial area found it hard to make an angry face. Their corresponding brain scans showed reduced activity in the areas of the brain that control emotions. They not only cannot express anger well but feel it less.

## Words

There is, too, the issue of the misuse of words: on that matter there is a clear distinction between the words uninterested and disinterested. To be uninterested is to be careless of considerations, and definitely not interested. To be disinterested is to have no benefit from the outcome, but still to be interested in what is taking place – just as a judge is interested but disinterested. Another instance of the misuse of a word is 'enormity': one should use the word to mean morally reprehensible, not one of magnitude.

There are some ideas that will plainly have few adherents. Among them is the idea that the dispossessed should have determinative power. Since they are not an organised group, as well as being marginal members of society, it is rather unlikely that such an idea would find approval. Of a lesser kind is the concept of the divine right of kings, which has long been abrogated in Western societies although there are a few residual elements of it elsewhere (Thailand for example).

Most recently the trend has been seen as in Westernised society as the rule of law, of universal enfranchisement, and of parliamentary democracy. More recently it has accommodated the abolition of serfdom and of slavery; yet more recently it has taken to anti-discrimination legislation. To this cheering news we might add a list of the improvements mankind has wrought.

Overall here we assert that communication is the very essence of social life: without it one would be bereft of one of its most significant parts. A point related to this is that of attractiveness, the main point here being that unattractive people suffer disadvantages by virtue of their appearance. A report in *The psychologist* noted that the less attractive tend to be perceived as less smart and less sociable. Less attractive people have lower earnings, and attractive people enjoy social advantages (see Attractiveness in the References).

Given the spectrum of behaviour one might need training of certain kinds. For example, those who are too overtly aggressive may have behaviour modification: those who are underwhelming may be taught to be more assertive: those with excessive anger may have anger-management skills: the very essence of social life. All of this is predicated on the assumption that such skills are available. Where there is a gross breakdown in communication skills, as in deaf mutes, they must suffer inordinately. It is only when someone as bright as Helen Keller do we know how they feel.

With respect to training one would be cautious about subjecting such persons to someone who is unqualified. The danger here is the unaccountability of practitioners who are unqualified. It is not that accountability is all but it is, at least, a basic safeguard. That is one of the reasons for professional registration.

Where it is intentional, and with respect to lying, Ekman's (1985) work has received lay expression in Gladwell's *Blink* (2006). Both make the point that facial expressions, no matter how fleeting or complex, are a vital guide to social interaction. Ekman's work, aptly called *Telling lies*), explores those spontaneous, fleeting and non-stylised facial expressions where meaning can be communicated by telling micro-cues that are not ordinarily under conscious control.

Those languages which are spoken widely are English, Mandarin, and Arabic, where once the language of resort was, in the scholarly world, Latin: that is no longer the case. It is worthy of note that English is a flexible and evolving language, with Mandarin and Arabic a bit less so. It is the case that Mandarin is written by many but largely within the confines of China: and Spanish to both Spain and large tracts of South and Central America.

## *Translation*

Presumably one wonders how much might be lost in translation. Nevertheless, the actions speak for themselves, while recognising poor translation. One calls to mind an instance, in Central America. A translation was taking place. The original saying in Spanish was 'In the name of our Lord and Saviour thou resemblest thy maternal parent': it came out in translation as 'Jesus, you are like your mother' – which is not quite the same. Thus, to paraphrasing: one may, even though quite inadvertently, get the wrong idea about is being proposed. The main danger in such rephrasing is the possibility of mistaking the meaning. One calls to mind the instance of a conference in Russia in which there was a constant reference to 'water goats'. It turned out to be 'hydraulic rams'.

The worst experience of all is being attributed with a point of view which is the reverse of the position being held. A related problem is being in error and having to publish a retraction. This can not only happen, but could indicate a fundamental honesty which, in the long run, may reflect well on the retractor.

### Voice

Another form of attractiveness is that of voice. Those who speak in fractured language, have voices that are harsh, piping or garbled are perceived to be less attractive. *The Australian Institute of Criminology* has a crime-prevention program for culturally and linguistic diverse member of the community (see AIC in References). It may have particular application for those from culturally and linguistically diverse backgrounds. Certainly, such a first step towards dealing with this would be to increase language fluency. One consequence of unattractiveness might be an increased possibility of behaving in an anti-social manner.

Being a good listener could well be inborn. Some people seem to attract those who want of talk, there are others who do not want to hear. One could imagine someone being attracted to a profession (psychiatry, say) in which they may either choose to listen or choose to talk. Having spoken to those who have visited psychiatrists they say that X is a good listener, or that they know more about Y than they care to know. In layman's terms 'such professionals get their jollies from ear-bashing patients'.

It is worthy of note that there are many forms of speech: they range from simple expository prose by presenting ideas to the unquestionably emotional. Writing a book is not the same as writing a thesis, in the latter one has a really restricted readership (supervisor and external examiners). Writing a poem is not the same as either, and writing a love-letter may have elements of poetry but is personal. Thus, one might conclude that there are different 'voices' for each style. What one might say may not be the same as what one would write.

## International Language

Without the requirement of taking part in the community there is no community. As such this is an argument against the use of ethnic enclaves wherein quasi-dwellers are not part of the larger body-corporate. We do need to recognise that cultural adjustment and imposition are significant variables in coping by expatriates. The most obvious challenge is that of language. Not being able to communicate ideas and information is a highly important variable.

Having a rudimentary knowledge of the language is vital, but that misses out on the nuances of speech. One could think of an argument that within a country one should be obliged to learn the language of that country – German in Germany, Persian (or Farsi) in Iran, English in the UK, French in France. Without such a requirement one would not be part of the broader community, would not understand signs, read about elections, keep abreast of local events, etc.

It is concluded that, as such, this is an argument against the use of ethnic enclaves wherein quasi-dwellers are not part of the larger body-corporate. In some countries there are enclaves who protect incomers from having to learn the local language: as such this is regarded as regrettable, and prevents those incomers from being part of that wider scope.

## Developmental Studies

It has been found in studies in developmental psychology that babies seem to have an inbuilt capacity for attending to faces and to facial expressions. The seminal work on this topic is Darwin's *The expression of emotion in man and animals* (first published in 1872). It had the explicit aim of demonstrating phylogenetic continuity. That work was completed at a time when experimental methods were less sophisticated than they are now. In the intervening 140+ years or so we have developed a better understanding than we had then. Darwin explained the continuity between humans and other animals in terms of underlying principles. In its way, this later work is of as much significance as *On the origin of species* (first published in 1859).

The principles expressed by Darwin are based upon the 'constitution of the nervous system', and our biological heritage. These expressions are part of our biological nature and are significant in adaptation. Darwin's conclusion was that these expressions of emotion stemmed from teeth shown in anger and were a precursor to biting; as he put it, the 'sneer is a civilised snarl'. Some expressions may no longer serve a direct biological purpose but still have communication value.

### *Assumptions*

One may take some assumptions and reverse their implied threat. The writer recalls an instance of travelling from Honolulu to Melbourne and was assigned a smoker's seat, but was allergic to smoke. After declining to sit the stewardess threatened to call the captain. The appropriate response was 'what an excellent idea, get him immediately': thus, the threat was turned into a solution.

China has resumed control over Macao and Hong Kong, as per the international agreement. Notwithstanding, China's record in Tibet is not admirable. Against this one must put the upgrading of the silk road. This is to be put against the lower regard for human rights. As one Chinese national put it to this author – it is necessary to have total control in a country as large and diverse as China, but one might question the need for such a large political entity. It is such debates that we need to consider such.

Here one must keep a sense of balance. The absence of human rights in China is to be put against the gains that they have achieved (in contradiction of the UN expressions on *Human Rights*). The desire to rebuild the road through Bokhara and Samarkand is economically admirable, and its commitment to energy without coal is to be admired. Further, their staunch resistance to corruption is to be admired. Yet further, China is not in the top ten of commercial whaling, as Japan now does in defiance of international law. In all of this one must maintain a sense of balance. One might give regard to the essence of human rights. It is a matter of determining priorities, particularly with respect to the separation of powers.

## Media

One of the most recent developments is that of the internet and of email. Indeed, one of the aspects of the internet is the factor known as 'those who prefer things to people'. On the internet it is easy to now send a brief message. The previous protocols of having to send the usual courtesies is now abrogated: one may use a simple salutation or a simple message, where before it was considered a discourtesy not to use an accepted formula for addressing others.

Using the internet via the iPod or computer as an information source has distinct advantages, one of main one being that it provides up-to-date information on subject not covered by the encyclopaedia, or is of wayward thought (such as the name of an actress), or is of more recent origin. A second advantage of the iPad over the encyclopaedia is its compact shape and its portability. One would have to hold that the iPad (or the iPhone) is one of the best inventions of the century.

One has to be aware that two items make scholarship more instant. What previously took months to do now one can do in a day. The use of the internet in locating and using articles is immeasurably quick. Further, in drafting an article (book, poem, essay) one can see it instantly on the word processor, and amend at will: it no longer needs to be retyped and retyped but can be done so promptly (what would Dickens' output have been had he had a word processor?).

One may glean not only information but also vicarious experience in reading. Indeed, the use of printed material is one of the boons of such. In addition to reading one has different styles of reading. This may take the form searching for material in Google-Scholar (with abstracts first to assess their relevance) to reading plays or novels for both information and experience. To reiterate the main point here, it is to gather both information and experience. That is also true of seeing plays in order participate in the shared experiences being portrayed by the actors.

## Cultural Differences in Communication

One needs to recognise that there are vast cultural differences in communication, quite apart from language. Such differences inhere in the assumptions made about a host of issues. Among them are the dimensions of individuality – collectivity, attitudes to death and dying, religious tolerance, and sex differences. The largely Western societies that foster the influence of women have that larger talent pool to draw on, and do. Do unto others as you would have them do to you may be called equality: as such the freedom of conscience, of assembly, and of religious freedom is of paramount importance (Trigg 2012).

There are several ways of being misunderstood. One is by poor expression, another is by way of ambiguity, another is not understanding the nuances of what is being expressed. Who expresses an idea may also be influential. For example, a simple factual statement from a medical specialist to a patient has a different context to one where one is in-private conversation with a friend just trying out, of kicking ideas around. Women in many cultures do not have the believability as do men, they being less convincing than are men, or so it is alleged.

Lutz (1991) outlined the special difficulties facing Turkish women migrating to the Netherlands, but her argument may have wider application. The confounding issue here is the mistaken identification of the subjugation of women with a specific religion. Lutz pointed out that men are the reference point in a wide range of cultures, religious and non-religious, and it is in such a context that women's status is set. It is in such enclaves that such subjugation may persist. Among the many disadvantages attendant upon being a female they are mentioned below.

## Styles and Skills

Suppose a tennis star opposes homosexual marriage, and quotes the bible in justification, but is criticized. The view held here is that, with freedom of speech, all ideas are available, the refutation is easy enough, either on grounds of evidence/logic, or on grounds of the right to a belief for which there is no evidence.

There are different styles and skills in communication. In neuro-linguistic programming there is emphasis upon the preferred modality (sight, hearing, touch, etc). In that system one might hear of 'I see what you mean', 'I hear you', and, and 'I will be in touch'. In other words, it is the study of neural mechanisms, of how brains acquire and store knowledge of the languages that we speak and comprehend. It is an account of what happens in the brain as we understand and remember, as well as its use in everyday life.

It is also an account of how competently we communicate. That extends to how well one writes. There are those who find it relatively easy to write, and others who find it a burden. One of the common phobias in Western society is the prospect of speaking in public. There are those who read widely and well, but do not so speak: there are those who find searching for information a real burden. In the matter of supervision of theses and professional experience this could be a significant variable, but perhaps less so than the record of successful supervisions.

There are studies in which talking and/or writing have been conducted, but the problem there is that such effect may wash out when considering the neuro-linguistic style of the participants. It is clear that a comparison of talking versus writing is a worthwhile study, but more so if the personality is an input. Of the different reasons for talking there are many such: one might characterise the different reasons as being:

- The 'getting it off your chest'. In this the aim is to unburden the mind, and includes such items as confession
- Making an observation or giving a point of view, perhaps in answer to a question
- Expressing thoughts and/or feelings. Here the aim is to give voice to thinking.

- Expressing wants or needs. Here the aim is to give voice to what is wanted.
- Being in the position of a supplicant. Examples here are being in a job interview or asking someone for something that you value.

This category of expression is essentially one-sided: they have something in their power to give and you are the supplicant who wants it. A conflict situation in which there is a disagreement. This applies particularly to non-resolvable cases. In extreme cases the contestants are implacable, mostly so when the civilised conclusion is 'we will have to agree to disagree'. It is quite likely, in such extreme cases, that it will end a friendship if the altercation goes beyond civilised bounds.

## What Makes a Good Communicator?

It is a good guide to an important principle, that being a good listener is the high road to being a good communicator. There are, of course, other factors that come into play, among them are:

- Use non-verbal communication appropriately. In other words, the body language should be consistent with what you are saying.
- One has in mind that being a good communicator is to be both friendly and confident.
- Being clear and concise is another prerequisite. While being that being open-minded, empathic, and respectful is most appropriate.
- Unless it is called for by the occasion being friendly and informal is the preferred mode.

## Six Degrees of Separation

This idea was first put forward by a Hungarian author (Karinthy) in 1929, although this is disputed. He believed that most people could be connected with anyone else in the world by the use of an intermediaries). In 1967 Stanley Milgram made the idea famous in the English-speaking world by a series of experiments. What is significant here is the closeness of the human family.

The connectedness of humanity is an idea first investigated by Milgram in 1967, and then empirically by Travers and Milgram (1969) in an appropriately named 'the small world problem'. They sent several hundred letters to a randomly selected group of people in an American city other than the one in which they lived. Milgram gave each of his recipients of his letter, and a target person, and asked them to get in touch with the target. The information given was name, occupation, and location. If the recipient of his letter did not know the target they were asked to intermediaries whom did know to effect an introduction. About 64 such chains reached their target, and for each the average number in the chain was six (hence six degrees of separation). The finding of an average of only six intermediaries separate us from anyone else gives credence to the notion that it is 'a small world'.

One bears in mind that this is an American study, and its findings may not be applicable elsewhere. What makes a corporation successful is its connectedness. Many companies have subsidiary suppliers (car-making, for example), and each section produces their contributory product at the right time. None of this would work without connectedness – horizontal rather than vertical.

One might speculate of the effect this might have upon the world-wide-web. The present author has found this to be slightly more difficult: the less famous the person the more degrees of separation. For example, it is easier to get in touch with the Canadian Prime Minister, the Archbishop of Canterbury, and the German Chancellor than it is to get in touch with the Head of the Sanitation Department at Lille, the Head of the London Underground, and the Head of a State school in Pretoria, or the captain of the Chilean warship that patrols the Straits of Magellan.

## *Music as Communication*

Music may be regarded as a basic form of communication. There is no reason to suppose that music should be regarded as being different from poetry. In music it is essentially non-rational, and appeals to our emotional side. One might, for example, have nonsense syllables set to poetry provided they scan, rhyme, or whatever is the criterion. Music is, essentially, about following the rules of musical composition. It should be both euphonious and satisfying.

The area in which women do not seem to shine is in that of being musical composers. In the well-respected Oxford companion to music (1979, 10th edition) and there are four pictures of women: they are, respectively, Plate 3 (opposite p.32) to Frances Clarke (propounder of music appreciation): St Cecilia, patron saint of music: Plate 32 (opposite p.161) to Maria Hackett, encourager of music: plate 54, opposite p.336 to Ethel Smith – for whom there is no entry: plate 153, opposite 976 for her contribution to the tonic Sol Fa: and to Amy Beach, who composed the Gaelic Symphony.

This is out of a total of 378 pictures of male composers this amounts to 1%. If one were to take Amy Beach as the only genuine composer, then the proportion is 0.26%. That said it is noted that women are famous as singers, performers, actresses, professors, surgeons, writers, etc.; in fact, any other field of endeavour. It cannot be that they lack opportunity since many had leisure time: and many were well instructed.

One would also have to note that some composers were born poor. Some examples are Debussy, Schubert, and Haydn. Many were feckless with money, Wagner and Mozart for example. It does seem that money is not a composer's forte. Perhaps some women felt compelled to masquerade as men. It is also possible that some musical themes were taken by men of recognised genius. In the case of Mozart's sister, Nannerl, herself an accomplished musician, it may be that Mozart appropriated some ideas of Nannerl's into his own music. It is unlikely that we will ever know.

One might also ask is it the case that women were instructed in music, which does appear to be the case. One might also ask if some women did not have time enough to compose, which is not so. Did they have the compulsion to compose, and that appears, superficially, to be likely. In the absence of other evidence, it does seem to be a relevant conclusion that it is a finding that requires an explanation. Could it be that women were traditionally considered to be unmusical, and thus used men as an identity? Could it be that women were not encouraged? One seeks for an explanation.

## Taking out Anti-feminine Bias

There are ways of taking out bias, and increasing the talent pool by 50%. among them are:

- Interview prospective musicians behind screens
- Have fewer portraits of male predecessors
- Block out names of candidates
- Ban headshots
- In recruitment, not be influenced by unimportant issues, such as colour of jacket, or affiliations.
- Be aware that attractive people are considered to be more worthy
- Purge discriminatory language from job adverts (except for obvious exceptions such as actresses, toilet attendants, etc.

All of this amounts to a particular mindset. If one can do that the rest may well follow. One, too, is mindful that some religions do not allow women as priests, rabbis, imams, etc. Here the question is, should they be compelled (or not compelled), by legislation, to conform to equality.

## Choosing a Course of Study

If one wished to study this topic further there are a number of options available, depending upon the aspects chosen. It might be language, facial recognition, facial expression of emotion, voice, or non-verbal communication. If, and when, an aspect is chosen to study. Further, one may choose the topic as an abstract academic one, or one worthy of study in its own right, or the sociology of language. With such qualifications in mind one could select a course either on-line or by attending. The options are available, further such courses may or may not charge a fee. Prospective student readers are encouraged to be specific in their requirements.

## Conclusions

There is a need to be alert to be alert to the different forms of communication: it may be voice, facial expression, non-verbal communication, media, etc. To be thus alert is to be forearmed. In particular, one is alerted to formal and informal means of communication, of verbal and non-verbal communication. Not only does the communication matter but so too does whoever give it utterance. In the case of interviewing prospective job interviewees there are ways of making the process more objective: suggestions for improvement are given.

One may study communication in its wider sense, but it is more likely to be addressed as a single entity. There is a notion that one communicates more readily, if one takes into account differences in personality. One should be alert to the commitment one must bring to that approach: although there is no definitive statement about which approach is best, notwithstanding, being sensitive to language and responses is a good start.

The use of consistency in communication is enhanced by the consistency of the communication process.

# Chapter 8
# Corruption

## Introduction

This chapter aims at enhancing the understanding of corruption: in doing so it makes the point that corruption is not a single entity, but is comprised of different aspects. In so doing this chapter argues that an entity is definable, and particularly where it is part of a larger concept. Perhaps one of the better-known definitions of corruption, according to the Shorter OED, is 'The destruction or spoiling of anything, esp. by disintegration or by decomposition with its attendant unwholesomeness; and loathsomeness; putrefaction'. It is thus seen as a decomposition and loathsome. This is rather less help than we would wish as it fails to tell us what it means in specific terms, it does not help in telling us of the larger picture.

What is particularly difficult here is the cultural differences. What may be corrupt in one culture may not be in another. As values vary, one is put in the difficult position of deciding which set of values should prevail. As it stands one of the reference points is the United Nations *Declaration of Human Rights*. Although those precepts cover some items they do not cover all, from which is follows that one must decide on the values that hold across cultures.

One of the concepts that seems particularly valuable is that of fostering equality, another is that actions, if made public, would receive wide acclaim (presuming that there is a moral majority). Yet another is that it is a breach if one uses public office for private gain. One would be inclined to add another, that of violent, or of devious, interventions, as well as tolerating subversive political acts. This is problematic in that there are occasions when violence in pursuit of worthy aims is the only solution.

There the difficulty is that one has to decide what are worthy aims. The Japanese attempts to dominate the Pacific and the attendant atrocities in the Second World War may seem a worthy aim to defeat, but other cases less clear cut. What, for example, would one make of a tyrant trying to hold on to power by being ostensibly democratic?



R. Francis, *Equality in Theory and Practice*,
https://doi.org/10.1007/978-981-15-3488-1_8

## *Definition of Corruption*

From the above considerations it is clearly difficult to define corruption, covering as it does, countries and any types of breach. One form of possible corruption is that some multi-national corporations have greater wealth than do many sovereign states, yet they are not subject to the democratic ballot box. Such wealth disparity is a characteristic of economies as well as of nations. Looking at the index of wealth-disparity one notes that too great a disparity may be construed as corrupt: too little removes the incentives to acquire wealth. Indeed, Wilkinson and Pickett (2009) concluded that nations that have a smaller spread of wealth, on average, do better, although the criterion may be problematical. Perhaps one could hold that the criterion is equality, although that may be a circular argument.

While these definitions give us related manifestations they do beg further questions. On the matter of what it all means we do need to recognise that all ideas need to be interpreted. There are some cases where interpretation might produce different meanings. Teenage pregnancies, for example, could be the norm in some societies, making use of welfare payments in another, and an unwillingness to contemplate marriage in a third.

That situation is rather different from one that constitutes corruption. It is argued below that corruption is dimensional rather than absolute. Along the definitional dimension one might consider a case such as permitting a proportion of overseas aid to go in corrupt payments in order for anything to be done in the target country. Without such corrupt payments it would be unlikely that any aid would be delivered, there being blocks to ensure their continuation. The continuation of such payments may be regarded as corrupt, and is thus the dilemma. Along that dimension we have the case of clerical staff spending excessive amounts on administration, thereby depriving the needy of help. This shades into moral judgments about issues as:

- Should one foster the economy by the doubtful technique of reducing taxes on business? (the so-called trickle-down effect).
- What percentage of GDP is it appropriate to donate to overseas aid as distinct from assisting current citizens?
- Should education be secular, at least to first degree level, and funded from the public purse?
- In the funding of medical services should prisoners be given free treatment
- Does one get international companies to pay a just proportion of tax?

## *Hong Kong Anti-corruption Commission*

One of the first bodies to counter corruption was in the Hong Kong police force. The original and highly effective body to combat corruption was the *Hong Kong Independent Commission Against Corruption* (see Hong Kong in References). Further, it was one of the first governmental anti-corruption bodies, set up when

Hong Kong was still, and is not now, a British colony. On the Hong Kong website there is an understanding of the ordinance:

> Public servants (for definition of "public servant", please refer to the Text of the Law) and it includes prescribed officers, as well as those employees of public bodies, and includes employees of such powers as bus companies and hospitals. These issues are subject to the proscribed from accepting bribes. Those public servants are to be castigated by Sections 3, 4, 5 and 10 of Prevention of Bribery Ordinance whereas employees of such entities as power companies and bus companies are subject to Sections 4 and 5.
>
> Section 3 does not allow and prescribed officer to solicit not accept any bribe without the special permission (presumably in writing) without the express permission of the chief executive.
> In Section 4 deals with any public servant who solicits or accepts any kind of reward during the execution of his duties is guilty of an offence.
> Section 5 deals with 'any influence' shall not only be guilty but the offeror shall also be guilty.
> Section 10 describes who maintains a standard of living or who has substantial assets that are not 'commensurate' with his salary will also be guilty of an offence.

It goes on to outline what is meant in the Act. In the Ordnance the items given are that an 'advantage' includes not only money but also includes such issues as gifts, loans, etc, and it specifically excludes entertainment. By entertainment the Ordinance means the provision of drink and food for the 'occasion when it is provided. This may be unclear but the officer concerned will form judgement. Basically this amounts to someone in a like situation of performing their duties.

What the Anti-corruption commission does it does well: where it is wanting is the definition of other forms of corruption. The issue of non-material gain, should be included in any formal definition. What is essential is that the United Nations agree on what constitutes corruption.

All of this is predicated on the assumption of non-guilt on the part of the recent protests by the conventional freedoms which were current on the assumption of innocence which was once formerly enjoyed by the inhabitants of Hong Kong. We shall have to wait and see how it works out under the current regime. The contention of the authors of the protest enjoin us to consider the breaking of the 1997 agreement that it would have preserved the freedoms that were enjoined before the handover. The 'one country – two systems' appear to have been breached ahead of time It may well be that either side could prevail, but that remains to be seen.

## *Transparency and Courtesy*

The organization, *Transparency International* (TI), was founded by Peter Eigen in Germany in the early nineties (for their origins see Transparency in References). The website of TI has much useful information. Among such is that of the perception of corruption in countries of the world. It is worth looking at how corruption relates to other variables, such as wealth disparity, the availability of cheap labour, political disempowerment, and to the wish to migrate to countries with better opportunities. The *Transparency International* website also publishes a *Corruption Perception Index.*

The index lists the criteria as being composite, a combination, which draws on corruption-related data, and is also derived from 'experts living and working in the countries and territories evaluated'. It will be noted that it is a perception of corruption rather than actual behavioural measurements, but is the best indicator we have from a reputable institution. The question of why it is, is based only on perceptions is convincingly answered on the TI website. It is noted from their website that some countries have a high level of corruption. Such countries have a poor quality of life, and are commonly suppliers of emigrants who wish for a better life. This assumes that corruption is one of the drivers that engender emigration, a point yet to be established.

TI is one of the few institutions devoted to uncovering corruption, and publicising where it occurs. It is an institution that plainly sets out to root out such corruption. In addition to their annual reports there is a weekly bulletin put out by that organisation. One of its main precepts is that corruption flourishes in secrecy, and the antidote is transparency. What is of special interest is the reporting of perceived corruption in different countries. It is clear from that perspective that some countries report more corruption than do others, and it is a persistent effect. It is to be noted that the report is one consistent with the accepted definition, involving the aspects mentioned in this chapter.

One of the conventional courtesies of life is that of equal treatment or tending to informational equivalence. On the matter of courtesy in meetings one does, rightly, give courtesy to other members, and to attribute proper motives to their expressions: not to do so might be treated as a lower form of corruption. One might record dissent on an issue but only on grounds of values rather than on personal friendship or animosity. For that reasons the right of reply is a means of ensuring that the interlocutor is not suppressed (Francis and Armstrong 2012).

The right of reply is also critical on occasions of such issues as book reviews. While a reviewer may get it wrong, or is biased in some way, the right of reply acts as an assurance that both sides are heard. In all things, balance is required. While we may say that every silver lining has a cloud, on this occasion the reverse is true. It is thus that courtesy requires that all sides be heard, and that no-one forces their views on another, although rational persuasion is quite in order.

## *Corruption Types*

A list of corruption items is given below. The one that is quite controversial is that of blasphemy. Should one be allowed to convert from one religion to another. This is one of the moral dilemmas so endemic to the human condition. According to a website (see Apostasy in References) the reputed *Pew Research Center* lists the countries, and also makes a distinction between apostasy laws and blasphemy laws. One of the many difficulties here is that of curbing the use of ridicule as a weapon against claims. One would have to wait and see how it works out.

While one can see the power of ridicule, to use too lightly is to bring accepted views into disrepute. It is borne in mind the Charlie Hebdo case in Paris in 2015. The satirical magazine Charlie Hebdo published a cartoon satirising a religious leader. The claim of Charlie Hebdo was, and is, that ridicule is one way of being critical of the Abrahamic religions (Judaism, Christianity, and Islam). It is, in fact, a paper devoted to irreverence, and believes that satirising and ridicule are often allegedly the only way to point out inconsistencies in doctrine.

In the event a group broke into the Charlie Hebdo office and murdered 12 people, and injured another 11. The point here being that one should not criticise. It is a case of free speech versus blasphemy, yet another moral dilemma, and goes to the heart of the issue. Should one consider this as an act of personality rather than as a religious scruple? The question now is 'is blasphemy to be regarded as corruption, or not?' – another truly moral dilemma.

## Casualisation of the Workforce

Most recently, and in many Westernised countries, there has been a casualisation of the workforce; the move to having employees become sub-contractors to avoid leave pay, etc.; wage disparities whereby the salary of CEOs runs into millions of dollars while workers are retrenched; the exportation of jobs to low-cost countries; the importation of labour which may be pressurised to forego some earned wages. This amounts to an increase in wages disparity, with consequential losses to equality. It is curious yet understandable that employers wish to lower the standards of payment to workers to the lowest level while employees press for the work to be adequately rewarded.

It is the growth of the union movement, of collective bargaining, that drives the impetus to better conditions. One of the most damning indictments of inequality is that of international conglomerates (for example) that have such economic power as to subvert the will of the people. Such organisations often have the economic power and political power that are accorded to few nations.

We need to recognise that people are ends in themselves rather than ciphers in someone else's plan. The equality thus enjoined means that each person is treated as an end in themselves. It would absurd not to point out that people are often employed to perform relatively menial tasks, what is unacceptable is then always treating them as personal ciphers. With economic resources at their disposal they are vulnerable to a superordinate's whim. It is thus that some form of sanctions for misbehaviour, and some form of security of income is essential, as is the following of certain procedures before possible dismissal.

We must also recognise that people are used for all sorts of tasks that are someone else's idea of fostering growth. What we must recognise is that when it comes to human values people are to be treated as ends in themselves. While they are used as subjects, the suggestion is that when it comes to affairs that interfere with profit people are treated as sentient beings with lives of their own.

There too might be forms in which the inducement is non-material, and may be a promise of support on another issue, a promise to keep silent on a second issue, or to favour a particular appointment, or to gain promotion. All of which may be done by way of untraceable bribes. For example, a friend of the author's made a trenchant criticism of a local council policy. He was advised that if he withdrew his objections then he would get a favourable deal when he went to trade his car in. No part of this transaction was traceable because it was seemingly above board and involved several business entities (he did not succumb to their offers).

## Bribery

Corruption may take the form of bribery, which we define as often involving a secret inducement. It is the offer of corrupt payment to produce an end that is inconsistent with morality and with many country's laws. In the case of bribery, that too may take both material and non-material forms. To require a payment by a country to secure a contract may be the norm in some places, but by Western standards is inadmissible. The Bible quotes several comments on bribery. To take three instances. In 1 Samuel 8:3 it notes

- And his sons walked not in his ways, but turned aside after lucre, and took bribes, and perverted judgment.

  In Job 15: 34 it is stated

- … for the congregation of hypocrites shall be desolate, and fire shall consume the tabernacles of bribery.

  In Psalms 26:10 it is stated

- In whose hands is mischief, and their right hand is full of bribes.

Such quotations clearly deplore the use of bribes. That is also true of the Koran where, in 2: 188 it is held that

- … and eat up not one another's property unjustly (in any illegal way eg. stealing, robbing, deceiving, etc), nor give bribery to the rulers (judges before presenting your cases) that you may knowingly eat up a part of the property of others sinfully'.

The Torah, in the strictest sense, is the first five books of Moses (Genesis, Exodus, Leviticus, Numbers, Deuteronomy). Bribery is deplored there: particularly bribing judges, as it '… blinds the eyes of the wise'.

It is clear that bribery is deplored in the Torah, the Bible and the Koran. That is also true of any form of corruption (hypocrisy, for example). Such words as 'forgery' and 'nepotism' do not appear in the Biblical Concordance. One presumes that they are similarly deplored. The same is true in the Koran, the words 'forgery' and 'nepotism' do not appear in the on-line Concordance. This is no indication that they are not to be condemned. The absence of evidence is not the same as the evidence of absence.

The analysis of corruption is given elsewhere, but suffice to make one further point: it has been shown that happiness and equitability are positively related, as reported in the World Happiness Report (see Table 12.1). There, the countries with the greatest happiness are also the ones with the greatest equality (Scandinavian countries are top-ranking). For the meek to inherit the earth the greedy will be forced to yield.

## Conflict of Interest

Plainly a conflict of interest is against ethical principles. One cannot properly act as judge in one's own cause: to be disinterested (as distinct from uninterested) it is vital to make the best impartial judgment. The famous statue on the Old Bailey is of the scales of justice weighing matters. In business terms one should not only declare an interest but also absent oneself from the deliberations and resolution on such issues. Where one has an interest, and it means that one must absent oneself often from consideration: it is doubtful if one ought to be a member of a body from which one must be so absent so often.

This applies not only to business but also applies in other realms. For example, in the academic world one could imagine the wife of a head of department being enrolled in a final honours course, a department which the husband heads. The head of department would, quite rightly, absent himself while the grade of honours was considered. What is doubtful is where the wife had no alternative places in the same city. In the event a husband would, quite properly, have absented himself from consideration of what class of honours to award, but that bypasses the question of the propriety of enrolling at that institution in the first place.

### *Cultural Mores*

Among such issues are not only those of basic values processes but also those of lack of traffic sense, and of appropriate cultural mores such as the use and treatment of public toilets, and spitting in public. While it might argued that a basic knowledge of the language of the country is important, so too might we argue that various forms of non-verbal communication be instructed. One of the major benefits of multiculturalism is the promotion of tolerance for diverse way, and that is to be admired, provided that no such ways are injurious to health. From such consideration arises the notion of cultural differences in standards.

Perhaps the closest to the present study is that of Dimant et al. (2013), that study looked at the influence of corruption for 111 nations for the years 1985–2000. Their conclusion was that 'Corruption is among the push factors of migration'. They also noted its deleterious effects on skilled migration, diminishing educational returns: it seems to have a smaller effect on the less well-educated. In our terms we would call the adverse effects of the brain-drain, a point is confirmed by Cooray and Schneider (2014).

While not clearly documented, they concluded a causation factor but wish to go no further than correlation. What is important to note is that study involves a different database, with the same result. It also adds a dimension to the percentage of the population born overseas and living elsewhere. The presence of corruption in a country is a significant impulse to go to a more favoured one (see also the chapter on Culture). For this analysis the present writer selected ten host countries and ten donor countries. It will also be seen that the percentage of the foreign-born is greatly different as between donor and host countries (see Table 8.1 below). The difference here is that the percent of the population overseas-born is given in the OECD website.

It will be seen that, as the population of donor countries is 1 or fewer, it is not possible to calculate coefficients. Also, the correlation of corruption with the size of the population, and does not reach the set 1% level. What does emerge is that, regardless of the percentage of the locally-born, there seems to be a relationship between the two types of countries corruption (there is a significant difference between the two types countries [donor and host], which is highly likely

Source: Population: http://www.pewglobal.org/interactives/migration-tables/
Source: Corruption: https://www.transparency.org/country

**Table 8.1** Emigration from corrupt donor countries to host countries

| DONOR | | | HOST | | |
|---|---|---|---|---|---|
| Country | Corrupt | % local born | Country | Corruption | % local born |
| Afghanistan | 16 | 1 | Australia | 77 | 29 |
| D. Rep. Congo | 20 | 1 | Canada | 81 | 21 |
| India | 41 | **1** | Denmark | 88 | 11 |
| Indonesia | 38 | 1 | France | 72 | 12 |
| Iraq | 18 | 1 | Germany | 80 | 15 |
| Mexico | 28 | 1 | Italy | 52 | 10 |
| Morocco | 43 | 1 | Netherlands | 82 | 12 |
| Nigeria | 27 | 1 | NZ | 87 | 23 |
| Philippines | 36 | 1 | UK | 80 | 13 |
| Vietnam | 33 | 1 | USA | 71 | 14 |
| Means | 30 | 1% or less | Means | 77 | 16 |

Countries chosen at random as preferred donor and host countries
Source: Population: http://www.pewglobal.org/interactives/migration-tables/
Source: Corruption: https://www.transparency.org/country
There is no overlap in the corruption score.
The donor country's highest score is lower than the host countries lowest score
There is a significant difference on both the corruption scores and the birthplace scores

The proposition investigated is that people migrate away from countries that are corrupt and immigrate to countries less corrupt. It will be seen that the percent of the overseas born is far greater in host countries, and distinctly lower in donor countries: it does appear that migrants may wish to go to donor countries. It is important to note that average corruption level is considerably 'better' for host countries than is so for donor countries. One must regard that as at least a significant correlative of the wish to migrate.

## Deceit and Underhandedness

Then there are offences involving deceit: they include the list: blackmail, extortion, forgery, and the like. Blackmail and forgery are unmistakeable cases. The issue of hypocrisy runs to the principle of the abrogation of law, as mentioned above. Blackmail is clearly a criminal offence, and payments in order 'keep quiet' as blackmailers find it too lucrative to desist. It does, however, put blackmailers at risk of being murdered.

Here blackmail is a kind of extortion: at a more extreme expression is the concept of extortion. There one finds the exertion of duress to produce some end that is not in keeping with accepted moral values. At the extreme is takes the form of blackmail for money. It runs through such issues as duress to reach a convenient solution to such relatively minor issues as enforced tipping. In the latter case one might encounter a restaurant this adds a percentage to the bill as a 'required' gratuity, even if the service is bad. At the other extreme is the requirement of a payment to do, or not to do, something. Thus, it is that extortion may take any one of a number of grades.

What is important here is often the threat of revelation. It does, of course, put the extortionist at risk of being killed in order not to reveal the incriminating information. They run serious risk of reprisals from those extorted, not the least of which is the extortionist facing trial in a criminal court. The one danger here is that the victim of extortion may have something serious to conceal that would otherwise become common knowledge.

### *Dimensionality of Corruption*

It is held above that corruption is not an entity but, rather, a dimension. A clear example is a government official being paid a corrupt payment to approve a building project that would not otherwise be approved. At the other end of the spectrum is a political decision to charge full fees for a university education. That is not corruption, but is a policy decision. However much one may disagree (if you think education is expensive try the cost of ignorance) it is a matter of policy and outlook. If one were to put a marker at one end of the spectrum a corrupt bribe, and policy decisions at the other we could, for example, have a seven-point scale:

Bribery decisions 1 2 3 4 5 6 7 Policy issues

Corruption may be manifest in its various forms. For that reason, and for other compelling economic and political reasons, migration shows itself to be an important response. Corruption, it is argued, is an important variable, but not the only one, that moves people to emigrate. There may be substantial cultural differences, and obviously so, particularly as they affect business. What is less appreciated is that the differences may be due to moving from an urban village culture and moving people to large conurbations.

Again, one of the difficulties here is deciding on the degree of corruption. If one were to take (say) the acceptance of bribes as an instance the population expectation of its propriety would vary substantially. Taking an instance from a realistic situation, one could imagine that a small jet-plane was purchased for the project, quite legitimately. On completion of the project, the plane was then sold to a local political minister for a knock-down price, it being understood informally that it was part of the deal.

## Hypocrisy

Hypocrisy is one offence that is difficult to accommodate. In its basic form it is an abrogation of the rule of law, particularly law requires that all are treated as equal, not 'one law for me and another for you'. One is concerned that there are elements of hypocrisy in certain international situations. Having the atomic bomb includes Russia, the United States of America, Britain, France and China. Four countries have declined to sign, Israel, India, South Sudan, and Pakistan. According to the latest website, North Korea has withdrawn, and is a non-signatory.

Would it be an example of hypocrisy for any of those countries rebuke another country for having the nuclear weapons of mass destruction, as has been done to North Korea? The secretion of money corruptly obtained while in office, and in the face of vehement denials of impropriety, is another example. Yet another example is, it would ill-become a legislator to berate business for not being ethical enough. That point is particularly apt in the light of broken political promises. Such a senior minister should not admonish business for not being ethical if the legislature is allowed to break promises to the electorate. History is replete with such examples of hypocrisy.

Such hypocrisy is one of the most difficult to fit into a definitional framework. For example, given that business is governed by legislation, to what extent should the legislature prevail upon business. An ancillary question is, if the legislature does not govern business, who will? In politics dilemmas abound: should one take course of action X instead of Y? Should the government have a commercial policy on Z?

Does one cast one's vote knowing it will make no difference, or does one cast it according to one's wishes.

Such issues are the essence of control, and they involve both substantive and procedural matters: instances of the former include such issues as permitting the trade in human organs, the sanctions to be available to counter smuggling, and the manner in which the government of the day fosters ethical behaviour. There is nothing in the least corrupt about legislatures debating issues: it is exactly what they are designed to do, and one cannot fault them on that issue, all provided it is done in an open and honest manner.

The notion that one should preach one thing and practice another is not acceptable, particularly when it involves self-aggrandisement and the solicitation and exercise of power. The notion of 'practice what you preach' points to an absence of equity in relationships. To espouse one set of principles and act on another may be regarded as the essence of hypocrisy. The 'do as I say' rather than 'do as I do' captures it well: the inconsistency of statements and actions is the very essence of the principle.

The disjunction between what is said and what is done may be hypocrisy. As La Rochefoucauld has remarked 'hypocrisy is the tribute that vice pays to virtue'. Such hypocrisy is, rightly, lowly regarded, and for good reason: the main reasons being both inconsistency, and that of being morally improper.

## Loyalty

For example, in Medieval times serfs and vassals swore allegiance to their liege-lords. That often implied that their children were so bound. It is thus that the principle of loyalty to oath (express or implied) would be at odds with the principle of self-determination. We presently have the conventional dilemma of where primary loyalty lies (is a politician primarily responsible to his/her electors or to the country as a whole, or do they allow their personal views influence their vote?).

Among the questions we might ask are:

- Is the first loyalty of a commercial board to be that of maximising profit?
- Where loyalty to a close friend or relative is at odds with loyalty to the law, which should prevail?

When moral dilemmas are posed the questions are often conflated into one. For example, if a potential migrant wants a better working and family life the questions are:

- Why do you want to leave rather than stay and improve your country
- Where do you want to go?
- Why are you allowing tyrants to drive you out?
- Are you a genuine refugee?
- Why did you choose the target country?

- What will happen when you are intercepted?
- What are the risks and what are the potential benefits?

There is a set of questions rather than a simple answer. Moral dilemmas abound in payments, allegedly corrupt. Where corruption does occur, it will be inevitable that there will be those who resist. Exactly what form the resistance should take, the personal consequences of so doing, and its long-term effects are all considerations. We do need to note that without such reporting it is extremely improbable that any improvement would occur. To be a whistleblower is to court economic disaster. Perhaps some variant of the American reward as a proportion of the money saved by the whistleblower could be a start, although one is mindful of the consequences to false reporting.

## Misuse of Power

The misuse of power is another and significant means of corruption. In the Alice books, the *Queen of Hearts* most famous line was 'Off with their heads' upon every caprice of disapproval (indeed, she does not say much else). Where political power is vested in someone not subject to the law there is the capacity, and likelihood of misuse, as does every tyrant. Feeling to be above the law is a recipe for autocracy or a feeling that the law is for others, but not one's self. For example, the idea that a particular group forbids the reporting of offences to authorities is offensive. To do so is an abrogation of the rule of law and, as such, profoundly disturbing. Clearly this us related to hypocrisy

### *Towards a New Definition*

A more inclusive definition of corruption would include: the misuse of public (or private) office for personal gain, and fosters deceit. The notion of corruption as grabbing, and as development, has been addressed by Soreide and Williams (2015). A non-material instance is the usurpation of political power and influence. The notion of corruption transforms into policy decisions, and thence to moral judgments. Amongst other things rather than being restricted to the use of a two-valued system of corruption, one might consider corruption to be dimensional. Indeed, there are works that give an account of the law on deceptive and misleading conduct (Lockhart 2015). Further, an account of the concept of money (and its corruption) is given in Martin (2013).

The working definition by Jain (1980) concerned the misuse of office. That definition is an excellent start. What we would add now is the notion of the misuse of office with elements of deceit, and a lack of consideration for others as being equal. To this we would have to add hypocrisy. The essence of corruption involves inequity, bad-will, and a lack of concern for the welfare of others. It is recognized that there are various other studies and approaches deserving of serious consideration. For example, there is a Dutch study (De Graaf and Huberts 2008) portraying the nature of corruption using a case study design. They offered nine propositions concerning corruption. Among them are that it can be a slippery slope, that aside from material gain it can include lack of love, friendship, or status, and may also include the desire to impress. Such propositions are most helpful.

There are other studies that deal with specific areas, police for example (Porter and Warrender 2009), and some that deal with particular aspects of corruption, in one case that of bribery (see Herrera et al. and Bribe Payers Index in References). Using that bribe payers index, which 'ranks the likelihood of companies from 28 leading economies to win business abroad by paying bribes'. The 2011 data gives the top (best) ranks to the Netherlands, Switzerland, Belgium, Germany, Japan, and Australia, in that order. The six bottom ranks are occupied by Argentina, UAE, Indonesia, Mexico, China, Russia. As the 2011 report noted, the cases of China and Russia were particularly influential, and would need to be assessed over time in order see if there was an improvement. Such conclusions, as were drawn, point to the need for ongoing monitoring. Further, it noted that bribery was relatively present in business dealings, with differentials for the various business sectors (agriculture, mining, finance, etc).

The conclusions concerning bribery, in addition to the specific conclusions, may also be a guide to general corruption. Of equal interest in the useful consideration of what it might mean in a cultural context (Pillay and Dorasamy 2010). Their approach is to provide links between national culture with the 'pervasiveness and arbitrariness of corruption' in national institutions.

This present work represents yet another approach to an understanding of corruption. In the wider context one might hold that one expects consistency: for ethics gives us two significant contributions. One is that it provides a consistency with certain rules; the second is that all behaviour conforms to agreed canons of value. An instance of inconsistency is the attitude of some anti-abortionists. Even if one agrees with their stance is that all life is sacred. Where it becomes inconsistent is their killing of practitioners who perform abortions – it is not a reverence for life.

## United Nations

That seems to be in contradiction to the UN *Declaration of Human Rights* It is curious that some nations are members of the UN and subscribe to the UN *Declaration* yet continue to defy the principles to which they subscribe. Some countries with missions to the UN, while not regarding the principles, appears to be hypocritical (see the UN website for evidence of Missions to the UN). Is it a case of having them in tent spitting out, rather than outside the tent spitting in? Are such countries allowed to remain in the hope of being subject to benign influence? Once again this is a matter for judgement.

Fundamental here is the need for a wide-ranging debate on the issues of (say) population policy. It would include such issues as infrastructure, regional growth centres, how much to go towards bettering the lives of citizens as compared to helping other countries, and should migrants be allowed to congregate in ghettos or enclaves. One might argue that charity begins at home: conversely one might argue that any prosperous nation has an obligation to provide assistance to those less fortunate. It is just such conclusions as are at the heart of judgment.

Among the issues that produce ethical dilemmas is that of an actual case in which a philanthropist offered a bonus to a footballer if his team won. The offer of a bribe intended to be certain of a loss would clearly be corrupt. If, on the other hand, the team is genuinely playing to win the bonus is simply an added inducement. To be thus charged with corruption on the latter account is a real legal and moral dilemma. This issue of bonuses being a significant part of commercial activity.

Here the question arises about corruption 'what can be done?' The sub-questions are what can be done legally? What can be done as a matter of social engineering?, and would one contemplate using legal but non-moral actions? One of the enduring dilemmas in morals is that of deciding whether it is improper to make current moral judgments against previously held values standards. In this there is often a conflict of loyalties.

## Conclusions

As mentioned in text and, as Lord Acton noted, 'power corrupts and absolute power corrupts absolutely' is strongly endorsed. With respect to corporate governance one might look at the functioning of UN governance principles, and see what instruction it may offer. Among the just criticisms that might levelled at that body is the existence of the Security Council with its right to veto proposals, regardless of motives, and may be for motives not connected with the issue, and designed to further some other end. Having fixed terms for legislative members, non-extendable, should put a curb on entrenched power, and would curb such excesses as now occur.

It is concluded here that corruption has many aspects and is manifest as a dimension rather than an entity. Further, corruption is significantly correlated with the action of migration. In this the notions of both transparency and accountability are paramount, as is parliamentary democracy and the rule of law. What is plain is that there ought to be a clear international understanding of the nature of corruption, followed by a formal definition. To be clear, it is not the only definition of the urge to migrate, there may well be other factors. It is only after such international agreement that one can move to eradicate corruption. The tentative re-definition offered is:

> The misuse of office, the assumption of power, avoidance of conflict, of interest, and involving hypocrisy.

# Chapter 9
# Politics

## Introduction

The idea of political power by individuals is an appealing one, particularly in countries devoted to the rule of law. Where political power is available through the ballot box it then needs to give to every citizen the right to select. There are, however, some features of many civilised countries that run counter to the precept of representatives being there for those who elected them. Among the features of political life there are several that deserve mention. They include the issues of the structure of parliaments, procedures for getting things done, and how appointments are made and terminated.

There is an amusing note about capitalism being defined as the exploitation of man by man, whereas socialism is quite the reverse. Socialism has had many proponents, many of them well-intentioned: perhaps the most famous is Karl Marx. His seminal work, *Das Kapital* represents a watershed in that it gave rise to one of major world revolutions. The dictatorship of the proletariat turned out to be the tyranny of a dictator, as it did in Russia. Since then various forms of socialism have been tried. In a modified form socialism has a place: the Scandinavian models seem to work well, as does the form in the UK wherein there is a mixed system having the benefits and drawbacks of such an implementation. That is so, even to the point of having a national health service, as does Canada for example.

In a highly controversial book, *The open society and its enemies*, that author (Popper 1945) called Plato a fosterer of the closed society (see Fascism and Popper in References): one might question the idea that his approaches are 'irrational'). The notion that men are born with souls of the appropriate kind determine whether they will be wise rulers. It is quite understandable that Popper should be so taken against fascism as he was one such to suffer at their hands. The idea that Plato, together with Hegel and Marx, formed a triumvirate dedicated to dictatorship of the proletariat.

Such views were not without their critics, and a reading of the work, and its critics would be an appropriate complement. What we have seen is the effects of fascism



R. Francis, *Equality in Theory and Practice*,
https://doi.org/10.1007/978-981-15-3488-1_9

which, on the evidence, runs counter to equality. In there is an ethos, such that certain countries seem to have a penchant for a particular type of government, Russia being one example with the persuasive Rasputin, and the undemocratic Stalin, and recent events.

Whichever approach we use it is not just a matter of introducing a system but, rather, how it fits into the culture, and its acceptance by the general population. There will always be exploiters of any system: there are always those who seriously disadvantage those needing help. Some aspects of political life seem to be banned from comment: thus, in Thailand, it is legally forbidden to be critical of the king.

There is a story about fasces – the bundle of sticks that occur in the Aesop fable. In that story a father of warring sons took a bundle of sticks and asked each of them to break the bundle – and they could not. When the sticks were taken out individually they were able to break each quite easily. The moral of that story, and there is always a point, that treated as a group they were powerful. One of the difficulties here is that the treating the whole enhances the power for good: it also enhances the power of evil.

The world outlook is inevitably modelled by prevailing approaches such as postmodernism, virtuality, ideology, information theory, behaviourism, chaos theory, and Realpolitik. In international affairs, historical circumstances have often dictated the direction of international relations – and, indeed, of foreign policy. The colonialist era necessarily had implications for power, for foreign policy, and for trade. It also had a significant impact on human rights movements.

Other eras have made for categorisation: the Hegelian dialectic, thesis and antithesis. Examples of categorisation are those of Western capitalism. the communist bloc, or resource rich and resource poor. One questions whether political parties serve any purpose other than being a forum for the well-placed and powerful. One of the main arguments in favour of political parties is that in unity there is the strength to effect legislation. One of the arguments against is the possibility that it could be used as a forum to prosecute sectional and personal interests.

Alliances will form but, hopefully, they would be shifting ones, geared to common views of legislative solutions. One would 'lose' the 'platform' that are espoused by parties as part of their electoral manifesto, but since there is no common legal obligation to keep political promises.

## Structural Approaches

First, as to the structure of legislatures. One of the prime considerations is whether one should have a bicameral legislature. The existence of an upper house (house of review) certainly has the merit of containing the excesses of the legislature. That is virtually denied where a political party has control of both houses. When someone is elected to the legislature they are there to serve those who elected them. If, for example, a prospective candidate were to be elected, and then found to be a religious maniac who refused to represent the interests of his/her electorate how would that play out? Should elected candidates be obliged to represent their electorates' interests, or should they act on conscience and lead, should they respond to bigotry? One can readily imagine cases where a convinced electorate would have declined a particular policy, but later came to endorse it (see Runciman 2008).

There can sometimes be a conflict of interest. Among the more obvious ones is having a direct financial interest in the deliberation, and not absenting oneself. A less likely one is to, for example, having an interest in negative gearing (a policy decision to allow deductions from one's salary as an offset to other, possibly real estate losses). In such cases voting in favour of a policy where there is a clear conflict of interest should be banned.

Another structural consideration is that of lobbyists. Here the question is 'should they be there at all?' The argument here is that individuals elect their representative, who then expects them to put forward their interests. The question is why pressure groups (such as certain professions, or interest groups) can afford to bring pressure to bear? It is their capital resources that make it so, while the electors do not commonly band together except at election times. At budget times the announcements about tax changes is given in the budget speech, thus it is a matter of timing. Presumably this is because it gives no alerting to interested parties: forewarning is forearming.

## National Matters

Power and hegemony are significant themes, as is the constant tension over the competition between the right to national determination and the necessity to demonstrate the legitimacy of government by reference to democratic processes. Those of an ideological bent will see political relations perhaps as part of the global struggle between social classes; or see international relations as Freudian psychoanalytic concepts writ large; or as being invested with the concepts of symbols, perceptions and images played out on a larger scale.

In order to know the will of the people one must, of necessity, canvass all of those eligible. Thus, in some countries, voting is compulsory (at least going to the polling booth and taking a voting form is so). Without such a safeguard one may be fined for not voting. The argument that it is 'my democratic right not to vote' seems to be negated by knowing that voting is an issue of fundamental importance. The notion that one might not vote is contrary to the principle that the most important political decision we ever make is choosing our legislature. In this, one's voice should be heard. Among such concerns is that there is no compulsion to vote (save in just over 20 countries).

One cannot opt out of issues such as paying tax, or taking part in the census yet many countries do not have a compulsion to vote. Of the various states in the world a few require citizens to vote on the government they want. It is curious that the most fundamental choice, that of choosing the legislature, should not be subject to the same strictures. It is held that such sacrifices as have been made to ensure universal suffrage deserve an accolade rather than being ignored. Voting, it is held, in a somewhat imperfect world, does seem to be the best approach to determining the people's will. As Churchill once said, democracy is the worst system in the world – except all the others.

The question arises that should the young or the older have a greater vote? Young people have a greater stake in the future, but older people have seen more and have a better appreciation of nuances. It is very difficult to determine, and thus the solution is not to discriminate. One presumes that while it is true that the young have a greater stake in the future it presumes that the older do not. Yet one could argue that they are equally concerned that their grandchildren inherit a just world. Equality implies that *all* are equal.

## Political Remedies

### *Reliance on Consultants*

A recent trend in many Western governments is to rely less upon the civil services and more upon 'independent' consultants: of course, they are properly bound to secrecy. Nevertheless, that trend increases the prospect of governments to find answers favourable to what they propose. It also increases the power of lobbyists, who work behind the scenes. Lobbying in the public domain may be just the evident tip of what is a major business (have the gamekeepers turned poachers?). What this amounts to is that money, as may be the case, exerts an undue influence on government.

A yet further issue is that of having political parties. If the elected representatives were to do as they were bidden (and who would do the bidding?) then there would be no need of parties as such. It is true that without party policy little would be done, but would that would be a bad thing? Common interest groups would form, but only for issues. In some places, political parties are banned: on this one would need assurance as to their motives. To be banned for honourable reasons may be acceptable; to be banned because they are a threat to the reigning junta may be quite another thing. There are some states and territories that do not have political parties. Monarchies such as Oman and Qatar have banned political parties; other monarchies, such as Kuwait, do not recognise political parties, but voting blocs are permitted.

Some territories of states that do recognise political parties, and have no political parties (such as the Falklands of the UK, and the North-West Territories of Canada). Other sovereign states (such as the Federated States of Micronesia) do not have them. The pros and cons of such an arrangement is given in the paper on Constitutional reform (see that term in References).

## Sortition

There is a process called 'sortition', which is a process using random sampling to make governmental decisions (government by jury). It consists of an alternative process, apart from government by parties, for legislating matters into law. Elections may be considered to part of an oligarchy (as the ancient Greeks believed), or part of an arcane and mysterious process for which the electorate may be barred. For the more modern view see Sutherland, and van Reybrouck, 2016, in References.

There is a concern that legislatures are worthwhile, noting that there is an encouragement to be adversarial because the major parties face each other. One could envisage using either a horseshoe shaped arrangement, or even randomising seats. Certainly, the writer's experience in various sized committees verify that oppositional seating produces an adversarial effect.

Recent experience has shown the disaffection with the current political process. The election of Donald Trump has shown such disillusion, and the relative disengagement from political elections. Such notions as 'fake news' and 'post-factual' comments are now part of the process. Further, electing a president of some kind is strictly for the wealthy, electioneering being an expensive process. As an alternative one could imagine a process of 'sortition', although that would not satisfy the question of who is to be the 'leader'. By way of contrast one might consider having professional jurors, those who are skilled at sifting evidence and arriving at considered decisions: the basis of a novel by Neiderman (2008).

## Acting on the Wishes of the Electorate

On the matter of procedures one should be able to rely on representatives to act according to the wishes of those who elected them. On the matter of conscience votes it should up to the house itself, on a non-party vote, to decide which issues require a non-party issue to be debated – not up to the party itself. Conscience votes could be decided by the legislature itself. Necessarily it would involve each issue to be decided by the house before the debate takes place.

It is only in recent times that universal franchise was given to all citizens. For example, there were university constituencies in. the UK wherein (from 1603 to 1950) two members were elected to represent, respectively, Cambridge and Oxford, and was dispensed with only recently (in 1950). In universal suffrage, the right to vote, was extended to all citizenry. That right, to be meaningful, is not restricted by race, sex, belief, wealth, social status, or affiliation. It is instructive to note that the first country in the world to allow all men to vote was France in 1792, and the first country in the world to allow women to vote was New Zealand in 1893.

Universal franchising, giving all adults the vote, has had a turbulent history. It has been a progressive series with each battle being hard-fought, even to the point where one of the most prominent and tireless campaigner was Emily Pankhurst. The suffragette Emily Davison threw herself to her death in front of the King's horse at the 1913 Derby. Women over the age of 21 gained the right to vote in Britain in 1928. Clearly there are substantial national differentials.

## Political Rectitude

Political rectitude is a modern force of considerable persuasive power. It was ever thus, but simple facts find modern expression. The notion of being 'politically correct' is one that may mar the capacity to invoke change. There are some issues that seem to be made for debate. In this one is aware of the issue of free speech versus the right not to be offended. It is a constant source of accomplishment that any idea may be challenged, particularly when dogma changes into anathema.

The formation of the UN just after World War II was a most impressive enterprise. Notwithstanding the difficulties it has experienced, the allegations of inefficiencies of administration, and the occasional over-riding that occurs, it is a main hope for improvement. It stands as an international beacon for fair dealing, and for moral intervention. The UN's constitution, with a Security Council, with special powers accorded to some states, could be improved, as could special observer status.

Following the first World War an inter-governmental organisation, called the *League of Nations* was founded. It was an outcome of the Paris Peace Conference that ended World War One. Moving from London to Geneva, and had the brief of being a forum for the resolution of international disputes. The three main proponents of the League were the American President, Woodrow Wilson, David Lloyd George of the UK, and George Clemenceau of France (although, curiously, the United States was never a member even though it sympathised with many of its aims).

One of the sticking points of view what that the covenant of the league should be linked to the Treaty of Versailles. The subsequent difficulties of that, and other problems, showed the Treaty to be unenforceable, resulting in its eventual demise as an effective organisation. Italy left the League in 1937, and in 1938 Britain tried the appeasement policy (without success) – ending its life in 1939 when war broke out. It met finally in 1946 and abolished itself, and closed its doors in Geneva. Plainly it had failed.

As early as 1943 it was decided at the Teheran conference, by Britain, Russia and the United States that there should be a new and more effective organisation, to be called the United Nations. That came into effect after World War II, and was originally based in Geneva, and subsequently in New York. It is inevitable that political compromises will be a part of UN politics: it would be absurd to pretend otherwise.

The United Nations excludes Antarctica, gives the Vatican observer status, and considers Taiwan as administered by China. It does give recognition of the Palestinian Territories by allowing the Palestine Liberation Organisation observer status. There are, no doubt, arguments to change the status of many things.

All of this suggests that radical reform is needed: the principal one being to the UN. Their power and influence, particularly in the case of non-conforming states, could be immense. In this one has scantier regard for politicians than was formerly the case. As Ray Simmonds so aptly put in a letter to a newspaper 'When one politician accuses another politician of being a hypocrite is this a believable accusation or hypocritical accuracy'. What is difficult here is that any proposal to change the rules whereby all nations would have equal say would be defeated by the veto power. Further, many member states are themselves dictatorships that abrogate the freedoms of which the United Nations is a supporter.

Having noted that it is incumbent upon us to reconsider the principles that underlie the notion of the UN. Admirable though they may be one could well imagine a modified and superior structure. For example, dispensing with the Security Council would be one option, thereby ensuring that voting was both democratic and binding, and without veto powers.

There are a number of suggestions wherein reform would be widely acclaimed, and justifiably implemented. Thus, the suggestions are ones that should engage the assembly, and subject to those members who are deserving of inclusion (see Veto powers at UN in References). Among the issues that are of serious political concern must include:

- All politicians should reflect their nation's electoral wishes, rather than fostering views that reflect their own views rather than pursuing their own (democracy in action).
- All members should conform to the UN precepts. Until that is done member states should be excluded: they should follow the UN *Declaration of Human Rights* (or not).
- The Security Council should be disbanded. The current five nations is a post-war relic, and consists of five nations is a post-war relic (China, France, Russia, the United Kingdom, and the United States).
- What is non-democratic and egalitarian is that the Security Council has the right of veto over any proposal and which could, thereby, prevent the adoption of any substantive proposal.

What is curious is that France is a member of the Security Council, but was a defeated nation in World War II, with Paris occupied by Nazi German, and the declaration of the state of Vichy (a common name for the French state which was headed by Marshal Petain in the second world war). It largely consisted of southern France and parts of the territories of North Africa). One could well ask why it was not so for Holland, or Poland, or Norway?

One could well imagine that the UN would have an upper house that represented a different constituency. For example, there could be members whose brief it was to care for the plight of indigenous peoples, of minority groups such as the Rohingya, and the Kurds and Gypsies. It could also consist of membership of nations likely to disappear under the encroaching sea, due to global warming. Were such a body to exist it could well have power over the deliberations of the main assembly. It could, for example, return Bills to the lower house for re-consideration: it would thus be a balance check on the main assembly.

One is mindful of the need, in some cases, to act quickly. For such circumstances, it could be at the call of an emergency meeting to empower the Secretary-General to act immediately.

Given that the present arrangement favours the Security Council it could well be necessary to abolish the present UN and reconstitute the body under a different name, thereby depriving the five permanent members of their veto powers, and by instituting an 'upper house' system. The merits of an upper house, a house of review, is that it does curb power.

The original concept of having it on neutral territory has much to commend it. Not the least of those problems is the perception that it does not favour any particular point of view.

Amongst other things, one could engineer a revisitation to the UN *Declaration of human rights*. One admires the 30 points of the United Nations *Declaration of Human Rights*. Even when one might question some of the propositions it is still an outstanding document. Among the propositions made, as the Bard observed, 'more in the breach than in the observance'.

Along the improvements that might be wrought are:

- With respect to the 30 propositions it could, for example, ensure that the term man and mankind are equally applicable to women.
- Article 4 on the banning of slavery. There are grades of subservience and the proposition ought to distinguish them. For example, the 'owning' of one human by another is banned in all countries, but that does not stop debt slavery, indentured labour, or the 'owning' of child labour. That proposition needs to be made more explicit.
- Article 5 bans 'cruel and unusual punishments'. One is minded of the Kumari case where sisters were condemned to by punished by rape for a perceived misdemeanour by their brother. That village elders could even contemplate such an action strains belief, even though they later retracted (see Kumari in References).
- Article 9 holds that no-one should be subjected to arbitrary arrest, detention or exile. That is contradicted by the capture and imprisonment of those in Guantanamo Bay who were not given the benefit of a civilian trial, which also contradict the principles expressed in Article 11, clauses (1) and (2). It needs universal application to all member states.
- One ought to be able to decline nationality. Article 15, sub clause (2) holds that no-one should be arbitrarily deprived of nationality – yet that is proposed by some nations. It could be redrafted to include countries who confer unwanted nationality on the unwilling.
- Article 26, clause (1) holds that 'elementary education shall be compulsory', which is not universal: and that same clause holds that higher education should be on the basis of merit, whereas it is now becoming more the ability to pay, or not to incur severe debts – a topic that needs further debate.

## Special Cases

### *Women's Votes*

Women who were householders in the UK, over the age of 30, and met certain property qualifications got the vote in 1918, but it was not until 1928 that women over the age of 21 got the vote. It is clear that the move to voting equality was a somewhat turbulent process. As one cannot distinguish voting capacity it is evident that it should be of universal application. Without that freedom one is in the position of trying to make discriminations by tacit criteria: who would decide?

### *Independence*

What is particularly interesting here is, for example, the right to separate from the state, and set up a new one. Such, for example, is the case in Spain where the Catalans wish to be separate, but are forbidden by the Spanish government. Here the question is 'what does one do in such circumstances?' A similar situation is also applicable to the Kurds.

The notion of protected disclosures is a vexing one. For example, it is considered appropriate to have cabinet documents secret as it may inhibit discussion of controversial topics. On the other hand, the 'commercial in confidence' provision should be available to the public on the grounds that it is public money that is being spent. That applies particularly to contracts once they are entered: no provision of secrecy may be applicable.

The next issue is equally contentious. It is, quite rightly, an offence to mislead the legislature. What is not understandable is that it is not an offence to mislead the electors who put them there. Broken promises make a mockery of statements and can only lead to contempt for parliamentarians.

One ought, for example, to be able to trust the word of an elected representative. If a formal promise is made one ought to be able to trust those elected to honour it. Thus, one would expect promised legislation to be introduced into the legislature (such as instituting a system of universal health cover for citizens), even if any upper house were to reject it. Similarly, if one promises not to introduce legislation, on a topic, that promise should be honoured (not to legislate for a Goods and Services Tax or VAT, for instance).

It is regrettable that parliamentary members sometimes follow the dictates of their own consciences rather than the will of their own electorate. Further, the existence of political parties with a legislative platform, will produce policies of which some will be acceptable to some, and others not. It is worthy of note that British origin countries (at least) still seat members in opposition. Since they face each other it is an invitation to be confronting, as has already been noted. Certainly, the writer's experience in various sized committees verify that opposition seating produces an adversarial effect.

Recent experience has shown the disaffection with the current political process. Electing a president of some kind is strictly for the wealthy, electioneering being an expensive process. As an alternative one could imagine a process of 'sortition'.

## *Incumbency*

In genuine democracies there should be a limit on having any incumbent in power for more than (say) ten years. To make that a longer period is to entertain the distinct possibility is that they will misuse that position to foster their own interests. The question here is, should that apply only to persons who are presidents, prime ministers, and governors-general. This idea was stimulated by the Mugabe case. He had, until very recently, been in power for 37 years; in fact, since independence in 1980.

One of the main arguments against leaving incumbents in power for too long is that they have the chance to form unholy alliances, and even change the rules that allow them to remain. Against this is the democratic means of removal. On balance the argument of stopping improper alliances, and allowing aspirants their chance outweighs the idea of incumbents remaining (on the grounds of efficiency). What is problematic here is, first, how long the strictures should be: the second is the idea of getting rid of the unworthy. It might also be added that it may deprive us of the talents of the worthy, and do so by democratic votes.

The Speaker of the Legislative House is a most important position. For it to be non-partisan then one should have some distinguished and clearly neutral person in that position. It would be regarded as heinous if a judge were to be partisan in hearing a case. By the same token one expects neutrality to be a requirement of such a position and, to be quite safe, of limited time-tenure. In the Westminster system the Speaker is commonly a member of the ruling party, and should thus not be appointed.

The appointment of a prime minister or president is, in some countries, at the behest of the party, and in the party room. In the case of the United States the election of a President is by way of electoral college votes rather than popular vote. One can see a case for giving power to someone elected to that position by ballot, whether by an untrammelled vote by the legislature or by popular ballot.

Perhaps one might (waywardly) suggest that a prime minister should be elected by parliament as a whole, and on a conscience vote. As above, the procedure by which a President is appointed is also contentious. One would have to recognise that many eminently suitable candidates would be reluctant to submit themselves to electioneering. To put the decision in the hands of, effectively, the leader of the party is to give extraordinary power to one person.

One significant finding is that individuals are dispensable. Where someone has been in power too long it seems to be an invitation to loss of insight. Extended incumbency of many years must give pause to advocates of democracy. Such a situation presents them with an unrivalled opportunity to gather colleagues, to engineer elections, and to use state resources to further their own interests. It is not being suggested that any individual behaves in such a manner but, rather, that it is a non-democratic process. The principle that no one is indispensable seems to be a good one. One might suggest that ten years in a job is quite enough time. It is worthy of note that Presidents of the USA may only be elected twice, and thence no more.

The power to ban from office anyone (say) who has been in office for more than (say) ten years, is that it may lead to corruption but, rather, that it is a means of minimising that corruption does occur. Even where the democratic process is in place one is concerned that coercion and corruption may be evident in the electoral process. One thing is plain, those who stay too long in come to believe in their essentialness: witness, Stalin in Russia, Duvalier in Haiti, Castro in Cuba, Mugabe in Zimbabwe, and Pinochet in Chile. That point does not seem to be true of constitutional monarchies as, for example, in the UK, Holland and Sweden. In those instances, it is true that monarchies persist, but their power is severely restricted: their role to provide continuity, and to advise but not determine.

## *Gay Marriage*

On such issues as 'gay' marriage it is of such fundamental social importance that the people should decide: thus, there is a need for a referendum (with appropriate constitutional change) to decide, particularly in those jurisdictions where a plebiscite outcome is not binding. It is argued that such a fundamental change requires the assent of the people by way of a referendum. If the constitution needs amendment then so be it. To have a political party decide that something so fundamental is contrary to democratic ideals. One might argue for marriage-equality. One could equally well argue for marriage-complementarity: it is entirely up to the electorate to decide.

The issue here is that it is being proposed that so fundamental point as family-matters should be the subject of a referendum. On that subject of framing questions to be put one might consider giving options rather than a simple answer to a single question. For example, one might convert a question such as 'should homosexual marriage be permitted' to 'how is marriage to be defined', thence to a series such as 'should homosexual marriage be legal' and 'should it have a name different from marriage?' Additionally, one might ask, 'should polygamy and polyandry be permitted' and 'should it have a distinguishing name?' With that the corollaries to be spelled out, such as 'should multiple wives all claim welfare benefits'. While one is about it a pronouncement on dowries would be welcome (see Marriage in References).

## Health and Education

Two of the most pressing dilemmas are health and education. The questions of value here are 'Should one provide medical help where problems are generated by smoking but they refuse to give it up?' (or is self-help a condition of intervention?). The basic premise here is whether self-help is a prerequisite. One might ask if co-operation is a prerequisite of caring and attention.

Moving to education, here it is argued that various cultures have forms of concern: particularly in the payment for education. The costs do vary: in Germany, for example, they regard a first degree education as an excellent investment and fosterer of talent. In the United States of America one must take out a substantial loan to go to university – particularly so for entry into the prestigious schools. This is a policy matter and deserves a thorough debate in the legislature. The provision of free tertiary education is of merit in that it is a career open to the talents. Against it might be said that education confers privilege that must be paid for. These contrasting views represent two different ways of looking at the world. One could be guided by the self-help principle: on the alternative system, the state minds the vulnerable – whether they have helped themselves. We might enquire whether these contrasting systems tend to equality. One is mindful of the precept that 'God helps those who help themselves'.

## Moral Obligations

One of the significant determiners of democracy is that of the ballot box. It is thus that one has a moral obligation to resist one-party rule. Perhaps one might consider them to be not so much revelations as tyrannies. To ask common humanity to become perfect is to ask them to abandon the human condition, to rise above existential angst, and to be what they are not. Apocalyptic views on humanity may be dangerous, and may be doomed to failure but that is not a reason for not trying. Without aspirations to improvement, rather than aspirations to perfection, we would be less than we are: with such aspirations, we take on the process of improving without falling into the error of believing it to be too readily achievable.

There are nations with a lesser regard for human rights. The rise of non-democratic regimes may be viewed with caution. China has resumed Hong Kong and Macao peacefully, but has invaded Tibet. Most recently they have attempted to assume control the South China sea by building artificial islands. Against we might note their plan to mechanise the Silk Road and make it more suitable for heavy traffic. The Chinese government also has generally improved the lot of the working public. One has to separate the admirable from the not-quite-so-admirable – always a difficult task. Most recently it has confirmed Xi Jinping, Secretary of the Communist Party of China, for life. This is a disconfirmation of the principle that democracy consists, among things, of a means of getting rid of unworthy leaders. We shall have to see how it works out.

Prosperous nations incur a moral obligation to help those less favoured. That said it is to be strongly noted that such aid should be with a view to making them prosperous and independent rather than continually assisting to preserve a non-functional style of life. We recognise the humanitarian crisis, and should be able to help. On a sense of balance, one cannot take into most-favoured nations all who wish to migrate: on the other hand, one has an obligation to help those in less favoured circumstances. Balanced against those who flee war or economic privations is to put the needs of the host country and its citizen's wishes. The importance is for legislators to bear in mind their responsibility is to the people who elected them – their voting citizens.

Not to do something to help is morally poor; to allow-in as immigrants could be to the detriment of the existing citizenry. One form that help might take is for the relevant legislature to allow in a proportion of extreme cases. To that could be added to the old *Colombo Plan* idea that the host country would educate incomers who, in turn, incur an obligation to take their education and experience back to their native lands, and, thereby, effect an improvement.

There are occasions on which morals may supervene. For example, the removal of urban level-crossings may yield a business case for a return of only 75 cents in the dollar, yet the non-business case (such as saving lives) may come to dominate the discussion. Another instance is that an endangered species of native animal may result in job losses: notwithstanding, the argument for the preservation of native species may supervene.

## *Whistleblowing*

Prime amongst such motives is a clear definition. To that end the first item one needs is a clear definition, bearing in mind the cultural differences and attitudes. It is suggested that the UN is in such a unique position.

Amongst the significant questions one might as a legislator perform are the ones below:

1. Define corruption
2. What makes an effective whistleblower regime?
3. how does one legislate for whistleblowing?
4. Review the current legislation
5. How does one give economic and social protection to the whistleblower?
6. What has been found to work in current legislation?
7. How does one encourage whistleblowing?
8. How to distinguish the genuine from the false whistleblower (who acts from selfish motives)?
9. What are the current challenges.

10. What are some of the current challenges? (including protecting disclosure where possible)?
11. Tie any fine to the subject's income.
12. Consider the idea of rewarding the whistleblower with a proportion of the money saved.
13. Have a court decide on penalties and bans
14. How does on prevent retribution?

Given these salient questions how does an evoked response sound?

## *General Observations*

The question here is, what are the benefits of capitalism. Among other things it does seem to be associated with greater freedoms, as power is divided. It also provides the benefits of differences wherein someone from an underprivileged background can succeed economically. In that sense is allows the freedom of choice, and contributes to the notion of allowing natural selection a freer rein. Intermediately, it consists of those who are part wealth creators and part rent seekers (those whose skills consist of appropriating the money of other).

At its worst it consists of those whose maxim is 'profit at any price', coupled with nepotism. Thus, the mass of workers need adequate protection. Karl Marx was skilled at the analysis of the problem, but regrettably a poorer provider of solutions. The difficulty here is that capitalism may need more control, rather than dumping, particularly applicable to those of psychopathic tendency.

In the sequel to World War II it is easy to comprehend the appeal that peace movements had, and the implications of that for moral philosophy. With this went a demonstrated commitment to internationalism, and a commitment to such bodies as the League of Nations and, eventually, the United Nations. Most significantly, to the beneficial moral stature that such bodies bring to bear, and to the immense good they do through sub-organisation – such as work with refugees, and with health, both in the provision of critical information as well as the provision of practical help (Global peace, also Peace in references).

The obvious destructive power of the atomic bomb had made it imperative to consider power ratios, it also gave rise to significant movements such as the *Campaign for Nuclear Disarmament* (CND). In all of this we should not lose sight of the impact that the release of significant documents had upon human and international relations theory. The revelation of the political background of the Russian revolution, the now availability of Nazi archives, and the post-Glasnost release of significant documentary archives from Eastern Europe are all relevant. What has come to be appreciated in recent times is the importance that attaches to the concept of multiple-causation. It is a timely antidote to the more simplistic notion.

The idea of preventing World War III has intrigued many, and given rise to books on the subject. One might argue that to prevent another world war there must be a co-ordinated approach. A grand strategy would include comprehensibility, open discussion, consistency, and attention to the realities of change and the effectiveness of detentes. The use of economic sanctions, and of armed intervention, is a part of what we do. What we may do with yet more force is to see the examples set by secular saints. It is proposed here that while we must recognise the role of economic and military force, the use of moral force is less obvious and, in the longer term, more enduring.

## On Being Cautious

There are various restrictions that may be placed on uncurbed political power. Even in court judges always have one eye on the appellate jurisdiction. Thus, one is reminded that a need to be appealable by reference to a Constitution, and is done by the highest court in the land. It is thus that there is an external reference point. The critical item here is that no-one has unbridled power in any genuine democracy.

Other curbs on unchecked power is the ballot box. At the next election, any political party that offends at the electorate thereby suffers defeat. Further, any politician who grossly offends the electorate, by gross moral turpitude, may be impeached. An ultimate sanction is that of mass protests, usually at the street level. We have seen such actions in recent times, and can testify mainly (though sometimes not) to their effectiveness. One is mindful of the uncurbed power of prime ministers (in going to war, for example), It would be politically monstrous if no curbs were to be placed on significant politicians.

### *Independence*

What is particularly interesting here is, for example, the right to separate from the state, and set up a new one. Such, for example, is the case in Spain where the Catalans wish to be separate, but are forbidden by the Spanish government, and in accordancd with the Constitution. Here the question is 'what does one do in such circumstances?' A similar situation is also applicable to the Kurds.

The notion of protected disclosures is a vexing one. For example, it is considered appropriate to have cabinet documents secret as it may inhibit discussion of controversial topics. On the other hand, the 'commercial in confidence' provision should be available to the public on the grounds that it is public money that is being spent. That applies particularly to contracts once they are entered: no provision of secrecy may be applicable.

The next issue is equally contentious. It is, quite rightly, an offence to mislead the legislature. What is not understandable is that it is not an offence to mislead the electors who put them there. Broken promises make a mockery of statements and can only lead to contempt for parliamentarians. One ought, for example, to be able to trust the word of an elected representative. If a formal promise is made one ought to be able to trust those elected to honour it. Thus, one would expect promised legislation to be introduced into the legislature (such as instituting a system of universal health cover for citizens), even if any upper house were to reject it. Similarly, if one promises not to introduce legislation, on a topic, that promise should be honoured (not to legislate for a Goods and Services Tax or VAT, for instance).

It is regrettable that parliamentary members sometimes follow the dictates of their own consciences rather than the will of their own electorate. Further, the existence of political parties with a legislative platform, will produce policies of which some will be acceptable to some, and others not. It is worthy of note that British origin countries (at least) still seat members in opposition. Since they face each other it is an invitation to be confronting, as has already been noted. Certainly, the writer's experience in various sized committees verify that opposition seating produces an adversarial effect.

Recent experience has shown the disaffection with the current political process. Electing a president of some kind is strictly for the wealthy, electioneering being an expensive process. As an alternative one could imagine a process of 'sortition'.

## *Women's Votes*

Women who were householders in the UK, over the age of 30, and met certain property qualifications got the vote in 1918, but it was not until 1928 that women over the age of 21 got the vote. It is clear that the move to voting equality was a somewhat turbulent process. As one cannot distinguish voting capacity it is evident that it should be of universal application. Without that freedom one is in the position of trying to make discriminations by tacit criteria: who would decide?

## *Health and Education*

Two of the most pressing dilemmas are health and education. The questions of value here are 'Should one provide medical help where problems are generated by smoking but they refuse to give it up?' (or, is self-help a condition of intervention?). The basic premise here is whether self-help is a prerequisite. One might ask if co-operation is a prerequisite of caring and attention.

Moving to education, here it is argued that various cultures have forms of concern: particularly in the payment for education. The costs do vary: in Germany, for example, they regard a first-degree education as an excellent investment and fosterer of talent. In the United States of America one must take out a substantial loan to go to university – particularly so for entry into the prestigious schools. This is a policy matter and deserves a thorough debate in the legislature. The provision of free tertiary education is of merit in that it is a career open to the talents.

Against it might be said that education confers privilege that must be paid. These contrasting views represent two different ways of looking at the world. One could be guided by the self-help principle: on the alternative system, the state minds the vulnerable – whether they have helped themselves. We might enquire whether these contrasting systems tend to equality. One is mindful of the precept that 'God helps those who help themselves'.

## *Moral Obligations*

One of the significant determiners of democracy is that of the ballot box. It is thus that one has a moral obligation to resist one-party rule. Perhaps one might consider them to be not so much revelations as tyrannies. To ask common humanity to become perfect is to ask them to abandon the human condition, to rise above existential angst, and to be what they are not. Apocalyptic views on humanity may be dangerous, and may be doomed to failure but that is not a reason for not trying. Without aspirations to improvement, rather than aspirations to perfection, we would be less than we are: with such aspirations, we take on the process of improving without falling into the error of believing it to be too readily achievable.

There are nations with a lesser regard for human rights. The rise of non-democratic regimes may be viewed with caution. China has resumed Hong Kong and Macao peacefully, but has invaded Tibet, and has aspirations to invade Taiwan. Most recently they have attempted to assume control the South China sea by building artificial islands. Against we might note their plan to mechanise the Silk Road and make it more suitable for heavy traffic. The Chinese government also has generally improved the lot of the working public. One has to separate the admirable from the not-quite-so-admirable – always a difficult task. Most recently it has confirmed the Secretary of the Communist Party of China may be appointed for life. This is a disconfirmation of the principle that democracy consists, among things, of a means of getting rid of unworthy leaders (see incumbency, above). We shall have to see how it works out.

Prosperous nations incur a moral obligation to help those less favoured. That said it is to be strongly noted that such aid should be with a view to making them prosperous and independent rather than continually assisting to preserve a non-functional style of life. We recognise the humanitarian crisis, and should be able to help. On a sense of balance, one cannot take into most-favoured nations all who wish to migrate: on the other hand, one has an obligation to help those in less favoured circumstances. Balanced against those who flee war or economic privations is to put the needs of the host country and its citizen's wishes. The importance is for legislators to bear in mind their responsibility is to the people who elected them – their voting citizens.

Not to do something to help is morally poor; to allow-in as immigrants could be to the detriment of the existing citizenry, and might also change the nature of the existing society. One form that help might take is for the relevant legislature to allow in a proportion of cases. To that could be added to the old *Colombo Plan* idea that the host country would educate incomers who, in turn, incur an obligation to take their education and experience back to their native lands, and, thereby, effect an improvement.

There are occasions on which morals may supervene. For example, the removal of urban level-crossings may yield a business case for a return of only 75 cents in the dollar, yet the non-business case (such as saving lives) may come to dominate the discussion. Another instance is that an endangered species of native animal may result in job losses: notwithstanding, the argument for the preservation of native species may supervene.

## Whistleblowing

Whistleblowing is one of the most important functions in rooting out corruption: for that reason one should put advantages in the way of those who blow the whistle. The only qualifier there is to have in place sanctions for those who, in blowing the whistle, are clearly motivated of malice. Amongst the significant questions one might ask a potential whistleblower to perform are the ones should be selected to have a freer rein. Intermediately, it consists of those who are part wealth creators and part rent seekers (those whose skills consist of appropriating the money of others). At its worst it consists of those whose maxim is 'profit at any price', coupled with nepotism. Thus, the mass of workers do need adequate protection. The difficulty here is that capitalism may need more control, particularly applicable to those of psychopathic tendency.

In the sequel to World War II it is easy to comprehend the appeal that peace movements had, and the implications of that for moral philosophy. With this went a demonstrated commitment to internationalism, and a commitment to such bodies as the League of Nations and, eventually, the United Nations. Most significantly, to the beneficial moral stature that such bodies bring to bear, and to the immense good they do through sub-organisation – such as work with refugees, and with health, both in the provision of critical information as well as the provision of practical help.

The obvious destructive power of the atomic bomb had made it imperative to consider power ratios, it also gave rise to significant movements such as the *Campaign for Nuclear Disarmament* (CND). In all of this we should not lose sight of the impact that the release of significant documents had upon human and international relations theory. The revelation of the political background of the Russian revolution, the now availability of Nazi archives, and the post-Glasnost release of significant documentary archives from Eastern Europe are all relevant. What has come to be appreciated in recent times is the importance that attaches to the concept of multiple-causation. It is a timely antidote to the more simplistic notions.

The idea of preventing World War III has intrigued many, and given rise to books on the subject. One might argue that to prevent another world war there must be a co-ordinated approach. A grand strategy would include comprehensibility, open discussion, consistency, and attention to the realities of change and the effectiveness of *detentes*. The use of economic sanctions, and of armed intervention, is a part of what we do. What we may do with yet more force is to see the examples set by secular saints. It is proposed here that while we must recognise the role of economic and military force, the use of moral force is less obvious and, in the longer term, more enduring.

## On Being Cautious

There are various restrictions that may be placed on uncurbed political power. Even in court judges always have one eye on the appellate jurisdiction. Thus, one is reminded that a need to be appealable by reference to a Constitution, and is overseen by the highest court in the land. It is thus that there is an external reference point. The critical item here is that no-one has unbridled power in any genuine democracy.

Other curbs on unchecked power is the ballot box. At the next election, any political party that offends at the electorate thereby suffers defeat. Further, any politician who grossly offends the electorate, by gross moral turpitude, may be impeached. An ultimate sanction is that of mass protests, usually at the street level. We have seen such actions in recent times, and can testify mainly (though sometimes not) to their effectiveness. One is mindful of the uncurbed power of prime ministers (in going to war, for example), It would be politically monstrous if no curbs were to be placed on significant politicians.

## Conclusions

Some of the imperfections of the present political setup are considered and solutions proffered for consideration. One is mindful of the notion that political systems adapt and evolve: as such, the present system is seen as in need of improvement. In the end the first point is to recognise is the need for change. Whatever solutions are being canvassed they must be debated widely. Not only for the sake of transparency but also to accommodate the wide range of ideas. It is only by such open-ness that just solutions will be found.

# Chapter 10
# Sex Differences

Here the issues are those affecting the role that women play in the community. Among those problems here are those of cultures that suppress women, that require them to wear a face veil, and discourage them for going out without a male relative as escort. At the other more moderate end of the spectrum there is the unconscious bias against women in Western society wherein they have a 'glass ceiling' as a barrier to promotion.

Iceland was the first country to elect a female Head of State, several others have had female prime ministers, Britain has a female head of state (as well as a female Prime Minister) and who is also head of the Anglican Church: Israel, Sri Lanka, and India have all had female prime ministers, and Australia has had a female prime minister, and a female Governer-General.

It bears repetition that some unlikely issues occur. For example, Ruanda has the most impressive record with respect to female members of the legislature (see Women in the legislature in References). What is most interesting here is that those countries have not become disaster areas.

Women's role in the criminal justice system is far less than it is for men, some sub-groups have special problems in being wayward. As was mentioned above, in the competition for equality it is worth noting that despite the controversy of redefining marriage there was never a suggestion that female homosexuals should be treated any differently from males. The issues that need to be canvassed widely are 'should marriage be confined to one man and one woman – or not'. 'Should polygamy and polyandry be recognised formally – or not', and 'what is the minimum age for marriage?' 'Should polygamy and polyandry be considered at the same time', and 'should there be a different name for different forms of marriage?' (see Marriage in References).



R. Francis, *Equality in Theory and Practice*,
https://doi.org/10.1007/978-981-15-3488-1_10

## Issues Differentially Affecting Women

### *Facial Recognition and Communication*

We have to recognise that women are more attentive to faces than are men. In the case of women it is often the case, at least in Western societies, that a little lipstick goes a long way.

Prosopagnosia is a condition where the ability to recognise faces is significantly impaired (although the recognition of other objects seems to be normal): it is, in other words, a form of face blindness. A socially disabling phenomenon, it must cause distress to sufferers, although many learn to cope. A complementary condition is one known as 'Möbius Syndrome' in which a paralysis of cranial nerves leads to sufferers losing the capacity for facial movement and expression (see Cole and Spalding 2009). The absence of the capacity to provide facial cues is both distressing for the sufferer and, in the longer term, makes them unable to take up professions in which interaction is critical – medicine, psychology, the ministry, law, teaching.

It is salutary in passing to draw parallels between an incapacity to communicate via facial expression, and the denial of facial feedback arising from wearing a veil. More importantly, an inability to communicate via facial expression could lead to misunderstandings that may then lead to offending. One might argue that, where women are adversely discriminated, one might even up the score by providing the veil. The difficulty here is that such an approach is historical (they have been adversely discriminated) – but not provide a justification for continuing such discrimination.

Interpersonal distance, and percentage and direction of gaze are further examples of non-verbal communication that may be the subject of inter-ethnic misunderstanding. One wonders how often annoyance, availability and comprehension are misinterpreted in inter-ethnic conversation, and to what extent that generates criminal acts.

It is, of course, quite possible that misunderstanding gives rise to misinterpretation of such issues as gestures, implicit understanding, and inappropriate actions. Sexual misbehaviour may result from a misunderstanding of such norms. For example, it was recorded that in the past, Italian workers were astonished to discover that if they became sexually involved with a girl under 16, their willingness to marry her, or the fact that she was already depraved, does not absolve them from guilt, as was the case according to Italian law (Ferracuti 1968, p.23).

Since the wearing of the veil is required in some cultures one is prevented from even guessing when they are lying. Ekman's work has received lay expression elsewhere. He makes the point that facial expressions, no matter how fleeting or complex, are a vital guide to social interaction. His work explores those spontaneous, fleeting and non-stylised facial expressions where meaning can be communicated by telling micro-cues that are not ordinarily under conscious control.

The use of face coverings by females in some cultures is contrary to the usual norms and forms of social interaction. Much of our social life depends upon facial recognition, on feedback in conversation, and in mutual gaze; without these our social life is impoverished, and an advantage is conferred on the covered one, who has access to information denied to her interlocutor. It also has criminal implications. If people were to be permitted to wear a total facial covering, it could conceal the identity of someone intent on committing an offence. One might debate such an issue in the conventional parliamentary way. The recent and temporary use of face masks then partially obviates that point.

Here the issues involve not only facial recognition but also facial expression. Much of our social interaction is based on reading clues from others: their appearance and movement are as important in communication as the words they use. Our social interaction is predicated on being able to see faces, interpret expressions, and interact. *The Man in the Iron Mask* is a literally faceless character, the *Elephant man*, with his horribly disfigured visage, was the subject first of horror, then of pity.

To indicate particular emotions we 'pull a face', in showing courage we 'face the music', and withdrawal from sociability involves 'self-effacement'; in Blake's *Songs of Innocence* pity has a human face. Additionally, the vast international cosmetics industry provides a material testament to the importance we attach to the face. As W.H. Davies so aptly put it in his poem, 'What is this life if, full of care, we have no time to stand and stare'. The apt couplet here is 'No time to wait till her mouth can/enrich that smile her eyes began'.

There is a view, held in a few countries, that a rejected suitor should take revenge on rejection by ensuring that their prospective partners deserve retaliation. It commonly takes the form of throwing acid into the faces of the rejecting partner. The 'reasoning' behind this is that no other man will find them attractive, having been rejected by a 'good' prospect (see Acid attacks in References). It is thus that such a fundamental change as recognising the commonly accepted definition of 'marriage' would be resolved. Whichever way the electorate voted it would make it more readily acceptable as it would represent the wishes of the electorate.

Women are just over half the population of the world yet are subject to entrenched discrimination in some cultures, and even in some organisations. One particular problem exists for those from cultures with a history of subjugating women where they are treated as chattels. Even where such women migrate they do so as adjuncts to the males who control their lives. Women, as much as men, should have the right to terminate any relationship without retaliation. The notion that women are killed every day by former partners is a deeply regrettable thought. Women have traditionally been subjugated: it is also the case that women were treated differently in places of worship: the notion of inferiority seems to have been bred into them (see Discrimination against women in References)

## Female Genital Mutilation

One particularly salient cultural example involves female genital mutilation (FGM). There is constant debate about the rights and consequences. In most Westernised countries there is an absolute prohibition. Clearly the main aim of a clitoridectomy is to make sexual pleasure absent, and thereby promote sexual fidelity (see female genital mutilation in the References). As the practice is so widespread one does not see it as a religious problem as one that has its roots in culture: further, one never knows what those subject to the procedure would have thought had they not been mutilated. Western females who, for instance, wish to have their labia surgically reconfigured at least freely choose the procedure as adults. Moreover, it is performed under proper hygienic surgical conditions. In the case of genital mutilation in some ethnic groups there is the very real danger of infection, shock and death.

When a parallel is drawn between circumcision and female genital mutilation it is often argued that the parallel does not exist. Circumcision has been practiced for thousands of years without seemingly ill effects, and with no diminution of sexual pleasure (but how would one know?). Further, those cultures that practice it have a reduced incidence of AIDS. There is an inclination to make a metaphorical connection but, as is often said, every metaphor is a limping one (see Circumcision in references).

Writers on the subject of the sexual mutilation of girl babies who have interviewed girls so treated have noted that some of the recipients of that treatment, when grown up, do not all seem to resent it, and do not think of it as mutilation. Nevertheless, it is contrary to Western ways and law, and just because some of those so treated do not resent it, it is no reason to permit the procedure. It appears that millions of women, mainly in Africa, have been subject to this procedure. It was outlawed in Sweden in 1982, the first Western country to do so. Many other have now followed, and it is now banned, or covered by existing legislation in many countries.

## Fertility and Population Growth

It is totally unrealistic to ask people to cease sexual activity: one might as well order the tides to stand still. To that end we need to recognise that there are pressure groups and religious organisations that are opposed to birth control, and there is a need to have their influence moderated. We should recognise the once reasonable rule of not procuring abortions in that day and age. It acted as a precaution against the use of abortifacients available at that time.

It does appear that high population growth rate relates to various dysfunctional aspects of society. This being so, then containing population growth is imperative:

one means of containing population growth is encouraging the practice of contraception. Given that people will not forgo sexual intercourse we can only be concerned with outcomes. There are forces opposed to such contraception – largely those of the fundamentalist disposition.

The scholarly account of classical attitudes to modern issues was given by Wilkinson (1979). It retails the views of the ancients regarding fertility. Mention was made of the concern about over-population in Malthus' essay of 1798, and reference made to Symonds in 1891 writing of '… our age when habitable portions of the globe are rapidly becoming overcrowded'. The author of the article recounts the various methods of birth control, dwelling particularly on infanticide. Amongst the merits of infanticide are the sex of the child is known and, secondly, it favours the life of the mother, (leaving out the obvious distress of the mother). In addition to 'exposure'. Among the methods of birth control given were:

- Acidulous medicaments
- Diuretics
- Emetics
- Jumping
- Lifting heavy weights
- Malnutrition
- Pessaries
- Pressure in certain areas
- Punching
- Purgatives
- Riding in a cart along a rough road
- Surgical interventions

Given that the rate of population growth is related to dysfunction then containing the growth rate is an imperative. It is incumbent upon the proponents of population policy growth to provide a re-consideration. The concept of 'populate or perish' is still a debate that we need to have. We also need to note the notion that, in some cultures, more children means a better chance of surviving older age. In countries where children are a form of social security there is a need to provide social security: more children does not mean 'better'.

To these issues we might couple a governmental policy of not encouraging fertility. Withdrawing government subsidies to young families might have an effect: families with young children would be economically disadvantaged and would, understandably, regard their deprivation as one that supports the more affluent, by having more substantial resources. In other words, the short-term and the long-term consequences seem to be irreconcilable. To hold that population growth is 'only X per cent' is to ignore the problem of compound growth. To this problem we must add the increased consumption of natural resources, and the consequence of waste disposal and of pollution (see Fertility and population growth in the References).

## Rape

Rape is a heinous offence, and particularly so when the woman is impregnated by the rapist. In 2011 it was reported that, in Afghanistan, a woman, Gulnaz (see References), was raped by a cousin's husband, had become pregnant and had given birth to the child. She was imprisoned for adultery, and would only be released on condition that she marry her rapist. To draw attention to this gross abrogation of human rights. A film was made, but political pressure to have it banned created another furore (see Gulnaz in References).

In a 2015 case of Meenakshi Kumari in the Indian state of Uttar Pradesh to be raped as punishment. She was 23 and the same fate awaited her 15 year-old sister. The precipitating offence was that her brother ran off with a woman of lower caste. They themselves are Dalits (formerly called the 'Untouchables'). The couple were hiding in New Delhi, and have real difficulty returning to their village. These cases are excellent examples of the clash of ethnic ways with the laws of civilised nations (see Kumari in References).

A family may decide that a female who has committed a sexual misdemeanour should be killed to preserve the family 'honour'. It is hard for the Western mind to comprehend that one could kill one's own child (see 'Honour killing' in References). Cultures that highly value female virginity and chastity may resort to killing when a female family member is thought to have 'dishonoured' the family. In one case a Middle Eastern man tried to hire someone to kill his niece, who was in a relationship with the follower of another religion. The father argued that the family shame and the niece's forgiveness should mitigate his sentence (see R v Qutami [2001] NSWCCA 353).

## Trafficking

Despite this bleakly economic justification for prostitution the notion of human trafficking is morally repugnant, despite it being a global phenomenon. Any activity that involves threat, deception, coercion or fraud is contrary both to law and to notions of justice. That is not to say that women should not engage in prostitution if they so wish: what is to be condemned is when it involves any form of exploitation. That cold account of prostitution in no way diminishes the case against women being forced into brothels. The UNODC has even produced a 'toolkit' to prevent trafficking in people (see the toolkit to combat trafficking in persons and human trafficking in the References.).

This comes to the heart of the problem, that of trafficking in humans. Such problems are commonly associated with sexual exploitation, the exploitation of children, forced marriage, forced labour and organised crime. Virtually every country in the world is affected by these crimes. The challenge for all countries, rich and poor, is to target the criminals who exploit desperate people and to protect and assist victims of trafficking and smuggled migrants, many of whom endure unimaginable hardships in their bid for a better life.

As the United Nations agency focusing on the criminal justice element of these crimes, UNODC has made great efforts against human trafficking and the smuggling of migrants, underpinned by the UN and its protocols on trafficking in persons and migrant smuggling. One account of human trafficking addresses the specific issue of trafficking for sexual purposes. Goodey (2003) focused upon the issue of victimhood, and on responses to sex trafficking within the European Union. The study's main concern was transnational crime, and the criminal justice system's reaction to women who are trafficked for sexual purposes. Goodey argued for a three-pronged attack on the problem: prevention, prosecution and protection. The conventional threefold approach of 'migration-crime-security' should, she further argued, be balanced by a fourth element – victimisation.

## Suffragism

Universal franchising, giving all adults the vote, has had a turbulent history. It has been a progressive series with each battle being hard-fought. Women over the age of 21 gained the right to vote in Britain in 1928. Clearly there are substantial national differentials. The first marker was New Zealand being the first self-governing country in the world to give women the vote (in 1893) (see previous notes).

## Forced Marriage

Of a lesser effect, possibly, is that of forced marriages. This should be distinguished from arranged marriages (see also Arranged marriages in References) where the participants are willing. In forced marriages, there is duress that is scarcely different from that caused by human trafficking. Civil governments have warned that new laws might be needed to stop teenagers being flown to other countries and forced into marriage. Such offences would, in effect, be punished as sex trafficking, and attract a substantial prison sentence, and may constitute a breach of human rights. Their parents often claim to arrange a marriage, many without their knowledge, to protect them against promiscuity and other Western vices. Who knows, they may work out well (see Forced marriage in the References).

### Violent Offences

Cases of violence occur in many families, and one has to recognise that males are commonly stronger than females. That is not say that violence against males never happens, but it is far less common. Recent world interest in domestic violence has rendered it more public and possibly better treated. Particular courts may imprison people for violence, or for breach of issues such as non-intervention orders (see Domestic violence , and Easteal 1994 in References). In 'civilised' societies violence against women is seen as contemptible, despite the fact that some members of such 'civilised' societies regard it as their right.

## Ambiguous Data

### *Prostitution*

Prostitution is another social indicator: some prostitution may be voluntary: other incidences are cases of procurement. The pressure exerted on girls and women to become prostitutes must be greater where there is economic deprivation. There probably is also a relationship between prostitution and drug abuse. As both prostitution and drug abuse are illegal in many jurisdictions: many drug abusers must resort to gaining a quick and untaxed income to support an expensive habit. Further, drug-addicted prostitutes are more likely to be regarded as outcasts even by such marginal groups as addicts who do not prostitute themselves or, conversely, prostitutes who do not take drugs (see Aoyama 2009).

Societies undergoing rapid industrialisation prostitution serves an economic function in two ways. In the first place, it helps to maintain a required workforce of young single men who do not then have to seek a wife and who might otherwise leave. In the second place, it allows entrepreneurs to extract large profits from the exploitation of the prostitutes, thus providing the entrepreneurs with capital that they may then use for other investments that are more acceptable to the general populace (to give a more cold-blooded view).

### *Polygamy*

As a generic term polygamy may take any one of three forms. One is one husband have multiple simultaneous wives; a second form (and less common) is that of one wife having multiple simultaneous husbands (commonly called polyandry): the third form is that of group marriage where the family consists of multiple husbands and multiple wives. These latter two are far less common.

In some cultures, polygamy is permissible. Having said that, it can be noted that although polygamy is legally impermissible it can be achieved de facto. Consider a man married according to law, who deserts a wife and takes on a common-law wife. Further, suppose that the de-facto wife bore him two children, giving further solidity to the union. The man has, in effect, two spouses. It would be a matter for the courts to consider the division of property, the legality of the assumed partnership and loyalty that is owed. Where there is a punishment for polygamy, it would be difficult to decide on the relative rights of a legal spouse and a common-law spouse (see Polygamy in references).

## *Imprisonment and Faith*

Yet another disadvantage suffered by women is that of imprisonment. Women of cultural and linguistic diversity (CALD) are often isolated and marginalised in prison, and thus receive more punitive treatment than the general prison population. There has recently been an increase in imprisonment for women, with a disproportionate number being from CALD backgrounds.

It has been observed that there is a short supply of interpreters, which may have an adverse impact on access to both legal advice and contact with their families. Concern has also expressed, with anecdotal evidence, about the difficulties faced by those of minority faiths in being able to practise their religion. These difficulties are exacerbated by a corresponding lack of post-release services and assistance (see Francis 2014b in References).

Women who are from an alien culture and imprisoned may suffer distinct disadvantages. The reason for so many being imprisoned in certain countries is gambling debts, and charges often relate to drug dealing and theft occasioned by a need to pay off the loan sharks who funded their gambling habit. A disposition to social isolation, to perceiving gambling as a means of acquiring wealth and a lack of language skills make these women ready targets.

One might, or might not, regard gambling as deviant behaviour, but it certainly has clear social consequences. Gambling may be as varied as football match fixing, cockfighting, casinos, online gambling websites, and betting on horse races. One of the problems is how to distinguish marginal gambling from such issues as quasi-economic forecasting and betting on the stock market (for an account of Violence against women see that entry in References). Yet further one could readily envision circumstances where being in prison deprives them of their spiritual comfort, and the right to attend those entities they worship.

## *Law and Custom and Norms*

Clearly law and custom are interactive, even though distinguishable. Further, both involve value judgements, and thus ethical and moral issues. We may distinguish law from custom in several ways.

- Law is explicit whereas custom is tacit
- Legal breaches invite formal sanctions: custom uses informal sanctions
- Customs evolve whereas law can be changed upon the instant
- Jurisprudence in many places hold that if it is not prohibited by law it is permissible: not so with custom
- Custom can be enshrined in law: law over-rides custom.

Judges must also decide on cases of breaches of normative principle, with a view to stopping it, despite whatever cultural traditions may be involved. We also need to recognise that our experience in dealing with native lore and law: imposing Western standards was not always successful (for further information see Violence against women in the references).

The view of women in some cultures stems from a view that women are, at best, human inferiors: they are viewed more as objects than as fellow humans. In 'civilised' societies violence against women are seen as quasi-contemptible, despite the fact that some members of such 'civilised' societies regard it as their right. In some cultures, however, physical punishment may be considered a norm. In dealing with special cases the plight of women is a difficult and compelling issue.

The vulnerabilities to which they are prone are various, and are mentioned below as examples of the constant adverse discrimination that women suffer. Segrave et al. (2009) provide an empirical and criminological work relating to the rights of women in Serbia, Thailand and Australia that ranges widely over the issues affecting sex trafficking. Their work provides accounts of processes and outcomes, as well as narratives about trafficked women, their advocates, policymakers and the criminal justice system (see also Women's rights in References).

The difficult situation of women from 'traditional' cultures wherein they were considered second-class citizens could be compounded by the loneliness of having no job or wider community contact; they can be additionally alienated by having a lesser command of English, or of the country's language. Differential access to services, and a disposition not to use them, could all combine to make life distressing. Lutz (1991) mentions barriers to obtaining referrals and services, and to the need for culturally appropriate services, all of which deserve a mention, as do diagnostic issues. Do unto others as they would have them do to you is a call to equality. Freedom of conscience and of assembly is important in fostering inclusion, and does so in the context of religious freedom (Trigg 2012).

As mentioned, there are various ways of taking out bias in business (for example). Among them are to do what the Vienna symphony orchestra did, and interview players behind a screen to determine only their musical ability. Other ways are to have fewer portrait of male predecessors, block out the names of candidates, ban headshots in job applications, thereby increasing the pool of talent by a substantial margin.

In recruitment one may be influenced by unimportant issues, such as colour of jacket. In business recruitment, it is noted that attractive people are considered to be more worthy. This purging of sexist language from job adverts will have the same effect of increasing the talent pool. The exceptions to this are such obvious exceptions as requiring a sex-appropriateness for actresses, toilet attendants, etc. From this should it be taken that women should not be excluded from being ordained as clergy (or not)?

## The Use of Referenda

Indeed, there is a view that there should be a referendum for such change. If a referendum is the only means of changing the Constitution then so be it. One could readily imagine that one might be given a variety of options: for example, in the one referendum one might be asked if one supported same-sex marriage. At the same time one could be asked if the voter favoured polygamy, polyandry, cohabitation, and the like. Thus, the ballot paper would canvass options such as:

Do you think that homosexuals should be allowed to marry
Yes [ ]. No [ ]

If they formalised their union do you think that they should have another term instead of 'marry'
Yes [ ]. No [ ]

Do you favour polygamy?
Yes [ ]. No [ ]

If you favour polygamy should wives have multiple claims?
Yes [ ]. No [ ]

Do you favour polyandry
Yes [ ]. No [ ]

## Conclusions

There are many ways in which women suffer adverse discrimination. They include rape, prostitution, genital mutilation, forced marriage, polygamy, and the special difficulties of imprisonment. At a lesser level it is so that even in many Western societies women earn less than do men, and have 'glass ceiling' to break. As we saw in the McSally case, political intervention can make a real difference.

In some cultures they have to wear a face veil, a circumstance that a legislature may wish to change, because of the entrenched attitude to women. It also cuts them off from facial recognition, and prevents them from interacting with facial expressions. That is a stricture that applies only to women. It is not that women should duplicate men's roles: it may be it is that they should be equal, but complementary.

It is possible that historical reasons dictate current practices. For example, do duennas in Spain result from the Arab influence when the Iberian peninsula was substantially occupied? We must conclude that religion and culture are often confused wherein culture may dictate more than is dictated by particular religious precepts. What may be religiously acceptable may be at odds with what cultural expectations express dictate (or imply). It is concluded that, notwithstanding anything else, there is no reason to practise adverse discrimination.

Are women's judgments better than those of men? It is question of fact rather than a question of perception. Among the propositions advanced is that decisiveness is a quality most admired in a leader. Women are more collaborative, which may be seen as a sign of weakness. Who found that women and men react differently to stress. Women tend to make smart decisions whereas men adopt more of a gambling attitude. Women tend to have their decisions more scrutinised than do men (see Ahl 2006). The overall conclusion must be that women still are adversely discriminated.

# Chapter 11
# Slavery

This concept of outright ownership of another human being has been around for millennia. It was a feature of both classical Roman and Greek, of whom Aesop was probably the most famous (see Aesop in References). In the ancient world slavery was part of life. They were acquired either through debt slavery, or as a punishment for a crime, or by being captured as prisoners of war. The implication of ownership was also that masters had the capacity to make freemen of slaves. One of the enduring dilemmas was whether the children of slaves were, themselves, subject to enslavement. It is ironical that the last country on the planet to outlaw slavery was, itself, one of the main sources of supply for enslavement.

One of the basic questions here is how one accounts being enslaved. It is probable that such definitional accounting may account for some of the apparent disparities. Even so it is appropriate to remember that slavery does exist still, and represents a factor to be deplored. According the UN human trafficking is defined as

> … the recruitment, transportation, transfer, harboring, or receipt of persons by improper means (such as force, abduction, fraud, or coercion) for an improper purpose including forced labour or sexual exploitation.

The question arises as to what, exactly, is slavery? How do we know when it is not slavery? The essential issue here is that it is not any form of slavery where one person cannot exert undue pressure on another: every individual is, allegedly, a free agent to do as they wish. From this it follows that slavery exists in degree, thus there are degrees of slavery ranging from outright ownership as a chattel to relatively minor forms of duress. Later in this chapter there will be an analysis of grading degrees of slavery. Manumission of slaves occurs when the master frees them voluntarily: emancipation occurs when the legislature so determines it: that process is also called ‘abolition of slavery’.



R. Francis, *Equality in Theory and Practice*,
https://doi.org/10.1007/978-981-15-3488-1_11

## Historical Comments

Evidence that slavery has existed from time memorial. Despite this it is relatively uncommon among hunter-gatherer people, even though requiring crops to be harvested, and menial labour to be performed. It is with the growth of economics, and of the need for tractable labour, that slavery grew. It has proliferated in places such as ancient Egypt, Ancient China, and various other ancient civilisations, such as Iran, the Roman Empire, the old Caliphates, and pre-Columbian America, not to mention modern instances.

Another instance is that of Passover which is the story of the exodus of the Jews from slavery in Egypt. A more recent instance was the case of Haiti, led by Toussaint L'Ouverture (in 1804) the state of Haiti was declared as the first state that did not account race as a determinant of social status. Although Toussaint L'Ouverture did not live to see it. There are also cases of historical interest wherein slaves rose in revolt against their 'masters'.

This idea of classes of people was expressed in classical Spartan times by the division into Spartiates (men of equal status – the ruling class of Sparta). Below them were the 'peroikoi' – freemen but not citizens – (but not slaves/serfs). The helots were the 'lower' orders. This notion of classes of people is what made the system undemocratic. In the city-state of Athens there were the 'upper' class (the Athenians), the Middle class (the Metics), and even the slaves had grades. This idea of classes of people also found expression elsewhere, and is totally contrary to the modern notion of 'one-person-one-vote'.

With the invention of the notion of idea that there are men of bronze, men of silver, and men of gold. It is as though it was an inherent characteristic. If a man of bronze (say) had the characteristic to be man of silver, it were better that he should wait for an opportunity to become a man of gold (say). Some writers call this the 'myth of metals'. Worth to the polis is determined by what kind of 'soul' he possesses, and determines worth. 'Gold souled' people are suited to rule, and 'bronze souled' people are there to obey. Different 'souled' people should not 'taint' the other class.

In this one is reminded of Plato's *Parable of the cave.* – one of his most important contributions. We do not see the world as it is but, rather, as a shadow-show. Plato imagines imagined that prisoners are in a cave, and unable to turn their heads. Behind them is a fire and puppeteers who present puppets so that only the shadows of the puppets are visible. What the prisoners see is simply the shadows of the puppets – not the thing-itself. It is thus for many, who do not know that they are perceiving mere shadows, and mistaking it for the real thing. It is thus for so many issues wherein we see no reality, only the shadow show.

It may be thus with slavery: we do not see the harm caused by such a discriminatory practice. Historically speaking there have been revolts of slaves who, understandably, objected to their enslavement. Perhaps one of the most famous is the revolt of the slaves in 73 BC under the leadership of Spartacus, He was a freeborn Thracian, and an auxiliary in the Roman army, eventually captured and sold into slavery. As a Roman gladiator he must have learned something of tactical soldiering. As many as 120,000 slaves were eventually in his army when, finally, he was defeated due, in part, to the might and resources of the Roman empire. To have held the Roman army at bay for over two years was a remarkable achievement.

Turning now to the Old Testament: there is inconsistency in the views expressed. For example, in Leviticus 25:44–46 it was noted that

- Both thy bondmen, and thy bondmaids, which thou shalt have, [shall be] of the heathen that are round about you; of them shall ye buy bondmen and bondmaids

whereas in Exodus 21:16 it was noted that

- And he that stealeth a man, and selleth him, or if he be found in his hand, he shall surely be put to death.

Whereas in Exodus 21:2 there is a finite time for enslavement

- If thou buy an Hebrew servant, six years he shall serve: and in the seventh he shall go out free for nothing'.

It was also possible that people sold themselves into slavery. In the *New Testament* there is a reference to Luke, the beloved physician. St Luke may have been born a slave. It was common for families to educate slaves in medicine to that they could fulfil the role of medical adviser to the family. In the Gospel according to St. Mathew (6:21, KJV) he held that:

- No man can serve two masters: for either he will hate the one, and love the other; or else he will hold to the one, and despise the other. Ye cannot serve God and mammon.

One might reasonably hold that Jesus, though he repeatedly denounced sin as a kind of moral slavery, did not rail against slavery. That point may also be true of the New Testament authors. One might argue that Jesus himself neither approved nor disapproved of slavery as an institution. In a paper published in *Evangelical Quarterly*, Giles (1994) noted that, while he often encountered it, 'but not one word of criticism did the Lord utter against slavery'. Many of Jesus' stories are set in a slave/master situation, and involve slaves as key characters. Giles notes that these circumstances were used by pro-slavery apologists in the nineteenth century to suggest that Jesus approved of slavery. This critique of Christendom could, conceivably, be used as a justification for the continuation of slavery.

## William the Conquerer

It is noted that there has been an unsteady progress toward eliminating slavery, and a consideration of various timeline websites show the constant move to eradicate slavery. Among the moves to abolish slavery are the revolt of the slaves under Spartacus, William the Conquerer's prohibition on the sale of heathen slaves to non-Christians, the eighteenth century successful revolt of the slaves on Haiti in 1804, with the establishment of the first independent black state outside Africa, the successful passing of legislation by Britain (thanks to the persistence by Wilberforce in 1833 – the year of his death). That idea is pursued by, for example, by Brazil which, in 1850, declared slavery to be form of piracy. As a conquerer, William 1st issued edicts such as that:

- I prohibit the sale of any man by another outside the country on pain of a fine to be paid in full to me.

and

- Let Christians not be sold outside of the land or to heathens:

and

- … but if he, who wishes to make his serf free, hand him over to the sheriff by his right hand in full assembly, he must proclaim him quit of the yoke of his servitude by manumission, and show him free ways and gates and give him arms, viz. lance and sword; finally the man is made free

The establishment of a slave-free state in Haiti was established by Toussaint L'Ouverture in the 1790s and the Wilberforce legislation in1833 ended the slave trade in all British countriesThe Wilberforce legislation, for example, held that

- Whereas divers Persons are holden in Slavery within divers of His Majesty's Colonies, and it is just and expedient that all such Persons should be manumitted and set free,

It will be seen that the timeline has a distinctly chequered history, with abolition being tried time and again. It is only in recent times that it has become an articulated concern that Western thought deplores. It seems to be initiated largely on conscience grounds, and is a largely European concern.

## Enslaving Africans

The idea of enslaving Africans was started in the fifteenth century, allegedly by the Portuguese, although it had been extant since the time of early civilisations. It appears to be the first consistent and wide-scale and genuine effort to make money. The Portuguese supposedly started exploring the West African coast with minor effects; that is until the development of plantations in the Americas and, notably, the Caribbean.

With the development, and profit, to be made the trade rapidly grew. What follows is predominantly a European solution to the problem, as the references to the Greeks, the Romans, the Incas and the Aztecs, the King James Version of the Bible (KJV), the early founders of America, and the Europeans all had slavery, including the first American President (George Washington).

It is thus that elimination of slavery culminated in the *League of Nations,* in 1926 made it necessary for member states to ban slavery and forced labour in their territories. Slavery was defined as the status or condition of a person over which the powers of ownership are applied. It was noted that slave trading involved the capture, selling, or transport of enslaved people, and went on to define forced labour as a "condition analogous to slavery" that had to be regulated and eventually stopped.

It will be noted that a parallel formulation in the UN banned slavery outright, as defined in Article 4. It will be noted that slavery may take any number of different forms. If one were to be of such a mind, the lowered grade of women as inferior to men, then one would classify being a woman as a form of enslavement. Witness the recent abolition of law whereby, in India, of the wives of Moslem men being divorced by saying the Talaq three times. (see Divorce in Islam in References).

## Definition of Slavery

The use of the word 'Slavedom' refers to the condition of enslavement, the term 'slave-driver' is taken to mean driving the worker to the point of exhaustion, similarly a 'slavey' is someone who is there to work and has no time for human contact. To slave is to be a drudge. Modern slavery is defined as:

One who 'possesses or controls another person in such a way as to significantly deprive that person of their individual liberty, with the intention of exploiting that person through their use, profit, transfer or disposal'.

## Villeinage

In the early Middle Ages there was a concept called villeinage, by which we mean the tenure by which a villein held land and tenements from a lord. Thus, the lord had the power and the land, but who were freemen in other respects. Thus, they were a hybrid with respect to freedoms. Serfs, on the other hand, were agricultural labourers bound by the feudal system, and tied to working on the lord's estate. The liege-lord held the right to recruit fighting men to fight his wars. Taking all of this into account shows clearly that it was a form of slavery.

One might inquire how this is different from modern conscription. The answer lies in the democratic process whereby the ballot box is supreme. While young men and women are recruited for the armed forces they do have a vote on whom they elect. That movement of lowering the age of suffrage to that of recruitment is a result of such a democratic process. In other words, the 'citizens' were not free in that they owed allegiance to someone else. One might enquire how that is different from today's allegiance to the state. One major difference is that, in civilised countries one is permitted to change allegiances, and free to leave.

## Human Trafficking

Yet another modern instance adds to the formidable list of disadvantages for prospective enslavement. Out of a parlous situation, people from North Africa get put-to-sea by traffickers to get to Europe. They have one outboard motor, insufficient fuel, an overloaded boat, and a 300-mile journey. Many drown and many are rescued by patrol vessels from Europe. In a recent book by Napoleoni (2016), she outlined the profit to be made from trafficking, and outlined the hypocrisy of Somali pirates' self-justifying. Her main account is of the profit to be made by trading in humanity (her book is appropriately called *Merchants of men*). The dealership in humans is now one of the most profitable in the world, and includes kidnapping for ransom to fund illegal enterprises.

A penultimate instance is that one may investigate supply chains to ensure that it does not involve exploitation of unwilling workers. A question here is 'should a country have a modern slavery Act to stop such practices?'. For example, a worker used n-hexane to clean tablet and phone screens. It is toxic but cheaper than the alternative, but causes damage to the central nervous system. Companies should know their supply chains in order to prevent such abuses. It has even been suggested that cheating on paying the minimum wage should be a criminal, and potentially, an imprisonable offence. The three principles relevant here are:

- Transparency
- Knowledge
- Accountability

For this to happen there must be law of compulsion to know, to be transparent, and to be accountable. This example is that of working for sub-standard pay. The modern instance is that of illegal immigrants working for sub-standard pay. The employers threaten to report them if they do not agree. It is thus that duress is placed on contenders with a dire threat for non-conformance. It is fitting that investigative journalists have uncovered such flagrant breaches of human rights.

### *Economy*

As such the slaves were a significant part of the economy, and the enslavement of captives of war added to that economy. The much-vaunted Greek democracy that was considered particularly Grecian was, in fact, based on slavery. To Greek citizens, the notion of 'the good' was to have time for contemplation: the idea of having such time for contemplative activities was the aim of the good life. To facilitate that enterprise there had to be workers/slaves.

Classical Greek culture rested on having slaves. It is not surprising that there were periodic revolts: they ranged from the revolt of the slaves under Spartacus in the first Century BC to the more legislative approach of William Wilberforce in the early nineteenth Century. It will be seen that it is an important part of the economy from city-states to empires: it gave leisure time to those allegedly free to think higher thoughts. It is interesting to observe that there are dire predictions of what will happen (and probably would not) if slavery were totally abolished.

There are several factors that make slavery possible: one such is the growth in population: more people mean more to enslave. The second reason is the prospect of migration: the move from rural environments to urban ones means that the naive migrant is readily exploitable by shady dealers. Such traffickers speak the local language, are more sophisticated and greedy: the vulnerable, have no money, no friends, and no family. The third reason is that of no national laws, or police protection, for the vulnerable. A fourth reason is that there is adverse discrimination with the basis of race, religion, caste, skin colour, etc.

## *Countries*

It is interesting to note that countries that formerly supplied slaves from Africa now county as countries that are still involved in slavery. In 2007 Wood wrote a book in which she was commissioned by a production company to write a book on places named Victoria. The first part of her work was a visit to what is now Ghana, the place most common to the recruitment of slaves. Among the harrowing tales of enslavement, and the way that they were treated is the way that locals were complicit in recruitment: it is a testament to the indifference that profit generates. As she noted (p.20); 'People sold their brothers and sisters, their friends, then they started raiding weaker tribes and villages so they could trade the people for guns, and so on'.

## *Press Ganging*

Another instance is that due to the growth of British naval power, at the end of the Eighteenth Century and early Nineteenth Century, British naval ships recruited their sailors by way of press gangs. The basic aim was to get prospective sailors to sign up. There were two basic methods of recruitment into the navy: one was volunteers, which is an obvious recruitment strategy. The second was 'pressing': by which it is meant they were 'prest', at the time it meant a loan or an advance, taking the King's shilling (enlisted). There were officers at every seaport, which was an alternative to being on half pay. The regulating officers hired some 'hard men' who formed 'gangs' (thus becoming 'gangers') with the aim of 'recruiting' potential sailor aged 18–55, although that was a lenient expression. Although the aim was recruit those with naval experience that was a kindly expression. It might also be mentioned that being press-ganged was a way of being free of debtor's prison as the navy protected men from his creditors provided the debt was under 20 pounds.

### *Blackbirding*

One of the further instances of a form of slavery was that of 'blackbirding' in Australia. Between 1863 and 1901 there were more than 60,000 workers from the south sea islands recruited to work on the sugarcane plantations in Queensland. The methods of recruitment ranged from open adverts to trickery and coercion. It was called 'indentured labour' and was a form of slavery 30 years after slavery was illegal in the British Empire. Curiously it was the 'white Australia' policy on immigration that put an end to it rather than a moral qualm. One of the saddest parts of that enterprise was the expulsion of the children of such 'blackbirders' who were forcibly repatriated.

## Contemporary Example

Effectively slaves were made of the myriad children who were lied to and transported to Canada, and Australia in – 100,000 of them, a scheme founded by MacPherson in 1869. The aim was to populate Canada, Australia, New Zealand, and South Africa with 'good' white settlers. What is worse, is that some were lied to, being told that their parents were dead. That scheme persisted in the earlier part of the last century, and finished just after WW2 or so it is alleged. Presumably, one could say the same of the early convicts: their enslavement may have been temporary but it was an extra punishment to take them from their known places in life.

## UN Declaration

Notwithstanding, in the UN *Declaration of Human Rights* of 1948 the first Article holds that all human beings are born free and equal in both dignity and human rights. It goes on to assert that they are endowed with conscience and reason, and should behave toward others in a spirit of brotherhood (if one can overlook the sexist language). The second Article holds that everyone (without exception) is entitled to the freedoms, without any kind of distinction (race, colour, sex, language, religion, etc). Nor is it determined by country or territory.

It is clear that slavery is forbidden. Despite those propositions Article 4 is quite specific that no-one shall be held in slavery or servitude. The precept is quite distinct: 'slavery and the slave trade shall be prohibited in all their forms'. Article 5, amongst other things, prohibits the use of 'degrading treatment or punishment'. Article 9 holds that no-one should be subject to 'arbitrary arrest, detention or exile' – which slavery most certainly is.

'All men are created equal' is a principle noted in the USA Constitution, but the enaction of a constitutional amendment may have no consequences. The American

Constitution (in Sect. 9) guarantees that no Bill of Attainder shall be passed (Sect. 9 (3)) holds that 'No Bill of Attainder or ex post facto Law shall be passed' (a Bill of Attainder holds that an act of the legislature being guilty of some crime without a fair trial: in effect it amounts to a loss of civil liberties). That proviso needs a justification in terms of Guantanamo Bay.

There people are imprisoned without trial. Considering that such people may not have broken any law of their country of citizenship, nor the law of any country that they were in. They were 'rendered', a euphemism that means captured in a foreign country and taken to Guantanamo Bay prison. That action is a blot upon the reputation of the United States of America, and substantially a diminishes their reputation for open dealing. As such it makes a mockery of their Constitution, and diminishes them in the eyes of others. On the other hand, one cannot fight with one hand tied behind one's back. The current systems of safeguards may (or may not) be adequate for dealing with terrorists: As ever, it is a moral dilemma of the most pressing kind. Perhaps there might be a solution that we have yet to discover.

## Law

Slaves were under property law – not humanitarian law. It is thus that choosing laws to suit the occasion was endemic. The legislative approach is exemplified in the case of William Wilberforce: a man of conscience the formal end of slavery was accomplished legislatively. The notion of one human being owned by another was, to him, morally abhorrent. William Wilberforce was a dedicated Christian whose conscience would not let him rest from righting wrongs. (he was born in 1759). His interests included the abolition of the slave trade, the improvement of factory conditions in Britain, and the founding of the society for the prevention of cruelty to animals (preceding the Royal prefix, eventually given by Queen Victoria).

### *Wilberforce*

Wilberforce's early attempts to halt the trade in humans met with little success, but eventually his persistence paid off. After many attempts to get legislation through Parliament he finally succeeded in the year of his death in 1833. This led to the ending of slavery throughout the British Empire. As an elected member of Parliament, he campaigned for 18 years to have the slave trade ended, and did so by continuously introducing anti-slavery motions in Parliament. Here the gradualist approach was most successful. First there was a ban on slave ships, then a ban on recruiting slaves, then a ban on new ownership then, finally, a ban on slavery. In 1807 the slave trade was finally abolished even though it failed to free those then currently enslaved. The final Act to free slaves throughout the British empire was proclaimed in 1833. It is fitting that such a reformer be buried in Westminster Abbey.

It is worth noting that there was a developing indignation about slavery such that in 1799 Lloyds of London stopped insuring slaves against 'natural death, ill-treatment or … throwing overboard'. Attention is also drawn to the Maroons who, in Jamaica, escaped slavery and sought refuge in the mountainous interior, forming communities of refugees. There are other forms of contribution to the slavery debate: among them is the analytical approach of Hobhouse whose contribution is mentioned elsewhere in this work. The main point here was its his analysis of specific plants on slavery. He showed the effect that the adoption of such plants had on the concept of equality, particularly in such issues as the potato famine in Eire and the use of slavery in the development of the sugar cane industry.

## Websites

### *Borgen Surveys*

For a different perspective, the Borgen surveys note the following:

- An estimated 29.8 million people live in modern slavery today
- Slavery generates $32 billion for traffickers globally each year
- Approximately 78% of victims are enslaved for labour, 22% of victims are enslaved for sex
- 55% of slavery victims are women and girls
- 26% of slaves today are children under the age of 18

### *End Slavery Now*

This website cites examples of slavery, it is that worldwide slavery is about 21 million. That is a figure that is at variance with other websites. Perhaps one of the reasons is that different definitions are used. This is an estimate based on what is slavery. One might agree that the following are all components:

- Domestic servitude
- Sex trafficking
- Forced labour
- Bonded labour
- Child labour
- Forced marriages

It is noted that child usage (or abusage) is one of the preceding listed ones. Nevertheless, profit seems to be one of the prime motives. To these rephrased principles we would add a ban on working for sub-standard pay. In such circumstances the person who is not allowed to work more than a set number of hours, or the employer threatens the employee to report them to immigration authorities unless they agree to being paid less, or employees are obliged to hand over some cash, a ready source of money-income for the unscrupulous.

According to the Free the Slaves website new slavery is now cheaper than paying a living wage, and slaves are readily disposable. It was held that in '… in 1850 an average slave in the American South cost the equivalent of $40,000 in today's money. Today a slave costs rather less about $90 on average worldwide'. This website cites examples of slavery, it is that worldwide slavery is about 21 million. That is a figure that is at variance with other websites. Perhaps one of the reasons is that different definitions are used. This is an estimate based on what is slavery. One might agree that the following are all components:

- Domestic servitude
- Sex trafficking
- Forced labour
- Bonded labour
- Child labour
- Forced marriages

It is noted that child usage (or abusage) is one of the preceding listed ones. Nevertheless, profit seems to be one of the prime motives. To these rephrased principles we would add a ban on working for sub-standard pay. In such circumstances the person who is not allowed to work more than a set number of hours, or the employer threatens the employee to report them to immigration authorities (unless they agree to being paid less, or employees are obliged to hand over some cash), a ready source of money-income for the unscrupulous.

## *Free the Slaves*

According to the Free the Slaves website new slavery is now cheaper than paying a living wage, and slaves are readily disposable. It was held that in '… in 1850 an average slave in the American South cost the equivalent of $40,000 in today's money. Today a slave costs about $90 on average worldwide'. This site nominated four kinds of slavery: labour, sex, forced marriage, and child. Also, according to that website, there are at least four factors that have an impact on slavery, they are:

- Population: the explosive growth in population, the existence of natural disasters, and exploitative opportunities make slavery more rife.
- Migration: millions are on the move seeking a better life, but find themselves in situations where they are far from home. One of the consequences is that they

find themselves without family support and trusted people – and thus are vulnerable.

- Corruption: In places where corruption is rife this leads to exploitation and enslavement.
- Adverse discrimination. This can lead to adverse discrimination based on gender, race, tribe, and caste.

Such a possibility as exists, makes it ripe for exploitation.

## *The Global Slavery Index*

According to their website, 58% of those living in slavery are in five countries. Those countries with the highest estimated prevalence of slavery, in proportion to the population, are:

- North Korea
- Uzbekistan
- Cambodia
- India
- Qatar

Such countries as the Scandinavian countries, Ireland, Austria, the USA, Canada, Australia, and New Zealand are economically wealthy, are low-level conflict-prone, are stable politically, and are happy to legislate against slavery not-withstanding the fact that the estimates are not always consistent it does appear that millions are enslaved.

As the Global Slavery Index stated 'Slavery isn't a mere historical relic, in 2016, around 40.3 million men, women and children from every part of the globe were victims of modern slavery'. It is unfortunate that it is also reported that 45.8 million people are enslaved. By way of contrast one might note that the Index to that useful work is a breakdown of country by country, as well as by region.

When considering estimates it is noted, with some pleasant surprise, that Brazil figures prominently and favourably. The remaining countries are, essentially, in Northern Europe. Looking at the map it seems that those countries left are former British colonies (Canada, Australia, New Zealand, and the United States). What one might make of that is problematical.

There is an estimated breakdown wherein five countries are nominated as having 58% of the slaves: India, China, Pakistan, Bangladesh, and Uzbekistan. Put another way one might note that the proportion of the enslaving nations, first is North Korea, where over 4% of the population is enslaved. Uzbekistan and Cambodia come, respectively, second and third. Slavery also accommodates such notions as forced labour, trafficking in persons, and forced marriage.

### *The Walk Free Foundation*

The Walk Free presents that there 40.3 million are currently enslaved, the majority in slave labour. It will be seen that such records may not be entirely consistent, particularly with respect to the number enslaved. Perhaps that is due to the application of the different definitions of slavery. Notwithstanding, is does point to enslavement as requiring constant monitoring.

## Commentary

The essential point is that enslavement is both profitable, and minimises disruptions in the workforce. Despite variations in profit it is noticed that, no matter what the profit, it is still profitable. One would have to conclude that there are discrepancies in the number of slaves worldwide, the numbers and proportions in each country, and the profits that slavery generates for traffickers. Notwithstanding such discrepancies it is a matter of serious concern that such slavery exists at all, and whether or not the profits that they generate, are accurate. The simple fact remains that slavery should not exist, and that there should be no profit in trafficking humans.

There are some distinguishing features; for example, there are alleged reports of government-sanctioned forced-labour camps, while North Korean women are the subject of forced marriage and of sexual exploitation in parts of the world. It is recorded that in one country there is forced labour during the cotton harvest. Some of those countries make low-cost labour available for consumer goods for marketing in the First World.

To the conventional definitions of slavery one might also include that of debt slavery. What we might note that, In terms of profit, human trafficking ranks third, behind drugs and arms trafficking. What follows is an indication of how the anti-slavery movement has progressed. This presentation is comprised of several other tables. It shows that progress in eliminating slavery is both slow and uneven in progress. One of the more convincing websites, among many, is the *Global Slavery Index* in that it lists the criteria for slavery, and provides justification for each inclusion.

## Grading of Slavery

It is argued here that slavery may take any one of several forms, and results in a gradation of forms of slavery. It is thus argued that the grades are:

- Worst: Outright ownership: Killing without sanction: Progeny enslaved
- Outright ownership: Sanctions for killing slaves: Progeny not enslaved

- Temporary forced enslavement (press gangs; blackbirding)
- Indebtedness with duress (extreme poverty)
- Minor indebtedness with pressures to conform.

For a further account of how one might quantify slavery see the section on quantification.

## Conclusions

What is clear is that so few of many countries are free of slavery. Rankings are based on three factors: a country's estimated slavery prevalence by population, a measure of child marriage and a measure of human trafficking. It is further noted that there are substantial variations as between nations and cultures. It was held by moral reformers that, at its most extreme, there is outright ownership, even to the point of being able to kill a slave and suffer no sanctions. Such slave owners also owned the progeny of slaves. In the ancient feudal system fiefs owed allegiance to their liege lords, and thus were bonded across generations. This grades down to lifelong servitude; to sexual slavery (including *jus primae noctis* and *droit de seigneur*); to temporary slavery (as was practised by Press Gangs); to threats (such as paying less than the minimum award wage – with the distinct probability of deportation). It is thus argued that slavery is on a continuum ranging from the most extreme form of slavery to that of being indebted to another.

Some form of duress will, no doubt, always be with us. What is quite unacceptable is the idea that one person should own another. As already mentioned, Articles 1 and 2 of the UN *Declaration of Human Rights* imply it. Further, it is quite specific in Article 4 of the UN *Declaration of Human Rights*, and underlines the concept of the power of legislation and education combined. The legislative force gives us the abhorrence of human beings owned by another. Legislation, quite sensibly, goes through progressive steps.

It will be seen that various countries legislated against the slave trade: it was not the province of one country to lead. What was international was to legislate against the slave trade, and the importance of going through a series of steps to achieve that end. The notion of one person owning another has contemporary abhorrence in Western eyes, but is a view that is not universally held. Taking the contemporary condition into account it is surprising that slavery should exist in the world today, various websites, although not always congruent, do indicate that it is still a problem, particularly at the extreme.

The essential element here is freedom of choice. One cannot choose to be financially independent, but one can work towards it: one cannot choose to be born somewhere: and one cannot choose to have a skin of a particular colour.

On the other hand, one can choose to follow a particular religion, a culture, or a set of precepts. It is argued that everyone should be free to choose what they believe, but never impose it on others. Taking that principle, it has been a continuous struggle to abolish slavery. Bearing in mind the caveats it is unlikely that debt bondage can be totally eliminated, but the more extreme forms of slavery can be eliminated. Slavery is to be condemned on moral grounds.

# Chapter 12
# Quantification of Social Variables

## Happiness

The aim of this particular exercise was twofold: firstly, to look at happiness in relation to other social variables; the second was to look at inter-connectedness. As the subject relates being contented with one's lot it is a worthy cause to investigate. On the *Happiness* criterion the formal definition given on the website is 0 = worst possible life, and 10 = best possible life, and the scores are so given.

It is noted that the method used was to aim for about 30 nations. That method then involved taking the first listed nation, then every fifth one, and with a listing of the last nation. In the event we ended up with the most common number being 33 (with an occasional one with data not listed). The results of that survey are given in Tables 12.1 and 12.2. The results show that happiness (being content with one's lot) related happiness strongly to longevity, peace, education, and lower corruption. It also revealed that longevity also related strongly to both education and corruption, as did peace and lower corruption and education and corruption (see Heyneman 2004 in References).

The main point of the exercise was to look at correlations in order to gain a first insight. The justification for using happiness as the main variable was to look at the contentment-with-lifestyle. In order to get a wide spread, and to approach a reasonable distribution in the array it was necessary to have thirty in each group. In the event there were enough sovereign states listed.

The first one in happiness was chosen, and then numbers five, ten, fifteen, etc., ending with the last one listed. That produced a list of 33 countries. The only exception was that the Gini Index was four countries short and thus had 29 countries, and three others had an N = 32. Here the correlations are given in relation to happiness, with the appropriate degrees of freedom being applied in each case.

As these are correlations one cannot say which causes which, or it may be mediated by some superordinate factors: nevertheless, it does give clues as to what conclusions one may draw, leading on to hypothesis-testing.



R. Francis, *Equality in Theory and Practice*,
https://doi.org/10.1007/978-981-15-3488-1_12

**Table 12.1** Happiness and other variables

| | Happiness | Longevity | Gini index | Peace | Education | Gender | Corruption |
|---|---|---|---|---|---|---|---|
| Country | | | | | | | |
| Finland | 7.632 | 81 | 21.5 | 1.515 | 0.815 | 42 | 85 |
| Switzerlnd | 7.487 | 82.6 | 29.5 | 1.373 | 0.844 | 32.5 | 85 |
| Australia | 7.272 | 82.3 | 30.3 | 1.425 | 0.927 | 28.7 | 77 |
| Germany | 6.965 | 80 | 27 | 1.5 | 0.884 | 30.7 | 81 |
| UAR/UAE | 6.724 | 77.7 | * | 2.245 | 0.673 | 22.5 | 71 |
| Chile | 6.476 | 78.9 | 50.5 | 1.595 | 0.746 | * | 67 |
| Guatemala | 6.382 | 72.6 | 53 | 2.245 | 0.484 | 12.7 | 28 |
| Malaysia | 6.322 | 75.2 | 46.2 | 1.637 | 0.671 | 10.4 | 47 |
| El Salvador | 6.167 | 74.9 | 37 | 2.239 | 0.563 | 32.1 | 33 |
| Kuwait | 6.083 | 78.2 | * | 1.909 | 0.646 | 3.1 | 39 |
| Lithuania | 5.952 | 75 | 37 | 1.732 | 0.877 | 21.3 | 59 |
| Mauritius | 5.891 | 75.8 | 35.9 | 1.547 | 0.718 | 11.6 | 50 |
| Kazakstan | 5.79 | 71.1 | 26.3 | 1.992 | 0.762 | 27.1 | 31 |
| Peru | 5.663 | 74 | 45.3 | 1.986 | 0.664 | 27.7 | 37 |
| Libya | 5.566 | 76.7 | * | 3.358 | 0.698 | 16 | 17 |
| Pakistan | 5.472 | 68.1 | 30.7 | 3.058 | 0.372 | 20.6 | 32 |
| Tajikistan | 5.352 | 68.1 | 32.6 | 2.263 | 0.639 | 19 | 21 |
| Morocco | 5.254 | 77.1 | 40.9 | 2.004 | 0.468 | 20.5 | 40 |
| Jordan | 5.161 | 74.8 | 39.7 | 2.087 | 0.7 | 15.4 | 48 |
| Vietnam | 5.102 | 73.7 | 37.6 | 1.919 | 0.513 | 26.7 | 35 |
| Bulgaria | 4.933 | 74.7 | 37 | 1.631 | 0.749 | 23.8 | 43 |
| S Africa | 4.724 | 63.8 | 62.5 | 2.324 | 0.695 | 42.1 | 43 |
| Laos | 4.623 | 64.6 | 36.7 | 1.8 | 0.43 | 27.5 | 29 |
| Bngladesh | 4.5 | 73.4 | 32.1 | 2.035 | 0.447 | 20.3 | 28 |
| Cambodia | 4.433 | 64.9 | 37.9 | 2.065 | 0.495 | 20.3 | 21 |
| Zambia | 4.377 | 52.7 | 57.5 | 1.786 | 0.591 | 18 | 37 |
| Myanmar | 4.308 | 68.2 | 38.1 | 2.179 | 0.371 | 10.2 | 30 |
| Uganda | 4.161 | 55.9 | 39.5 | 2.182 | 0.479 | 34.3 | 26 |
| Guinea | 3.964 | 64.6 | 39.4 | 1.93 | 0.294 | 21.9 | 27 |
| Afghan | 3.632 | 51.7 | * | 3.567 | 0.365 | 27.7 | * |
| Syria | 3.462 | 75.1 | 35.8 | 3.814 | 0.553 | 13.2 | 14 |
| Cntrl Afr R | 3.083 | 52.8 | 43.6 | 3.218 | 0.318 | 8.6 | 23 |
| Burundi | 2.905 | 60.9 | 42.4 | 2.641 | 0.37 | 30.4 | 22 |
| | | 0.79 | −0.34 | −0.60 | 0.77 | 0.20 | 0.79 |
| Corr/hpns | 33 | 33 | 29 | 33 | 33 | 32 | 32 |
| **Meaning** | Happiness | Higher numbers are happier | | | | | |
| **Source** | | http://worldhappiness.report/ed/2018/ | | | | | |
| **Conclusion** | | Immigrants match natives with respect to happiness | | | | | |
| **Meaning** | Longevity | Average age at death | | | | | |

(continued)

**Table 12.1** (continued)

| | Happiness | Longevity | Gini index | Peace | Education | Gender | Corruption |
|---|---|---|---|---|---|---|---|
| **Source** | | https://www.cia.gov/library/publications/the-world-factbook/rankorder/2102rank.html | | | | | |
| **Meaning** | Equality | (Gini) perfect equality = zero. Max inequality = 100 | | | | | |
| **Source** | | https://www.cia.gov/library/publications/the-world-factbook/rankorder/2172rank.html | | | | | |
| **Meaning** | Peace | Iceland is the most peaceful at 1.111 Syria the least peaceful. Higher Nos = less peaceful | | | | | |
| **Source** | | http://visionofhumanity.org/app/uploads/2017/06/GPI17-Report.pdf | | | | | |
| **Meaning** | Education | Mean & expected years of schooling. | | | | | |
| **Source** | | http://hdr.undp.org/en/content/education-index | | | | | |
| **Meaning** | Gender | % of women in the legislature | | | | | |
| **Source** | | | | | | | |
| **Meaning** | Corruption | | | | | | |
| **Source** | | Transparency.com | | | | | |

There were some surprises, Rwanda being top of the list with respect to the proportion of female members of the lower house, with Bolivia and Cuba being respectively second and third, Namibia coming in fourth. While we acknowledge that it is simply a correlation, no necessary meaning is attached to it, but it could generate hypotheses.

Overall one is obliged to conclude that these are simply correlations. One may mediate the other (in either direction), or the relationships are the result of some other variable (as the sale of surfboards in Malibu in the United States may inversely relate to the sale of snow skis in Melbourne, Australia – mediated by the weather). Nevertheless, the picture that it seems to build is that contentment with one's lot is a combination of longevity, longer schooling, and lower corruption. Better schooling also seems to be related to lower corruption. It is as if they form a significant combination (although this could be a mistaken conclusion),

From this one might also note that too much happiness may lead to complacency. It is worth noting that the tests were, overall, most conservative, being two-tailed, and with unequal variances. The statistics were done by using Excel to calculate both the correlations between happiness and each of the listed variables for both the high and the low groups.

The websites are as listed in the references, with what the numbers mean in each case. As the table shows, where data is missing the most conservative substitution is made in order not to give a false positive. It will be noted that the correlations are between 'happiness' and each of the other variables. To reiterate, it is to be noted that the definition of 'happiness' is where 0 equals the worst possible life, and 10 equals the best possible life.

The selection of the groups was to indicate a variety of social variables, and each tested for statistical significance to see which was worth pursuing. The overall

**Table 12.2** Intercorrelations

| | Happiness | Longevity | Gini index | Peace | Education | Gender | Corruption |
|---|---|---|---|---|---|---|---|
| Happiness | * | 0.793 | −0.338 | −0.603 | 0.765 | 0.197 | 0.792 |
| Longevity | * | * | −0.458 | −0.452 | 0.677 | 0.005 | 0.613 |
| Gini | * | * | * | 0.139 | −0.241 | −0.179 | −0.291 |
| Peace | * | * | * | * | −0.538 | −0.538 | −0.662 |
| Education | * | * | * | * | * | 0.253 | 0.737 |
| Gender | * | * | * | * | * | * | 0.391 |
| Corruption | * | * | * | * | * | * | * |
| **Conclusions** | | | | | | | |
| **Happiness-Longevity** | | | 0.001 | Happiness is related to Longevity | | | |
| **Happiness-Peace** | | | 0.001 | Happiness is related to peace | | | |
| **Happiness-Education** | | | 0.001 | Happiness is related to education | | | |
| **Happiness-Corruption** | | | 0.001 | Happiness is related to low corruption | | | |
| **Longevity-Education** | | | 0.001 | There is a strong relationship between longevity and education | | | |
| **Longevity-Corruption** | | | 0.001 | There is a strong relationship between longevity and low corruption | | | |
| **Peace-Corruption** | | | 0.001 | There is a strong relationship between peace and low corruption | | | |
| **Education-Corruption** | | | 0.001 | There is a strong relationship between education and low corruption | | | |

These data form a cluster of variables that are indicative of what makes life favourable for humanity
The chosen data is 0.6 and above
That is particularly so for being content with one's lot in life, and with the other mentioned strong variables

picture that emerges is that of a correlational study, which may lead to the formulation of appropriate hypotheses. One such hypothesis may be that contentment with one's lot in life is comprised of a combination of longevity, peace, education, and lower corruption. One technique for evaluating the power of each is that of discriminant analysis (see Happiness in Index and Appendices).

## Further Quantification

Moving now to the issue of quantification in general it is noted that the quantification of ethics makes it more precise, allows for operational definitions, and permits us to compare and contrast the different ways of considering ethical issues. The provision of quantitative techniques encourages us to consider such simple techniques as asking, How much would I need to pay you to do X?, to the more sophisticated techniques, such as paired comparisons. By considering such issues we come to a better understanding of what constitutes the nature of judging according to value systems. One may make decisions according to various principles.

There are so many things in the world that we admire, but seemed unable to measure. Take, for example, the instance of precision in measuring precisely the value of certain ethical values. The instance given in the Appendix shows that to be a precise amount for a particular group.

One of the common criticisms of ethics is that it is imprecise. As Lord Kelvin once remarked, if something exists it exists to some amount, and is therefore potentially measurable. The quantification of ethics fulfils that aspiration in that it makes it more precise, allows for operational definitions, and permits us to compare and contrast the different ways of considering ethical issues.

The provision of quantitative techniques encourages us to consider such simple techniques as asking, 'How much would I need to pay you to do X?'. By considering such an issue we come to a better understanding of what constitutes the nature of judging according to value systems. One may make decisions according to various principles. One example is 'I would rather play golf than play chess'. It will be argued in this work that an ethical issue may be so quantified.

Quantification may sometimes act as a guide to the importance of an issue. For example, in recently past times the amount of money spent on foreign wars could be far more than is spent on medical matters and unemployment benefits combined. The criteria of financial success in business might be expressed as hourly return per employee, or capital value increase, or gross product, or market share, or turnover. One of the questions to ask is, does the size of misdemeanour matter? Are arms manufacturers ethical by delivering quality goods at a reasonable price and on time? Is selling a lot of alcohol worse than selling a bit of heroin? The answers to such questions should enlarge our understanding of what we regard as important.

## *Principle*

An example of a moral precept is 'my moral action will always be in accord with the principle of preserving and fostering equality'. A moral absolute would be (I would sacrifice my only son rather than lose my faith in God) or (I would not sacrifice my son for anything, including a love of God). An absolute moral value would be, thus, I would not betray my child for anyone, anything, or any amount of money.

## *Comparisons*

Human judgment about values is a bit more problematical. However, there are ways of operating. One technique is to invoke comparisons. For example, using a fine balance of probabilities, one could hold that I would rather play tennis than tiddleywinks, to use a non-moral instance. A moral instance would be I assign the only available dialysis machine to patient X rather than patient Y, on the basis of the principle Z.

Comparisons of moral dilemmas (could I more easily solve the issue preferring to change careers rather than change houses in another city?). Thus, the provision of quantitative techniques encourages us to consider such simple techniques. Using money as a common denominator, one might come up with the idea that it might be used as a means of quantification. The provision of quantitative techniques encourages us to consider such techniques as posing, (for example: how much would you be prepared to pay to destroy my marriage?).

One of the simplest techniques is to use money as the reference point. Using money as a common denominator, one might ask, for example, to ask how much you would charge a bank to make all women staff wear purdah (or at least some form of modest veil). How much would a citizen take to dispense with periodic elections? How much to betray your country to a foreign power? Thus, the quantification of ethics fulfils that aspiration in that it makes it more precise, allows for operational definitions, and permits us to compare and contrast the different ways of considering ethical issues.

## Ranking and Rating

Another way of looking at values is to consider rating principles. For example, one might regard telling lies as less important than cheating a friend. For example, one might rate little white lies as one on a ten-point scale, but deliberate deceit as seven or eight. One might also rank such breaches, saying that cheating outranks lying. One might, too, be concerned at the kind of lie. For example, giving an over-indulged compliment may be regarded as less heinous than telling an outright lie concerning a financial dealing.

## Paired Comparisons

A more complex measure is that of paired comparisons. The use of paired comparisons is useful for those occasions where the number of dilemmas is small. In principle, it holds that every instance of moral dilemma is compared to every other one In order to determine their importance. Suppose that there are (say) five examples which need to be ordered in terms of importance. This is a technique whereby every principle is comparison to every other principle. For that reason, it is suitable only for relatively few principles.

## Other Techniques

There are several techniques of numerical analysis that could be of further use. These include hypothesis testing, discriminant function, and factor analysis. Dealing with each in turn, and starting with hypothesis testing. There is a convention in the behavioural sciences that if the odds against it being a random event are better than one in 20 (the 5% level of significance) then one accepts the hypothesis. That said it is still noted that one could be still mistaken. It takes much more robust testing to ensure that the phenomenon is a real one.

### *Methodological Issue*

To take a practical example: In the work on sensory isolation it was hypothesised that certain cognitive and emotional changes occurred as a result of isolation. John Zubek, a Canadian researcher, using an ingenious experimental design, showed that the effects were due, instead, to the fact of being immobilised. What had previously been mistakenly attributed to the effects of isolation were attributable to some other factor. In the case of isolation: the subjects were, incidentally, kept immobile. It is thus that robust testing, a questioning attitude, and the willingness to admit that one's previous efforts were in error, is paramount.

## Discriminant Analysis

In discriminant analysis one is doing what one commonly does professionally – assess the weight of items. On the court bench, for example, a magistrate or judge assesses the weight of different factors such as guilt, remorse, the weight of evidence, etc. before deciding on the appropriate penalty. In medicine a GP will assess the weight of different symptoms before deciding what is important. In everyday life, a father will decide what proportion of time should be devoted his son, an anthropologist will decide on the attribution of a skull as belonging to a particular tribe where there are prominent supra-orbital ridges, prominent cheekbones, the location of the ears, etc.

It is fortunate that such a technique is available that assigns weights to different factors. Thus, an anthropologist might assign a weight of two to prominent supra-orbital ridges, but a weight of only one to prominent cheekbones, and half-a-point to ear location. The technique is variously called discriminant analysis or discriminant function, and involves solving simultaneous equations.

## Factor Analysis

Factor analysis also deserves a mention. Imagine a Martian coming to earth and wanting to discover how many factors may be used to describe the minimum of issues to describe a box. Having made all the possible measurements he (or she, or it) finds that many are correlated, and only three matter, length, breadth, and depth. That is what factor analysis does – discover the minimum number of factors that relate to description. Having sought a minimum solution: one is then put to identify those factors. That naming is then found by insight.

## National Character

It is noted that statistical indicators may be used to assess national character. One significant work in this field is by Lynn (1971). The general thrust of this work, and others of its genre, is that social statistics may be used imaginatively to resolve such questions as: How can we objectively evaluate national character? What is the general attitude to topics such as abortion? How can we assess approaches to health prevention issues? From such analyses one can gauge general tendencies. For example, we can use the prevalence of the use of anti-depressants to draw a conclusion (see Anti-depressants in References): we can assess religiosity by attendance at religious services and we can assess literacy by the use of educational indicators.

## *Delphi Technique*

Yet another means of quantification is to use the Delphi technique (a variant of the nominal group technique-NGT). Both techniques utilize structured groups, the use of facilitators, group brainstorming, etc. The differences include that in the NGT there is one round per session whereas in the Delphi methods there may be two or more rounds over a longer period. In the NGT there is identification whereas in Delphi there can be anonymity. Such a difference may seem a negligible one, but one combines the methods to best effect.

The most useful consideration is use them as you see fit. There can, of course, be a fusion of the methods. In any case it is one way of getting answers to difficult and ambiguous questions. It is used as an analytical tool to make forecasts of issues characterized by complexity and uncertainty. It utilizes the principle that several heads are better than one, and that a sequence of attempts to solve the problem is superior to a one-shot approach. It is, in other words, a reiterative technique.

To work this technique a reference group is chosen to select (say) the important ethical principles that should appear in the company or professional code. The group is asked to write down, without reference to each other, the principles they consider to be most important; they are then asked to rank them in order of importance, one being the most important. The group mediator then asks for the principles and enters them on a board, visible to the group, ending up with a list of ethical principles. With this comprehensive list the mediator then asks, for each principle, how many ranked it first, then how many ranked it second, then how many ranked it third.

Giving a value of 5 to first rank, a value of 4 to second rank etc., allows us to derive a value for each principle. It will be seen that the adopted technique requires several 'rounds' in order to make proper use of its potential, and used reiteratively. There are practitioners now that use computerised systems to record responses and rapidly (almost simultaneously) identify the issues and the priority of importance of those issues to the group. The technique should properly be called the nominal group technique.

One of the main aims of this device is to set out the goals and objectives; to consider a wide array of possible choices; to order those choices for importance; identify group values; gather whatever facts might be available, and use all of them, to come to a conclusion. This technique is also invaluable where a pooled judgement is considered appropriate. It also makes better use of those with special expertise. This technique commonly uses the sequence of:

- Identifying the issues
- Identifying the options
- Determining the initial position
- Consulting and then reordering, with reasons being given

- Reiterating the results, with further discussion, with explanations for disagreements
- Evaluating the underlying reasons, restructuring the evidence.

There are practitioners now that use computerized systems to record responses and rapidly (almost simultaneously) identify the issues and the priority of importance of those issues to the group (see Appendix Table A1).

Examples of Moral Dilemmas

Minimizing tragedy
I assign the surgery for X rather than patient Y on the basis of Z.

And general guidance

Prudence (do not over-drink).

A Moral Precept

My moral action will always be in accord with the principle of preserving and fostering equality.

On parental concern there is:

Would I sacrifice my wife rather than lose my children?

Size or importance of the misdemeanour

Is cocaine dealing less moral than selling tobacco? Are arms manufacturers ethical by delivering quality goods at a reasonable price and on time? Is selling a lot of alcohol worse than selling a bit of heroin?

## Conclusions

All of the predictions come in the expected direction, being content with one's lot involves the following conclusions, based on correlations of 0.6 or better.

Happiness-Longevity
Happiness-Peace
Happiness-Education.
Happiness-Corruption

Longevity-Education
Longevity-Corruption

Peace-Education.
Peace-Corruption

Education-Corruption

These data form a cluster of variables that are indicative of what makes life favourable for humanity. That is particularly so for being content with one's lot in life, and with the other mentioned strong variables. These data obtained was the latest as available as at 8/11/2019. See table below for basic data.

It is hoped that this analysis will give rise to new hypotheses. It is further argued here that being quantitative about morals has real merit. It brings some precision to moral judgments, and brings order into a field that has been rather imprecise. Among the techniques available are those of the importance; money motives, ranking, rating, the Delphi technique, and paired comparisons, as well as for other more sophisticated methods of approach. For the stated reasons the value of moral culpability is made quantifiable. For further reading see Wacks (2012).

# Chapter 13
# Theories

## Introduction

Human judgment about values is problematical. How much more is the resolution of moral dilemmas. Before embarking on aspects of morals there should be some qualifications entered. Among other things we must assert that moral laws are mutable. We have firm views of evidence-based medicine, and have cause to be very grateful for it. And now to the view that morals, too, change, largely as a result of rethinking issues. This is illustrated by reference to three instances – abortion, dying with dignity, and the treatment of animals. Three such examples are given:

## Classical Theories

There are various theories of morality, including *Virtue ethics, Utilitarianism, Consequentialism* and the like. Each of these approaches will be considered to see which best concludes on moral theory. An essential part of moral theory is to hold that such an approach is one that eventually triumphs over such issues as economics or technology. The blistering attacks sometimes mounted against equality seem to stem from 'practical' issues, and the notion that privilege prevails over morality.

Here it is argued that morality is prime. In the quest for justification of morality over practicality it finds expression in such fields as asylum seekers, work experience, social policy, and the treatment of prisoners – in other words, the treatment of the vulnerable. There are some aspects of morality that appear to be difficult to grasp. One is the capacity to categorise assumptions. An attempt is made to both identify, and to resolve this categorisation issue.



R. Francis, *Equality in Theory and Practice*,
https://doi.org/10.1007/978-981-15-3488-1_13

## Virtue Ethics

This is an Aristotelean notion, and a genuine contribution, whereby virtues are seen as emphasising character, and aspects of mind. The merit of this approach is that it considers both personal and civic virtues. They are to be seen, amongst other things, as contributing to community benefit: they should, and do, contribute to political and civil order. Virtue is seen as influencing other actions, such as attitudes, interests, wishes, and expectations.

It is thus that we could characterise Virtue Ethics as teleological, as governed by the end to be achieved. For Aristotle there are two fundamental parts: the rational and the non-rational. Our rational part is characterised by the rational part by logic, truth, and evaluation: the non-rational part by desires and wants. Rather than reduce the Aristotelean view prefers to cultivate the virtuous individual. Here the point of seeking the good is for character training, for others, and for the body civic.

A more analytical appraisal might give the assignation as political virtues (such as respect for the law), the communal values (such neighbourliness and charity): the intellectual virtue (such as curiosity and thoughtfulness); and the moral virtues (such as honesty, decency, and courage). As we have those whose cognitive ability is so negligible as to regard them as imbeciles, so too are those whose moral notions as to regard them as moral imbeciles (see the section on 'personality'). Their notions of such concepts as altruism and of selfless contributions, and of charity, are so miniscule as to regard the ordinary person's view of them as unbalanced. This view of ethics is a persuasive approach.

## Kantian Analysis

By way of contrast we note that, according to Kant, morality consists not in the result but, rather, in the intention. This principle, known as the 'categorical imperative', may be called the imperative of morality. Right action, so Kant argued, is not based on intuition or inclination but, rather, is based on law determined by reason. The human conceptual apparatus may know its form and limits; knower and known are interdependent. This view was regarded by Kant as a refutation of extreme empiricism and of scepticism. In essence, the view holds that one should act as if the underlying principle is one that should govern our moral actions.

## Deontology

This approach emphasises the duties enjoined on incumbents. Its emphasis lies on conforming to rules and guides. It is duty based and is given as a set of guides of moral behaviour. The emphasis here is upon duties. One should behave in a manner such that it is one that emphasizes devotion to duty – whatever the duty is. One is enjoined to do one's duty: it calls to mind Admiral Nelson's admonition 'England expects, this day, that every man do his duty'. The difficulty here is that the deontological approach emphasises duties, without specifying what those duties are.

## *Utilitarianism & Hedonism*

This approach is a consequentialist approach that emphasises outcomes. It is eminently practical in that it compares consequences. This notion has a long history, and is traceable back to the Epicureans. In more recent times its explication is attributable to John Stuart Mill. Mill was a nineteenth century thinker who was both a philosopher and a social reformer: he wrote extensively on logic, political economy, liberalism, and ethics. His book, *On liberty and utilitarianism*, is still widely cited in political and ethics debates. The central thesis of which is that the only justifiable reason for interfering with the liberty of action of any mature and reasonable person is to prevent harm to others (one would have to qualify that by mentioning justifiable harm, as in self-defence). As Oliver Wendell Holmes is credited with saying, 'the liberty to swing your fists ends where your neighbours nose begins'.

In Utilitarianism the guiding principle is the greatest happiness of the greatest number. It is postulated that happiness is the greatest good. States should aim to maximise happiness – the greatest good is to maximise happiness of the greatest number. To this writer it fails to give appropriate recognition to the rights of minorities. One could imagine the greatest happiness of the greatest number would involve prejudice and adverse discrimination against a minority group. The lesser numerically is not the lesser morally. If one were to hold that the majority would get pleasure from persecuting a minority that would not make it morally right. It would, indeed, be remiss not recognise that consequences are of direct relevant to morality.

There has been an attempt to rectify this by the proposal of Act Utilitarianism. In this latter development, the principle is that a person's act is moral if it produces the best moral outcome. This is to be distinguished from Rule Utilitarianism in which an action conforms to a rule that leads to the greatest good. It, too, suffers from the same fate of begging the question of 'what is the greatest good?' What we need are substantive precepts that tell us what is the greatest good. This leads to the consequence that there must be moral precepts that are superordinate to specific instances. One might even argue that religion may be the basis of morality: one could equally well argue that morality precedes religion, and that religion was used to buttress the idea that it was of divine origin – an interesting speculation.

## *Consequentialism*

Here one is concerned to look at outcomes. Taking into account the idea that consequences matter, one is put into the position that outcomes are crucial. That is a position that is difficult to counter. One is concerned that the time-frame may be critical.

What is critical here is that the longer view must be taken rather than the short-term one. One could well imagine that in business a fly-by-operator could milk funds and then abscond: that is inconsistent with the notion that the long-term view is that repeat business comes from being an open and honest operator. In essence, the Consequentialist view is that no system can ignore the consequences.

## *Pantisocracy*

No account would be complete without mention of the movement called Pantisocracy. This view, dreamed up jointly by Samuel Taylor Coleridge and Robert Southey, and was a government by all. They contended that in any egalitarian community all should have a chance of governing. It is a system of government where all rule equally. They believed that the ownership of personal property, in that system, a group of educated individuals would cede their property to the common good, and would labour for the community as a whole (just a few hours per day).

It was hoped that the scheme would find wider acceptance, and form a basis for an improved society. Just such a scheme foundered on two bases: one was the failure to recognise 'freeloaders', the uncommitted 'users'; the other was disillusionment with the ideals of the French revolution. Regrettably it was an idea doomed to failure because of the variety of humans, there being users and contributors. It is noted as one of the necessary hypotheses of Darwinism that there must be variety, lest one has no choice.

## The Naturalistic Fallacy

The original assertion that the naturalistic fallacy was made by Hume in the Eighteenth Century, and was reiterated by Moore, in his 1903 book *Principia ethica.* It holds that one cannot derive an 'ought' from an 'is'. In other words, the view holds that ethical statements cannot be derived from factual terms (thus one cannot hold that it is a moral statement that because an issue is pleasant it is, therefore, moral). The distinction has become one whereby there should be one between logical and analytical. In essence, it points to the unique nature of morality. Turning now to more contemporary approaches, the first of which is an account of economic justification for improving the lot of all people.

## Modern Approaches

Three modern issues come to mind. One is the advent of the new threat of 'terrorism': the second is the use of 'drones' to spy on people, the third is data matching. Each of these requires may require the advent of new principles, or they may be covered by previously enunciated principles. For example, the principle that there may be no further intrusions into personal privacy may cover it.

Taking the threat of terrorism, for example: the idea that one may detain on grounds of suspicion may be out-of-order. One might argue that terrorists have won if we concede to their demands that governments should 'take control'- it is yet another moral dilemma. The second issue is one of drone 'strikes'. Suppose that a group are secreted with one hostage, does one 'sacrifice' the hostage on the grounds of overall justice, or does one protect the hostage. The third instance is that of data matching. Suppose one puts into a computer the tax returns, the claims on social security, lifestyle equivalence, etc. does one then draw conclusions previously unavailable? Or does one protect individual privacy with a principle.

In each of the instances one might consider reconsidering the principle at issue, and decide whether a new precept is required. In exactly the same way one might consider whether self-driving cars should have a moral compass, If one were, for example, to avoid a crash by killing two children or, alternatively, three adults of indeterminate age: which would one choose? It is just such dilemmas that require is to make moral choices.

Conspiracy theories are those which are not disputed by contrary facts, thereby leading to the conclusion that the proponents are fundamentally irrational. Evidence-based explanation are commonly to be preferred. If one were to set out the arguments in favour of equality the ideas that it promotes talent, no matter where it appears.

### *Rawls*

In his writing, Rawls (1971), advanced some propositions on the ethics of equality. Amongst them are:

- Each person has an equal right to the most extensive system of equal basic liberties compatible with a similar system of liberty to all.
- The 'difference principle': social and economic equalities are to be arranged so that they are both (a) the greatest benefit to the least advantaged, and (b) attached to offices and positions open to all under conditions of fair equality and opportunity.

This view is a virtual denial of the merits of *Utilitarianism*. Such a view holds, under *Utilitarianism,* that the aggregate of happiness is determinist, and could be used to support slavery. A second objection is that it fails to account for freedoms (such as the rule of law) which we hold dear. The Rawls account thus takes individuals as moral beings, and is based upon two major principles: (1) that every person has the equal right to basic liberties, always subject to the freedom of others. (2) Where there are social and economic inequalities they should be arranged such that they are an advantage of all, and that positions are open to all.

The first proposition entails free speech (subject always to reasonable rebuttal), and regulates the social and economic world, and this first principle has ascendancy over the second principle. It is thus seen as espousing individual freedoms as paramount (and always subject to the curtailment of the freedom of others). For Rawls the idea of 'Justice as fairness' is paramount.

Given the current state of the world one must recognise that economic inequality prevails, and that some trade-off is required. The view that such freedoms are defined in political terms means that it ignores the reality of such differences as personality. One is mindful that there is such a range of personality that there are leaners and lifters, users and genuine cases, exploiters and saints. How one distinguishes between genuine cases and users is an ever-present problem.

## The Rio Declaration

The Rio Declaration of 1992, although not binding, was a statement on the UN Principles, and reasserted its affirmations. The 27 Principles ranged from Principle 1

- Human beings are at the centre of concerns for sustainable development. They are entitled to a healthy and productive life in harmony with nature.
- Which now speaks of 'human beings' rather than 'man' (being a synonym for humanity). The Principles, was allied to the notion that it is necessary to have 'Information for decision-making', and covers such issues as poverty, education, health, indigenous issues, and desertification. It was pleasing to see a reaffirmation of the basic principles (see Rio Declaration in References).

## Kohlberg

On the subject of moral developmental stages in humans Lawrence Kohlberg (see References) has argued that the development of moral stages in a child goes through phases. These are listed as pre-conventional, conventional, and post-conventional, and each of these phases has two steps. The sense of morality thus proceeds from obeying authority figures to the development of conscience, and a critique of moral rules. Amongst the critiques of this approach is that of assuming that what is true of

American white males is universally true, a point yet to be demonstrated, but one cannot imagine it being false (see Kohlberg in References)..

## Parfit

Reference is made to the work of Parfit, whose work should be of substantial help to those specialising in ethics. His 2011 book deals with the problems of ethics from the point of view of a philosopher

## Temkin

It will be readily seen as an argument in favour of equality. The argument is a basic proposition which gives more power to the vulnerable. That conclusion is also drawn by Temkin in his book, appropriately called *Inequality,* published in 1993 it outlines the case in favour of all humans being equal. As was mentioned above, Temkin's (1993) question is fundamental, and questions when is one situation worse than another with respect to inequality? He imagines three situations: many are free and prosperous and few badly off; a number are not free or well off; and a situation where the number of well off and badly off are about equal. Just such a question invites us to examine our views about the nature of morality.

## Haidt

The work of Haidt (2012) is valuable in that it poses some very difficult questions. One of his instances is that an owner's dog is killed outside the home and so they take it inside and cook it. The question here is 'is anything wrong with the action as the dog is already dead (and succulent). Another question is where a man buys a chicken and has sexual intercourse with it before cooking and eating it. One is reminded of a problem of a brother and sister who had sexual intercourse: the sister was on the pill and the brother had had a vasectomy. Is there anything morally amiss here? One can understand, in the latter case, the possibility of a damaged child, but that is remote in the extreme. Is the taboo a generalizable one?

One of the striking illustrations that Haidt uses is that of Armin Meiwes who put an advert in a paper advertising for someone to be slaughtered and eaten. He did receive a number of responses. Having selected the person, he then cut off pieces of the victim and left him to bleed to death in the bath: then cooked and ate pieces of his body. In the event he was retried, and eventually convicted of murder, and sentenced to life imprisonment (see Meiwes in References).

As Haidt noted elsewhere in the book, the brain of a neonate is flexibly wired rather than hard wired – hence the human tractability. His views are that intuitions come first, reasons second. There is, he holds, that there is more to morality than harm and fairness. His book, following Darwin, is essentially, about group behaviour as it relates to morality – and thus to how we polarize issues. Morality has more than one matrix, further, we have the power to transcend selfishness.

## Distributive Justice

A more sophisticated analysis of this principle involves distributive justice. There are at least three aspects to this view. One is that everyone gets equal shares no matter what (simple equitability); the second is that people get shares according to their contribution (commercial equitability); and the third is that people get shares according to need (the socialist model).

It is doubtful if the second of these issues is perceived as just in the political sense in that it may be perceived that all are contributors to the national common wealth. Getting shares according to need, does provide for those less fortunate but it also affords an opportunity to those able to exploit social welfare. One would guess that the political view of distributive justice would be an amalgam of the first and third points – simple equitability being easier to understand and manage. In this, one needs to bear in mind that misfortune is not the same as injustice.

Distributive justice consists in considering several related questions. Its main concern is the fair distribution of goods, although that may be extended to non-material justice. It considers such questions as 'Should it be each according to their contribution?' 'Should it be to each according to need?' It is such questions that lie at the heart of fairness.

## Social Attitudes

There has been a diminution of violence of centuries. Among such motives are those of commerce (which divides power), feminisation, the escalation of reason, literacy and mobility (what was called cosmopolitanisation). Most importantly Pinker's data include such items as the decline in nuclear weapons interest, the number of deaths in each war, the length of military conscription, and the disapproval of spanking in the U.S., New Zealand, and Sweden.

As evidence for the diminution of violence over the centuries one might point to the movement to abolish capital punishment. The now non-use of the iron maiden, the rack, public beheadings and hangings, and breaking on the wheel is evidence enough. As mentioned elsewhere in this work, it is curious beyond belief that we could have engaged in torture for theological disagreement, for having opinions contrary to those in authority. Life is no longer solitary, poor, nasty, brutish, and short. All of this means that more tender personalities may now flourish.

## Attitude to Death

With the advent of the case for the diminution of cruelty one might also re-consider attitudes to death. Being deprived of life must give pause to the incautious as well as to the cautious. The case for changing attitudes to death has been considered by Aries. As he noted, attitudes to death were static, and then something triggered a change. Aries outlined approaches death with an analysis of four periods: tamed death, one's own death, thy death, and forbidden death. In his analysis, he drew on ancient manuscripts, and on ancient characters. As we note, being alive has become more precious, as evidenced by the Wilkinson & Pickett book as well as by the changed attitudes to cruelty, as outlined by Pinker (also see Death and, separately, Kubler-Ross in References).

It is also appropriate to reiterate that several jurisdictions have legislated to make an easeful death for those who are terminally ill and wish for an end to their pain and suffering. One would wish for appropriate safeguards to ensure that it is their own decision, arrived at without pressure from anyone. That appears to have been done. It is also worthy to recall that those jurisdictions that have so enacted found that the 'peaceful pill', as it came to be called, was used less often than was expected. The effect seemed to be that it was an option not often used: it seemed to act as deterrent rather than an enhancer, by way of giving the sufferer comfort as an available option.

## Numerology

When Martin Gardner was the contributor to 'Mathematical Games' in the magazine *Scientific American* (1960) he posed an interesting instances of numerology. One was the numerological significance of 13 to the composer Wagner. There are 13 letters in his name: he was born in 1813 (add the digits and it comes to 13: he composed 13 works: *Tannhauser*, his greatest work, was completed on an April 13th: he finished *Parsifal* on January 13th 1882; *Lohengrin* was first heard by him in 1861, exactly 13 years after his composition; he died on a February 13th.

Another instance is that 666 (the mark of the beast) is the sum of the integers on the roulette wheel (1–36). The instances that Gardner gives include the significance of the founder of Seventh Day Adventism, and the emperor Napoleon. One is beset with the puzzle of whether they are contrived instances, or something meaningful: one has an impression of scepticism on the part of that author (see Gardner in References).

## Social Indicators

Of a different kind of book, (Wilkinson and Pickett 2009) was entitled *The spirit level.* What is important is the subtitle which they describe as why more equal societies almost always do better on desirable social indicators. Their thesis is that equality engenders improvement in the quality of life. It is, in other words, desirable to foster equality. One might argue that without economic equality there can be no social equality: a point well-taken.

As those authors point out, once the wealth of the populace reaches a certain level it no longer produces longevity. To that it should be added that, after a certain point, it no longer produces greater felicity. The increase in depression and anxiety is upon us in the Western world, and no less in the third world although for different reasons.

We do need to bear in mind that those authors live and work in Britain; as such they live in a society which is relatively obsessed with social status. Notwithstanding, their analysis is an objective one that covers more than one country. Their substantial argument is that countries with greater equality do better: indeed their book is subtitled why *equality is better for everyone.* The subtitle gives the subject matter of the work. It deals with topics as compelling as trust, women's equality, income, and the Development Index.

Their argument traces the development of equality through the divine right of kings (and, as they say, it was arbitrary), the development of democracy, equality before the law, the legal abolition of slavery, through the universal franchise to 'include non-property owners and women'. It is picked up by such issues as free education, health matters, protection of the rights of employees, tenants, and covers such topics as adverse racial discrimination

Most recently it runs counter to the resistance to marriage equality. With this goes the notion of being tolerant of diverse views. One might characterise this as a dual contradiction: one the one hand there is an increasing tolerance of diversity; and advocates an increase in trust.

The tolerance of diversity leads to a more nuanced view of 'keeping up with the Joneses'. The existence of the super-rich creates an attitude of 'I want it too'. It does appear that some countries are outliers. In terms of violence, the gun lobby, police shootings, and the general attitude to violence as a 'solution'. One calls to mind a discussion of author with an Australian senator. Her analysis was that some countries such see 'violence as a solution, we see it as a problem', that despite the many merits of such societies.

The Wilkinson & Pickett book endorses the concept of equality as a means of improving the quality of life of us all. Their work purports to be one whereby it endorses the concept of increasing equality on the grounds of objective criteria. Those same arguments could also apply to the moral argument. In that same book, they instance the case of the Exxon Valdez spillage four fifths of respondents said that the country should pursue environmental protection 'regardless of cost. 'Taken literally, that meant that they were to shut down all schools, hospitals, and police, and fire stations, stop funding social programs, medical research, foreign aid, and national defence, or raise the income tax to 99%, if that is what it would have to cost to protect the environment'.

It is to be noted in social attitudes there are some desiderata. One outstanding instance occurred when the present author was a student in New Zealand. There was a plan that NZ would educate qualified people on the clear understanding that would return home, and take the benefits of their education with them.

## Applications

The income of the world's powerful people exceeds that of many sovereign states: more importantly, their influence is far wider than their financial means. The control that they exercise is worldwide and connected to information technology and the flow of information. Control of the media, powerful lobbying capacity, and quasi-monopolistic power are instances. It is difficult to quantify the power that some exercise. For example, how is one to decide how powerful is Queen Elizabeth II as head of the Commonwealth? How powerful is the *Secretary General* of the United Nations? How powerful was an author such as Charles Dickens? How powerful was Gandhi? Mandela? How powerful was the founder of *Amnesty International,* or how powerful is the *Red Cross*?

It is difficult to imagine that the man-in-the-street having the same power as a billionaire. For one thing, the billionaire would have access to the best legal operators, and could pay, which the man-in-the-street could not afford. Notwithstanding, naming and shaming in the press could have a demonstrable effect. Plainly the conclusion is that money conveys power, but so does position, and so too does moral stature.

Taxation may be one of the lesser reasons to invest in certain countries. Among the important factors are political stability. Economists are justifiably taken less seriously than they should be since they ignore a basic fact of life. The relationship between income and life satisfaction is curvilinear rather than a straight correlation. Once the income reaches a certain level money matters less. What does matter is personal security, the rule of law, social connections, and the like.

## Moral Dilemmas

Dilemmas abound in real-life, and often require moral resolution. Thus, in medicine, one might have the dilemma of 'should I assign the only dialysis machine to patient X rather than patient Y on the basis of Z?' In crime one might have the police dilemma of arraigning someone whose offence is legally required to be indicted, but where there is justice to be accorded by ignoring it (as is the possible, although unlikely, in the case of someone illegally killing a known hitman). One might argue that the court should decide, but that may be a doubtful and cumbersome process. Indeed, it is the basis of many plays and TV dramas. One calls to mind the film Sophie's choice, in which she is to lose one of her children to the Nazi regime on entering Auschwitz. Such dilemmas are a common feature of those involving values.

One of the basic propositions or hypotheses of Darwinism is that there needs to be a variety in order for selection to take place. It is thus that we will always be psychopaths and saints. Given that, then legislation will always be needed to contain the excesses of greed while not such strictures would apply to those of a more saintly disposition. The role of education converting potential psychopaths cannot be overemphasised. One would hope that saintliness would become the default position.

The state has precedence in terms of power: that is why it is important to redress that imbalance by such issues as, in court, the presumption of innocence until proved guilty; the state must make its case, rather than the assumption of guilt. That point is temporarily suspended while the prosecution is making its case. A fair trial consists of an independent expert deciding after hearing both sides.

Look at the consequences of streaming in education. Finland has virtually few private schools, is non-competitive, as distinct from (say) the UK which has a tiered system. Compare this to the UK, which funds and fosters private schools where one might have the facilities of a five-star resort and another can barely afford the basic requirements.

Among the advantages of a good education is that meritocracy is fostered. There are characters who are non-competitive and therefore lose out. Even so, that principle leaves out those who are co-operators at the expense of those who are competitive. Germany and Slovenia, for example, have both abolished fees for undergraduate tertiary education: but its critics speculate that they fund something for which they derive no direct benefit. As a matter of principle, the notion that it fosters equality of opportunity and prevents the non-consideration of going to university on the grounds of poverty may seem to be worthy causes.

## Whistleblowing

Whistleblowing may be defined as an act designed to report an unethical breach, motivated by the need to act in the public interest. They initiate of their own volition something that breaches the rules of open-ness and honesty. Such a definition fails to accommodate the notion that actions can be maliciously brought, and may be in retaliation for some real or imagined slight.

The notion that one could report misdemeanours is entrenched in our system. For example, suing a tobacco company could have serious repercussions for one's career as they have virtually unlimited resources for expert legal teams.

One must recognise that there is a plethora of legislation in the Western world to govern whistleblowing, but it is largely ineffective due to there being unofficial means of retaliation. One of the few cases where it is effective is under court protection, and cedes a profit to the whistleblower a proportion of the sum saved – a source that provides a financial independence to a potential whistleblower: this is really a task for an independent audit committee.

There is a special problem in the case of journalists. Among such, is that of preserving the anonymity of sources. If such sources were revealed it could place the whistleblower's job in jeopardy. What makes this especially difficult is that, in some jurisdictions, a public servant who discloses unauthorised information could be imprisoned – and thus the moral dilemma. That problem is compounded by the knowledge that phone calls may be traceable.

## Religious Encyclical

It is not a matter of surprise that a major religious movement should have expressed itself in explicit terms. The general notion of the 'brotherhood of man under the fatherhood of God' is an older one. The explicit statement of recent age was that of Pius Xl. *On the unity of the human race*, although written in 1939 was unpublished until recently (see Passalecq and Suchecky 1997). That document holds and advocates the common humanity. There were, understandably, statements about the special role of the Roman Catholic Church, with views as seen by Pius XI.

In the Encyclical there followed statements about the bankruptcy of the mechanical-atomistic approach, deceptive promises of material well-being: the bankruptcy of equality falsely based on capital: dissociation through the acquisitive instinct: the developing destructive role of private property: excessive dependence on the state and the growing power of the state; totalitarian states, economic collectivism; and misplaced authoritarianism. The work concludes with Revelation's testimony and the unifying power of redemption.

That document noted strongly that humanity is united by a common nature. Unity is to be gained, amongst other things, through work, the family, religion, and by the character of the state. The document speaks against racism, and against dysfunctional forms of the state. It is easy to see the reaction to the social and political context in which this Encyclical was written; it is also clear about the timeless issues that confront those who assert a common humanity.

The work was commissioned by Pius XI as he saw war approaching, and the racial issues which attached to that imminent conflict. The work has several articles which give the context of the writing of the article, which was drafted by a Jesuit Priest at the request of the Pope. The work is an understandable mixture of theological issues (such as the right of religious worship), and secular ones (such as territorial nationality).

## Physical Constants

The value of pi – and every other mathematical constant is what it is, and no legislation is going to change it. The Medieval schoolmen did an analysis of logic, and came to the conclusion that of the many ways of writing a syllogism only a limited small number are valid (as distinct from true, validity being whether the conclusion follows from the premises). It parallels the findings in mathematics wherein the ancient Greeks, and Arab astronomers, discovered the regularity of the rules which apply to the physical world, and show the regularity with which one can make inferences.

## Assumptions as Critic

The writer recalls talking to the criminologist Gordon Hawkins, amongst other things he was a book critic. When asked what he assumed when picking up a book to review he said that the writer had convinced the publisher to send it for review, and the reviewers had given it favourable comment. Gordon Hawkins said that he was convinced by that evidence, and would look for merit. If he could not find it he was duty-bound to say so. When asked if it happened often the reply was that it was rare.

## By Elimination

I only know two tunes: one of them is 'songs my mother taught me, and the other one ain't'.

## Assumption of Equal Competence

Some issues rest upon different assumptions. An instance is a ship's officer being asked by the captain at what time there would be one fathom under the keel on a rising tide. The calculation was simple and involved finding the state of the tide at the primary port, calculating the delay at the secondary port. The ship drew 24 feet at the stern and so needed a 30 foot depth on a rising tide (so that in the event of stranding it would float free). Having noted the time the captain said to the officer to go down to the local brothel and get the sailors out. Here the assumption was that competence in one field would be competence in another.

## The Offensive Prize

There is a branch of logic that deals with the syllogism. There is a particular syllogism with a suppressed premise, it is called an enthymeme (see Sinclair 1951 in References). In a university competition, when the writer was an undergraduate, the one that won the 'most offensive' prize was 'I have tried to be a good Christian, but cheerfulness keeps breaking in'.

## The Basis of Humour

Assumptions as a basis of humour. First example, English comedian looking up at the Royal box and saying 'That reminds me, I must buy some stamps': second example, an aspirant young actor gets role as part of husband and goes home to tell his father. The father replied that next time he hoped his són would soon get a speaking part.

## Wrong but Socially Useful

A useful working principle, acknowledged to be totally wrong but socially useful. (eg. everyone knows the law). If ignorance were a defence it would be universally used (I am sorry your honour, I did not know that killing was a crime).

## Challenging Assumptions

Expressed and challenged assumptions. For example, Kepler's showing that Aristotle's view that all celestial motion was circular was in error. Kepler's showing that the path of planet in orbit is an ellipse, with the sun at one focus. Second example: Semmelweis' showing that going from corpse dissection to delivering babies without prior scrubbing and disinfecting would result in infant deaths. He was declared mad and incarcerated – then vindicated by the Pasteur demonstration of the basis of infection.

## Knowability

Some things may be known eventually (the other side of the Moon: once we did not know, now we do). Some things will never be known (eg. One day, while driving through the city in December the local blood bank had a sign that read 'b ood bank'. Was it a pun [noel], or was it an accident, we will never know.

## The Missing Item

The one major item missing, and most important here, was the assumption, that I know that I am right. The notion that one has one's own direct line the 'the truth' is a dangerous assumption, and has led to death for many, heresy for example).

## Comment on Theory

Despite such repressive regimes there are principles underlying our behaviour, and they do not vary much, even though the means of expression may differ. There is small merit in committed conceptual views, such as those of Jung or Behaviourism, games theory, or bio-genetics, done to the exclusion of rival theories and in a doctrinaire manner. There is no attempt at psycho-archaeology in an endeavour to explain particular actions or attitudes, on the part of individuals. What does seem important is that theological and philosophical, and should not be subject to restraints imposed by logic.

There are those who would lay claim to special knowledge, the so-called gurus. One would not put Jung in the company of Jim Jones (see the Jones website in References). Jung has, amongst other things, provided us with psychological insights such as the concept of Introversion / Extraversion, archetypes, the collective unconscious, and (with Freud) the concept of synchronicity. Jones was responsible for over 900 deaths at Jonestown in Guiana.

Hitler is not accorded the positive accolades that we accord to Francis of Assisi. Even the widely popular Indian gurus vary: Maharishi Mahesh Yogi seemed to have been a genuine giver whereas Baghwan Shree Rajneesh managed to make himself wealthy (amongst other things, he owned a large collection of Rolls Royces), and some held him in alleged scorn for his lack of a coherent doctrine as well as for his sexual exploitation (see Rajneesh in References).

Some obvious beliefs of another age need to be rebutted. For example, that the Black Death in Europe was caused by wearing fashionable pointed shoes, that one could be prevailed upon to restore sight, and that it would work instantly, that one is willing to hold contradictory views in popular sayings 'out of sight out of mind' and 'absence makes the heart grow fonder', and that many people report hallucinations whereas in fact they are relatively commonplace (where the popular belief was that it was confined to the mentally unstable). The major point here is that by doing such challenging is the only way to discover the small percentage that leads to better understanding.

## Rationality

By way of comparison, the rationality of man, as distinct from less rational beliefs assumed that model, as mentioned by Adam Smith in his book *The wealth of nations* (1776). In economic behaviour this assumes that the rational model is an appropriate one. One cannot have an economics based on rationality for we live in an irrational world. The notion that humanity is entirely rational in economic behaviour is to be challenged: the existence of fashions, and of fads is evidence enough. There it was assumed that rational self-interested man is the appropriate model. That quite ignores the importance of unpaid labour, of love, of caring, and of genuine concern. Economic man, in particular, has a particular and unsustainable view of what is alleged to move us. Hume's work makes a similar point (see Hume in References). In one of his most famous passages he noted:

> Reason is, and ought only to be the slave of the passions, and can never pretend to any other office than to serve and obey them.

## Logical Paradoxes

A logical paradox is one that is a contradiction. For example, the Cretan paradox. 'Epimenides is a Cretan, and said all Cretans are liars'. If he is telling the truth then he is lying (If all Cretans are liars then he, as a Cretan, is a liar and cannot be believed even though he is telling the truth). If he is lying, as a Cretan allegedly does, then he is telling the truth, that not all Cretans are liars. Another example is the statement that I am not making a statement when plainly one is (perhaps one solution to this paradox is a statement cannot make a statement about itself).

### *Easterlin Paradox*

The Easterlin paradox was named after the economist Richard Easterlin (see References). He suggested that a higher level of a country's per capita gross domestic product did not correlate with greater self-reported levels of happiness among citizens of a country, in contrast with people inside a country. Later research has questioned whether Easterlin's conclusions about the non-correlation were accurate.

While there have been justifiable criticisms, it may be true that a curvilinear relationship may hold for certain categories of people. As Kahneman and Deaton (2010) concluded, '... high income buys life satisfaction, but not happiness, and low income is associated with both low life evaluation and low emotional well-being'.

## *The Cantril Ladder*

In addition to that concern there is, too, the notion that there is a ladder (called a Cantril ladder) that gives a simple measure of happiness. Denmark, Switzerland, and Iceland are included in the tops: of the bottom three of 53, Ecuador, Belize, and Japan are in the bottoms (see World Happiness in References). By way of comparison the UN report on happiness (see Cantril in references) the top three are Norway. Denmark, and Iceland with the bottom three of 155 are Tanzania, Burundi, and the Central African Republic.

## *The Research Paradox*

One of these is what a concept which Grabosky (1996) called 'paradoxical cause'. The essence of that concept is that one intends to produce one outcome and the reverse is found. He provides several instances. One of them is the Hillsboro Stadium disaster in the UK in 1989. Barriers where put up to from crowd control but, in the event acted as barriers in which 96 people died and incurred 766 injured.

A second instance is that of being 'tough' on crime, with the consequence that prisons are full: a third instance is where wherein more prohibitions are seen as a challenge to authority, as precepts to be flouted and challenged: or in medicine where a drug (such as benzodiazepines) may cause criminal behaviour rather than the main effect of sedative or muscle relaxants. It is worthwhile to note that one must be open to finding the reverse consequences to what one expects. It is so often the case that the evidence runs contrary to received opinion. It is thus that science progresses.

It is concluded that paradoxes often require an empirical solution. A most recent case is that of deciding whether one ought to keep taking antibiotics until finished, or should one stop when its effect has been achieved. On the one hand it is supposed to ensure the demise of all infections; on the other hand it may lead to the development of a more virulent strain of bugs. Thus, some paradoxes may be resolved empirically while others may be formally logical (as in the hare and the tortoise): they are similar in style to oxymorons.

## Description of Minimal Principles

It is thus that consideration needs to be given to the notion of equality as a quantifiable moral value. In an ideal world one would be able to express the basic propositions of morals. It is only by considering each factor that we may improve, and that includes modifying the list the following list. This list will, inevitably, be constantly subject to modification, the general point being that it represents a first cut of the principles which underlie a code of ethics (as distinct from a code of conduct). It was held (see above) that moral principles are constantly subject to modification, and so it should be.

- Dignity
- Equitability
- Prudence
- Honesty
- Open-ness
- Goodwill
- Suffering alleviation

## Excellence

If one knew what excellence was, it would be an admirable goal to which one might aspire. Given a limited definition it might be said that it is getting something done to a high level of expertise. One of the characteristics of excellent professionals is that they feel they live in an imperfect world: things are rarely as good as they should be. Given the frailties of human nature, the demands of time and of competing values, the solutions to almost all problems are less than perfect.

Their self-perceived inadequacies will become evident to the external critic. An essential precondition of intellectual or artistic eminence is the vision to see how things might be – to have an insight into ways of doing things better, of perceiving failings, and the power to persuade others. This power to persuade may need to be exercised in the face of determined resistance – the will to go ahead despite powerful opposition. With such a view goes what seems a paradoxical humility. Knowing how things ought to be induces in first-rate professionals the idea that they must cope in a flawed world. This imperfection may be seen as something that invites adverse judgement. Exactly who is to bring judgement, or why such a judgement might be brought, is not fully explained. It is the inchoate sense of imperfection that lies at the heart of the concern. Lesser operators do not seem to be troubled by the notion of imperfection, and therein may lie the core of the issue.

A renascent interest in corporate performance may be driven by commercial imperatives. As competition increases so too does the need to strive for excellence.

It is curious that we expect, and get, 'total quality management' (TQM) in symphony orchestras (no sour notes, excellent performance, prompt starting, etc). Why can we not get the same from car repair garages, computer repair people, and airlines? Perhaps it is the 'luxury' nature of the product that demands such quality; one would not otherwise pay such money for a non-necessity.

Cormack (1991) has asked the pertinent question as to whether Western values are consistent with the search for excellence. He concluded that there is such a set of values, and identified them as being as follows: the inherent value of mankind; people are seen as an asset, what they are, and what they can become. It is our destiny to serve and to improve. The joy of good work; the satisfactory completion of something demanding brings fulfilment. The importance of service is not only service to customers, it is service to all – customers; neighbours; subordinates, etc. It is better to give than to receive; performance is judged by the stewardship of assets.

In most professional work excellence is judged, in part, by the ethical codes. Excellence is, however, more easily recognised than codified. It is seen as a journey as well as a destination; a process as well as an achievement. As Peters and Austin so aptly put it, '... excellence happens when high purpose and pragmatism meet'. Judgments are not made on single issues, but on overall evaluation. The difference between statesmen and party hacks is that the former has a broader vision, substantial confidence in their own quite proper insights, a constructive approach, and a moral tone to their views and behaviour.

The judgement of how well such criteria have been satisfied must be left to those fitted to judge. Exactly who such judges might be is a matter for debate. It may be that outsiders are best equipped. For instance, pilots may not be the best judges of aircraft design, vignerons not the best judges of wine, nor surgeons the best judges of the desirability of surgery, although it is recognised that they do have a role to play.

There are some forms of professionalism in which sheer competence and artistry are sufficient; musicianship, for example. In most forms of professionalism, however, values become significant. We do not accord to dictators the notion of excellence, despite their efficiency, dedication and list of accomplishments. Those to whom we accord excellence have commonly acted according to commonly accepted ethical standards.

Over recent decades various theories of management have, as one of their unstated premises, the search for more ethical ways of doing things. Team work theories, Theory X and Theory Y, primary social motives, and the application of Swedish and Japanese methods have a common motivation. One of the characteristics of excellent professionals is that they feel they live in an imperfect world; things are rarely as good as they should be. Given the frailties of human nature, the demands of time and of competing values, the solutions to almost all problems are less than perfect.

It is worth noting that the companies on the Peters and Waterman criteria were also market leaders in their respective and diverse fields. Excellence, including ethical excellence, is clearly profitable. To achieve potential, some values need to be emphasised and these include:

- The value of personal worth and self-esteem based on the uniqueness, significance and importance of the individual;
- the value of loving our neighbours, of esteeming them and promoting their growth and well-being rather than pursuing our own interests at the expense of those around us;
- the value of community and the responsibility of businesses to take the social and human dimension into their areas of shareholder accountability;

There is a caution that striving for excellence may produce disillusion: take the example of a child driven to educational perfection by ambitious parents. The stress, the deprivation of childhood pleasures, and the due sense of proportion would be lost in the search for educational excellence. In international relations, the search for excellence in political systems could lead to intolerance of those who are striving for social justice in a less pressing fashion.

Notwithstanding, with this caution in mind we might conclude that we are able to recognise the presence of excellence, but may doubt whether a quantified judgement can be made. Like love and enmity, wealth and poverty, rain and shine, we know it when we see it. Excellence is both an achievement and a form of dedication, perhaps of passion. Although it is not possible to pronounce upon all its attributes, it might best be captured by the notion that excellence is a process as well as an achievement; ethics is one of the travel documents, as well as the destination.

## Conclusions

Of the various views one is sympathetic to the concept of virtue ethics, with the proviso that the virtues are explicated, and subject to modification. That proviso also applies to deontology. The Kantian view is one whereby it is held to be desirable that actions become guides to future actions; that one should act as if the principle behind that action should be a general guide.

The *Utilitarian* view fails to give sufficient attention to the rights of minorities, partially rescued by the notion of *Act Utilitarianism.* An act is moral if it produces a moral outcome (whatever a moral outcome might be). Clearly one ought to be able to specify what is moral. In *consequentialism* one cannot imagine a moral act without a moral consequence: in that the *consequentialists* are right, as is also the case with deontologists. For both the *deontologists* and the *consequentialists* one ought to be able to specify the code of morality before accepting their propositions.

Modern contributors, they see equality as a desirable aim: it is as if they hold it to be a self-evident truth. That is so for such theorists as Rawls, Kohlberg, Parfit, Temkin, and Haidt: in effect, they hold that same proposition, that moral dilemmas are inherently pervasive and are thoroughly worthy of our attention.

# Chapter 14
# General Conclusions

There are, as we have seen, a variety of theories from which to choose. This account has speculated about which account best fits the facts, It does appear that each account (Malthus, Darwin, Lovelock, Hobhouse, and all the theorists, as well as modern theorists all have something important to say. The general contributions that each make is valuable, and adds to our some of knowledge and explanation. This account also makes a contribution in terms of providing a different perspective, and of how quantification may be an additional tool.

The theorists all provide useful approaches that provide explanations, save that the Hedonistic calculus (and *Utilitarianism*), which do not seem to accommodate the rights of minorities. That is partially redressed by the provision of *Act Utilitarianism*, defined as producing the best possible results in that specific situation. Here the problem is 'best'. *Rule Utilitarianism*, on the other hand, holds that moral rectitude depends upon the adequacy of the rules that allow it to make the greatest good. As with medicine, one must be impressed by an evidential base.

Of the various approaches to moral theory one is attracted to all of them save the notion of 'the greatest happiness of the greatest number'. There the problem is the rights of minorities: partially redeemed by the idea of *Act Utilitarianism.* Friedman (2000) made that point when he wrote on globalisation; that it involves not only the development of communications, global trade, and improved technology, but also the persistence of our tribal roots and ancestral connections: a point that is captured by Friedman in the title of his book *The lexus and the olive tree*. Verifiable truth is one of the bulwarks of freedom, and often one of the means of being critical of governments.

The process currently called 'political spin' is putting a politically beneficial interpretation on seemingly adverse events. For example, the notion of revising the visa system by dispensing the idea of foreigners taking local jobs. What may happen is that one visa system is replaced by another which may still allow foreigners who receive less pay. With respect to pollution issues one may argue that an oil spillage could benefit the local economy by creating jobs. The idea that, in biblical terms, the



R. Francis, *Equality in Theory and Practice*,
https://doi.org/10.1007/978-981-15-3488-1_14

statement that if a man smiteth thee, turn the other cheek. That could be interpreted to mean 'never let anyone hit you in the same place twice'.

In all of this there an instance of the misuse of words. People who terrorise are called terrorists, but why it should include the murder of the innocents is an eternal mystery, and one of our first tasks is to try and understand what it is that justifies it. This is one of the mysteries of motivation: there must be an explanation somewhere.

On another note one calls to mind the recent instance is that of a group seeking national independence. The case of the Catalans seeking independent national status are prevented by the Spanish government, and with the justification of being in accord with its Constitution: thereby making independence impossible. How one becomes an independent state is highly problematical. Use of the law to prevent independence was met with the might of the overarching state. The same issue applies to a proposed Kurdish state, separate from Iraq (and, indeed, to any other region wishing for independence). The one that was successful was South Sudan becoming independent of Sudan, and in the light of a bloody war. Under such circumstances it is difficult to see how any area, region, of quasi-state may become independent.

## Factors in Equality

There are a number of factors that may influence equality: apart from the twin processes of legislation and education are those of political arrangements and of personality. At the national level one might be concerned at the idea that lobbying is done at all. Bearing in mind that MPs are responsible to their electorates it does seem odd that their loyalty should be to a party line rather than to the people who elected them, although it may be argued that 'a party' represents certain aspirations. It is thus that the notion of having lobbyists may be inappropriate, an interesting question. At the general level one might (or might not) be concerned that all refugees are welcome, and that may be at odds with the idea that political decisions affecting the electorate (and the country) should be at variance with the welcoming-all argument. This is clearly a debate that every country should have.

It is instructive to note that human values follow a normal distribution. At one extreme is that of personal psychopathy where a dominant individual misuses power to foster their own interests and ideas. At the other extreme are those whose saintly style is constructive, helpful, and well-intentioned. While we can do less about the dominating psychopath we can, and should, provide the safeguards of the rule of law. The requirement that no-one may occupy a position of political power for more than an agreed period (restricted incumbency), and that member-nations of the UN may be required to conform to all of the principles lest they be expelled.

## Solutions

The absolute amount of pain and suffering might be increased due to the growth in population. Against this is to be put the diminution of violence. Overall the conclusion would have to be that the diminution of violent extremes must be seen, overall, as beneficial. As was mentioned, we longer shove little boys up chimneys, we no longer kill people for theologically disagreeing with the status quo, we longer break on wheel those who dissent on the complexities of royalty.

Several things need to be done, and this is entirely a matter for debate in the legislature. One is to control population growth: another is to ensure equality of all – including women: the third is to include all sentient beings in the press for equality. Here is the main point is that morals should be normative rather than peripheral. Politically speaking, some countries have gone to the extent that choosing a government is a crucial issue, and have legislated to make voting compulsory. Just as one cannot choose to ignore being taxed or being required to take part in a census; the choice of legislature is yet more important.

## Theories

The views of Aristotle, Kant, Parfit, Temkin, Kohlberg, Haidt, Rawls, distributive justice, etc. are all evidence that people have excellent insights into the basis of ethical behaviour. Even though some may be subject to reasonable criticism. The view of Aristotle on virtue ethics is an interesting twist on what is a significant worldview. Indeed, one writer has argued that it is the exercise of virtues that produces happiness - an interesting twist on virtue ethics.

One view advocates the socialist model. There is no reason to believe that minding the vulnerable would not work in a large society: the second argument that it is socialist to which the appropriate reply is 'and so it should be, to mind the vulnerable'. One of the problems here is that the 'vulnerable' will also include those who exploit the system. How to distinguish the genuine from the users is a perennial problem.

There are different perspectives that one may use in looking at the equality issue. Among them are physical, psychological, social, cultural etc. Each of these deserve a comment. One has a clear impression of the influence of physical factors on the development of such issues as the viability of this planet, slavery, space travel, and Darwinian adaptation. Human judgements are always subject to error, and to change as values change. Separate may not be equal: equality looks to social connections – not separations. One cannot always argue the Nuremburg defence (I was only following orders). There are some principles of human behaviour that appear to be universal. One is that a loss is more serious than a gain, other things being equal (witness the number of suicides during the great depression of 1929).

Another principle appears to be 'Who cares the least then controls the relationship', and finds expression in many human enterprises, and range from international agreements to personal and intimate relationships. It has its origin in those having the least to lose are likely to engage in conduct that is both riskier and more beneficial to them. Having little to lose means that actually losing is of lesser consequence.

Additionally, we have seen William James' views on habit, which he described therein as being the 'enormous flywheel of society'. As he concluded, it is better that those accustomed to one way of doing things do not move careers. How else would we have people doing disagreeable jobs? All this so long as barriers are not placed in the way of career change.

One of the characteristics of excellent professionals is that they feel they live in an imperfect world: things are rarely as good as they should be. Given the frailties of human nature, the demands of time and of competing values, the solutions to almost all problems are less than perfect. A not uncommon expression of their concern is captured in the phrase 'they will find me out'. Their self-perceived inadequacies become evident to the external critic. An essential precondition of intellectual or artistic eminence is the vision to see how things might be - to have an insight into ways of doing things better, of perceiving failings, and the power to persuade others.

## Psychological Contributions

One would have to conclude that psychology has something to offer, but only if it is evidence-based: the insights provided must bear relationship to observed fact. To that we must add that such insights should be original and worthwhile: such ideas as the significance of the number seven by Miller (see Miller 1956), or by the obedience studies (Milgram 1963) (see also Haney, Banks & Zimbardo 1973: Zimbardo et al. 2000), and the phi phenomenon.

Humans come with differing senses of power and determination. This power to persuade may need to be exercised in the face of determined resistance - the will to go ahead despite powerful opposition. With such a view goes what seems a paradoxical humility. Knowing how things ought to be induces in first-rate professionals the idea that they must cope in a flawed world. The wish of tyrants is an imposition of ideas onto the larger political canvas, and presents one person's view of how things ought to be (and also provides a means of lining the pockets of dictators).

## Hidden Truths and Research

With respect to 'hidden truths' there are some ways of determining what is really going on. For example, there is an elementary consideration in research that one matches data. It is not good, for instance, in comparing those who live on main roads compared to those who live (say) 300 metres away without matching for age and health. One would not, for example, compare younger people living away from main roads with those of distinctly older people living on main roads: hidden truths are more subtle.

Matthews (1998) has outlined what he calls 'data sleuths': one may make inferences about missing data. An instance that he gives is that of 'capture - recapture' wherein they infer 'ghost populations'. To take an instance that he gives suppose one is to gauge the number of prostitutes abroad in a city. They go out and find prostitutes; a few weeks later they go out and 'recapture' prostitutes. The prospect of finding the same ones is more likely when the number is small: the larger the number available the less likely it is that the same ones would be encountered.

This can yield an estimate of the size of the population. That same principle, derived from ecology, may be applied to any population. In the ecological instance by the 'capture and recapture' method. Animals in the wild are tagged, with a subsequent recapture to determine the prospect of getting the same animals twice. It is recommended that the different kinds of equality be approached in its own best way.

## Moral Dilemmas

The notion that just eight people control as much wealth as the poorest half of the world's population, roughly 3.6 billion people. Put another way 62 people own as much wealth as the poorest half of the world's population: the tiny richest percent own/control more than the entire remainder is a significant part of the story, but not all. If economic growth were the only criterion one could reasonable ask if inequality was a brake on growth. The essence of a moral question is with reference to a value, to a moral virtue, or to a codified system of ethics. The work of Stiglitz is an example of how much this disparity counts.

Life is replete with moral dilemmas. For example, in medicine should one deny medical treatment to those who refuse to help themselves, but still expect excellent treatment? (e.g. smokers who will not give up the habit). Should one be obliged to take migrants who are displaced in countries wherein we have militarily intervened? (see References). Should former colonial citizens be given the nationality of the centre of the empire? In the long-term, moral persuasion supervenes, and unjust laws resisted.

Some people love people, others love humanity but not people (and some like both and some like neither). This relates to short term help versus long-term strategy. It is known that some are concerned with long-term effects (such as a burgeoning population) whereas others are directly concerned to help those in immediate need. How and why is life a constant tension between the individual and the collective? Does one help individuals in the here and now, or have the long-term view (such as birth control)? Does one do both?

## Naturalistic Fallacy

This is an instructive instance that brings to bear the naturalistic fallacy. That point argues that one cannot derive an 'ought' from an 'is' – a point well taken and dealt with in text. In this work, it is argued that the 'is' of equality ought to be an 'ought': it is a guiding principle that deserves special attention, and one that invests other ideas, and is the connection between the French revolution case cited and the concept. The 'ought to be equal' becomes the guiding principle, provided that it is goal that one works towards rather than seen as an achievement.

## Politics

In politics there are a number of suggestions for improvement. One is the obvious examples of parliamentary democracy, and the rule of law. Without such guides there is being subject to the 'whim of iron' of tyrants. A similar kind of solution is that of lobbyists. Why they should exist at all is a worrying question. It is noted that members of a legislature are elected to represent the interests of those who elected them: they are not presumably there to respond to the blandishments of pressure groups – yet another moral dilemma. In response to those members of the legislature who pursue their own standards rather than those of the electorate may not be elected at the next election, but that is no guarantee. Lobbying for money, particularly from overseas interests, is bribery.

No one spends money without the expectation of reward. Politically speaking, there is a problem in countenancing the notion of lobbyists. Our political representatives are there to represent their constituents, not as a means of pursuing their own special interests. It is difficult to see the justification of political lobbyists, notwithstanding their entrenched position. Constituents are meant to be the supporters of their political representatives, not supporters available to special interest groups: yet another debatable topic.

Yet another political issue is that of members of a legislature itself. One might ask if electing members of a legislature is the best form of democracy: the answer may be 'no'. There could be other superior methods, including the use of 'juries', a group of randomly selected people deliberate on an issue and come up with conclusions – a process called 'sortition'. One writer referred to the Ancient Greeks, and how they did it, and asks the serious question of what is applicable to small city-states is appropriate to larger democracies? That book is one of questioning the current evaluation of 'democracy', and how it might be improved. He noted, with castigation, that political parties may be corrupt – van Reybrouck (2016) called it decolonising democracy.

Another issue is that of climate change. The lip service given to scientific evidence is only token: if one were to attend to the scientific evidence (such as the melting of the polar icecaps) one would be concerned about the role that population growth, and the use of fossil fuels use, reduction might be effective. The use of available natural-energy sources has much to commend it.

## *Population Policy*

Having a population policy is a must. One debates the unbridled growth of the population, notwithstanding the wishes of developers. Although technology may be increase and improve the provision of food and the disposal of waste there is a limit to what this planet can support. This is one topic worthy of serious debate.

Excessive fertility is seen as one of the major problems of the world. In addition to the burgeoning of humanity there is the added problem of compound growth. It will be seen that to have many children is seen, in a number of cultures, as being 'worthy' and potent. To curb this desire, it is clear that the twin approaches of education and legislation are necessary. One also has in mind that fundamentalist views that forbids contraception may have to change.

It is clear that legislative discouragement is effective, as is the non-provision of family allowances. In addition to the burgeoning of population growth, and so does the problem of the supply of food, water shortages, as well as those of sewage and waste disposal. The banning of excessive packaging would be a good start. Additionally, one recognises that a major attitudinal change, as well as that of practicalities, is necessary. For example, the notion that one has children to care for one in one's age has to be replaced by a system that guarantees care in one's age rather than being reliant on children.

## *Rights*

The types of rights may be regarded as belonging to a specific category. For example, one may regard a roof over one's head is a right, having an adequate income as another right, being allowed to vote, to be treated as an equal before the law, and with right to a free education (provided one is properly prepared for tertiary education). One may further consider rights to a minimum of free medical attention.

What a gap there is between wealth and poverty. The increasing gap between rich and poor may be changing. One must view such a conclusion not only in terms of material possessions and income but also in moral terms. The fight for equality before the law, the provision of basic services, such as medical attention, are an important part of such considerations.

Among the less considered rights is that of a right to accommodation. While it is recognised that one cannot require ownership the question remains, do people have a right to be housed. In general, one must also be attentive to such issues as female equality, universal suffrage, the rule of law, of parliamentary democracy, and of the diminution of violence as a 'solution'. Equality without economic equality is lesser, and should also be manifest in well-being. This stereotypes economic indicators, and fails to measure what is important to us. Finance is a crucial part of commerce, but there is more to a well-functioning economy than is usually measured.

The idea that CEOs deserve a high salary is a myth. One is taken with the notion that a CEO cannot be paid more that (say) ten times the pay of the lowest paid worker may have merit. It would certainly ensure that no-one was underpaid. This is to be paired to the idea that one should never underpay workers. Notionally one would make it an imprisonable consequence to underpay workers and thereby deprive them of the their legislatively justified salary. To threaten them with legal action might extend the jail time.

## *Social Approaches*

The current barriers are mainly mental ones. One is persuaded by the evidence that current pressing problems are of several kinds, including the treatment of women as second-class citizens, of the climate-change deniers, and the problem of over-population, all of which have been outlined. The 'trickle-down' argument does appear to foster inequality in that it boosts such inequality at the expense of common humanity.

The social approaches are in a similar vein. Here the value shades from the psychological (the individual being in a social situation to the actual social situation itself). It also shades, at the other end of the spectrum, into such issues as prejudice and togetherness. There are two main conclusions here. One is, that some instances of cultural practices are utterly contemptible (as in Suttee, and so-called 'honour killing'): the second is that greater equality results in substantial improvements on the various social indicators (as Wilkinson and Pickett 2009, have shown).

It is not being suggested that national obsessions are typical of certain countries: what is being suggested is the there are some issues that are clearly characteristic of certain countries, although they may not be the only obsessions. In the United Kingdom it is (amongst other things) with social class, in the United States it is (amongst other things) a formally and legislative obsession with guns. In presenting such a list one necessary ignores the benefits which such a culture confers.

With respect to theory we conclude that the 'invisible hand' of Adam Smith does not appear to operate in the moral realm. It was intended to describe the unintended consequences of social benefits that flow from individual action. It is, in other words, a means of balancing out demand and supply. It is somewhat regrettable that its application to morality is not as effective.

Sometimes that interest is theoretical (or at least never came to practical fruition), as was the case with Fourier and St. Simon. Practical outcomes were evident in the Quaker families of Cadbury, Fry, and Rowntree who set up ideal working conditions and treated employees as valued people rather than economic tools. As mentioned elsewhere in this work, that idea was also given practical expression in Robert Owen's factory in New Lanark in Scotland, by various co-operative movements throughout the world, and now finds its largest expression in the Mondragon enterprise in Spain (see Mondragon in References).

A renascent interest in corporate performance may be driven by commercial imperatives. As competition increases so too does the need to strive for excellence. Altruistic behaviour towards non-kin should be reciprocated and beneficial. If one knew what the criterion of excellence is it would be an admirable goal to which one might aspire. Given a limited definition it might be said that it is getting something done to a high level of expertise. It has been observed that an excellent plumber is very much more admirable than is an incompetent philosopher.

In commenting on that issue, the point was made by Peters and Austin (1985) that any society which downgrades excellence in plumbing because it is a relatively humble activity, yet tolerates shoddy philosophy because it is a lofty activity, will have '... neither good plumbing nor good philosophy. Neither its pipes nor its theories will hold water'.

Kohlberg set out to schematize the development of the moral sense. He started with the simplest view that characterized the most primitive stage. His view sets out a developmental sequence, and is essentially rational. If one were to level a criticism of the approach it is that what may be true of America may not be true of the rest of the world. Having noted that, it would be hard to imagine the approach being so wildly in error.

## *Women and Fertility*

Here there is a moral dilemma of whether one should require by law that women as well as men should be ordained in religions that otherwise maintain such a ban? It is a contrast between the secular and the divine. On the one hand it prevents the equalisation of the sexes; on the other hand, it interferes with the rights of religious freedom: a truly difficult dilemma.

Of the techniques that seem to work is the enactments of the legislature. Banning the discrimination against women would be a start, banning the use of face veils and headscarves, making equal pay mandatory, and giving them equal opportunity are all indicated. That would, thereby, include the talents of fully half of the human race. It is just such issues that are fully deserving of legislative debate.

## *Relation to Religion*

One of the interesting speculations is whether morals derive from religion, or whether religion was one of the ways of attributing to it some divine provenance. In other words, it is possible that morality may be man-made (or not), and of human origin. As was noted, moral dilemmas abound, and are the basis of many acted scripts. Such concerns are also evident in real-life situations. For example, is it worse to kill a policeman or a member of the public? On one view, it is worse to kill a policeman as they represent the law, and murder strikes us as anarchistic. On the other hand, one might argue that the police understand the risks, and therefore the risks are understood and should be borne. On the equality view all murders are illegal killings: on one view, no matter who dies, they should be considered as equal.

A point worthy of note in any consideration is substantial asymmetry, evident not only in paradoxes but elsewhere also. For example, the notion that certain individuals deplore people dying with dignity, and insist that their ideas should take precedence over everyone else's. They insist that their view should prevail, even when those not of that view do not insist that fundamentalists should follow the more moderate view. It is an interesting example of an unbalanced questioning. One might say that, on the other hand, the process invites consideration of appropriate safeguards. Here, as in other areas, a sense of balance is required.

### *The Republic Debate and Referenda*

There are implications for nuances that often turn out to be critical. For example, in the question of 'should we become a republic' (if not already one) turns out to be 'how should a national president be elected?' To that we can add that in terms of fairness and justice, should we be more concerned with restorative justice than with retributive justice? One of the common nuances is that migrants are so enamoured of their new country that they are prepared to tolerate circumstances that would send a native-born angry at the erosion of civil liberties, those hard fought, and won, freedoms. Migrants, being pleased at their improved situation might be less concerned: yet another truly modern dilemma. The simplistic idea that Referenda should be one question is now dated. The idea is to canvas alternatives, such as how should a President be elected by the legislature on a conscience vote, by the legislature on a party vote, by the people, write in another method, etc.

## Oxymorons and Paradoxes

One is minded of oxymorons – contradictions in terms (in Shakespeare's Romeo & Juliet he describes 'parting is such sweet sorrow'), and Tennyson's 'faith unfaithful kept him falsely true'. Other examples are 'seriously funny', 'deafening silence', and 'pretty ugly'. The idea of asymmetry is critical to this point. The instances given in the previous paragraphs do make the point of asymmetry. An instance is that of toleration: does one tolerate the intolerant. If the general principle is 'no' then one is breaching the rule: if 'yes' it is taking tolerance to the extreme. The lack of symmetry here is the extreme of toleration brings in train what is clearly a breach of acceptable codes of conduct. If one is dedicated to non-violence it prohibits the use of force, even in self-defence. The concept of non-violence bans even moderate force, no matter what the circumstances.

## The United Nations

With respect to the United Nations, one of ideals of the world is the notion that there are agreed principles which have been presented as 30 propositions of the UN (the rightly acclaimed *Declaration of Human Rights*). That is not to say that all is sweetness and light. First, one could well imagine that the Security Council – with its power of veto – should be abolished. Second, there could be an upper house (a house of review) which has a different electorate.

## The Indigenous Peoples

One of the pressing problems is the plight of the indigenous people: thus, the problems of the North American Indians, the Aborigenes of Australia, and the original natives of Brazil. Yet more complicated is that one indigenous peoples replaced another, as was the case of the Maoris allegedly replacing the Moriories in New Zealand (although that is in dispute). Notwithstanding, what runs to the heart of the matter is, what rights do native peoples have when confronted with a race that more advanced technologically. Should they conform to modern standards, and join the twenty-first century, or should they be allowed to retain their traditional way of life: truly a dilemma.

One of the options is that It may be comprised of major disadvantages groupings such as the Kurds, the Palestinians, Aboriginal peoples Amerindians, native South Americans, for instance. Third, those members of the UN who do not conform in all respects to the *Declaration of Human Rights* in all respects, could have their membership suspended until they did so. Not only in terms of legislation but also be active in the seriousness of their pursuit of wrongdoers.

## The Moral Personality

Indeed, on the aspects of the moral personality one could well imagine developing a test of such: one bears in mind the distinction between emotional intelligence and other forms of intelligence. In the former one may be alert to emotional concerns perhaps, at its most cynical, as being for selfish motives: in the latter one is ever mindful of the moral implications, and acts accordingly.

One of the difficulties is that it requires not so much a statement of intention, but one of actual behaviour: thus, the strong preference for a behavioural rather than a pencil-and-paper test. We must ever bear in mind the point made in the individual differences chapter: that there is a broad spectrum of differing humanity, ranging from saints to sinners, lifters and leaners.

Exactly who is to bring judgement, or why such a judgement of morally uplifting might be brought, is not fully explained. It is the inchoate sense of imperfection that lies at the heart of the concern. Lesser operators do not seem to be troubled by the notion of imperfection, and therein may lie the core of the issue. To redress that imbalance it has been put, by a fictional Irish bartender, 'The job of the newspaper is to comfort the afflicted and afflict the comfortable'

## Types of Inequality

Here there are such questions concerning absolute and relative poverty. The question is 'should people have enough' and leave room for the supremely wealthy, or should it be equal in all respects? Is that something to be emulated? The push for equality begs the question, are we talking about absolute or relative poverty. Here the question is, should people have enough? (whatever 'enough' may mean).

It is thus that we recognise the various types of equality need to be discussed and resolved (e.g. education, opportunity, sex related, politically apt, social outcomes, equality before the law, etc.). It is noted that post-dictions (as distinct from predictions) are of lesser value, yet are a guide to future action. One of the few things that we could hold is that, without climate change firmly on the agenda, natural disasters will be exacerbated. That is particularly so with the increase in population, leading to more people being affected, as well as the prospect of increased publicity.

One of the pressing questions is 'should we go for equality of opportunity, or for quality outcome'. Given that some would not press for opportunity: it is relatively urgent that opportunities should be firmly on the social agenda. On one view equality of opportunity is a minimum requirement lest we squander nascent talent. Apart from material disparities one must also be attentive to such issues as female equality, universal suffrage, the rule of law, of parliamentary democracy, and of the diminution of violence.

One must also view such a conclusion not only in terms of material possessions and income but also in moral terms. The struggle for equality before the law, the provision of basic services, such as medical attention, are an important part of such considerations. The notion that a handful of people own as much wealth as the poorest half of the world's population prevents true equality. That is a significant part of the story, but not all. Do we go for total equality in all respects. The gap between rich and poor is fostered by some governments, and treated in a pejorative manner by others. The poorest person on earth has nothing: the richest controls \$105 billion. Notwithstanding, it is changing, with some aspects being plainly ahead of others.

# Final Commentary

Some problems are more acute than others: amongst seen as current are the issues of preserving the environment, preventing climate change as much as possible; the issue of the downgrading of women (and thus losing half the competence of the gene-pool); next is the reform of government, particularly reform of the UN (for example, ejecting those who do not conform). This procedure would also give consideration to alternative forms of democracy. By means least, are the myriad of problems entailed by population growth. Further, should one go for equality of opportunity or of equality of outcomes. Here it is argued that efforts should be rewarded: in that sense equality of opportunity is a must.

Further, the twin processes of legislation and education have much to commend them. It is unreasonable to think that some will be richer than others: what can be done is to ensure that such twin processes contain the excesses of the few.

Good may come of unjust laws being broken, evil may come from bad laws being kept: no longer do we forbid trade unions, fail to give universal franchise, and no longer condone slavery. It is seen that there is a continuous movement to abolish the death penalty (at least in the longer term). This should percolate down to repressive regimes via the trickle-down effect, no matter how minimal. In the long-term, morals trumps economics, but we may need to speed the process by way of legislation and education. We conclude that equality is a desirable goal, that there has been an erratic movement toward, and with increasing success. We must also conclude that the idea of equality is buttressed not only by social indicators but also by moral argument

In summary one must say that, eventually, moral argument wins. To this we should add that the UN is in urgent need of reform; that women are also to be treated as first-rate humans; that excessive population growth is seen as a significant problem; and that education and legislation are the methods by which one may bring it about, particularly using the gradualist approach. One can never get true equality, but that is no reason to give up trying. There are some features that stand out starkly in this analysis. It is argued here that the twin arguments of improving the quality of life, and of moral input are the twin buttresses. Among the most pressing concerns about equality is that violence is a last resort – not a first one.

Some forms of equality are more readily achieved than are others. For example, it is easier to legislate for ‘one man one vote’ than it is for financial equality (the wealthiest person in the world is a CEO, and who controls over a 100 billion dollars). One recognises that such considerations may run counter to some forms of recognised religions, but that will be part of the debate. It is recognised some forms of government are superior to others, at least in both political and human terms, and are to emulated.

In choosing a criterion by which one can judge one bears in mind the need to choose an appropriate one. What is a criterion, and what does it change? For example, one table might use various criteria to look at accident rates; an example is of passenger miles, or driver miles, or time on the road. It is thus that the choice of whether one is effecting an improvement depends on the choice of what is being measured. If one were to debate the foregoing it would go some way toward fostering equality. It is a matter of concern at the criteria used. For example, on the removal of level crossings one might be concerned with how many minutes of driving time might be saved. Instead the criterion might be how many lives are saved by controlled crossings.

Trickle-down effect leads to an increase in inequality. A moral choice is often one where one has to choose the lesser of two evils. Of the various forms of equality, one must consider it in its various manifestations: educational / financial / gender / equality before the law / equality of outcomes / social standing, etc. Some such are more readily achievable than are others, a point that deserves strong recognition, starting with the suggestions given above.

If one were to recommend to a government on what was needed there is an obvious answer; two items. One is a commitment to human rights (with its concomitant ancillaries); the other in the form of an anti-corruption commission. It is only by adopting such measures can one be assured of an appropriate outcome. It is recommended that legislatures debate such issues, bearing in mind that the selection of a criterion-measure is fraught with difficulties. One should keep trying and testing and arguing. If there is one impressive argument it is that morality and its consequences has increasing salience.

## Recommendations

First one would recommend that the problem of the veto be abolished. It is possible that it could be used for purposes other than what was intended. Second, the UN should be located in a neutral country (such as Switzerland or Sweden). It is recognised that it was, once, located in Switzerland – and should be relocated again. It is only by such means would it achieve its purpose of being seen as neutral. Third, the notion of being unforgiving is offset against the idea of requiring all members to conform to the precepts of the UN (or does the UN hope to influence the non-democratic regimes by having them onside (is it better to have them outside the tent spitting in, or better to have them inside the tent spitting out?).

At the national level there is a pressing need to have people governed by a Constitution. It is no good having a Constitution if it is ignored by the *status quo.* It is mandatory to have it applied consistently. On voting one would wish to see it done on a non-work day. The idea of having it on a weekday prevents many from taking time off work in order to vote. Further, every citizen should be on the roll. It is recognised that some jurisdictions even allow permanent residents to vote. As a matter of importance, it should rank number in compulsory voting. There is no more important decision to be made as to the selection of the next legislature. That is a matter for the country concerned. This should be one of the rules of law. It is, again, no good having a rule of law when, for example, hypocrisy denies it (one rule for me, another for you).

With this goes respect rather than reverence. There is a polite fiction that the royal family are ‘different’: they are also funded from the public purse: that is a justification provided some purpose is found. For example, it is not that it gives more power to one person, rather it cuts up the power by requiring ‘royal assent’ or ‘presidential agreement’.

With this goes a requirement: that of an investigative body and an express doctrine of human rights. As to the first it should be totally independent and requiring no exceptions (and would include parliamentarians, police, the judiciary, etc.).

Also, at the national level, is the issue of state school education. One could well imagine a place where the state runs the only school system. By such means may we ensure that all schools are properly funded and managed. There is a denial of privilege for those attending a non-state school, with the consequence of all requiring a commitment to state education without the deprivation of funds for the needy.

A final point is that the face-covering veil should be outlawed by the state. The idea that it applies to females only is anathema, further it denies the right to interpret reactions to commentary. The face being the main means of gauging reaction. On those twin grounds there is a case for banning. The case for requiring quotas for females has much to commend it. Banning the use of headshots, interviewing aspirant musicians behind screens, and requiring no indications of sex in job interviews should be mandatory. In terms of principle one is persuaded by the idea of ethical gradualism, and the power of education. As one is learning, only flagrant breaches of any code require prosecution. What is required is that the rule of law be mandatory, no exceptions permitted.

Above all, one needs two interdisciplinary and totally independent bodies: one of them is the indispensable charter of human rights (rather than legislating to fiddle on the fringes in legislating religious freedoms), other is the right to unfettered examination of ALL social institutions (police, courts, prisons, parliament, etc.) there should not be ANY exceptions. It is imperative that the members be totally independent of ALL other influences.

In most professional work excellence is judged, in part, by the ethical codes. Excellence is, however, more easily recognised than codified. It is seen as a journey as well as a destination; a process as well as an achievement. As Peters and Austin so aptly put it, ‘... excellence happens when high purpose and pragmatism meet’. Judgments are not made on single issues, but on overall evaluation. The difference between statesmen and party hacks is that the former has a broader vision, substantial confidence in their own insight, a constructive approach, and a moral tone to their views and behaviour.

There are some forms of professionalism in which sheer competence and art, dreamtime, and artistry are sufficient; musicianship, for example. In most forms of professionalism, however, values become significant. We do not accord to dictators the notion of excellence, despite their efficiency, dedication and list of accomplishments. Those to whom we accord excellence have commonly acted according to commonly accepted ethical standards. Over recent decades various theories of management have, as one of their unstated premises, the search for more ethical ways of doing things. Team work theories, Theory X and Theory Y, primary social motives, and the application of Swedish and Japanese methods have a common motivation.

One of the characteristics of excellent professionals is that they feel they live in an imperfect world; things are rarely as good as they should be. Given the frailties of human nature, the demands of time and of competing values, the solutions to almost all problems are less than perfect. The current commitment to total quality management, and best international practice, is a recent expression of that idea, transferred to the business context. There is no doubt that quality sells goods and services: it benefits an organisation in the longer term, but not the shorter term.

Excellence may be construed in the negative rather than the positive sense. A story that illustrates the unusual employment of the negative is that of a job applicant who, when asked to nominate two referees of good standing, named the Commissioner of Police and the Chief Magistrate. On the applicant's return interview he was told that neither the Commissioner nor the Chief Magistrate had ever heard of him. 'There,' said the applicant triumphantly, 'isn't that an excellent reference?' It is worth noting that the companies on the Peters and Waterman criteria were also market leaders in their respective and diverse fields. Excellence, including ethical excellence, is clearly profitable. To achieve potential, some values need to be emphasised and these include:

- The value of personal worth and self-esteem based on the uniqueness, significance and importance of the individual;
- the value of loving our neighbours, of esteeming them and promoting their growth and well-being rather than pursuing our own interests at the expense of those around us;
- the value of community and the responsibility of businesses to take the social and human dimension into their areas of shareholder accountability;

There is a caution that striving for excellence may produce a distortion. Take the example of a child driven to educational perfection by ambitious parents. The stress, the deprivation of childhood pleasures, and the due sense of proportion would be lost in the search for educational excellence. In international relations, the search for excellence in political systems could lead to intolerance of those who are striving for social justice in a less formal fashion.

Notwithstanding, with this caution in mind we might conclude that we are able to recognise the presence of excellence, it is possible that a quantified judgement can be made. Like love and enmity, wealth and poverty, rain and shine, we know it when we see it.

Excellence is both an achievement and a form of dedication, perhaps of passion. Although it is not possible to pronounce upon all its attributes, it might best be captured by the notion that excellence is a process as well as an achievement; ethics is one of the travel documents, as well as the destination. That same point is true also of morality. We shall argue that equality is a desirable moral quality, for both moral and non-moral reasons.

## Ethics Is a Changeable Condition

The notion that precepts may change is evident, express or implied. Works common to the area question whether equality is desirable. If it is then what type of equality to which we should aspire. Temkin's question is fundamental, and questions when is one situation worse than another with respect to inequality? He imagines three situations: many are free and prosperous and few badly off; a number are not free or well off; and a situation where the number of well off and badly off are about equal.

At first glance it would seem that a minority are strongly disadvantaged, the second is where many are oppressed, the third is where the oppressed and the free and prosperous are about equal. Here the fundamental question is 'are they equal'. Parfit's cases pose similar problems. In his work, that of a philosopher, many issues are canvassed, and some solutions contemplated. It is a work that would be of inestimable value to specialists in philosophy. Haidt's (2012) contribution to the debate on equality has his suggestions as sixfold, they are:

- Care (as distinct from harm)
- Fairness (as opposed to cheating)
- Liberty (as opposed to oppression)
- Loyalty (as opposed to betrayal)
- Authority and respect (as opposed to subversion)
- Sanctity (the opposite of degradation)

The basic message here is moral precepts may well change: what is acceptable at one time may be quite unacceptable at another. His approach puts less pressure on rationality and more on intuition, and may be subsequently modified by discussion. Three recent decisions have played a part in denying the previously endorsed principles: one is the notion of being terminally ill and allowed, with physician help, to die with dignity: a second one is that of putting legislative strictures on the treatment of animals: a third is the right to abortion under certain specified conditions (for example, in cases of rape). Such instances serve to remind us that moral precepts are fluid, and in constant need of re-consideration. It will be seen in the text that various views, the basis of morality are canvassed: all have merit, some more than others.

## Two Types of Intervention

The two tried and successful methods of social change are education and legislation. It is thus one might argue that early experiences are determinative, thus the value of education. Under such a view one can see the argument in favour of banning private schools, done on the grounds that having them promotes a sense of privilege and fosters inequality: history is replete with instances of creative genius that knows no origin.

With respect to legislation its power is in endorsing or banning certain actions, actions that have a significant effect. The notion that law-abiding is a prerequisite, one can see the power that such an approach had. Clearly there is much to overcome, but one would wish to see steady progress. Legal equivalences need to be matched by economic ones. There is still much to be done, but much to be accounted as genuine progress. One would hope that such legislation would be evidence based.

Of all the techniques that seem to work the one of gradualism takes precedence. No matter what the circumstances being gradual, and moving from one improvement to the next seems to meet with success. In professional work the one qualification that is enjoined is that some heinous and flagrant breaches should result in being struck off the register of both professional and as trustworthy. Notwithstanding, a gradual approach appears to be the one workable solution to social problems, while recognising that breaches of significant magnitude are deserving of legal sanctions.

One would envisage the setting up of agencies with a particular brief: and to do so with the specific brief of following moral rather than 'practical' situations. Thus, one would be devoted to jobs that did not involve the manufacture or sales of arms; nor follow the idea of setting up coal mines, or not allow land degradation. Just about all advances and benefits to the human condition are attributable to human well-intentioned intervention. This is true of everything from water supplies to high-level cultural pursuits, from health to improved environments. Such improvements would not happen were it not for those reformers who felt that they had a responsibility to humanity to improve the lot of their fellow-creatures. Thus, we might say that human rights have a complementary side - that of human responsibilities.

## The Overall Conclusion

The overall conclusion to be reached here is that, in the longer term, morals triumphs over economics. For example, slavery is now outlawed in every sovereign state (notwithstanding, slavery persists to this day). It is an irony that one of the countries strongly opposed, and indeed was engaged in a revolt against enslavement, is now one of the countries reputedly has one of the largest portions of enslavement. It is clear that the United Nations is implacably opposed to enslavement and carries it into one of the 1948 principles (Article 4).

What every country need are two issues: one is a bill of human rights; the second is a body of investigators. The first is an expression of basic human rights, written into the Constitution and free from the depredations of the law, and protected from those who would argue that it is open to interpretation. The second feature is an independent body that is capable of investigating breaches of the Constitution, and does so without any exceptions (police, the judiciary, parliamentarians, etc.).

It is also worth noting that in the third paragraph of the Preamble it refers to 'man' rather than to humanity. One presumes that this is meant in the generic sense whereas, as seen in the chapter on sex differences (it would have been improved by the clear understanding of 'man' embracing 'woman') as a fundamental press for equality. It is suggested here that voting power includes both men and women. It is only thus may one determine the wish of the electorate. There are arguments in favour of such a conclusion, but the most fundamental is that of morality: people should be equal, taken as a basic proposition. Because we may or may not ultimately succeed is no reason to stop trying to improve on the situation.

Written in 2019

# Appendix

**Table A1** Paired comparisons: example from the Delphi (or the nominal group technique). Here the presumption is that each variable is compared to each other variable: thus Principle 1 is compared respectively to Principle 2, 3, 4, & 5: Principle 2 to Principle 3, 4, & 5: Principle 3 to 4 & 5: and Principle 4 to Principle 5. The weighted results are from one of the comparisons. The weighted principles that emerge from one such analysis are:

| | Principle 1 | Principle 2 | Principle 3 | Principle 4 | Principle 5 |
|---|---|---|---|---|---|
| Person 1 | 5 | 2.5 | 2.5 | 5 | 4 |
| Person 2 | 5 | 3 | 1 | 2 | 4 |
| Person 3 | 4 | 1 | 3 | 2 | 5 |
| Person 4 | 3 | 2 | 4 | 1 | 5 |
| Person 5 | 2 | 4 | 3 | 1 | 5 |
| **Weighting** | 19 | 12.5 | 13.5 | 11 | 23 |
| **Order** | 2 | 4 | 3 | 5 | 1 |

The presumption is that the 1st ranking is worth more than a second ranking and so we weight the ranks. A 1st ranking gets a weighting of 5, a second ranking a weighting of 4, and third gets 3, and so on. This is rather like the way in which punters and tipsters on horse races have places weighted. If we add the weighted scores (bolded) we arrive at a weighting of those principles for that group. We may well find that financial probity scores highest, and honesty second (or the reverse). Openness and conflict of interest rank third equal. If need be, these numbers can be manipulated statistically. In this case it will observed that Principle 5 wins (whatever Principle 5 may be).

It is seen that a simpler, but less intuitive way, would be for the ranking of 1 for prime position, 2 for a second, and 3 for a third, etc. In such a case to lowest number would rank first, the second lowest would rank second, etc. It is noted that the paired comparisons technique is suitable only for a comparison of a relatively small number of variables, its main advantage is that it is a systematic way of ensuring that each Principle is compared to every other Principle.



R. Francis, *Equality in Theory and Practice*,
https://doi.org/10.1007/978-981-15-3488-1

The rule is that 5 variables in the paired comparisons set yields 10 comparisons: 6 variables yields 16 comparisons. From this it emerges that the addition of an extra variable increases the number of comparisons from 5 variables = 10 comparisons to 8 variables = 28 comparisons. Thus, the addition of an extra variable from 4 comparisons adds:

4 variables = 6 comparisons
5 variables = 10 comparisons
6 variables = 15 comparisons
7 variables = 21 comparisons
8 variables = 28 comparisons
9 variables = 36 comparisons

The assumption is made that comparing (say) 1 & 2 is the same as comparing 2 & 1. This may or may not be justified, but it is a reasonable assumption. For a guide the numbers are given above.

It is clear that it is a thoroughly systematic technique best suited to a limited variable array. Those wishing to learn more of this technique are recommended to consult books on group techniques. One good example contains several instances of the kind of problem for which the use of the Delphi technique is readily applicable. This a ready means of identifying the salient issues: it could also be used to compare such issues as honesty, promise keeping, hypocrisy, etc. To work this technique a reference group is chosen to select (say) the important ethical principles, that could then appear in the professional or company code.

As the reader will have gathered, this argument is a plea for more equality. It is incumbent on political experts to recognise that although we may not achieve true equality in our lifetime that is no reason for its non-attempt.

# References[1]


Ahl, H. (2006). Why research on women entrepreneurs needs new directions. *Entrepreneurship Theory and Practice, 30*(5), 595–621.

Albert, A. (1985). *Selective toxicity*. London: Chapman & Hall.

Allport, G. (1955). *Becoming*. New Haven: Yale UP.

Antidepressants. https://www.medicalnewstoday.com/articles/248320.php

Aoyama, K. (2009). *Thai migrant sexworkers: From modernisation to globalisation*. Basingstoke: Palgrave Macmillan.

Apostasy. http://www.pewresearch.org/facttank/2016/07/29/whichcountriesstilloutlawapostasyandblasphemy/

Aries, P. https://www.penguinrandomhouse.com/books/4744/the-hour-of-our-death-by-philipe-aries-translated-from-the-french-by-helen-weaver/

Arranged marriages see also 'forced marriage'. https://www.newidea.com.au/arranged-marriage-is-it-the-same-as-a-forced-marriage

Ashley, J. (1992). *Acts of defiance*. London: Penguin.

Attractiveness. (2006). *The Psychologist. 19*(4), 199.

Australian Institute of Criminology [AIC]. https://aic.gov.au/search/node/cald

Axelrod, R. (1980). *The evolution of cooperation*. New York: Basic Books.

Ball, P. (2016, April 4). How human sacrifice propped up the social order. *Nature*. https://www.nature.com/news/how-human-sacrifice-propped-up-the-social-order-1.19681. Accessed 1 May 2019.

Bangerter, A., & Heath, C. (2004). The Mozart effect: Tracking the evolution of a scientific legend. *British Journal of Social Psychology, 43*, 605–623.

Behrendt, L. (2003). *Achieving social justice: Indigenous rights and Australia's future*. Annandale: Federation Press.

Benedict, R. (1947). *The chrysanthemum and the sword*. London: Secker & Warburg.

Birx, H. J. (2005). *The encyclopedia of anthropology*. Thousand Oaks: Sage.

Blackmore, S. (1999). *The meme machine*. Oxford: Oxford University Press.

Bogumil, D. D. (2001). Attribution and reciprocity in international relations: The attribution reciprocity model. *North American Journal of Psychology, 3*(3), 463–481.

Bouazizi, M. https://www.britannica.com/biography/MohamedBouazizi

Bribe Payers Index. https://www.transparency.org/research/bpi

Brinkman, R., & Kirschner, R. (2012). *Dealing with people you can't stand*. New York: McGraw Hill.


[1]All websites and references checked as at 20/12/2019.



R. Francis, *Equality in Theory and Practice*,
https://doi.org/10.1007/978-981-15-3488-1

Cadbury, D. (2012). *Chocolate wars*. New York: US Public Affairs.
Callinicos, A. (2000). *Equality*. Cambridge: Polity Press.
Cantril, A. H. http://news.gallup.com/poll/122453/understandinggallupusescantrilscale.aspx
Cherry, S. (2016). Lust and gluttony may be obvious sins. But do not forget control and certainty. *Cambridge Alumni Magazine*. Easter, Issue 78.
Christie, R., Geis, F. L., Festinger, L., & Schachter, S. (Eds.). (1970). *Studies in Machiavellianism*. New York: Academic.
Circumcision. https://www.mayoclinic.org/tests-procedures/circumcision/about/pac-20393550
Citizens Bank of Canada: Since changed it name to Vancity Community Investment Bank. https://www.vancitycommunityinvestmentbank.ca/#copy
Cole, J., & Spalding, H. (2009). *The invisible smile*. Oxford: Oxford University Press.
Connors, M. K., & Hewison, K. (2008). Thailand's 'good coup': The fall of Thaksin, the military democracy. *Journal of Contemporary Asia, 38*(1), 110.
Constitutional reform. https://www.google.com.au/search?source=hp&ei=dS78Xdz5GdXA3LUPkKiziAk&q=democracy+without+political+parties&oq=Democracy+without+political+parties&gs_l=psy-ab.1.0.0j0i22i30l2.3096.27289..32833...0.0..0.1694.15147.0j6j10j11j1j1j3j1j2......0....1..gws-wiz.......0i131.H0BiuRj8__o
Cooray, A. V., & Schneider, F. (2014). *Does corruption promote emigration? An empirical examination* (IZA discussion Paper No. 8094). SSRN: http://ssrn.com/abstract=2424193
Cormack, D. (1991). *Excellence at work*. Corby: British Institute of Management.
Corruption: Transparency International. https://www.transparency.org/news/feature/corruption_perceptions_index_2016. (Higher numbers = lesser corruption)
Corruption. www.transparency.org/country
Darwin, C. (1859). *On the origin of species*. London: John Murray.
Darwin, C. (1872). *The expression of emotion in man and animals*. London: HarperCollins.
Davies, J. B., Sandstrom, S., Shorrocks, A., & Wolff, E. N. (2008a). *The world distribution of household wealth* (WIDER Discussion Paper, No. 2008/03). Helsinki: UN University/Leibnitz Information Centre for Economics. Also at https://www.econstor.eu/bitstream/10419/84667/1/659523361.pdf
Davies, J., Llberas, R., & Shorrocks, R. F. (2008b). *Measuring the global distribution of wealth*. https://www.oecd.org/site/worldforumindia/Davies.pdf
de Graaf, G., & Huberts, L. W. J. C. (2008). Portraying the nature of corruption using an explorative case study design. *Public Administration Review, 68*(4), 640–653.
Death. http://users.clas.ufl.edu/davidson/arch%20of%20death/week%2011/aries%201974.pdf
Declaration of Human Rights. https://www.un.org/en/udhrbook/pdf/udhr_booklet_en_web.pdf
Denniss, R. (2016). *Econobabble: How to decode political spin and economic nonsense*. Carlton: Black Inc..
Dimant, E., Krieger, T., & Meierricks, D. (2013). The effect of corruption on migration. *Applied Economics Letters, 20*(13), 1270127.
Discrimination against women: (see also Women's rights). https://www.pciglobal.org/discriminationagainstwomen/
Displaced persons. http://www.unhcr.org/558193896.html
Divorce in Islam. https://www.alislam.org/islamiclawsayatullahalialhusaynialsistani/divorce
Domestic violence. http://www.unwom-en.org/en/whatwedo/endingviolenceagainstwomen/factsandfigures
Dorling, D. (2012). *No nonsense guide to equality*. Oxford: New Internationalist.
Easteal, P. (1994). Addressing violence against women in the home: How far have we come? How far to go? *Family Matters, 37*, 8693.
Easterlin, R. https://esrc.ukri.org/about-us/50-years-of-esrc/50-achievements/the-easterlin-paradox/
Education, schooling in years. https://www.infoplease.com/world/world-statistics/school-years-around-world

Education: UN Development Program. http://hdr.undp.org/en/content/educationindex. (higher numbers = longest [best] education)

Education and corruption: See Heyneman.

Ekman, P. (1985). *Telling lies: Clues to deceit in the marketplace, politics, and marriage*. New York: W.W. Norton & Company.

Enslaving nations. https://www.forbes.com/sites/niallmccarthy/2016/05/31/the-countries-with-the-most-people-living-in-slavery-infographic/#1fa347d21b12

Equality of the sexes in the Torah. http://thetorah.com/genderequalityatcreation/

Erikson, K. (1966). *The wayward puritans*. New York: Wiley.

Face recognition. (2009, July). *The Psychologist*, 571.

Facing up to expression. (2015). *The Psychologist*. 28(9), 701.

Fascism and Popper. https://www.iep.utm.edu/popp-pol/

Female genital mutilation (FGM). http://www.meforum.org/1629/isfemalegenitalmutilationanislamicproblem

Ferracuti, F. (1968). *European migration and crime: Collected studies in criminological research*. Strasbourg: Council of Europe.

Finzi, E. (2013). *How Botox affects our moods and relationships*. Basingstoke: Palgrave Macmillan.

Fogarty, M. P. (1963). *Working together: A commentary on the Marlow declaration*. Oxford: Catholic Social Guild.

Folbre, N. (1994). *Who pays for the kids? Gender and the structures of constraint*. London: Routledge.

Forced marriage. https://www.google.com/search?client=firefoxbd&q=forced+marriages

Foreign born population. http://www.pewglobal.org/interactives/migrationtables/

Fragile states index. http://fundforpeace.org/fsi/2017/05/14/fsi2017factionalizationandgroupgrievancefuelriseininstability/

Francis, R. D. (2014a). Assumptions and deeming. *Journal of Financial Crime, 21*(2), 204–214.

Francis, R. D. (2014b). *Birthplace, migration, and crime*. Basingstoke: Palgrave Macmillan.

Francis, R. D., & Armstrong, A. F. (2012). *Meetings: Formal rules and informal guides*. London: Anthem Press.

Frank, R. H. (2016). *Success and luck: Good fortune and the myth of meritocracy*. Princeton: Princeton University Press.

Frankfurt, H. (1987). Equality as a moral ideal. *Ethics, 98*(1), 21–43.

Friedman, T. L. (2000). *The lexus and the olive tree*. New York: Anchor Books.

Gangestad, S. W., & Scheyd, G. J. (2005). The evolution of human physical attractiveness. *Annual Review of Anthropology, 34*, 523–548.

Gardner, M. (1960, January). *Mathematical puzzles and games*. Numerology. Scientific American.

Gender gap: Interparliamentary union. https://www.undp.org/content/dam/undp/library/Democratic%20Governance/Global_Parliamentary_Report_English.pdf

Geneva Convention. https://www.redcross.org.au/get-involved/take-action/take-action-on-an-issue/what-is-international-humanitarian-law?gclid=EAIaIQobChMIxqLB2p_D5gIVzhwrCh3wTw-TEAAYASAAEgLR7fD_B

Giles, K. (1994). The Biblical argument for slavery: A case study in hermeneutics. *Evangelical Quarterly, 66*(1), 317.

Gulf states. https://www.chathamhouse.org/research/regions/middle-east-and-north-africa/gulf-states

Gladwell, M. (2006). *Blink*. London: Penguin.

Global Peace Index: Institute for economics and peacehttp://visionofhumanity.org/app/uploads/2017/06/GPI17Report.pdf.

Goleman, D. (1997). *Emotional intelligence*. New York: Bantam Books.

Goodey, J. (2003). Migration, crime and victimhood: Responses to sex trafficking in the EU. *Punishment & Society, 5*(4), 415–431.

Grabosky, P. N. (1996). Paradoxical cause. Unintended consequences of crime prevention. In R. Homel & R. Clarke (Eds.), *Crime prevention studies* (Vol 5). Administration, compliance and governability program. Research School of Social Sciences. Australian National University.

Guantanamo Bay. https://theintercept.com/2019/08/30/guantanamo-bay-press-restrictions/ and https://casebook.icrc.org/case-study/united-states-habeas-corpus-guantanamo-detainees

Gulf states GDP and population. https://www.chathamhouse.org/research/regions/middle-east-and-north-africa/gulf-states

Gulnaz. https://edition.cnn.com/2015/04/07/asia/afghanistan-gulnaz-rape-marriage/index.html

Haidt, J. (2012). *The righteous mind: Why good people are divided by politics and religion.* New York: Pantheon.

Hammersely, R., Khan, F., & Ditton, J. (2002). *Ecstasy and the rise of the chemical generation.* London: Routledge.

Happiness. http://worldhappiness.report/ed/2018/ (higher numbers = happiest)

Hare, R. D. (1991). *The hare psychopathy checklist revised.* Toronto: MultiHealth Systems.

Hayek, F. A. (1960). *The constitution of liberty.* Chicago: Chicago UP.

Hearnshaw, L. S. (1951). Exploring the intellect. *British Journal of Psychology, 42*, 315–321.

Herrera, A. M., L. Lijane, and P. Rodriguez. Bribery and the nature of corruption.

Hess, E. H. (1965). Attitude and pupil size. *Scientific American, 212*(4), 46–54.

Heylighen, F. *The science of self-organization and adaptivity.* http://pespmc1.vub.ac.be/Papers/EOLSSSelfOrganiz.pdf

Heyneman, S. P. (2004). Education and corruption. *International Journal of Educational Development, 24*(6), 637–648.

Hilton, J. *Lost horizons* (any edition).

Hobhouse, H. (1985). *The seeds of change.* London: Sidgwick & Jackson.

Hofstede, G., Hofstede, G. J., & Minkov, M. (2010). *Cultures and organisations: Software of the mind.* New York: McGraw Hill.

Hong Kong. http://www.icac.hk/en/law_enforcement/acl/poborcps/index.html and http://www.icac.org.hk/en/law/law/index.html; https://www.gov.hk/en/about/abouthk/factsheets/docs/icac.pdf

Honour killing. https://www.unodc.org/documents/justiceandprisonreform/UNODC.CCPCJ.EG.8.2014.2English.pdf

Human Relations Area Files. http://hraf.yale.edu/about/; http://hraf.yale.edu/wpcontent/uploads/2013/11/HRAFUserGuidev1.pdf

Human trafficking. https://www.unodc.org/unodc/en/humantrafficking/whatishumantrafficking.html

Hume, D. (1739, 1740). *Enquiries concerning human understanding.* Oxford: Clarendon Press.

Huxley, A. (1954). *The doors of perception.* London: Chatto & Windus.

International convention on refugee rights and statelessness. http://www.unhcr.org/enau/1951refugeeconvention.html

Jain, A. K. (1980). *Economics of corruption.* New York: Springer.

James, W. (1981). *Principles of psychology.* Cambridge: Harvard UP.

Jones, D. (2013). Social evolution: The ritual animal. *The Lancet, 493*, 470–472.

Jones, J. https://www.biography.com/people/jimjones10367607

Justman, S. (2005). *Fool's paradise: The unreal world of pop psychology.* Chicago: Ivan R Dee.

Kahneman, D., & Deaton, A. (2010). High income improves evaluation of life but not emotional wellbeing. *Proceedings of the National Academy of Science, 107*(38), 16489–16493.

Kohlberg, L. https://www.google.com/search?client=firefoxbd&q=kohlberg

Kringelbach, M. L., & Berridge, K. C. (2010). The functional neuroanatomy of pleasure and happiness. *Discovery Medicine, 9*(49), 579–587.

Kubler-Ross, E. (2011/1997). *Living with death and dying.* New York: Touchstone.

Kumari, M. https://www.amnesty.org.uk/india-dalit-sisters-protection-raped-punishment-brothers-crime*

Lanchester, J. (2010). *Whoops!* London: Allen Lane.

Laski, M. (1961). *Ecstasy*. London: Cresset Press.

Lea, S., Burgoyne, C., Webley, P., & Young, P. (2002). The economy. *The Psychologist, 15*(1), 1820.

Lester, D. (2013). Measuring Maslow's hierarchy of needs. *Psychological Reports, 113*(1), 15–17.

Levitt, S. D., & Dubner, S. J. (2005). *Freakonomics: A rogue economist explores the hidden side of everything*. New York: Harper Collins.

Lloyd, T. (1991). *The 'nice' company*. London: Bloomsbury.

Lockhart, C. (2015). *The law of misleading or deceptive conduct* (4th ed.). Chatswood: LexisNexis.

Longevity. https://www.cia.gov/library/publications/theworldfactbook/rankorder/2102rank.html (average age at death)

Lorenz, K. (1949). *King Solomon's ring*. London: Routledge.

Lovelock, J. E. (1979). *Gaia: A new look at life on earth*. Oxford: Oxford University Press.

Lovelock, J. E. (1982). *The ages of Gaia*. New York: Norton.

Lovelock, J. E. (2000). *Homage to Gaia*. Oxford: Oxford University Press.

Lovelock, J. E. (2006). *The revenge of Gaia*. Melbourne: Allen Lane.

Lutz, H. (1991). The myth of the 'other': Western representation and images of migrant women of so called 'Islamic background'. *Review of Sociology, 2*(2), 121–137.

Lynn, R. (1971). *Personality and national character*. Oxford: Pergamon.

Mabo case. https://aiatsis.gov.au/explore/articles/mabo-case

Macchiavelli, N. (1532). *The prince*. (various reprints).

Malthus, T. (1798). *An essay on the principles of population*. London: Johnson.

Marmot, M. (2005). Social determinants of health inequalities. *The Lancet, 365*(9464), 1099–1104.

Marriage. http://www.theguardian.com/world/2011/dec/01/afghanwomanfreedmarryrapist

Martin, F. (2013). *Money: The unauthorised biography*. Oxford: Bodley Head.

Maslow, A. http://psychclassics.yorku.ca/Maslow/motivation.htm

Matthews, R. (1998, May 23). Hidden truths. *New Scientist*, (2135), 28.

Mayer, A. E. (2007). *Islam and human rights*. Colorado: Westview Press.

McSally. http://edition.cnn.com/2002/US/01/24/airforce.suit.saudi.cnna/index.html?related

Meiwes, A. https://www.theguardian.com/world/2003/dec/04/germany.lukeharding

Milgram, S. (1963). Behavioral study of obedience. *The Journal of Abnormal and Social Psychology, 67*(4), 371–378.

Milgram, S. (1967). The small world problem. *Psychology Today, 2*, 60–67.

Miller, G. A. (1956). The magical number seven plus or minus two: Some limits on our capacity for processing information. *Psychological Review, 101*(2), 343–352.

Missions to the UN. https://www.un.org/globalcall/content/united-nations-missions

Mondragon. https://www.mondragon-corporation.com/en/about-us/

Moore, G. E. (1903). *Principia ethica*. Cambridge: Cambridge University Press.

More, T. (1903). *Utopia*. Chiswick Press (London: Translated from the Latin).

Morris, D. (1977/2002). *Peoplewatching: The Desmond Morris guide to body language Jonathon Cape*. London.

Mugabe. https://www.biography.com/political-figure/robert-mugabe

Murdock, G. P., & Provost, C. A. (1973). Measurement of cultural complexity. *Ethnology, 12*(4), 379–392.

Napoleon, did he abolish slavery. https://www.biography.com/political-figure/robert-mugabe

Napoleoni, L. (2016). *Merchants of men*. New York: Random House.

Naughton, J. (2001). *A brief history of the future: From radio days to internet years in a lifetime*. New York: Overlook Press.

Neiderman, A. (2008). *Deadly verdict*. London: Severn house.

Nwanna, G. I. (1998). *The do's and don'ts around the world: A country to culture social taboos, and etiquette*. Baltimore: World Travel Institute.

Olds, J., & Milner, P. (1954). Positive reinforcement produced by electrical stimulation of septal area and other regions of rat brain. *Journal of Comparative and Physiological Psychology, 47*(6), 419–427.

O'Neil, C. (2016). *Weapons of math destruction*. London: Allen Lane.

Orwell, G. (1941/2018). *The lion and the unicorn*. London: Penguin.

Oxford companion to music. (1979). (P. A. Scholes, Ed., 10th ed.). Oxford University Press, Oxford.

Pakistan's mission to the UN. http://www.pakun.org/Pakistan%20at%20the%20UN/

Parfit, D. (2011). *On what matters*. Oxford: Oxford University Press.

Parkinson, B. (2017, June). Faces in the wild. *The Psychologist*, 59–64.

Passalecq, G., & Suchecky, B. (1997). *The hidden encyclical of Pius XI*. New York: Harcourt Brace.

Pavlov. https://www.revolvy.com/main/index.php?s=Pavlov%27s%20typology&item_type=topic

Peace. http://visionofhumanity.org/app/uploads/2017/06/gpi17report.pdf

Peters, T. J., & Austin, N. (1985). *A passion for excellence*. New York: Random House.

Peters, T. J., & Waterman, R. H. (1982). *In search of excellence*. New York: Harper Business.

Peterson, J. B. (2018). *Twelve rules for life: An antidote to chaos*. Toronto: Random House.

Phillips, L. D., & Wright, G. N. (1979). *Cultural differences in the assessment of the communication of uncertainty*. London: Social Science Research Council.

Pillay, S., & Dorasamy, N. (2010). Linking cultural dimensions with the nature of corruption: An institutional theory perspective. *International Journal of Crosscultural Management, 10*(3), 363–378.

Pinker, S. (2011). *The better angels of our nature: The decline of violence in history and its causes*. Harmondsworth: Allen Lane (Penguin).

Polygamy. https://www.google.com/search?client=firefoxbd&q=polygamy

Popper, K. (1945). *The open society and its enemies*. London: Routledge.

Porter, L. E., & Warrender, C. (2009). A multivariate model of police deviance: Examining the nature of corruption, crime and misconduct. *Policing and society: An International Journal of Research and Policy, 19*(1), 79–99.

Qutami, R. V. (2001, June 28). New South Wales Court of Criminal Appeal, NSWCCA, p. 353.

Rajneesh.https://www.carmrades-blog.com/all-articles/2016/10/2/the-story-of-the-rolls-royce-guru

Rawls, J. (1971). *A theory of justice* (Rev. ed. 1999). Boston: Harvard UP.

Refugees and stateless persons. https://treaties.un.org/pages/ViewDetailsII.aspx?src=TREATY&mtdsg_no=V3&chapter=5&Temp=mtdsg2&clang=_en

Ridley, M. (1996). *The origins of virtue*. London: Viking.

Rio Declaration. (1992). Earth summit. Rio declaration and forest principles. *UN Conference on Environment and Development UNCED*.

Rizzolati, G., & Craighero, L. (2004). The mirror-neuron system. *Annual Review of Neuroscience, 27*, 169–192.

Ruhe, J., & Lee, M. (2008). Teaching ethics in international business courses: The impacts of religions. *Journal of Teaching in International Business, 19*(4), 362–388.

Runciman, D. (2008). *Political hypocrisy: The mask of power, from Hobbes to Orwell and beyond*. Princeton: Princeton UP.

Salerno, S. (2005). *Sham: How the selfhelp movement made America helpless*. New York: Three Rivers Press.

Seale, C. (2000). Changing patterns of death and dying. *Social Science and Medicine, 51*(6), 917–930.

Segrave, M., Milivojevic, S., & Pickering, S. (2009). *Sex trafficking: International context and response*. Cullompton: Willan Publishing.

Seligman, M. E. P. (1972). Learned helplessness. *Annual Review of Medicine, 23*, 407–412.

Seligman, M. E. P. (2002). *'Authentic' happiness*. New York: Simon & Schuster.

Seligman, M. E. P. (2011). *Learned optimism*. New York: Knopf Doubleday.

Sheldrake, R. https://www.sheldrake.org/research/morphic-resonance

Sinclair, W. A. (1951). *Traditional formal logic*. London: Methuen.

Singer, P. (1976). *Animal liberation*. New York: Harper Collins.

Singer, E., & Hudson, V. (1992). Conclusion: Political psychology/foreign policy, the cognitive revolution, and international relations. In E. Singer & V. Hudson (Eds.), *Political psychology and foreign policy*. Boulder: Colorado: Westview Press.

Slavery. Borgen project: https://borgenproject.org/10statisticsonslaverytoday/; End Slavery Now: https://www.endslaverynow.org/learn; Free the slaves: https://www.freetheslaves.net/; Global slavery index: http://www.globalslaveryindex.org; Walk free: https://www.walkfreefoundation.org/aboutus/

Smith, A. (1776). *The wealth of nations*. London: Methuen.

Smith, N. (2011). *Basic equality and discrimination: Reconciling theory and law*. Farnham: Ashgate.

Smith, P. B., Dugan, S., & Trompenaars, F. (1996). National culture and the values of organisational employees. *Journal of Cross-Cultural Psychology, 27*(2), 231–264.

Social determinants of Health. http://www.who.int/social_determinants/sdh_definition/en/

Soreide, T., & Williams, A. (Eds.). (2015). *Corruption, grabbing and development*. Cheltenham: Edward Elgar.

Stiglitz, J. E. (2013). *The price of inequality*. London: Penguin.

Stivers, R. (2008). *The illusion of freedom and equality*. Albany: State of NY press.

Stohl, M., Lichbach, M. I., & Grabosky, P. N. (2017). *States and peoples in conflict*. London: Routledge.

Storr, A. (1996). *Feet of clay: Saints, sinners and madmen: A study of gurus*. New York: Free Press.

Sutherland, K. (on sortition). https://www.newdemocracy.com.au/docs/researchpapers/What%20Sortition%20Can%20Do%20PSA.pdf

Swami, V., & Furnham, A. (2007). *The body beautiful*. Basingstoke: Palgrave Macmillan.

Temkin, L. S. (1993). *Inequality*. New York: Oxford University Press.

Teplov B M. (1964). *Pavlov's typology* (J. A. Gray, Trans.). New York: Macmillan.

Thomas, M. S. C. (2017, May). A scientific strategy for life chances. *The Psychologist, 30,* 22–25.

Toffler, A. (1970). *Future shock*. New York: Bantam Books (Random House).

Transparency International (history). https://www.transparency.org/files/content/ourorganisation/ShortBio_PeterEigen_EN.pdf

Transparency International/country (on corruption). www.transparency.org/country

Travers, J., & Milgram, S. (1969). An experimental study of the small world problem. *Sociometry, 32*(4), 425–443.

Trigg, R. (2012). *Equality, freedom, and religion*. Oxford: Oxford University Press.

UNODC: Toolkit to combat trafficking in persons. https://www.unodc.org/unodc/en/human-trafficking/2008/electronic-toolkit/electronic-toolkit-to-combat-trafficking-in-persons%2D%2D-index.html

Utopia. https://www.sparknotes.com/philosophy/utopia/summary/

Van Reybrouck, D. (2016). *Against elections: The case for democracy*. Oxford: Bodley Head.

Vancity bank. https://www.vancity.com/

Veto power at UN. https://www.securitycouncilreport.org/un-security-council-working-methods/the-veto.php

Violence against women. http://www.who.int/mediacentre/factsheets/fs239/en/

Volkswagen. https://www.google.com/search?client=firefox-b-d&q=vw+martin+winterkorn+ceo

Wacks, R. (2012). *Understanding jurisprudence*. Oxford: Oxford University Press.

Watts, D. J. (2003). *Six degrees: The science of a connected age*. London: Heinemann.

White, J., & Taft, S. (2004). Frameworks for teaching and learning business ethics within the global context: Background of ethical theories. *Journal of Management Education, 28*(4), 463–477.

White, S. G. (2007). *Equality*. Cambridge: Polity Press.

WHO. (2003). https://www.google.com/search?client=firefox-b-d&q=World+Health+Organisation

Wilkinson, L. P. (1979). *Classical attitudes to modern issues*. London: Kimber.

Wilkinson, R., & Pickett, K. (2009). *The spirit level: Why more equal societies almost always do better*. London: Penguin.

Winchester, S. (2002). *The map that changed the world.* London: Penguin.
Women in legislature (%). http://archive.ipu.org/wmn-e/classif.htm
Women's rights. https://www.globalfundforwomen.org/womenshumanrights/
Wood V (2007). *Victoria's empire.* London: Headline Publishing.
Wootton, B. (1963). *Social science and social pathology.* London: Allen & Unwin.
World Bank comments on corruption. https://www.worldbank.org/en/topic/governance/brief/anti-corruption
World Happiness Report. http://worldhappiness.report/
World population. https://www.worldometers.info/world-population/
World's worst sound. http://mentalfloss.com/article/13065/11worstsoundsworld
Zhou, Y., Divya, J. S., Topping, K., & Todman, J. (2008). Theoretical models of culture shock and adaptation in international students in higher education. *Studies in Higher Education, 33*(1), 63–75.
Zimbardo, P., Maslach, C., & Haney, C. (2000). *Obedience to authority: Current perspectives on the Milgram paradigm.* New Jersey: Erlbaum.
Zimmer, C. (2008 October 15). *Darwin would have loved Botox.* Discover (the magazine of science, technology, and the future).

# Index

**A**
Abortion, 2, 13, 28, 30–32, 117, 142, 174, 179, 217
Accountability, 7, 96, 118, 156, 199, 216
Aesthetics, 25–26, 38, 91–92
Africa, *see* Sub-Saharan Africa
Altruism, 42–43, 46, 47, 58, 180
Animals, 13, 21, 25, 44, 51, 70, 98, 131, 136, 159, 179, 205, 217
Apartheid, 12, 72
Apparent movement, 39
Aristotle, 54, 56, 180, 193, 203
Assumptions, 49, 54–56, 63, 75, 89, 95, 98, 99, 118, 179, 222
Aversions, 44

**B**
Ballot box, 8, 106, 119, 130, 133, 135, 137, 155
Becoming, 51, 84, 126, 143, 157, 202
Bible (the), 19, 33, 100, 110, 154, 183, 184
Binet, 56
Blackbirding, 158, 164
Botox injections, 95
Brain development, 24
Breaking on the wheel, 186
Bribery, 107, 110–111, 114, 117, 206
Business decisions, 84–85

**C**
Capitalism, 69, 119, 120, 132, 136
Capture - recapture, 205
Challenging assumption, 193
Charlie Hebdo, 53, 109
Chartism, 79
Children transported, 158
Chocolate, 24, 78
Churchill, 47, 122
Climate change, 5, 19, 30, 68, 70, 206, 208, 212, 213
Cocoa, 23, 24, 78
Code of conduct/code of ethics–distinction, 2, 3, 64, 80, 89, 197
Coffee, 23
Cohabitation, 149
*Colombo plan*, 131, 136
Colonial past, 31
Commerce, 19, 89, 208
Commonwealth (the Old), 47, 49, 76, 111, 131, 136, 152, 153
Commonwealth of nations, 15, 61
Communication, 33, 40, 84, 91–104, 140–146, 201
Communism, 69
Compulsory voting, 214
Conclusions, 13, 14, 16–18, 32, 39, 47, 48, 53, 62, 67, 69, 75–76, 82, 89, 92, 93, 98, 101, 103, 104, 111, 117, 118, 137, 149–150, 164–165, 167, 169, 174, 176–177, 183, 203, 205–209, 211–219
Conflict of interest, 88, 111–113, 121, 221
Conscience vote, 123, 128, 210
Consequentialism, 179, 181–182
Conspiracy theories, 183
Constitutional change, 129
Contraception, 28, 31, 32, 143, 207
Corruption, 6, 10, 11, 57, 61, 83, 98, 105–114, 116–118, 129, 131, 136, 162, 167, 169, 171
Cotton, 23, 24, 163


R. Francis, *Equality in Theory and Practice*,
https://doi.org/10.1007/978-981-15-3488-1

Courtesy, 14, 55, 61, 66, 74, 86, 94, 99, 107–108
Cross-cultural socialising, 74
Culturally adverse discrimination, 64, 94, 140, 148, 150
Culture, 11, 24, 25, 34–37, 40, 49, 50, 61, 63–76, 92–94, 100, 105, 112, 114, 117, 120, 130, 134, 139–144, 147, 148, 150, 156, 164, 165, 207, 208
Culture and race confounded, 63

**D**
Darwin, 9–10, 20–23, 46, 47, 98, 201
Darwinism, 21, 182
Data matching, 15, 67, 183
Death, 11, 33, 34, 41, 45, 46, 53, 69, 99, 124, 142, 153, 154, 159, 160, 213
Deceit, 10, 113–114, 116, 172
Declaration of human rights, *see* UN Declaration
Definitions of corruption, 105
Delphi technique, 175–177, 222
Deontology, 180–181
Developmental studies, 98–100
Dimensions of corruption, 106, 112–114, 116, 118
Distributive justice, 203
DNA, 19
Drones, 67, 183
Dying with dignity, 2, 179, 210

**E**
Econo-babble, 88
Economic commentators, 13, 34, 88, 152, 213
Economic imperialism, 34
Economic power, 8, 12, 34, 109
Ecstasy, 35–38
Education, 7, 31, 32, 44, 62, 81, 83, 85, 86, 106, 113, 126, 130, 131, 134–136, 164, 167, 171, 184, 202, 207, 213, 215, 217
Emoji, 94
Emotional intelligence, 60, 211
Empathy, 34, 44, 50, 60
Enfranchisement, 95
Ethical personality, 56
Eugenics, 20, 28
Excellence, 6–7, 44–45, 52, 82, 83, 209, 215, 216
Expatriates, 73, 75, 97
Eysenck Personality Inventory, 56

**F**
Face, 93, 94, 98, 140, 141
Face and culture, 61, 66, 69, 70
Face veil, 139, 150, 209
Facial expression, 21, 93–96, 98, 103, 104, 140, 141, 150
Factor analysis, 173, 174
Factors in business, 84
Failed states, 15, 54, 83, 124, 181
Faith, 147, 172, 210
Fasces, 120
Fascism, 119
Fashions, 40, 41, 50, 64, 78, 216
Female genital mutilation, 142, 143
Female prime ministers, 139
Fertility, 29, 142–143, 207, 209
Forced marriage, 145, 149, 160–163
Franchising, 123, 145
Freedom of expression, 85
Freud, 194

**G**
Gaia, 9, 22, 23
Gambling, 147, 150
Gay marriage, 129
Gaze, 92, 94, 140, 141
Generous spirited, money mean (GSMM), 52
Gestures, 21, 92, 93, 140
Gifts, 3, 87, 107
Gini index, 20, 31, 167
Glass ceiling, 18, 87, 139, 149
*Golden rule*, 8
Grading of slavery, 163–164
Gradualism, 1, 215, 218
Gross domestic product (GDP), 11, 82, 83, 106
Guanxi, 76
Gulf states, 11, 29
Gurus, 45

**H**
Habit, 59–60, 63, 146, 147, 204, 205
Haidt, 12, 13, 203, 217
Happiness, 111, 167–171, 181, 184, 201, 203
Health, 24–25, 83, 86, 111, 119, 127, 130, 132, 134–136, 174, 184, 205, 218
Hedonism, 181
Hierarchy of needs, 38
Hobhouse, 20, 23–24, 160, 201
Homosexual, 139, 149

Homosexual marriage, 100, 129
Hong Kong, 98, 106–107, 130, 135
Honour killing, 144, 208
Human Relations Area Files, 75
Hume, 182
Huxley, 36, 37
Hypocrisy, 54, 110, 113–116, 118, 156, 214, 222

I
Imprisonment, 86, 126, 147, 149
Income disparity, 8, 31, 212
Independence (political), 7, 8, 11, 12, 14, 23, 25, 26, 29, 40, 44, 49, 56, 61, 62, 66, 67, 70, 80, 87, 92, 98, 105, 107, 113, 114, 119–125, 127–129, 132–134, 136, 137, 144, 149, 180, 181, 184, 201, 202, 204, 206, 213, 216
Indigenous, 30, 64, 125, 184, 211
Inequality (types of), 53, 56, 71, 106, 112, 207, 212, 217–218
International language, 97
Introversion/Extraversion, 55
Island states, 5

J
Jung, 194
Just war, *see* War (just)

K
Kant, 180, 203
Keller (Helen), 38, 95
Kohlberg, 184–185, 203, 209
Koran (the), 33
Korte's laws, 39

L
Language, 25–27, 40, 63, 65, 73, 88, 92, 95–97, 99–101, 103, 104, 111, 147–149, 157, 158
Law and custom, 148–149
Legislation/parliament, 159
Lobbying, 7, 29, 122, 202, 206
Longevity, 167, 169, 171
Lorenz, 44
Lovelock, 9–10, 20, 22–23, 201
Luck, 58, 59, 62
Lying, 96, 140, 173

M
Mabo, 30
Machiavellianism, 59
Malthus, 20, 29, 143, 201
Maps, 15, 27, 93, 162
*Marlow Declaration*, 77
Marxism, 10
Maslow, 38
Media, 5, 27, 66, 69, 74, 84, 85, 93, 99, 104
Mill, J.S., 181
Minimal principles, 197
Minnesota Multiphasic Personality Inventory (MMPI), 56
Mirror neurons, 25
Misuse of power, 116–117
Möbius Syndrome, 140
Modern approaches, 183–184
Mondo Cane and Mondo Pazzo, 70
Mondragon, 36, 37, 209
Money matters, 81–83
Moody
  Standard & Poor, 88
Moral approaches, 15, 60
Moral dilemmas, 30, 108, 109, 115, 116, 118, 159, 172, 173, 176, 179, 183, 205, 206, 209
Moral obligations, 130–131, 135–136
Moral personality, 211–212
Mozart effect, 74
Multi-culturalism, 65, 70
Musical ability, 148

N
National character, 50, 174
National obsessions, 208
Naturalistic fallacy, 182, 206
Neuro-linguistic programming, 100
Neurology, 36, 37
New Lanark, 36, 37, 77–78, 208
Nominal group technique, 175, 221
Non-verbal communication, 56, 92–94, 101, 103, 104, 111, 140
Numerology, 187

O
Obedience, 14, 33, 204
Old boy network (the) Guanxi, 76
*Open society and its enemies*, 119
Organisational commitment, 71, 72, 132, 136, 216

**P**
Pain and suffering, 17, 203
Pair by pair comparisons, 171, 173, 177, 221, 222
Paradoxes, 46, 210–211
Parfit, 12, 185, 203, 217
Parliamentary democracy, 95, 118, 206, 207, 212
Pavlov, 50
Peace, 3, 17, 31, 33, 35, 37, 46, 74, 124, 132, 136, 167, 171
Personality, 7, 12, 38, 49–62, 66, 68, 73, 100, 104, 109, 180, 184, 202
Phi phenomenon, 39, 204
Physical abuse, 61
Physical factors, 19, 49, 203
Pleasure centres, 35
Political power, 8, 13, 61, 109, 116, 119, 133, 137, 202
Political rectitude, 58–59, 124–126
Polyandry, 129, 139, 146, 149
Polygamy, 28, 129, 139, 146–147, 149
Pop psychology, 1, 64
Population, 2, 5, 8, 11, 12, 17, 19, 20, 27–31, 66, 72, 79, 85, 112, 114, 118, 120, 141–143, 147, 157, 161, 162, 164, 203, 205–207, 212, 213
Power of veto at UN, 125
President, 123, 124, 128, 129, 134, 154, 210
Press gangs, 61, 157, 164
Prime Minister, 24, 102, 128, 133, 137
Prisoner's dilemma, 42–43, 70
Privacy (nothing to hide), 11
Projective tests, 56
Prosopagnosia, 93, 140
Prostitution, 28, 144, 146, 149
Psychopathy, 8, 55, 57–58, 202

**Q**
Quakers, 9, 24, 78, 208
Quantification, 85, 164, 167–177, 201

**R**
Race and culture confounded, *see* Culture and race confounded
Racial dilemmas, 30
Racism, 3, 21, 30
Ranking, 70, 164, 172–173, 221
Rape, 13, 47, 85, 126, 144, 149, 217
Rating, 88, 172–173, 177
Rationality, 13, 53, 57, 217
Rawls, 183–184, 203
Reading, 94, 99, 119, 141, 177
Referenda, 149, 210
Religious views, 28
Representing the electorate, 120
Ridley, 42, 46
Rio Declaration, 184
Rituals, 29, 70
Robotics (advent of machines), 86
Rorschach, 56

**S**
Salary disparity, 109
Seattle (Chief), 3–4, 7, 107, 216
Semmelweis, I., 53
Sex, 16, 28, 29, 31, 65, 87, 99, 123, 139–150, 158, 160, 161, 212, 215, 219
Shangri La, 16, 17, 36, 37
Sharpeners and levellers, 50
Singer, 43, 102
Six degrees of separation, 101–103
Slavery, 2, 5, 11–14, 61, 66, 69, 95, 126, 151–165, 184, 203, 213, 218
Slavery and economics, 152
Slavery and morals, 2, 13, 213, 218
Slavery and UN Declaration, 12, 66, 126, 158, 164
Slavery grading, 163
Slavery websites, 160
Smith, A., 83, 195, 208
Social determinants, 25
Social indicators, 146, 208, 213
Sortition, 123, 128, 134, 206
Speaker, 128
Standard of living, 107
Statistics, 31, 169, 174
Strategic decisions, 89
Stremes, 85–87, 89
Sub-Saharan Africa, 5, 70
Succession planning, 87
Suffering, *see* Pain and suffering
Suffrage, 79, 122, 123, 155, 207, 212
Sugar, 23, 160
Sybil (the), 49

**T**
Taxonomy of cultures, 75
Tea, 23, 24
*Teflon factor*, 51
Temkin, 12, 203, 217
Temporal integration, 52

Terrorism, 67, 183
Thematic apperception test (TAT), 56
Theories of ethics, 2
Theorists, 20–25, 32, 51, 52, 54–59, 201
Thermic law of delinquency, 26
Time (aspects of), 38, 39, 41, 53–55, 58, 60, 66, 76, 99, 117, 120, 142, 179, 180, 211
Timeline for abolitionism, 154
Times out of sequence, 41
Tolpuddle martyrs, 79
Torah (the), 79
Trafficking in humans, 144
Transparency, 6, 107–108, 112, 118, 137, 156
Treating workers well, 78
Tsarist rule, 10
Types of corruption, 108–109
Tyranny, 10, 45, 119, 130, 135

**U**

*UN Declaration of Human Rights*, 12, 61, 66, 70, 117, 125, 126, 158, 164
UN reform, 213
Uninterested vs disinterested, 95, 111
Unionism, 77, 79–80
University fees, 113
UN membership, 211
UN power of veto, 211
Upper house, 120, 125–127, 134, 211
Usurpation, 61, 116
Utilitarianism, 179, 181, 184, 201
Utopia, 16–17, 36–38, 46, 47

**V**

Veils (face), 3, 20, 43, 61, 66, 69, 70, 92–95, 114, 123, 134, 140, 141, 204, 215
Villeinage, 155
Violence, 1, 4, 11, 17, 26, 45, 47, 67, 70, 105, 146–148, 203, 207, 212, 213
Virtue ethics, 179, 180, 203
Voice, 39, 92, 96–97, 100, 101, 103, 104, 121
Volkswagen GDP, 81

**W**

Wandering gene, 25
Wanderlust, 25
War, 17, 20, 28, 31–34, 46, 49, 57, 63, 67, 70, 105, 124, 125, 131–133, 135–137, 151, 156, 202
War (a just), 122
Wealth, 6, 8, 9, 20, 23, 27, 32, 40, 79, 83, 84, 106, 107, 123, 132, 136, 147, 205, 207, 212, 216
Wealth of Nations (the), 83, 195
What can be done about corruption, 118
Whistleblowing, 131, 136–137
Wilberforce, 14, 154, 156, 159–160
Wilkinson & Pickett, 14, 106, 208
Winds, 26
Women, 2, 4, 8, 16, 18, 30, 43, 64, 67, 70–73, 93–95, 99, 100, 102, 103, 123, 124, 126, 127, 134, 139–150, 155, 160, 162, 163, 172, 203, 208, 209, 213, 219

MIX
Papier aus verantwortungsvollen Quellen
Paper from responsible sources
FSC® C105338

If you have any concerns about our products,
you can contact us on
**ProductSafety@springernature.com**

In case Publisher is established outside the EU,
the EU authorized representative is:
**Springer Nature Customer Service Center GmbH**
**Europaplatz 3, 69115 Heidelberg, Germany**

Printed by Libri Plureos GmbH
in Hamburg, Germany

Rees, R. J. (2005). *Interrupted lives: Rehabilitation and learning following brain injury*. East Hawthorn, Australia: IP Communications.
Rocchio, C. (2004). *Ketchup on the baseboard: Rebuilding life after brain injury*. Youngsville, NC: Lash & Associates Publishing/Training Incorporated.
Sherry, M. (2006). *If I only had a brain: Deconstructing brain injury*. New York, NY: Routledge.
Silver, J. M., McAllister, T. W., & Yudofsky, S. C. (2011). *Textbook of traumatic brain injury*. Arlington, VA.: American Psychiatric Publishing Inc.
Skloot, F. (2004). *In the shadow of memory*. Lincoln NE: University of Nebraska Press.
Strand, M. (2004). *Meditations on brain injury*. Zotolla Publishing.
Thomas, A. (2006). *A three dog life: A memoir*. San Diego, CA: Harcourt.
van Maanen, J. (2011). Ethnography as work: Some rules of engagement. *Journal of Management Studies, 48*(1), 218–234.
Wagner, J. (1993). Ignorance in educational research or, how can you not know that? *Educational Researcher, 22*(5), 15–23.
Wallace, C. A., & Bogner, J. A. (2000). Awareness of deficits: Emotional implications for persons with brain injury and their significant others. *Brain Injury, 14*(6), 549–562.
Widdershoven, G. (1993). The story of life: hermeneutic perspectives on the relationship between narrative and life history. In R. Josselson & A. Lieblich (Eds.), *The narrative study of lives* (Vol. 1, pp. 1–20). Newbury Park, CA: Sage.
Winslade, W. J. (1998). *Confronting traumatic brain injury: Devastation, hope and healing*. New Haven, CT: Yale University Press.
Woodruff, L., & Woodruff, B. (2008). *In an instant: A family's journey of love and healing*. New York, NY: Random House Trade Paperbacks.
Yudofsky, S. C., & Hales, R. E. (Eds.). (2008). *The American Psychiatric Publishing textbook of neuropsychiatry and clinical neurosciences* (5th ed.). Washington, DC: American Psychiatric Publishing.

# Chapter 2
# Understanding the Assumptions of Major Models of Disability Theory

*Everything is vague to a degree you do not realise till you have tried to make it precise.*

Bertrand Russell.

## 2.1 Introduction

The Foreword introduced ABI through Durham's personal experience. The co-author, Ramcharan, has been involved in funded disability research for 25 years. He was involved in research of the All Wales Strategy for the Development of Services to Mentally Handicapped People [*sic*] 1983 (see Felce et al., 1998) and co-directed the Learning Disability Research Initiative, a two million GBP strategy involving thirteen projects designed to support implementation of Valuing People (2001), a national intellectual disability government policy in England (see Grant & Ramcharan, 2007). Paul's work for over a quarter of a century has melded an interest in the everyday life experiences of people with a disability (Ramcharan, Roberts, Grant, & Borland, 1996), and advocacy and voice (Goodley & Ramcharan, 2010). The interest in everyday lives and the everyday struggles faced by people with disabilities was a key basis upon which this exploration of the life experiences of people with ABI was both interesting and, at the same time, challenging. Durham's work was, therefore, immediately of interest leading to both his supervision of her Ph.D. and his contribution to this volume. Both share the passion to seek to change lives for people whose struggles are grounded in their social circumstances as much as their biology.

Chapter 2 provided a review of Websites, books and blogs written by people with ABI, supplemented by a consideration of the information and resources most readily available to people with ABI.

The period over which mending bodies and re-establishing basic skills take place can be variable. One guide to TBI suggests written by a neuropsychologist using 'psychological tests' suggests that



C. Durham and P. Ramcharan, *Insight into Acquired Brain Injury*,
DOI 10.1007/978-981-10-5666-6_2

> research on these tests indicate that for two years following a head injury, there is evidence of improving scores. After this period…I can no longer see large changes in scores (http://www.tbiguide.com/getbetter.html)

More importantly, many people with ABI recount this as an early inpatient response to the question of how long it would take them to get better. From the perspective of the professional (the outsider), this time frame is 'golden' insofar as the greatest recovery is presumed to happen within this time, and it attracts the greatest professional input designed to mend bodies and re-establish basic skills. It is analogous to the 'golden hour', directly after a traumatic injury when there is greatest likelihood that prompt treatment will prevent death. Although recognising its limitations, we shall for brevity, therefore, use the term 'golden period' to refer this two-year period, or thereabouts, directly after the person acquires their brain injury.

We also use this term to contrast with the views of people with ABI. As shall be seen, from the perspective of the person with ABI (the insider), this period is far from golden—it is the 'dark hole period'—the time of greatest pain, loss and despair as Durham has found in her continued engagement with people with ABI over the years.

Depending on the cause of the brain injury, for example, a car accident or a fall causing broken bones some people with ABI are hospitalised. Others suffer brain injury and it is not diagnosed, and/or they are not hospitalised. Some spend a short time, others months or years in hospital depending on their injuries and/or severity of the brain injury. Except for people with severe brain injury, at some time during the 'golden period/dark hole period' of medical and rehabilitative attention, most people with ABI go home to their communities where they have to mend their 'fractured lives'. Examples of information and resources that are typically available for people with ABI and their families have been examined, but from what source does this information come? Upon what assumptions is it based? This is the question that preoccupies us in the following three chapters.

We show that many of the categories of understanding in the information on Websites are drawn from what might collectively be termed a biopsychosocial model encompassing a majority medical model input. We also argue that this more formal academic engagement around ABI has significant blind spots, that it is preponderantly negative, that it predisposes to only certain professional interventions and that in so doing it misses solutions to the everyday support required once a person moves home from hospital or rehabilitation. By exploring the underlying theory, models and information, this review seeks to re-frame the approach on sound alternative assumptions, and to further inform and populate the methodological tool *Keys to the ABI Cage* that is used in this study.

In the first section of this chapter, some of the theoretical frameworks around disability are discussed and two broad categories are identified, the body-object view of ABI and the body-subject view of ABI. The dominance of the body-object view, it is argued, is not inconsequential. The results of such a view continue to objectify people, to obfuscate any interest in the complexity of their everyday lives and, as a result, to miss what is most important—the person behind the theory and behind the actions consequent to the theory when applied. The remainder of this chapter will then examine features and assumptions of the body-object view, including research into ABI, leaving a focus on building the body-subject view for the chapter to follow.

## 2.2 Differences in Perspectives of Disability

> Man has become less rational than his own objects, which
> now run ahead of him, so to speak, organising his surroundings
> and thus appropriating his actions,
> Jacques Baudrillard.

As already mentioned, it is all too easy to slip into a view that damaged brains produce damaged emotions, damaged behaviour, damaged communication, damaged interaction…damaged people…disabled people. The following introduces philosophies and ways a person with ABI can be viewed.

### *2.2.1 The Body-Object Model*

> *'The body is our general medium for having a world'*
> MauriceMerleau-Ponty, *Phenomenology of Perception.*

The roots of the distinction upon which we draw in this volume have a significant past, lying in broader philosophy, at least since the Enlightenment.

Naturalism and idealism as competing epistemologies have been in contention since Schelling, Kant and the later phenomenologists starting with Husserl who questioned Descartes proposition about the measurement of the object world through science. The competing traditions pit the pursuit of the factual world in the capacity of science to intercept, define and hence find meta-theory, against the idealist view that the reality of external objects cannot be subject to proof. The idealists' world is mediated by our consciousness, and it is only through such consciousness and intention that the world comes into existence.

In this way, even the hard fact of a 'stone' is not, for the idealist, defined through its scientific properties, its physical properties, chemistry and origin (igneous formed from fire and sedimentary formed from the compacting of layers). Rather, the stone may be the object of an aesthetic interest, and it may be a weapon in certain circumstances, evidence of the likelihood of a particular presence such as oil or gold, and so forth. In this way, the stone exists only by the intention of its use, by the conscious intention of the actor.

From one point of view, what is important for the purposes of this volume would be the external and defined fact of acquired brain injury. From another point of view, what is important is how we come to know acquired brain injury through consciousness and experience. The result of our epistemology is consequential to our understanding of the world, our ontology and, more importantly to the choices we make in intercepting and working upon that world. As Merleau-Ponty (2002) argues 'to understand is to experience harmony between what we aim at and what is given, between the intention and the performance—and our body is the anchorage in the world' (Merleau-Ponty, 2002, p. 167).

According to the French phenomenological philosopher Merleau-Ponty (2002), the view we have of the body plays a foundational role in the way we understand and engage with the world. He wrote of difference between the 'body-object', as determined and predicted by medical science, as the outsider's perspective, and the 'body-subject', as the body as we experience it, the body that gives meaning to the world around us, as the insider's perspective. An outsider or etic (Pike, 1954) description of an observed behaviour or belief often holds a different perspective or philosophy to that of an 'insider' (emic) (Pike, 1954). Just as body-object proponents rely upon Cartesian dualism and the separation of the body as an external object from its observation, so the body-subject proponents see object and subject as one and the same, i.e. as people see things, so they are.

However, even within the bifurcated category, body-object or body-subject, which is used to structure this and the following chapter, there are many different philosophies, 'models' or belief systems that have evolved, define and fundamentally affect the way in which the individual with ABI is viewed and treated. Perception of ABI is dictated by the dominant belief, model or 'lens' through which the individual, the medical or rehabilitation professional, family member, friend or the general public views, considers, assesses, or judges the person with ABI. These different beliefs can affect the way outsiders regard and behave towards the person with ABI.

Disablement models that developed in the twentieth century 'defined the meaning of terms we use every day, and that do not always exert a positive effect upon the people to whom such terms refer' (Masala & Petretto, 2008, p. 1242). So before reviewing the ABI literature, it is essential to discuss the place of theoretical systems in research. As a researcher, do such frameworks dictate the approach and limit what I want to observe or measure? Should a theory be used as an apparatus to interpret a person's world? Or should we be looking in our data for the ways in which people themselves construct their own realities and mould something out of these accounts? These questions are not inconsequential because they have a bearing upon how interactions take place between people, one party to this interaction being a person with ABI. It is, therefore, also relevant to the method employed in any study of people with ABI including the present study.

Below, we demonstrate the points made above by exploring and considering varying theoretical views of disability and their corollaries and consequences.

### 2.2.2 The Moral Model

The first and oldest model of disability is the moral model. In this view disability is a defect caused by a moral lapse or sin….it brings shame to the person with the disability, (Olkin, 1999, p. 25)

*"Macbeth: How does your patient, doctor?*

*Doctor: Not so sick, my lord, as she is troubled with thick-coming fancies that keep her from rest.*

*Macbeth: Cure her of that! Canst thou not minister to a mind diseased, pluck from the memory a rooted sorrow, raze out the written troubles of the brain, and with some sweet oblivious antidote cleanse the stuffed bosom of that perilous stuff which weighs upon her heart.*

*Doctor: Therein the patient must minister to himself."*

—William Shakespeare, Macbeth

People with disabilities have been recognised as 'different' and treated according to such differences for many centuries. Recognition and veneration through the ages, of 'gifted' savants with prodigious abilities beyond the population at large (Treffert, 2014) and, since Athenian times[1] (Penrose, 2015) a consistent recognition and support for those disabled in the military service of their country, represent but a small minority of cases resulting in 'positive regard'.

More often than not the effect of such 'difference' has resulted in treatments that have produced troubled lives, impoverishment and a life quality for which none of us would choose to queue. Through the ages, people with disabilities have, *inter alia*: been seen as 'possessed' or 'children of the devil' (leading to exorcism, bloodletting and being burnt at the stake); subject to infanticide (and death); treated as freaks (leading to fair game for circus sideshows, commodification and humiliation); perceived to belong to the class of 'moral degenerates', (such as prostitutes, criminals and beggars who have traditionally attracted the interest of the corrective services); argued to be a threat to the national gene pool (leading under a eugenic argument to both mass murder in Nazi concentration camps and to enforced separation of males and females in institutions); rated as 'unemployable' (leading to their occupancy of poor houses and later institutions); and, latterly, accepted to be legitimate beneficiaries of welfare (having to declare their disability to access additional support services), (see e.g. Thompson, 2010; Metzler, 2013; McClimens & Richardson, 2010; Nielson, 2012; Bogdan, 2014).

For most of history, humanity has perceived the trouble as lying with the person with a disability whether by possession, incapacity to work, moral degeneracy and

---

[1]Penrose, in his interesting comparison between the Athenians and Spartans, shows how much more sympathetic the Athenians were, than the Spartans. He argues that '…in Sparta, the failure to recognise the disability caused by impairment was a harsh form of prejudice…The Athenians allowed disabled veterans and others to be exempted from military service and to collect a pension, whereas no consistent record of exemption is extant from Sparta' (Penrose, 2015, p. 522).

more recently in their biology. How might we better understand this sad history, through which the morality of public and Government views have separated, labelled and denigrated one significant group of humans? One way is to consider the links between Government, economy, knowledge and public sentiment (McClimens & Richardson, 2010).

The lack of engagement of Governments and people with disabilities prior to the middle ages meant that the treatment of people with disabilities was likely to be a product of community sentiment. Such sentiment would have been diverse across regions, but would almost inevitably have included issues around systems of religious belief on the one hand and economic security on the other. Given the unpredictability of agrarian modes of production and technology, capricious climates and insecure tenancy, the economic circumstances were often highly testing.

The confluence of living on the edge of survival, alongside religious views of possession might, in the absence of other options have led to people with disabilities being left to die or to infanticide or exclusion, e.g. being treated as possessed. The very survival of people with disabilities was, therefore, at issue and exacerbated by very low levels of medical proficiency. Often, the family mediated the experience of relatives with a disability by controlling interaction with the rest of the community. Families, it should be noted, have consistently been a vital support mechanism through the ages. But for people with disabilities, life was tough and, for many, all too short.

The emergence of new nation States in Europe in the middle ages saw the protection of land for the nobility, giving rise in 1325 to *Prerogativa Regis* (in the prerogative of the monarch) in which land was held for 'idiots and natural fools' for the land-owning classes, though no provision was made for those without land. In the absence of such support from families, people with disabilities were likely to be driven to vagrancy, prostitution or shelter in the monasteries from which they were 'sent to beg "cap in hand"—the source of the term Handicap—for charity' (Ramcharan, 2016).

The moral model of labelling views the person with a disability as being responsible for both disability and the treatment accruing given the adopted moral position. The religious model has, in the past, been an extreme model where disability is viewed as punishment by God, or a supernatural force and was common in the Middle Ages and particularly during the Inquisition. It was often seen as resulting from their immoral actions the person or those of their parents. Although the moral model of viewing ABI can be seen as ignorant, some insiders privately still hold onto this perception (Durham, 1997). This influences well-being and self-efficacy for people with ABI. Some outsiders behave towards insiders, people with ABI, as if they are being punished by God, or because they had 'asked for it' by engaging in reckless behaviour, driving dangerously or taking drugs, for example (Durham, 1997).

It was not until the Elizabethan Poor Laws in the UK in 1601 that the roots of welfare can be identified. The landed gentry now operated in smaller identified areas termed parishes. Since taxes were essential for parishes to thrive, it became necessary to identify the 'impotent poor', i.e. those unable to be economically productive.

The resultant laws represented the first recognition of the State's responsibility to support the deserving poor. To be deserving of 'alms' or handouts, it was, therefore, necessary to be defined or to self-define as disabled, a welfare model that lasts in some shape or form to the current day. By doing so, the government social policy and administration of disability separated people with disability from the population at large providing a serviced existence for those eligible.

The alms offered from the earliest times were not enriching but based on the principle of less eligibility, i.e. that they would not match the level of wages for employment (Claeys, 2000). Furthermore, this 'economic model' distinguished between the 'employed, unemployed and unemployable' (Scull, 1989, p. 219). In this model, the person's inability to work and the consequences of this for the individual, employer and Government are established as a basis for social policy. This model was used primarily by policymakers to assess distribution of benefits and to counter fraudulent claims, but this model can lead to confusion and lack of coordination in disability policy. Another important dimension of this model is that by declaring themselves disabled, the person effectively declares themselves unemployable, the result of which means they are more likely to be confined to the financially disadvantaged sectors of society or, later, institutions.

More particularly, from a social policy perspective, the person with ABI is seen as a victim of circumstances, deserving pity and the recipient of charity due to the tragedy of their disability. The emergence of the Poor Laws in the UK, for example, demonstrate how the tragedy/charity model of the 1800s involved the transfer of the responsibility of giving alms from the Church to the government. Workhouses run by local governments housed the unemployable and in some cases the unemployed. The charity model views the disabled including those with ABI as having a tragic, negative and miserable existence. Through raising money and resources, somehow the suffering and sadness of the disabled person's lives would be reduced (Oliver, 1990, p. 1; Swain & French, 2004). This model lasted for nearly two centuries, although both the Enlightenment and industrialisation played a significant role in once more changing the living circumstances of many people with disabilities.

The advancement of science as the Enlightenment unfolded, heralded longer working hours and progressively harder manual labour in the industrial sector, as well as the growth of bureaucracies and more 'brain work'. Agriculture was increasingly mechanised and people moved in droves to cities to provide industrial labour. States too, were changing. Having established the place of alms or welfare, there was now a gradual extension of suffrage, i.e. voting rights. The Poor Laws in the UK from 1834 reflected this widening suffrage and the need to cater for more than just the landed classes led to a focus on the interests of the wider citizenry. Since all men would vote[2], it was necessary to appeal to all groups including people with disabilities.

[2]In the late eighteenth century, the western USA and some northern European countries gave women the vote. The full right to vote in Australia came with Federation in 1901. In the UK, it was not until 1928 that women had the same voting rights as men and in Switzerland, not until 1971.

While the workhouses provided temporary and low-quality housing for those temporarily out of work, people with disabilities and mental illness posed a problem for Governments and were expensive to house on a continuous basis. For example, as Richardson (2005) argues

> Capitalism therefore sought to remove, control and discipline those who would not or could not conform to new working practices by introducing new secular controls…Between 1720 and 1825, 150 hospitals were built in England to cater for the rising numbers of sick poor (p.71).

These asylums were seen to be placed where the concentration of residents allowed scientific discoveries to be applied more systematically. The seminal work of Seguin and later others on how education could achieve change in the behaviour and abilities of people with disability was revolutionary. While the emergence of modern medicine and psychiatry saw medical staff placed in control of such asylums, Dykens (2006) argues that Seguin's idea of the training school which through education delivered people with disabilities back to community life was adopted quickly but that,

> ..over time these schools changed dramatically. With the realization that students were not being cured, schools became less educational, larger and more custodial..institutions became places to keep persons away from a less forgiving and accepting society, (2006, 185).

McClimens and Richardson (2010) posit that up to and during the mid-1900s many people who had disabilities either died when they were young or lived their lives hidden away in institutions or their homes. In the first half of the twentieth century, both the moral and the early medical models were firmly entrenched in western culture and people with disabilities remained segregated from society (Mackelprang & Salsgiver, 1999). 'Segregation was considered a caring policy in a society which did not care about disabled people…. but World War 1 produced hundreds of thousands of people with disability—who took on the role of the worthy poor' (British Broadcasting Corporation, 1999, cited in Mackelprang & Salsgiver, 1999, p. 7).

Large institutions situated 'around the bend' (and out of sight, the source of this euphemism describing the insane) now operated to cure and to train the lunatics and mental defectives, at least those who did not remain with their families. Bracken and Thomas (2001) argue that in some ways, having been given positions of leadership within the institutions, that psychiatry was borne out of the institutions, rather than the other way around.

The early period in the emergent leadership of the medical profession was also influenced towards the end of the 1800s by Mendel and Darwin in relation to heredity and Binet in relation to intelligence. It may have seemed at the time that the

---

(Footnote 2 continued)

Prior to that age restrictions applied (making their voting numbers smaller than men) and various property or rate paying requirements which prevented their suffrage.

potential of biological science was limitless and that, almost inevitably, the source was individual deficit or pathology. Consequently, the eugenics movement argued that people with disabilities were weakening the national gene pool. Separation of the sexes in the institutions and mass sterilisations followed and continued in some places up to the 1960s (Stubblefield, 2007).

However, the most egregious of the eugenics policies under Nazism saw many hundreds of thousands of people with disabilities gassed in the concentration camps. The repercussions of the Second World War for disability cannot be underestimated. The 1948 Universal Declaration of Human Rights emerged in large part as a response to the experience of Nazism. Not long after, Goffman's (1961) work on asylums and Barton's (1959) on institutional neurosis changed public sentiment and pointed to the regimentation, Spartan conditions and cruel treatment experienced in the asylums. While survival rates improved, inmates' experiences are widely recognised as being extreme and catastrophically damaging. Not surprisingly the latter half of the twentieth century has seen deinstitutionalisation and resettlement in the community under a series of 'community care' initiatives hand-in-hand with normalisation theory.

While normalisation proposed (Wolfensberger 1973; 1983) that people should lead as normal and socially valued lives as others in society, it remained difficult to establish among such diversity what represented a norm and, indeed, what was socially valued. More fundamentally, the welfare model continued. To be able to qualify for welfare payments, people had to declare themselves as a person with a disability in order to access services. That many of these policies were exclusive and segregated meant a 'parallel' existence for those so labelled. Thus, while being on a disability register accorded them rights to welfare, it also separated them into a system of off the shelf disability—only services which kept them segregated from the community, leaving the exhortations of normalisation unfulfilled.

Normalisation had observed the application of a host of stereotypical labelling over the ages: 'perpetual child' 'an object to be pitied' 'brave but pitiable', 'objects to raise money for'; 'a menace or threat to society' or 'people to be feared' (Wolfensberger, 1973). People with disabilities have often been portrayed as deviant in the literature, films and television. Bogdan and Biklen (1993) suggest that most monsters are in fact persons with disabilities. Mary Shelley's Frankenstein published in 1818, for example, portrays such monstrosity as a reflection of the potential of the possibilities of science. People with disabilities have been perceived as: 'sick', 'needing special treatment for which they should be thankful', a 'burden to society—they never quite fit in', 'ugly and sexless', 'incompetent', 'freaks' 'cursed by God', or in terms of disability was a 'gift or test from God' (Gill, 1993, pp. 12–15).

It is easy to see that the fundamental view held by persons within society will lead to actions that reflect such views. People act rationally, but do so in a way that reflects the premise upon which that rationality is based. The perception of the person with a disability being a menace or threat would lead to the persons so labelled being distanced from society. The view that the disabled person's body and biology are broken and need to be mended would lead to the primacy of the medical professions in their lives. For the person on the receiving end of such views, the effect of such labels cannot but affect their own self-concept and their reaction to it.

### 2.2.3 The Medical Model

> For too long a time–for half a century, in fact–psychiatry tried to interpret the human mind merely as a mechanism, and consequently the therapy of mental disease merely in terms of technique. I believe this dream has been dreamt out. What now begins to loom on the horizon is not psychologized medicine but rather those of human psychiatry.
>
> —Viktor E. Frankl, Man's Search for Meaning

The emergence of the medical model alongside the large institutions noted earlier had established a significant medical leadership by the turn to the twentieth century. Rollin (2003) usefully reviews a plethora of treatments for those illnesses recognised by the profession in the UK at the time. Rollin argues dominant treatments to be abstention and 'cold turkey' for alcoholics, hypnotism for the neuroses (i.e. neurasthenia, a 'ragtag' of symptoms causing lassitude and, hysteria) and 'moral treatments' for the insane designed as 'palliatives for symptoms'. Such palliation was likely to encompass systems of physical restraint such as padded cells and straitjackets, chemical restraints available at the time and a number of exploratory approaches such as music, cycling, 'hypodermic injection of brain extract',[3] Indian hemp[4] and opium.[5]

Rollin asserts 'The composite picture of psychiatry in Britain at the end of the Victorian era and a little beyond is chiefly one of unremitting gloom' (2003, p. 298). Certainly, the effect on inmates would have been nothing short of catastrophic to their lives and freedoms. The early testing of treatments seems to have been based upon trial and error more than science, and institutional inmates were the guinea pigs for new treatments. A more systematic approach to the classification of diseases and to treatment was to emerge in the two decades that followed.

Bracken and Thomas (2001) point to the seminal work of Karl Jasper's highly influential *General Psychopathology*, first published in 1913, and to its phenomenological backdrop. Jaspers built his work on the seminal phenomenological writings of Edmund Husserl who had argued that by the process of 'bracketing out' surrounding contextual issues, it was possible to access the phenomenon at issue.

Unlike the vast majority of major phenomenological writings that came later, Husserl, who had started as a scientist, maintained a Cartesian view of the world in which mind and matter remain separate. Most later writings in phenomenology posited that the subject and object world were one and the same, that 'as I see things so they are'. This latter position allows an explanation of the meaning of behaviour in terms of the contextual social, environmental and other factors, making these central to understanding explaining human behaviour and the impact on the person. But Husserl's adoption of a Cartesian position was to have a profound effect on Jasper's work.

---

[3]Lancet 3 February 1891.

[4]BMJ, 4 July 1890.

[5]BMJ, 18 March 1893.

In Jaspers' view, the bracketing out of contextual factors led to a focus upon the 'form' rather than 'content' of the individual psyche. So, for example, hearing voices is not of interest in terms of content of those voices but, rather, that there is no stimulus (form) that accounts for the voices. In many ways, phenomenological reduction here ironicises the patient's experience. That is to say, although the medic uses their experience as reported, the model of 'science' is still used to judge whether there are grounds for hearing such voices. In the absence of such grounds, the conclusion is that the cause must be organic and, indeed, faulty.

Despite this, Bracken and Thomas say that Jaspers's comprehensive work on 'form' established the groundwork for the Diagnostic and Statistical Manual used in the USA to date. More importantly, the underlying assumption of form is that it is disordered individual cognition that must be addressed—that the fault lies in the biology of the individual. Importantly, in making a case for a new direction for mental health they argue that,

> Both supporters and critics of psychiatry agree that the discipline is a product of the European Enlightenment and the movement's preoccupations with reason and the individual subject. Although a critical, postmodern position does not mean rejecting the Enlightenment project, it demands acknowledgement of its negative as well as positive aspects. It means questioning simple notions of progress and advancement and being aware that science can silence as well as liberate, (Bracken & Thomas 2001: 724).

As shall be seen, it is these silences that are those being attended to through this study.

The traditional medical model, therefore, places the source of the problem with the person with the disability and stresses the importance of finding a cure or, by taking a moral position on what is 'acceptable' behaviour, helping the person be more 'normal' (Mackelprang & Salsgiver, 1999; Olkin, 1999). Disability was seen as a medical problem, as a

> defect or failure of a bodily system and as such is inherently abnormal and pathological. The goals of intervention are cure, amelioration of the physical condition to the greatest extent possible and rehabilitation...persons with disability are expected to avail themselves of services offered to them and to spend time in the role of patient or learner being helped by trained professionals, (Olkin, 1999, p. 26).

More importantly, the engagement of the medical profession with what is now termed ABI was about to take on a particular urgency. The links between the emergence of medicine and the Great War 1914–1918 cannot be underestimated as the crowds of injured returned from the fronts in Europe, 'the earliest disability policies of the twentieth century around ABI were entrenched in a medical model primarily focused on the physical restoration of individuals who had suffered some sort of physical trauma or impairment as a result of war' (Blessing, Golden, & Bruy'ere, 2009, p. 2).

Prior to the twentieth century, there was a high mortality rate of people suffering from ABI but improvements in care made during World War 1 reduced the death rate (Boake & Diller, 2005). As argued below, the Second World War also produced significant leaps forward in classifying and treating such head injuries.

Even more recently the Iraq and Afghanistan conflicts, blast injuries caused by war have led to significant new research into brain function (Belanger, Kretzmer, Yoash-Gantz, Pickett, & Tupler, 2009; Jones, Fear, & Wesseley, 2007).

The medical or biomedical model of disability has had dominance in the public's perception of disability. The medical model has regarded disability as a defect or sickness that must be cured through medical intervention. It focuses on, for example, training the body to walk and limbs to work again, in order for the person to be able to accomplish everyday tasks; therapy to assist speech; and training to be safe, inside and outside the safety of home or a rehabilitation hospital.

Although ABI does not feature in the early disability literature, it was perhaps seen in those times as manifested in physical impairment and mental impairment. It was not until the mid-twentieth century that it began to have an identity of its own. After 1948, under World Health Organisation auspice the International Classification of Diseases (ICD) and a significant number of reclassifications have taken place since. Similarly the USA, which also had its own history of classification, launched the Diagnostic and Statistical Manual (DSM) with an additional focus on clinical use in 1952, at the same time WHO published ICD-6. This new classification drew on classification work by the Veteran's Administration working with World War II veterans. A vital turn at this point was the move to a biopsychosocial model on the basis of the work of Adolf Meyers who saw mental disorders as individual reactions to biological, psychological and social factors.

The International Classification of Impairments, Disabilities and Handicaps (ICIDH) which complements the ICD classification plays a similar role in grounding the biopsychosocial model. While the recognition of ABI as a medical issue first and foremost came at the turn of the twentieth century, it was not until much later that it was formally incorporated within a disability model. In 1980, the World Health Organisation described:

> Impairments as any loss or abnormality of psychological or anatomical structure or function; disability as any restriction or lack of ability (resulting from an impairment) to perform an activity in the manner or within the range considered normal for a human being; and a handicap as any disadvantage for a given individual, resulting from impairment or a disability that limits or prevents the fulfilment of a role that is normal for that individual. (WHO, 1980, p. 14)

Looking at the history of professions and their legitimacy, it may be that the capacity of medicine to work on the brain and the injured body together gave the category of ABI a life of its own. In a useful editorial of the *American Journal of Psychiatry*, for example, Yudofsky and Hales (2002) speak of three classifications addressed by psychiatry (mood, affect, thought and behaviour), neurology (motor and sensory) and neuropsychiatry (attention, alertness, perception, memory, language and speech, intelligence, cognition and motivation). People with ABI may fit under the disability or handicap classification, but it was not until 1993, at a meeting on ABI held in Oxford (UK), that the International Brain Injury Association was formed to encourage global exchange of information, to support research, provide training and to advocate for brain injury (International Brain

Injury Association, 2011). But the move to clarity around the classification of brain injury has been slow.

ABI itself has really only recently been adopted in the DSM and ICD classifications. Wortzel and Arciniegas (n.d) review this history. The DSMIII (American Psychiatric Association, 1980) spoke of 'post-concussional syndrome' but not traumatic brain injury or head injury; traumatic brain injury like acquired brain injury however when using initials TBI and ABI DSM II-R (American Psychiatric Association, 1987) identified only 'head injury' as an etiologic factor for delirium and organic personality syndrome; DSM IV (American Psychiatric Association, 1994) and DSM IV TR (American Psychiatric Association, 2000) use the term 'head trauma' in narratives describing delirium, amnestic disorder, dementia, cognitive disorder (not otherwise specified) and personality change. DSM V (American Psychiatric Association, 2013) TBI and neuropsychiatric sequelae are detailed and criteria for diagnosing an injury event as TBI are offered. This is considered within a framework of neurocognitive disorders and includes a long list of behavioural disturbances (delusions, hallucinations, mood disturbance, affective lability, agitation, disinhibition, wandering, apathy) and the co-occurrence with neurocognitive symptoms (depression, irritability, fatigue, headache, photosensitivity, sleep disturbance).

Wortzel and Arciniegas (n.d.) usefully summarise the DSM approach. In this model, they use the preinjury, injury and post-injury time frames to consider the focus of rehabilitation professionals in four key areas.

- **Cognition**—including impaired arousal or attention, slow processing, memory disturbance, communication issues, apraxia, visuospatial and executive dysfunction.
- **Emotion**—incorporating pathological effect, depression, anxiety, irritability and anger, agitation and aggression;
- **Behaviour**—including disinhibition, apathy, sleep disturbance, fatigue and headaches;
- **Sensorimotor function**—including pain, visual problems, dizziness/vertigo and seizures.

The classifications in the DSM as described above perhaps give a clue about the focus of the current model. It remains unclear whether this approach is biopsychosocial in that many of the social aspects of lives are ignored. First, even were the focus to have a social dimension, this seems to be likely to be in the hands of the medical and rehabilitation staff to establish and to work upon. Secondly, the model is based on a normative framework of cognition, emotional behaviour and sensorimotor function. This means some interpretation is required to assess what is (the person presenting) and what ought to be (the 'normal' person). Thirdly, the focus on what 'ought to be' implies efforts to use all medical and rehabilitative efforts to achieve this norm, a largely de facto biomedical approach. Fourthly, the body-object approach—the biomedical model—imposes power differences between professional and client (Sherry, 2006; Smart, 2009).

> There may be important weaknesses and limitations of the Biomedical Model which are less visible and rarely acknowledged, but have far greater implications…prejudices and discrimination towards people with disabilities has developed not in spite of but because of it, (Smart, 2009, p. 4).

The 'golden period/dark hole period' of which we spoke in the introduction to this chapter, that two-year window in which such change is taken to be possible, therefore establishes a focus premised upon pathology. In this volume, as will be seen, life after that 'golden period/dark hole period' now needs to be similarly transcended to engage with the latter end of a 'recovery model', that is, with re-engaging in everyday life.

### 2.2.4 The Social Model

Some models have sought to provide grand or all-encompassing theories around disability. In recent years, the social model of disability has posed a significant challenge to the medical model as a global theoretical framework for understanding disability (Barnes, Oliver, & Barton, 2002). The social model thesis separates the impairment from disability.

> Impairment—lacking part of or all of a limb, or having a defective limb organism or mechanism of the body.
>
> Disability—the disadvantage or restriction of activity caused by contemporary social organization which takes no account of people who have physical impairments and thus excludes them from mainstream social activities. (UPIAS, 1976, quoted by Oliver, 1990, p. 11.)
>
> Disability is something imposed on top of our impairments by the way we are unnecessarily isolated and excluded from full participation in society. Disabled people are therefore an oppressed group in society. (UPIAS, 1976 p. 4)

In this model, the impairment is seen as a characteristic, feature or attribute that affects an individual's mind or body function as a result of an injury, genetic make-up or disease. In contrast, disability is seen as socially constructed. Society is built for the able-bodied, and so it discriminates against people with impairments. It creates disadvantage through attitudes and culture (e.g. negative images in the media) that reinforces stereotypical views of incapacity, inaccessible environments (e.g. homes, businesses, transport, workplaces, education) and organisations that do not question discrimination nor provide accessible environments. Since these barriers are socially produced, they are subject to socially produced solutions.

But there are some limitations to the social model. For example, Shakespeare and Watson (2001) argue that the social model has not so much as replaced the medical model but has simply placed a higher emphasis on addressing disability as a social issue. They go on to explore the background to British academic and political debates over the social model and argue that the time has come to move beyond this position. Three central criticisms of the British social model are presented and focus on the issue of impairment, the impairment/disability dualism and the issue of identity. It is suggested that an embodied ontology offers the best starting point for disability studies, and some signposts on the way to a more adequate social theory of disability are provided.

Indeed, the impairment/disability distinction remains unresolved and fails to establish an embodied ontology (i.e. the disability identity itself). In reflecting this embodied ontology, common identity and action through disability pride has been proposed (Morris, 1991), while intersectionality, the combination of excluded identities (disability, ethnic minority, LGBTI among others) has been a focus for others (Caldwell, 2010). Looking at the history of labelling by others, as discussed above, the embodied ontology or body-subject view is potentially hugely important. Shakespeare (2006) suggests that the way forward lies in a combination of the medical and the social model and new ways of thinking. The issue of impairment, the impairment/disability dualism and the issue of identity are included in the criticisms of the British social model and echo the breakdown of Shakespeare's relationship with the UK disabled people's movement as disability studies became too reliant on political rhetoric and ideology (Shakespeare & Watson 2001). Shakespeare states that 'there is no qualitative difference between disabled and non-disabled people because we are all impaired in some form, some more than others' (2002, p. 27).

However, the very act of saying the word 'disability' may not be helpful. If there is no qualitative difference, as Shakespeare suggests, then why is it we still recognise a group of people with disabilities versus the rest of society? The issue is borne out in the tone and focus of disability studies literature. Longmore (2003), Garland-Thomas (1997a) and Sherry (2006) argue that the social model of disability focuses upon physical disabilities, while cognitive impairments such as brain injury are overlooked. Chappell posits that ABI is marginalised within the social model and states 'some of the arguments emanating from within the social model are assumed to refer to all disabled people, when in reality they do not' (1998, p. 212).

Oliver (2004) acknowledges five common criticisms of the social model (of which he was the main architect): it ignores or is unable to deal adequately with the realities of impairment, it ignores the 'pains' (Oliver, 2004, p. 8) of both impairment and disablement, it is unable to incorporate other social divisions, disabled people are viewed as 'other' (Oliver, 2004, p. 9) and it is inadequate as a social theory.

More recently, the social model has generated a number of radical critiques posing various alternative terminologies around people with a disability. Abberley (1999) asserts 'a liberative theory' of disability requires the posing of values counter to the classical sociological and revolutionary consensus, the assertion of the rights of the human 'being' against the universalisation of human 'doing' (p. 14). Finkelstein (1980, 1993) argues that 'the predominant factor contributing to the disablement of different groups is the way in which people can participate in the creation of social wealth' (Finkelstein, 1993, p. 12).

Oliver (1990) posits that the comprehensive materialistic account of the creation of disability places ideology at the centre of arguments about disability. In the above models, the assumptions underlying the role of the State/society and the body-object, even though not a medical model, are no less likely to have huge ramifications on the persons so-defined.

The problems of many of these attempts to distinguish groups of people with disabilities are that they rely on prior meta-theoretical categories. Moral classification supports the treatment of people as sinners; medical classification establishes the grounds for medical intervention; the social model establishes the grounds for access while failing to explore limitations to the accessibility argument for some. The arguments around 'embodied ontologies' are vital for they fire off the quotidian narratives of day-to-day life and experience, and the collective and synthesised narratives these represent.

For example, Nussbaum (2001) argues that over time people adapt to deprivations which despite best attempts, they fail to escape. In such circumstance, there is an 'adaptive preference' to a life denuded of the potential many of us would continue to fight for, leaving the person 'satisfied with their lot'. Bourdieu's seminal work on the ways in which societal structures rub up against human agency is useful to this debate on ontology, disability, identity and adaptive preference (e.g. Bourdieu and Wacquant, 1992; Bourdieu, 1994). It was established earlier that the principle of less eligibility in which welfare is always lower than employment income and that many of the services to people with disabilities run parallel to generic services for the population as a whole. Each of us brings a number of capitals to bear in our struggle to flourish, and this is true for all humans.

In the absence of additional support from family or others, the economic capital wielded by people with disabilities under a welfare model is likely to be severely limiting; in services that are often still closed, social capital for people with disabilities is limited to those in closed services. Such capital does not afford an expansive network of reciprocal support out of which to build a flourishing community. Moreover, the person has very little symbolic capital (power) given their place within the systems of power (field) operated by staff within such settings.

The structure of State welfarist policy, therefore, bears down upon the person in such a way as to limit the extent to which their combined capitals, their habitus, can be used in pursuit of their life's ambitions. Over any protracted period, such limitations produce a way of being, what Bourdieu terms a 'disposition' which is reflected in the ways in which people act. This establishes their ontological view of the world and of their identity. In the face of additional discriminatory, hectoring and rejecting behaviours by the community, people with disability begin to embody their social practices as what they have come to expect from the world. Such embodied practices may come to reflect Nussbaum's adaptive preference behaviours in which the loss of hope that there can be change for the better is exemplified in limited personal choices and ways of being.

For people with ABI, the challenge to the person's ontology and identity can be particularly important. From the start, there is an additional potential struggle with the embodied practices of life's disposition to date, compared with the need to establish one that is new. It is, therefore, absolutely essential that from the start those interactions, those services, those relationships in the person's life are formed to establish the embodied practices of inclusion and of dignity. It was one of the necessary features of this research to draw upon what we know about people with ABI to structure the research approach to do no harm at minimum, but to work in an inclusive way that treats participants with dignity.

## 2.3 Recapitulation

In this chapter, we have summarised a number of assumptions underlying major models of disability and demonstrated that in all disability theory models there can only but be assumptions. It has been seen that such assumptions are the basic premise upon which social action is based: assume possession by the devil, then treat such possession; assume biological cause, then address the biological cause; assume social exclusion through inaccessible environments, then create ones that are accessible. Two further points are necessary to make in relation to the discussion above.

First, since the introduction of welfarist models disability theories may have characterised differences across a range people with disabilities, but the administration of disability under welfare policy still means that to access services, it is necessary to declare or be declared as a person with a disability. This is true even under the radical National Disability Insurance Scheme in Australia in which access to those assessed as having 'significant and enduring' disabilities makes available individualised funds that, at least theoretically, can be used to purchase services of people's choice.

It should be noted at this point that at any one time 19–20% of the population of any country may have disabilities, more in countries where there has been conflict. Many of these people live full lives, are employed, home owners and live in relationships of their choice. So, not all people with disabilities are registered for the provision of disability services. Systems of rationing, therefore, still mediate those who are 'deserving' and those who are not. For those that are, lives are dictated by the availability of health and social care services and by other defined rights to services.

For many years, such services have almost inevitably been segregated and run parallel to the policies and services available to other citizens (e.g. in terms of schooling and employment) maintaining the long discrimination between those who work, as independent from those who are deemed to be unable to do so. Redefining people with disability as 'citizens' with rights to a minimum level of outcome or in some other way that affords them as humans a fundamental right to a good life could have huge impacts. This relates to the second point.

In all the models considered above, the medical model has perhaps provided a classificatory system that separates out ABI most. As shown above, many of the arguments within the social sciences seek broader theoretical formulations of disability that are all inclusive. Importantly, also all the models reviewed take the behaviour of others as a predicate to the theory of disability. Having defined the disability, the consequences of mundane interactions are seldom linked back to the theory itself. Disability theory has as yet to systematically explore the behaviours of professionals or members of the community as the subject of understanding. So, for example, what would be the point of making roads and buildings accessible if those around still treated you with disdain? Of what use would it be to mend a body if the professionals treat you in an undignified manner? Even if psychiatry grew from phenomenological roots, even if social constructionism reflects the social model, the everyday experiences and interactions of people with disabilities have been subservient to broader theoretical formulations and this remains a yawning gap, a blind spot, the 'tiger hidden in the foliage'.

It is now time to focus on the everyday and mundane life experiences of people with ABI. In phenomenological terms, a move to the lifeworld (Lebenswelt) rather than that of the bracketing Husserl recommended is required, an engagement with the natural attitude (Schutz & Luckmann, 1973), and the inter-subjectivities of everyday life and experience are necessary. But, as already established, to do so requires at the very least to ensure the approach does no harm and takes into account as much as is known about people's experiences in such a way as to engage in a research process that is at once positive, based on dignity and which helps participants to engage with the reconstruction of ontologies, identities and embodied practices, of hope. This study seeks this path.

Nevertheless, there is knowledge from each of these perspectives that is useful. In what follows, we seek to draw upon the collection of body-object knowledge in Chap. 3 and body-subject knowledge in Chap. 4 to further instruct us as to how the Cage should be populated. Once again, in these chapters we separate out these instructional findings into shaded Headwork boxes that inform Keys to the ABI Cage and to the processes used to engage people with ABI as research participants.

## References


Abberley, P. (1999, April 15). *The significance of work for the citizenship of disabled people*. Paper presented at the University College, Dublin. Retrieved from http://www.leeds.ac.uk/disabilitystudies/archive/abbarley/sigofwork.pdf

American Psychiatric Association. (1980). *Diagnostic and statistical manual of mental disorders DSM-III* (3rd ed.). Washington, DC: American Psychiatric Association.

American Psychiatric Association. (1987). *Diagnostic and statistical manual of mental disorders DSM-III-R (3rd ed. rev.)*. Washington, DC: American Psychiatric Association.

American Psychiatric Association. (1994). *Diagnostic and statistical manual of mental disorders DSM-IV* (4th ed.). Washington, DC: American Psychiatric Association.

American Psychiatric Association. (2000). *Diagnostic and statistical manual of mental disorders DSM-IV-TR* (4th ed. rev.). Washington, DC: American Psychiatric Association.

American Psychiatric Association. (2013). *Diagnostic and statistical manual of mental disorders DSM-V* (5th ed.). Washington, DC: American Psychiatric Association.

Barnes, C., Oliver, M., & Barton, L. (2002). *Disability studies today*. Cambridge, MA: Polity.

Barton, (1959). *Institutional neurosis*. Bristol: Stonebridge Press.

Belanger, H. G., Kretzmer, T., Yoash-Gantz, R., Pickett, T., & Tupler, L. A. (2009). Cognitive sequelae of blast-related versus other mechanisms of brain trauma. *Journal of the International Neuropsychological Society, 15*(01), 1–8.

Blessing, C. J., Golden, T. P., & Bruyère, S. M. (2009). Evolution of disability policies and practices in the United States: Implications for global implementation of person-centered planning. In C. A. Marshall (Ed.), *Disabilities: Insights from across fields and around the world* (Vol. 3: Responses: Practice, legal, and political frameworks, pp. 1–16). Westport, CT: Praeger.

Boake, C., & Diller, L. (2005). History of rehabilitation for traumatic brain injury. In W. M. High (Ed.), *Rehabilitation for traumatic brain injury* (pp. 3–13). Oxford, England: Oxford University Press.

Bogdan, R. (2014). *Freak Show: Presenting human oddities for amusement and profit.* Chicago, IL: University of Chicago Press.

Bogdan, R., & Biklen, D. (1993). Handicapism. In M. Nagler (Ed.), *Perspectives on disability: Text and readings on disability* (2nd ed., pp. 69–76). Palo Alto, CA: Health Markets Research.

Bourdieu, P. (1994). Structures, habitus, power: Basis for a theory of symbolic power. In N. B. Dirks, G. Eley, & S. B. Ortner (Eds.), *Culture/power/history: A reader in contemporary social theory* (pp. 155–199). Princeton, NJ: Princeton University Press.

Bourdieu, P., & Wacquant, L. (1992). *An Invitation to reflexive sociology.* Chicago, IL: Chicago University Press.

Bracken, P., & Thomas, P. (2001). Postpsychiatry: A new direction for mental health. *British Medical Journal, 322,* 724–727.

Caldwell, K. (2010). We exist: Intersectional in/visibility in bisexuality and disability. *Disability Studies Quarterly, 32*(1). doi:10.18061/dsq.v30i3/4.1273

Chappell, A. (1998). Still out in the cold: People with learning difficulties and the social model of disability. In T. Shakespeare (Ed.), *The disability reader: Social science perspectives* (pp. 207–231). London, England: Cassell.

Claeys, G. (2000). The "Survival of the Fittest" and the origins of Social Darwinism. *Journal of the History of Ideas, 61*(2), 223–240.

Durham, C. (1997). *Doing up buttons.* Ringwood, Australia: Penguin.

Dykens, E. (2006). Toward a positive psychology of mental retardation. *American Journal of Orthopsychiatry, 76*(2), 176–193.

Felce, D., Grant, G., Todd, S., Ramcharan, P., Beyer, S., McGrath, M., et al. (1998). *Towards a full life: Researching policy innovation for people with learning disabilities.* Oxford: Butterworth Heinemann.

Finkelstein, V. (1980). *Attitudes and disabled people: Issues for discussion.* New York, NY: World Rehabilitation Fund.

Finkelstein, V. (1993). The commonality of disability. In J. Swain (Ed.), *Disabling barriers: Enabling environments* (pp. 9–16). London, England: Sage.

Garland-Thomas, R. (1997). Integrating disability studies into the existing curriculum. In L. J. Davis (Ed.), *The disability studies reader* (pp. 295–306). New York, NY: Routledge.

Gill, C. (1993). Isolation: Confronting the painful social realities that come with disability. *Mainstream, 9*(1), 18–25.

Goffman, E. (1961). *Asylums: Essays on the social situation on mental patients and other inmates.* Harmondsworth: Penguin.

Goodley, D., & Ramcharan, P. (2010). Advocacy, Campaiging and people with learning difficulties. In G. Grant, P. Ramcharan, M. Flynn, & M. Richardson (Eds.), *Learning disability: A life cycle approach.* London: Open University Press and McGraw-Hill Educational.

Grant, G., & Ramcharan, P. (2007). *Valuing people and research: The learning disability research initiative overview report.* London: Department of Health.

International Brain Injury Association. (2011). *History of IBIA.* Retrieved from http://www.internationalbrain.org/?q=history

Jones, E., Fear, N., & Wessely, S. (2007). Shell shock and mild traumatic brain injury: A historical review. *American Journal of Psychiatry, 164*(11), 1641–1645.

Longmore, P. K. (2003). *Why I burned my book & other essays on disability*. Philadelphia, PA: Temple University Press.
Mackelprang, R. W., & Salsgiver, R. O. (1999). *Disability: A diversity model approach in human service practice*. Pacific Grove, CA: Brooks/Cole.
Masala, C., & Petretto, D. R. (2008). From disablement to enablement: Conceptual models of disability in the 20th century. *Disability Rehabilitation, 30*(17), 1233–1244. doi:10.1080/09638280701602418.
McClimens, A., & Richardson, M. (2010). Social construction and social model: Disability explained? In G. Grant, P. Ramcharan, M. Flynn, & M. Richardson (Eds.), *Learning Disability: A life cycle approach*, pp. 19–33. Maidenhead, England: Open University Press and McGraw-Hill Educational.
Merleau-Ponty, M. (2002). *Phenomenology of perception* (C. Smith, Trans.). London and New York: Routledge Classics.
Metzler, I. (2013). *A social history of disability in the middle ages: Cultural considerations of physical impairment*. New York, NY: Routledge.
Morris, J. (1991). *Pride against prejudice: Transforming attitudes to disability*. London, England: Women's Press.
Nielson, K. E. (2012). *A disability history of the United States*. Boston, MA: Beacon Press.
Nussbaum, M. (2001). Adaptive preference and women's options. *Economics and Philosophy, 17,* 67–88.
Oliver, M. (1990). *The politics of disablement*. Basingstoke, England: Macmillan.
Oliver, M. (2004). If I had a hammer: The social model in action. In J. Swain (Ed.), *Disabling barriers: Enabling environments* (2nd ed., pp. 7–12). London, England: Sage.
Olkin, R. (1999). *What psychotherapists should know about disability*. New York, NY: The Guilford Press.
Penrose, W. D. (2015). The discourse of disability in ancient greece. *Classical World, 108*(4), 499–523.
Pike, K. L. (1954). Language in relation to a unified theory of the structure of human behaviour, Vol. 1. Glendale, CA: Summer Institute of Linguistics (The Hague, The Netherlands: Mouton, 1967
Ramcharan, P. (2016).*Understanding the NDIS: a history of disability welfare from 'deserving poor' to consumers in control*, The Conversation, July 6th. Retrieved from http://theconversation.com/understanding-the-ndis-a-history-of-disability-welfare-from-deserving-poor-to-consumers-in-control-58069
Ramcharan, P., Roberts, G., Grant, G., & Borland, J. (1996). *Empowerment in everyday life: Learning disability*. London: Jessica Kingsley.
Richardson, M. (2005) Critiques of Segregation and eugenics. In G. Grant, P. Goward, M. Richardson & P. Ramcharan (Eds) *Learning Disability: A life cycle approach to Valuing People*. Open University press and McGraw-Hill Educational.
Rollin, H. R. (2003). Psychiatry in Britain one hundred years ago. *British Journal of Psychiatry, 183,* 292–298.
Schutz, A. & Luckmann, T. (1973). *The structures of the life-world*. (R.M. Zaner & H. Tristan Englehardt Trans.). Evanston, IL: Northwestern University Press.
Scull, A. T. (1989). *Social order/mental disorder: Anglo-American psychiatry in historical perspective*. Berkeley, CA: University of California Press.
Shakespeare, T., & Watson, N. (2001). The social model of disability: An outdated ideology? *Research in Social Science and Disability, 2,* 9–28.
Shakespeare, T. (2006). The social model of disability. *The Disability Studies Reader, 2,* 197–204.
Sherry, M. (2006). *If I only had a brain: Deconstructing brain injury*. New York, NY: Routledge.
Smart, J. F. (2009). The power of models of disability. *Journal of Rehabilitation*, *April–June*, 1–11.
Stubblefield, A. (2007). Beyond the pale: Tainted whiteness, cognitive disability and eugenic sterilization. *Hypatia, 22*(2), 162–181. doi:10.1111/j.1527-2001.2007.tb00987.

Swain, J., & French, S. (2004). Whose tragedy: Towards a personal non-tragedy view of disability. In J. Swain (Ed.), *Disabling barriers: Enabling environments* (2nd ed., pp. 34–40). London, England: Sage.

Thompson, M. (2010). Disability, psychiatry and eugenics. In A. Bashford & P. Levine (Eds.), *The oxford handbook of the history of eugenics* (pp. 116–134). Oxford, England: Oxford University Press.

Treffert, D. A. (2014). Savant Syndrome: Realities, Myths and Misconceptions. *Journal of Autism and Developmental Disorder, 44*(3), 564–571.

UPIAS. (1976). *Fundamental principles of disability*. London, England: Union of the Physically Impaired Against Segregation.

Wolfensberger, W. (1973). *The principle of normalization in human services*. Toronto, Canada: York University Campus, National Institute on Mental Retardation.

Wolfensberger, W. (1983). Social role valorization: A proposed new term for the principle of normalization. *Mental Retardation, 21*(6), 234–239.

World Health Organisation. (1980). *International Classification of Functioning, Disability and Health (ICIDH-2)*. Geneva, Switzerland: WHO.

Wortzel, H. S. & Arciniegas, D. B. (n.d.). The DSM-5 approach to evaluating traumatic brain injury. Veterans Affairs and Rocky Mountain MIRECC.

Yudofsky, S. C., & Hales, R. E. (2002). Editorial: Neuoropsychiatry and the future of psychiatry and neurology. *American Journal of Psychiatry, 159,* 8.

# Chapter 3
# Body-Object Knowledge and Its Relevance

> *In nothing do men more nearly approach the gods than in giving health to men.*
>
> Cicero

## 3.1 Introduction

Having laid out assumptions of disability models in the last chapter, we are nevertheless convinced that these models can contribute something to our interest in focusing on the lives and experiences of people with ABI. As such, in this chapter, we explore some of the significant findings from the medical and biopsychosocial models and then translate these into concepts that informed and which helped us to populate our methodological tool, 'Keys to the ABI Cage'. We follow up in Chap. 4 by undertaking a similar review of literature and its relevance around the body-subject approach.

It should be observed that huge research resources are committed to biopsychosocial model research and treatments over the 'golden period/dark hole period'. Moreover, we shall see that the 'deficit', broken bodies, broken minds focus has fed into Web resources as reviewed in Chap. 1.

Seeking to maximise people's capacity to function through medical means is essential, but there are other issues that need to be considered for the person to learn to feel and fare better in the community. Significantly less research takes place in this domain, a place where, after leaving hospital or rehabilitation, they must spend the rest of their lives. A cursory review of medical model research, its focus, nature, character and its effects is undertaken below. This literature will focus upon the physical and emotional issues that the medical model seeks to address. At relevant points grey textboxes are used as Headwork, to demonstrate how the information informed the Keys Study methodology.



C. Durham and P. Ramcharan, *Insight into Acquired Brain Injury*,
DOI 10.1007/978-981-10-5666-6_3

## 3.2 ABI and the Medical Model Findings

Millions of dollars are spent on research into ABI, and millions of dollars are spent on rehabilitation programs. The professional has a potentially vast array of data at their fingertips as there are a plethora of tests they can administer to people with ABI, as will be demonstrated in the following section.

Truism though it be, it needs stating that most practitioners function in the way in which they have been educated and trained (Smart, 2009, p. 3). A search of major medical, rehabilitation and nursing journals demonstrates that the majority of ABI studies follow quantitative approaches. In undertaking this review of the literature, a number of Web engines were used that included: Informa Healthcare; PubMed; ProQuest; Wiley Online Library; Taylor & Francis online; ScienceDirect; Google Scholar; Web of Science; Ovid Medline; Ingenta Connect; SAGE Journals online. The search strategy entailed using the following fundamental words: quantitative studies, brain injury, ABI, traumatic brain injury, TBI, and these in combination with each other and with IQ loss, memory loss, depression, fatigue, coping, pain, cognitive rehabilitation therapy, self-awareness, post-traumatic stress disorder, learning disorders, tests, scales, measures and questionnaires.

A review of the above journals was undertaken by looking at ABI-specific studies in the past twenty years (between 1991 when Durham sustained ABI and 2011, when the original Ph.D. study was being undertaken). It is 20 years since Durham suffered ABI and the authors therefore held a keen interest in developments made over that period of time. The review also examined articles in the *Journal of Sociology and Social Welfare, Journal of Poverty, Journal of Social Work* and the *International Journal of Intercultural Relations*, which were more social science-orientated journals but when searched were found to carry ABI-relevant studies.

Quantitative journal articles were reviewed to establish an objective perspective of difficulties/differences and deficits of ABI to (a) provide a background to problems participants may experience, in order to inform the method employed and the tone of this study; (b) examine issues identified by professional studies, which could inform the 'talk-about' cards; (c) identify issues that could be addressed in the ABI learning resource and (d) to look for similarities and differences to issues identified in qualitative studies and books and blogs written by people with ABI. As neither Durham or Ramcharan are rehabilitation professionals, a review of studies involving specific rehabilitation programs was not taken.

The assessment of ABI and its associated co-morbidities were found to occupy a significant number of studies, many of which replicated Website contents presented in Chap. 1. However, the co-morbidities themselves were a significant proportion of the literature and they fell into a number of categories. Ten of these categories, the main ones identified, are used as subsections in the review that follows, and they fall into areas relating to psychiatry, neurology and neuropsychiatry. It will not have escaped the reader's attention that these very much mirror the pathological and negative approach and cover areas set out in the neat summary of medical interests presented by Wortzel and Arciniegas (n.d.) in the last chapter. Where relevant, some of the methods of individual assessment are also mentioned because they are part and parcel of the approach that turns the ABI into an object, the body-object, to be more precise. Needless to say, some of the more established assessment approaches have a longer history than the 20-year search dates.

## 3.3 Some Categories of Body-Object Research

In what follows, consideration of each area of literature is supplemented by Headwork boxes to inform the Keys Study, our study of everyday lives, in a way that was likely to support people to feel and fare better.

### *3.3.1 IQ Loss After ABI*

Intelligence quotient (IQ) loss represents one of the primary tools through which the medical and associated professions have estimated the effect of ABI. Not surprisingly, a significant number of assessment methods were found in the literature review, though we do not explore these in detail here. Rather, findings are reviewed and include, inter alia: people with ABI have a mean loss of 14 points of Full Scale IQ from estimated preinjury baseline and they show no evidence of recovery 20 months later (Parker & Rosenblum, 1996); performance IQ score on the Wechsler Adult Intelligence Scale-Revised emerged as the most significant predictor of return to work/school following brain injury (Ip, Doran, & Schentag, 1995). Kay and Lezak (1990) posit that traditional intelligence tests, devised using artificial tasks that emphasise old learning, are not an indication to how the person will function with everyday tasks. An average IQ score can mask severe differences—the person can be performing in a superior range on some tasks, but be severely impaired on others and have trouble with memory, planning and self-monitoring (Fig. 3.1).

I can't understand; I can't do things I used to; I can't think properly; I've lost my job;

**Fig. 3.1** Headwork 1: 'Talk-about' cards relevant to the literature on IQ loss

### 3.3.2 Memory Loss After ABI

There were numerous studies around *memory* and ABI in the literature reviewed—working memory, prospective memory, deficits in attention and memory, bilateral damage to important structures of the brain and ways to improve prospective memory (Fleming, Shum, Strong, & Lightbody, 2005; Gil, Caspi, Ben-Ari, Koren, & Klein, 2005; Raskin & Sohlberg, 2009; Roche, Fleming, & Shum, 2002; Roche, Moody, Szabo, Fleming, & Shum, 2007; Sunderland, Harris & Baddeley, 1983). Memory impairments are among the greatest impediments to people returning to work, but may be one area of cognition that can respond to restorative intervention (Raskin & Sohlberg, 2009), a point we shall rely upon and which is further discussed in Chap. 6 in relation to learning.

Findings from these studies highlight difficulties people with ABI experience with encoding, performance and executing phases of prospective memory, which is the foundation of an intention and remembering to perform the intention. Evaluation of the effectiveness of rehabilitation methods, the frequency of memory lapses and working memory difficulties were identified. Schacter and Slotnick (2004) state that memory can be 'distorted' while Schacter, Chiao & Mitchell (2003) posit that '…not only is our sense of self based on memories of past experience…but our retrieval, recollection, and reconstruction of the past is, reciprocally, influenced by the self' (p. 227). The authors conceptualise this with a metaphor of 'The Seven Sins of Memory' or 'flawed memory experiences' (Schacter et al., 2003, p. 227) which include, transience (refers to forgetting over time), absent-mindedness (refers to lapses of attention), blocking (temporary inaccessibility of stored information), misattribution (attribution of memories to incorrect sources or believing you have seen/heard something you haven't—distorted misinformation), suggestibility (distorted or invented including bias) and persistence of memories (unwanted recollections for example with post-traumatic stress disorder).

If memory cannot be relied upon (Schacter et al., 2003) how reliable are the test results of people with brain injury? Could their assessment results differ on another day, or another hour of the day? For the purposes of this study, all these factors were considered (Figs. 3.2 and 3.3).

Data collection must assist participants to access memories by:

- Having an in-built way to help them focus on remembering.
- Developing a new strategy to assist them to discuss their memories or their experience in a positive way.
- Engaging sensory, short-term, long-term and prospective memory.
- Ensuring participants do not feel foolish: they will need prompts to help them to remember issues and also some way to prompt them so that they will remember what they are talking about.

**Fig. 3.2** Headwork 2: The memory difficulties of the participant should be considered in the method of data collection

I forget my name; I forget where I live; I've lost my memory; I've lost my friends; I've lost my job; I can't talk properly; I forget what things look like; I'm dependent; I get lost; I have to do lots of tests;

**Fig. 3.3** Headwork 3: 'Talk-about' cards relevant to the literature on memory loss

### *3.3.3 Depression/Suicide After ABI*

Depression and suicide were also well represented among the articles reviewed. Clinical studies have reported high rates of suicide attempts (18%) and clinically significant suicidal thoughts (20–21%) (Simpson & Tate, 2002). The prevalence, symptoms, significance of cognitive impairment and depression and suicide have been widely reported (Fann, Uomoto, & Katon, 2001; Hoofien, Gilboa, Vakil, & Donovick, 2001; Jorge, Robinson, Moser, Tateno, Crespo-Facorro, & Arndt, 1993; Jorge, Robinson, Moser, Tateno, Crespo-Facorro, & Arndt, 2004; Kreutzer, Steel & Gourley, 2001; Rapoport, McCullagh, Streiner, & Feinstein, 2003). These studies employ a range of formalised objective assessment measures (Figs. 3.4 and 3.5).

Data collection must help participants feel comfortable by:

- Taking place at a location where the participant feels comfortable — a local library, coffee shop etc.
- Helping them feel 'safe' by explaining several times what they will be asked to do
- Allowing them to take their time
- Letting them lead the discussion
- Allowing them privacy — they must not be 'pushed' to divulge private things
- Having ways to redirect negative thinking by reviewing positive things they have achieved
- Demonstrating understanding about their challenges
- Making it a positive process by not 'threatening' their self confidence by pointing out their deficits
- Giving them positive ideas to think about as they remember their difficulties

**Fig. 3.4** Headwork 4: The depression and emotional fragility of the participant should be considered in the method of data collection

Sad; Depressed; Distressed; Frustrated; Angry; Have to do lots of tests

**Fig. 3.5** Headwork 5: 'Talk-about' cards relevant to the literature on depression

### 3.3.4 Fatigue After ABI

A large number of scales have been developed that attempt to measure the nature, severity and impact of fatigue. Dittner, Wessely and Brown (2004, p. 157) report details of 30 scales and recommend that scales are selected to suit the clinician's needs and that existing and new scales are developed and validated.

Fatigue greatly influences the post-ABI life of the person, and there have been innumerable studies employing different ways to measure and compare fatigue between people with and without ABI. There were many surveys, interviews, questionnaires and scales for the researcher to employ. Once again though these are subject to comment, it is the findings that preoccupy us here. Findings of these studies, which include those conducted with people who have ABI, report significantly greater levels of fatigue than the general population, increased daytime sleepiness, lack of energy and exhaustion (Borgaro, Baker, Wethe, Prigatano, & Kwasnica, 2005; La Chapelle & Finlayson, 1998; Olver, Ponsford, & Curran, 1996; Ziino & Ponsford, 2006a, 2006b) (Figs. 3.6 and 3.7).

Interview/data collection must be of a suitable length of time so participants are not distressed by fatigue.

- Opportunity for participants to take a break – a coffee break.
- Interview broken into segments – each segment discussed so they can see progress.
- By using objects/cards/pictures and words they obtain input not just in words.

**Fig. 3.6** Headwork 6: The fatigue of the participant should be considered in the method of data collection

I can't do the things I used to do; I've lost my job; I've lost my friends; I have to do lots of tests

**Fig. 3.7** Headwork 7: 'Talk-about' cards relevant to the literature on fatigue

### 3.3.5 Coping Strategies of People with ABI

Studies around emotions and coping (Bornhofen & McDonald, 2008; Pagulayan, Hoffman, Temkin, Machamer, & Dikmen, 2008), emotional and executive functioning (Douglas, 2010; Garcia-Molina, Bernabeu, Guitart, & Roig-Rovira, 2010) have examined ways people cope with ABI. During rehabilitation, and post-rehabilitation, studies have been conducted into community programs (Vander Laan, Brandys, Sullivan, & Lemsky 2001; Ylvisaker, Feeney, 1998), intimacy

(Aloni, Keren, Cohen, Rosentul, Romm, & Groswasser, 1999; Gill, Sander, Robins, Mazzei, & Struchen, 2011), assessing care and support needs (Ladanyi & Elliot, 2008; Turner-Stokes, Williams & Johnson, 2009). Studies into peer support suggest that peer support can enhance coping and can also help offset loneliness and the disruption of social support that can be associated with brain injury (Hibbard et al., 2002; Struchen, Davis, Bogaards, Hudler-Hull, Clark, & Mazzei, 2011).

There have also been studies of people with ABI that have investigated coping strategies and relationships between coping, apathy, depression, denial and avoidance and emotional adjustment (Anson & Ponsford, 2006a,b; Curran, Ponsford & Crowe, 2000; Ownsworth, Desbois, Grant, Fleming & Strong, 2006; Ownsworth, Fleming, Strong, Radel, Chan & Clare, 2007).

High levels of emotional distress have been shown to affect coping; higher levels of depression were associated with coping strategies characterised by worry, wishful thinking and self-blame; strategies that focus on problem-solving and having a positive outlook were related to lower anxiety levels. Major coping types identified include emotion-focused, problem-focused, perception-focused and avoidance coping. Once again inventories with good statistical properties were widely used in these studies (Fig. 3.8).

| **Coping strategy identified in literature** | **Examples of 'talk-about' cards** |
|---|---|
| Avoidance coping | Going out, staying home |
| Problem focused | Doing hard things, achieving hard things, Seeing some progress, Doing things I couldn't do before |
| Emotion focused | Talking |
| Peer support | My family, my friends, what others with ABI have done |
| Health Professionals | Doctor; Occupational Therapist; Counsellor; Health Professionals |

**Fig. 3.8** Headwork 8: 'Talk-about' cards relevant to the literature on coping

Chapter 4 will review qualitative studies around coping, resilience and quality of life.

### *3.3.6 Pain Following ABI*

The incidence of pain following brain injury shows that chronic pain is a significant problem in mild, moderate and severe TBI (Lahz& Bryant, 1996); that shoulder pain after TBI is a clinical issue that has not been well researched or recognised (Leung, 2006) and that pain is quite common because the nature of many ABIs being the result of accident (Sherman, Goldberg & Bell, 2006) (Fig. 3.9).

I have terrible pain; I've lost my job.

**Fig. 3.9** Headwork 9: 'Talk-about' cards relevant to the literature on the consequences of pain

### *3.3.7 Self-awareness After ABI*

Self-awareness is another important area that has been the focus of studies examined in the review. Fleming, Lucas and Lightbody (2006) posit that self-awareness is a complex phenomenon that impedes the rehabilitation process and outcome. Their study provided an individualised program to improve self-awareness. These programs were successful but, in all four cases, were accompanied by anxiety. Ownsworth et al., (2007) studied awareness and long-term adjustment, and different awareness typologies were identified. Individuals with good self-awareness and high defensiveness demonstrated the most favourable outcomes. Ownsworth, Desbois, Grant, Fleming and Strong's (2006) study of the associations between self-awareness and emotional wellbeing empirically supported the theoretical view that an increase in self-awareness is associated with improved employment status. Fleming and Ownsworth's 2006 review of awareness interventions in brain injury rehabilitation was conducted because '…unawareness related to brain injury has implications in rehabilitation, functional outcomes, and the emotional well-being of clients' (Fleming & Ownsworth, 2006. p. 74).

Lam, McMahon, Priddy and Gehred-Schultz (1988) posit that self-awareness increases participation in rehabilitation and Ezrachi, Ben-Yishay, Kay, Diller and Rattok (1991) link self-awareness to successful community and vocational reintegration. A correlation has also been found between self-awareness and emotional distress (Fleming, Lucas, & Lightbody, 2006; Fleming & Ownsworth, 2006; Fleming, Shum, Strong & Lightbody, 2005; Fleming & Strong, 1999; Fleming, Strong, & Ashton, 1998; Lezak & O' Brien, 1988; Roche, Moody, Szabo, Fleming & Shum, 2002).

Research has shown that clients with better self-awareness of their impairments have better participation or involvement and compliance in rehabilitation (Fleming

Interview/data collection must be allow for participants to become aware of the difficulties they experience, explore how they feel because of their ABI and coping strategies they use successfully.

- Opportunity for participants to see what some people with ABI have experienced
- Interview needs to be divided into sections to focus upon before moving to another sections.
- Objects/cards/pictures and words utilized to assist them to reflect.

**Fig. 3.10** Headwork 8: Participants may lack self-awareness therefor the method should assist them to reflect

et al. 1998, 2005). Thus, there is a complex interaction between self-awareness and compliance. Self-awareness and compliance will be issues to address in the Keys Study (Fig. 3.10).

### 3.3.8 *Post-traumatic Stress Disorder After ABI*

Studies also evaluate the relationship between acute stress and post-traumatic stress, memory and amnesia (Bryant & Harvey, 2000; Harvey & Bryant, 1998 1999; Gil, Caspi, Ben-Ari, Koren and Klein, 2005). There are other studies about persistent post-concussive symptoms and post-traumatic stress disorder (PTSD) as a consequence of war by Schneiderman, Braver, and Kang (2008); Hoge, McGurk, Thomas, Cox, Engel and Castro (2008) and Ohry, Rattok and Solomon (1996). Bryant, Marosszeky, Crooks, Baguley and Gurka (2000) investigated the effect of PTSD on rehabilitation after severe ABI. Once again scales with strong statistical properties were adopted in all these studies (Fig. 3.11).

Interview/data collection must be take into account the participant may be suffering prom PTSD – they must be treated with respect, kindness, they should direct the interview with what they wish to talk about, they must be put at their ease, the interview must be non-threatening..there must be no right or wrong answers – they must feel success

**Fig. 3.11** Headwork 9: Trauma can play a part in how participants react in interviews

### 3.3.9 *Learning Difficulties After ABI*

Studies suggest learning difficulties can result from ABI through the combination of cognitive, memory, sight, hearing and understanding impairments that result from damage to the brain. There are many studies in regard to such learning disabilities: Siegal (1989, 1999), Sternberg and Spear-Swerling (1999), Stanovich (1991), Swanson (1993a, b), Wagner and Garon (1999) and Wong (1996). This topic will be examined at length in Chap. 5, which focuses upon education and learning (Fig. 3.12).

Interview/data collection must be take into account the participant may have comprehension and learning difficulties therefore learning principles must be employed

**Fig. 3.12** Headwork 10: Participants may have comprehension and learning difficulties

### 3.3.10 Cognitive Rehabilitation Therapy

Perhaps one of the closest links between therapeutic intervention and re-engagement in everyday life was in the area of cognitive rehabilitation therapy. Several articles were found in the review of this area. Cognitive rehabilitation therapy is a process of re-learning cognitive skills that have been changed or lost because of damage to the brain cells or chemistry. It involves education about cognitive weakness and strengths, process training—practicing cognitive skills, strategy training and functional activities training. Harley et al. describe it as 'reinforcing, strengthening, or re-establishing previously learned patterns of behaviour, or establishing new patterns of cognitive activity or compensatory mechanisms for impaired neurological systems' (1992, p. 63).

Giles (2010) conducted one of the largest randomised controlled trials of rehabilitation after traumatic brain injury to examine the theoretical relationships between cognitive and functional rehabilitation. The study added to the evidence base supporting neurofunctional intervention in addition to standard care in improving independent living skills in people with moderate or severe TBI.

Schoenberg et al. (2008) compared outcomes of patients who received computer-based cognitive therapy with participants who received face-to-face speech–language rehabilitation and established that similar outcomes at a similar cost were the result. Carney et al. (1999) ascertained that specific forms of cognitive rehabilitation reduce memory failures and anxiety and improve self-concept and interpersonal relationships. Cernich, Kurtz, Mordecai, and Ryan (2010) explain current treatment options, and Grealy, Johnson and Rushton (1999) used exercise and virtual reality to improve cognitive function. They concluded that exercising in a virtual environment offers the potential for significant gains in cognitive function. Yet Kay and Lezak (1990) warn against 'The Rehab Wizard'—where people with brain injury and their families feel let down by the belief that cognitive retraining would be the answer to behavioural and cognitive difficulties.

The links between cognitive function and re-engagement with everyday life are obvious. The objective measurement, based upon pre-established understanding of cognition, establishes an important framework through which to maximise cognitive functioning. However, the objectification of the person's cognitive skills can miss the connections between cognition and other aspects of the person's life, and the person's view is an important feature as a focus for re-engagement in everyday life. Cognitive rehabilitation therapy involves professional intervention, and there are computer-based programs that can be used by the person once they have returned home. In Chap. 5, more will be said of the links between cognition, learning and ABI.

### 3.3.11 Other Areas of Focus in Studies

Studies of the 'effect of ABI on the family' of people with ABI examine the needs of the family members of patients with severe TBI. Bond, Draeger, and Mandleco and Donnelly (2003) concluded that 'the need to know, the need for consistent information and the need to make sense of the experience was vital' (Verhaeghe, Defloor, & Grypdonck, 2005).

There are also studies that touch upon social identity and social support, which have been viewed from different perspectives with various discoveries. These include the following: cognitive deficits have been found to bring the person closer to family (Haslam, Jetten, Postmes & Haslam, 2009); identity crisis and disruption associated with ABI (Teasdale & Engberg, 2001) and social isolation and a relaxed way of living in rural areas has been found to accommodate the fatigue of the person with ABI (Jones & Curtin, 2010). Community integration involving relationships with others, independence in one's living situation and activities to fill one's time have been recommended in McColl et al.'s (1998) study.

## 3.4 Some Reflections on Quantitative Body-Object Research

More needs to be said about the body-object literature as a collective body of knowledge and its relevance relationship to the present study.

The studies above show particular foci, most of which are based around deficits. Another indicator of the breadth and depth of interest was the range of topics investigated in research articles in the *Journal of the Australian Society for the Study of Brain Impairment* in the two years following the above literature review: memory (23 articles), communication (10), cognition/motivation (9), community rehabilitation support (8), rehabilitation outcomes (5), residential care (4), executive function (4), anxiety (4), social behaviour (3) and family (3). Two or less articles were found on: neural cells/genes, physical fitness/leisure activities, behavioural change, goal setting, depression, dementia, emotional adjustment, emotional impact hospital to home, occupational issues, early recovery rates, reasoning and positive psychology. The authors understand that approximately 90% of articles published in this journal have been quantitative studies.

As demonstrated by information under the 'Headwork' headings, the development of *Keys to the ABI Cage* drew upon this literature. The literature review was used to inform the process through which to engage people with ABI so as to do no harm. It was anticipated that they might be suffering from IQ loss, memory impairment, depression (even suicidal thoughts), fatigue, lack of self-awareness, post-traumatic stress disorder, difficulty coping and pain. Thus, it was acknowledged that we would be approaching and engaging fragile, vulnerable people to reflect upon their ABI experience.

The 'talk-about' cards, which were a central part of the process, 'translated' difficulties participants may be experiencing, and the differences between their pre- and post-ABI life into everyday, colloquial comments upon which they could choose to reflect if they wished.

However, the approach of the medical model is that 'defects or failure of a bodily system are detected and … goals of intervention are cure, amelioration of the physical condition to the greatest extent possible' (Olkin, 1999, p. 26). The literature reviewed has demonstrated how specific difficulties/differences/deficits have been separated for specific examination by experts in various fields. But it is the *combination* of the *total* of the overlapping difficulties/differences/deficits that affect the lived experience or lifeworld of people with ABI. Moreover, these must be set against the positive aspects of their lives, which are seldom if ever mentioned.

The importance of the difficulties/differences/deficits (IQ and memory loss, depression, cognitive rehabilitation therapy, fatigue, lack of self-awareness, post-traumatic stress, coping and pain) cannot be ignored. These topics focus upon and consider answers to blank spots, areas that have been identified as some of the things that are more likely to be found among people with ABI. However, these studies above are largely second-order accounts, which may fail to establish the self-reported impact and meaning from a person-first perspective.

Tests for IQ or memory loss are *not the same* as the initial medical tests conducted in the acute hospital stage to determine the damage to the person's brain (e.g. magnetic resonance imaging; computed tomography or computerised axial tomography; electroencephalogram; position emission). These medical tests are used to 'prove' the physical brain has been damaged.

It is more difficult to prove ABI through IQ and other tests, and tests may not identify how the person feels because of their ABI. Some people feel uncomfortable about others judging and knowing about their difficulties, and there are many reasons why a person may perform a test badly or well at the time of these tests. These reasons might include, inter alia, motivation, whether or not they are having a good or bad day, time of day the test is given and so forth, but test results are taken to be of great importance when used in legal proceedings. The body-object perspective investigated by these studies 'filters down' to be reported in Web-based material, as the basis for information in many brain injury support Websites. For the person with ABI, reading about possible difficulties/differences/deficits can be valuable because they provide information so they realise they are not imagining things and that they are not alone, but there may be little information to aid or help the person adapt, cope and re-engage in life, and the reporting may reinforce the view that they are 'more damaged' and 'less normal' than the rest of society. A positive approach would at very least address the issues of coping and adaptation more systematically as well as listing and describing deficits.

Viewed from the 'body-object' perspective, ABI leads to the assumption that a formulaic piece-by-piece response by medical and rehabilitation practitioners is all that can be done. But, as will be shown, this perspective is problematic as the approach is one based on defining problems and not about examining the positive aspects of the person's life.

The nature of data collection, where the person with ABI may be treated as 'the object' of professional and professionally shared expertise, may further disempower the individual. Most importantly, this medical model of research is transposed into the rehabilitation setting, where the issues of the inequality of power between the professional and the client are taken as a given. The professional (the expert with all the knowledge) administers a test or questionnaire (that may have been trialled and developed in studies), and the client, the person with ABI, is required to comply and answer the predetermined test questions. Because, for example, injuries from of a motor vehicle accident may involve compensation, the client may feel under additional pressure to comply to complete tests.

There are, then, further issues that inform the present study which are informed by the processes involved in research and practice adopted by the body-object approach (Figs. 3.13 and 3.14).

- Because of the number of 'tests' given to people with ABI, the method employed in this research should *not* be like a test.
- The method should give the interviewee the power to choose issues to discuss and whether or not to disclose information.
- The participant should hold the power, be in control.
- The method should focus upon things the interviewee does to help themselves.
- Engagement with the method should have a positive outcome.
- The method should acknowledge that the interviewee has many challenges, and acknowledge that having ABI is difficult.
- The method should foster hope and empower people to share with others the ways they tackle their difficulties.
- The method must be user friendly, easy, use non medical language and be nonthreatening.
- Participants must not feel they 'have' to participate in this study, they must not be bullied or coerced to participate.
- Participants will be the 'expert'.
- The possible emotional fragility and fear of new situations will need to be addressed.

**Fig. 3.13** Headwork 11: Reflecting on body-objects tests and this study

Participants must be comfortable being engaged in this study by:

- Helping them to understand what is required of them.
- Helping them to understand why they are participating – the purpose.
- Ensuring they don't feel foolish: they will need prompts to help them to remember issues and also some way to prompt them so that they will remember what they are talking about.
- Ensuring that they can reflect upon their experiences (including their deficits) in a way that does not upset them.

**Fig. 3.14** Headwork 12: Participants should feel comfortable

Chapter 1 pointed to other important issues (love, hope, courage, determination, etc.) that affect the lifeworld of people with ABI, both in hospital and once they leave the hospital or rehabilitation setting. These could be regarded as blind spots. These factors are not generally the focus of quantitative research (nor rehabilitation); indeed, they may not be issues that can be addressed by medical professionals, but that does not mean that these issues are not vital to the individual as they re-engage with life. Indeed, as suggested earlier using the notion of 'embodied practices', it is vital to ensure that the life experiences from the earliest stage prepare the person for a life of hope and not of resignation. The Keys Study intended to identify things that had helped people with ABI to learn to feel and fare better and to share these collective concepts.

One more point should be made. The focus of literature reviewed above predominantly covers the 'golden period/dark hole period' when the person with ABI has most contact with professionals who can 'make a difference', the period over which it is believed that body can be 'salvaged' and 'repaired'. But, to reiterate, the consequences of ABI remain with the person for many years, or a lifetime, not just the 'golden period/dark hole period'. In spite of the tremendous advancement in knowledge gained about ABI, there is little information available about the way people with ABI understand their new situation, or how they feel about rehabilitation, or being involved with research studies or how they regain their sense of identity, or things they can do to help themselves.

## 3.5 Recapitulation

Quantitative body-object literature provides empirical data about particular difficulties/differences/deficits for people with ABI. The systems of classification established in the medical model have been criticised because of their focus on 'mending' bodies and brains while missing the everyday and mundane lives produced by the recurrent and prolonged engagement with the medical and rehabilitation professions. The empirical studies reviewed have, like the assessments of clinical professionals led to the development of questionnaires, standardised measures, scales, tests and collateral reports to determine deficits in order to identify the impairment of the person with ABI, and to assess areas for improvement in a time-controlled manner with results that can be shared and understood by other professionals. But 'learning to improve' or 'learning to live again' does not cease for the person with ABI once their engagement with the professions has diminished or ended. Indeed, it might be argued that the importance of re-learning in situ, where they re-engage with their everyday lives, is important as well as the initial professionally dominated period.

From the literature reviewed in this chapter, it has been found that people with ABI are known to lack self-awareness, and they can experience memory difficulties and can become distressed when they become aware of their difficulties and limitations. These issues were considered in the development of *Keys to the ABI Cage* method, which aimed to provide a positive experience for participants as 'Headwork' in this chapter has demonstrated. Examples of 'talk-about' cards informed from the quantitative, body-object literature, allowed the participant to reflect upon their own experience, by exploring both the positive as well as the negative aspects of their life world. Involvement in the Keys Study was not as confronting or challenging as an IQ test for example as participants had seen the Cage model, been shown a Power Point presentation explaining what they would be asked to do to reflect upon and speak about their experience.

The Keys Study was designed to access the first-person experiences of people with ABI. Participants were not obliged to understand and answer questions. As it presently stands, the quantitative, outsiders', body-object, medical model may not fit the needs of the fragile participant experiencing multiple challenges.

The period of re-learning for people who acquire an ABI lasts a lifetime, yet few studies examine the period post-professional input. The Keys Study focused on the period when people were learning to re-engage with the complexities of their relationships and home lives after the 'golden period/dark hole period', implying that the methodology sought to adopt an approach in which there was a learning element. Chapter 5 will examine literature about learning.

Finally, the approach adopted did not accept that body-object-based information exhausts the information that should be publicly available. Indeed, such information may be counterproductive to personal identity and the views others have of relatives with an ABI. In his study, Sherry (2006) suggests:

> … a need for the theoretical revision of both the medical and social models of disability. Issues of rights, inclusion, respect, and diversity are often marginalized within the medical model, where the focus is on labelling the 'deficits' of an impaired body. Likewise, issues of identity, embodiment and human agency are often sidelined in the social model, where the focus is on identifying disabling barriers, often from a structuralist or materialistic perspective, (Sherry, 2006, p. 203).

Taking into account Sherry's recommendation, the following chapter will examine the body-subject, qualitative literature.

## References

Aloni, A., Keren, O., Cohen, M., Rosentul, N., Romm, M., & Groswasser, Z. (1999). Incidence of sexual dysfunction in TBI patients during the early post-traumatic in-patient rehabilitation phase. *Brain Injury, 13*(2), 89–97.

Anson, K., & Ponsford, J. (2006a). Coping and emotional adjustment following traumatic brain injury. *The Journal of Head Trauma Rehabilitation, 21*(3), 248.

Anson, K., & Ponsford, J. (2006b). Evaluation of a coping skills group following traumatic brain injury. *Brain Injury, 20*(2), 167–178.

Borgaro, S. R., Baker, J., Wethe, J. V., Prigatano, G. P., & Kwasnica, C. (2005). Subjective reports of fatigue during early recovery from traumatic brain injury. *Journal of Head Trauma Rehabilitation, 20*, 419–425. doi:10.1097/00001199-200509000-00003

Bond, A. E., Draeger, C. R. L., Mandleco, B., & Donnelly, M. (2003). Needs of family members of patients with severe traumatic brain injury: Implications for evidence-based practice. *Critical Care Nurse, 23*(4), 63–72.

Bornhofen, C., & McDonald, S. (2008). Emotion perception deficits following traumatic brain injury: A review of the evidence and rationale for intervention. *Journal of the International Neuropsychological Society, 14*(4), 511–525.

Bryant, R. A., & Harvey, A. G. (2000). New DSM-IV diagnosis of acute stress disorder. *American Journal of Psychiatry, 157,* 1889–1890.

Bryant, R. A., Marosszeky, J. E., Crooks, J., & Gurka, J. A. (2000). Posttraumatic stress disorder after severe traumatic brain injury. *American Journal of Psychiatry, 157*(4), 629–631.

Carney, N., Chesnut, R. M., Maynard, H., Mann, N. C., Patterson, P., & Helfand, M. (1999). Effect of cognitive rehabilitation on outcomes for persons with traumatic brain injury: A systematic review. *The Journal of Head Trauma Rehabilitation, 14*(3), 277–307.

Cernich, A. N., Kurtz, S. M., Mordecai, K. L., & Ryan, P. B. (2010). Cognitive rehabilitation in traumatic brain injury. *Current Treatment Options in Neurology, 12*(5), 412–423.

Curran, C. A., Ponsford, J. L., & Crowe, S. D. (2000). Coping strategies and emotional outcome following traumatic brain injury: A comparison with orthopedic patients. *The Journal of Head Trauma Rehabilitation, 15*(6), 1256–1274.

Dittner, A. J., Wessely, S. C., & Brown, R. G. (2004). The assessment of fatigue: A practical guide for clinicians and researchers. *Journal of Psychosomatic Research, 56*(2), 157–170. doi:10.1016/S0022-3000(03)00371-4

Douglas, J. M. (2010). Relation of executive functioning to pragmatic outcome following severe traumatic brain injury. *Journal of Speech, Language, and Hearing Research, 53*(2), 365.

Ezrachi, O., Ben-Yishay, Y., Kay, T., & Diller, L. (1991). Predicting employment in traumatic brain injury following neuropsychological rehabilitation. *The Journal of Head Trauma Rehabilitation, 6*(3), 71–84.

Fann, J. R., Uomoto, J. M., & Katon, W. J. (2001). Cognitive improvement with treatment of depression following mild traumatic brain injury. *Psychosomatics, 42,* 48–54. doi:10.1176/appi.psy.42.1.48

Fleming, J. M., Lucas, S. E., & Lightbody, S. (2006). Using occupation to facilitate self-awareness in people who have acquired brain injury: A pilot study. *Canadian Journal of Occupational Therapy, 73*(1), 44–55.

Fleming, J., & Ownsworth, T. (2006). A review of awareness interventions in brain injury rehabilitation. *Neuropsychological Rehabilitation, 16*(4), 474–500.

Fleming, J. M., Shum, D., Strong, J., & Lightbody, S. (2005). Prospective memory rehabilitation for adults with traumatic brain injury: A compensatory training programme. *Brain Injury, 19*(1), 1–10.

Fleming, J., & Strong, J. (1999). A longitudinal study of self-awareness: Functional deficits underestimated by persons with brain injury. *Occupational Therapy Journal of Research, 19*(1), 3–17.

Fleming, J. M., Strong, J., & Ashton, R. (1998). Cluster analysis of self-awareness levels in adults with traumatic brain injury and relationship to outcome. *The Journal of Head Trauma Rehabilitation, 13*(5), 39–51.

García-Molina, A., Bernabeu, G. M., & Roig-Rovira, T. (2010). Traumatic brain injury and daily life: The role of executive function. *Psicothema, 22*(3), 430–435.

Gil, S., Caspi, Y., Zilberman, B.-A., Koren, D., & Klein, E. (2005). Does memory of a traumatic event increase the risk for post-traumatic stress disorder in patients with traumatic brain injury? A Prospective Study. *American Journal of Psychiatry, 162,* 963–969. doi:10.1176/appi.ajp.162.5.963

Giles, G. M. (2010). Cognitive versus functional approaches to rehabilitation after traumatic brain injury: Commentary on a randomized controlled trial. *The American Journal of Occupational Therapy, 64*(1), 182–185.

Gill, C. J., Sander, A. M., Robins, N., Mazzei, D., & Struchen, M. A. (2011). Exploring experiences of intimacy from the viewpoint of individuals with traumatic brain injury and their partners. *Journal of Head Trauma Rehabilitation, 26*(1), 56–68. doi:10.1097/HTR. 0b013e3182048ee9

Grealy, M. A., Johnson, D. A., & Rushton, S. K. (1999). Improving cognitive function after brain injury: The use of exercise and virtual reality. *Archives of Physical Medicine and Rehabilitation, 80*(6), 661–667.

Harley, J., Allen, C., Braciszeski, T., Cicerone, K., Dahlberg, C., Evans, S., et al. (1992). Guidelines for cognitive rehabilitation. *NeuroRehabilitation, 2*(3), 62–67.

Harvey, A. G., & Bryant, R. A. (1998). The relationship between acute stress disorder and posttraumatic stress disorder: A prospective evaluation of motor vehicle accident survivors. *Journal of Consulting and Clinical Psychology, 66*(3), 507–512.

Harvey, A. G., & Bryant, R. A. (1999). Dissociative symptoms in acute stress disorder. *Journal of Traumatic Stress, 12,* 673–680.

Haslam, S. Alexander, Jetten, Jolanda, Postmes, Tom, & Haslam, Catherine. (2009). Social identity, health and well-being: An emerging agenda for applied psychology. *Applied Psychology: An International Review, 58*(1), 1–23. doi:10.1111/j.1464-0597.2008.00379.x

Hibbard, M. R., Cantor, J., Charatz, H., Rosenthal, R., Ashman, T., Gundersen, N., et al. (2002). Peer support in the community: Initial findings of a mentoring program for individuals with traumatic brain injury and their families. *The Journal of Head Trauma Rehabilitation, 17*(2), 112–131.

Hoge, C. W., McGurk, D., Thomas, J. L., Cox, A. L., Engel, C. C., & Castro, C. A. (2008). Mild traumatic brain injury in US soldiers returning from Iraq. *New England Journal of Medicine, 358*(5), 453–463.

Hoofien, D., Gilboa, A., Vakil, E., & Donovick, P. J. (2001). Traumatic brain injury (TBI) 10-20 years later: A comprehensive outcome study of psychiatric symptomatology, cognitive abilities and psychosocial functioning. *Brain Injury, 15*(3), 189–209.

Ip, R. Y., Dornan, J., & Schentag, C. (1995). Traumatic brain injury: Factors predicting return to work or school. *Brain Injury, 9*(5), 517–532.

Jones, J., & Curtin, M. (2010). Traumatic brain injury, participation, and rural identity. *Qualitative Health Research, 20*(7), 942–951.

Jorge, R. E., Robinson, R. G., Moser, D., Tateno, A., Crespo-Facorro, B., & Arndt, S. (2004). Major depression following traumatic brain injury. *Archives of General Psychiatry, 61,* 42–50.

Jorge, R. E., Robinson, R. G., Starkstein, S. E., & Arndt, S. V. (1993). *The Journal of Neuropsychiatry and Clinical Neurosciences, 5*(4), 369–374.

Kay, T., & Lezak, M. (1990). The nature of head Injury. In D. W. Cothell (Ed.), *Traumatic brain injury and vocational rehabilitation* (pp. 21–65). Monomonie, WI: Research and Training Centre, University of Wisconsin-Stout.

Kreutzer, J. S., Steel, R. T., & Gourley, E. (2001). The prevalence and symptom rates of stroke in older adults. *Psychosomatic Medicine, 63,* 210–215.

La Chapelle, D. L., & Finlayson, M. A. (1998). An evaluation of subjective and objective measures of fatigue in patients with brain injury and healthy controls. *Brain Injury, 12,* 649–659.

Ladanyi, S., & Elliott, D. (2008). Traumatic brain injury: An integrated clinical case presentation and literature review: Part II: The continuum of care. *Australian Critical Care, 21*(3), 141–153.

Lahz, S., & Bryant, R. A. (1996). Incidence of chronic pain following traumatic brain injury. *Archives of Physical Medicine and Rehabilitation, 77*(9), 889–891.

Lam, C. S., McMahon, B. T., Priddy, D. A., & Gehred-Schultz, A. (1988). Deficit awareness and treatment performance among traumatic head injury adults. *Brain Injury, 2*(3), 235–242.

Leung, J. (2006). *A prospective comparative study of shoulder pain after TBI & cerebrovascular accident: Final report to motor Accident Authority of NSW.* Retrieved from http://www.lifetimecare.nsw.gov.au/FileHandler.ashx?name=Brain%20Injury/A_Prospective_Comparative_Study_pdf

Lezak, M. D., & O' Brien, K. P. (1988). Longitudinal study of emotional, social, and physical changes after traumatic brain injury. *Journal of Learning Disabilities, 21*(8), 456–462. doi:10.1177/002221948802100802

McColl, M. A., Carlson, P., Johnston, J., Minnes, P., Shue, K., Davies, D., et al. (1998). The definition of community integration: Perspectives of people with brain injuries. *Brain Injury, 12*(1), 15–30.

Ohry, A., Rattok, J., & Solomon, Z. (1996). Post-traumatic stress disorder in brain injury patients. *Brain Injury, 10*(9), 687–695.

Olkin, R. (1999). *What psychotherapists should know about disability*. New York, NY: The Guilford Press.

Olver, J. H., Ponsford, J. L., & Curran, C. A. (1996). Outcomes following traumatic brain injury: A comparison between 2 and 5 years after injury. *Brain Injury, 10,* 841–848. doi:10.1080/026990596123945

Ownsworth, T., Desbois, J., Grant, E., Fleming, J., & Strong, J. (2006). The associations among self-awareness, emotional well-being, and employment outcome following acquired brain injury: A 12-month longitudinal study. *Rehabilitation Psychology, 51*(1), 50–59.

Ownsworth, T., Fleming, J., Strong, J., Radel, M., Chan, W., & Clare, L. (2007). Awareness typologies, long-term emotional adjustment and psychosocial outcomes following acquired brain injury. *Neuropsychological Rehabilitation, 17*(2), 129–150.

Pagulayan, K. F., Hoffman, J. M., Temkin, N. R., Machamer, J. E., & Dikmen, S. S. (2008). Functional limitations and depression after traumatic brain injury: Examination of the temporal relationship. *Archives of Physical Medicine and Rehabilitation, 89*(10), 1887–1892.

Parker, R. S., & Rosenblum, A. (1996). IQ loss and emotional dysfunctions after mild head injury incurred in a motor vehicle accident. *Journal of Clinical Psychology, 52*(1), 32–43.

Rapoport, M. J., McCullagh, S., Streiner, D., & Feinstein, A. (2003). The clinical significance of major depression following mild traumatic brain injury. *Psychosomatics, 44*(1), 31–37.

Raskin, S. A., & Sohlberg, M. M. (2009). Prospective memory intervention: A review and evaluation of a pilot restorative intervention. *Brain Impairment, 10*(1), 76–86. doi:10.1375/brim.10.1.76

Roche, N. L., Fleming, J. M., & Shum, D. H. K. (2002). Self-awareness of prospective memory failure in adults with traumatic brain injury. *Brain Injury, 16*(11), 931–945.

Roche, N. L., Moody, A., Szabo, K., Fleming, J., & Shum, D. (2007). Prospective memory in adults with traumatic brain injury: An analysis of perceived reasons for remembering and forgetting. *Neuropsychological Rehabilitation, 17,* 314–334.

Schacter, D. L., Chiao, J. Y., & Mitchell, J. P. (2003). The seven sins of memory. *Annals of the New York Academy of Science, 1001*(1), 226–239. doi:10.1196/annals.1279.012

Schacter, D. L., & Slotnick, S. D. (2004). The cognitive neuroscience of memory distortion. *Neuron, 44*(1), 149–160. doi:10.1016/neuron2004.08.017

Schneiderman, A. I., Braver, E. R., & Kang, H. K. (2008). Understanding sequelae of injury mechanisms and mild traumatic brain injury incurred during the conflicts in Iraq and Afghanistan: Persistent postconcussive symptoms and posttraumatic stress disorder. *American Journal of Epidemiology, 167*(12), 1446–1452. doi:10.1093/aje/kwn068

Schoenberg, M. R., Ruwe, W. D., Dawson, K., McDonald, N. B., Houston, B., & Forducey, P. G. (2008). Comparison of functional outcomes and treatment cost between a computer-based cognitive rehabilitation teletherapy program and a face-to-face rehabilitation program. *Professional Psychology: Research and Practice, 39*(2), 169–175.

Sherman, K. B., Goldberg, M., & Bell, K. R. (2006). Traumatic brain injury and pain. *Physical Medicine & Rehabilitation Clinics of North America, 17*(2), 473–490.

Sherry, M. (2006). *If I only had a brain: Deconstructing brain injury*. New York, NY: Routledge.

Siegal, L. S. (1989). IQ is irrelevant to the definition of learning disabilities. *Journal of Learning Disabilities, 22*(8), 469–478. doi:10.1177/002221948902200803

Siegal, L. S. (1999). Learning disabilities: Issues in the definition and diagnosis of learning disabilities. A Perspective on Guckenberger v. Boston University. *Journal of Learning Disabilities, 32*(4), 304–319. doi:10.1177/002221949903200405

Simpson, G., & Tate, R. (2002). Suicidality after traumatic brain injury: Demographic, injury and clinical correlates. *Psychological Medicine, 32*(4), 687–697.

Smart, J.F. (2009). The power of models of disability. *Journal of Rehabilitation*, *April–June*, 1–11.

Stanovich, K. E. (1991). The sociopsychometrics of learning disabilities. *Journal of Learning Disabilities, 32*(4), 350–361.

Sternberg, R. J., & Spear-Swerling, L. (Eds.). (1999). *Perspectives on learning disabilities: Biological, cognitive, contextual*. Boulder, CO: Westview Press.

Struchen, M. A., Davis, L. C., Bogaards, J. A., Hudler-Hull, T., Clark, A. N., Mazzei, D. M., et al. (2011). Making connections after brain injury: Development and evaluation of a social peer-mentoring program for persons with traumatic brain injury. *The Journal of Head Trauma Rehabilitation, 26*(1), 4–19.

Sunderland, A., Harris, J. E., & Baddeley, A. D. (1983). Do laboratory tests predict everyday memory? A neuropsychological study. *Journal of Verbal and Learning Behaviour, 22*(3), 341–357. Retrieved from http://dx.doi.org/10.1016/S0022-5371(83)90229-3

Swanson, H. L. (1993a). Executive processing in learning disabled readers. *Intelligence, 17,* 117–149.

Swanson, H. L. (1993b). Working memory in learning disability subgroups. *Journal of Experimental Child Psychology, 56,* 87–114.

Teasdale, T. W., & Engberg, A. W. (2001). Suicide after traumatic brain injury: A population study. *Journal of Neurology, Neurosurgery and Psychiatry, 71,* 436–440. doi:10.1136/jnnp.71.4.436

Turner-Stokes, L., Williams, H., & Johnson, J. (2009). Goal attainment scaling: Does it provide added value as a person-centred measure for evaluation of outcome inneurorehabilitation following acquired brain injury? *Journal of Rehabilitation Medicine, 41*(7), 528–535.

Vander Laan, R., Brandys, C., Sullivan, I., & Lemsky, C. (2001). Integration through a city-wide brain injury network and best practices project. *NeuroRehabilitation, 16*(1), 17–26.

Verhaeghe, S., Defloor, T., & Grypdonck, M. (2005). Stress and coping among families of patients with traumatic brain injury: A review of the literature. *Journal of Clinical Nursing, 14*(8), 1004–1012.

Wagner, R. K., & Garon, T. (1999). Learning disabilities in perspective. In R. J. Sternberg & L. Spear-Swerling (Eds.), *Perspectives on learning disabilities* (pp. 83–105). Boulder, CO: Westview.

Wong, B. Y. L. (1996). Teaching low achievers and students with learning disabilities to plan, write, and revise opinion essays. *Journal of Learning Disabilities, 29*(2), 197–212. doi:10.1177/002221949602900209

Wortzel, H. S. &Arciniegas, D. B. (n.d.). The DSM-5 approach to evaluating traumatic brain injury. Veterans Affairs and Rocky Mountain MIRECC.

Ylvisaker, M., & Feeney, T. J. (1998). Everyday people as supports: Developing competencies through collaboration. In M. Ylvisaker (Ed.), *Traumatic brain injury rehabilitation: Children and adolescents* (2nd ed., pp. 367–384). Boston, MA: Butterworth-Heinemann.

Ziino, C., & Ponsford, J. (2006a). Selective attention deficits and subjective fatigue following traumatic brain injury. *Neuropsychology, 20,* 383–390. doi:10.1037/0894-4105.20.3.383

Ziino, C., & Ponsford, J. (2006b). Vigilance and fatigue following traumatic brain injury. *Journal of the International Neuropsychological Society, 12,* 100–110. doi:10.1017/S1355617706060139

# Chapter 4
# The Body-Subject Perspective of ABI—A Literature Review of Qualitative Studies

> People create reality and their lived experience as they reflect on, interact with and respond to others; thus reality is fundamentally inter-subjective. Only theories that take into account this inter-subjective nature of human experience can understand, explain, and illuminate how people create their social and personal realities.
>
> Prus

## 4.1 Introduction

Thus far, we have created Headwork boxes that inform the content and processes of 'Keys to the ABI Cage' by reviews of information on Websites and body-object literature. Unlike some of the personal narratives reviewed in Chap. 1, the predominant focus of Websites and the body-object approach was found to be deficit-based. The blank spot (Wagner, 1993) was that these approaches were blind to anything outside of the syllogism that starts with 'mending broken bodies' as a premise.

We argue there is a need for a 'paradigm shift' (Kuhn, 1962) to supplant present theories because they no longer speak to the concerns of practising scientists (Terre Blanche & Durrheim, 1999, p. 4) and practitioners, and those who live every day of their lives with ABI. As Sandberg and Alvesson (2011) say, there is often a need to 'reframe' a research area rather than simply to point to 'gaps in the literature'. The body-object perspective, the medical model, focuses on mending deficits and does so by isolating different aspects of the person affected by ABI as shown in Chap. 3. Saxe, in the nineteenth-century poem 'The Blind Men And The Elephant', points out that the beast was more than the sum of its parts that people think they can 'see' when in fact they are 'blind' or unaware, and they speak knowledgeably about that which they do not know. This poem articulates how the person with ABI and indeed professionals may view the way they are treated as just isolated 'bits' of themselves, rather than taking them as a whole person. This poem could be viewed as a metaphor for the body-object view—it does not see the person as a whole person.



C. Durham and P. Ramcharan, *Insight into Acquired Brain Injury*,
DOI 10.1007/978-981-10-5666-6_4

### The Blind Men and the Elephant: John Godfry Saxe (1816–87) (see Saxe, 1995)

It was six men of Indostan
To learning much inclined,
Who went to see the Elephant
(Though all of them were blind)'
That each by observation
Might satisfy his mind
The First approach'd the Elephant,
And happening to fall
Against his broad and sturdy side,
At once began to bawl:
"God bless me! But the Elephant is very like a wall!"
"….like a spear!" "….like a snake!" "….like a tree!" "….like a fan!"
So oft in theologic wars,
The disputatants, I ween,
Rail on in utter ignorance
Of what each other mean,
And prate[1] about an Elephant
Not one of them has seen.

### Elephant: Christine Yvonne Durham after John Godfry Saxe

The outside of an Elephant
Is made up of different parts
But that's not all Elephant is, Elephant has mind and heart
Elephant's more than leg and trunk and hide and eyes and meat.
Elephant's more than tail and ears and side and tusk and feet.

In circus, zoo, and forest too
Elephant works in fields and more
A family pet, a faithful friend,
He can run amok and gore.
Carrying tourists, logs or heavy loads, his attributes are many

But rogue and wild, and strong and huge, Elephant's very scary!
Why, oh why, I ask you,
Does this massive wrinkly beast
Disobey his master

[1]Prate—to talk foolishly or at length about something.

Or sit upon a seat?
He sways and dances (it is true) when tethered to a stake
When looking into all of this, of sense we cannot make

The essence of the Elephant
Is mighty hard to find
It's not locked up in books or film
Or held in someone's mind
If only Elephant could speak, and tell us what he knows
Then, and only then, could we discover how he goes.

In this light, 'mending bodies' is not the *only* way to perceive ABI, nor treat people with ABI, and as will be demonstrated in this chapter, the body-object approach misses a large portion of the phenomenon that is of importance to the insiders, to people with ABI who question 'Will I *ever* feel better?' 'Will life *always* be this awful?' 'I'm lost, how can I find myself?' (Durham, 1997).

This study was approached from the insider's perspective and author Durham placed herself as a 'visible researcher' (Denzin, 1997), exploring the insider's, body-subject, emic view introduced in Chap. 1. As joint authors, we will commence by considering the person with ABI as being *more* than the sum of their parts. Subsequent to introducing phenomenology in Chap. 3, the concept of 'intentionality' will be revisited and its links with qualitative academic literature and with feminist perspectives drawing upon personal narratives and insider's views will be explored as an alternative.

This chapter will establish the place of this study within the body of work of qualitative body-subject research: research that focuses on ways people experience ABI. The review of qualitative studies, together with the perspectives discussed in this chapter, informed the methodology employed in the 'Keys Study'. Chapter 5 will continue to provide a background to the methodology by reviewing relevant learning theories and concepts from educational literature.

### 4.1.1 Intentionality: Another Way to Consider ABI

In Chap. 3, the place of phenomenology as an alternative ontology to those grounded in a scientific or the hypothetico-deductive model was introduced. Two requirements for a study methodology follow. First, if phenomenology is a suitable ontology (philosophy of being), then what is its epistemology—its philosophy of knowledge? Secondly, and subsequently, how can such an epistemology be operationalised?

Phenomenology, a philosophical movement of the early twentieth century, had immense influence on continental Europe. Developed as a theory of knowledge by Edmund Husserl (1859–1938) in his book *Ideas: A General Introduction to Pure Phenomenology* (1913), it offers a descriptive analysis of 'essences' in general. 'Essences' (from the Greek *eidos* 'form'—exceptionally vivid visual or auditory images that allow detailed recall of something previously perceived) were not only objects (such as an object of sense-perception) but also acts of consciousness. The phenomenologist must 'bracket', suspend judgment or perform an 'epoché', the 'natural attitude' to the world. Phenomenology asserts that through 'eidetic' or 'intuitive' approaches we have knowledge of the *essential features* of the lifeworld, which phenomenologist's term 'essences'.

One of the major presuppositions of phenomenology is that people have an intention to an object. As already argued, the seemingly hard fact of a stone might, given differing intentionality, for a physicist a series of atomic and subatomic forces —for a petroleum prospector, a focus for analysis of hydrocarbon presence—for an artist, its aesthetic—or for a person being attacked, a source of defence. The intentionality towards the stone is defined in its usage. The phenomenological researcher tries to find the essence of a phenomenon from a particular perspective— in this case from the experiences of people with ABI. This does not involve an hypothesis or preconception but focuses on the 'how' and 'why' of everyday intuitive lived experience—again, in this instance of the experience of ABI—rather than the 'how much' or 'how many' of the scientific positivist position.

Since the second century, when problems of brain injury were first recorded, people were searching for a way to make 'broken heads' 'better'. The old nursery rhyme 'Jack and Jill' (1795) tells the story of two children who went up and fell down a hill—Jack fell down, and broke his crown, and went to bed to mend his head with vinegar and brown paper (an old remedy used to treat wounds, bruises and other injuries). This study aimed to find a new way to help 'mend' broken heads.

An alternative and more sinister origin of this rhyme, suggests another theory about the head, and offers another way to view brain injury. 'Jack and Jill' is claimed to tell the story of King Louis XVI's (Jack's) beheading (lost his crown) followed by Queen Marie Antoinette (Jill) whose head came tumbling after. The executioner held Louis XV1's severed head aloft, by the hair, to allow the head to gaze on its body as consciousness was believed to remain for at least eight seconds after beheading until lack of oxygen caused unconsciousness and eventual death.

For many people, ABI is akin to 'losing their head'. Like King Louis's eyes gazing at its own body, they can observe their own body and life, but they are quite disconnected from it. In a split second mind, memory, movement and hope can vanish leaving the individual with ABI profoundly damaged, unable to understand, unable to call on prior knowledge, unable to find a way forward. It is as if they have 'lost' their head, 'lost' themselves, and 'lost' their life as they knew it. Over time, they can spiral down feeling discouraged, desperate, humiliated, worthless and disorientated (Durham, 1997) because to improve cognitively and physically is a long, slow process.

Phenomenology is a philosophy in which a person reflects and speaks about their interpretational narrative of their experience (Giorgi, 1985a, b). Each person is unique and they can engage in personal understandings and discovery and explore the meaning of that experience. Above we can see two competing narratives in relation to Jack and Jill. Neither may be wrong—each differs given how we intentionally engage with the rhyme, whether an historical allegory or as a narrative on the contemporary treatment of the day.

The contention in this book is that, like the blind men approaching the elephant, 'mending bodies' by adopting a singular and biomedical intentionality misses the whole and ignores the experiences of people with ABI as they seek to re-engage with their everyday lives.

This study posed the question: Given new understandings of the experiences and intentioned actions of people with ABI, can we find a new or different way to reconnect head, body, life and dreams for people who suffer from ABI?

We have sought to show above how a phenomenological ontology (a philosophy of being) gives rise to a study epistemology (a philosophy of knowledge) and an alignment has been established between these in opposition to a positivist stance. However, for an empirical study, a philosophy of knowledge has to be operationalised—to be translated into a methodology. Van Maanen (1990), writing about phenomenological research in education, relates 'experience' to our direct acquaintance of things, the intuitive qualities, impressions of, description of and interpretation of the everyday. But this leaves open how we ask about this experience. What questions and approaches should be used? Giorgi (2009, p. 122) argues that 'What one seeks from a research interview in phenomenological research is as complete a description as possible of the experience that a participant has lived through'. Furthermore,

> Asking for a situation is vital since the discovery of the meaning of the phenomenon (later in the data analysis) needs to have been connected to a specific context in which the phenomenon has been experienced (Englander, 2012, p. 13).

The present research benefited from Durham's experience of ABI both personally and as discussed previously her long engagement with people with ABI over many years. The research questions therefore reflected this prior understanding of 'context' as a basis for the development of a research approach and 'questions' capable of understanding the experience of ABI among the study sample. They also drew upon the systematic study of literature grounded in a supervisory relationship with Ramcharan for the purposes of gaining a doctoral degree by research.

As with all other humans, our actions as writers and researchers are therefore themselves intentioned. If first-person ontologies are given primacy, it is not only to fill a gap and to achieve paradigm shift. It is also to hear the voice of people with ABI and to ensure our research conduct achieved dignity and respect, and did no harm.

In this respect, it has been argued that 'only qualitative analysis can accurately capture the complex pattern of an individual life without violating the integrity of life or dehumanizing the individual' (Kotre, 1984, p. 3).

Renzetti and Lee (1993, p. 6) assert that 'extreme sensitivity is needed in the conduct of research that intrudes into the private lives or deeply personal experiences of the research participants'. Feminist advocates of qualitative methods have argued that 'individual women's understandings, emotions, and actions in the world must be explored in those women's own terms' (Jayaratine & Stewart 1991, p. 85). 'Such methods are consistent with the ways in which research participants are treated and the care with which researchers attempt to represent the lived experience' (ibid., p. 90). For feminists, this involves being cognisant of issue of power and patriarchy.

The majority of participants in this study—those with ABI and people who care for and support other people with ABI—were 'vulnerable', 'difficult to access', 'invisible' 'hidden' and 'hard to reach' (Stone, 2005). From previous chapters, it has been demonstrated that this was to be 'sensitive research' (Wellings, Branigan, & Mitchell, 2000, p. 256) with vulnerable people (Liamputtong, 2007). Their 'invisibility' could have included their marginality, lack of opportunity to voice their concerns, fear of their identity being disrespected, stigma attached to their social conditions, heavy responsibilities and scepticism about being involved in research (Birman, 2005; Fisher & Ragsdale, 2005; Stone, 2005). The present research therefore aimed to provide a time and place for conversations, described by Robertson and Webber (2000) as 'deep and meaningful conversations about life experiences, many of which have not previously been voiced' (pp. 531–532) and research with '…potential consequences or implications, … directly for the participants…' (Sieber & Stanley, 1988, p. 49).

Oakley (1981) suggests the 'goal of finding out about people through interviewing is best achieved when interviewer and interviewee is non-hierarchical and when the interviewer is prepared to invest his or her own personal identity in the relationship' (p. 41). A rapport and understanding of the individual participants was developed over the period of contact, the phone calls and the interview. Specific encounters were particularly upsetting and are etched in memory for the interviewer Durham, and Ramcharan who had access to the data transcripts. The powerlessness, frustration, perception of being 'taken advantage of' or being 'ripped off' by 'the system' affected some participants profoundly. This was one issue in this study that was underestimated.

Feminist studies also point to experiences of oppression (Mies, 1983: Peter 2000; Fraser and MacDougall 2016) within the research process and the importance of reflexivity or recognition of self in the research process. This is the opposite of Milgram's (1974) famous study of 'obedience' that relied on the abstract authority of the 'scientist', which is an example of research design that depends on *maximising* the hierarchical distance between researcher and research participant. Moreover, in line with arguments by Jayaratine and Stewart (1991), the research topic was selected to have potential to help people with ABI; the Keys Study aimed at specifically determining information that would be most useful and have positive impact; the method was designed to be appropriate to ask questions of vulnerable people; and the answers and data collected would be to assist people with ABI.

The Keys Study was sensitive research into vulnerable people, and to reduce the power differential between researcher and researched, a research approach capable of achieving this was needed. As such, we adopted a narrative research method involving principles of motivational interviewing, which is a directive, client-centred counselling style for eliciting behaviour change by helping clients explore and resolve ambivalence (Rollnick & Miller, 1995). Using this method, the participant was placed in control to speak about what, from a plethora of potential topics, they considered important. The relationship between the interviewer and interviewee was more like a partnership rather than expert/non-expert interaction.

In the Preface to this volume, the 'Keys to the ABI Cage' was presented. It will have been noted from Chaps. 2 and 3 how we used Headwork boxes to guide the relationships between researcher and participants during the development of the data collection method. "Keys to the ABI Cage" as presented in the introduction to this volume is the result. However, there is one further set of literature which informs our approach, the qualitative, body-subject, emic or insider's perspective which is reviewed below.

## 4.2 ABI from the Qualitative Body-Subject, Emic, Insider's Perspective

Having explored some phenomenological assumptions, we now explore how a view grounded in experience was created for the Keys Study.

Rees (2011), in his book "Out of Calamity", depicts people with ABI as whole people with many facets. In his narratives about people with ABI, Rees tells the story of Phillip, a young man whose parents are delighted when they come across notes that he has scribbled: in their eyes this is an indication of improvement. But

> his mother's claims about his improvement has raised a few eyebrows among the more prescriptive and sceptical professionals…(who said) anyway his mother is not objective and doesn't know what she is talking about (Rees, 2011, p. 60).

*From the perspective of the insider*, 'those professional gainsayers, and there are many of them…' (Rees, p. 64) can impact upon the individual. In considering Joe, another person with ABI, 'few (professionals) if any gave Joe any hope' (Rees, p. 79); fortunately Joe received kindness and understanding from the hospital cleaners. 'Joe's serious injury, isolation, lack of hope, let alone activity had drained his strength'. These quotes provide an example of how some people with ABI and their family perceive their treatment by professionals; their need to be listened to, their point of view taken into account, even small positive issues to be considered and their need for encouragement and hope.

As explained in Chap. 1, one reason for undertaking this study was conversations with hundreds of people with ABI who have attended Durham's presentations or workshops, told her that they felt, and still feel powerless. They lacked encouragement and hope. Simon (all names in this volume are pseudonyms) stated: 'They (the professionals) thought I was stupid but I'm not, I'm just slow.' Mark remarked: 'The medical viewpoint is that people with ABI don't have insight. This is not true…we do have insight…we have to re-assess our own lives'. But the body-object perspective can take away hope and further disempower the person with ABI, who, with 'King Louis XV1's gaze' (or the gaze of the decapitated head surveying the person they once were) may see themselves as no longer an individual, as a 'retard', 'object of pity' among many other disparaging labels.

The body-object language such as 'physical problems' does explain the consequences to the person, who may feel unintelligent and dumb: Jo-Anne said: 'I can't walk normal and I fall over. I feel stupid'. Jo-Anne, together with the majority of people with ABI would not have used the word 'cognition' before their ABI, so terms such as 'cognitive impairment' need 'translation' so that people like Jo-Anne can understand how having cognitive impairment can impact on their everyday life. Terms such as 'behaviour impairments' or 'personality dysfunctions' may not explain that a person with ABI might feel out of control and do crazy things that they would not have done prior to their ABI.

At writing workshops, Peter made the observation: 'When I get mad I do mad things: I threw my new typewriter in the river because the Keys weren't in alphabetical order!' demonstrating, in a humorous way, that later he had insight into what was normal/not normal and the affects of anger and frustration. Max remarked 'When I was mad I chased an emu', indicating he also had insight into 'foolish things' he could do when he was angry. Phillip said: 'I need a "cone of protection" like Maxwell Smart, to keep out my anger', showing he had considered his anger problem and found a 'socially acceptable' way to describe it. Martin divulged that 'I'm not mad. I just pretend to be'—demonstrating he was aware of 'what's what', and 'who's who' but that he could only accomplish his ends through extreme behaviour. These comments support the findings of Egan et al. (2006)'s study, who found that people with ABI are capable of greater insight, reflection and humour than indicated in previous research.

Lack of 'Choice', lack of 'Being in Control' and lack of 'Power' may not feature in lists of impairments, but people with ABI are acutely aware that ABI brings with it loss of choice, loss of power to have a say in what they want to do. Poignant statements such as from Atticus: 'The moment my stroke hit me in the back paddock I lost my choice'; Adrian, 'I felt disempowered in rehab. If you stay disempowered they keep their jobs'. These statements about the predicament of powerlessness of people with ABI have been expressed at a number of ABI support meetings.

People with ABI listen to other people with ABI; there is understanding and a bond. Felicity said: 'It's helpful to know others have the same experience'; Pip remarked: 'It's good to know someone understands'; Ian thought: 'There's a lot of wisdom in this room full of people with brain injury, a lot of experiences'; John explained by saying: 'I can feel what you say mate'; Pru commented: 'I want to be seen as me, an individual, regardless of any disability'.

The research tool Keys to the ABI Cage demonstrated empathy with the ABI experience.

The body-subject view which would support such voices also fits with the seminal ideas of phenomenology offering 'an interpretative approach to social reality and the lives experience of human beings' (Holloway & Wheeler, 2010, p. 3).

Qualitative research comes in many forms, but data has priority; it is initially broadly focused, process orientated, context-bound, and involves getting close to data (Holloway & Wheeler, 2010, p. 10). The focus is on the emic; 'thick descriptions' (Geertz, 1973) which are detailed portrayals, interpretations and the uncovering of feeling and meaningful behaviours; the researcher–researched relationship is based on the concept of equality as human beings; the researcher is visible and is the main research 'tool'.

The use of qualitative research has only recently begun to populate the literature around ABI, but is quickly growing (see, e.g. Sample & Darragh, 1998;

Albrecht & Devlieger, 1999; Darragh, Sample & Krieger, 2001; Levack, McPherson, & McNaughton, 2004; Howes, Benton & Edwards, 2004, 2005; Jumisko, Lexell, & Söderberg, 2007; Lorenz, 2010a, b; Uprichard, 2010; and Lloyd, Gatherer & Kalsy, 2006).

## 4.3 Qualitative Academic Research: The Insider's Experience from the Outsiders' Perspective

A formal literature review up to the time of the study in 2011[2] was undertaken using 12 web search engines. Main terms qualitative studies, narrative, lived experience, quality of life, coping, resilience and brain injury yielded 24 studies many of which revealed blind spots not covered in conventional quantitative approaches. These blind areas contributed to the method of *Keys to the ABI Cage* and the 'talk-about' cards that populated the cage and offered participants focal points for their narrative.

This literature, produced largely through open-ended and semi-structured interviews and narrative first-person accounts, illuminate the person with ABI's own perspective and lifeworld. Gelech and Desjardins (2011, p. 62) posit that although concepts of the personhood of the individual as 'lost' or 'shattered' have dominated discussions in the literature, this 'perspective is a crude representation of the post-injury experience of self, and the aspects of stability, recovery, transcendence and moral growth are also involved in this process'. Like Rees, they show how the complexity of 'personhood' cannot be subsumed under a single concept and is dynamic as opposed to being fixed and, as such, must develop during and post the rehabilitation experience.

This involves *relational* concepts of self: comparing the present self with the past self, the self in relation to others or the self as improving over time (Nochi, 2000). Nochi's categories of the positive self include the 'self as better than others' with ABI; the 'grown self' in which the new ABI self is seen as having grown in relation to their past self; the 'recovering self' in which progress is being made; the 'self living in the here and now', in which people see themselves as normal; and the 'protesting self' who find ways to function best given life's challenges. Nochi demonstrates how, using these categorisations, the person can come to terms with their new self.

Kendall and Muenchberg (2009) suggest that there is a significant process of grieving for the loss of the old identity and the construction of a new identity. In the examination of 52 biographical accounts by people with ABI, they isolated a number of coping strategies: personal discovery (learning about self), goal-directed (practical problem-solving), control and independence, purpose (believing their

[2]The more recent literature will be explored further in the discussion chapter later and any new findings interpolated with the recommendations for practice.

injury had a purpose), spiritual, social coping (using support networks), focusing on each day and not long term, persistence and hard work and use of emotional coping and seeing the lighter side. The strategies are not mutually exclusive and focus on an 'opportunity structure' for rationalising the new self in a new environment. In some ways, both Nochi and Kendall and Muenchberg's strategies are generic in that they have relevance to us all. What is different is that acquiring an ABI may change the distance for accomplishment. As argued of Borudieu in Chap. 3, new circumstances require a person to find new personal and social, economic and symbolic resources to pursue lives they choose. Linge (1990) usefully argues that a focus on small achievements helps in this regard.

Indeed, the study by Jumisko et al. (2009), in their examination of 'what it means to feel well', points to the importance of becoming familiar with the new self, together with showing strength and resolve, re-establishing a sense of control, being close to someone and feeling 'good enough'. This work mirrors the salutogenic theory first posited by Antonovky (1979). Antonovky argued that a 'sense of coherence' was essential to the management of stress and to coping and as a precursor to better health. However, it is not just health that is as issue for many people with ABI. Levack et al. (2010), in their meta-analysis of 23 studies, also emphasise areas of the new self. They point to disconnects between mind–body, the pre- and post-injury identity, social situations and emotional supports. These factors test the reconstruction of self-identity and reconstruction of both personhood and 'place in the world'. For Levak, Kayes and Faydl (2010), it is the internal and external resources on which people with ABI can draw, that is vital. Yet discovering these new resources may be problematic too without additional support.

Examining coping themes not present in quantitative coping inventories, Karpmann et al. (1986) identify a number of characterising features that are largely about personal qualities and values: hope and optimism, determination, self-evaluation, new attitudes to life, new support networks and religion. But, as pointed out by both McColl et al. (1998) and Turner et al. (2007), people need to find solutions in their own peculiar and individual circumstances. Turner et al. (2007) suggest that this means a need to work with individual experiences as a focus for rehabilitation. But if this focus on the individual is important to the rehabilitation professional, it must be *more important* to the person as they seek to re-enter life without professional input. Even more importantly, Kendall and Terry (2008) found that while coping produced benefits in short- and long-term functioning, it did not necessarily contribute in the same way to wellbeing and faring well. This significant finding represents a blind spot in the literature, especially for people after the 'golden period/dark hole period'.

The focus on adaptation and coping styles in the literature reviewed in Chap. 3 focused around professional practice, and how the professional orientates towards delivery of care and support. The collective work around personal accounts speak of the place of love, hope, faith, of the importance of nurturance, social and support networks, of knowledge and personal skills in engaging with the practicalities of everyday life challenges. They speak of relational thinking of the new and old self, the self as changing and of the connection of the self to others. These and many more feature as the internal and external resources and personal qualities that can be drawn upon from an everyday repertoire, so the person can learn to cope and learn to feel and fare better.

By exploring the subjectively meaningful experience of people with ABI, the qualitative studies establish a multitude of perspectives with a dominant focus of coping, adaptation and recovery. Some of the studies have an interest in further clarification of conceptualisations that might contribute to professional practice in varying ways. Featuring in this way are the elucidation of coping themes that can be operationalised using coping inventories (Karpmann, Wolfe & Vargo, 1986); coping styles that allow professionals to orientate towards different responses by people to the acquisition of brain injury (Kendall & Muenchberg, 2009); coping styles that go hand-in-hand with people feeling 'at ease' with themselves—successful styles of coping (Nochi, 2000); coping and adaptive responses in targeted areas such as community inclusion (McColl et al., 1998), employment (Oppermann, 2004) and in the transition from hospital to home (Turner et al., 2007).

On the basis of the reviewed studies, a number of points informed the development of *Keys to the ABI Cage* and to the methodological procedure used in this study. The boxes are at times repeat concepts previously discussed, these important concepts that apply to ensuring the wellbeing of participants as they (a) engage with this study and (b) return home to continue to struggle with their ABI (Figs. 4.1 and 4.2).

Taking place at a location where the participant feels comfortable — a local library, coffee shop etc.
Helping them feel 'safe' by explaining several times what they will be asked to do.
Allowing them to take their time.
Letting them lead the discussion.
Allowing them privacy — they must not be 'pushed' to divulge private things.
Having ways to address 'Faulty Thinking' to redirect negative thinking by reviewing positive things they have achieved.
Demonstrating understanding about their challenges.
Making it a positive process by not 'threatening' their self confidence by pointing out their deficits.
Giving them positive ideas to think about as they remember their difficulties.
Making interview/data collection must be of a suitable length of time so participants are not distressed by fatigue.
Giving opportunity for participants to take a break — a coffee break.
Breaking Interviews into segments — each segment discussed so they can see progress.
Using objects/cards/pictures and words they obtain input not just in words.

**Fig. 4.1** Headwork 15: Strategies in the method employed to help them feel better/cope better

1. Difficulties and differences:
I've lost the 'old' me; I don't 'know' the 'new' me; I forget my name; I forget where I live; I've lost my memory; I've lost my friends; I've lost my job; I can't talk properly; I forget what things look like; I forget what you're saying or I'm saying; I've lost my freedom; I'm dependent; I get lost; I have to do lots of tests; I can't understand; I can't do things I used to; I can't think properly.
2. How I feel can LOCK me in the ABI Cage:
Sad - Depressed; Distressed; Disappointed; Mad - Frustrated; Angry; Nuts/crazy; Bad - Guilty, Bad - I say and do the wrong thing; Bad - I don't understand; I feel crushed; I feel scared; I hate myself; I feel hopeless (the experts can't fix me).
3. Keys that can RELEASE me from the ABI Cage:
Love, Having Hope, My family, my friends, what other people with ABI have done, encouragement, animals, talking, sport, flowers,going out, exercise, sport, staying home, cup of coffee, doing hard things, achieving hard things, stretching my comfort zone, seeing some progress, doing things I couldn't do before, my doctor, my occupational therapist, my counsellor, health professionals.

**Fig. 4.2** Headwork 16: 'Talk-about' cards allow participants to reflect on issues

## 4.4 Narrative as the Insider's Perspective of ABI

> By words we learn thoughts, and by thoughts we learn life.
>
> Jean Baptiste Girard
>
> For me, words are a form of action, capable of influencing change. Their articulation represents a complete, lived experience.
>
> Ingrid Bengis

Life stories are important to everyone as they provide an opportunity for the person to express who they are, their sense of self and they also allow others to understand who we are and how we got that way (Linde, 1993; Widdershoven, 1993). Narratives can reveal the personal, situated and practical aspects of coping and show that coping with ABI is not a single event but 'coping as inseparable from their existence' (Marshall, 2009, pp. 137–138). When writing about life stories of people with learning disabilities (*sic* intellectual disabilities) Atkinson (2010) states that stories can help us trace an otherwise hidden history, treat people as 'expert witnesses', enable people to represent themselves as fully rounded human beings, show the beginnings of a resistance movement, encourage historical awareness and reflexivity (Atkinson, p. 7). Atkinson suggests life stories are particularly important 'because often people have been silent, or silenced, while other people—families, practitioners, historians—have spoken on their behalf' (2010, p. 9). People with ABI have similar experiences and by telling their stories they gain a voice.

The books written by people with brain injury and their families (Chap. 1) demonstrated the need of people to tell of acquiring their injury, to show they have gained wisdom from their experience, helped others by passing on advice, encouraged them and offered an uplifting story about the importance of love, courage and hope. These three words are the insiders' perspectives of the important issues that help people endure/cope with brain injury. But these are metaphysical words, not recorded on medical reports, government documents or quantitative research papers. Yet such concepts lying within a humanist frame are as crucial to a person's life as a mended body. These concepts are also both positive and powerful and are the antithesis to the negativity of the fixing broken bodies approach characterised by much of the body-object writing.

There is a saying 'beauty is in the eye of the beholder'. We argue that in a similar way a blind spot is in the eye of the beholder. People with ABI and family who write books about their experience do so in order to illuminate issues, thoughts *they believe that other people do not see*; in other words blind spots. They bring to light things they perceive to be hidden issues of the ABI experience.

However, research into ABI narratives is not straight forward as asserted by Tidwell et al. (2009). Making sense of and organising information from narrative is not easy. 'Quite unlike its pristine and logical presentation in journal articles…real research is often confusing, messy, intensely frustrating and fundamentally non-linear' (Marshall & Rossman, 1999, p. 21).

Some of this complexity has been addressed in the professional and academic literature as discussed below.

### 4.4.1 Narrative to Reveal the Insider's Perspective: Books Written by Professionals

Accounts by professionals have commonalities to the books, web articles and blogs as discussed in Chap. 1 and as outlined by Atkinson above.

Brain injury professionals use narrative as a powerful method to confront the reader with the realities of life for the person with ABI. Rees (2011) expresses the bewildering world of the person with brain ABI illuminating the blind spot that positive interactions with others are important.

> Negative interactions, or perceived negative interactions, increase the person's perception of threat and can turn simple frustration into aimless rage. Alternatively, sustained positive exchanges between the environment and brain can help the person develop awareness and socially acceptable behaviour. (Rees, 2011, p. 107)

Rees also demonstrates their intelligence, feelings and awareness of their difficulties, inter alia:

> I am well aware that they regard me as intellectually inadequate compared to them p. 17.
>
> My fear of rejection isolates me p. 17.
>
> She talks in riddles although there is a consistent theme of her 'quest for the elusive true self' p. 21.
>
> Progress is a balancing act p. 64.
>
> The visiting psychologist or social worker who just wants to test Michael and produce a report which is invariably negative. Because they identify his deficiencies as they call them…it's the lack of positive input which fosters ignorance. Ignorance leads to lack of understanding and being ignored p. 141.
>
> Sometimes we were advised that Ben was 'plateauing'. That's another expression that defies accurate definition and is not helpful for someone striving to recover p. 151.

Rees has shone a light upon blind spots that are not the focus of medical model research. The main themes that have come out of his work are:

> people with ABI can be aware of their own perceived deficits and aware of how other people view them
>
> being brain injured can cause shame and frustration
>
> people with ABI want to be the same as other people
>
> people with ABI are isolated and lonely
>
> recovery may involve good and bad days, one step forward, one step back
>
> definitions such as 'plateauing' are not helpful
>
> it is not easy to remain positive.

Mason (2008), an ABI Case Manager, writes of the courage of people with ABI as they 'put the pieces together', their perseverance, everyday struggles, search for help and hope for recovery. He writes of the harsh realities endured by the mounting number of ABI survivors whose lives may be unravelling. Here again, we read of the importance of hope, courage and the importance of giving people a voice to tell their story to restore their dignity.

Laskowski (2003) wrote his book after hearing poetry written by a man with a severe ABI and felt 'stunned and ashamed', to find he was surprised by the 'intelligence and feeling' expressed in the poetry. His fictionalised journal focuses upon the everyday struggle to communicate and be intimate with others, the person's efforts to free himself from chains of his caregivers and return to normal life.

Driscoll and Straus's (2009) stories of American soldiers with TBI and PTSD present us with yet another set of blind spots. Military personnel train so hard they may cut off their emotions to do what they are told, which can come back and haunt them. They can feel like they are 'stained' by their war experience that they have 'blood on their hands' (Driscoll & Straus, 2009, p. 68) and this can affect their progress. Several of the issues identified by military personnel could be applied to other people with ABI—low tolerance of things other people did and telling it as they saw it. They Driscoll and Strauss write of a man with TBI in a supermarket remarking 'Lady, if you hit him (small son) again I'll break your arm and shove it up your ass. You should spend less time on the phone, and more time taking care of your kid'. Driscoll and Straus identified that one of the biggest challenges of ABI is mustering 'the courage to allow others to help you even when you feel unsafe' (2009, p. 73).

References to children with ABI have been purposely omitted, but because a story book for children was to be written as a component of the final ABI learning resources—for Henry Stewart Talks UK and the book 'Unlocking My Brain Through the Labyrinth of Acquired Brain Injury' (Durham, 2014), a search was conducted to locate books that use narrative to explain ABI to children. Picture story books for children included Snyder's (1998) '*Elvin, the Elephant Who Forgets*', Leaf and Widucki's (1988) '*Susan's Dad: A Child's Story of Head Injury*' and Moulton's (1986) '*My Friend Lucy*' and Parker's (2005) '*The Get Well Soon...Balloon!*'.

## 4.5 Recapitulation

This chapter has shown that intentionality is central to this study, which is based on the premise that meaningful behaviour is best grasped through the person's narrative, through their own voice being heard.

It was likely that participants would express widely varied everyday experiences and respect for this diversity was vital. It was important to assist the participants to express how the challenges they faced could be offset by positive factors in their lives, particularly in their lives after the 'golden period/dark hole period'.

In order to learn to feel better, learning to cope and adapt are essential. The review of qualitative studies and material written by people with ABI proposed that it was important to incorporate metaphysical concepts (love, hope, support and courage) in order to fully encompass the phenomena of coping. These factors have a knock-on effect on the methods and procedures to be adopted and more of these are considered in Chap. 6.

Through the examination of body-subject or emic perspectives, qualitative studies and narratives, another picture has emerged of the way the person with ABI can place their lives in the light while themselves growing in the process. From the insider's perspective, involvement in qualitative and quantitative studies involves issues of power, control and opportunities to speak about what is deeply meaningful. Participant experience for those involved in quantitative studies where tests, scales and questionnaires are used differs from those involved in qualitative narrative studies, where the person would have the opportunity to express their opinions and reflect on their experience. It can be seen that some of the research topics discussed in the quantitative studies in Chap. 3 (e.g. depression, self-awareness, coping, peer support and social identity) have also been identified in qualitative studies, where the studies reviewed, focused upon coping, rather than deficits.

This review has also shown there is a large amount of information from the insider's perspective not readily available to people with ABI or their families, unless they subscribe to academic journals that report on findings of studies. Tragically, the insight, wisdom or blind spots identified in this literature are not readily available to assist the person with ABI to have hope and understanding. This material does not appear to be translated nor does it trickle down to ABI support organisations' Websites to the same extent as data obtained from quantitative studies. Additionally, like the insiders' perspective information in Chap. 1, this information is available only for 'seekers'. Many people with ABI would not have the computer or other skills or resources to sift through and find the resources that would help them. Indeed, some people with ABI do not have computers and remain isolated from the communities in which they live.

The findings from the qualitative studies echo Durham's experience about the importance of love from family and friends, a hope and belief that life for people with ABI had been spared for a purpose, to help others with ABI as was the case with author Durham. The findings from these studies also provide positive encouragement and hope for the person with ABI.

The Keys Study set out to determine whether there was a way to assist participants with ABI to reflect and 'discover' these perceptions/beliefs/strategies *for themselves*, to join the metaphysical with concepts and ideas that support them to feel and fare better.

Given the changes to identity, circumstance and context, the interface for reflection and learning becomes absolutely essential to the Keys Study and warrants further attention. The joining of metaphysical concepts with everyday life experiences is a product of lifelong learning. But for the person with ABI who is challenged to relearn (and to do so with as a new identity, with changed personal and social resources) as quickly as possible, they need a learning tool to assist them to reflect and learn. Based upon the difference between what a student can learn without help and with help, the Keys Study therefore essentially drew upon Lev Vygotsky's seminal work on the 'zone of proximal development'. Under this conception, different resources are used as scaffolding to support learners to independently find their own solutions. The case of re-learning for people with ABI represents a unique problematic challenge and requires the study to address learning principles in its approach to data collection.

In conclusion—How can people with ABI and their families learn of the good news—all the data about things that can positively affect their endurance/coping/recovery? How can people with ABI construct their own knowledge about ways of coping with ABI? This question will be explored in Chap. 5, a chapter devoted to learning principles.

## References

Albrecht, G. L., & Devlieger, P. J. (1999). The disability paradox: High quality of life against all odds. *Social Science and Medicine, 48*(8), 977–988.

Antonovsky, A. (1979). *Health, stress and coping*. San Francisco, CA: Jossey-Bass Publishers.

Atkinson, J. (2010). Narratives and people with learning disabilities. In G. Grant, P. Ramcharan, M. Flynn & M. Richardson (Eds.), *Learning disability: A lifecycle approach* (pp. 7–19). Maidenhead: Open University Press and MacGraw-Hill Educational.

Birman, D. (2005). Ethical issues in research with immigrants and refugees. In J. E. Trimble & C. B. Fisher (Eds.), *Handbook of ethical research with ethnocultural populations and communities* (pp. 155–177). Thousand Oaks, CA: Sage Publications.

Darragh, A. R., Sample, P. L., & Krieger, S. R. (2001). 'Tears in my eyes 'cause somebody finally understood': Client perceptions of practitioners following brain injury. *The American Journal of Occupational Therapy, 55*(2), 191–199.

Denzin, N. K. (1997). *Interpretive ethnography: Ethnographic practices for the 21st century*. Thousand Oaks, CA: Sage.

Driscoll, P. P., & Straus, C. (2009). *Hidden battles on unseen fronts: Stories of American soldiers with traumatic brain injury and PTSD*. Philadelphia, PA: Casemate Publishers and Book Distributors.

Durham, C. (1997). *Doing up buttons*. Ringwood, Australia: Penguin.

Durham, C. (2014). *Unlocking my brain through the labyrinth of acquired brain injury*. Sydney, Australia: Ventura Publishing.

Egan, J., Chenoweth, L., & McAuliffe, D. (2006). Email-facilitated qualitative interviews with traumatic brain injury survivors: A new and accessible method. *Brain Injury, 20*(12), 1283–1294.

Englander, M. (2012). The interview: Data collection in descriptive phenomenological human scientific research. *Journal of Phenomenological Psychology, 43,* 13–35.

Fischer, C. B., & Ragsdale, K. (2005). Goodness-of-fit ethics for multicultural research. In J. E. Trimble & C. B. Fisher (Eds.), *Handbook of ethical research with ethnocultural populations and communities* (pp. 3–25). Thousand Oaks, CA: Sage.

Fraser, H., & MacDougall, C. (2016) Doing narrative feminist research: Intersections and challenges. *Qualitative Social Work,* 1–15.

Geertz, C. (1973). Thick description: towards an interpretation theory of culture. In C. Geertz (Ed.), *The interpretation of cultures: Selected essays* (pp. 3–30). New York, NY: Basic Books.

Gelech, J. M., & Desjardins, M. (2011). I am many: The reconstruction of self following acquired brain injury. *Qualitative Health Research, 21*(1), 62–74.

Giorgi, A. (1985a). Phenomenological psychology of learning and verbal tradition. In A. Giorgi (Ed.), *Phenomenology and psychological research* (pp. 23–85). Pittsburgh, PA: Duquesne University Press.

Giorgi, A. (1985b). Sketch of a psychological phenomenological method. In A. Giorgi (Ed.), *Phenomenology and psychological research* (pp. 1–21). Pittsburgh, PA: Duquesne University Press.

Giorgi, A. (2009). *The descriptive phenomenological approach in psychology: A modified Husserlian approach*. Pittsburgh: Duquesne University Press.

Holloway, I., & Wheeler, S. (2010). *Qualitative research in nursing and healthcare* (3rd ed.). Chichester, West Sussex, England: Wiley-Blackwell.

Howes, H., Benton, D., & Edwards, S. (2004). Women's experience of brain injury: An interpretative phenomenological analysis. *Psychology & Health, 20,* 129–142.

Howes, H., Edwards, S., & Benton, D. (2005). Male body image following acquired brain injury. *Brain Injury, 19*(2), 135–147. doi:10.1080/02699050410001720077

Jayaratne, T. E., & Stewart, A. J. (1991). Quantitative and qualitative methods in the social sciences: Current feminist issues and practical strategies. In M. M. Fonow & J. A. Cook (Eds.), *Beyond methodology: Feminist scholarship as lived research* (pp. 85–106). Bloomington, IN: Indiana University Press.

Jumisko, E., Lexell, J., & Söderberg, S. (2007). Living with moderate or severe traumatic brain injury: The meaning of family members' experience. *Journal of Family Nursing, 13*(3), 353–369. doi:10.1177/1074840707303842

Jumisko, E., Lexell, J., & Söderberg, S. (2009). The meaning of feeling well in people with moderate or severe traumatic brain injury. *Journal of Clinical Nursing, 18*(16), 2273–2281.

Karpman, T., Wolfe, S., & Vargo, W. J. (1986). The psychological adjustment of adult clients and their parents following closed head injury. *The Journal of Applied Rehabilitation Counselling, 17,* 28–33.

Kendall, E., & Muenchberger, H. (2009). When systems hurt rather than heal: Outcomes following psychological injury at work. In C. Marshall, E, Kendall, R. Gover & M. Banks (Eds.), *Disability: Insights from across fields and around the world* (Vol. 3, pp. 145–154). Westport, CT: Praeger Publication.

Kendall, E., & Terry, D. J. (2008). Understanding adjustment following traumatic brain injury: Is the Goodness-of-Fit coping hypothesis useful? *Social Science and Medicine, 67*(8), 1217–1224.

Kotre, J. (1984). *Outliving the self: Generativity and the interpretation of lives*. Baltimore, MD: Johns Hopkins University Press.

Kuhn, T. S. (1962). *The structure of scientific revolutions*. Chicago, IL: University of Chicago Press.

Laskowski, T. (2003). *Every good boy does fine*. Dallas, TX: Southern Methodist University Press.

Leaf, L. E., & Widucki, L. (1988). *Susan's dad: A child's story of head injury*. Emeryville, CA: Meadowbrook Rehabilitation Group.

Levack, W. M. M., Kayes, N. M., & Fadyl, J. K. (2010). Experience of recovery and outcome following traumatic brain injury: A metasynthesis of qualitative research. *Disability and Rehabilitation, 32*(12), 986–999.

Levack, W., McPherson, K., & McNaughton, H. (2004). Success in the workplace following traumatic brain injury: Are we evaluating what is most important? *Disability and Rehabilitation: An International, Multidisciplinary Journal, 26*(5), 290–298.

Liamputtong, P. (2007). *Researching the vulnerable: A guide to sensitive research methods*. London: Sage.

Linde, C. (1993). *Life Stories: The creation of coherence*. New York, NY: Oxford University Press.

Linge, F. R. (1990). Faith, hope and love: non traditional therapy in recovering from serious head injury: A personal account. *Canadian Journal of Psychology, 44,* 116–129.

Lloyd, V., Gatherer, A., & Kals, S. (2006). Conducting qualitative interview research with people with expressive language difficulties. *Qualitative Health Research, 16*(10), 1386–1404. doi:10.1177/1049732306293846

Lorenz, L. S. (2010a). Discovering a new identity after brain injury. *Sociology of Health & Illness, 32*(6), 862–879. doi:10.1111/j.1467-9566.2010.01244

Lorenz, L. S. (2010b). *Brain injury survivors: Narratives of rehabilitation and healing*. Boulder, CO: Lynne Rienner (not sure which of these refs are relevant)

Marshall, C. A. (2009). *Disabilities: Insights from across fields and around the world.* Westport, CN: Praeger.

Marshall, C., & Rossman, G. B. (1999). *Designing qualitative research* (3rd ed.). Thousand Oaks, CA: Sage.

Mason, M. P. (2008). *Head cases: Stories of brain injury and its aftermath*. New York, NY: Farrar, Straus and Giroux.

McColl, M. A., Carlson, P., Johnston, J., Minnes, P., Shue, K., Davies, D., et al. (1998). The definition of community integration: Perspectives of people with brain injuries. *Brain Injury, 12*(1), 15–30.

Mies, M. (1983). Towards a methodology for feminist research. In G. Bowles & R. Klein (Eds.), *Theories of women's studies* (pp. 117–139). Boston, MA: Routledge & Kegan Paul.

Milgram, S. (1974). *Obedience to authority: An experimental view*. London, England: Tavistock.

Moulton, G., & Van der Loo, J. (1986). *My friend Lucy*. Markham, Canada: Scholastic TAB.

Nochi, M. (2000). Reconstructing self-narratives in coping with traumatic brain injury. *Social Science and Medicine, 51*(12), 1795–1804.

Oakley, A. (1981). Interviewing women: A contradiction in terms. In H. Roberts (Ed.), *Doing feminist research* (pp. 30–61). Boston, MA: Routledge & Kegan Paul.

Oppermann, J. D. (2004). Interpreting the meaning individuals ascribe to returning to work after traumatic brain injury: A qualitative approach. *Brain Injury, 18*(9), 941–955.

Parker, V. S. (2005). *The get well soon...Balloon!*.Wake Forest, NC: Lash & Associates Publishing/Training Inc.

Peter, E. (2000). The politicization of ethical knowledge: Feminist ethics as a basis for home care nursing research. *Canadian Journal of Nursing Research, 3*(3), 103–118.

Rees, R. J. (2011). *Out of calamity—Stories of trauma survivors*. Stepney, Australia: Axiom Australia Publishing.

Renzetti, C. M., & Lee, R. M. (1993). *Researching sensitive topics*. London, England: Sage.

Robertson, J. M., & Webber, C. F. (2000). Cross-cultural leadership development. *International Journal of Leadership in Education, 3*(4), 315–330.

Rollnick, S., & Miller, W. R. (1995). What is motivational interviewing? *Behavioural and Cognitive Psychotherapy, 23*, 325–334.

Sample, P. L., & Darragh, A. R. (1998). Perceptions of care access: The experience of rural and urban women following brain injury. *Brain Injury, 12*(10), 855–874.

Sandberg, J., & Alvesson, M. (2011). Ways of constructing research questions: Gap-spotting or problematization? *Organization, 18*(1), 23–44.

Saxe, J. (1995). The blind men and the elephant. In M. Gardner (Eds.), *Famous poems from Bygone Days* (p. 124). Courier Dove Publications. ISBN 978-0-486-28623-5

Sieber, J. E., & Stanley, B. (1988). Ethical and professional dimensions of socially sensitive research. *American Psychologist, 43*(1), 49–55. doi:10.1037/0003-066X.43.1.49

Snyder, H. (1998). *Elvin: The elephant who forgets*. Youngsville NC: Lash and Associates Publishing Training Inc.

Stone, S. P. (2005). Reactions to invisible disability: The experience of young women survivors of hemorrhagic stroke. *Disability and Rehabilitation, 27*(6), 293–304.

Terre Blanche, M., & Durrheim, K. (1999). Histories of the present: Social science research in context. In M. Terre Blanche, K. Durrheim, & D. Painter (Eds.), *Research in practice: Applied methods for the social sciences* (pp. 1–16). Cape Town, South Africa: University of Cape Town Press.

Tidwell, D. L., Heston, M. L., & Fitzgerald, L. M. (2009). *Research methods for the self-study of practice*. Dordrecht, The Netherlands: Springer.

Turner, B., Fleming, J., Cornwell, P., Worrall, L., Ownsworth, T., Haines, T., et al. (2007). A qualitative study of the transition from hospital to home for individuals with acquired brain injury and their family caregivers. *Brain Injury, 21*(11), 1119–1130.

Uprichard, S. (2010). *Experiences of the process of adjustment to a brain injury: An interpretative phenomenological analysis* (Unpublished Doctoral thesis). University of Hertfordshire. Retrieved from http://hdl.handle.net/2299/452

van Maanen, M. (1990). *Researching lived experience: Human science for action sensitive pedagogy*. Albany, NY: State University of New York Press.

Wagner, J. (1993). Ignorance in educational research or, how can you not know that? *Educational Researcher, 22*(5), 15–23.

Wellings, K., Branigan, P., & Mitchell, K. (2000). Discomfort, discord and discontinuity as data: Using focus groups to research sensitive topics. *Culture, Health and Sexuality, 2*(3), 255–267.

Widdershoven, G. (1993). The story of life: Hermeneutic perspectives on the relationship between narrative and life history. In R. Josselson & A. Lieblich (Eds.), *The narrative study of lives* (Vol. 1, pp. 1–20). Newbury Park, CA: Sage.

# Chapter 5
# Reflection, Understanding and Insight from the Educational/Learning Perspective

> *Every function in the child's cultural development appears twice: first, on the social level, and later, on the individual level; first, between people (interpsychological) and then inside the child (intrapsychological). This applies equally to voluntary attention, to logical memory, and to the formation of concepts. All the higher functions originate as actual relationships between individuals.*
>
> Lev S. Vygotsky

## 5.1 Introduction

Responses from people who read *Doing Up Buttons* (Durham, 1997) and *Unlocking My Brain through the labyrinth of ABI* (Durham, 2014) demonstrated firstly that people could *learn* and reflect upon their own life by reading of the physical, emotional, social and metaphysical things that affected the quality of life and well-being of someone else, as they adapted and adopted coping strategies to re-engage in their new life. Additionally, there is a need for material that deals with the reconstruction of the 'whole person', or self, following ABI. This implies the particular relevance and importance of learning in the lives of people with ABI during rehabilitation and after leaving hospital when support and resources may be withdrawn. This is an area yet to be fully researched and in which much remains to be done.

Several authors who write about ABI state the need for people with ABI to 're-learn' (Durham, 1997; Freeman, 1998; Lewis, 2004; Rees, 2005). As has been shown, it can be difficult to locate 'easy to read' information that employs educational principles to inform, motivate and encourage people with ABI to *learn* to understand their lifeworld. Their quality of life and well-being is affected by the physical, emotional, social and metaphysical things (existence, cause and effect and possibility). Certainly, the predominant messages in the grey literature (e.g. ABI support Websites) have previously concentrated on the medicalised diagnostic 'problems' identified in Chap. 1.



C. Durham and P. Ramcharan, *Insight into Acquired Brain Injury*,
DOI 10.1007/978-981-10-5666-6_5

Much of the seeker information on Websites provides information that is of this banking type, providing 'the facts' about ABI. But, as we have demonstrated, facts are uni-dimensional in perspective and can lack connection to people's realities. Only recently have the stories of people with ABI demonstrated that encouraging people to write of their ABI experience, not only helps the writer 'sort out their thoughts' but can help people learn about vital issues as they reflect and reconstruct themselves and their lives.

In terms of learning, Freeman (1998) usefully states that:

> Medicine has very little to offer (to help the person function as independently as possible) in this direction. The way forward lies in education… in fact the medical model, as well as being superfluous in many cases and at most times in a person's life, is also often counterproductive to follow. The medical model sees the patient as subservient to the professional. It sees the power of recovery lying in the hands of the physician, whereas the power for recovery lies within the injured person as they relearn their daily living skills… Education is the key, (Freeman, 1998, p. 14).

Durham yearned for a book to help her learn about, and understand, some of the ramifications of ABI, the consequences of injury to her brain. She was terrified when she could not figure out what to do, and when she found herself intentionally doing something senseless. She did not understand why her head instinctively told her body to react in a certain way. An example is one day, crossing the railway tracks on her way to school, the boom gate came down to signal an approaching train. She did not know what to do and was astonished to find herself running across the tracks in front of the oncoming train. It sped past with only a whisker to spare. 'You stupid idiot', she told herself 'Why on earth did you do that?' It took days of puzzling before she figured out an explanation of why she had done such a dangerous thing. She realised that she had been frantically searching her mind for what it meant when a horizontal barrier was placed across your path. Somewhere in her subconscious, she remembered the ribbon at the finish of a running race when she was a child at school. She must have thought that a boom gate was like a finishing line of a race and this is the reason she ran. Other examples such as the 'drop your handbag' when traffic lights turn green were equally as puzzling though less dangerous. But when 'wires are crossed' thinking about 'what is normal' becomes a real issue.

Frequently, cognition problems only surface once rehabilitation has been completed, when the person moves into a re-engagement with their social, familial lives and within their localities. The person may not have the words to explain problems, or they may feel too ashamed to confess that they feel either stupid or crazy. For Durham, shame played a role when not knowing what to do and where to get information about doing crazy things. The logic was 'Crazy people do crazy things, I do crazy things therefore I must be crazy or insane'. If only there were narratives about the experiences of other people with ABI, and the strange things they did (in books or blogs that now exist), Durham would have seen the connection between her actions and the man who stopped at a puddle because he did not know what it was, or the person who chased emus, or the man who threw his typewriter in the creek because the Keys were not in alphabetical order. Similar narratives would convey some comfort and recognition that others had these problems. But education is more than information; it involves the learner *doing* something—engaging, making sense of, making connections, applying and considering how they can use their new understanding.

Vygotsky's'(1978) 'zone of proximal development' where a learner can achieve learning with the assistance of scaffolding from the teacher or a peer, and where the scaffold is slowly removed (as scaffolding is removed from a building when construction is complete), offers potential. As explained below, the Keys Study, therefore, drew upon a number of educational and learning principles to provide scaffolding to support learning, and to apply this learning to action, and thus achieve more autonomy and independence.

Once again, as the discussion unfolds, relevant Headwork will point to how the literature informed the methodological approach and procedure. As in the previous chapters, this will be highlighted in separate shaded boxes.

## 5.2 Scaffolding Learning: The Place of, Educational Theories, Motivation and Flow

In order to discover, realise or understand, children, adults and people with brain injury, all need to be absorbed and actively engaged in their learning. This study developed *Keys to the ABI Cage* with the aim of motivating participants to reflect and learn more about ABI and things that helped them to learn to feel and fare better. Mirroring the arguments in Chaps. 3 and 4, philosophies/models/beliefs or paradigms in education are changing from those focusing on 'being taught', the analytic-empirical-positivist-quantitative paradigm (where the person believes that a separate material reality exists apart from the beliefs of the individual, group or societies—similar in concept to the medical model) to 'learning on your own with guidance', the constructivist-hermeneutic-interpretativist-qualitative paradigm (Schubert & Schubert, 1990). In this latter paradigm 'Truth is a matter of consensus among informed and sophisticated constructors, not correspondence with an objective reality.' (Guba & Lincoln, 1989, p. 44).

In the constructivist model, there is a significant critique of what Freire (1974) calls 'the banking model' in which education becomes an act of depositing knowledge, in which the students are the depositories simply memorising and repeating what has been deposited and teachers the depositors of the knowledge. Rejecting this model has led to different positions. For example, critical-theory, neo-marxist and postmodern-praxis focus upon 'questions of power, control, and epistemology as social construction with benefits to some and not to others' (Muffoletto, 1993, p. 4).

As Freire goes on to say:

> They (students) do, it is true, have the opportunity to become collectors or cataloguers of things they store. But in the last analysis, it is men/women themselves who are filed away

> through the lack of creativity, transformation, and knowledge in this (at best) misguided system. For apart from inquiry, apart from the praxis, men/women *cannot be truly human* [our emphasis]. Knowledge emerges only through invention and reinvention, through the restless, impatient, continuing, hopeful inquiry men/women pursue in the world, with the world, and with each other. (Freire, 1974, p. 58).

Others argue for modes and tools to better understanding and more effective problem-solving (Reeves, 1996), a point premised on seminal authors such as Kolb (1984) and Lewin (1890–1947). This is an important point that fits well with the more constructivist approaches to contemporary learning theory. In their seminal work, Bloom (1956) developed a taxonomy exemplifying the process of learning through stages: from remembering, to understanding, to applying, then analysing, evaluating and then creating once again. Learning must be tied to actions ultimately, but must, too, be open to change.

So the question arose as to how the research could incorporate learning that had the potential to change how each person acted as a result of engagement.

In summary the study, which employed *Keys to the ABI Cage* as a method, was firmly positioned within the experiential learning theory: learning is a process grounded in experience, where learning is a holistic process of adaptation to the world (Freire, 1974; Kolb, 1984). From within such a paradigm, learning is a process of creating knowledge through the transformation of experience. The success of the Cage would recognise the importance of internalising knowledge and learning in pursuit of social activity, life transformation, and would attempt to scaffold learning (Vygotsky, 1978) and have implications for practice.

But in what does such scaffolding consist? This is discussed below.

### 5.2.1 Motivation and Engagement as Crucial Elements in the Learning Process

Engaged students want to learn. Many people with ABI are not ready to learn for many reasons. For example, they may not acknowledge that they have ABI, they may still want to be (and pretend to be) as they were, or they may feel there is stigma attached to having ABI (e.g. they feel they are different and 'dumb').

Csikszentmihalyi (1990, 1997) posits that 'flow' happens when the person becomes so absorbed in an engaging and interesting task that action and awareness merge. According to Wlodkowski (2008) in order to foster flow, firstly the goals must be clear and compatible, allowing the learner to concentrate even when the task is difficult. This links to 'negotiated curriculum theory', where goals are negotiated with the person. Secondly, the feedback is immediate, continuous and relevant so that the learner is clear about how well they are doing. Thirdly, the challenge carefully balances skills and knowledge while stretching the learner's capacities (Wlodkowski, 2008, pp. 267–268). These concepts were incorporated into *Keys to the ABI Cage* tool to establish flow.

If students are to work through Bloom's taxonomy as described previously (Shulman, 2002; Coates, 2005, 2010; Krause & Coates, 2008), 'motivation is the portal to engagement' (Barkley, 2010: p.15).

So how is it possible to support such motivation? As early as 1932, Piaget (1932) stressed the importance of experiences as the learner makes connections in an atmosphere of play with the teacher's role as facilitator, mentor, consultant and coach. The notion of 'playfulness' is at the heart of many contemporary learning approaches as exemplified in scaffolding using enhanced online and computer-simulated learning environments (Delen, Liew & Willson 2014; Duffy & Azevedo 2015). These studies demonstrated more engagement with learning resources and particular improvements for students assessed as being less motivated prior to the intervention (Duffy and Azevedo 2015).

However, such engagement is often influenced by self-perceptions and expectations as shown in Fig. 5.1.

*Keys to the ABI Cage*

- captured the attention and curiosity of people with ABI.
- provided an example of what it's like to have ABI.
- showed them their input was important.
- simplified the complexities of ABI into three themes reflecting the 'talk-about' cards.
- adopted a method that was an unexpected, fun and different way to examine a serious issue.
- was used in a way that participants received constant feedback that they were doing well.
- was implemented such that participants received constant feedback that they were doing well.

**Fig. 5.1** Headwork 17: How Keys to the ABI Cage addressed the issue of motivation

### *5.2.2 Engagement Is Influenced by Expectations and Self-perceptions*

From educational theory, we learn that in order for the learner to engage in learning, they need to believe that success will result from their effort. '[People] need to have confidence that, if they put in the effort, they can succeed. If there is no hope, there is no motivation' (Barkley, 2010, p. 11). Motivational theories that address student expectations include self-efficacy theories, attribution theory and self-worth models (Cross & Steadman, 1996). Self-efficacy theories state that the learner's belief about their ability to succeed has *greater importance* than either skill level or task difficulty (Bandura, 1971, 1997; Corno & Mandinach, 1983). If the person has confidence in their ability to perform a task, they will be motivated to engage in it. This theory holds an important message for professionals working with people with ABI.

In the present study, participants were introduced to *Keys to the ABI Cage*, with a PowerPoint presentation explaining the three-step way of looking at ABI. They then examined the *Keys to the ABI Cage* model—looking at the different 'talk-about' cards and the numerous different objects. This process showed the participant how ABI can affect people, how people feel about ABI, and factors that help people cope using everyday (non-medical) language.

By rehearsing the method with the participants in several different ways (seeing and touching) and reviewing the PowerPoint introductory digital storage disc, participants could see that they could contribute and succeed in sharing their thoughts. As the participants identified issues that affected them, they were led to discover factors that had helped or could help them in the future. They isolated strategies through which they could help themselves. This approach assisted them to have success in their own learning. On many occasions participants said 'You'll understand…you have brain injury'. There was relief that they could open up and voice their issues and not feel ashamed (Fig. 5.2).

However, as argued below, perceptions of success and failure are also important particularly for people with ABI given their circumstances. The person with ABI may have experienced failure in every attempted task—in many things they *do, inter alia*—they cannot walk, talk or even eat properly. The individual may also face failure in everything they *think,* they do not know what day it is, they forget names (including their own name), they do not know what a cup or a hairbrush is and they cannot follow conversations. They attribute failure (and the resultant

*Keys to the ABI Cage*:

- recognised the importance of involvement and participation for learning to take place.
- was devised to assist the participant to become involved and participate, and think about their experience.
- gave everyday examples and used everyday things to show that the task was not difficult or complicated.
- used simple structure (1. Difficulties and Differences, 2. Feelings and 3. Keys) that could be used for further reflection not only in the 'classroom' (the research location), but also outside the parameters set for the research study.
- ensured participants were not coerced to answer specific questions but to simply tell the parts of their story they wanted to share using the tool as a prompt.
- engaged the participants because it was interesting and different.
- gave participants control over the direction of the interview.

**Fig. 5.2** Headwork 18: Keys to the ABI Cage addresses the issue of engagement

feelings of being dumb or stupid) to nearly everything. It was recognised that having such attributes could affect their willingness to engage with *Keys to the ABI Cage* and the study.

Weiner's (1985) attribution theory states that students attribute success or failure according to their perceptions of why they might have succeeded or failed in the past. Weiner suggests that success or failure of tasks can depend on factors that include ability, effort, luck, fatigue, ease or difficulty of the task. If 'success' depends on attributes over which the person believes they have control, such as putting in an effort, a hypothesis was made that students (people with ABI) would be more likely to have confidence to be involved with the task rather than when success depends on external conditions over which they have no control, such as the difficulty of the exam (test, questionnaire).Weiner's attribution theory suggests that the person with ABI, whose cognition, emotions, memory and confidence is damaged, may believe that failure is most likely because they attribute the situation to be dominated by *external (outside the person)*, *unstable (the outcome is not as intended)* and *uncontrollable* factors. They are not 'in control'.

In order to counteract these factors, the persons with ABI involved with this study were informed in the advertisement, and during the preinterview phone conversations, that their personal insights were important, their comments were valuable and that they would be able to choose what they said. Barkley (2010) has

*Keys to the ABI Cage*:

- used an original method so that participants would not think 'last time I did a test/questionnaire I failed, or I felt a failure.'
- employed many different ways so the person could feel successful — from putting a card in a box to discussing their experiences.
- was implemented to encourage and praise participants for their wisdom/personal insights.
- had no right or wrong answers.
- was developed so that success was built into the tool.
- placed participants in control of what they wished to talk about.
- looked interesting and fun thing to engage with;
- helped the participant understand what they were asked to do;
- provided constant positive reinforcement that they were doing well;
- did not ask difficult questions;
- made easy requests about what to do (place a card or talk about an issue) and, gave them choice about the topics they wished to talk about.

**Fig. 5.3** Headwork 19: Keys to the ABI Cage addresses the issue of attribution of success

also shown how ‘success’ is built into a task: when there is no right or wrong answers, the person is encouraged and praised for their wisdom and the person has the power to control the discussion (Fig. 5.3).

Associated with promoting success in learning as described above is the fear of failure. Evasion can be a powerful strategy to maintain control for students who do not feel it possible to gain from learning. In the absence of personal control, Barkley (2010) posits that these students have a ‘low level of confidence and expectancy of failure [that] have placed them in a state of almost chronic disenchantment’ (Barkley, 2010, p. 14). These learners recognise the value of learning to accomplish a task, but feel incapable because they ‘aren’t certain of what to do or how to do it or they doubt they can do it’ (Barkley, p. 14).

The interview aimed to have participants involved in reflection, not involved in trying to figure out how to evade questions they did not wish to speak about.

The importance of preserving the participants’ self-worth was essential to all discussions relating to failure, success and having control. Cross and Steadman (1996) describe ‘failure-accepting students’ who are resigned to failure. They feel hopeless and respond to learning tasks with indifference (Cross & Steadman, 1996). To cope with failure in daily life, people with ABI need to accept failure as a minute-by-minute, hour-by-hour occurrence rather than as defining who they are.

When some students do not succeed, they would rather let people think they are *lazy* (question their effort) rather than think they are *dumb* (question their ability). Some students do not even try because they believe there is a low possibility of success—Covington (1993) refers to these students as ‘failure avoiders’. Similarly, people with ABI have to overcome their abhorrence of admitting they do not know how to do up their buttons or tie their shoelaces and their self-worth and self-esteem is affected by their differences and difficulties. Fear of failing and being seen as dumb can block and inhibit learning.

*Keys to the ABI Cage* method was developed to allow the participant to preserve their self-worth because the tool acknowledged their enormous challenges in an

*Keys to the ABI Cage*:

- had clear study goals and aims.
- employed steps to reflect upon th ings that positively affected their lifeworld.
- led participants to see that they could understand more about their ABI through reflection.
- offered immediate, continuous and relevant feedback so that the participant was clear about how well they were doing.
- supported reflection on personal experience and carefully balanced skills and knowledge while stretching the participant’s capacities to reflect.

**Fig. 5.4** Headwork 20: Keys to the ABI Cage addresses the issue of self-worth

empathetic way and asserted that they had special insight and wisdom, which they were invited to share with others with ABI. Self-worth models put forward the hypothesis that people are strongly motivated to preserve their self-worth (Fig. 5.4).

### 5.2.3 Active or Experiential Learning

'Active learning' principles were used in *Keys to the ABI Cage*. Learning is taking an idea or concept and making it part of the personal knowledge and experience of the learner. This is done by connecting concepts and 'accommodating' (Barkley, 2010)—fitting or altering the existing structure to accommodate the new learning and action as a result.

People grasp new information in different ways: some 'through experiencing the concrete, tangible, felt qualities of the world', relying on their senses and 'immersing themselves in concrete reality'; some through 'symbolic representation or abstract conceptualisation—thinking about, analysing or systematically planning'; some through watching others and reflecting on what happens—reflective observation; some 'jump right in and start doing things—active experimentation' (Kolb et al., 2000, pp. 3–4).

Coulson and Harvey (2013) propose a model of scaffolding reflection for experience-based learning: over four stages students need to be 'supported to reflect', to 'reflect for action', to 'reflect in action' and then to 'reflect on action'. This model links learning to change through reflection and offers maximum agency to the person to convert thoughts to actions over time—to explore the 'dropped handbag at the traffic light' and to apply new forms of action to see what works.

The plasticity of the brain, may, over time, offer new neural pathways that create a learned behaviour or a recognition, and there is a need to stop and think, or provide a new cue for the person's actions. For the purposes of this research, *Keys to the ABI Cage* offered an innovative tool with recognisable metaphors (crushed cans, pigs that fly) and a series of 'talk-about' cards that reflected common experiences from which each person could reflect, and then through reflection, formulate new ideas about their lives and how they act. The approach also fits with Vygotsky's idea of the zone of proximal development, leading to more independent and autonomous change based on reflection and learning.

People with ABI who may have an unreliable memory might panic when they forget what they were told or instructed to do. But having the Cage in front of them and 'talk-about' cards in their hands, they had a way to review the issues that led to certain conclusions as they figured things out for themselves. Additionally, people with ABI may become paralysed when trying to judge if they did give the correct answer, so they needed to know that it was okay to revisit their ideas (Fig. 5.5).

Keys to the ABI Cage:

- used concrete experiences of touch, and seeing, and talking as a basis for the participant to share observations and reflections.
- allowed more abstract concepts explored from which they could draw implications for action, serving as guides to create new experiences.
- engaged participants' senses. They saw and touched the symbols and 'talk-about' cards, they could observe what issues others had had, and were keen to add their own thoughts.
- was an exciting and different experience.
- engaged the participant in reflection and allowed pauses for reflection.
- supported engagement with the materials and encouraged understanding and higher order thinking (analysis, synthesis and evaluation).
- gave participants something to do (physically) as they shared and discussed ideas - employing active learning techniques to support engagement and learning
- allowed the participant to feel and do (accommodating), think and do (converging), think and watch (assimilating) and feel and watch (diverging)(Kolb, 1984).

**Fig. 5.5** Headwork 21: Keys to the ABI Cage addresses the issue of active learning

### *5.2.4 'Flow'*

*Keys to the ABI Cage* was also devised to encourage what Csikszentmihalyi (1990, 1997) terms 'flow'. Flow happens when the person becomes so absorbed in an engaging and interesting task that action and awareness merge. According to Wlodkowski (2008) in order to foster flow, firstly the goals must be clear and compatible, allowing the learner to concentrate, even when the task is difficult. This linked to 'negotiated curriculum theory', where goals are negotiated with the person. Secondly, the feedback was immediate, continuous and relevant so that the learner was clear about how well they were doing. Thirdly, the challenge carefully balanced skills and knowledge while stretching the learner's capacities (Wlodkowski, 2008, pp. 267–268). These concepts were incorporated into *Keys to the ABI Cage* tool to establish flow (Fig. 5.6).

*Keys to the ABI Cage*:
- had clear goals.
- used cards to help participants concentrate even when thinking about hard things.
- gave control about what they want to talk about.
- offered immediate, continuous, and relevant feedback.
- challenged the participant and carefully balanced between what the participant kneow while stretching them to think more about issues.

**Fig. 5.6** Headwork 22: Keys to the ABI Cage addresses the issue of 'flow'

### 5.2.5 *The Theory of Association*

No single teaching and learning strategy is applicable to all people. It is necessary to differentiate sufficiently to allow differing engagement styles. de Sousa's (1987) theory of association was implemented in *Keys to the ABI Cage* where a combination of pictures, symbols, objects and words was used to provide a framework to support the participant's ideas. The participant was assisted to emotionally respond to the process by the purposeful use of humour and *Keys to the ABI Cage* being 'different' and eye-catching and a unique way to revisit their ABI experience in a safe space. Emotions were acknowledged as an important element in the whole ABI experience, as emotions can influence transfer and obtaining attention.

Brain scans have shown that retention can be improved when new learning makes sense and it can be connected to experience (Barkley, 2010). Memory difficulties affect every aspect of learning new information. By embedding strong emotional context, repetition and visual imagery learning was more likely to become part of long-term memories. Pictures and objects were used to help the participant make connections so they could make sense of and retain more than by simply reading or being told information.

As retention of the learning needs 'adequate time to process and reprocess information so that it can be transferred from short-term to long-term memory…this requires time and usually occurs during deep sleep' (Barkley, 2010, p. 23). By allowing participants to reflect further upon their concepts, they were given 'Some Further Thoughts' sheets so that they could record any further thoughts they had in the days following the interview (Fig. 5.7).

*Keys to the ABI Cage*:
- allowed the participant time to think/understand.
- repeated information to allow time for assimilation.
- engaged the participant by allowing them to examine the association between difficulties or challenges and how they felt.
- used pictures/objects/symbols so the participant could put the concepts together.
- added 'Some Further Thoughts' sheets to allow time for further reflection.

**Fig. 5.7** Headwork 23: Keys to the ABI Cage addresses the issue of theories of association

### 5.2.6 *Learning in a 'Community*

Many people with ABI feel as if they are the only person to experience what they experience. Knowing others in the community share common experiences can help them to feel less isolated. Barkley (2010) writes about the importance of promoting synergy between motivation and active learning through creating a sense of classroom 'community'.

In this study, a sense of community was used—not in a classroom, but with connecting the participant to the ideas and thoughts of other people with ABI—a 'Community of people with ABI'. Much of what has been written about learning communities was applied to this study to develop a group of connected people with shared interests, goals and responsibilities towards one another (Brophy, 2004); the words on the 'talk-about' cards were from other people with ABI, and they were helping to develop material/resources to help others with ABI (Fig. 5.8).

*Keys to the ABI Cage*:
- gave them a sense of belonging to a group of people facing similar challenges.
- established a 'community' feeling, a resource from people with ABI for people with ABI.
- emphasised the values of the participant's insight to help others with ABI.
- allowed the participant to come to the conclusion that they are not alone or isolated with their issues.
- supported self-reflection in a malleable way to allow any issue the person wanted to 'get off their chest' to be talked about.

**Fig. 5.8** Headwork 24: Keys to the ABI Cage addresses the issue of participants feeling they are part of a community of people with ABI

Howe (2013) provides a useful argument that scaffolding should be presented as a 'support for the reconciliation of conflicting perspectives' and we have seen, how for people with ABI, such conflicts may seem pervasive. In this light, each person struggles for meaning through their interactions with peers, networks and with formal learning. For many people with ABI, there are significant 'conflicting perspectives' at a time when they are more likely to have fractured social networks and peer groups. Consequently, people with ABI have found through Durham, and with excitement, that others have similar experiences, that there is some possibility of alliance and of empathy. Slovak et al (2016) show how sharing the scaffolding across the students and the home can support socio-emotional learning by reinforcing new skills and actions. The relevance *of Keys to the ABI Cage* may, therefore, not just rest with this study. As argued in Chap. 9, its relevance and the relevance of other scaffolding underscores the vital learning that should be central in the lives of people with ABI in their homes, networks and, as importantly, within services.

We have considered above the 'motivational factors' that contributed to the development of *Keys to the ABI Cage*. But there are also vitally important aspects to cognition and learning which also needed to be taken into account. These are set out below.

## 5.3 Educational Theories About Cognition and Learning

In order to engage with *Keys to the ABI Cage*, 'cognitive' skills are required. The participant needs to think about concepts, reflect and express their opinion. But as covered earlier, people with ABI may have cognitive problems that include difficulty with short-term memory, concentration, confusion, slow thinking, slow processing of information, difficulty understanding, planning, organising, problem-solving, rigid concrete thinking and mental fatigue. We also learnt that impairment of memory is a significant impediment to people with ABI who are returning to work; however, memory can help through programs designed to assist memory (Raskin & Sohlberg, 2009). *Keys to the ABI Cage* was developed to support the individual whose slow thinking and poor memory may limit their understanding and problem-solving.

### *5.3.1 Cognition*

In the following sections, different approaches to cognition are used to inform the further development of *Keys to the ABI Cage*. Given different approaches, this section is meant to draw upon leading paradigms within learning and rehabilitation practice.

### 5.3.2 *Cognitive Rehabilitation*

Cognitive rehabilitation is an established branch of rehabilitation where the individual practices various cognitive tasks to help attention, memory and other problems with thinking. This may include doing arithmetic, solving logic puzzles and working on concentration and communication skills and executive functions.

Sohlberg, and Mateer (2001) explain that just as cognitive abilities overlap each other they are also influenced by emotional difficulties such as anger, anxiety or depression, behavioural difficulties such as impulsivity, frustration and physical problems such as impairments to movement, sensory changes, headaches and pain. The authors suggest that the artificial distinction among cognition, emotion and motivation has been steadily 'eroded' but

> it is still common in rehabilitation texts to see box diagrams in which cognitive problems are dealt with in cognitive rehabilitation and/or speech therapy, emotional and behavioral problems are dealt with in some sort of affective rehabilitation therapy (e.g., group counselling, individual psychotherapy); and physical problems are dealt with through medical management and occupational rehabilitation specialists…. Although the notions of inter-disciplinary or even trans-disciplinary treatments attempt to bridge and coordinate various approaches, there has been very little written on or investigated with regard to how to practice this philosophy in patient interactions and not just in a paper trail, (Sohlberg & Mateer, 2001, p. 9).
>
> This, they argue, should not simply be the domain of collaborating professionals.

More recently, we have begun to reap the rehabilitation benefit from collaborating and forming partnerships with families and caregivers, (Sohlberg & Mateer, 2001, p. xi). See Fig. 5.9.

*Keys to the ABI Cage*:

- took account of the emotional, cognitive and physical difficulties of participants.
- provided a framework to anchor information.
- provided clear instructions.
- built errorless learning into the tool.

**Fig. 5.9** Headwork 25: Keys to the ABI Cage addresses issues from cognitive rehabilitation

### 5.3.3 *Cognition/Thinking Involves Steps and Skills*

Compared with cognitive rehabilitation, education views cognition within a framework of providing a scaffold or framework for learning. Anderson and Krathwohl's taxonomy (2001) seen in Fig. 5.10 is a revised form of Bloom's Taxonomy of Learning (1956) introduced earlier. While it is tempting to view or treat the following taxonomy as a linear process for learning, this should be avoided. For example, inquiry or problem-based learning approaches often start at the complex end of the taxonomy ('create') to stimulate learning, and then work 'backwards' to examine the issue and deepen learning.

Learning involves:

- *'Remembering'* involves recognising (identifying) and recalling (retrieving) information. This starting point can prove to be difficult when memory is affected.
- *'Understanding'* involves the person constructing meaning from information: interpreting, illustrating, classifying, summarising, inferring, comparing and explaining.
- *'Applying'* involves using the knowledge or procedure to a new situation or event.
- *'Analyzing'* involves breaking the material or concept into parts by differentiating, organising and attributing.
- *'Evaluating'* involves making judgments based on criteria and standards by checking and judging.
- *'Creating'* involves putting elements together to form a functional whole; re-organising elements into a new pattern or structure — generating ideas — hypothesising, planning — designing and producing — constructing.

**Fig. 5.10** Anderson and Krathwohl's learning taxonomy (2001)

It could be generalised that good thinking involves gaining insight of an issue in order to have foresight to tackle similar issues. Thinking back to Durham's experience with 'drop your handbag' reaction to a green traffic lights or 'running in front of an oncoming train' reaction to a boom gate, she needed to understand by remembering, understanding, applying, analysing, evaluating and creating to develop ways to talk to herself next time she saw a traffic light or boom gate, and when she was confused about what to do.

*Keys to the ABI Cage* used a cognitive process:
*Remembering*: Start by obtaining simple remembering and recall of information.
*Understanding*: Lead participant to make show they understand a concept by telling a story to illustrate the point.
*Applying*: Use the concept to make connections and apply the information to another idea. Explore and analyse the consequences of the information, and select other issues to distinguish a point.
*Evaluating*: helping participant make a judgement about the issue by checking and judging.
*Creating*: generating ideas about how the information could be used in the future, hypothesise, and plan for a further time.
Encourage synthesis where information gained can allow insight and foresight into problems.
Involving different ways of engaging with the material, recalling, talking about, applying a concept to something else, connecting, comparing and analysing the material until the person can talk about possible issues for the future and what to do about them.

**Fig. 5.11** Headwork 26: Keys to the ABI Cage provides steps for participants to engage in higher order thinking

People with ABI need to learn to strengthen their cognitive skills across the lower order and higher order thinking spectrum. In using tools that are underpinned by such principles, people with ABI can then begin to engage with the variety of cognitive thinking levels (Fig. 5.11).

### 5.3.4 Learning Styles

There are various approaches or ways of learning (Kolb, 1984). The way that a person concentrates takes in, understands and stores and remembers new information is defined as their learning style. Honey and Mumford (1982) posit that students learn best when they have an experience, they review the experience, they draw conclusions from the experience, then plan the next step. This draws upon the concept of the student as 'activist', 'reflector', 'theorist' and 'pragmatist'. Such a learning style approach was employed in *Keys to the ABI Cage*. Participants created their own knowledge by exploring the ideas drawn from other people with ABI and the ABI literature (Fig. 5.12).

*Keys to the ABI Cage.*

- gave participants the experience of seeing the Cage, and watching the digital storage disk.
- helped them to review from their personal perspective.
- encouraged them to draw conclusions from the experience and then plan how they could deal with issues and emotions in the future.

**Fig. 5.12** Headwork 27: Keys to the ABI Cage provides an experience for participants to review

### 5.3.5 Multiple Intelligence

Multiple intelligences are a theoretical framework for defining/understanding/assessing/developing people's different intelligence factors. In his seminal work, Gardner (1983) conceptualised multiple intelligences as a framework that defines how we think, how we come to understand our world or how we generate knowledge. With Gardner's hypothesis in mind, *Keys to the ABI Cage* addresses many of these 'intelligences' in helping participants understand and generate knowledge (see below) Fig. 5.13 employment of Gardner's Multiple Intelligences in Keys to the ABI Cage.

| Gardner's Multiple Intelligences | Person's Preferred Learning | How the Cage used the Intelligences |
|---|---|---|
| 1.Visual spatial intelligence | The person likes drawing and remembers visual landmarks | The Cage used spatial concepts, visual landmarks: it was a visual and memorable 'landmark'. |
| 2.Verbal/linguistic intelligence | The person likes to think in language or metaphor | Engaging with the Cage involved using spoken and written language, and engaging imaginatively with metaphor through the spoken word |
| 3. Logical/ mathematical intelligence | The person likes to compare and/or categorise information | Engaging with the Cage provided an opportunity to compare and categorise information:the person could compare, categorise and 'measure ' their own and other people's experiences of ABI. |
| 4.Bodily kinaesthetic intelligence | The person finds meaning in movement and touching | Engaging with the Cage involved touching, and moving: touching the objects in the Cage, moving things about in the Cage, holding and placing the cards. |
| 5.Musical/ rhythmic intelligence | The person learns through rhythm and music | There was a rhythm established – the participant took up and placed the cards. |
| 6.Interpersonal intelligence | The person sees the idea from another person's perspective | Engaging with the Cage led the participant to see the concepts from the perspective of other people with ABI. The 'talk-about' cards held experiences from others and the CD recounted Durham's own personal experience. |
| 7.Intrapersonal intelligence | The person is aware of their own strengths, weaknesses and feelings and has insight | Engaging with the Cage led the participant to become aware of their strengths, weaknesses and feelings and develop insight through the three main questions. |

**Fig. 5.13** Summary of Garner's multiple intelligences and how they were used in the Cage

| | | |
|---|---|---|
| 8. Naturalist intelligence | The person has a keen interest in the world of nature | The photos of the Cage outside involved the world of nature.The bird, rocks and other contents were part of an 'eco-system' and used this as a metaphor for their experiences. |
| 9. Spiritual/ existential intelligence | The spiritual meaning of life is important to the person. | Engagement with the Cage provided an opportunity for the participant to discuss their spiritual meaning of life. Metaphor was used. |

**Fig. 5.13** (continued)

As shown, 'multiple intelligences' present a panoply of vehicles through which learning can best be accomplished rather than a single theory reliant upon a limited range of learning styles. In this sense, the approach offers a means through which people can meaningfully engage using the learning style they find most appropriate to their own engagement with knowledge. It is argued that the concepts of learning styles and multiple intelligences can be helpful when working with people with brain injury because the person may have difficulty comprehending words, they may be suffering from aphasia to some degree and memory difficulties may limit their ability to remember the topic under discussion. By holding the 'talk-about' cards in their hands, they had a prompt for what they were talking about.

Applying the concept of multiple intelligences to this study, a hypothesis is made that some people might find the physical presence of the Cage and handling the artefacts (symbols) more helpful, while others might participate better with the digital storage disc, visual version in which the written word is required to express their response. *Keys to the ABI Cage* appealed to and sought to engage all of Gardner's multiple intelligences.

The models of disability outlined in Chap. 2 established pretheorised versions of reality which, it has been argued, imposed, as a priority, a framework of meaning. These assumptions would guide us to ask only certain questions that come from the premises of these theories and reflect their assumptions. The phenomenological stance allows the data from people with ABI to 'speak for itself', to establish their meaning and, from this, to ground our understanding in those areas that have meaning and relevance to those with ABI rather than a theory imposed by 'experts' without consultation.

## 5.4 Recapitulation

This chapter has identified the literature in the field of education that was considered when devising *Keys to the ABI Cage*. A foundation of this study was that people are different, they learn in different ways and that different things can affect their learning.

*Keys to the ABI Cage* was devised to address people who are logical, critical, realistic and accurate by using structured activities, allowing them to deal with the information sequentially, analytically, logically, factually and verbally. *Keys to the ABI Cage* was also devised to address the learning needs of people who learn through intuition, imagination, seeing the big picture, trying to understand and by discussing and sharing ideas. It is acknowledged that the issues discussed in this chapter may not be a prime consideration of ABI research, nor may the issues be the foremost focus in rehabilitation. This may be because of pressure of time constraints, limited funding, lack of resources, an absence of guidelines and the absence of appreciation of the significance of motivation and educational and learning principles.

But it is nevertheless essential that learning is seen to be particularly important to people who have to build new lives, build new identities and discover actions that help them cope on a day-to-day basis.

The aim of the Keys Study was for the individual to achieve understanding and insight into ABI, so they can learn to feel and fare better and make the best of living with ABI. This study aimed to access the lifeworld of people with ABI by inviting them to talk about their life in terms of a 'commonwealth of concepts' displayed visually in the tool, *Keys to the ABI Cage,* or, indeed to add to these concepts. It also offered a model for thinking through lives in terms of actions to adopt that would support them to fare better. Learning is, as pointed out early in this chapter, vital to humans choosing how to act.

Finally, this chapter has brought a constructivist learning theory into alignment with a phenomenological and constructivist epistemology as outlined in Chap. 3 and how this has informed Keys to the ABI Cage, the study methodology. It has shown how, all of us—families, friends, or human service professionals—can listen to the lifeworld and experiences of people with ABI and **WE CAN LEARN FROM PEOPLE WITH ABI**, how to help them and others with ABI feel and fare better. Chapter 6 will explain the methods used for this study, synthesising information about education from this chapter with information about ABI obtained from the literature reviews in Chaps. 2–4. Interpretative phenomenological analysis (IPA), the method used to analyse the data, will be explained, and an example of how IPA was used will be provided. Chapters 7 and 8 will then present the analysed findings.

## References

Anderson, L. W., & Krathwohl, D. R. (Eds.) (2001). *A taxonomy for learning, teaching, and assessing: A revision of Bloom's taxonomy of educational objectives*. Boston, MA: Allyn & Bacon (Pearson Education Group).

Bandura, A. (1971). *Social Learning Theory*. New York, General Learning Press.

Bandura, A. (1995). *Self-efficacy in changing societies*. Cambridge, England: Cambridge University Press.

Bandura, A. (1995). *Self-efficacy: The exercise of control*. New York, NY: W.H. Freeman.

Barkley, E. F. (2010). *Student engagement techniques: A handbook for college faculty*. San Francisco, CA: Jossey-Bass.
Bloom, B. S. (1956). *Taxonomy of educational objectives: The classification of educational goals, Handbook I: Cognitive domain*. London, England: Longman.
Brophy, J. E. (2004). *Motivating students to learn* (2nd ed.). Mahwah, NJ: Lawrence Erlbaum.
Coates, H. (2005). The Value of student engagement for higher education quality assurance. *Quality in Higher Education, 11*(1), 25–36.
Coates, H. (2010). Development of the Australasian Survey of Student Engagement (AUSSE). *Quality in Higher Education, 60*(1), 1–17.
Corno, L., & Mandinach, E. B. (1983). The role of cognitive engagement in classroom learning and motivation. *Educational Psychologist, 18*(2), 88–108.
Coulson, D., & Harvey, M. (2013). Scaffolding student reflection for experience-based learning: A framework. *Teaching in Higher Education, 18*(4), 401–413.
Covington, M. V. (1993). A motivational analysis of academic life in college. In J. C. Smart (Ed.), *Higher education: Handbook of theory and research* (Vol. 9, pp. 50–93). New York, NY: Agathon Press.
Cross, K. P., & Steadman, M. H. (1996). *Classroom research: Implementing the scholarship of teaching*. San Francisco, CA: Jossey-Bass.
Csikszentmihalyi, M. (1990). *Flow: The psychology of optimal experiences*. New York, NY: Harper and Row.
Csikszentmihalyi, M. (1997). Intrinsic motivation and effective teaching: A flow analysis. In J. L. Bess (Ed.), *Teaching well and liking it: Motivating faculty to teach effectively* (pp. 72–89). Baltimore, MD: Johns Hopkins University Press.
Delen, E., Liew, J., & Willson, V. (2014). Effects of interactivity and instructional scaffolding on learning: Self regulation in online video based environments. *Computers & Education*, 312–320.
de Sousa, R. (1987). *The rationality of emotion*. Cambridge, MA: The MIT Press.
Duffy, M. C., & Azevedo, R. (2015). Motivation matters: Interactions between achievement goals and agent scaffolding for self-regulated learning within an intelligent tutoring system. *Computers in Human Behavior, 52*, 338–348.
Durham, C. (1997). *Doing up buttons*. Ringwood, Australia: Penguin.
Durham, C. (2014). *Unlocking my Brain: Through the labyrinth of Acquired brain Injury*. Edgecliff NSW: Jane Curry Publishing.
Freeman, E. A. (1998). *Brain injury & stroke: A handbook to recovery*. Sydney, Australia: Hale & Iremonger.
Freire, P. (1974). *Pedagogy of the oppressed*. New York, NY: Continuum.
Gardner, H. (1983). *Frames of mind: The theory of multiple intelligences*. New York, NY: Basic Books.
Guba, E. G., & Lincoln, Y. S. (1989). *Fourth generation evaluation*. Newbury Park, CA: Sage.
Honey, P., & Mumford, A. (1982). *The manual of learning styles*. Maidenhead, England: Peter Honey.
Howe, C. (2013). Scaffolding in context: Peer interaction and abstract learning. *Learning, Culture and Social Interaction, 2*(1), 3–10.
Kolb, D. A. (1984). *Experiential learning: Experience as the source of learning and development*. Englewood Cliff, NJ: Prentice Hall.
Krause, K., & Coates, H. (2008). Student engagement in first year university. *Assessment and Evaluation in Higher Education, 33*(5), 493–505.
Lewis, J. (2004). *Mind how you go!: A post-stroke path through the maze of mind, body, emotion and spirit*. Charnwood, Australia: Ginninderra Press.
Muffoletto, R. (1993). *Schools and technology in a democratic society: Equity and Social Justice*. Paper presented at the Annual Conference of the Association for Educational Communications and Technology, New Orleans, LA.
Piaget, J. (1932). *The moral judgement of the child*. London, England: Routledge & Kegan Paul.

Raskin, S. A., & Sohlberg, M. M. (2009). Prospective memory intervention: A review and evaluation of a pilot restorative intervention. *Brain Impairment, 10*(1), 76–86. doi:10.1375/brim.10.1.76

Rees, R. J. (2005). *Interrupted lives: Rehabilitation and learning following brain injury*. East Hawthorn, Australia: IP Communications.

Reeves IT_FORUM listserv (1996, Feb 21) http://www.educatipnau.edu.au/archivesCP/Refs/reeves.paradigms.html

Schubert, W. H., & Schubert, A. L. (1990). Alternative paradigms in curriculum inquiry. In H. J. Walberg & G. D. Haertel (Eds.), *The international encyclopedia of educational evaluation* (pp. 157–162). New York, NY: Pergamon.

Shulman, L. S. (2002). Truth and consequences? Inquiry and policy in research on teacher education. *Journal of Teacher Education, 53*(3), 248–253.

Slovák, P., Rowan, K., Frauenberger, C., Gilad-Bachrach, R., Doces, M., Smith, B., … Fitzpatrick, G. (2016, February). Scaffolding the scaffolding: Supporting children's social-emotional learning at home. In *Proceedings of the 19th ACM Conference on Computer-Supported Cooperative Work & Social Computing* (pp. 1751–1765). ACM

Sohlberg, M. M., & Mateer, C. A. (2001). *Cognitive rehabilitation: An integrative neuropsychological approach*. New York, NY: Guilford Press.

Vygotsky, L. (1978). Interaction between learning and development. In M. Gauvain & M. Cole (Eds.), *Readings on the development of children* (pp. 34–40). New York, NY: Scientific American Books.

Weiner, B. (1985). An attributional theory of achievement motivation and emotion. *Psychological Review, 92*(4), 548–578.

Wlodkowski, R. J. (2008). *Enhancing adult motivation to learn* (3rd ed.). San Francisco, CA: Jossey-Bass.

# Chapter 6
# Capturing Insights

*The doctor may also learn more about the disease from the way the patient tells the story than from the story itself.*
James B. Herrick.

## 6.1 Introduction

We have identified in previous chapters difficulties and problems associated with ABI from the literature. We have also emphasised the blind spot relating to a positive model of ABI which seems all but absent from the literature to date. In adopting a method that supports people to feel and fare better, and which is itself ethical in its approach, we have adopted van Maanen's concept of 'Headwork' to provide a catalogue of important issues and statements that informed the 'talk-about' cards and that 'did no harm'. A number of criteria therefore needed to characterise this study:

- to preserve the rights, privacy, dignity and wellbeing of participants.
- to approach brain injury from the insider's body-subject perspective—Durham's role was as a *person with brain injury and a visible researcher.*
- to adopt *a constructivist paradigm* of education, where the individual themselves 'constructs' knowledge, with guidance. Knowledge produced was of *direct benefit to people with brain injury*, to adopt a *positive* as well as a negative focus.
- to respect participants as 'whole' human beings and acknowledge their courage and perseverance (they would not be defined only by their difficulties, differences and deficits).
- to select adults at least two years post brain injury who are no longer in the rehabilitation setting.

Below, we make a formal introduction to the study methodology.



C. Durham and P. Ramcharan, *Insight into Acquired Brain Injury*,
DOI 10.1007/978-981-10-5666-6_6

## 6.2 Keys to the ABI Cage—Contents of the Method

*Keys to the ABI Cage* was displayed at the end of the Foreword. The Cage itself was used in face-to-face meetings but, for people in rural areas, a PowerPoint version was created and distributed on a DVD. The PowerPoint presentation included slides with Durham's voice-over. Additionally, three orange-coloured slides were situated after each of the three topics on the 'talk-about' cards. When the participants came to an orange slide, they were asked to pick up the 'What ABI means to me' sheets and answer the question that corresponded to the 'talk-about' cards (Themes were as follows: Difficulties and Differences, Feelings and Keys). For both groups, the face-to-face group and participants living in rural areas then, three themes about issues were addressed as shown in Fig. 6.1.

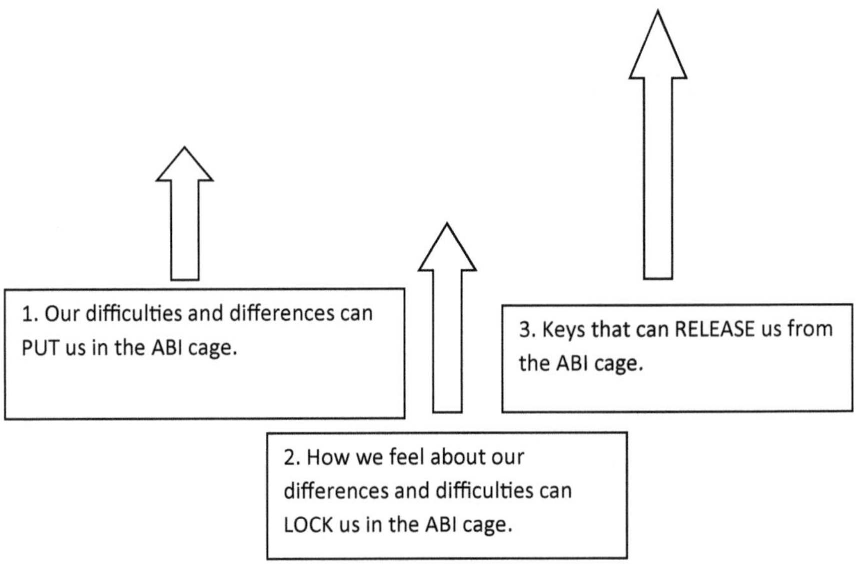


**Fig. 6.1** Three research themes Keys to the ABI Cage

## 6.3 Alternate Ways to Conduct the Interview

'Handy Thinking Tools' were prepared to provide an alternative structure for the interviews for participants who did not appear to understand or enter into the spirit of 'Keys to the ABI Cage', and/or for participants who became 'stuck' on a particular problem or issue. Both 'Handy Thinking Tools' and 'Keys to the ABI Cage' are learning/discovery tools to assist the unpacking of the many facets of ABI: to provide a structured framework to build a discussion, to jog memory (before answering open-ended questions) to encourage reflection, self-discovery, thinking what coping strategies are used and could be used in the future, to provide a positive interesting experience, to lead the participant to learn new tools to use in their daily activities to understand issues and problems.

All participants responded well to 'Keys to the ABI Cage' except one participant who became stuck on the words on one 'talk-about' card part way through the interview using 'Keys to the ABI Cage'. Handy Thinking Tools was also used in discussions along with 'Keys to the ABI Cage' at a second meeting with ABI support groups. Professionals were introduced to Handy Thinking Tools and found them a valuable resource for discussions.

Method B: Handy Thinking about what it is like to have ABI

Handy Thinking Tools are tactile, tangible, mnemonic devices that utilise senses of touch, sight and hearing to reinforce analytical, practical, creative thinking about an issue or problem. Participants can learn to 'count on their fingers'—digits of the hand can be used as symbols to prompt specific questions. Handy Thinking Tools can help in brainstorming and understanding of issues, and lead to the individual finding solutions and making informed decisions (Fig. 6.2).

**Fig. 6.2** Handy Thinking® Tools

1. THUMB: Pigeonhole it: Ask 'What is it like to have ABI?' (Sort, organise and group the problem or issue).
2. POINTER FINGER: Point out the facts: Ask 'What are some facts that you know about ABI?' 'What facts would you like to know about having ABI?' 'What do you do/say to yourself to help you cope with your ABI?'
3. MIDDLE FINGER: Find the Feelings: Ask 'What are some of the feelings you have about having ABI?' 'What do you do/say to yourself to help you cope with your feelings about ABI?'
4. RING FINGER: Judge the issue: Ask 'What are the Good, Bad and Curious things about having ABI?' 'What are the bad things about having ABI?' 'Is there anything good that has come out of you having ABI?'

5. LITTLE FINGER: (this finger needs GROWTH—Great Original Wise Thinking) Ask 'What have you discovered?' 'What has helped you cope with your ABI?' 'What could you do to help yourself in the future?' 'What advice would you give to someone with ABI?'

Method C: Advice to a friend with ABI

If the participants do not become engaged with either 'Keys to the ABI Cage' or 'Handy Thinking Tools' about what it is like to have ABI, they might be having difficulties with one of the following issues or problems, or another similar problem. Their problem could be written on a 'talk-about' card and then they could talk about the issue. This method was prepared but not used in the Keys Study as Keys to the ABI Cage was readily adopted by the participants.

Once they had unpacked the issue, it was anticipated that participants might wish to engage with 'Keys to ABI Cage' or talk about ABI using 'Handy Thinking Tools'.

The following issues have been identified in workshops with people with ABI over the past 15 years. If the participant did not want to talk about their own issues of ABI, they may be happy to give advice to one of the following 'people'. 'Talk-about' cards could be looked through and a problem tackled to break the ice and get the participants talking.

Using 'Handy Thinking Tools', the participant could choose one of these problems or issues to unpack:

1. Crushed
   Sally: 'I hate myself, I'm a waste of space'. Paul: 'I don't think I'll ever feel better. Will I?'
2. Temper
   Sean: 'The OT kept telling me I wasn't trying enough. It made me mad'.
   Jim: 'How can I deal with my temper?'
3. Sad
   Sam: 'I can't stop crying. I'm so sad'.
   Phillipa: 'How can I deal with my sadness—I've lost myself and my life!'
4. Bad thoughts
   Dean: 'I can't let go of awful thoughts'.
   Brian: 'My thinking—sometimes I think I'm crazy. I don't understand'.
   Heidi: 'I keep jumping to conclusions. I was convinced my husband was having an affair—I saw it in a dream'.
5. Understanding
   Mark: 'How can I learn to understand again?'
   John: 'I can't understand what people say. I feel stupid'.
6. Memory
   Christopher: 'I can't remember what day it is or even my own name. What can I do?' Mary: 'I've forgotten how to tell the time, what money is and how to work change out in a shop. What things could help me?'

## 6.4 The Sample

### 6.4.1 Sample Sizes

This study was primarily about the experiences of people with ABI at least two years post acquiring their brain injury. These people were engaged in their everyday lives once again. Confidence in the findings of the study was enhanced by triangulation of data—the employment of three different types of participants (sources) and two methods of data collection.

Participants were to include 30 people with ABI, five people who care for and support people with ABI (Note not referred to as carers—as the word carer implies unequal power) and five professionals. The latter two groups were included for the purposes of data triangulation (Denzin, 1970) and the different methods established methodological triangulation (Lincoln & Guba, 1985) to test the tool in different formats.

Data saturation was sought by the selection of the number of participants with ABI (Glaser & Strauss, 1967; Strauss & Corbin, 1998). This saturation ensures trustworthiness since no new concepts are obtained from additional interviews once saturation is reached. Various arguments have been made about what size sample achieves saturation (Mason, 2010; Morse, 1994; Creswell, 1998; Bertaux, 1981; Smith, 2004; Smith & Eatough, 2008). Given our wish to exemplify diverse experiences as well as collective experience, we established a sample size of 30 as noted above.

However as Durham still experiences difficulty with counting, in error, 36 people with brain injury were interviewed for the study, (in this case much to her supervisor, Ramcharan's, satisfaction and mirth).

### 6.4.2 Type of Sample (Inclusion Criteria) of Participants with ABI

As the main aim of this study was to do no harm to participants, ethical considerations informed the inclusion criteria: participants with ABI and people who care for people with ABI needed to be willing to reflect on the ramifications of ABI without becoming too distressed; if a person with ABI was taking part in the study, the person who cares for and supports them could not take part in the study, or vice versa. Participants needed to be able to understand the Plain Language Statement about the study, and be able to participate meaningfully with words or actions; they needed to be between the ages of 19 and 60 years; they should not be in a fragile state, stressed or in the midst of a crisis, nor awaiting a court case related to any accident associated with their ABI in 2009 (the year the interviews were conducted). Participants needed to be willing to have the interview tape-recorded. In order to reassure participants that their privacy would not be invaded, they were specifically *not* asked their age, occupation and so forth and all data was deidentified and circumstances sufficiently disguised so as not to give away their identity. The participants with ABI were to be between 2 and 14 years post-injury. The majority of participants with ABI were in their 20s and 30s, their brain injury was caused by a motor vehicle accident (i.e. brain injury acquired from the year 2000 plus), and they acquired their brain injury between two and eight years previously.

Participants were recruited from information placed in a broad range of brain injury support group newsletters and websites in both city and rural areas. A major feature of this research is that it had no connection to 'traditional' sources of participants where the participant may have felt services/support could be compromised by their statements.

We have decided not to follow convention and detail demographic and disability characteristics of the sample. Disability (what impairments each person has), under a social model, is considered less important than the experiences they related around their struggles with everyday life. Given the analysis undertaken, we considered ex post facto what role demographics would have played in our analysis. The answer was that they would have played very little part—the focus was on the recurrence of themes in their experience which they guided in the choice of 'talk-about' cards which were selected from the ABI Cage. The small study sample would also have made it difficult to make sense of causation or even influence sufficient to satisfy a scientific critique. In some senses the gratuitous use of data not used later seemed to us an unusual approach for these reasons.

The sample was therefore a non-probability sample and was purposive, requiring participants with particular characteristics to participate in the study. The sample might also be categorised as a *criterion* sample in that only a specific group, a group that met the study criteria from among the ABI population, was recruited for the study.

The sample resultant from the above approach is summarised in Fig. 6.3 in which we identify the data collection strategies used across each participant group.

| Group | **Method** | **People with ABI ($N = 36$)** | **Family carers** | **Professionals** |
|---|---|---|---|---|
| A | Interview only | 10 | 5 | 5 |
| B | Reflection Kit plus Interview | 10 | | |
| C | Reflection Kit only | 16 | | |

Group A = Interview only — 10 people with ABI, five people who supported and cared for other people with ABI and five professionals.

Group B = Reflection Kit plus an interview — 10 people with ABI

Group C = Reflection Kit only — 16 people with ABI.

**Fig. 6.3** Methods of data collection

## 6.5 Interviews and Their Importance

It will be noted that the data collected from the PowerPoint Reflection Kit came in written form and this did not allow the same detail nor discussion that might have been used in a face-to-face interview. The approach therefore allowed some comparison of the two approaches. Ideally interviews would have been preferred and the opportunity to engage in narrative and life story discussions. As argued previously, learning often takes place in interaction and discussion with others through a process of reflection and then safe testing out of ideas and actions.

Life stories are important to everyone as they provide an opportunity for the person to express who they are, their sense of self and allow others to understand who we are and how we got that way (Linde, 1993; Widdershoven, 1993); therefore, *Keys to the ABI Cage* was developed to scaffold the person's thinking to tell the story of their experience.

Such interviewing involves unpacking and exploration of the participant's experiences and lifeworld and led to greater understanding. Creswell's (1998) 'qualities of caring' was adopted: which the participant was viewed as a valued person, their comfort and security was paramount. The interviewer gave freely of themselves in conversation (Creswell, 1998). The researcher listened carefully, to 'hear' data, to have an 'ear' for what the participants were saying and focused on what they found to be important or unimportant in their search for meaning (Hermanowiscz, 2002). The interview was limited to one hour rather than a maximum of 90 min (Seidman, 2006), because people with ABI may be experiencing fatigue, emotional, cognitive and physical difficulties, and difficulty travelling to an interview. Pre- and post-interview phone calls allowed rapport to develop, and 'Some Further Thoughts' sheets gave the participants time to reflect on issues after the interview. Seidman's tips to direct the interview (2006, pp. 81–93) were followed. These included: Respond to the interviewee, but do not lead the response to the question; Do not interrupt the participant while they are speaking; Ask them to tell a story about a particular part of the experience. Be patient; do not fill the silences—give them time to think and respond.

## 6.6 Keys to the ABI Cage—The Study Procedure

Brain injury support organisations were contacted by phone and asked to place an advertisement in their newsletter. People with ABI, family carers and professionals were all invited to ring and register their interest, and they were then contacted by phone. If they fitted the inclusion criteria, they were sent a letter that set out the inclusion/exclusion criteria and Plain Language Statement which detailed the research, and two Informed Consent Forms to be witnessed (one to keep and one to send to Durham). Once the signed consent sheet was received, Durham phoned and negotiated a time for the interview or discussed sending the Reflection Kit. In the case of interviews, a telephone call was made the day before the interview to make sure it was still suitable and to remind them of the time and place of the meeting.

Interview procedure:

If a face-to-face interview was being undertaken, the following were taken by car and assembled at the interview location if possible (on several occasions, the cage was assembled on the footpath or car park as it was too bulky to be assembled in a coffee shop):

- *Keys to the ABI Cage*, complete with walking stick, pole and 'talk-about' cards.
- Two boxes (one labelled 'Do' and the other box 'Don't') and a second set of the 'talk-about' cards.
- A laptop computer with the PowerPoint® presentation 'Introduction to 'Keys to the ABI Cage' ready to use.
- The recording device.
- The signed and witnessed Ethics Consent Form returned to Durham.
- The evaluation form.
- A 'Some Further Thoughts' sheet and self-addressed stamped envelope.
- Take-home information about who to contact if the participant was upset by revisiting their past experiences.

When the participant arrived, Durham introduced herself and her husband Edward who drove her to each interview. Edward then moved to an area out of the way but within sight of (but out of hearing range). The interview commenced with a brief chat about previous phone conversations, and the participant was put at their ease. Coffee was ordered (if in a location where coffee was available).

Consent and permission to audio record the interview were then confirmed, and the voice recorder was switched on. In the face-to-face interview setting, Durham introduced the participant to the *Keys to the ABI Cage* model as they viewed the digital storage disk on a laptop computer. This described the three-step process (Fig. 6.1) of the interview to familiarise them with the concept and what they would be asked to do.

They participant then examined the cage and 'talk-about' cards to further become familiar with the concept and with what they would be asked to do.

Reflection Kit procedure:

In the first contact once interest had been registered by a prospective participant, Durham asked the participant if they had a computer, if they knew how to insert and use a digital storage disk and if they were willing to participate in this way (with or without an interview). After they had read the Plain Language Statement and returned the signed, witnessed Consent Form, a package was assembled and sent by mail. This included an instruction sheet for using the Reflection Kit, the digital storage disk, 'What ABI means to me' sheets and a stamped addressed envelope to return the completed sheets.

Having established rapport in the interviews or by phone with those who were sent the DVD Reflection Kit, the data collection began around the three themes.

Theme 1. 'Our Differences and Difficulties Can PUT us in 'the ABI Cage'

This sign can be seen hanging on Durham's old walking stick horizontally inserted into the left side of the cage, along with black-backed 'talk-about' cards (black symbolising the negative) held in plastic pockets (Fig. 6.2). Like the two other themes described below, the choice of 'talk-about' cards for this theme was drawn from the literature reviewed in Chaps. 3–5 (and summarised in shaded Headwork boxes across chapters), from public information and from personal and wider experiences of people with ABI.

Participants were invited to pick those cards relevant to them (either in interview or in the Reflection Kit) and place them in a 'Do' and 'Don't' box. Participants could talk about the comment, or something the words reminded them of, *if they wished to do so*. The cards and other objects in the cage were employed to provide interactive prompts for participants to think about and talk about their own chosen concepts and ideas.

The tool was 'organic'. The 'talk-about' cards allowed participants to 'wander' through the concepts as they chose, make connections and change their mind after further reflection. In the first section, 'Our Differences and Difficulties can PUT us in the ABI Cage', participants added the following statements to those already provided, which were turned into 'talk-about' cards over the period of the 30 interviews: 'I don't know "new" me'; 'I've lost "old" me'; 'Police'; 'Lawyers'; 'Isolated'; 'Very, very, very cold' (Fig. 6.4).

Theme 2 'How We Feel About Our Differences and Difficulties Can LOCK us in 'the ABI Cage'

Hanging **inside** the cage were red-backed 'talk-about' cards (red for emotions), hung on hooks held by bird-shaped mirrors—to remind people to look and reflect. Words on the 'talk-about' cards (Fig. 6.5) were drawn from the literature (see Headwork in previous chapters). Additionally, there were also objects that were metaphors or symbols—a crushed Solo® drink can (to symbolise a crushed life), a snuffed out candle (a finished life) and a toy snake (people are scared of me). The same procedure applied to choosing cards and discussing their meaning. Titles on the cards used are shown in Fig. 6.5.

Theme 3 'Keys Can RELEASE us from the ABI Cage'.

This sign can be seen on the right side of the cage at the top of the long wooden pole with golden keys attached to it (Fig. 6.6). The pole was crowned with a wooden pig with flywire wings—a flying pig—symbolising achieving the impossible. Hanging on the pole were white-backed (white symbolising the positive) 'talk-about' cards fixed to a rigid Perspex sheet. These cards had mini-objects attached to them

**Fig. 6.4** 'Talk-about' cards—Theme 1: Our differences and difficulties that PUT us in the ABI cage

**Fig. 6.5** 'Talk-about' cards—'How we feel about our difficulties and differences can LOCK us in the ABI Cage'

(e.g. sun for sunshine, mushroom for nature, tiny cup for coffee, a tiny dog, 'stretching my comfort zone' had a rubber band wound around it). This captured the interest and attention of participants and caused a lot of smiles. These particular cards focused on those factors that help to 'RELEASE' people from the cage.

This list contained a wide range of things in order to show participants that there were *many* things that can help us feel better, or factors that have a positive effect

**Fig. 6.6** 'Talk-about' cards —Keys can RELEASE us from the ABI Cage'

on our lives (Fig. 6.6). When participants held the stack of cards denoting *Keys to the ABI Cage* that could release them from the cage, they became aware of the large number of 'Keys' that could help them feel and fare better, shown in Fig. 6.6.

Figure 6.7 shows the approach used in both interviews and in the Reflection Kit.

At the conclusion of the interview participants; completed a brief evaluation sheet; were given the 'Some Further Thoughts' sheet, and a stamped self-addressed envelope; a sheet of phone numbers of people to contact if they became upset as a result of participating in the study; and 'Hope Stone', This was a black polished river stone with a star affixed to, This was a meaningful symbol of the hard things (the stone was a hard thing) people with ABI can tackle and a coloured message that they can find ways to reach for the stars.

Participants were contacted by phone on the day following interview, or when Durham received 'What ABI means to me sheets', and again one week later to make certain that participants were not troubled by their participation. A thank you card was sent. This contained two coloured photographs—one of the 'ABI Cage' and another of the 'Pole of the Flying Pig'—showing some of the Keys that can release us from the ABI Cage, and additionally a bookmark of coloured paper with the phone numbers of professionals for them to contact in case they were/became upset as a result of their participation in the study.

Eight participants returned 'Some Further Thoughts' sheets and had put an effort into relating issues they had previously forgotten to mention. Two others just wrote a few words, ten did not return the sheets. There was a great variation in the quantity and quality of data collected in the interviews and Reflection Kit. This will be discussed in Chap. 9.

| ***Keys to the ABI Cage*** **Acquiring better insight into what it's like to have ABI** |
|---|
| *The words on these 'talk-about' cards are things people have talked to me about (and I've experienced myself.) You are invited to talk about these things. 1. How you are **different** to how you were,and the **difficulties** you have. |
| 2. How you **feel about your differences and difficulties.** |
| 3. Things that have helped you **cope** with your ABI. |
| *I had my world turned upside down when I had a terrible car accident. |
| *Every day I still struggle to live with pain from my injuries, ABI, double vision and memory problems. So I do understand what life is like for you. |
| *I felt frightened and bewildered. I didn't want anyone to ever feel as lost and scared as I was. So I wrote *Doing Up Buttons*. |
| *Here are my doves Lovey Dovey and Cloud. They couldn't walk or fly properly so they weren't proper birds. I felt wasn't a proper person — I couldn't even do up my buttons!! We were a good team! |
| *When I went on television to talk about my book I would put them in a cage to take them to television studios. |
| *ABI is just like being put in a cage. It feels like the cage is locked and the key is thrown away. There seems to be no way out. |
| *But pigs can fly! I have tried to stay hopeful! I decided to use (1) My old walking stick, (2) Lovey Dovey's Cage, (3) A flying pig, to help you explain what living with ABI is like for **<u>you</u>.** |
| *Picture of the Cage |
| *Our Differences and difficulties can PUT us in the 'ABI Cage' |
| 'Talk-about' cards:Our Differences and difficulties can PUT us in the 'ABI Cage' |

**Fig. 6.7** Introductory digital storage disk and Reflection Kit: *Stars* indicate individual slides and the words on the slides

| |
|---|
| I forget where I live, I have terrible pain, I can't walk properly, I dribble and choke when I eat, I forget my name, Rehab, I forget what things look like, I've lost my freedom – I can't drive, I look like I'm drunk, I laugh and cry at the wrong time, I can't talk properly, I can't do things I used to do, Having to see lots of doctors, I've lost my family, I've lost my job, I can't do up my buttons, Having to do lots of tests, I've lost my friends, I can't eat properly, My hands don't work properly, I'm dependent and get lost, I've lost my memory, I feel sick and dizzy, I fall over and walk into walls, I forget what you're saying or I'm saying, I've lost myself, I look different, I can't see properly I can't think properly. |
| *<u>How we feel about our differences and difficulties can 'LOCK' us in the ABI Cage:</u> |
| 'Talk-about' cards How we feel about our differences and difficulties can 'LOCK' us in the ABI Cage. |
| Bad: guilty, say and do the wrong thing, don't understand.<br>Sad: depressed, disappointed, distressed.<br>Mad: angry, frustrated, 'crazy' and 'nuts'.<br>Hopeless – the experts can't fix me, crushed, scared, I hate myself. |
| *Keys that UNLOCK 'The ABI Cage' These things help us cope: |
| Talk-about cards: Keys that unlock 'The ABI Cage' These things help us cope: |
| Having hope, Staying home, Exercise, Books, Stretching out of my comfort zone, Making things, Talking, My family, What other people with ABI have done, My OT, Going out, Saying I CAN do it, My Counsellors, Sport, The sea, Doing things I couldn't do before, The country, My garden, Helping, My doctor, Seeing some progress, A cup of tea /coffee, Time passing ,Talking books, Encouragement , Love, A treat, Sunshine, Being useful, |

**Fig. 6.7** (continued)

| |
|---|
| Growing things, My sense of humour, My health professionals, My friends, Flowers, Religion, A picnic, Books, Stretching out of my comfort zone. |
| *Now we are going to look at **your** experience and things that have helped **you** turn a piece of poo into a rose.<br>***HOPE= Help Other Possibilities Emerge"** |

**Fig. 6.7** (continued)

## 6.7 Ethics

Ethical considerations were of implicit in the study design as emphasised in preceding chapters. The Keys Study sought to establish a balance between risk and benefit, both in the process of doing the work, and in terms of the long-term gains (i.e. means and ends). We sought to achieve benefit for study participants and public good by making the study findings relevant to the wider population of people with ABI. We also sought to ensure the benefit produced was at all times as high as could be managed within a research process which the RMIT Human Research Ethics Committee would approve.

Ethics may also apply to the researchers too.

As a person with ABI, Durham still experiences difficulties with double vision, memory, understanding time, numbers, juggling a number of tasks at the same time and fatigue. Organising just two interviews a week, packing the car, arranging driving support from Durham's husband for trips of up to two hours to the interview, conducting the interviews, and all the administrative work such as transcribing and organising interviews were emotionally and physically draining and took their toll.

All-in-all significant difficulties were experienced by Durham in juggling so many different tasks at the same time.

Halfway through the interviews, an ethical issue arose, which required attention, and the study was suspended for a period of three months while this was resolved. The suspension of the interview programme meant some people were already in the 'pipeline'. It was important to honour the agreement to involve them in the study.

Unfortunately, the issues that involved the suspension of the study led to reluctance to make contact with participants at the conclusion of the study or at the time of writing this book in case there could be another incident. This is unfortunate as it was intended to present the findings of the study to participants and send them a copy of *Unlocking My Brain* to ask for their comments.

## 6.8 Analysing the Data

In total, over 150,000 words of transcripts of data were transcribed from the recorded interviews, Reflection Kit 'What ABI means to me' sheets and 'Some Further Thoughts' sheets that were returned after the interview. The most data recorded was from the interviews. The breadth and depth of data from both the Reflection Kit 'What ABI means to me' sheets and 'Some Further Thoughts' sheets reflected the individual and their understandings, i.e. some interviews and Reflection Kits and sheets obtained amazing insights but others did not.

A software programme was not used for analysis to be true to phenomenology. This phenomenological study had been about 'humanness': the method that data was gained through interviews and conversations, with Durham's role as a subjective actor, rather than a detached and impartial observer (Moustakas,1994; Plummer, 1983; Stanley & Wise, 1993). Participants had freely shared their deep metaphysical suffering, and Durham was concerned that a software programme might not capture the pain, shame and hope expressed by the participants.

### *6.8.1 The Phenomenological Approach to Data Analysis/Understanding*

In phenomenology, 'Meaning is central, and the aim is to try to understand the content and complexity of those meanings… through a sustained engagement with the text and a process of interpretation' (Smith & Osborn, 2003, p. 66). The analysis therefore searched through dialogue to uncover connections between issues and emotions, issues and insight, and issues and how people coped or survived.

Phenomenological reduction involves leaving theoretical speculation behind and 'bracketing', cutting through the taken-for-granted and conventional wisdom about what it is like to have ABI—the blank spots. Instead, it focuses on the participant's personal perceptions, understandings and knowledge—blind spots. Data analysis moulds 'meaning from narrative' (Moustakes, 1994) from the 'clay' of the words participants used to describe their everyday, mundane, quotidian experiences.

Several approaches to analysis of the data were trialled but rejected. Colaizzi's (1978) seven-stage model proved too unwieldy and confusing; The approach of Diekelmann et al. (1989) was rejected given it was formulated for use by a research teams; Giorgi's (1985a, b) four stages of reading to make sense of the whole, failed sufficiently to explore meanings behind the expressions. This brought us to the interpretive phenomenological analysis (IPA) of Smith (1996).

Smith's (1996) interpretative phenomenological analysis (IPA) was eventually selected for several reasons. First, the interviews themselves were from an insider's perspective and IPA is concerned with a person's *personal perception and account* of ABI (an event), rather than attempting to make any essentialist statement about ABI (the event itself) (Smith, 1996). IPA involves interpretation. As an insider,

Durham was in a good position to interpret statements: 'explain the meaning, bring out the meaning, act as an interpreter'.

Secondly, IPA focuses on the *narrative* and involves formulating the connections between issues, emotions, insights and survival.

Thirdly, IPA allows flexibility of approach and delves deeper than quantitative measurement, thus enriching the ABI literature.

Finally, Smith's method encompasses many methodological translations of phenomenology, those that were rejected as described previously.

| Smith's & Osborne's Stages | Approach Used |
|---|---|
| Stage 1. Looking for themes 'in the first case' for each individual participant. | Transcripts read a number of times. Became familiar with the account. Comments noted in margin. Reflection<br>Constant comparison. |
| Stage 2. Clustering themes in the first case to find emergent themes.<br>Each individual participant. | In other margin record emerging theme titles. Move response to slightly higher level of abstraction. Transformation of initial notes into themes. |
| Stage 3. Clustering of emergent themes to find overarching themes.<br>Master list of combined emergent themes from all the participants. | Look for connections between themes.<br>Try to make sense of the connections between themes — check with transcript. Cut and paste to compile directories of participants phrases that support related themes. Extracts moved, condensed and edited. |
| The process was repeated for each of the46 transcripts. | Once each transcript had been analysed by the interpretative process, a final table of superordinate themes was constructed. |
| Stage 4. Clustering of overarching themes to find super ordinate themes. | Examination of overarching themes — looking at richness of passage, how the theme helps illuminate other aspects of the account, prevalence of the theme and impact on the individual of the theme. |
| | Once superordinate themes were identified earlier transcripts were reviewed in light of the superordinate theme. |

**Fig. 6.8** Smith and Osborne's stages and approach used

Transcripts of participants with ABI, then transcripts of mothers and wives who care for and support family members with ABI, finally professionals' transcripts were analysed to support data triangulation and to demonstrate different ways people perceive factors that influence the lifeworld of people with ABI. The analysis followed the staged process described in and Smith and Osborne (2008), first for one transcript, and then repeating the procedures for each transcript; identifying themes in the first case which were revisited and clustered together to form *emergent themes* if they repeated across participants. These themes were further clustered together to form *overarching themes*, which were finally clustered into *superordinate themes*. An example of this process is shown below as explained previously in.

### 6.8.2 *Applying Smith and Osborne (2008): A Worked Example*

The approach used is summarised as previously explained in Fig. 6.8.

The following short example relates to things that negatively affect the lifeworld of participants with ABI. The same approach was used in relation to all data across each of the three study focus areas and each of the three participant groups.

Stage 1 **'Words in the first case' (the participant's direct words)**

Sally's transcript was read and reread to identify factors that had a negative impact on her lifeworld. These were underlined and notes made.

> It was many months…I think it was my GP, that actually diagnosed me. I think she said 'are you angry?' and that was one of my biggest problems. Cause I couldn't control my anger (9). I don't think I realised that, because I didn't know what was going on those first few months. But then I ended up getting referred to do rehab, so I was there for 6 months.

Among all the underlined passages was one statement 'I couldn't control my anger' (Sally statement 9), and this example will now be used. This statement is shown in Fig. 6.9 with an emergent theme shared by other participants—'anger' and 'lack of control' and an overarching theme that seemed to hold all of these themes in the first case.

Stage 2 **Clustering of emergent themes**

Sally's emergent themes of 'Anger' and 'loss of control' were now cut and pasted onto a master list of emergent themes of all the participants with ABI (Fig. 6.10).

Stage 3 **Clustering of emergent themes to make overarching themes**

Sally's statement demonstrated that her inability to control her anger had a negative effect on her lifeworld. Implicit were several comparisons—between the 'old' Sally, who could control her anger, and the 'new' Sally who could not control her anger; and between Sally who could not *trust herself* to control her anger versus

| Underlined points Themes in the first case – Sally's words | Emergent Themes | 1.1.1.1 Overarching themes |
|---|---|---|
| *1.1.1.2 Step 1:*<br><br>1.1.1.3 <u>I couldn't control my anger</u>(9)(the ninth statement in Sally's transcript )<br><br>*1.1.1.4 Step 4:*<br><br>1.1.1.5 *To check if Sally couldn't control her anger would this af[illegible] her so that s[illegible] she had 'lost' her old self, and didn't feel 'normal'* | *Step 2:*<br><br>Anger<br>Lack of control | *Step 3:*<br><br>Loss of my 'old' self<br>Loss of feeling 'normal' |

**Fig. 6.9** Themes in the first case, emergent and overarching themes

the one that did. It might be assumed that she felt this loss of control and anger was not 'normal' and that, as a result, she did not feel normal. Clustered with similar statements from other participants with ABI, the consequences of Sally's inability to control her anger therefore clustered together to form the emergent themes:

(i) Loss of identity: the phenomena of the 'new' and 'old' me.
(ii) Loss of understanding.
(iii) Loss of trust—I can't trust myself.

Anger
Frustration
Loss Of Trust

Loss of Identity: The 'New' And 'Old' Me:**Comparisons**
    Depression
Can't Understand
Can't Control Emotions
    Disappointed
    Distressed
Crazy/Insane
Guilty
Stupid/Bloody Idiot
Embarrassed
Disempowered

**Fig. 6.10** Emergent themes from several participants, including Sally's 'Anger'

The transcripts of other participants were then revisited using a constant comparative approach, and similar themes were clustered together to make the overarching theme 'Loss of self' 'loss of the 'old' me'. Figure 6.11 shows themes at the varying levels.

Stage 4 **Clustering of overarching themes to make superordinate themes**

This process was repeated as the clustered overarching themes were cut and pasted together to form the superordinate themes, umbrella themes capable of holding several overarching themes together under a single category. In this case, Sally's frustration and concern about her inability to control her anger contributed to the Blind Spot 'Syndrome' or 'Conglomeration'. The consequences of ABI can result in the person with ABI being (not just feeling) Afraid, Ashamed and Isolated. This belief is in their 'blind spot'. They are not aware of these as factors, that they are feeling afraid, ashamed, isolated.

The 'essence' of the lifeworld of people affected by being unable to control their anger is very complicated and through reflection, as seen in this example, people engaged in the interview had the chance to reflect and to learn through the process.

| Superordinate Themes | Overarching Themes | Emergent Themes |
|---|---|---|
| 1. 'The Blind Spot Conglomeration'. Consequences of ABI can result in the person with ABI being (not just feeling) Afraid, Ashamed and Isolated but this is in their 'blind spot' and they are not aware of these factors that influence their wellbeing. | 1. Loss of 'self' loss of the 'old' me | (i) Loss of identity:the phenomena of the 'new' and 'old' me: Comparisons |
| | | (ii) Loss of understanding |
| | | (iii) Loss of trust: Can't trust myself, other people, the experts, fate/God/luck |
| | | (iv) Loss of faith/Religion/ being punished by God |

**Fig. 6.11** Superordinate, overarching and emergent themes

## 6.9 Recapitulation

This chapter has discussed *Keys to the ABI Cage* metaphor/tool and has pointed to the three themes focused upon in the interviews and a number of 'talk-about' cards that variously populate both the physical cage and the Reflection Kit. Data collection, sample size, type of sample, the interview procedure, the Reflection Kit procedure, ethical considerations of this study and the method employed (IPA) to interpret and analyse the data have also been considered.

The analysis of the resultant data illustrated using a worked example how one comment from just one of the 46 participants could, using a constant comparative method of data analysis, be placed in emergent and overarching themes through the process of analysis

It is now time in the following two chapters to present a summary analysis of all the transcripts in relation to the three study themes and from the point of view of the three sample groups—people with ABI, their carers and professionals.

## References

Bertaux, D. (Ed.). (1981). *Biography and society: The life history approach in the social sciences (SAGE Studies in International Sociology)*. London, England: Sage.

Colaizzi, P. F. (1978). Psychological research as the phenomenologist views it. In R. S. Valle & M. King (Eds.), *Existential-phenomenological alternatives for psychology* (pp. 48–71). New York, NY: Oxford University Press.

Creswell, J. W. (1998). *Qualitative inquiry and research design: Choosing among five traditions*. Thousand Oaks, CA: Sage.

Denzin, N. K. (1970). Introduction. In N. K. Denzin (Ed.), *Sociological methods. A sourcebook* (pp. 471–475). Chicago, IL: Aldine Publishing.

Diekelmann, N., Allen, D., & Tanner, C. (1989). *The NLN criteria for appraisal of baccalaureate programs: A critical hermeneutic analysis*. New York, NY: National League for Nursing.

Giorgi, A. (1985a). Phenomenological psychology of learning and verbal tradition. In A. Giorgi (Ed.), *Phenomenology and psychological research* (pp. 23–85). Pittsburgh, PA: Duquesne University Press.

Giorgi, A. (1985b). Sketch of a psychological phenomenological method. In A. Giorgi (Ed.), *Phenomenology and psychological research* (pp. 1–21). Pittsburgh, PA: Duquesne University Press.

Glaser, B. G., & Strauss, A. L. (1967). *The discovery of grounded theory: Strategies for qualitative research*. Chicago, IL: Aldine.

Hermanowicz, J. C. (2002). The great interview: 25 strategies for studying people in bed. *Qualitative Sociology, 25*(4), 479–499.

Lincoln, Y. S., & Guba, E. G. (1985). *Naturalistic inquiry*. Newbury Park, CA: Sage Publications.

Linde, C. (1993). *Life stories: The creation of coherence*. New York, NY: Oxford University Press.

Mason, M. (2010). Sample size and saturation in PhD studies using qualitative interviews. *Forum Qualitative Sozialforschung/Forum: Qualitative Social Research, North America*. Retrieved from http://www.qualitative-research.net/index.php/fqs/article/view/1428/3027

Morse, J. M. (1994). Designing funded qualitative research. In N. K. Denzin & Y. S. Lincoln (Eds.), *Handbook of qualitative research* (2nd ed., pp. 220–235). Thousand Oaks, CA: Sage.

Moustakas, C. E. (1994). *Phenomenological research methods*. Thousand Oaks, CA: Sage.

Plummer, K. (1983). *Documents of life: An introduction to the problems and literature of a humanistic method*. London: Unwin Hyman.

Seidman, I. (2006). *Research: A guide for researchers in education and the social sciences* (2nd ed.). New York: Teachers College Press.

Smith, J. A. (1996). Beyond the divide between cognition and discourse: Using interpretative phenomenological analysis in health psychology. *Psychology and Health, 11*(2), 261–271.

Smith, J. A. (2004). Reflecting on the development of interpretative phenomenological analysis and its contribution to qualitative research in psychology. *Qualitative Research in Psychology, 1*(1), 39–54. doi:10.1191/1478088704gp00409

Smith, J. A., & Eatough, V. (2008). Interpretative phenomenological analysis. In W. Stainton Rogers & C. Willig (Eds.), *The SAGE handbook of qualitative research in psychology* (pp. 179–192). Los Angeles, CA: Sage.

Smith, J. A., & Osborne, M. (2003). Interpretative phenomenological analysis. In J. A. Smith (Ed.), *Qualitative psychology: A practical guide to research methods* (pp. 51–80). London, England: Sage.

Stanley, L., & Wise, S. (1993). *Breaking out again: Feminist ontology and epistemology*. London, England: Routledge.

Strauss, A., & Corbin, J. (1998). *Basics of qualitative research: Techniques and procedures for developing grounded theory* (2nd ed.). Thousand Oaks, CA: Sage.

Widdershoven, G. (1993). The story of life: Hermeneutic perspectives on the relationship between narrative and life history. In R. Josselson & A. Lieblich (Eds.), *The narrative study of lives* (Vol. 1, pp. 1–20). Newbury Park, CA: Sage.

# Chapter 7
# Understanding What Negatively Affects the Lifeworld of People with ABI

> *I cannot conceive of a greater loss than the loss of one's self respect.*
>
> Mahatma Gandhi
>
> *She took a step and didn't want to take any more, but she did.*
>
> Markus Zusak

## 7.1 Introduction

We have demonstrated that many accounts of ABI place theory as subject and experience as a predicate. The medical privileges mending broken bodies and on occasions some psychological help, however for many people, very little more than what can be done to practically mend such bodies is considered; the social model privileges how disability is socially constructed under the banner of 'accessibility' and hence limits its interests to these premises.

We have asked an alternative question in this book. We have asked participants, more than two years post-acquiring their brain injury about how their experiences, can help us understand how best we might respond to assist people with ABI to re-engage with the social world and environments of their everyday lives.

We have shown how "Keys' to the ABI Cage' was borne out of Durham's wide-ranging experience with people with ABI, from what is known in the literature and from an educational perspective which scaffolds learning and motivates engagement. We have shown how in this study all of this was achieved in a way that helped people to feel and fare better and in a way which conferred dignity and respect on those who participated.

This chapter and the following chapter will use interpretative phenomenological analysis (IPA) outlined in Chap. 6 to examine factors that negatively and positively affected the lifeworld of a person with ABI, where the place of intentionality is a vital component of the process. Others might choose to cluster or collapse the data in a different way. This interpretative analysis did not focus on every theme that emerged from the data, rather, themes were purposefully chosen because of their relevance to the research question—to discover factors that had a negative effect on



C. Durham and P. Ramcharan, *Insight into Acquired Brain Injury*,
DOI 10.1007/978-981-10-5666-6_7

the lifeworld of people with ABI, and to discover what the data suggests about their learning experience.

In what follows we present the lifeworld, the everyday experience, of people with ABI for a sample of people post-rehabilitation to exemplify the lives, the struggles and the successes that characterise their existence.

However, a note should be made about the narratives of participants. Despite the focus being post the 'golden period/dark hole period', the affect of rehabilitation on their lives was considered and shown to have a huge impact on their later experiences back in the community. 'Rehab' was just one of 60 'talk-about' cards, which many participants chose and placed in the 'Do' box—it was yet another way their life might have been 'different' since their ABI. While this study had no intention of critiquing or analysing rehabilitation, most participants had a plethora of comments to make and stories to tell about 'rehab' which amounted to it being, for them, more a 'dark hole' than a 'golden period'.

This chapter will demonstrate that people with ABI can learn to have self-awareness, not in a linear straightforward way, but by a process of 'learning', or 'constructive circumambulation'- by being supported through scaffolding to circle (or visit and review their experience) and recircle themselves: to reflect upon, build upon and learn from their experiences.

A labyrinth—a winding, twisting path walked to aid reflection—explains the right brain, creative process of "Keys' to the ABI Cage'. The process involves imagery, imagination and intuition and an opportunity to vew and review an issue form several directions in several time frames. A labyrinth is different to maze as a maze has just one solution. A labyrinth presents a puzzle to be solved—requiring logical, sequential analytical left brain thinking where memory is vital to emerge.

*Keys to the ABI Cage* method provided the 'path' like a labyrinth for participants to 'walk' to tell stories to aid them to reflect on things that had a negative and positive effect on their life. Insiders (people with ABI) and outsiders (family members and professionals) were included for the purpose of triangulation.

This chapter will commence with the superordinate (main) themes and summarise how these were populated by giving examples from the overarching and emergent themes identified in participants' narratives (see Chap. 6, Fig. 6.6). This is the reverse to how the analysis was achieved, i.e. it started with words in the first case, clustering them into emergent themes, clustering these into overarching themes and finally superordinate themes. It should be noted that neither the superordinate nor overarching themes were on the 'talk-about' cards rather the findings from using these cards could be clustered into these themes.

While we cannot say that the themes exhaust all narratives from all people with ABI, we can propose that for this sample of 36 people with ABI the themes derive from their narratives and, that as the work continued, fewer and fewer new themes emerged. This provides some confidence that the data was becoming saturated for this sample and that we can confidently report the recurrence of experience of study participants.

## 7.2 Factors that Negatively Affect the Lifeworld of Participants with ABI

> Long term recovery from brain injury is not a medical problem...Medicine has very little to offer in this direction. The way forward lies in education...the power for recovery lies within the injured person as they relearn their daily living skills. Education is the key, (Freeman, 1998, p. 14).

The arrangements and methods for this study have been premised on these words. Two superordinate themes were eventually identified as characterising *overall*, the things that negatively affected the lifeworld of people with ABI:

- 'ABI damages not only the person's brain, body and beliefs, it also damages their hope, honour, trust, safety and security';
- And 'Learning with ABI is hard labour—it is a struggle to learn when the person is afraid, ashamed and isolated'.

In the remainder of this section, these emergent themes and their relation to the four overarching themes are explored. The superordinate and overarching themes are shown in Fig. 7.1.

### *7.2.1 Loss, Lost and Trapped*

The majority of participants told stories to illuminate the overwhelming effect of being a 'different' person as they struggled to function. They were overcome not only by physical, mental, communication and emotional difficulties and pain but they were also overpowered by a sense of loss.

| **Superordinate Themes** ⇦ | **Overarching Themes** |
|---|---|
| | 1. Loss, lost and trapped |
| ABI damages not only the person's brain, body and beliefs, it also damages their hope, honour, trust, and safety and security. | 2. No longer a 'normal' human being |
| | 3. Damage from emotional fallout |
| Learning with ABI is hard labour | 4. The rehab experience didn't suit me |

**Fig. 7.1** Study superordinate and overarching themes

> I wish I could have one more day without a brain injury just to be the person that died once more — to be with my family the way I used to.

In their struggle to make sense of themselves, most participants told stories about how they constantly compared their old and new self: how they thought they deserved to be treated by people including by their family, friends, health and legal professionals and how they perceived that they were actually treated; and their slow recovery progress compared to the effort they were making. Many stories demonstrated that life prior to their ABI seemed 'more fair' than their post-ABI life, where they had no choice and little power. The complexity was in many ways, therefore a product of comparing a *new with an old me* as shown in Fig. 7.2.

The difficulties expressed in Fig. 7.2 also cut the person off from normal people, isolating them, making them feel like an alien. Without a personal identity and clarity over their own self, the presentation of self becomes impossible and the self becomes constructed to reflect and respond to the ways others treat them. This 'looking-glass self' was not a self with which the person felt happy! A sense of bewilderment, loss and confusion because of what people said and of the 'stranger' who had taken over their body and life was complicated and demanded all their attention.

> When I don't understand what people are saying I feel frustrated … embarrassed

Self-doubt was common with self-trust a casualty as well as trust in other people, experts, fate or luck.

> I'm frightened because I can't trust myself and I can't trust other people and I can't trust health professionals.

Indeed a third of participants felt 'scared' or had 'lost trust' in their families. Fred was 'physically attacked…smacked by my wife'. Melissa was distressed that her parents would accuse her of being lazy but she was trying hard and suffered

| 'Old Me' | 'New Me' |
|---|---|
| 1. I could walk, drive, work, go out, socialise, travel. I could chose to do anything I wanted to | I can no longer do these things. With my loss of physical, cognitive skills difficulties I've lost my choice — I have no power |
| 2. I could talk, listen and understand | I can't talk, listen understand and I have great difficulty communicating |
| 3. I could eat easily | I don't know when I'm hungry, I have difficulty chewing, swallowing — I can't smell or taste my food |
| 4. I could see | I can't see properly |
| 5. I could cope with life | I can't cope with life and fatigue plagues my day — I get exhausted trying to cope with all by difficulties. This limits my life |
| 6. I could control my emotions | I can't control my emotions I make a fool of myself crying when I shouldn't |

**Fig. 7.2** Comparisons to the 'Old' and 'New' me taken from the data

from 'bad fatigue'. A majority lost trust in their friends who said they 'seemed OK'—Pete wished he could reply 'Oh yeah. Swap places with you, then.'

Distress was expressed at the perceived lack of understanding from professionals and at the pessimistic prognoses they delivered. Their stories inferred that they thought professionals would be 'the one group of people who would understand'. More is said of the professional group later.

For those who had religious beliefs, this had both a negative and positive impact on their lifeworld. Some participants had *lost trust in God,* and many were struggling to make sense of why God was punishing them, or they queried whether God had caused their ABI to teach them a lesson, or if they could trust God to protect them in the future.

> Man plans — God laughs.

The loss of trust (in themselves, others, God and the future) negatively affected their lifeworld.

As we proceed in this chapter, we shall highlight the inherent forms of learning that can be identified in the narratives as exemplified in Fig. 7.3.

**To query, to ask questions about trust and fairness, to remember the 'old me' and make comparisons with the 'new me'**

**These demonstrate how participants were employing cognitive processes ..interpreting, comparing, explaining and making judgments. They show how they circle around discussion of their reality to make sense of it. They are circumnabulating on the basis of their construction of their reality.**

**Fig. 7.3** Examples of people with ABI 'learning'

### *7.2.2 No Longer Like a 'Normal' Human Being*

Statements from participants indicated a degree of insight into the changes they were grappling with and the ability to compare themselves to a 'normal' human being. But none of the participants referred to themselves as disabled, although Goodley's (2011, p. 1) statement 'to be disabled evokes a marginalised place in society, culture, economics and politics' could be applied to them. However, as they told stories and compared themselves to other 'normal' people, this comparison had a negative effect on their lifeworld.

The four emergent themes: 'Can't function normally', 'Can't understand and communicate normally', 'Can't control my emotions normally' and 'weird and abnormal issues' clustered together to form the overarching theme 'I'm not like a 'normal' person any more'.

Having balance problems and being 'clutsy', 'dodgy' and 'fineline' made activities such as walking, driving, socialising and travelling a problem with impaired vision accentuating these issues for some. Several participants described how in the early months after their injury, they were 'freaked out', frightened and disturbed when they lost the basic 'normal' ability to know how and when to eat.

> I forgot to eat. I didn't have any appetite; I didn't know when I was hungry and when I wasn't.

They found themselves dribbling and choking, because their 'brain had forgotten how to tell the throat how to swallow'. Meg still felt like a 'freak' as she still had to put her fingers down her throat to help herself swallow. Loss of smell and taste was further proof that they were no longer 'normal'. Despite fatigue, many participants had difficulty sleeping at night or, as one participant expressed it, her brain 'could no longer go to the place of sleep'.

The inability to speak so that other people could understand was very upsetting.

> I have a great deal of trouble enunciating words — people find it hard to understand me

*Holding* the 'talk-about' card with a topic in their hands helped some participants to *hold* a conversation about how they had difficulties speaking, listening and understanding. Several participants discussed their puzzling inability to use the telephone, yet they did not remember this or 'have the words to ask for help' at an appropriate time.

> It's weird telling you … because you understand what I'm talking about … But then you forget that you couldn't remember to use the phone, so you couldn't actually get any help anywhere, because you couldn't remember what you couldn't remember. I think, looking back now, I thought there was something really bad, wrong, and that I'd better not tell anyone. No, not that I shouldn't tell anyone, but that I was embarrassed, ashamed … I don't know, I think I was terrified.

The perceived 'lack of normality' also stretched to controlling emotions, a category sufficiently large and important to stand on its own. Emotional outburst, uncontrollable laughing or crying was referenced many times:

> I cried all the time…at the drop of a hat. I was very emotional

> I went sort of the opposite, I just found everything hilarious. I was really extreme. I'd sit there and just laugh at everything. Well, I couldn't help myself.

The participants spoke of perplexing 'invisible' issues—'left neglect' where they ignored the left side of their body; double or distorted vision; and not knowing who was talking.

> If I was granted a wish today, it wouldn't be to have my sight back. It would be 'can I have my left side back, to make me whole again'. But the loss of sight I can overcome, workaround. The left loss…

> If a person was in the blind spot, I didn't know that they were there…I couldn't see them, but my body could sense they were there and I'd move away, so I was forever falling over. So I'd say … "walk over there, you're on top of me, get away from me", and she couldn't understand.

The overarching theme 'Not like a normal person anymore' therefore encompassed everyday functions, understanding and communicating, emotional control and weird issues and had a significant impact of their everyday lives. When taken together as a complex, these issues produced lives in which, without support and understanding, it became difficult to move forward with even the day-to-day decisions much less those pervasive choices that one makes to seek a better life (Ramcharan et al. 2013). Once again learning took place during the interviews (Fig. 7.4).

### 7.2.3 *Grappling with Emotional Fallout*

All participants identified with the 'Sad', 'Mad' and 'Bad' 'talk-about' cards and their subsections. The employment of these three small everyday words provided a 'softly softly' approach, a non-psychological, non-professional way to broach profound, personal, serious matters. Participants 'got' the way the words were used, and the words got them talking. Several participants requested the cage door be

**Fig. 7.4** Examples of people with ABI 'learning'

*n/learning: participants demonstrated a depth of recognition about their lifeworld and they could understand things were not 'normal'(a comparative approach) and they made judgements, checked and evaluated, classified and came to conclusions about their action (a performative approach).*

Reflecting Anderson and Krathwohl's (2001) model, of learning they were seeking to remember, understand, applying, analysing, evaluating and then (re) creating.

unlocked so they could remove and hold the crushed drink can saying 'This is me, my life'.

Many participants expressed *disappointment* with themselves and their lives, because they could now no longer achieve their dreams, the fact that day-to-day survival was difficult, that financially their future was changed for the worse: that they no longer had careers they had loved, marriages had broken down—life was no longer predictable or controllable.

> Disappointed is an interesting word, it's too mild for what I felt. I was probably disappointed with myself, disappointed with the doctors, and disappointed with everyone and everything for a while.
>
> Um, sad, distressed, and absolute abject despair and futility. Because I think brain injury it's the unknown as well.
>
> I'm so disappointed with life — my illness wasn't my fault.

They were ashamed and disappointed. They talked about feeling depressed, hating themselves, having contemplated suicide or disappearing, feeling powerless and the reluctance of professionals, family and friends to discuss their suicidal feelings. Many participants also identified with the 'distressed' 'talk-about' card—that the ABI experience was distressing.

Anger was a big problem for many participants, and they told stories of their terrible anger and rage. Anger was expressed at the way they had been treated by professionals.

> I was very angry, I had terrible anger
>
> I'm so angry at the way I was treated — all professionals, even alternative ones are arrogant.

Another participant explained about their terrible uncontrollable anger where they wanted to put their hand through a glass window, and how they would kick things and hit their partner.

However the majority of respondents reported they had feelings of frustration, they felt annoyance rather than anger—at themselves, at situations they were put in because of having ABI and their loss of choice.

> Probably mad/frustrated — that's brain injury in a nutshell.
>
> Oh God I was really frustrated.
>
> It drives you to distraction… trying to make your brain work.

All participants placed the 'Frustration' 'talk-about' card in the 'Do' box. 'Mad/frustrated—that is brain injury in a nutshell' and their stories told of the struggle of trying to cope with a brain and body that does not obey the person—of when they cannot understand why they behave in a certain way, when they are forced to rely on others, or to complete ordinary tasks when they are blind.

Many participants said that in the years following their accident they had believed they had gone mad or insane that they often questioned if they were crazy, mad or nuts. They thought that everyone else was mad: Sharon said she thought the professionals were trying to make her feel insane on purpose, or, surmised that was what they were doing, was 'part of a stupid IQ assessment'. These participants were profoundly affected by believing they were insane.

Most participants expressed *guilt* in some story or other—either about pain they were causing their family who they felt they had 'let down', for what they had put their family through, because they had not avoided the accident, because they could not make themselves better or because they had 'let' their ABI affect their life too much.

> I feel guilty because I can't trust myself — I'm not dependable — with good and bad days my thinking works in stops and starts.
>
> I feel bad because I'm slow and I can't concentrate, I can't understand things.

Over half the participants felt guilty they had not 'tried hard enough to make themselves better' as they grappled with the emotional fallout of ABI.

Many male participants expressed feeling like a 'bloody idiot' when they did or said the wrong thing, poor balance and unsteady gait led to accusations of being intoxicated, stereotyped as a loser and declined entry to bars. Women felt bad about other issues such as doing and saying the wrong thing; one participant elegantly called this the 'loss of social graces'; others would query if the inappropriate action was due to their ABI or whether they were 'just stupid?' Not being able to complete simple tasks such as doing up their buttons resulted in them 'feeling pretty stupid actually', being embarrassed because they were 'slow and can't concentrate or can't understand things'. The participants were ashamed, afraid and isolated as a result of their emotional fallout.

The stories told, when taken together, indicate an unremitting struggle to claim (back) an identity; they speak of the anger and frustrations of seeking to be understood and to understand others; they speak of the unremittingly negative responses and rejection of who they are and how they are; so too do the stories highlight how this reduces their mobility, their social interaction and accessing physical environments. In each life area, the downward spirals which interconnect us to being social and to being human are crushed. The frustrations, the emotion represent a cry of hope against the barrage of negative events in their lifeworld (Fig. 7.5).

**Fig. 7.5** Examples of people with ABI 'learning'

| |
|---|
| Cognition/learning: remembering, understanding, analyzing, evaluation were again demonstrable as THE modus operandum, the very essence of their struggle to square learning and action as acceptable to others and to themselves. |

## *7.2.4 The Rehab Experience Didn't Suit the Individual*

As mentioned earlier, this study did not set out to critique rehabilitation. An unexpected outcome of the study was over half the participants expressed opinions about how upsetting they had found the rehabilitation experience.

Reviewing the data revealed issues around a perceived lack of understanding of the professional. Use of power, and concepts such as truth, fairness and justice in treatment, had a profound long-term ramifications on many participants' sense of wellbeing. Some participants had forgotten what was *said* and *done* in rehabilitation, but not how rehabilitation made them *feel*. They talked about people and events they did not want to think about, but found they could not forget. This will be further examined in Chaps. 8 and 9.

The following long quote has been included because the perception this participant had about the rehabilitation experience still upsets her years later and it encompasses many of the participants' comments:

> Rehab was so awful actually I don't…it's something I don't talk about, I don't think about, if I do, I cry…I've always believed it was my own fault that I didn't like rehab. In terms of that, I was in a terrible place, so it was always going to be bad…I was suffering…anywhere would be bad…but this was worse. 'Cause it was bad at home, but this was really bad. And I think it's the way, it's a system that… it's a hierarchy, it's really structured, it's really rigid, there's rules, there's no compassion, there's no understanding, it's not about the individual, it felt like you were in a factory…that you were just being pushed through, you were a number…you were just on this treadmill.

The majority of participants were informed that the brain heals for up to two years, and then they 'plateau out'. This two-year rule took away their hope: 'I was told all through my rehab and from other doctors, that the brain will only heal in the first two years, and after that there's not much healing that happens'.

A few participants said they had been damaged twice—firstly by ABI, and secondly by rehab.

Cognition/learning: remembering, understanding, analyzing, judging, evaluation were again demonstrated

It is important for the powerless to exert their own influence on situations, on other's views and actions toward them. When such views and actions were imposed by others, they ignored the emotional state and showed disrespect and 'trust', a central and important context for joint learning, was lost, and identities damaged.

**Fig. 7.6** Examples of people with ABI 'learning'

In rehab I felt like a meal ticket.

… they were just like a Nazi camp to me …

I wanted it to be about me. Well, all our problems were different. And I don't like group therapy.

Some of those experts that I saw…didn't inspire … they made it harder

Rehab was a waste of time.

My OT was hopeless — it just didn't fit with what I felt I needed.

I wasn't wanting an OT and I didn't want to do the exercises.

I didn't like anything done in groups.

[Health professionals]…anyone who has made a difference? Nup sorry

Professionals from rehab centre I don't think played a huge role in my acceptance … They focused on the physical

If all the health professionals were sitting there I'd just (acts holding a gun) blow them away…all fucking useless.

Less than being a 'golden period', rehab as an experience for many was a 'dark hole' the memory which many participants sought to repress. As emphasised in Chap. 10, professional empathy was sadly missing. The struggle to exert their own influence on the process was denied by the system, and they were powerless to change how people treated them.

*Note* Positive comments about rehabilitation will be identified in the following chapter (Fig. 7.6).

### *7.2.5 Recapitulation*

Most participants 'got it wrong', no matter what they did, many had only limited success and some were worn out with the struggle and were frozen. Chap. 8 will examine factors identified by participants that helped to counteract the paralysing effect of ABI—factors that helped them to live and learn.

Throughout the interviews, many participants modified their statements as they reflected further about an issue. Most surprising were two participants who had stated that they had suffered from depression and been suicidal until recently. But later in the interview, they stated that they now realised that ABI had been the *best* and *worst* thing that had happened to them in their life. As will be seen in the following chapter, great challenges and satisfaction are not mutually exclusive.

## 7.3 Mothers and Wives': Factors that Have a Negative Impact on the Life of Their Loved Ones

Participants included three mothers of sons with ABI, Molly and Sue (pseudonyms, as for all participants) whose sons were in their twenties. Molly cared for her son at home, Sue's son lived independently and both sons had support from formal carers. Jane's son, a young teenager, was at school. Also included in this group were two wives, Jo whose husband had suffered his ABI several years ago and whose life had established a form and rhythm to accommodate his disability and Liz who was still learning to put in place structures to support her husband. These five women had had their lives totally disrupted by the ABI suffered by their loved one, and they shared the common goal to provide a lifeline, to protect, encourage and support their loved one; and factors that affected their son or husband also affected them. Emergent themes were clustered from the plethora of issues, difficulties and differences they identified. The analysis proceeded in the same way as previously outlined.

### *7.3.1 Factors that Negatively Affect the Lifeworld of People with ABI from the Perspective of Mothers and Wives*

The three overarching themes, the 'lack of understanding and guilt'; 'being judged by others and the stigma of ABI'; and 'sadness for the future', collapsed down to the superordinate themes: 'It's very hard being a person with ABI'; and 'It's very hard caring for and supporting a person with ABI'. This is shown in Fig. 7.7.

### *7.3.2 Lack of Understanding and Guilt*

All the mothers and wives spoke about how medical terms are hard to understand and the difficulty they had obtaining information that they could understand, their need of information for family, friends, and school and sporting groups. They stated that they needed training so that they could learn how to help their loved one.

| Superordinate Themes | ⇐ | Overarching Themes |
|---|---|---|
| It's very hard being a person with ABI. | | 1. The lack of understanding and guilt |
| It's very hard being a carer of a person with ABI. | | 2.Being judged by others and the stigma of ABI |
| | | 3.The sadness for the future |

**Fig. 7.7** Mothers and wives: overview of findings

> I mean medical terms are hard enough if you don't have a brain injury but if you have an injury it becomes like a second language because I know a lot about medical terminology because I've done a medical receptionist's course but before I did it, if you look at the medical terms… you don't know unless you've studied it …so imagine someone with an ABI it's like hello, I don't know what you're talking about …

They all felt helpless in the early days in the hospital. '*I needed information and training*'. They were not advised what they could or should do; they felt 'thrown in the deep end', and spoke with regret and anguish '[I] didn't know what I was doing'. Some said that they did not understand about ABI and one thought he would 'grow out of it' or 'get better' despite his mother being told 'this is as good as he's going to get'.

> But it's mind boggling, I mean you're there with your loved one and there's all these IVs and everything going on and these machines beeping and you think there really needs to be a non medical way to explain things…

Based on a belief that rehabilitation would make all the difference, these women tenaciously fought for rehabilitation for their loved ones. Molly and Liz even fought for rehabilitation where they were told there would be no benefit, taking extreme measures to learn how to care for them, even getting their private health insurance to pay for some time in a rehabilitation hospital so that they could learn how to physically care for them.

Despite this trust in the system, they reported 'very little rehabilitation of the mind...is this a cup or a toothbrush?… but not a lot'. Sue spoke about how the rehabilitation experience for her son involved too much time with no activity, which led to bad habits such as smoking. If therapies had appealed to her son, his outcomes might have been better. The mothers' emphasis on rehab highlighted that, for them, such rehab would give the person maximum chance to improve or get better. Any mother would want this. But in placing the emphasis here, it identified rehab as a singular hope, one tied just to mending bodies as well as an approach incapable of addressing needs in the social realm subsequent to this phase. Sue, a mother with a son in his early twenties, identified a plethora of issues with which she had to juggle. He was not a child, he had both good and bad days and he wanted his independence: this was a

> 'recipe for disaster… he blew his settlement trying to buy affection and loyalty'. 'Drugs — psychosis — from then on it has been hell — he couldn't cope — life lost all reality — Everything he used to do and his dreams were gone' (Sue).

Liz's problems were becoming more apparent as her husband spent more time at home after leaving hospital.

> I kept asking myself is it behavioural or is it something wrong with his head? Is it going to improve? (Jane).

Jane's son was refusing to attend school, and Molly had fought and won many battles with authorities. Jo had experienced problems with the legal system, and friends were loath to testify in her husband's defence. The five women had coped with and swallowed many 'bitter pills'.

### 7.3.3 *Being Judged by Others—The Stigma of ABI*

A further theme related to being judged by others. Here, the stigma of ABI and the distress of loving a person with ABI were found to be fundamental issues.

> I know a lot of people who've never heard of ABI they wouldn't have a clue…

> I want people to understand — more education about ABI — it would even be nice to have a TV ad…something about ABI, you know.

All the women had stories that clustered into how difficult it was when people did not understand about ABI. It was particularly upsetting when family and friends could not or would not acknowledge or were in denial about their son's/husband's difficulties. Jane spoke about how she was having trouble getting her son to go to school because of comments made by the teacher who told her son's classmates that her son was just lazy, and the teacher aide she had fought so hard to get, would be sent on errands rather than assist her son. Sue's son had a 'sort of aide' when he tried to go back to university but the aide did not understand about ABI. All the women said they want more people to understand, and they wanted more education about ABI.

Having their son or husband accused of being drunk was a common occurrence. Sue spoke about 'the worst moment of my life' when a neighbour accused her son of being drunk and said to her 'you must be so embarrassed by your son'. Unsteady gait caused rejection, criticism, venom and stigma. Having a stick was seen as a way to show the son had a problem. Jo's husband was told he was drunk at the supermarket, and people had taken advantage of him and short-changed him.

Stories emerged about how friends and strangers perceived them as 'pretending' or 'cheating' to get an advantage. This was very upsetting. Jo's friends, who were to be a witness in her husband's court case, privately told her that there was nothing wrong with her husband now. Strangers had made similar comments when they saw a disability sticker on their car or when they were in disabled seats at concerts.

> We've been to concerts — people say "What's your disability?" And he say's "I've got an ABI" and they say, "You're standing up, you're walking you're talking, you're fine".

### 7.3.4 *Sadness for the Future*

Mothers and wives spoke about how their life now revolved around the needs of the person with ABI. Some mothers of sons with ABI spoke about the added difficulty of trying to support their husbands as they slowly came to terms with their son's brain injury, cope with the needs of their other children as well as considering if it was possible for them to continue to work perhaps in a part-time capacity.

> Because you're Mum you fall into the habit of treating them as children, wanting to 'fix' them, and that's really difficult not to do. I constantly get reminded by my son now "Mum you're doing it again" (laughter) so I have to stop and think.

The two mothers of the older sons were concerned about what would happen to their sons when they die. They felt pressured to put things in place so that their sons would be supported.

Sue spoke about her son's loneliness, his relationships that have ended in disaster and her sadness at watching him with his brother and his nieces, and she could see that look 'I'll never have this'. She was acutely aware of all the things his life lacked and was saddened to think that he would always be on his own with no love. She said:

> T.S. Eliot — my biggest metaphor for ABI is the Hollow Man … between the idea and the reality, between the motion and the act is the shadow (chasm), and that for me was with my son. He'd agree "I can do that, yes I'll do that" — but the next day — nothing, no memory of it, no motivation no capacity and that becomes incredibly frustrating.

There was a sense of loss for the future and a sadness for the mothers and their sons too.

> No girlfriend — no grandchildren. As a mother it's sad to think he'll be on his own — no love — how do you replace that?

> My son's had a few tries at relationships but they've ended in disaster so I think he's signed off from that…

> On the love angle, we had a little granddaughter born recently … seeing my son with his brother and his nieces you could see that look "I'll never have this" and he doesn't drive

> because he can't, he's got so many lacks in his life comparative with—and I know comparisons are odious but I just wonder….

Another mother had to make the decision to turn off her son's life support. She spoke of her anguish:

> As a mum it was the hardest thing…we told him that we really love him and we'd give him that choice and every one of us did that with him — they turned off the life support and he began breathing for himself … he has fought so hard to be here.

### 7.3.5 *Recapitulation*

It is very hard being a person with ABI, and it is very hard caring for and supporting a person with ABI. But once the whole story of the experience of the mothers and wives is considered in Chap. 8—'Factors that positively affect the lifeworld'—this experience will be seen to be not all negative and need to be balanced with positive factors as discussed later.

It will be observed that there were many commonalities of issues identified by people with ABI, and mothers and wives of other people with ABI. These included the difficulty understanding ABI and the need for information in non-medical language. Shame and guilt was felt by both groups, and the stigma of ABI played a role in negatively affecting their lifeworld. The mothers and wives demonstrated that they believed that rehabilitation was vitally important. This belief in the effectiveness of rehabilitation was not identified by over half the participants with ABI, who were disappointed in their rehabilitation experience. The participants with ABI identified problems with rehabilitation that the carers had not identified.

## 7.4 Professionals: Factors that Have a Negative Impact on the Life of Their Clients

Professionals representing over 70 years of experience working with people with ABI had a wide range of different philosophies. Each person brought the expertise of their training and their experience to the study.

They were interviewed in order to triangulate the data about factors that they thought had a negative impact on their client's life, and also to obtain their feedback about *Keys to the ABI Cage* information/learning tool and if it could be of benefit to their clients.

### 7.4.1 Factors that Negatively Affect the Life of People with ABI

Following the same approach as previously, the views of professionals' emergent, overarching and superordinate themes could best be expressed by one professional with the simple words 'Brain injury is a bugger'[1] expressing her frustration, and admission of defeat that trying to help people was complicated and difficult, Fig. 7.8.

**Fig. 7.8** Professionals: factors that negatively affect the life of clients with ABI

| Superordinate Themes | Overarching Themes |
|---|---|
| ABI is a bugger | 1. The losses of ABI |
| | 2. People don't understand ABI |
| | 3.Emotional challenges |

### 7.4.2 The Losses of ABI

Professionals spoke about the loss of life as they knew it, including loss of physical and cognitive skills.

> (my client) has been locked up in a secure ward in a rehab hospital for 8 years.
>
> …he forgets things, he laughs, he cries.
>
> He's a very cluey guy, and has lots of embedded knowledge (but can't read)

Kirsten spoke of the losses associated with ABI—that her clients feel they have lost everything.

> Recognise that there is a lot of loss — I think like they feel they've lost everything from relationships to especially work, driving a car, having to start all over again.

[1]Bugger is an Australian colloquialism meaning complete frustration in this context.

Mary identified that there was a limitation on understanding, so that clients relied on trust because they had lost the mental resources to raise an alarm if they were being poorly treated and that they had lost the ability to know when they had been diddled or tricked. She stated that no one deals with their distrust of themselves.

> Distrust … they can't trust themselves — others.
>
> They may have a 'chip on their shoulder', but no one deals with that.

### 7.4.3 *People Don't Understand ABI*

Professionals stated that, in the main, the general public does not understand ABI. Several professionals spoke of general practitioners who had little knowledge about ABI, and clients with ABI having poor experiences with medical professionals, and the way staff can treat young people like children.

> The person with brain injury may have experienced many people who do not understand ABI.
>
> I know lots of people, lots of GP's who don't understand ABI.
>
> A lot of people with brain injury have had a lot of poor experience with the medical profession.
>
> I've noticed with X over the years that he does have quite a mistrust for medical professionals and I've met other clients like that and that's based on the poor relationships they've had whether it's with GPs, or psychiatrists, psychologists….

Four of the professionals identified that medical jargon is actually useless to people with ABI and their families in the long run.

> It is useful in giving a diagnosis, **but it doesn't explain what it means for the life of the person** [our emphasis] and it's actually quite useless information for families — education is much broader than just information.

Several professionals spoke about the isolation of the person with ABI that there was misunderstanding within families and that people with ABI can lose contact with their friends, they cannot relate to their friends and, moreover, their friends have nothing to say to them and they have nothing to say to their friends. This even occurred with some families.

> There can be a lot of misunderstanding, even within families.
>
> Families split up, divorce…
>
> They need advice to see a counsellor for marital problems: marital counselling but people don't know that stuff and how are they ever gunna know that stuff if someone isn't there to tell them
>
> People with ABI don't want everything all at once— show them (a model of the) brain, take them apart, show them where damaged.

Phyllis said people who had not been involved with the health system before were given too much information all at once and that 'social workers like to tick boxes and you only have certain amount of time with the client'.

> They (the client) didn't hear it…they weren't in the space where they could hear it.

Ben was concerned that some people with ABI fall

> somewhere in the cracks between the criminal justice system and the Mental Health Act, which doesn't seem to cater for either of them very well.

Once people with ABI are discharged from the health system, unless they have been linked up to some other agencies before discharge, they are left to sink or swim. Phyllis talked about the need to have an agency to support people once they had left hospital.

> Once they're discharged from the health system, unless they've been linked up to some other agencies before discharge they are left to sink or swim.

### 7.4.4 Emotional Challenges

Professionals identified that people with ABI can suffer from depression and emotional problems.

> I think it's almost irrefutable…certainly the research shows that if you've got an ABI your incidence of depression and other mental illnesses is very high.

> They can have very bad weeks this makes them very fragile…emotional problems.

> There's the down side of getting really depressed about the problems, but there's the up side of these are all the amazing things of how you cope.

> 'We have lots of trouble modulating inappropriate behaviour…he realises…then he forgets…and he says "ooh sorry".' 'There can be a lot of misunderstanding, even within families.'

> They can't relate to their friends because their friends have nothing to say to them and they have nothing to say to their friends.

All the professionals spoke about the incidence of depression and other mental illnesses associated with ABI and how their clients' bad weeks can make them very fragile. Judy, Kirsten and Mary said that some clients try to pretend they are okay but they slip up; women are concerned that they look different. All professionals spoke about how their clients were isolated from their family and friends.

Not all professionals identified all the losses and difficulties that people with ABI identified; although as a *group,* most of the difficulties were discussed. Areas of expertise were apparent by the comments from the group of professional participants.

### *7.4.5 Brain Injury Is a Bugger*

The factors that negatively affected the lifeworld of clients with ABI, the losses of ABI, people don't understand ABI and the emotional challenges collapsed down to the superordinate theme: 'Brain injury is a bugger'.

As mentioned above, the professionals as a collective group identified most of the issues identified by the people with ABI, and mothers and wives. However, this translated into a rather different approach. This approach, the blind spot, was their focus on the deficits and crucially the absence of focus on how these deficits affected the hope and honour of the person or on their ability to learn. There was not a focus on teaching the clients to understand, patience or the motive to recognise the person as a human first and not a subject of their professional practice. Several practitioners focused on 'fixing' and not on issues around fear, shame, trust and power. A blind spot of some professionals was the fear and shame of the person with ABI and how this impacted on their lifeworld, and which they failed to see.

## 7.5 Recapitulation

By using IPA analysis, this chapter has identified the ways in which ABI is experienced by people with ABI, by family carers and by professionals. The triangulation of data that might confirm the common themes and experiences has actually only partially accomplished this task. Indeed, while there were some common categories of experience between the groups, there were also uncommon categories or blind spots.

Common categories identified were the physical, cognitive and emotional losses and challenges of ABI. The issues were complicated; they overlapped and affected other issues. The collective and catastrophic affect to the person's life was identified by all groups, as was the isolation of the person with ABI.

However, participants with ABI reported their loss of trust and hope, and their shame and humiliation had a profound effect on their lifeworld. It should be noted that a pathological and deficit approach is unlikely to endear professionals to the person with ABI unless that person has accepted and reflected on ways to build upon what skills they have to feel and fare better in their lives. Sadly, the majority focus on such deficits as a basic assumption for professional action is the obverse of what people with ABI need to feel better about their damaged selves. A mindset change is required of professionals to acknowledge the feelings of the person with ABI alongside trying to 'fix' their body and mind—empathy is essential (see Chap. 10). The participants with ABI were aware they had many blind spots. This included being able to understand ABI and the consequences of ABI to them; they needed to understand their emotional reaction to situations, their shame, their belief they were insane, their loss of trust of themselves and others. But in the negative cycle of interconnected events, interactions and emotions, their capacity for hope and their pursuit of a full life became a casualty of the unremittingly negative feedback from many quarters.

One interpreted blind spot was the participant with ABI's belief that it was the 'professional's job was to cure them'—the same way as you go to a doctor to get medication or surgery to 'get better'. A second important interpreted blind spot was their inability to see *they* could play an active, indeed a lead, role in helping themselves.

The statements made by the participants with ABI reported in this chapter demonstrate that they had awareness and insight into things that negatively affected their lifeworld. As demonstrated at various points, the implicit struggles with elements of learning were an essential aspect used by them in seeking to adapt to new lives, identities, relationships and environments. But there was very little technical know-how used to scaffold this learning, nor recognition of its centrality by any of the participant groups. In the face of huge amounts of new information, people with ABI felt swamped by their experience. But some participants had moved from feeling that life was not worthwhile to feeling that life was worthwhile, and a few participants felt enriched by their struggle.

Thus, these negative themes are not the whole story—participants with ABI had also discovered 'Keys' to release themselves from the 'ABI Cage'—these discoveries will be explained in the following chapter. In discovering Keys over time, each was demonstrating the capacity of human will to fight their way through, to reflect, to learn and to formulate new actions which confer upon them a sense of belonging and fulfilment.

This chapter has shown the often catastrophic, always challenging and complicated nature of ABI, and a conclusion could be reached that the story of people with ABI is bleak and hopeless. In Chap. 8, this view is tempered with the positive experiences of data from the three participant groups.

However, looking more closely are other messages.

It can be seen from the narratives in this chapter that participants with ABI were implicitly comparing perceptions, ideas and actions almost continually. For example, comparisons of self and identity:

> I wish I could have one more day without a brain injury…

Comparisons on their metaphysical and moral compass:

> I'm frightened because I can't trust myself and I can't trust other people…

Comparisons of how they are and what they are struggling, through reflection, to be:

> It drives you to distraction…trying to make your brain work

and so forth.

Their statements were not mechanical and unchanging e.g. I am x, I think y and I do z. Rather people explored what x, y and z they were and how they might be x1, y1 and z1 in the context of their everyday spaces and interactions. Their statements were, then, 'constitutionally comparative', comparing options about identity, about social actions and so forth. In being so, it can be asserted that they were *comparing* concepts, ideas and actions. One can see the similarities between this as a form of learning and Anderson and Krathwohl's (2001) learning taxonomy described earlier.

Furthermore, the complex of concepts established '*mini-hypotheses*' about how to feel and fare better in the world. In Austin's (1962) words, the concepts were '*performatives*'—more than just words, but words that implied chosen social actions. This *constructive circumambulation* from the Latin *circum* around plus *ambulātus* to walk is used to describe looking at an issue by reflecting on it from different points of view—moving round the problem and actions taken, then reflecting on the action to redefine issue and further action that could be taken in a circular, not a linear way. This is the very essence of learning and explains its centrality to growth for people with ABI as they re-engage their communities.

Sadly, since trying out new actions often 'goes wrong', the negative feedback of others who do not understand the struggle of ABI leads to criticism and rejection as shown in this chapter. This has a major effect on the person. They may lose the capacity to circumambulate and think: it is better to be me in my isolation than to be me in interaction with others (perhaps leading to depression); or, it is better to express my frustrations in ways in which people pay attention than to remain quiet (often leading to accusations of challenging behaviour); or, it is simply better to be with others who understand (ABI support groups).

What is missing in services is the understanding that is necessary to house this learning safely and in place, i.e. within the networks and supports relationships that constitute the person's interactional life. Making the person safe to try, and to make mistakes, is what establishes the grounds for continued reflective circumambulation. While people with ABI, indeed all of us, may not reach a solution through our efforts, we will reach that one which is best in supporting us to feel and fare better safely without damage to how we define ourselves.

Chapter 8 continues to exemplify these themes but relating to the things that free people from the ABI Cage. The ideas are further discussed in Chap. 9.

## References

Anderson, L. W., & Krathwohl, D. R. (Eds.). (2001). *A taxonomy for learning, teaching, and assessing: A revision of Bloom's taxonomy of educational objectives*. Boston, MA: Allyn & Bacon (Pearson Education Group).

Austin, J. L. (1962). *How to do things with Words*. Cambridge, MA: Harvard University Press.

Freeman, E. A. (1998). *Brain injury & stroke: A handbook to recovery*. Sydney, Australia: Hale & Iremonger.

Goodley, D. (2011). *Disability studies: An interdisciplinary introduction*. London, England: Sage.

Ramcharan, P., Leighton, D., Moors, R., Laragy, C., Despott, N., & Guven, N. (2013). *It's my choice toolkit*. Melbourne: Inclusion Melbourne and RMIT University. Available at: http://www.inclusion.melbourne/wp-content/uploads/2013/06/Its_My_Choice_Vol1_web.pdf

# Chapter 8
# Factors that Positively Affect the Lifeworld of the Person with ABI: 'Keys' for Change

> *The greater the obstacle, the more glory (or satisfaction) in overcoming it.*
>
> Molliere

## 8.1 Introduction

It is with relief that at last we come to the heart and purpose of this study—to find the factors that have a positive effect on the lifeworld of people with ABI—love, hope, understanding, empathy and humanity.

This chapter provides some noteworthy information for professionals so they can see the importance of showing their insight and understanding and provide easy to understand explanations so that people with ABI do not feel beaten and broken by the system.

Since these areas are largely unreported, these factors did not draw on academic notions such as quality of life, coping or resilience but drew on the views of people with ABI, the wives and mothers and the professional participant narratives.

As with Chap 7, people with ABI identified a wider range of factors than some of the family members or professionals. The latter groups addressed the issue with directness: they had definite established opinions. Once again participants with ABI did not address the issue of helpful things in a linear straightforward way, but in a roundabout way, by using 'talk-about' cards in telling stories, making connections, revisiting ideas, changing their ideas—a process of 'constructive circumambulation'—circling themselves and reflecting on, changing their mind, and learning from thinking about their experiences.

Chapters 6 and 7 explained the way in which the analysis was carried out. There were 35 'talk-about' cards under the heading Keys to the ABI Cage and these included 'My Doctor', 'My health professionals', 'My OT', 'My Counsellor'. It



C. Durham and P. Ramcharan, *Insight into Acquired Brain Injury*,
DOI 10.1007/978-981-10-5666-6_8

needs to be noted that medical and rehabilitation professionals need to inform their clients that they cannot 'fix' them as medical professions can 'fix' other ailments like removing an appendix, inserting a pacemaker or prescribing medication that cures cancer.

The person with ABI needs to be enlightened and encouraged to understand that they need to be *actively* involved in learning to live with ABI. They need to learn to understand, accept and adapt from as early a time post-injury as possible. They need to be counselled to understand that many things can bring satisfaction to life, even though at the time they wish they could be the 'old me' in their 'old life'. Stories of how other people with ABI have coped could be useful in this regard.

## 8.2 Factors that Positively Affect the Life of People with ABI

Chapter 7 identified just some of the perplexities and complexities of ABI for the person with ABI that leads to unsatisfactory lives. Keys are things that help people with ABI to move from being *unsatisfied* in their life after acquiring their ABI, to being *satisfied* (at least to some extent) with their life. Keys to the ABI Cage therefore represent an amalgamation of participants' perceptions, opinions, emotions and identified factors that positively affected their lives.

This study has established that there are a plethora of Keys that can help people with ABI unlock the ABI Cage and release them from feeling imprisoned.

As the overarching themes, Keys are phenomena that people with ABI can use to play an active role in helping themselves to find ways to cope with or live with the challenges of ABI. Keys are active not passive. Keys require the person to have 'active acceptance', the will and courage to accept Keys proffered by family, friends and professionals. Other Keys need the curiosity and effort of the person to find ways to regain their identity and reach some form of new equilibrium.

The data led us to two superordinate (main) themes that positively affect the lifeworld of the person with ABI. Firstly, there are many Keys that open the ABI Cage (help the person with ABI to feel and fare better). Secondly, constructive 'circumnambulation' learning can assist the person with ABI to help themselves to feel and fare better.

At end of Chapter 7 we observed that the narratives collected from participants with ABI were both constitutionally comparative as well as performative. In the narratives, we saw the struggles between ideas and perceptions and concepts that support a person to make choices about how to act in their everyday life. We continue to explore these ideas in this chapter. In this chapter, we also confirm 'constructivist circumambulation' as the second superordinate theme. Such learning can assist the person with ABI to learn to help themselves to feel and fare better. Figure 8.1 presents a summary of the overarching themes that dually made up both superordinate themes. We shall use the overarching themes, as before, as subsections to describe these findings.

| Superordinate Themes ⇐ | Overarching Themes 'Keys' |
|---|---|
| 1. There are many 'Keys' to open the 'ABI Cage'<br><br>2. Constructivist 'circumambulation' learning can assist the person with ABI to learn to help themselves to feel and fare better. | 1. Hope: Learned optimism/resilience /coping<br><br>2. Love<br><br>3. Learning to understand ABI and working things out<br><br>4. Learning to face the facts (acceptance)<br><br>5. Making progress: Brain injury is not all bad |

**Fig. 8.1** People with ABI: overview of findings of factors that positively affect the life of people wirg ABI

## 8.2.1 *Hope*

The overarching theme of 'hope' encompassed determination, wishful thinking and denial. Participants expressed the importance of believing ABI was not going to 'beat' them—they believed they would improve, though of what such improvement consisted was, as will be seen, as much to do with a fulfilled and satisfying life (acceptance and re-evaluating goals), as to do with a mended body.

The consequences of giving up hope would mean they would no longer struggle against their difficulties/differences/deficits.

> Um, I guess I don't use the word hope, I just think of it as bloody mindedness. Sheer determination, where I'm mad as hell and I'm not going to take this anymore.
>
> Hang on; I'm not going to let this beat me!
>
> Proving professionals wrong—I've proved them wrong in a thousand ways.
>
> There is nothing I can't do. I just haven't found a way to do it.

Once again the sense of movement, growth and change are encapsulated both successes despite challenges and others' views as well as hope for the future. They emphasise the constitutional comparison of concepts which 'define them as learners, doers, and as successful'. These are the basis of the hope we all carry, not just people with ABI.

Wishful thinking including not believing the opinion of professionals was voiced by some:

> They told mum that I'd never be able to walk again or do this or that or have children—Luckily I didn't believe them—you wouldn't want to believe would you! (laughter) (drove to the interview, was married with children).

> The doctor was quite adamant that after two years you've reached your peak—it took away all my hope—I was frustrated because I thought I was going to get better… but then I thought I'm going to improve…

Note that the things accomplished and valued were not about mending bodies. In the first quote, the person was married, could drive and had children. These represent the fulfilment of their capabilities, accomplishment despite the challenge or the opinions of medics or others.

Denial also played a role in improving their lifeworld.

> It just went in one ear and out the other,

> I've never thought about these things

Indeed, some found ways to manage despite their difficulties and excused such difficulties by saying 'everyone does silly things'.

For many of these participants, 'hope' involved what we have termed 'wishful thinking', because it involved a refusal to accept the considered opinions of professionals. Their refusal to accept that their life would be spent in a nursing home, in a wheelchair or that they could not have children assisted their recovery.

The majority of participants had refused to accept the 'two-year rule'. They had been informed that the progress will cease or slow down after the first two years but they refused to believe this. Indeed, our proposition is that this is an inimitably medical and rehabilitation view. It ignores all that is required in the social realm. The person's concept of self lies in their social and community lives, emphasising the need for medics to 'leave a space' for this, not to comment upon the body as if it were the world. Fixing bodies is a smaller part of a larger whole. Living lives well in spite of ABI is the key and requires learning and an empathy from professionals about what contributes to setting the conditions for engaging with such learning.

Hope encompassed many characteristics outlined in Seligman's (1998) 'Learned Optimism'—the participants had learned to tell themselves that just because they had failed at a given task this did not mean they would always fail in everything they attempted and they could 'excuse' their failure or blame something else. They coped and bounced back in a resilient way if hope was maintained.

Several participants talked about how they obtained comfort and security from their religious belief and that this was very important to them. However, concern that God was punishing them was frequently associated with religious belief. Nearly one-third of participants said that nature and the environment brought hope and comfort and a few participants spoke about seeking symbols to show they were: 'doing the right thing'. This search to confirm their existence and identity is very well rehearsed in existentialist writings, but clearly featured as an everyday experience for many in the study sample.

### 8.2.2 Love

Participants with ABI could be divided into two groups—half who spoke about how they were loved, supported and sheltered by their family and how their love for their family also caused them to work harder for the sake of their family—so they could have a life. For these participants, the love was of prime importance.

> Love is extremely important. I believe that if I didn't have my family and husband to come home to, I wouldn't have worked so hard—I don't think I did it for me, I did it so they could have a life…

and, another key releasing this person was,

> The understanding of my oldest and very dear friends and their ongoing support.

The other half of the participants, who did not identify love as a Key, told stories of how they were estranged through divorce, or misunderstanding or lack of understanding. Many in the latter group spoke of animals who loved them unconditionally and who gave their life meaning. Several participants stated that they would have killed themselves but for their love of their animals and the way their animals 'understood' and loved them—animals provided the unconditional love they needed to survive. Several participants identified that taking responsibility and caring for their animals had been very important.

> I could stay in bed but I have a big black muzzle [of her guide dog] nudging me saying get up and feed me.

> My dog understood that I was crook [Australian word for unwell] and stayed by my side.

> I think if I didn't have my three cats who loved me unconditionally, to talk to, I wouldn't cope at all.

> Taking responsibility and caring for something else (my animals)—I think it is very big.

> My cats saved my life. I would have 'disappeared' but for my cats.

Most participants identified things they loved doing, things that gave them satisfaction, and a purpose. The way they perked up and became enthusiastic about these things showed they were more than a diversion—they were fully engaged with their 'passion'.

A huge range of such passions were identified: painting, fishing, knitting, going to live shows, writing, going out for coffee or lunch. Some men were very passionate about watching sport, the gym and exercise. Many women participants said they had discovered (or learnt) that doing cross stitch/tapestry/knitting focused their thoughts, calmed them down and they felt productive as they watched their project progress. Several women referred to their craft as their 'security blanket' and they took it everywhere.

Participants could be divided into two groups - those who liked going out and those who liked staying home.

> I love going out—I'm terrified of my armchair
>
> I love going to live shows
>
> Going out to lunch on the weekend made me feel more normal
>
> Writing all my thoughts down—everything… and they say stop this lunacy and I say I can't stop…
>
> Painting—art is very important (couldn't draw before) colour gets me excited
>
> Ah, gardening is a new thing I've taken up that I find a lot of peace, as a therapy… it's a wonderful, wonderful thing
>
> A treat—yes—that's part of the life process—it has to be achieved—a prize at the end of something. You've achieved something so now you can have a treat. Big or not so big—a cup of coffee shared with friends or family
>
> Exercise—Yes so important — I'm convinced the exercise side of things reduced the severity of the damage that was done significantly.

The final category of things people love is things that give people a sense of satisfaction and purpose—helping others—particularly others with ABI. This was most important as it allowed the person to use their sense of empathy and humanity that has been perhaps newly acquired—it is a positive new gift they can give. Participants spoke with pride about their volunteering. May expressed it beautifully:

> I'm a volunteer I have a lovely lady to look after. She's lovely, she loves me, she's like a mum to me and I'm a mum to her.

Others expounded

> Helping people yea…!
>
> I volunteer to help people with disabilities 'cos I know what it's like to be in a wheelchair.
>
> Being useful—yes that's why I do so much—I refer to it as my sense of purpose.

It should not go without notice that what people share, brings people together. People with ABI share an understanding and in doing so understand that rejection by others hurts, that trust between people supports their interaction and growth, that giving of the self produces a sense of accomplishment among many other feelings. If we were to replicate services and relationships that carry similar such features, we might discover the 'pearls of wisdom' people with ABI are proffering to the rest of the world.

Love of people, pets and activities helped most participants belong and feel comfortable about themselves. Love by others and for other carried people from a life that did not seem worthwhile to a life with worth and purpose. Meaningful lives which made best use of capabilities and give life purpose were therefore central to feeling and faring better.

## 8.3 Learning to Understand ABI and Working Things Out

Learning to understand is at the heart of this thesis. It is not possible to 'give' people understanding—understanding comes from actively taking on board ideas and information, learning to make sense of ABI for themselves and trying out the ideas before once more adapting their understanding.

About a third of the group spoke about the importance of finding out what other people with ABI have done and the value of peer support. An ABI writing group helped people share ideas, learn new skills and express themselves. Some participants in 'seeking to belong' found joining ABI support organisations was helpful, yet others voiced the opinion they wanted to be normal, mixing with normal people.

> Gain as much knowledge as you can about your brain injury to help you understand...

> If I'd had the CD (Reflection Kit) earlier on it would have helped me to understand that I wasn't going mad. And it certainly would have given me another way of approaching things too. And perhaps to even ask more questions. Because if I knew that was the situation, then I could relate that to other areas...

> What other people with ABI have done—this is massive to me—peer support—my writing group

> What other people with brain injury have gotten up to, or survived. Um, it didn't help to start with, because I was too interested in myself. But later on, to read stories of people who've survived was good

> Meeting you (Durham) at a conference in Sydney was another moving point for me and the rest of my life, as I feel that it is the survivors who can talk the talk to get others back on their feet after an injury, because we can walk in their shoes.

All participants with ABI had struggled and were still struggling to understand ABI for themselves. Not one participant remarked 'I found this wonderful web site...booklet...I was given information from the hospital', or that 'Dr X explained ABI so that I suddenly understood'. No one spoke about understanding about ABI from information on brain injury support Websites or blogs, although now, eight years after the interviews, more people are searching the web.

All the participants wanted to find out more about ABI. About a third of the participants spoke about reading *Doing Up Buttons* and gaining greater understanding from reading the story—it helped them make sense of their own personal issues. Almost all the participants said that 'medical language' was not helpful in helping them make sense of their experience.

*Keys to the ABI Cage* helped many participants understand their ABI—one man said that he had ABI for 7 years and he denied it—but the Cage had 'showed him' (he had gained self-awareness) and he now acknowledged his ABI; another said if he had seen the Cage earlier it would have helped him to understand that he was not going mad, and would have given him another way to approach things and ask more questions; another participant commented 'It let me open up my own eyes'. Opening up my own eyes is a wonderful description of 'learning'.

Participants had discovered (taught themselves) a range of strategies through which they could work things out: for example, 'patience', 'minimal stress', 'simplicity', 'routine/organisation', 'structured living', 'quietness', 'a healthy diet', 'exercise', 'concentration' and 'tracking progress and achievements'. Notable here is that these categories do not differ from those that might benefit anyone let alone people with ABI. Participants also spoke about the effort required to teach themselves to make their body work again.

Try not to get impatient with myself

Never be afraid to ask for help or get something wrong

The more 'mistakes' I made the more I learnt and recovered. Getting as much help from as many people as possible always puts you in the best position possible

Whatever I'm doing gets all my attention

Writing…recording my thoughts, feelings and daily events

Tracking my progress and achievements

Facing the fact I need to rely on my palm pilot diary

Everything is 'slowly slowly' and time has changed

'I try to be the best I can at everything that I was good at before my ABI.'

'My short term memory is getting better… I have always practised my memory with mind games and developed strategies'

'Repetition with a new task or learning something different — repetition is the only way to cement it until it becomes part of the fabric of your life'.

The reader should be aware that implicit in these narratives is that participants had already remembered and understood concepts and had then gone on to apply, analyse and evaluate their actions. They were in effect reflecting - circumambulating through both self-reflection and then testing in order to create new ideas to move their lives forward. These implicit concepts so clearly demonstrated above align with Anderson and Krathwohl's (2001) learning taxonomy presented in Chap 5.

Twelve positive comments about specific rehabilitation professionals were obtained from transcripts of the 35 participants with ABI. Speech therapists, counsellors and psychologists were appreciated, and three men spoke about physical exercises being 'wonderful' or 'brilliant'.

I did a lot of intensive rehab…. physio exercises at the gym. I devoted all my time to doing that, last year 6 days a week. (man)

Rehab exercises was just brilliant (man)

My balance is a hundred times better with a lot of hard work and physios. (man)

I had a lot of rehab, it was extremely helpful. But taking control of it was… better. I was so determined to get home It was going to take too long to do it their way. It's a long time to sit, if you're just in hospital (woman)

The doctor treating me with respect and dignity that I was just like my old self

…but the head rehab doctor, she was excellent.

> …I was starting to realise then that something dire must have happened. Because, she (the doctor) came in and sat on the bed, took my hand and was very emotional. Which for a doctor, I thought was very surprising. She said "It's so great to see you back here, the way you are now, that's wonderful" and so on and so forth. And, from that day on, I had all the staff coming into see me, to tell me that they were all there to help me out and so on. Eventually I got up and started walking again, and doing all the rest of it.

> …she (the doctor) she thinks I've made a marvellous recovery and I think she's quite proud of that. Probably for her and her skills as well.

> I believe in God and I believe in doctors too and I believe in the wonderful kidney guy, and the neurologist I believe in him too and my GP–she's good.

Empowering the person with brain injury to have a say was important. One man spoke about how 'Letting me do what I want, and not what they think I want/need. One of my speech therapists used that theory on me and it allowed me to surge forward in my rehabilitation'.

### *8.3.1 Learning to Face the Facts (Acceptance)*

'Facing the facts (acceptance)' could be seen as a subset of the 'Learning to understand ABI and working things out', but it concerns a cluster of comments from participants about discoveries they had made about identity, self-belief, not giving up, a positive attitude and a sense of humour.

Accepting that the person is not the same as prior to ABI was mentioned often:

> Coming to terms with the fact that I'm not the same person anymore

> Redefining who I am and where I want to head to

> Admitting to myself I have shortcomings (short-term memory) and learning to employ strategies to assist me with coping with these shortcomings

> I now view the word from a changed perspective

> I have changed careers/job to a completely different area

Recognising the positive things that have come because of ABI:

> Changed me—learning new things

> I have a much greater understanding of life and people

> Learning to appreciate life

> Believe in yourself

> Looking at every part of my life post the brain bleed as a bonus

> Focusing on the small goals that achieve bigger goals

> It's like I'm constantly finding new aspects of myself

> Talking about things.

Again, just to reiterate, all of these quotes are about changing and reframing concepts and ideas about self and, as such, implicitly linked with (re)learning.

One man said ‘at least I’ve got some sense: a sense of humor!’ Several persons saw a sense of humour as important to their lifeworld, as ‘the best thing I’ve got going for me’, the ability to see the funny side of things or to be a ‘court jester’ to whom people came to share humour. This man had thought about ways he could get attention and prepared humorous things to say. By using their sense of humor, they gained value from being who they were rather than feeling the butt of other people’s mirth or disparagement.

### *8.3.2 Making Progress—Brain Injury Is not All Bad*

The burden of feeling ‘not normal’ and ‘different’ to others weighed heavily on many participants so being able to do normal things again was seen as a symbol of improvement and progress—and boosted their confidence, self-esteem and hope.

Participants spoke about making progress in big and small ways. A handful of participants spoke of the freedom of being able to drive again. It was an exciting part of recapturing their life in any way possible. For Mary, it was wonderful when she was actually able to put her left foot straight into her slipper. Others mentioned

> Being a basketball coach and instilling some of my training into the team
>
> Knowing I am making a worthwhile contribution at work.
>
> Returning to study
>
> Now I’m in a job that I love more than anything I’ve done. So I think this has given me the opportunities to make those sort of decisions, and it’s been a really powerful experience
>
> Getting my license again was freedom!

Achieving or doing hard or challenging things was also found to be a Key to the ABI Cage:

> Doing things I was told that I wouldn’t be able to do
>
> Stretching outside my comfort zone
>
> Being able to do things at work that are beyond my fellow peers
>
> I was proud I could teach therapists a couple of things on the computer.

Being able to work or be a volunteer, being able to make a worthwhile contribution and being able to reuse old skills in their new life led to participants move from feeling life was unsatisfactory to life was satisfactory. Some participants wanted to ‘give back’ to help others in the same predicament, felt they were now wiser as they had thought about and explored their lifeworld and had a much greater understanding of life and people.

> I’m glad this happened to me. My mother is horrified when I say that. But I would say that I haven’t changed as a person, but I’ve learnt something…a little more courageous…I think this has given me the opportunities to make those sorts of decisions and it’s been a really powerful experience and I’m glad it happened.

Some participants expressed how lucky they feel to have survived: it has given them a chance to start their life again, they feel special because they had experienced so many unique and valuable things, they believe they are a newer better person and have become more aware, for example of the environment, pollution, good friendship, humanity, volunteering, service clubs and general sharing. Some have become highly sensitive to many things such as noise, light, people, even feelings. Brain injury has been a really powerful experience for many of the participants.

> What I say to them now is, there are two selves, there's the person I was before, and no matter how much I grieve and think I've lost that person, I have not lost her. She's still here, she's just been pushed back by this new self. There's two selves, and there's this new self, and the two of them have to learn how to get along.

After discussing their experience, many participants described experiencing 'The Survivor's High':

> I am clearly meant to be in this world now and I have a responsibility to work on myself always to be living up to the best me I can possibly be
>
> I am so grateful that physically, thank God, I am OK, my spirit has been damaged, not broken, and it's up to me to make the most of the unpleasant challenge that has happened to me
>
> I have a desire to share my story and feelings with others so they too can appreciate the wonders of life and all the moments they have. If they had a difficult experience which challenged them, I am so happy to come talk to people and let them know they're not alone
>
> I was lucky (to have the right surgeon) I'm not scared, I should be but I'm not I should be dead but I'm not.' (brain tumour)
>
> I have to accept that I am newer better person and I have become more aware of the environment, pollution, good friendship, humanity to mankind, volunteering, service clubs and general sharing, better sailing skills amazing eh?.

### 8.3.3 *'Many Keys' and 'Constructivist Circumambulation'*

Participants identified a plethora of factors that helped them to feel and fare better. These are not only their Keys. They are the Keys, as will be described in Chap 9 which need to feature in all forms of professional services and supports.

These 'Keys' to the 'ABI Cage' covered a wide range of factors from humble everyday things, to things that gave their life meaning and purpose. They were pleased to identify 'talk-about' cards that were important to them and to tell stories about other hobbies or pastimes that brought them pleasure. Using 'Keys to the ABI Cage' to talk about their experience helped them to made sense of ABI and construct their own knowledge about things that helped them to feel and fare better. For many, it added to a learning journey that had already begun. But for many others, it represented a revelation which prompted then to think that starting such a learning journey was a Key to their growth.

Posit, if you will, that learning, relearning, seeing things anew, reframing our view of the world is the basis of moving forward in life, indeed growing. If this is accepted, then many people with ABI are required to do so in the most difficult of circumstances, from which there is little escape. If this is true, then it might be argued that the preponderance of people with ABI who struggle to re-learn will be greater than for the population at large. If this is the case, it might be argued they become deepened by their experience, a point to which we again refer later.

Once we recognise that some people with ABI have great insight into the ABI experience, **we** can learn from them. It is not just the case of their learning from us that is important.

### *8.3.4 Triggers and Turning Points*

This study also sought to try to find 'triggers', turning points or epiphanies when the participant came to the realisation that life was going to be bearable, that it was worthwhile living. As they engaged with *Keys to the ABI Cage,* participants told stories of such experiences. We will allow the participants to explain:

> Actually it was a flower that told me one day that the world is really worth being in. It was a memorable experience because I was walking around the side of my house and the world had been grey for a long, long time and I saw a red tulip, the bulb I'd put in a pot, and it had flowered red and honestly I stopped in my tracks, and it was like wow, and I'll never forget that, and the world then had colour.

> Yes yes I had a lightning bolt moment, an epiphany—in rehab I was in the ABI unit, surrounded by others—you start comparing yourself and you say "I'm not as bad as them", and my family was saying "Oh my God, she isn't really quite with it!" and I knew I could sit back and do nothing, and let people look after me and pamper me for the rest of my life, or I could take another road and have a life that I felt I had achievement in. I felt I was at the crossroads that it was up to me—one was the hard slog the other was the easy road but I don't think I've ever taken the easy road.

> I was told all through my rehab and from other doctors, that the brain will only heal in the first two years, and… I refuse to believe that and I feel very lucky that I refused. So that really helped me to think I could keep getting better. I still believe it.

> Believing the brain is a muscle—today the new term is neuro-plastic, but I was told all through my rehab and from other doctors, that the brain will only heal in the first two years…. That would be the one big change I would like to see in rehab or ABI treatment. I went for 10 years and I saw people who believed it—it was heartbreaking.

In this last quote, we can see that modern medical discoveries and theories such as arguments about the plasticity of the brain allow us not just to have hope, but also to act in ways that seek to accomplish outcomes through a rewiring of our brains and how they make connections between things, i.e. how people learn. If people with ABI are sentient beings, then they will continue to have this capacity. It is both false and wrong to assert that nothing can change post-hospital or rehab.

| Superordinate Themes | Overarching Themes 'Keys' |
|---|---|
| With love, hard work and the 'right' attitude his life can improve | 1. Love |
| | 2. Understanding — the 'right' information |
| | 3. Developing some quality of life for him |

**Fig. 8.2** Wives and mothers: overview of findings

Indeed, after the 'dark hole' of the first two years—the 'golden period' and rehab, the main work is still left to do.

## 8.4 Wives and Mothers: Factors that Positively Affect the Life of People with ABI

In this section, we proceed analysis of transcripts as for people with ABI and identified that love, understanding and developing quality of life were seen as central prerequisites to the superordinate theme that 'with love, hard work and the "right" attitude, it was possible to feel and fare better, i.e. to improve' (Fig. 8.2). The form of improvement, as shall be seen is, once again at odds in respect to a medical model only approach.

### *8.4.1 Love*

Family carers identified love as an essential overarching theme: Family, people who love them and people they love and things they love to do, categories replicating the views of people with ABI themselves which were presented at length earlier.

### *8.4.2 Information They Could Understand*

Once again, repeating the narratives of people with ABI, mothers and wives stated that it was vital to obtain information that they could understand, their relatives and schools and sporting clubs could understand—this was not simply information from a 'bunch of booklets' or the Internet as 'they repeat all the negative issues'.

> Information and not just give you a whole bunch of booklets—probably 5 months after his injury I started to read through some of these—my husband wouldn't. Reading them sort of throws you because you think "Oh my God is he going to be like this—like that? Is he going to end up that way?"

Family members of people with ABI thought that *Keys to the ABI Cage* would be a way to explain about ABI 'in a humorous way—with things their family member could relate to, things he could see and touch'.

As one mother put it:

> I've had great support from friends—but I don't think even my closest friends understand ABI or me—some days I'm just ragged; I need info for friends.

Mothers and wives talked about the breakthrough once their loved ones understood about ABI, developed some insight and then accepted assistance. Brain injury support groups and talking to others with ABI was seen as valuable ways to obtain understanding.

> He has developed some insight: He accepts assistance

> He accepts he needs to use his mobile phone

> [He] accepts it's good to talk to someone else with ABI.

Looking at the things people talked about, it is possible to see a movement away from information about the ABI to consideration of concepts together in interaction which are about how to establish meaning to life and in doing so, how to counterbalance the challenges faced. This is a source of information in the metaphysical realm of hope, love, trust and dignity as well as about the practical helping tasks.

### 8.4.3 Developing Some 'Quality of Life'

The mothers and wives of boys and men with ABI all identified that it was vital to find 'good' people who could help in different ways—a psychologist, a guardian (who took over managing Sue's son's life—'if she had not intervened he would be dead') who obtained 'proper' medication and accommodation.

Maintaining social ties requires helping loved ones develop confidence and self-esteem. These tenacious women carers spoke with pride about the way their family member coped

> …learning by his own mistakes, but not on tight leash…but supported and shadowed

> He works 16 h a week; Sympathetic understanding work is important

> You should see him on the phone 'I'm an artist now'… this has helped his self esteem—he feels like he's out there and contributing to society and he's made friends with others who have ABI, [with] similar injuries to himself, [it's] easier when people understand

> Whiteboards, he's only just started to use a diary, he couldn't before, he tried but he wouldn't know what day it was but now…
>
> …he lives with a mobile phone ringing…we just program it in and it rings and tells him what he does at a particular time.

Realisation that the lifeworld of their loved one was affected by their attitude led to comments such as: 'I need patience' and 'Every little thing is a gift'; 'I take it just one day at a time'; 'We're lucky to still have him'; 'Appreciate the small gains and events'.

### *8.4.4 Recapitulation*

'With Love, Hard Work and the "Right" Attitude, His Life Can Improve'.

Clarity over the importance of love, understanding and developing quality of life, even through small engagements that accomplish change, are what set the conditions for giving meaning to life and are separate from the cold and clinical environments of rehabilitation. They are also a necessary environment through which constructive circumambulation (replication of positive reflection leading to greater insight) can be engaged and which support positive change for people with ABI.

Learning together then was vital in creating new roles, tasks, expectations. These, as will be shown in Chap 9, become the habituated aspects that define new lives, relationships and communities which over time all concerned come to accept. It is true that sometimes these networks break down, but replacement networks which do the same are vitally important to rebuild. Life without a network of support, without love and without empathy is isolating and destructive to any person. But for those whose agency to search out and build such networks is not matched by the resources they have, no such new support networks can be built. This emphasises the need for competence and resources that are distributed to support people with ABI, perhaps more than for others as well as for services able to support such support building.

## 8.5 Professionals: Factors that Positively Affect the Life of Clients with ABI

As for participants with ABI and family members, we proceeded to interview and analyse transcripts for professionals who each brought to the study their expertise and experience about things that help people with ABI to learn to feel and fare better. They brought valuable insight into this area of the study. Overarching themes identified by clustering of emergent themes provided a new angle on the importance of the family, 'the support team' of the individual.

*Professionals: Overview of Findings*

<table>
<tr><th>Superordinate Themes</th><th>Overarching Themes</th></tr>
<tr><td rowspan="3">Group X:The professional provides guidance to fill the gap when the person leaves rehabilitation.<br><br>Group Y: The humanity of the professionals — they can help by encouraging hope, providing connection, socialisation and empathy, this can support the person to have a purpose, and break down isolation.</td><td>1. Group X - The gap is filled by professionals when the person leaves hospital/rehabilitation</td></tr>
<tr><td>2. Group Y - The person's hope, acceptance and attitude is important</td></tr>
<tr><td>3. Technology and specific social groups help both group X and Y</td></tr>
</table>

**Fig. 8.3** Professionals: overview of findings

It was anticipated that a triangulation of the data between professionals and people with ABI and family carers would lead to confirmation of views. However, divergent views among professionals and in comparison with wives and mothers called into question the use of triangulation as simply 'confirming themes'. The professional views fell into two groups:

X group focused on the place of the professional; while, Y group focused on the 'humanity' of the professional.

As previously, Fig. 8.3 presents an overview of the superordinate (main) and overarching themes.

### *8.5.1 Group X: The Professional Fills the Gap After the Person Leaves Rehabilitation*

Professional Group X saw that the most helpful thing for the person with ABI and their family was to have home visits by professionals to fill the gap between hospital and home and have regular contact with the family, to manage or address problems and make sure providers are doing the right thing.

> People with brain injury need help with not the medical needs but follow up needs—I think none of the current models work well that's why they often struggle and their families struggle because the health bit ends at whatever point they think that your rehab is finished...
>
> What we need to start saying is rehab doesn't start till 2 years or 5 years post-injury but we have this system where things have to be very set and very structured, again if you don't fit the pigeonhole you don't get...
>
> We need regular training for family carers. Current training is often just for the professional and service providers.

### 8.5.2 *Group Y: The Person's Acceptance and Attitude Is Important—Hope, Love and Dreams*

For Group Y, the person's hope, acceptance and attitude is important:

> People with brain injury need hope when the doctor says you're going to be a vegetable, or that you're only going to improve for 2 years or 5 yrs... people need to have hope
>
> His self worth—there's a light inside him it may be masking other issues but it's still a form of self-esteem
>
> ...once you provide situations for people to thrive in, they will do that, and I'm always amazed that how far that can go
>
> Medical jargon is actually useless to you in the long run...not in diagnosis but what it means for life it's actually quite useless information to families—education much broader than just information
>
> Help with the creation of purpose—purpose I think is an absolute key to everything we're doing
>
> The "switch" to get people going again. It's the same things that everybody else does—their kids, their partners, their work it's all those things that we all value—what makes me feel good. What makes me get out of bed every day and come to work?
>
> There's something about recreation... the sense of purpose is so enormous in human beings, that to have lots of time, and nothing to do with it, no sense of purpose, is worse... it's torture
>
> Some people might see it as a wake-up call. Like some people may lose their jobs would lose their self-esteem and would despair, and other people would say I get to spend extra time with my children and I think some people see it as that. It [ABI] can bring you to despair, or it can help you to refocus your life and priorities and there's something about your belief and faith or serendipity or whatever it happens to be... I've spoken to people for example, who have said I can't rush around so much, so I am able to listen more and that has opened huge opportunities for me

We have cited many quotes from professionals in Group Y because they saw the individual with ABI as working with the power to affect their outcome by working with hopes, dreams, understanding and purpose. These professionals identified that understanding the impact of ABI on the individual was an important component and that people needed education and supportive networks. This was much broader than about the getting better, about rehabilitation and overseeing providers. As examined in Chap 7, Group Y said that medical jargon is actually useless, not in diagnosis, but in what it means to life in the long run.

Clients might have information, but they cannot absorb it. They need be able to identify issues to tackle and what they will do to improve.

Some professionals identified how a sense of humour helped their clients and how, as professionals, they needed a sense of humour. Clients needed to think about 'alternatives to watching television'.

Professionals from Groups X and Y identified that Palm Pilots and mobile phones can be helpful if the person is able to use them. Several professionals stated that there needed to be more groups like Headway, where the person could go to just 'hang out'. In one country town location, a travel cost of $90 a week meant belonging to an urban group would not be viable financially, especially as a taxi was required to get the client to the centre. On the other hand, some people do not want to be in an ABI group. They want to be out with people in their communities and localities who reflect their interests and aspirations.

## 8.6 Recapitulation

This chapter has shown in spite of catastrophic, complicated affects of ABI, Keys can help the person move from being unsatisfied with their life during the months or early years after their ABI, to being *engaged* in thinking about the elements of a meaningful life. This study has established that there are a plethora of Keys that can help people with ABI unlock the ABI Cage so they can release themselves from feeling imprisoned and find a satisfaction in their lives.

The Keys exist in the metaphysical world as well as in the world of practical help and clinical attention to getting better. Indeed, the notion of getting better establishes a particular type of opportunity structure for hope that may never be realised. The meaning of hope, love, caring, trust and the warmth in offsetting the challenges lies deep in us all. The Keys are a way of understanding this and a way of beginning to see what is important to people and thus, what should then, also be important to professionals.

Keys 'open doors'. They are one step in the process of moving from one place to another. Keys involve a complex mix of coexisting perceptions, opinions, emotions and behaviours. Keys can be used by people with ABI so they play an active role in helping themselves to find ways to cope with or live with the challenges of ABI. These Keys can release people from feeling bleak about brain injury and beaten by brain injury, so they can make the best of brain injury. Keys are active not passive; all these Keys require the person to have active acceptance—the will and courage to accept Keys proffered by family, friends and professionals. Other Keys need the curiosity and effort of the person to find ways to regain their identity and reach equilibrium. The personal stories of participants with ABI revealed that, for some, the brain injury brought a fresh appreciation of life, an awareness of their strengths and weaknesses and wisdom.

Mothers and wives of people with ABI believed that love, understanding and patience could assist their loved ones and the development of lasting networks of support. Some professionals suggested professional expertise is valuable in guiding the person with ABI (and their family) on the ABI 'journey', while other professionals identified empathy and compassion as being of prime importance. All participants identified the importance of the person and their family gaining understanding about ABI.

It is thus that we have come full circle to the phenomenological heart of this study. This study commenced by explaining that it was going to look for a way to acquire better insight into ABI in order to find a way to help people feel (and fare) better.

Remembering and then 'understanding' was the common and universal theme that helped people move from feeling that life was not worthwhile to feeling that life was worthwhile. In order to 'understand' people need to work with Keys, *they* can identify and Keys that are meaningful *to them*. As the first step in Anderson and Krathwohl's learning taxonomy, remembering (identifying and recalling information) leads to the second step 'understanding' (interpreting, classifying, inferring, comparing and explaining), then applying the understanding to different concepts, then analysing, evaluating and finally creating (generating ideas and hypothesising).

From this study, a conclusion could be drawn that the usual information about ABI needs to be supplemented by linking in the underlying 'Keys' including the metaphysical concepts in order to support each person to feel and fare better. The metaphysical ideas around love, trust, resilience therefore become a necessary environment and context in which people learn and apply their ideas in interaction with others, in which they fail but come back with lessons that help them try again. The recurrent and endless attempts to 'try again' (Anderson and Karthwol's category of 'creating once again') are what place learning at the very centre of efforts to support people with ABI. Most importantly, 'trying again' represents ***every*** person's struggle to give meaning to their lives, to achieve their capabilities and help them to feel and fare better whatever the circumstances within which they live.

We can therefore now emphatically agree with Freeman's words that 'education is the key' and we shall further formalise this argument in the following chapter.

## References

Anderson, L. W. & Krathwohl, D. R. (Eds.) (2001). *A taxonomy for learning, teaching, and assessing: A revision of Bloom's taxonomy of educational objectives*. Boston, MA: Allyn & Bacon (Pearson Education Group).

Seligman, M. E. P. (1998). *Learned optimism.* New York, NY: Pocket Books.

# Chapter 9
# Discussion: Illuminating 'Blind Spots' for the Health Service Providers

*Long term recovery from brain injury is not a medical problem. What is needed is re-learning... the power of recovery lies within the injured person as they relearn their daily living skills. Education is the key,*

(Freeman, 1998, p. 14)

## 9.1 Introduction

In this chapter, we will draw together some of the threads of learning **we** have gained **from our study participants**. We shall employ a framework that acts as a heuristic to assemble the blind spots and blank spots that have been discovered. Along the way, we shall emphasise how this research has relevance to people with ABI, family carers and professionals. So, to house the findings in a synthesised manner, our first task is to adopt a heuristic framework that will support this intention.

Let us recall the importance of Edmund Husserl's phenomenology to our study, the importance of listening to the lifeworld of people with ABI and others as they ascribe meaning to their world. In identifying such meaning, we can identify grounds for their social action, i.e. why people act the way they do. Social action presupposes meaning—for example, if I give meaning to my identity as a non-racist, my social actions will reflect this 'reality', and vice versa.

Moran (2011) points to Husserl's 'phenomenology of habitualities' and argues that, 'Habit…for Husserl is intimately involved in the constitution of meaningfulness and forms of sense at all levels'. Once people pursue social action without having to think about the relevant action for that situation, they have formed a habit. Many of these habits are shared with others, making them cultural mores. In our own lives, consider our roles within our family, our work group and among friends.

We are not always 'mind readers', so, with just the smallest action, it is easy to cause offence. For example, not unpacking the dishwasher as our partner has anticipated or not following or showing appreciation for the sport/television



C. Durham and P. Ramcharan, *Insight into Acquired Brain Injury*,
DOI 10.1007/978-981-10-5666-6_9

program/film/food or music our friends value. Much of what we do is habitual, and we negotiate where to 'change expectations'.

We have seen in detail how people with ABI struggle with these habitualities as they re-engage in day-to-day life in their communities. Indeed, when habits cannot be applied by the person they become 'exposed', since they have to make a decision about how to act and respond without relying on that habit; the reactions of others to them in such circumstances, therefore, have a huge impact. The person with ABI becomes the 'looking glass self' seeking affirmation, guidance and information from others to gauge whether their own response and actions have been acceptable. So negative responses, and especially their reoccurrence, can be devastating for the person. Imagine being rejected or told you are wrong constantly. It is soul-destroying!

The notion of habitualities is vital to this chapter in two ways—on the one hand, it has the potential to explain 'blind spots'; on the other, the concept emphasises the importance of learning such habitualities as a precursor to people with ABI living an included life, developing a clear identity and to pursuing future hopes, dreams and aspirations.

Let us look at the relevance of habit to 'blind spots'. It is possible for two groups of people to have different habits. It is only the power one has over the other which allows those with power to define the 'reality' of that situation in terms of which actions are pursued. Any other interpretation is to the powerful party a 'blind spot'—they cannot see, or simply reject, the alternative view as well as those actions that the alternative view would warrant.

Thus, we have argued that a view of 'mending bodies' (tied up with an education drawing on a history of 'established' ideas) misses the vital stage of mending lives which lasts for a lifetime once people move back to their home and community. We have shown how the language and categories explaining ABI in many public information documents draw from the 'habits' of a 'mending lives' discourse. We can, too, see how the negative and pathological labels used in this narrative lead to particular professional actions to 'make the person (as close to) normal' again. All of these actions exist insofar as the professional has rights and authority to define 'the problem', to the extent that what is published on Websites recognises this authority and, insofar as the construction of services is based upon, and consequent to, the authorised professional definition of the 'problem'.

Pierre Bourdieu's work on *habitus* offers a very useful heuristic in this respect (Bourdieu & Wacquant, 1992). They argue that we have capitals (resources) that are economic, cultural, social and symbolic (to do with power) upon which we draw in our everyday lives. These capitals will differ among groups, between an Inuit Eskimo and an urban Londoner for example. In living in these contexts, we draw on the potential of the capitals to create our habits and, pursue our lives within the context of what we learn to be culturally and socially appropriate.

Thus, for example, the many words for 'white' which structure Inuit existence, survival and flourishing, will not be mirrored in the urban Londoner's understanding and culture. Collectively, the habits become a disposition (habituality), a way of being, and all social practices are embodied (i.e. internalised) as Inuit practice and culture. The Inuit use these categories with a great degree of expertise. A Londoner arriving and telling the Inuit they have it wrong and should act in a different way would likely not be taken seriously and left to his or her own devices if she/he continued to insist upon a different way of being or 'seeing whites' in this case. Within any cultural 'field' then, there is what Bourdieu terms symbolic capital, a relation of power that operates to maintain the disposition of the culture within any field of practice (i.e. in this case a tundra environment and community).

Now, apply this to people with ABI. It is likely that their capitals will change once they get back home; it is likely that they will require new supports to live a life of their own choosing; it is likely that their search for the embodied practices of their group will be affected by their injury, and it may be that unlocking their potential to adopt new identities given these changes may be problematic.

For people entering new lives, there is 'anomie' in which the person with ABI is alienated from their usual preinjury social practices, habitualities and moralities. For them, social practices are unknown by virtue of having to redefine their lives, spaces and their interactions with others. In such circumstances, the 'looking glass self' becomes more important. Since actions and relations are unknown, people are looking even more than may be usual for the confirmation and affirmation of others in terms of who they now are (identity)—in order to define themselves and how they act (social acceptance) in the future.

The social practices and identity, unknown to them, become known through others' responses to them. This research has demonstrated 'what is known and experienced' by different groups. In the first section of this chapter, we shall talk about the concomitant blind spots, particularly those which do not see, ignore or reject the lives and experiences of people with ABI. In doing this, we propose to ask the reader, professionals and families to **assume the position of 'the looking glass self'**. Of this, more shortly.

The second pre-eminent aspect of habit relevant to this thesis, and which is further explored in Sect. 9.3, is its relevance to the centrality of (re-) learning in the lives of people with ABI. If, as argued above, social practices are unknown and, if people with ABI have to find new replacement social practices, then inevitably (re-) learning is required to survive and to flourish.

It has been argued above that the disposition and embodied practices of any culture are tied up with an historical lineage of ideas; they are built from a recognition of the powerful (usually government) conferring the right of some people (usually professionals) to act using this established history of ideas; they are sustained around complex guilds and professional societies and complex organisational structures with governance that resists challenge. In short, the disposition and embodied practices of these groups are extraordinarily resistant to change. Foucault has argued that professionals given the power to act turn their clients into objects, i.e. clients become objectified and defined by the professionals' ideas through such 'dividing practices' (Foucault, 1982).

What we have shown in this study is the lack of clarity people with ABI have in relation to their disposition, their habitual and comforting place within family, home and community. We have also shown how this is often related to the struggles to adopt an identity of their own. Writing is now beginning to emerge around identity in a world of post-modernity. Ranieri and Pachler, for example, write that:

> In the fast-changing and uncertain world of late- or post-modernity, individuals need to continuously cope with new challenges; this condition requires them to develop a flexible identity and a dynamic ability of "being-in-the-world" (2014, p. 64).

Adding complexity to this task for people with ABI in relation to learning is that

> …content delivery as the dominant paradigm is no longer appropriate, a point argued by constructivist approaches to learning from Vygotsky (1931/1978) to von Glasersfeld (1995). To face the challenges of uncertainty and change in "liquid" modernity (Bauman 2000), learners require flexibility, and need to develop a dynamic ability to make sense of knowledge so they can deal with perpetual change (ibid).

Since learners are indeed immersed into an ever-changing world, the acquisition of static knowledge transmitted by the teacher or trainer is no longer sufficient for the learner to make sense of their dynamic experiences of the world—if it ever was. In other words, content delivery as the dominant paradigm is no longer appropriate, a point argued by many.

However, in their excellent article on a dialogical conception of habitus, Akrivou and San Giorgio (2014) suggest that Bourdieu's theory of habitus does not allow sufficiently for such change. They consider that 'transformative' learning takes place where trust is established between interlocutors in conversation and as accompaniers in social action.

Moreover, conversation partners gradually become less preoccupied with 'safe' habits and engage in reaching a 'shared truth' with regard to how to proceed in a shared quest for *die sache*—or the subject matter of inquiry (Gadamer, 1989; Gadamer & Lawrence, 1982; Kelly, 1988). For them, conversation represents the 'binding "play of persons"'—and this can only happen in trusting relationships since

> The quality of experiencing cognition is possible once a person freely "gives up" the safety of one's self authorship on the basis of solitary reason….the processual self emerges from a dialogical habitus experiencing an organic way of being complete in situ…This gradually develops a diverse set of the brain's cognitive pathways…we learn to skillfully *be* with experience (Akrivou & San Giorgio, 2014, p. 2).

Notable in this quote is the notion now gaining recognition from science in relation to the plasticity of the brain.

Post-modernity and identity and research around new identities in new e-media environments have recently been gaining more interest too. This idea of lifelong learning as an 'ability to see' draws on Heidegger's notion of 'being in the world' cultivating adult learners' dynamic abilities to be actively engaged with their thinking, acting and feeling. In doing so, they live 'authentically' as well as, flexibly, in the face of change. In this context, personal mobile devices have been viewed by some as suitable means of supporting individuals' adults' learning at any time, anywhere and across many contexts (Arrigo, Kukulska-Hulme, Sanchez, & Kismihok, 2013).

However, new technology may be a double-edged sword. Field and Lynch (2015) point to the 'liminal space' (Field & Lynch, 2015) between identities into which many young people now fall, observing of their study participants that,

> …they have in common a current inability to imagine the future; when asked about the future they speak of obstacles and of impossible situations which inhibit choice. They appear bound, immobilised. For some, life is to be coped with (ibid, p. 11).

The authors highlight the importance of learning in formal and informal environments and through 'communities of practice'. Looking at identity and cultural practices among young music learners, Lonie and Dickens (2016) show how some learning environments exclude young people as do some settings and some organisations. They show how by re-appropriating spaces for communities of practice the students in their study were able to encounter and learn new art forms across genres through self-directing social practices. It may not have escaped the readers' attention that some participants with ABI expressed similar sentiments about ABI support groups which they attended. Walsh, Muldoon, Gallgher, and Fortune (2015) in their study of 53 adult survivors of ABI in post-acute community rehabilitation argue the importance of social factors to well-being, a social cure (Jetten, Haslam, & Haslam, 2012). As they say,

> It seems that belonging to groups (affiliative identity) fosters perceptions of social support and that perceiving social support facilitates participation in activities which become internalised as social identities (self-as-doer identity) which in turn impact positively on psychological well-being. Our results suggest that looking to one type of social identity alone may not tell the whole story regarding relationships between social identity, social support and emotional status following brain injury, (Walsh et al., 2015, p. 566)

Stone, Underwood, and Hotchkiss (2012) talk about a 'relational habitus' in which learning is intersubjectively sustained through formal and informal communities. There are several implications from this emergent research for people with ABI. If learning is the key as Freeman argues, then people need to be supported to learn in environments in which they can feel safe and learn to trust those with whom they interact. Learning is based on deep relationships since it is only through encounters of trust that self-reflection ensues and actions change. Moreover, growing is better supported in relationships that last and where habitualities become shared over time. Some approaches since this study was completed begin to recognise these factors even within rehab practice. Sullivan, Gray, Williams, and Green (2014) suggest 'clinical implications for real life activities to be incorporated as part of rehabilitation' (p. 424); Lexell, Alkhed, and Olsson (2013) emphasise group rehab to give patients 'the tools they needed to change their everyday situation, especially in relation to gaining more knowledge and learning new routines and habits' (p. 536) where professionals, family and friends play crucial roles. The place of 'habits' in this proposition should be noted not least since predating any new habit is a lot of learning and a lot of practice!

Habits which have been glued together previously with a range of available resources and capitals are thrown into complete disarray when a person re-enters life in the community where new habits have to form in a coherent way to produce inclusion. The resources that are available are likely to be different and the demands on others similarly so. Amartya Sen, a Nobel Laureate for Economics argues that a person's capabilities are bounded within his or her circumstances. To live to achieve what one is capable of, to hope, to dream are a function of how the resources that are available will, or come to be, applied.

In these senses, the implications for services must be grounded in a series of principles relating to learning, to identity and to positive change based upon the lifeworlds of those with whom they engage, with whom they explore ideas in a trusted relationships. Moreover, the levels of support to provide the freedoms others take for granted should be designed to work towards situations in which sufficient supports are available not just to manage an austere existence, but to support hope, aspirations and growth.

We now have a framework for exploring blind spots and for exploring the practice relevance of the research findings. This occupies the following two sections.

## 9.2 Understanding Negative Blind Spots

This section explores the 'blind spots' identified in the Keys Study. Instead of presenting them as findings, we ask the reader, given what they have learned, to walk a mile in the shoes of people with ABI; we ask readers to empathise and to weave these new threads of understanding into a strong rope designed to support people with ABI to feel and fare better—to provide new 'scaffolding' that holds up the structures, processes and elements of a good life through learning.

It will be remembered from Chap. 3 that one phenomenological approach to the medical understanding of symptoms was that if there were no apparent explanations for their observations that they might be seen by medics as delusions or as hallucinations. Drawing on the phenomenology of Husserl (intended perception) and Merleau-Ponty (embodied perception), Fuchs (2005) writing about delusional mood and perception argues that there is an 'intimate connection with the world mediated by the lived body' (Fuchs, 2005, p. 138). Note here that this connection to the world changes if our body changes. For example, experience of stairs will change if, all of a sudden, one becomes blind or unable to walk.

To encounter such new embodiment and perception, we now ask the reader to place him or herself as a novice Eskimo, or, as a new village resident living in high and mountainous terrain, or, as a Bedouin—i.e. as a stranger (Schutz, 1944) in a new world in which movement, social interaction and perhaps language have changed. Flimsy as this metaphor may be, it may provide sufficient analogy to people with ABI, arriving in a new destination with no clear identity, being challenged by the terrain, and struggling to communicate in order to survive and flourish.

Imagine now that you are required to walk from the village to uphill pastures, or to go out and hunt seal in the ice or to successfully mount a camel to follow other Bedouin across a desert—you might struggle with thin air walking uphill, or end up in danger trying to walk on different forms of ice or fail miserably to get the camel to do your bidding and, further, to act in culturally appropriate ways since you have not the habitualities of that culture at your disposal. You may feel shame or loss of status, unable to control your body as you have been used to doing. If your fellow villagers, Eskimos or Bedouin tribesmen, show a lack of empathy and kindness; if they offer no support; if all you get is negative feedback; if you lack the esteem you have once had in your home environment—then you are, over time, likely to become exasperated and even angry.

When Websites and medics talk about challenging behaviours, it may be that these are produced by the reactions of others and are not only a function of the brain injury. It may be that these are wholly understandable as 'behaviours of resistance or protest' (Ramcharan, Nankervis, Strong, & Robertson, 2009). The cause of such behaviours needs to be understood by the professionals and families and others. Such behaviours may be wholly understandable. They represent the struggle to be human, to be accepted and to be treated with dignity.

The first 'blind spot', then, is that ABI damages more than just the brain.

As you employed the looking glass self in the examples above, you may have felt all those things felt by people with ABI in our study sample—fear of different types (being lost, left behind, in danger, unsure of who to turn to and so forth), shame (at the incapacity to know how to act, at gaining recognition and status, at lack of knowledge of practicalities), disappointment, distress, hopelessness (since you cannot yet choose how to act, how to communicate and how to flourish in your new environment) and loss of status (comparing the new you to the one you are now in your new environment and social group) along with anxiety, suspicion leading over time to a sense of hopelessness and even depression.

You may have felt guilt too. William James (1950) in the *Principles of Psychology* wrote about the 'fiendish punishment' experienced if people do not notice us or 'cut us dead'. James suggests that the consequences would be 'rage and impotent despair' (cited in de Botton, 2004), and the person with ABI may daily experience the 'torture' of being a 'nobody', being held in low esteem, invisible or ignored. Like our sample participants, you would be searching to understand what was 'true' in life—and what made you a valued human being at all.

The medical model too has the potential to classify these beliefs/feelings/perceptions in a negative light (see Chap. 3, Diagram 3.1). These symptoms are treated as the cause of the person's cognitive, behavioural and emotional problems.

What this study has shown is that in many cases they are not symptoms, but rather a perfectly reasonable and understandable response to the struggles of life. Adopting these symptoms as a cause leads to a downward spiral since the response is more negative feedback, maybe more medication, perhaps more specialist services trying to rid the symptomatology through regimes that incorporate testing and behavioural programs.

In this way, the medical model treats the effect of these interventions (behaviour, emotions, depression) as the cause of behaviour. What this study shows is that the cause also lies in the social realm, with the impassioned struggle to be human, to be social and to be included.

The second, and associated, blind spot in this study is the negative effects of rehabilitation for over half the participants in this study.

Taking up your 'looking glass role' where you left off, consider, if you will, how much courage it would take to resist the constant negative feedback in your social life only to find you are being subjected to countless medical and psychological tests, being told you are lying about your abilities or cheating to get a better life (monetary compensation). As a new Eskimo, tribe member or Bedouin, you are now subjected to tests to see why you are not 'normal'.

For many people in this study, the rehabilitation experience had been a real problem. It is no 'golden period' at all but a 'dark hole'. The protagonist in Graham Greene's story *The Moment of Truth* reveals that:

> …[he] thought doctors and surgeons are not necessarily good psychologists; perhaps, because their interests are so concentrated on the body that they forget the mind, they don't realise how much a tone of voice reveals to the patient. They say "there's always a good hope" but what the patient hears is "there is very little hope if any", (Greene, 1990, p. 37)

Participants in this study believed strongly that rehabilitation should not solely be about mending bodies, but about helping them understand ABI and themselves and building skills, talents and hopes through education and encouragement. Instead participants reported inter alia: being 'treated like a leper', being 'dumb and stupid'; feeling mistrust having been 'burnt' or 'tricked' when doing assessment tests in particular; feeling terms had been misused.

This feeling of being tricked was revealed very forcefully to Durham during the last stage of the first few interviews. Durham had made two sets of 'talk-about' cards that were very similar: 'Being useful' and 'Helping'; and 'A cup of tea' and 'A cup of coffee'. Durham was astonished that the first five participants all responded in similar vein to the following: 'Being useful is the same as helping!' 'A cup of tea or coffee—what's the difference—did you think I had forgotten I had already chosen one'. They explained that they felt they were being 'tested' and 'tricked', as they had been in rehabilitation tests and it took some time to repair the conversation and convince them that there had been no intention of tricking them. The 'Helping' and 'A cup of tea' cards were removed because the main aim of this study was to do no harm and not to upset the participants. This was the only example where the 'talk-about' cards distressed a participant.

People with ABI also reported being given IQ tests on several occasions and experienced negative emotional outcome from being obliged to complete tests that emphasised their impairments. Is the purpose of such tests to indicate their capacity to cope? If this is so, the people with ABI should have their test results explained to them and different ways of coping with their social networks explored. People need to be able to employ higher order thinking in order to identify strategies they use; however, learning about ABI, (re-)learning about manners and learning about 'faulty thinking' in an engaging way should play an important part of the rehabilitation experience.

Some emergent findings contest the assumptions of this IQ testing model. Gordon and Duff (2016) point out how important it is to learn contextually and with familiar partners (as opposed to IQ which simply tests the individual). They found using collaborative referencing (agreement on the label for novel shapes in their research) that recovering the agreed label reduced each time the task was repeated. One interesting finding was that when just one member of the ABI sample was provided a new partner, they too improved, indicating agreement was not based upon their memory, '…these results demonstrate the important role partners play in the communicative successes or failures of individuals with TBI in everyday interactions' (Gordon & Duff, 2016, p. 1482).

If such new ways of learning are peculiar to setting and interactants (as in your case of being an Eskimo, Bedouin or high plains villager), then there may be potentially limitless ways in which you might learn with and through others to establish you new habitualities, drawing on multiple intelligences, and in everyday settings and interactions. Mogensen (2016) drawing on neuroplasticity argues that the undamaged parts of the brain can be 'reorganised into new algorithmic strategies'… clinical outcomes may be a patient with different but as proficient mechanisms for cognition' (Mogensen, 2016, p. 429), i.e. the brain rewires itself to find a solution. He points to inexplicable and seemingly unimportant matters, such as a finger rather than a cross in a computer-simulated prism adaptation therapy experiment, as producing much better outcomes for no apparent reason. Much remains to be done to explore the potential of neuroplasticity, contexted cognition, new technologies for learning and social action which are anathema to the negative targeting of IQ and other tests which simply point to 'the' problem.

Given the emphasis of this book that 'learning is the key', it is not surprising that Durham and Ramcharan posit that much work needs to be done and that there is a significant need to prioritise research and practice in these areas.

For many people with ABI, their issues in rehab were described as 'minor', 'unimportant' or 'insignificant', while 'plateauing' was used to imply no further improvements were likely or expected. The turn of phrase 'you never will…' was often defeating leading to loss of motivation and hope.

By reason of the blind spots identified above, threats to the self-efficacy of participants, their belief in their capacity to achieve goals, were severely challenged. Verlinden and Brands (2016) have found that 'Control over interfering emotions and developing a sense of control and mastery over brain-injury associated symptoms seem to be of importance in the development of self efficacy…Treatment programmes should focus explicitly on reinterpretation of interfering thoughts and symptoms and the reinforcement of self-beliefs' (p. 604). The present authors would concur.

In the above two blind spots, we have shown how the continuous low level or direct negative reinforcement destroys a person's self-esteem, suspends their identity formation and destroys their trust in others. Participants in our study had 'proof' or reasons for many of their fears that affected their lifeworld, (see Sects. 7.2.1 and 7.2.2). From the perspective of the professional, some of the fears expressed by participants with ABI could be placed upon a sliding scale from extreme sensitivity, to paranoid, to delusional. However, in the same way we saw that avoidance could be a coping strategy (in Chap. 5) or used as a defensive function for retaining self-esteem (McKay, Langdon, & Coltheart, 2007). What can be seen by others as purely negative and/or destructive behavioural issues can be performing a very valuable and protective function for vulnerable people on the long-term road to learning to live with ABI.

Aristotle posits in *Nicomachean Ethics* that how one manages one's fear is a measure of courage. Positive psychologists have pointed to 'endorsed strengths' or 'encompassing virtues' such as wisdom, courage humanity, justice, temperance and transcendence, and how these define bravery, persistence and integrity, i.e. courage (Peterson and Seligman, 2004). It has been argued that a shift is required in terms of how rehabilitation practice produces improvements in well-being by working with such strengths and virtues (Evans, 2011). This is one important lesson for professionals—the need to adopt positive—psychology and strength-based (Connolly & Harms, 2015; Slade, Oades, & Jardin, 2017) models which build on strengths and which recognise causation in personal experience and not in organic abnormality.

Some approaches, suggested since the completion of this study, have started to reflect issues such as those outlined above. Perceptively, Ackroyd, Fortune, Price, Howell, Sharrack, and Isaac (2011) emphasise,

> raising clinician's awareness of the possibility of growth for their clients rather than working solely to "fix a problem". The social network surrounding the person with ABI may also provide an opportunity for the development of post-traumatic growth. Some recent research in people with other neurological illness suggests that growth in patients tends to be best predicted by growth in their partners and vice versa…thus a communal search for meaning seems to be a significant process by which growth may be maintained… building what is strong rather than solely striving to fix what is wrong. (p. 654).

Using 'compassion-focused therapy' Ashworth, Clarke, Jones, Jennings, and Longworth (2014) show how shame, self-blame and other emotional responses can be addressed in rehabilitation to support adjustment, to build trust in staff and to regain control. They speak of 'scaffolding' interventions for those not coping after injury. Fraas (2015) speaks of the growing recognition by clinicians of the importance of listening and responding to personal narratives, while Greenfield (2011) emphasises the need for clinicians to take a more phenomenological approach, to dialogue, explore changes in metaphor so as to support identity development, establish coping and promote advocacy.

The sense of loss you may now be feeling in your role as Eskimo, Bedouin or high mountain villager may be great. If you had been told you would never 'get better' or 'get the hang of your new role' you may lose hope, feel lonely and isolated. Our participants had a real distaste for being delivered such 'messages of doom'. Some studies have found improvements over time for people with ABI through involvement in the 'academy of life' (Bulinski, 2010) through improved self-efficacy (Cicerone & Azulay, 2007) or through attaining healthy and productive lifestyles (Corrigan, Bogner, Mysiw, Clincholot, & Fugate, 2001).

However, for many, the unrelenting negative responses may simply add to the destruction in their lives and of their lives. Moreover, it is a struggle to learn when the person feels afraid, ashamed, isolated and is trying to understand and cope with the ideas discussed above (see Sects. 7.2.1, 7.2.2, 7.2.3 and 7.2.4). Without support how can you get up a mountain where the air is so rarefied? Without support how would you handle the camel and pitch your tent; without support how would you navigate the dangers of different ice-flows and find your food? Moreover, without observing and learning and practice following others, your own identity within the social milieu and environment will remain perplexing if not opaque. You will not learn your place and develop your new identity without such learning.

In their important review summarising applied behaviour analysis and positive behaviour support, Ylvisaker, Turkstra and Coelho (2005) argue for a 'collaborative contextualised approach' encompassing: working in highly idiosyncratic contexts, where behaviours will be used (through situational training and coaching), with regular communication partners, 'so they can interact supportively and do not misinterpret or react punitively to awkward behaviours' (p. 264) allowing self-reflection and withdrawal if feeling stressed. Vitally, they argue that the 'application of a person-centred goal formulation framework, so that the individuals understand that their goal is "social success", not "social appropriateness", and counselling specifically designed to help the individual develop a personally compelling sense of self that includes positive social interaction strategies as a component' (p. 264). It seems to us that this represents very apposite advice given our study findings.

Some recent studies are recognising the importance of both positive psychology but also the importance of placing interaction in social contexts of everyday interaction. Martin, Levack, and Sinnott (2015) argue that

> that social identity and social connectedness ought to be primary foci of rehabilitation rather than matters only of secondary concern. Consideration needs to be given to both the environmental contexts and the intrapersonal strategies that support people who require residential rehabilitation services to achieve social connection, and thus their life goals, following a severe acquired brain injury, (p. 1234).

Some studies also recognise that it is important to work with family and friends too. For example, Andersson, Bellon, and Walker (2016) show how for children with ABI returning to school there is a need to support 'the family to adjust to changes and work towards the positive construction of new roles and identities following brain injury' (p. 838).

The third negative blind spot is that learning is hard labour.

Resume your Eskimo, Bedouin or high country native role, having now been there for a few days. How is it possible to learn all you need to do when getting mixed messages or being ignored? Through your isolation, shame and fear you may find it hard to learn—self-awareness of your unusual situation is a start and may also help in your understanding of the physical, emotional, cognitive and metaphysical challenges you are facing.

Participants with ABI in this study had a deep understanding of their situation: they could identify issues that affected them when they were provided with the scaffolding and the opportunity to discuss ideas through using *Keys to the ABI Cage*. They demonstrated that they could learn to acquire better insight into ABI using *Keys to the ABI Cage*. Learning theories, then, can be applied to assist each person with ABI to learn about and understand their ABI.

Participants spoke about not being in the right 'headspace' (see Chap. 7) to understand ABI in the 'information' that, in the past, had been given to them because they were 'trapped': swamped by their losses, no longer normal people and damaged from emotional fallout of feeling sad, bad and mad. They were ashamed, afraid and isolated and over half the participants were disempowered by their rehabilitation experience. Maybe at the time of their involvement in the Keys Study, two years or more post-injury, they were in the right 'headspace'; however, an hour spent with a bird cage let them open up their own minds to greater understanding of ABI.

Some participants admitted they had denied that they had ABI. Self-awareness is an important area that has been the focus of studies examined in the literature review in Chaps. 3 and 4. It is a complex phenomenon that can impede the rehabilitation process and outcome (Fleming, Lucas, & Lightbody, 2006; Lamberts, Fasotti, Boelen, & Spikman, 2016). Assisting people to understand and gain self-awareness both positive and challenging around their ABI in a constructive way was an important component of this study and also for learning.

The interviewed mothers and wives felt guilty that initially they were unable to understand ABI and may have done things differently had they such information. Statements made by professionals identified most of the physical and cognitive losses and some of the emotional difficulties. However, most professionals revealed a blind spot: they focused on 'fixing' the deficits of their clients without focusing on how these deficits affected their client's self-esteem and self-belief, their ability to learn, and eschewed discussion of issues of trust and power. Each client's fear and shame was not issues that were readily talked about. Learning could be termed a blind spot of the medical model, and it was not a focus of the professionals, nor the majority of studies about ABI.

The finding herein suggests that the headspace is not only about recognition of ABI and its affects. Trust through relationships where people can feel they can 'get it wrong' safely or 'confront themselves' is vital. Even before the process of learning then, preconditions such as building trust and self-awareness are necessary precursors to establishing a 'headspace' in which the person feels motivated to learn. This may be in short supply where the negative responses leave the person without hope that things can change. In your 'looking glass role', you may not have a common language with which to negotiate, to be heard nor to understand. In that role, you may be dependent upon support and would learn least through a didactic blackboard and chalk approach. As described in Chap. 5, you might fare better by drawing on other learning approaches—visual, kinaesthetic, music/rhythm and other forms of interaction drawing on other intelligences (Gardner, 1983).

Figure 5.1 presented earlier, outlines Anderson and Krathwohl's (2001) learning taxonomy with the fundamental elements being remembering, understanding, applying, analysing, evaluating and creating. In your "looking' glass role', you may already have been imagining the employment of these strategies. From the above, it can be seen that even reaching step 1, 'remembering', can be a problem when faced with the confusion caused by negative reactions, rejection and mixed messages. Embodied practices or habitualities are 'understood' through observing and/or modelling or experiencing the 'correct' ways to act in different circumstances within the cultural setting(s) occupied. The motivation to achieve such understanding may also be casualties where no matter what the person tries, they 'get it wrong'. This is exacerbated where the person is taught in inappropriate ways leading to further rejection.

An important finding of this study was that all participants—people with ABI, mothers and wives, and professionals—identified that there was a need for information in non-medical language that helps people understand and learn about ABI. All three groups stated that people with ABI, their families and the general public and some health professionals do not understand the ramifications of ABI. We have shown that there are presently some significant blind spots in the information that is available and that much of the information is couched in a negative manner which further accentuates difference and abnormality.

Further study is needed to determine different ways to identify suitable information for people with ABI, created in a way that is interesting to them and understandable. *Keys to the ABI Cage* used several metaphors and material objects (crushed cans and flying pigs as well as hope stones) to support reflection and understanding. There is potentially limitless artifice possible to engage people in ways that respect them as humans, that supports their reflections and which builds confidence. As we shall argue later, these must be a key to a 'positive learning' approach for people with ABI.

We shall attend to the 'analysing', 'evaluating' and 'creating' elements of Anderson and Krathwohl's (2001) learning typology in the following section.

At this point, it is sufficient to note that prior to engaging in learning there is a need to: build trust in relationships (prove empathy and understanding); build confidence, self-awareness and adaptation; offer a safe space to 'get it wrong'; and to support reflection on information that is made understandable and which reflects multiple intelligences.

But this does not explain either the content of a 'positive learning' approach or the processes. In the section to follow, we shall explore the remaining four blind spots in the light of our proposition about the centrality of learning to the lives of people with ABI. We shall synthesise findings in such a way as to begin to weave the threads together which will support people with ABI to feel and fare better.

## 9.3 Drawing on Positive Blind Spots

Above, we established the importance of *learning* to people with ABI faring and feeling better. Further, we have shown how negative blind spots simply reproduce anomie, trauma, difficult behaviours, rejection, isolation and loss of hope, self-esteem and confidence:

> …professionals often do not seem to realise that prolonged small traumas, for example ongoing experiences of failure or cumulative life events, might increase their vulnerability

> of developing PTSD-like symptoms…[trauma] That is, different kinds of problem behaviours can be considered as symptoms of PTSD, such as aggression and anger outbursts, self-injurious behaviour, non-compliance, social isolation, sleeping problems and restlessness…, (Mevissen & de Jongh, 2010, p. 308).

Such blind spots simply exacerbate or reproduce the very things they are supposed to address—they are 'brought forth by the healer'—i.e. are iatrogenic. They contribute to a 'headspace' that does not produce a motivation to learn. Indeed they can, in a worst case scenario, themselves be a source of trauma presaging

> …the effects of assaults on victims' sense of safety, trust and self-worth; their frequent revictimisation; and their loss of coherent self (van der Kolk, Roth, Pelcovitz, Sunday, & Spinazzola, 2005, p. 389)

In your "looking' glass role', you have been tested to see what is wrong with you, and you have been given negative feedback. What are you wishing for from your new friends and 'family'—what services would you choose and why? The participants in our study pointed to a number of things for which they yearned—to a number of blind spots in which the formal literature fails to engage substantively. These are explored below, and they are linked into the learning model being developed out of the findings of this study.

Blind spot 4 is the positive effect of 'humanity'.

People, as we have seen, cannot learn if they are in the wrong 'headspace'. Kirsten, a participant in this study, a professional with many years' experience working with people with ABI, remarked 'What I like about the stuff you are doing—the humanity of it—with all these things it's about humanity…'. She reflected upon the importance of hope and a sense of purpose. In your own new "looking' glass role', your sense of hope, (knowing there is no way back home), is to become part of your group and your culture, to thrive in your new world—to develop loving, reciprocal and valued relationships that make you feel good and make you want to be part of something, 'to get out of bed everyday', as Kirsten put it. Kirsten exemplifies the centrality of family friends, empathy, touch and reassurance.

Rees (2005) writes about 'connoisseurship' people who understand ABI and can assist people with ABI:

> The greater the number of persons who become connoisseurs, the greater is the chance of promoting understanding effective learning, and inclusion…Connoisseurs will have intimate familiarity with the phenomena of people with brain injury. They respect and are committed to their inclusion in society and understand the factors influencing rehabilitation. Connoisseurs typically present narratives that advance community understanding of the difficulties, but also the skills and talents, of people with brain injury, (Rees, 2005, p. 5).

In short, people with ABI require support from those who have sufficient knowledge of ABI, who understand the importance of inclusion and who treat them as equally human.

Put another way, the problem is not solely that of the person with ABI—it belongs to the people with whom they interact and the services and support workers too. Out of such core values comes the support that produces competence. As argued by Booth and Booth (1994), competence, therefore, should not be defined by *individual abnormality* and difference but by the distribution of supports available within family, friendships and society which helps each person to flourish. This 'distributed competence' model is about how we all flourish—since none of us on our own have the capacity to 'do it all ourselves'—we share the necessity of a 'civic duty' to share with others.

Consider the businesses and bankers, mechanics, service industries, educationalists, employers and others upon whom all of us rely, but 'take for granted', but who help us flourish. This is a hidden distributed competence upon which we rely. Similarly in your "looking' glass self', you too will want to rely on this distributed competence and you too will want to find the ways in which you can contribute something to your new 'tribe'—to be treated with dignity and as a human who has potential to contribute.

There are then, many Keys that open the ABI Cage, which is blind spot 5 as exemplified in so many ways by study participants as described in Chap. 8. The sixth blind spot is Keys that 'help in coping' and the seventh blind spot is 'optimism'. These blind spots are *insufficiently represented* in the literature on ABI. Figure 9.1 sets out the number of areas identified by research participants that act as Keys to the ABI cage relating to blind spots 5–7.

The lists in Fig. 9.1 present concepts at differing levels. Some are about attitudes (being positive, sense of humour); others are about outcomes (success, achieving

| | Additional Keys identified by participants over the study period were: |
|---|---|
| • Seeking social support<br>• Focusing on solving the problems<br>• Working hard to achieve<br>• Worrying<br>• Invest in close friends—engaging in particular intimate relationships—this strategy was not a common strategy<br>• Seeking to belong<br>• Wishful thinking<br>• Social action<br>• Tension reduction<br>• Recognising you are not coping<br>• Ignoring the problem<br>• Resisting self-blame<br>• Keep to oneself<br>• Seeking spiritual support<br>• Focusing on the positive<br>• Seeking professional help<br>• Seeking relaxing diversions<br>• Physical recreation | • Nature<br>• Animals<br>• Symbols<br>• Helping others<br>• Further study<br>• Achieving hard things<br>• Sense of Humour<br>• Employment<br>• Doing 'normal' things/feeling a 'normal' person<br>• Success<br>• Attitude<br>• Doing things for myself<br>• Feeling deepened through suffering |

**Fig. 9.1** Keys to the ABI cage

hard things); some are in the metaphysical realm (spiritual support, love and intimate relationships); activities, environments and sentience feature (nature, environments); personal development and achievement (achieve hard things, working hard to achieve things, further study); others relate to support (seeking social support, seeking professional help); and belonging and identity feature strongly as do the hope for doing normal things and feeling like a normal person.

There are signs that the literature since this study was conducted that is beginning to reflect some of these arguments. Levasseur et al. (2016), for example, use a Human Development Model-Disability Creation Process (HDM-DCP) drawing upon an anthropological model of human development and disability. This model shares the notion of habits that was central to the arguments made earlier on in this chapter. The model sees such habits as the result of the person's interaction with personal (identity, organic and capability factors) and with environmental factors (societal, community and personal). Habits cannot, therefore, form if factors prior to interaction remain confused or unclear, '…illustrating the circular and practical … dynamic and interactive process of disability and human functioning' (p. 638). This cyclical process has its similarities to our notion of 'constructive circumambulation'.

However, the model focuses on the individual without recognising that environmental, interactive, community and other concepts are interactively produced. It is the joint learning and distribution of competencies which makes a difference. Thus, the capacity of those close to create outcomes through interaction and to themselves learn how to do this is placed centre stage as a principle for service provision.

In short, none of the categories is any different from those we would expect of any of us. Why then should such hopes, aspirations and capabilities be so hard to achieve? Think again of your "looking' glass role'. Had you identified any of these as having potential to help you feel and fare better?

A positive approach to ABI would privilege these ideas and would do so among key people in the person's life.

*Keys to the ABI Cage* allowed people with ABI to easily identify phenomena that contributed to a satisfying life for them—to their psychological wellbeing, happiness and hope for the future. Yet the search for life satisfaction remains unresolved for many and in the literature too (Astrom, Asplund, & Aström, 1992). Participants emphasised the need to grow, to transform. Some were 'deepened by suffering' (Nietzsche, 1995). In the words of Helen Keller

> Character cannot be developed in ease and quiet. Only through experience of trial and suffering can the soul be strengthened, ambition inspired, and success achieved.

and Martin Luther King,

> Human progress is neither automatic nor inevitable… Every step toward the goal of justice requires sacrifice, suffering, and struggle; the tireless exertions and passionate concern of dedicated individuals.

Several participants felt that their life was enriched by their ABI experience; they now appreciated being alive, they were aware of their strengths and weaknesses and they now felt wise.

These beliefs or understandings also emerged through the interview process as a means of learning about ABI and applying new knowledge to themselves, reflecting on their life and gaining insight. This appeared to be a turning point for some participants in terms of their self-understanding and new pride in what they had achieved and overcome. The study identified that some participants had constructively circumambulated around the phenomena of ABI and worked things out for themselves: they had learnt that there were many Keys to the ABI Cage, that certain things affected their quality of life and that they had different ways of coping with their challenges. The 'powerful experience' of ABI had led them to acquire better insight into life. They felt wise. This is powerful information to pass on to others experiencing the life challenges of ABI.

The participants chose and talked about virtues and strengths such as: wisdom and knowledge, courage (accomplishing goals in the face of opposition), humanity (strengths of tending and befriending others), justice, (fairness), temperance (forgiveness and mercy, humility and modesty, self-regulation and self-control) and transcendence (appreciation of beauty, gratitude, hope, humour and playfulness and spirituality).Thus, subjective well-being is influenced not only by their physical, cognitive or emotional impairments but by their engagement with everyday life and relationships and by a focus on 'what is strong, not, what is wrong'. These findings have subsequently been made available to people with ABI with the publication of 'Unlocking my Brain through the Labyrinth of Acquired brain Injury' (Durham, 2014) to encourage them to reflect and gain insight and have their own 'Eureka moments'.

This process of 'analysing' that knowledge, the next in Anderson and Krathwohl's (2001) stages, was found in this study to be transformative—but maybe not immediate. It takes significant time, rehearsal and re-rehearsal to make sense of what it means in terms of relationships and place. For example, in distinguishing the many words for 'white' in Eskimo culture you may 'make many mistakes' before knowing which white makes igloos, which is a fishing hole, which is unsafe and so forth. This is why safe spaces for applying, evaluating and reviewing that knowledge are required. In doing so, patience is needed for while the brain may be plastic, it will take time for new neural pathways to turn rehearsal into habituality. It is also why in developing new relationships the distribution of competencies between people with ABI, family, services and others needs to be negotiated. But learning new distributions of competence is as much about *the learning of others* as it is about the learning of people with ABI. *Learning together*, therefore, needs to be in context and applied to goals that become agreed over time.

For many, both people with ABI and family carers, this new distribution of competencies requires adaptation and maybe even dealing with grief and loss. For example, the centrality of employment to people's identity and felt sense of accomplishment as well as the source of material comfort may be significantly changed (Sveen, Soberg, & Ostensjo, 2016). In the Keys study, five participants were working in different areas to their preinjury jobs, two participants expressed job satisfaction and four were studying. Some participants wished they could have career opportunities or work longer hours. Others who were not working wished to gain some employment and many had tried with great persistence to obtain work but could not.

Thus, unfortunately, few of the participants in the present study felt they had recovered sufficiently to be able to claim they had a 'healthy and productive lifestyle, or had returned to work'. If only two out of the 36 participants were satisfied with current employment, this is indeed a grim reality for the future of this group of people with ABI if life satisfaction and coping equates to being able to live as they had lived and worked before their ABI. Coming to terms with this and finding positive factors to balance out this part of their identity was clearly one of the harder things to accomplish for many people.

This finding was in agreement with the idea that although concepts of the 'personhood' as 'lost' or 'shattered' have dominated discussions in the literature, that this 'perspective is a crude representation of the post-injury experience of self, and the aspects of stability, recovery, transcendence and moral growth are also involved in this process'(Gelech & Desjardins, 2011, p. 62). Nochi's (2000) categories also show how a person can come to terms with their new self and develops new coping strategies as identified in Chap. 4 (Kendall, Kendall, & Muenchberg, 2009). It is also why Linge's (1990) suggestion to note and focus on small achievements is wise for all of us, people with ABI too.

*Keys to the ABI Cage* aimed to help people with ABI discover and come to terms with the new self (self-actualisation) by helping them to understand ABI, to feel safe, to belong to the 'brother/sisterhood' of people with ABI, to recognise their achievements and to have their achievements recognised by others. Identification of factors that positively affected their lifeworld assisted them to see their ABI experience with 'new eyes'.

Findings from *Keys to the ABI Cage* indicated few participants mentioned the word coping; however, they could nevertheless identify Keys what could be classified as coping strategies (see 8.2.3–8.2.7). Lazarus and Folkman's (1984) seminal work and Smith and Lazarus's (1990) work centres round the notion that emotions are influenced by evaluations (appraisals) of events that cause specific reactions in different people.

People with ABI in this study wrote about a wide variety of coping strategies—more extensive than those recorded in most coping self-report inventories (see Chap. 4), indicating that self-report inventories may fail to assess the full nature of coping. The problems associated with self-report inventories have been documented extensively in the literature, yet the use of these inventories to assess coping is still widespread (Kendall, Shum, Lack, Bull, & Fee, 2001).

Participants with ABI in the present study identified a plethora of unique ways to cope with multiple challenging situations at any one time; physical danger; emotional spin-offs including their loss of confidence and loss of trust; and their belief that they are sad, mad and bad, afraid, ashamed and isolated and fatigued.

This study unravelled complexity, whereas coping inventories do not. It allowed choice by the person of those things that they could or might use as 'appraisal' devices and buffers against stress. The Keys, therefore, allowed the collection of diverse experiences and provided grounds for choosing how people can engage. By drawing on the 'talk-about' cards, which represent the range of experience, people reflected on strategies and approaches they do not presently use but ones that may be open to them.

In the face of adversity, challenge and exclusion, it is hard to bounce back, to demonstrate resilience (Garmezy, 1991; Luthar & Ziegler, 1991; Masten, Best, & Garmezy, 1990). With the supports implied from our findings, some participants could be said to have displayed 'resilience'. Adversity can be applied to people with ABI, but competence is problematic if you are not competent to walk, talk, think or even eat as you once did. Positive adaptation involves skills, attitudes, awareness, acceptance of deficits and taking steps to adapt. These are not the normal attributes of a person whose life is changed by ABI.

Perlesz, Kinsella, and Crowe (1990) stated that few studies explore the experience of coping well and resilience after traumatic injury, and this still seems to ring true. Curran, Ponsford, and Crowe's (2000) study provided evidence that coping strategies are associated with emotional outcome, and Uprichard (2010), using the person-centred global approach, found that participants felt less valued and judged by society and wanted the focus to be on enablement rather than disablement. This is also a finding of *Keys to the ABI Cage* study.

The Resilience Research Centre (RRC) uses a more ecological and culturally sensitive definition of resilience. 'In the context of exposure to significant adversity, resilience is both the capacity of individuals to navigate their way to the psychological, social, cultural, and physical resources that sustain their well-being'(Resilience Research Centre, 2017). Given this definition and what was said about the use of *Keys to the ABI Cage* in providing a scaffold for coping, the same may be asserted around resilience. The Cage maximises the chance that people may find the resources through which to sustain their wellbeing.

The nature of this scaffolding and a reflection on 'Keys' to the ABI Cage is summarised below.

## 9.4 Scaffolding Learning—Summary for Readers, for People with ABI, Family Carers and Professionals

Scaffolding learning requires establishing the conditions to create a 'headspace' in which people feel motivated to learn. Building trust in relationships is the key to this as is patience and a safe space to try and to fail. Working on 'what is strong, not what is wrong' is crucial—a positive educational approach. The metaphysical concepts around love, intimacy, hope, beliefs, belonging and support are an essential holding environment in which all thriving is accomplished. Being negative, critical or providing complex or mixed messages or being punitive is counterproductive and is iatrogenic, contributing to loss of hope and, in worst case scenarios, to a feeling of trauma and abuse.

Learning is not a singular thing to make people 'normal'. To create new habitualities means working with people in their natural settings with their everyday relationships, families, friends and others. Normality is defined by the groups through their actions—trying to make the person fit with pre-existing habitualities is likely to fail and to stress all involved. Similarly, competence does not just adhere to the disability. Rather competence is distributed and all parties must learn how this new distribution of competencies will work for the benefit of the group and in a culturally sensitive manner. Whatever each person contributes, no matter how small should be valued as, ipso facto, their contribution to the groups and its identity. Moreover, each situation will be different and so will require a different approach.

Professionals need to plan for diversity and not establish prearranged approaches imposed by authority and without listening to the voices of people with ABI, those which ignore each person's peculiar circumstances, relationships and settings.

Since replicating pre-existing relationships is unlikely to work, adaptation, coping and resilience need to be major mechanisms through which all parties operate. This may also involve dealing with grief and loss.

In all forms of learning, a range of learning styles (intelligences) needs to be catered for in ways which make them understandable. The learning process that follows should draw on some of the concepts and any others that are not listed from this study as a positive mechanism for helping people to explore possibilities, options and their interconnections consistently.

The process of learning may be very slow and so patience is required. Understanding is supported by constructive circumambulation in which by drawing on appropriate concepts and ideas the person begins to test the complex interconnections making up their life. Habituated acts which glue people together in culturally acceptable ways take time to (re-)learn—rewiring the neural pathways may require rehearsal ad infinitum—but the brain has a plasticity the nature of which is as yet not fully tested, leaving hope that things can change.

Once understanding begins the opportunity to apply, analyse and evaluate follows naturally if the understandings have been worked upon in natural settings across the important relationships in each person's life. At this stage, and reflecting back on Bourdieu's concept of habitus discussed earlier, the stage of application, analysis and evaluation will draw upon all those resources—economic, social, cultural and symbolic, that are available and will seek to convert these into positive outcomes for the person and the groups within which they operate. It may be that in this approach the final element of Anderson and Krathwohl's (2001) approach—creativity—may become a function of all parties including the person with ABI as they draw upon, co-ordinate and apply the capitals they have to their best advantage. The role of professionals will be in supporting the *conversion of these capitals into outcomes*.

Finally, since all people are aiming to achieve what they can in life given their own gifts and capabilities, the journey itself is as important as the outcome. What gives meaning to life is that struggle to be all you can be given those capabilities. Even if you do not quite complete the journey, it should have been worth the struggle. Change and movement towards hopes, dreams and aspirations are all important. To bring us back to the starting point of learning, for people with ABI, many of these notions of life's possibilities have to be redefined to give life meaning—this means recognising the ABI and what is possible must be an essential starting point—then people can dare to dream. You may now relinquish your role as Eskimo, Bedouin or high plains native recognising how for you, as for people with ABI, what is left is 'hope'. Then, we can all weave the threads together in ways that help each person including those with ABI, to feel and fare better.

In Chap. 10 to follow, we reflect on some of the policy and practice recommendations for professionals, family carers and people with ABI. This is couched in terms of a message of hope rather than one which produces separation, anxiety, fear and hopelessness.

## References


Akrivou, K., & Di San Giorgio, L. T. (2014). A dialogical conception of *Habitus*: Allowing human freedom and restoring the social basis of learning. *Frontiers in Human Neuroscience,8,* 432. doi:10.3389/fnhum.2014.00432

Ackroyd, K., Fortune, D. G., Price, S., Howell, S., Sharrack, B., & Isaac, C. L. (2011). Adversarial growth in patients with multiple sclerosis and their partners: Relationships with illness perceptions, disability and distress. *Journal of Clinical Psychology in Medical Settings,18,* 372–379.

Anderson, L. W., & Krathwohl, D. R. (Eds.). (2001). *A taxonomy for learning, teaching, and assessing: A revision of Bloom's taxonomy of educational objectives.* Boston, MA: Allyn & Bacon (Pearson Education Group).

Andersson, K., Bellon, M., & Walker, R. (2016). Parents' experiences of their child's return to school following acquired brain injury (ABI): A systematic review of qualitative studies. *Brain Injury,30*(7), 829–838. doi:10.3109/02699052.2016.1146963

Ashworth, F., Clarke, A., Jones, L., Jennings, C., & Longworth, C. (2014). An exploration of campassion focused therapy following acquired brain injury. *Psychology and Psychotherapy: Theory, Research and Practice,88*(2), 143–162.

Aström, M., Asplund, K., & Aström, T. (1992). Psychosocial function and life satisfaction after stroke. *Stroke,23*(4), 527–531.

Arrigo, M., Kukulska-Hulme, A., Sanchez, I., & Kismihok, G. (2013). Meta-analyses from a collaborative project in mobile lifelong learning. *British Educational Research Journal,39*(2), 222–247.

Booth, T., & Booth, W. (1994). *Parenting under pressure: Mothers and father with learning difficulties.* Buckingham: Open Univeristy Press.

Bourdieu, P., & Wacquant, L. (1992). *An invitation to reflexive sociology.* Chicago, IL: Chicago University Press.

Bulinski, L. (2010). Social reintegration of TBI patients: A solution to provide long-term support. *Medical Science Monitor: International Medical Journal of Experimental and Clinical Research, 16*(1), PH 14–23.

Cicerone, K. D., & Azulay, J. (2007). Perceived self-efficacy and life satisfaction after traumatic brain injury. *The Journal of Head Trauma Rehabilitation,22*(5), 257–266.

Connolly, M., & Harms, L. (2015). *Social work: From theory to practice.* Port Melbourne, Australia: Cambridge University Press.

Corrigan, J. D., Bogner, J. A., Mysiw, W. J., Clinchot, D., & Fugate, L. (2001). Life satisfaction after traumatic brain injury. *The Journal of Head Trauma Rehabilitation,16*(6), 543–555.

Curran, C. A., Ponsford, J. L., & Crowe, S. D. (2000). Coping strategies and emotional outcome following traumatic brain injury: A comparison with orthopedic patients. *The Journal of Head Trauma Rehabilitation,15*(6), 1256–1274.

de Botton, A. (2004). *Status anxiety*. Camberwell, Australia: Penguin Books.

Durham, C. (2014). *Unlocking my brain: Through the labyrinth of acquired brain injury*. Edgecliff NSW: Jane Curry Publishing.

Evans, J. J. (2011). Positive psychology and brain injury rehabilitation. *Brain Impairment,12*(2), 117–127.

Field, J., & Lynch, H. (2015). Getting stuck, becoming unstuck: Agency, identity and transitions between learning contexts. *Journal of Adult and Continuing Education,21*(1), 3–17.

Fleming, J. M., Lucas, S. E., & Lightbody, S. (2006). Using occupation to facilitate self-awareness in people who have acquired brain injury: A pilot study. *Canadian Journal of Occupational Therapy,73*(1), 44–55.

Foucault, M. (1982). The subject and power. *Critical Inquiry,8*(4), 777–795.

Fraas, M. R. (2015). Narrative medicine: Suggestions for clinicians to help their clients construct a new identity following acquired brain injury. *Top Lang Disorders,35*(3), 210–218.

Freeman, E. A. (1998). *Brain injury & stroke: A handbook to recovery. Sydney*, Australia: Hale & Iremonger

Fuchs, T. (2005). Delusional mood and delusional perception: A phenomenological analysis. *Psychopathology,38,* 133–139. doi:10.1159/000085843

Gadamer, H. G. (1989). *Truth and method* (J. Weinsheimer & D. G. Marshall, Trans.). New York, NY: Continuum.

Gadamer, H. G., & Lawrence, F. G. (1982). *Reason in the age of science*. Cambridge, England: Cambridge University Press.

Gardner, H. (1983). *Frames of mind: The theory of multiple intelligences*. New York, NY: Basic Books.

Garmezy, N. (1991). Resilience in children's adaptation to negative life events and stressed environments. *Pediatric Annals,20*(9), 463–466.

Gelech, J. M., & Desjardins, M. (2011). I am many: The reconstruction of self following acquired brain injury. *Qualitative Health Research,21*(1), 62–74.

Gordon, R. G., & Duff, M. C. (2016). Incorporating principles of the collaborative contextualised intervention approach with the empirical study of learning and communication in traumatic brain injury. *Aphasiology,30*(12), 1461–1482.

Greene, G. (1990). *The last word and other stories*. Harmondsworth, England: Reinhardt Books.

Greenfield, B. (2011). Phenomenology as a philosophical orientation for understanding the transformative experience of disabling illness. *Topics in Stroke Rehabilitation,18*(1), 35–39.

James, W. (1950). *Principles of Psychology*. New York: Dover Publications

Jetten, J., Haslam, C., & Haslam, S. A. (2012). *The social cure: Identity, health and well-being*. Hove: Psychology Press.

Kelly, M. (1988). Gadamer and philosophical ethics. *Man and World,21*(3), 327–346.

Kendall, E., Kendall, M., & Muenchberger, H. (2009). Coping following traumatic brain injury: Lessons from autobiographical accounts. In C. Marshall, E. Kendall, R. Gover, & M. Banks (Eds.), *Disability: Insights from across fields and around the world* (Vol. 1, pp. 129–142). Westport, CT: Praeger Publication.

Kendall, E., Shum, D., Lack, B., Bull, S., & Fee, C. (2001). Coping following traumatic brain injury: The need for contextually sensitive assessment. *Brain Impairment,2*(2), 81–96.

Lamberts, K. F., Fasotti, L., Boelen, D. H. E., & Spikman, J. M. (2016). Self-awareness after brain injury: Relation with emotion recognition and effects of treatment. *Brain Impairment*, 1–8.

Lazarus, R. S., & Folkman, S. (1984). *Stress, appraisal, and coping*. New York, NY: Springer.

Levasseur, M., Pigot, H., Souture, M., Bier, N., Swain, B., Therriault, P., et al. (2016). Identifying participation needs of people with acquired brain injury in the development of a collective community smart home. *Disability and Rehabilitation: Assistive Technology,11*(8), 636–644. doi:10.3109/17483107

Lexell, E. M., Alkhed, A., & Olsson, K. (2013). The group rehabilitation helped me adjust to a new life: Experiences shared by persons with an acquired brain injury. *Brain Injury,27*(5), 529–537. doi:10.3109/02699052.2013.765598

Linge, F. R. (1990). Faith, hope and love: Non traditional therapy in recovering from serious head injury: A personal account. *Canadian Journal of Psychology,44,* 116–129.

Lonie, D., & Dickens, L. (2016). Becoming musicians: Situating young people's experiences of musical learning between formal, informal and non-formal spheres. *Cultural Geographies,23* (1), 87–101.

Luthar, S. S., & Zigler, E. (1991). Vulnerability and competence: A review of research on resilience in childhood. *American Journal of Orthopsychiatry,61*(1), 6–22. doi:10.1037/h0079218

Martin, R., Levack, W. M. M., & Sinnott, K. A. (2015). Life goals and social identity in people with severe acquired brain injury: An interpretative phenomenological analysis. *Disability and Rehabilitation,37*(14), 1234–1241. doi:10.3109/09638288.2014.961653

Masten, A. S., Best, K. M., & Garmezy, N. (1990). Resilience and development: Contributions from the study of children who overcome adversity. *Development and Psychopathology,2*(4), 425–444.

McKay, R., Langdon, R., & Coltheart, M. (2007). The defensive function of persecutory delusions: An investigation using the implicit association test. *Cognitive Neuropsychiatry,12*(1), 1–24.

Mevissen, L., & de Jongh, A. (2010). PTSD and its treatment in people with intellectual disabilities: A review of the literature. *Clinical Psychology Review,30*(3), 308–316.

Moran, D. (2011). Edmund Husserl's phenomenology of habituality and habitus. *Journal of the British Society for Phenomenology,41*(1), 53–76.

Mogensen, J. (2016). Cognitive recovery after acquired brain injury-neurocognitive mechanisms and their clinical implications. *Ec Neurology,3,* 428–431.

Nietzsche, F. (1995). *The birth of tragedy* (C. P. Fadiman, Trans.). Now York: Dover (original work published in 1872).

Nochi, M. (2000). Reconstructing self-narratives in coping with traumatic brain injury. *Social Science and Medicine,51*(12), 1795–1804.

Perlesz, A., Kinsella, G., & Crowe, S. (1999). Impact of traumatic brain injury on the family: A critical review. *Rehabilitation Psychology,44,* 6–35.

Peterson, C., & Seligman, M. E. P. (2004). *Character strengths and virtues: A handbook of classification*. Oxford, England: Oxford University Press.

Ramcharan, P., Nankervis, K., Strong, R., & Robertson, A. (2009). *Experiences of restrictive practices: A view from people with disabilities and family carers*. Melbourne: Department of Human Services. Available at, http://www.dhs.vic.gov.au/__data/assets/pdf_file/0008/608588/osp_experiencesofrestrictivepractices_pdf_0509.pdf

Ranieri, M., & Pachler, N. (2014). Inventing and reinventing identity: Exploring the potential of mobile learning in adult education. *Prospects,44,* 61–79.

Rees, R. J. (2005). *Interrupted lives: Rehabilitation and learning following brain injury*. East Hawthorn, Australia: IP Communications.

Resilience Research Centre. (2017). *What is resilience?* Retrieved from http://resilienceresearch.org/about-the-rrc/resilience/14-what-is-resilience

Schutz, A. (1944). The stranger: An essay in social psychology. *American Journal of Sociology,49* (6), 499–507.

Slade, M., Oades, L., & Jarden, A. (2017). *Wellbeing, recovery and mental health*. Cambridge UK: Cambridge University Press.

Smith, C. A., & Lazarus, R. S. (1990). Emotion and adaption. In L. A. Pervin (Ed.), *Handbook of personality: Theory and research* (pp. 609–637). New York, NY: Guilford Press.

Stone, L. D., Underwood, C., & Hotchkiss, J. (2012). The relational habitus: Intersubjective processes in learning settings. *Human Development,55,* 65–91. doi:10.1159/000337150

Sullivan, C. T., Gray, M. A., Williams, G. P., & Green, D. J. (2014). The use of real life activities in rehabilitation: The experience of young men with traumatic brain injuries from regional, rural and remote areas. *Australia Journal Rehabilitative Medicine,46,* 424–429.

Sveen, V., Soberg, H. L., & Ostensjo, B. (2016). Biological disruption, adjustment and reconstruction after mild traumatic brain injury. A focus group study. *Disability and Rehabilitation,* March 2016 doi:10.3109/09638288.2015.1129445

Uprichard, S. (2010). *Experiences of the process of adjustment to a brain injury: An interpretative phenomenological analysis* (Unpublished doctoral thesis). University of Hertfordshire. Retrieved from http://hdl.handle.net/2299/452

van der Kolk, B. A., Roth, S., Pelcovitz, D., Sunday, S., & Spinazzola, J. (2005). Disorders of extreme stress: The empirical foundation of a complex adaptation to trauma. *Journal of Traumatic Stress,18*(5), 389–399.

Verlinden, I., & Brands, I. (2016, January). The influence of cognitive complaints, cognitive performance and emotional distress on self-efficacy in patients with acquired brain injury. *Brain Injury, 30*(5–6), 604–604.

Walsh, R. S., Muldoon, O. T., Gallgher, S., & Fortune, D. G. (2015). Affiliative and "self-as-doer" identities: Relationships between social identity, social support, and emotional status amongst survivors of acquired brain injury (ABI). *Neuropsychological Rehabilitation,25*(4), 555–573. doi:10.1080/09602011.2014.993658

Ylvisaker, M., & Feeney, T. J. (1998). Everyday people as supports: Developing competencies through collaboration. In M. Ylvisaker (Ed.), *Traumatic brain injury rehabilitation: Children and adolescents* (2nd ed., pp. 367–384). Boston, MA: Butterworth-Heinemann.

Ylvisaker, M., Turkstra, L. & Cooelho, C. (2005). Behavioural and social interventions for individuals with traumatic brain injury: A summary of research and clinical implications, *Seminars on Speech and Language, 26*, 256–267.

# Chapter 10
# Parting Thoughts: Finding a Balance

*It isn't that they can't see the solution. It's that they can't see the problem.*

G.K. Chesterton

*The diseases of the mind are more destructive than those of the body.*

Marcus Tullius Cicero (106-43BC)

> While modern medicines may occasionally have an almost magical effect on a person's life, the time has come to move beyond our rather arrogant clockwork model of the brain, within which a clinician has only to isolate some faulty cognitive gear and repair it. We have to begin to think of the brain as a self-organizing ecosystem, one of such staggering complexity and delicate balance that almost any aspect of a patient's life may be relevant to a diagnosis or essential to treatment, (Ratey, 2001, p. 354).

## 10.1 Looking Back at Keys to the ABI Cage

We now turn full circle and reintroduce Keys to the ABI Cage that readers will first have encountered in the Foreword. We do so now to ask what lessons can be learned by people with ABI, professionals, family and other carers given the study findings. We concur with Sherry that 'there is a need for important, practical revisions in the way we understand and respond to the experience of brain injury' (2006, p. 212). At appropriate points, we offset to the right principles and findings to make them easier to identify and to seek to respond to Sherry's appeal.

### *10.1.1 Principles Induced from the Genesis of the Cage*

The birth of *Keys to the ABI Cage* emanated from the combination of Durham's own experience of brain injury (the cage being one symbol of that experience),



C. Durham and P. Ramcharan, *Insight into Acquired Brain Injury*,
DOI 10.1007/978-981-10-5666-6_10

a recapturing of her professional background in education and from filtering the views of the many hundreds of people with ABI responding to her first book 'Doing Up Buttons'. Further, though, it offered a mechanism to systematically collect data analysed in three areas reflecting a history of responses from people with ABI —'differences and difficulties that can PUT us in the cage'; 'how we feel about these differences and difficulties can LOCK us in the ABI Cage' and 'Keys that RELEASE us from the ABI Cage'. Perhaps most importantly, and yet often missed, the intention of the Cage to DO NO HARM was the most critical and fundamental contextual factor. It provided a non-judgemental context which treated people as humans and introduced artistry to engage people in a human way, with dignity and respect for what they bring to the world.

Even prior to generating the study findings then, the Cage had already built on personal history and experience and the public voices of people with ABI. Along with the study findings in this book, the importance of the Cage to Durham and to others with ABI is that it represents a 'confirmed and consistent' voice and view of people with ABI. Dismissing this voice would represent a dominant professional approach which uses 'dividing practices' (see Chap. 9) to maintain professional power and authority to act.

> Hearing the voices of people with ABI must be central to all endeavour which aims to support people to feel and fare better.
>
> Means are as important as ends. All services, supports and studies should aim to do no harm. This is not just doing no physical and biological harm; it is about doing no emotional and psychological harm also.

### *10.1.2 The Learning Dimension*

This study shows that people with ABI struggle with learning, but that this learning is as central to a better life as is the mending of their bodies. This learning is continuous—it takes place at a time when the personal resources are least available but when the changes in life, relationships, settings and contexts are at a demand that is anomalously and enormously high, given their changed circumstances.

> (Re)learning for people with ABI is continuous. It often occurs at a time when personal resources are at their lowest and learning demands relating to 'new bodies', new contexts, settings and relationships are at their highest.

It has been shown that all learners need to be motivated in order to engage in learning. The use of objects (e.g., the crushed soft drink can, the flying pig, the rubber band on the 'stretch outside my comfort zone' 'talk-about' card) created interest and the small objects on the Keys 'talk-about' cards (e.g., miniature watering can, dog, sun, moon, mushroom, flower) created amusement.

> Learning should not be arcane and tedious. There are always ways to inspire and excite so that people remain motivated to continue.

This all helped to maintain the focus and keep the session relaxed. Holding the cards in their hands participants remarked that they now realised that they had found ways to cope with many difficulties. This reflective activity appeared to be a powerful way for them to understand and acknowledge the things they had learnt to cope with. They felt empowered not only to speak about the words on the card, but to talk about things the words reminded them of—they decided what was important to discuss, not the interviewer's interests. Moreover, placing the cards in 'Do' or 'Don't' box focused their attention and gave them a physical way—an action—to express their thinking.

> I'm still walking round dragging my cage but I can see I'm getting somewhere (Participant with ABI)
>
> '...The 'talk-about' cards led to discussions and realisations' (Participant, professional).

Keys to the ABI Cage therefore admirably supported constructive circumnambulation through which people could explore ideas in a circular roundabout way through self-reflection. Offering 'talk-about' cards helped people reflect and build connections between things, as well as discovering new ideas which they could engage in their own time, drawing upon what was important to them.

In the interview situation, *Keys to the ABI Cage* allowed people with ABI to tell stories and share their experience.

> If I'd had the CD (Keys to the Brain Injury Cage) earlier on it would have helped me to understand that I wasn't going mad. And it certainly would have given me another way of approaching things too. Perhaps then I could have asked more questions. Because if I knew that was the situation, then I could relate that to other areas. It would have helped me tracking my progress/achievements (Participant with ABI)
>
> It sets things out, it's very interesting once you start realising it's a tool for reflection (Participant family carer).

The Cage therefore supported Anderson and Krathwohl's (2001) initial stages of learning—remembering, understanding and formulating new actions on the basis of their reflection.

> Once motivated, directing and controlling engagement in areas defined by the learner as important allowed reflection and linking of concepts and ideas (understanding). This 'constructive circumnambulation' led to hypotheses about how to organise new social actions in order to flourish in their everyday lives.

Some participants expressed relief when they held cards and remarked how comforting it was to learn that others have had these difficulties too—they had not been imagining things—they were not alone, they were not mad. This was a shocking revelation that people have gone through the 'health system' for several years and not understood that their difficulties were 'normal' for people with ABI. This burden should NEVER be placed on the shoulders of damaged people with ABI struggling with their own multiple burdens. The 'Reflection kit' (used on its own for country participants and used prior to the interview by over half the interview participants) and 'Some Further Thoughts' sheets (for all participants) proved to be of great benefit. Participants who had the kit prior to the interview were pleased to have had time to think about concepts so that they could re-engage and expand on the concepts at the interview. Although some people had forgotten what they'd written on the 'Reflection kit' sheets prior to the interview with the Cage they all said they valued the combination of kit, Interview and Further Thoughts sheets. Once again some participants greatly valued the 'Some Further Thoughts' sheets they took home after the interview and took time and effort to consider issues and ideas at greater depth.

The Reflection Kit and 'Some Further Thoughts' sheets were also useful with many who had written them being able to re-engage with the concepts many had forgotten between their writing and their participation with the Cage.

In approach and content, the Cage demonstrated respect and offered a way to establish mutual respect and empathy. It allowed metaphysical concepts, for example around love, courage, support and hope to populate the narratives—for participants to exemplify their sentience and their humanity.

> A vital characteristic of any learning environment is that it is imbued with humanity, respect for each person as a sentient being and one capable of empathy. No learning can usefully prevail under disrespect, duress or rejection.

Keys to the ABI Cage has several potential uses in its physical form or as a data storage disk. A learning resource, *Keys to the ABI Cage* could include a discussion starter for ABI groups, a learning tool for people with ABI and carers, a tool with sheets for personal reflection. *Keys to the ABI Cage* could be trialled as a useful tool to make sure the people with ABI/family carers/professionals were 'on the same page'—were aware of the major problems the person was dealing with. The Cage could be a useful to introduce health science students to ABI as well as professionals.

Durham was curious as to whether participants who were vision impaired would react to the tool but they carefully touched the cage and objects while they were described. One legally blind participant joked that the pig would have difficulty flying as she had felt the wings and said they were made from fly wire. This participant said that having a mental picture in her head of *Keys to the ABI Cage* helped her imagine her ABI. Additionally when she held all the 'Differences and Difficulties' cards she said, with obvious pride, that she had not realised how many issues she had coped with.

*Keys to the ABI Cage* was also trialled at three different ABI Support Group sessions. Each session had up to 15 people with ABI. The tool worked well in the group situation and encouraged group discussion. One support group wanted to use the digital storage disk with a group of people using computers at the centre, with the aim of viewing the digital storage disk again in a year's time to review the individual's progress. It is interesting to realise that there could be many different uses of the ABI Cage and the digital storage disk.

> … your cage is a wonderful example of feeling they are locked in and trapped in that cage and there is actually no way forward or out. I think you're right, I think human beings generally do have the ability to um to find a way forward um against all odds, that's what people with ABI tell you it was against all odds (Participant professional).

The Cage had some weaknesses. The logistics of packing up, moving and setting up the *Keys to the ABI Cage* was not easy, but the reaction by participants made the effort most worthwhile. Because of the bulk and large size of the cage (66 cm wide by 100 cm tall, the pole was 150 cm tall) it was not possible to take it into cafes or libraries for interview purposes. Moreover it represents just one of many potentially innovative ways to build the right resources to support learning.

Although introduced to groups since the study, the use of the Cage as a research study methodology has not yet been sufficiently tested over time as a means of scaffolding learning and as a support tool in the context of everyday service delivery. However, after work done subsequent to the study with professionals and ABI groups, the portents of success remain high. The Cage is just one of potentially many devices that may engage people with ABI in learning. What is important is that those who provide services and supports, understand the importance of learning as an essential part of their professional practice. Researchers, designers and innovators need to test further the potential of new forms of learning across media and across time.

> Teaching and learning should be a major element in the training of service professionals. New learning design and media, along with the Cage and any offshoots, should involve understanding about how people learn and teaching strategies to employ to make learning engaging and meaningful. Need to be implemented and tested further over time with people with ABI and the people who support them in their local environments.

Finally, the participants in this study were all able to speak for themselves and met other inclusion criteria around not presently being stressed or engaged in legal proceedings. While acknowledging this as a partial sample given the spread of ABI, we would assert that the common threads of learning, empathy and humanity that tie this study together are applicable to the many rather than the few. It is not the extent of the brain injury that has greatest import but, rather, the damage to life and humanity—if this is the case perhaps 'acquired brain injury' might be better cast as 'acquired damage to life and humanity'.

## 10.2 Implications of the Study Findings

This study has exposed the staggering complexity and delicate balance of the brain and also of that of the lifeworld of the person with ABI trying to cope with damage to their brain, body and beliefs; their hope, honour and trust, their security and safety.

Weighing up the plethora of complicated and complex difficulties participants with ABI experienced in their day-to-day lives, it appeared impossible that anything could balance the scales so that life could be tolerable. However, it was demonstrated that it was possible for some participants with ABI to achieve a balance and that the negative factors of physical, cognitive, emotional differences, difficulties and deficits of ABI could be balanced by the positive influences of hope, love, understanding, learning to work things out for themselves and even small everyday things. The latter were those crucial things that conferred a meaning and purpose to life that is essential in maintaining a positive stance.

Importantly, people with ABI and their families need to have some information about positive things they can do, so they can learn what other people with ABI have done to help themselves. A catalogue of coping strategies could be a valuable resource for people with ABI who have forgotten coping strategies they employed prior to their ABI. Further research is needed to find factors that help people with ABI, and help people with ABI learn about different coping strategies that could help them deal with their difficulties. We have, too, shown that learning needs to take place in context and with those who provide support over time. Learning is therefore not simply for the person with ABI but around finding new habits that support them as a group to survive and make the best of brain injury together.

Positive information from studies about ways people cope with ABI, ways to improve memory, manners and faulty thinking, factors that improve quality of life need to be 'translated' into everyday language and made available to the person who sustains a brain injury, their family and support organizations.

> All support for people with ABI should operate from a positive philosophy in which every engagement builds on strengths, in which every success no matter how small is celebrated and in which the contribution of the person within their network of social relations is recognised as a contribution to the group. People would benefit from a catalogue of coping ideas used by others translated into everyday language and made available in ways that support learning.

Since the completion of this study in 2012, many writers are making a case for such strengths-based approaches, such as in the Social Identity Model of Social Change (SIMIC) (Jetten, Haslam and Haslam, 2012), positive approaches (Evans, 2011; Martin, Levack and Sinott, 2015; Gan & Ballantyne, 2016), client centred practice (D'Cruz, Howie and Lentin, 2015; Barker et al., 2016), along with participatory and co-design approaches which transfer choice and control more firmly into the hands of the person with ABI him or herself (Knox, Douglas and Bigby, 2016; Hawley, Gerber and Morey, 2017) or which do so through self-help groups (Cutler et al., 2016; Gelech, Bayley and Desjardins, 2017).

It is worth noting that other discipline areas, such as mental health, have adopted such positive models—the recovery model in mental health.

However, the experiences of participants in our sample indicated that bio-pscyho-social approaches did not work on strengths and did not employ such positive approaches despite Hojat's (2016) argument that the model reflects the World Health Organisation's holistic definition of health as 'a state of complete physical, mental and social well-being and not merely the absence of disease or infirmity', (WHO, 1948).

The majority focus on pathology and abnormality and in service delivery therefore further damaged the person's self-esteem and confidence. The pathological focus also made its way into hard copy information and Websites, reinforcing difference and 'abnormality'. Furthermore, all participants with ABI, mothers and wives of people with ABI, and professionals stated that people with ABI, their families and the general public and some health professionals do not understand the ramifications of ABI, and that there is a need for information in non-medical language. Lack of understanding about ABI had a negative effect on the lifeworld of most of the participants with ABI. It was disappointing that so many participants had felt that they had gone mad or insane and did not realise the consequences of ABI, in spite of being involved in the medical system. Professionals need to provide the person with ABI and their family information presented in a way that they can *understand* ABI.

> From the earliest time after injury, whilst bodies mend to the extent possible, it is vital to build through a learning approach, empathy and dignity the grounds for a positive life. Information about ABI should emphasise these positive messages and the centrality of learning to accomplish lives and relationships through which the person can feel and fare better.

This study demonstrated the need of information in everyday language that is discussed with the person and their family, about the range of things that can improve the well-being, satisfaction and quality of life for person with ABI, and the importance of learning new things. Family members need to work with professionals in supporting and helping the person understand things they can do to help themselves live with ABI and to do so in the context within which they are being asked to live and flourish. Constructive information from other people with ABI about attitudes, understandings and emotions that have helped them learn to feel and fare better needs to be provided to the person and their family.

The person with ABI and their family need information about practical everyday things that can help them learn to feel and fare better. This includes the importance of finding an activity that the person loves doing (from knitting and sewing to gardening and playing computer games), the company and companionship of pets, and being able to contribute by helping at home and helping other people with ABI, i.e. to build a new culture habituated to all within their operating social and support network.

Love, hope, understanding and everyday things *can* help the person with ABI to make progress from a life that is unsatisfactory, when they feel imprisoned in the ABI Cage, to a more satisfactory life, when they have discovered Keys to unlock the ABI Cage. Yet, as this study has shown, people with ABI can continue learning even if it takes more time. That learning takes place in context and so implicates family members and others so that they too can learn, adjust, cope and thrive.

> All learning takes place in context. The aim should be to habituate learning within everyday social and support networks so everyone accepts their roles, their strengths and limitations. Supporting learning with information delivered in ways and formats that are understandable and which support the person to maximise their use of collective resources (capitals) in pursuit of individual and collective goals is vital to accomplish a life in which habituated actions support the person to 'know their world' and, in doing so, to fare and feel better in that world. There is a need for an "ABI educator" supporting the person and their family with this information and with skills in building stronger and more robust social and support networks.

There has been very little focus on the need to place such education at the forefront of service delivery for people with ABI in the community. One exception is Silvestro et al (2017) who, in a statement which very much reflects the argument of this volume, state that collaboration between medical and educational sciences provides

> ...a "functional synergy" permits the development of the person, and establishes an indissoluble link between functions and attitudes, thus allowing the achievement of the greater possible autonomy. In this way classical and pedagogical rehabilitation may be combined in a single concept of educational action. To realize this integrated educational process it is important to evaluate and promote awareness development, based on the possibilities of brain plasticity and on the presence of multiple intelligences skilfully in-tertwined each other. Therefore, self-awareness plays a prime role in educational actions for the rehabilitation of persons with severe ABI' (p. 82)

We suggest this as a major area for both research and practice in the future.

Looking at the themes already outlined above, there are many similarities between this and the 'recovery model' which has been widely adopted in mental health services. For example, Jacobson and Greenley (2001) identify internal conditions such as hope, healing, empowerment, connection and external conditions such as human rights, a positive culture of healing and recovery-oriented services as central to producing better outcomes. There may be much to be learned from such models and their recent development (Slade, Oades and Jarden, 2017).

In the present study, many participants with ABI stated that much of the information provided to them, especially while in rehabilitation, destroyed their hope. It is also false to see the rehab period as a 'golden period'. This may be so for mending bodies but it was seen by many participants as a 'deep dark hole'.

It should not be forgotten that people have to spend much longer outside rehabilitation and in their communities after discharge. This study provides evidence that people with ABI learn ways to adapt and cope with living with brain injury, year in and year out, so their life improves to some degree as the years pass. It is never 'as good as it gets' since things are always changing; a small gain is made here or there, circumstances change, people come and go and so forth.

If there was just one change that could happen from this exhausting and exhaustive study it would be that no one is ever told they will only improve for two or even five years as was the experience of many participants. The words 'vegetative state' and 'plateau' should not be used, other terms should be employed. The term 'mild ABI' does not adequately describe the difficulties a person may encounter, nor that an easy recovery will not necessarily follow, as is the case in most 'mild' illnesses. These three terms can have a negative effect on the lifeworld of the person with ABI.

> It is vital for professionals to provide feedback which sustains hope and motivates the person to continue learning. Too many professional especially in rehabilitation give the impression through their words that nothing can change once their work is through. This is simply untrue and has a huge impact on ongoing recovery. Words should always be chosen to support hope but to emphasise the need for continued effort over time.

The experience in rehabilitation, and thereafter especially given comments from participants about the negative impact of being required to complete a battery of tests, needs to be considered by professionals. If the person is given a test they should be given the opportunity to have their test result explained to them, along with positive action that will be taken by professionals to address the issue and things they could do to try to overcome the difficulty. This needs to be in clear written and verbal form. Further research into the value to the client of doing tests needs to be undertaken.

Studies need to be undertaken to ascertain the value to the *client* of IQ tests and whether there is a replacement for them. A hypothesis has been formed after interviewing people with ABI that if some of the time taken completing tests was spent *learning* about ABI, having difficulties explained, being given strategies to address issues, this could positively affect the lifeworld of people with ABI.

> In light of the findings of this study the relevance of recurrent testing of people with ABI needs to be reconsidered. Such tests should not defeat the person or act as a threat. When used, their use to the benefit of the person should be clearly articulated. More research is needed on the negative impact of these tests.

The renewed focus on biographical and narrative approaches (Greenfield, 2011; Lennon et al., 2014 and Fraas, 2015) can be equally as powerful and, if seen as part of the development of trust can deepen the relationships and understanding between professionals and people with ABI and the use of compassion as a form of therapy, (Ashworth et al., 2014). These are, it should be noted central elements of empathy as a fundamental principle underlying the therapeutic relationship.

Some participants believed that ABI was a really powerful experience that had let them experience unique and valuable things, so that they now had a fresh appreciation of life, they were aware of their strengths and weaknesses and were now a wiser, better person. The implications of these findings can provide a lifeline for people with ABI who are feeling swamped by things that negatively affect their lifeworld.

> The gap between what their lives were and what they become with ABI is more vast than the majority of people will experience. It is easy for people to fall into this chasm unless supported not to do so. Bridging this gap is 'fantastical' and doing so represents for many who do so a deepening for them and something from which we can all learn. This deepening also represents a painstaking reframing of life and its certainties, a huge feat of learning. Any successes in this struggle are grounds for celebration.

This study showed that there are many Keys to open the ABI Cage. Hope, love, learning to understand ABI, working things out for themselves and learning to face the facts were identified by participants as factors that helped them learn to feel and fare better. The crucial role of the empathetic professional was identified by all participants in this study. Hojat (2016) has emphasised that humans 'are evolved to connect together for survival. Among the factors that fulfil the human need for affiliation and connectedness are social institutions such as marriage, family, and social support network, including clinician-patient empathic relationships' (p. 17).

Drawing on a number of studies he shows how patient outcomes improve with empathy (though not necessarily with sympathy) and argues that this empathy binds the patient and professional in a bond of 'trust'. Such trust is best supported through empathic clinician engagement, 'listening with a "third ear" and "seeing with the mind's eye"' (p. 129) and where, 'the patient perceives the clinician as a helping member of a social support system…' (p. 189). For Hojath, then the science of medicine must work with '…the art of medicine (the psychological, social and interpersonal aspects of illness) merge into one unified holistic approach to patient care. Empathy is a key element in the holistic care system' (p. 72).

Professionals, service providers, rehabilitation hospitals and brain injury support organisations can all play a powerful, empathic, active role in assisting clients to understand their ABI and identify the things *the person finds helpful.* This study identified an abundance of issues around ABI and education as well as Keys that will support professional staff to play their role in the wider networks of support through which people with ABI will live the rest of their lives.

> Empathy plays a crucial role since it establishes the grounds for trusting relationships. Such trust is a prerequisite for people learning new roles and tasks within any naturally occurring support network. Strengthening the competence of this long term network of support is essential.
>
> Faring and feeling better takes place within everyday environments and relationships. Professionals need to demonstrate empathy and it should be a requirement of their practice expertise and monitored as a quality measure.

The tool, *Keys to the ABI Cage,* supported the participants with ABI to share their insight into ABI as they told stories about their experience and identified factors that negatively and positively affected their lifeworld. A conclusion that can be drawn from this study is that although people with ABI may be considered to lack self-awareness, participants demonstrated that by using *Keys to the ABI Cage,* they could reflect on their difficulties, differences and feelings and identify Keys—factors that could help them learn to feel and fare better in a constructive, positive way. The professional has an important role in assisting people with ABI to articulate their challenges to recognize ways to help themselves. The term ABI itself refers to the brain sustaining injury, but it been shown that the brain is but part of the 'person' that requires attention. In many ways, it is itself a misnomer. When we think of a person who is identified as having an ABI, we need to be thinking of the broad spectrum of their life and not just about 'mending' their brain and the physical losses of ABI. Mending lives is infinitely as complex and equally as important as mending brains and bodies.

> People with ABI have insight. Their struggle is equally about mending lives as it is about mending bodies.

This study has established that many people with ABI believe they are mad and bad and that they are afraid and ashamed. There is a stigma and humiliation associated with being a person with ABI. The emotional welfare of the person with

ABI should be of primary consideration for all contact by professionals, whether in the research, rehabilitation or medical setting.

To address this issue, the curriculum of the health professionals should concentrate on this issue, and professional journals and conference presentations should focus on the importance of 'humanity' as a basic value held by the brain injury professional. All professionals involved in this study could identify the physical and cognitive consequences of ABI, but they were not as focused on how the person with ABI felt as a whole person, not just a focus on the deficits of ABI.

For ethical and humane reasons all professionals working with people with ABI should have a 'reminder checklist' to refocus their attention on how the client may feel. The ABI professional needs to show humanity and understanding to their clients. This could enrich and strengthen the rehabilitation experience for clients. Professionals need to have a broader understanding of the consequences of ABI, not just their specific area of expertise. This also requires further investigation.

## 10.3 Study Limitations

With any study there are limitations, and this study is no exception. The study was completed in 2012 but data was collected in 2008–9. Further, the selection of participants at least two years post-injury meant that much data on the experience of services would have been prior to 2008 and, in many cases as far back as the year 2000. In this sense, the study findings may be somewhat dated. However, even as an historical record, the findings are important in locating key systemic and treatment issues which should form strong grounds for the development of future services. We have in Chaps. 9 and 10 sought to update the literature to point to new approaches and new ideas aimed at addressing some of the more challenging experiences of study participants.

The sample might be considered to be relatively small, though by being so, there were advantages. It was, for example, possible to collect far more data about the meaningful experiences of participants than would have been collected in larger samples using statistical data. So what we lost in sample size, we gained in the depth of data collected. The analysis was rigorous and in being so threw up recurrent themes which indicated that data saturation was reached. However, we recognise people responding to adverts on brain injury support groups and Websites may represent a sample skewed by such involvement. For example, it may have favoured those who were seeking information, knowledge or those finding it more difficult to cope.

We would say that if the study's aim was to seek generalization that this sampling strategy may not have been appropriate. However, since our aim to explore a collection of diverse experiences as far as was possible, we think we have accomplished this to a significant degree. There remain issues about those with ABI who are more isolated and who do not maintain contact with either services or with ABI groups and who would not have known about nor elected to participate in this study. For this hard to reach group, more research is required.

As will have been noted in Chap. 6, we resisted listing the 'characteristics' of the sample—their age, occupational, marital status or the impairments or struggles with activities of daily life they experienced. In looking back at the analysis of data and delivery of key findings, we can say that even were if we had done so it would not have produced gains to study findings. We have made some points along the way in which data comes from people of a certain age, gender and who have particular problems with daily life. These are made contextually, and we recognize the importance of these contexts. However, the main focus was to explore the repeated experiences of participants rather than focusing on how the plethora of demographic data might be relevant. Indeed, for a sample, this small that may have proved very difficult. Our proposition is that there was sufficient in the recurrence of themes to make the reporting of demographics details redundant. While against convention, we suggest it avoids gratuitous use of data that is given no further meaning in the analysis.

As with any interpretive method, it is easy to say that the data may be attended to with differing interpretive approaches. This is always a bone of contention. We do believe that the structure of the Keys to the ABI Cage and the opportunity for people themselves to guide the discussion were a notable benefit of this study. By the same token, the approach may not suit those who would rather have data collected in systematic categories in which the same areas of discussion were covered with each participant. Doing no harm was an important defining feature of this research, and we argue that by leaving the choice of 'talk-about' cards to the participants that they chose what was important to them. In doing so, they chose from a consistent series of themes. That makes their responses all the more meaningful.

## 10.4 A Final Few Words

This volume has used a plethora of analogies in order to provide new ways to consider ABI. It has proposed mindset changes to specifically allow the healthcare professional to revisit their concepts/mindsets/models when working with people with ABI.

The reader will be aware that a number of species of fish undertake migrations upstream, against the flow of the river to spawn and feed and to maintain genetic fitness within fish communities.

Bundles of branches were first used in France in the seventeenth century to create steps in steep channels or to allow fish to swim up waterfalls. Fish ladders or fishways are constructed today for this purpose. Fish negotiate a regulated upward flow, then have a calm pool to gather strength for the next upward push. In such a way the person with ABI can be empowered and assisted to take on the many challenges of a new lifeworld in steps with a calm period to gather strength for a further thrust. Having the opportunity to discuss their experience, tell stories and learn to understand about ABI can be the branches or fish ladders to assist their swim upstream and become 'adept in being brain damaged' (Skloot, 2004, p. 196).

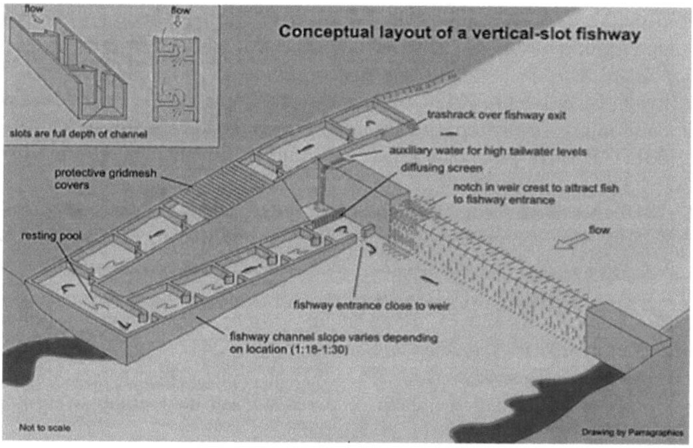


This book has shown that participants with ABI had insight into their difficulties, differences and feelings and the many Keys that opened their ABI Cage. As they reflected, they realised that their hope, acceptance and attitude (their mindset) had helped them to learn new ways to help themselves feel and fare better.

We believe that this study adds further to the growing calls for positive models not just in relation to people with ABI, but also for those with mental health (Slade et al., 2017), disability (Martz & Livneh, 2016) and across social work (Connolly & Harms, 2015). Furthermore, this study clearly shows how, by reflecting on how people with ABI perceive their lifeworld, we open up limitless possibilities for learning. In implementing these possibilities, much still remains to be done.

The study has shown that educational principles can be applied to empower people with ABI to learn to acquire better insight into ABI.

> The power of recovery lies within the injured person…Education is the key. (Freeman, 1998, p. 14).

## References

Anderson, L. W., & Krathwohl, D. R. (Eds.). (2001). *A taxonomy for learning, teaching, and assessing: A revision of Bloom's taxonomy of educational objectives*. Boston, MA: Allyn & Bacon (Pearson Education Group).

Ashworth, F., Clarke, A., Jones, L., Jennings, C., & Longworth, C. (2014). An exploration of campassion focused therapy following acquired brain injury. *Psychology and Psychotherapy: Theory, Research and Practice, 88*(2), 143–162.

Barker, R. N., Sealey, C. J., Polley, M. L., Mervin, M. C., & Comans, T. (2016). Impact of a person-centred community rehabilitation service on outcomes for individuals with a neurological condition. *Disability and Rehabilitation, 39*(11), 1136–1142. doi:10.1080/09638288.2016.1185803

Connolly, M., & Harms, L. (2015). *Social work: From theory to practice*. Port Melbourne, Australia: Cambridge University Press.

Cutler, M., Nelson, M. L. A., Nikoloski, M., & Kuliski, K. (2016). Mindful connections: The role of peer support group on the psychosocial adjustment of adults recovering from brain injury. *Journal of Social Work in Disability and Rehabilitation, 15*(3–4), 260–284.

D'Cruz, K., Howie, L., & Lentin, P. (2015). Client-centred practice: Perspectives of persons with traumatic brain injury. *Scandinavian Journal of Occupational Therapy, 23*(1), 30–38.

Evans, J. J. (2011). Positive psychology and brain injury rehabilitation. *Brain Impairment, 12,* 117–127.

Fraas, M. R. (2015). Narrative medicine: Suggestions for clinicians to help their clients construct a new identity following acquired brain injury. *Top Lang Disorders, 35*(3), 210–218.

Freeman, E. A. (1998). *Brain injury & stroke: A handbook to recovery.* Sydney, Australia: Hale & Iremonger.

Gan, C., & Ballantyne, M. (2016). Brain injury family intervention for adlolescents; A solution-focused approach. *NeuroRehabilitation, 38,* 231–241.

Gelech, J., Bayly, M., & Desjardins, M. (2017). Constructing robust selves after brain injury: Positive identity work among members of a female self-help group. *Neuropsychological Rehabilitation.* doi:10.1080/09602011.2017.1308872

Greenfield, B. (2011). Phenomenology as a philosophical orientation for understanding the transformative experience of disabling illness. *Topics in Stroke Rehabilitation, 18*(1), 35–39.

Hawley, L., Gerber, D., & Morey, C. (2017). Improving personal self—Advocacy skills for individuals with brain injury: A randomized pilot feasibility study. *Brain Injury, 31*(3), 290–296. doi:10.1080/02699052.2016.1250952

Hojat, M. (2016). *Empathy in patient care: Antecedents, development, measurement and outcomes.* New York: Springer.

Jacobson, N., & Greenley, D. (2001). What is recovery? A Conceptual model and explication. *Psychiatric Services, 52,* 482–485.

Jetten, J., Haslam, C., & Haslam, S. A. (2012). *The social cure: Identity, health and well-being.* Hove: Psychology Press.

Knox, M., Douglas, J. M., & Bigby, C. (2016). I've never been a yes person: Decision-making participation and self-conceptualization after severe traumatic brain injury. *Disability and Rehabilitation,* doi:10.1080/09638288.2016.1219925

Lennon, A., Bramham, J., Carroll, À., McElligott, J., Carton, S., Waldron, B., et al. (2014). A qualitative exploration of how individuals reconstruct their sense of self following acquired brain injury in comparison with spinal cord injury. *Brain Injury, 28*(1), 27–37. doi:10.3109/02699052.2013.848378

Martin, R., Levack, W. M. M., & Sinnott, K. A. (2015). Life goals and social identity in people with severe acquired brain injury: An interpretative phenomenological analysis. *Disability and Rehabilitation, 37*(14), 1234–1241. doi:10.3109/09638288.2014.961653

Martz, E., & Livneh, H. (2016). Psychosocial adaptation to disability within the context of positive psychology: Findings from the literature. *Journal of Occupational Rehabilitation, 26*(1), 4–12.

Ratey, J. (2001). *A user's guide to the brain, perception, attention and the four theatres of the brain.* New York: Pantheon Books.

Sherry, M. (2006). *If I only had a brain: Deconstructing brain injury.* New York, NY: Routledge.

Silvestro, D., Mazzeti, M., Melia, C., Stagno, M. T., Carlesimo, G. A., Bivoni, U., et al. (2017). Educational action in the rehabilitation of severe acquired brain injuries: The role of self-awareness. *Annali dell'Istituto Superiore di Sanità, 53*(1), 82–85.

Skloot, F. (2004). *In the shadow of memory.* Omaha, NB: Bison Books.

Slade, M., Oades, L., & Jarden, A. (2017). *Wellbeing, recovery and mental health.* Cambridge, UK: Cambridge University Press.

WHO. (1948). *Preamble to the Constitution of the World Health Organization as Adopted by the International Health Conference*, New York, 19–22 June, 1946; signed on 22 July 1946 by the representatives of 61 States (Official Records of the World Health Organization, no. 2, p. 100) and entered into force on 7 April 1948.

# Glossary

**Attribution theory** Students attribute success or failure according to their perceptions of why they might have succeeded or failed in the past (Weiner, 1985).

**Biopsychosocial model** the inconsistent interaction between biological, psychological and social factors. This model counters the biomedical model, which attributes disease to biological factors, such as viruses, genes, damage or abnormalities.

**Blank spots** is a term to identify an issue where enough is known about the issue to pose questions, to gather data to fill in the blank spot, as is used by quantitative research (Wagner 1993).

**Blind spots** is a term to name issues in which existing theories, methods and perception have not identified the issue. Enough is not known about the issue to even ask about, or care about the issue (Wagner 1993).

**Circumambulation** from the Latin *circum* around plus *ambulātus* to walk, literally means 'walking around'. In this volume, this term, which has been used by Jung and many religions, denotes a reflective, open approach to learning leading to construction for personal growth. This contrasts to being directed, or thinking that someone has an exact answer and course of action that will apply to your circumstances. The person looks at an issue by reflecting on it from different points of view—moving round the problem and actions they have taken, then reflecting on the action to redefine issue and further action. Circumambulation is taken in a circular, not linear way.

**Constructive circumambulation** We found that learning takes place as people 'circle' ideas *repeatedly to make sense of their world in order* to *test* action*s that work and allow them to gain* control over their lives. This we term 'constructive circumambulation'.



C. Durham and P. Ramcharan, *Insight into Acquired Brain Injury*,
DOI 10.1007/978-981-10-5666-6

**Fieldwork** to be immersed in, live with and like the people who are studied (van Maanen, 2011).

**Flow** when the person becomes so absorbed in an engaging and interesting task that action and awareness merge ( Csikszentmihalyi, 1990, 1997).

**'Grey' literature** the term used for information that is not in the mainstream published journal articles. These monographical narratives may be published by commercial publisher or self-published.

**Headwork** thinking about an issue making connections of how knowledge gained from the literature was analysed, evaluated and applied (van Maanen 2011).

**Insiders 'emec' perspective** this term is used in anthropology, social and behavioural sciences to research from the perspective of the insider—from within a certain group. In this study from the perspective of the person with brain injury (Pike 1954).

**Intentionality** meaningful behaviour based on the person's perception.

**Interpretative phenomenological analysis** a detailed exploration of how participants are making sense of their personal and social world. This is an experiential qualitative approach to research.

**Lifeworld (*Lebenswelt*)** the world of the person's lived experience (Husserl, 1952, 1962).

**Outsiders 'etic' perspective** this term is used for research from the outside, from the perspective of the observer, the researcher (Pike 1954).

**Phenomenology** philosophical reflective study of experience and consciousness from the first-person point of view (Husserl, 1913).

**Qualitative body-object model** the body as a subject—research explores intentionality—meaningful behaviour based on perception. Research exploring meaning in context. The approach is therefore more process-orientated, offering 'thick' description. Body-subject research around ABI is emergent with a focus upon identity, coping, adaptation, recovery and resilience. Much less research has been undertaken around the range of experiences and social lives of people with ABI.

**Quantitative body-object model** the medical model that primarily focuses on the body as an object to 'mend'.

**Textwork** writing after listening to and observing people to produce stories and narratives (van Maanen, 2011).

**The 'golden period'** We have employed this term to identify the time frame of two years directly after the person acquires their brain injury. From the perspective of the professional (the outsider), the greatest recovery is presumed to happen within this time. We have adapted this term from **the 'golden hour'**, the time directly after a traumatic injury when there is greatest likelihood that prompt treatment will prevent death. Note this term is used with the specific aim of drawing attention to the different convictions of the professional (the outsider) and the person with brain injury (the insider). For them, this is the **'dark hole period'**; this period is far from golden—it is the 'dark hole period'.

**'Thick' description** description that explains not just the behaviour, but its context, so that the behaviour can become meaningful to an outsider.

**'Zone of proximal development'** a learner achieves learning with the assistance of scaffolding from the teacher or a peer. The scaffold is slowly removed (as scaffolding is removed from a building when construction is complete) leading to more independent and autonomous change based on reflection and learning (Vygotsky, 1978).

MIX
Papier aus verantwortungsvollen Quellen
Paper from responsible sources
FSC® C105338

If you have any concerns about our products,
you can contact us on
**ProductSafety@springernature.com**

In case Publisher is established outside the EU,
the EU authorized representative is:
**Springer Nature Customer Service Center GmbH**
**Europaplatz 3, 69115 Heidelberg, Germany**

Printed by Libri Plureos GmbH
in Hamburg, Germany